Machiavelli

AND HIS FRIENDS

First Paperback Edition   ISBN 0-87580-599-X

Design by Julia Fauci

The Library of Congress has cataloged
the hardcover edition as follows:
Machiavelli, Niccolò, 1469–1527.
Machiavelli and his friends : their personal correspon-
dence / [Niccolò Machiavelli] ; translated and edited by
James B. Atkinson and David Sices.
        p.   cm.
Includes bibliographical references and index.
ISBN 0-87580-210-9 (alk. paper)
1. Machiavelli, Niccolò, 1469–1527—Correspondence.
2. Florence (Italy)—Politics and government—
1421–1737. 3. Intellectuals—Italy—Correspondence.
4. Statesmen—Italy—Correspondence. 5. Authors,
Italian—16th century—Correspondence.
I. Atkinson, James B., 1934–   . II. Sices, David.
III. Title.
DG738.14.M2A4   1996
945'.06'092—dc20   96-3106 CIP

This translation, authorized by Unione Tipografico-
Editrice Torinese, is based on *Opere di Niccolò Machi-
avelli; Volume terzo, Lettere,* a cura di Franco Gaeta
(Turin, 1984).

Portrait of Machiavelli courtesy of Al Ministero per i
Beni Culturali e Ambientali.

Letter by Machiavelli to Vettori (#244) published by
permission of the Houghton Library
(FMS Eng 1343 [13]), Harvard University.

To

Gretchen

Jacqueline

Andreas

Katrina

Nils

Harry

Laura

Anne

Andrew

Contents

Letter written by Niccolò Machiavelli to Francesco Vettori (Letter 244)

Preface

A few remarks about this edition are in order. We retain the somewhat artificial distinction, although it has its shortcomings, that Italian editors have made between Machiavelli's official correspondence and his personal letters. The line between the two is not always sharply drawn. Furthermore, not all the letters written in Machiavelli's hand from the period under consideration have been published in Italian. We have therefore based our text on the best available edition of Machiavelli's *Lettere*, which Franco Gaeta prepared as volume three of the *Opere di Niccolò Machiavelli* for the Unione Tipografico-Editrice Torinese in 1984. We have made some additions based on Giorgio Inglese's edition of the *Lettere a Francesco Vettori e a Francesco Guicciardini* (Milan: Rizzoli, 1989), whose notes were extremely helpful, and on the results of scholarship done since Gaeta's edition appeared. We have also consulted an earlier edition of the letters that Gaeta prepared for Feltrinelli in 1961.

The modern publication history of Machiavelli's letters begins with Edoardo Alvisi's edition, published in Florence in 1883 by Sansoni. This volume was used in large part by Gaeta in his 1961 edition. Once Gaeta's first edition of the letters was published, several Italian scholars were inspired to examine the correspondence more closely. Roberto Ridolfi wrote "*Per un'edizione critica dell'epistolario machiavelliano. La Lettera al Vettori del 20 aprile 1513*," in *La Bibliofilia* 68 (1966): pp. 31–50, and two more articles in *La Bibliofilia* 71 (1969): "*Le carte del Machiavelli*," pp. 1–23, and "*Contributi all'epistolario machiavelliano: la lettera del Vettori del 16 aprile 1523 nel testo originale inedito*," pp. 259–64. Meanwhile, another scholar, Sergio Bertelli, was preparing the way for his edition of the letters with "*Carteggi machiavelliani*," *Clio* 2 (1966): pp. 201–265, and "*Appunti e osservazioni in margine all'edizione di un nuovo epistolario machiavelliano*," in *Il pensiero politico* 2 (1969): pp. 536–579. The year 1969 proved to be significant for publication of works about the *Lettere*. First, Bertelli brought out his edition, the *Epistolario*, published in Milan by Giovanni Salerno; it was reprinted in Verona by Valdonega in 1982. Second, Paolo Ghiglieri issued an important study, *La grafia del Machiavelli studiata negli autografi*, published in Florence by Leo S. Olschki. In 1971, Mario Martelli wrote an article, "*Memento su un'edizione dell'epistolario machiavelliano*," in *La Bibliofilia* 73 (1971): pp. 61–79, and brought out his own edition of Machiavelli's works, *Tutte le opere*, published by Sansoni in Florence, which included a careful reexamination of the available texts of the letters. The Gaeta edition that we have followed, published in 1984, relied heavily on Martelli's work, although Gaeta modernized Italian spelling.

Many of Machiavelli's letters, as published in Alvisi's 1883 text, were translated by Allan Gilbert and published on three separate occasions: first by

Packard and Company in a 1941 publication, *The Prince and Other Works*; then by Capricorn Books in 1961, as *The Letters of Machiavelli*; and finally by Duke University Press in 1965, in volume two of Gilbert's three-volume *Machiavelli: The Chief Works and Others*. In 1988, the University of Chicago Press reprinted the text used for the Capricorn edition, which appeared in *The Chief Works and Others*. Sixteen of Machiavelli's letters, translated by J. R. Hale in *The Literary Works of Machiavelli* in 1961 for Oxford University Press, were reprinted by Greenwood Press in 1979.

The headnotes in this volume are designed primarily to help set the stage for important events occurring during Machiavelli's troubled times. In some cases, because of the relatively small number of letters occurring within certain periods of time, we have combined two or more years into a single group; in a few of these cases the headnotes have not been divided by year. The headnotes attempt to place both the people and the places referred to in the correspondence in a historical framework. They thus, incidentally, provide a somewhat distorted biography of Machiavelli, since they are governed by the needs of the letters and not by the needs of a balanced overview of his life and times.

The footnotes are designed to elucidate material not generally known except to specialists in Renaissance Italy or in the Italian language. Those notes that Gaeta prepared for his 1984 edition were the most useful and are acknowledged by parenthetical citation. Also helpful were the notes Ezio Raimondi prepared for his *Opere di Niccolò Machiavelli*; we consulted the seventh edition, published in Milan in 1976 by Mursia, and have indicated them by parenthetical citation. We should also mention that two reviews of Gaeta's 1984 edition helped us with both the text and the notes: the first by Filippo Grazzini, which appeared in *Lettere Italiane,* 36, 4 (October–December) 1984, pp. 605–609, and the second by Giorgio Inglese, which appeared in *La Bibliofilia* 86 (1984): pp. 271–280. Numerous other sources consulted in writing the footnotes are arranged according to their abbreviations listed at the back of this edition. The Works Cited pages should not be construed as an exhaustive bibliography, because many important studies concerning Machiavelli and his milieu are absent from it. To acknowledge the source for each fact drawn upon in the notes is a task that is next to impossible. They are prepared, however, in good faith and with apologies in advance for sins of both omission and commission.

The index is meant to guide the reader in locating specific people and events. It attempts to regularize spelling, because the correspondents are not always consistent. Names appearing in the introduction to the volume and in the headnotes are indicated in boldface type to distinguish them from references in the actual correspondence. Thus the reader may more easily follow the careers of individuals in their historical context as well as observe the possible evolution of their characters as they are mentioned throughout the text of the letters.

Finally, a word about the translation itself is necessary. In order to maintain consistency in the voices of the letter writers, David Sices translated the letters to Machiavelli and James B. Atkinson translated those from him. Each of us reviewed the other's work, but, in the main, the final version represents the understanding of the person responsible. We have attempted to make these letters readable and enjoyable while staying as close as possible to the original Italian text. The several entire letters translated from the Latin, as well as Latin words and phrases in Italian letters, appear in italic print in this edition. Two other typographic indications are square brackets and the use of angle brackets to designate coded material. Unless otherwise noted, square brackets signify either emendations made by the translators or ellipses in Gaeta's text. We follow Gaeta's indications and insert angle brackets to alert the reader about phrases in code; the point at which the coded material ends, however, is not always evident from Gaeta's text. The notes, headnotes, and introduction were prepared by James B. Atkinson.

In closing, we would like gratefully to acknowledge the assistance of Andrew Feldherr of the Department of Classics at Dartmouth College, as well as generous grants from Dartmouth College's Ramon Guthrie Fund and Office of the Dean of the Faculty, and a publication grant from the National Endowment for the Humanities to Northern Illinois University Press. We would like to express our gratitude to Patricia Carter of Baker Library at Dartmouth College for her great help in obtaining source and secondary materials and to Wendy Warnken of Northern Illinois University Press for her sensitive and meticulous participation in the execution of our project.

Introduction

As the familiar litotes would have it, "Niccolò Machiavelli needs no introduction." Everyone has a sense of who he is and why he is important. To a broad audience, *The Prince* and *The Discourses* have long revealed a vital thinker about politics and history. Perhaps it is useless to "introduce" a writer who has been both reviled and revered for almost five centuries.

Machiavelli is not widely known as a writer of letters. Indeed, making his acquaintance may be a new experience for many readers, who will find his personal correspondence articulating urgent preoccupations and exposing facets of his personality not always present in the standard fare of university curricula. There is ample evidence in his letters, to be sure, of his shaping ancient and modern history to his own advantage and of refining his thoughts on politics for clarity and subtlety. But a less familiar Machiavelli shines through his letters: Machiavelli the literary artist, Machiavelli the storyteller, Machiavelli the playwright, Machiavelli the self-fashioning portraitist, Machiavelli the practical joker. In other words, a self-conscious Machiavelli emerges.

There are a few correspondents in these letters who need some introduction. Biagio Buonaccorsi, Filippo Casavecchia, Miguel de Corella, Luigi Guicciardini, Agnolo Tucci, Giovanni Vernacci, and Agostino Vespucci become familiar in reading their letters. Others will be in less need of an introduction. The reader's sense of such well-known contemporaries as Francesco Vettori, Piero Soderini, and Francesco Guicciardini will become more intimate than it previously was, however, in the context of these letters. We comprehend these individuals and their times better once we see them grappling with everything from abstractions such as Fortune and the ideal state to such quotidian matters as office politics and sex. The Machiavelli who receives reports about the yields of his harvests, who voices anxieties about tax increases, who in one breath tells his young adolescent son to "study, do well, and learn, because everyone will help you if you help yourself" and in the next breath advises him about how to handle an ornery young mule (Letter 328)—this Machiavelli is less likely to be seen as the "murtherous Machiavil" of Shakespeare's Richard, Duke of Gloucester (3 *Henry VI*, 3, 2, 193).

Thus, the process of introducing the reader to Machiavelli's personal correspondence is here reversed. In addition to introducing individuals, some familiar and some not, and highlighting their thought processes and their personality traits, these personal letters perform their own introduction. They acquaint us better with the entire context in which this correspondence was created. Valuable to readers of literature, history, and politics, Machiavelli's letters have long been recognized as the testing ground for ideas that he developed more fully in his political and historical writings. As they articulate and shape new directions in his thinking, they also react keenly to his correspondents. It is within the lively interplay of the letters that the resilience of Machiavelli's mind is often most evident and most exciting.

We cannot ignore the value of the context in which these letters were created. To assess the context properly, we must begin on its periphery by discovering more about Machiavelli's correspondents and his friends. Then we shall be better able to observe how he consciously uses his letters to create a self-portrait and to refine his thought—often simultaneously. Finally, we can center our focus on the informing significance that this context has for Machiavelli.

MACHIAVELLI'S CORRESPONDENTS AND FRIENDS

Not all of Machiavelli's correspondents are of equal significance. Some, such as Don Micheletto (Miguel de Corella), are no more than casual acquaintances writing about side issues of their official concerns. Others, such as Giovanni Vernacci and Francesco Soderini, though important to Machiavelli's personal or political life, are infrequent correspondents. Vernacci, a relative, plays the role as much of confidant as of friend—much more sincerely than Vettori and Guicciardini do, considering their fraught relationships with Machiavelli. Cardinal Francesco Soderini is a remote but powerful admirer of Machiavelli's projects for a militia. Filippo de' Nerli, in contrast, is such an ambivalent admirer of Machiavelli that he may not even properly be termed a "friend." But the loyalty and devotion of friends such as Filippo Casavecchia and Biagio Buonaccorsi to Machiavelli is unimpeachable; as is true of all good friends, however, they must be accepted with their warts. The better-known Francesco Vettori and Francesco Guicciardini have their warts too, but they are essential sparring partners and animating participants in this correspondence. Whatever their shortcomings, each person has his intrinsic worth and is essential to filling in the interstices that exist in the correspondence.

The hapless Don Micheletto was a Spaniard who served Cesare Borgia as lieutenant and later, in 1507, Machiavelli as leader of his prized Florentine militia. Despite weaknesses of language and style (Letters 146 and 147), he urgently needs to convince Machiavelli that he is in the right. Imagine dealing with someone who, in the middle of a convoluted explanation, writes about his relations with both Machiavelli and the Signoria:

> If it should seem to you that I have sinned by the Holy Spirit in this part, I pray Your Lordship to tell those people who have related this matter to you, along with Your Lordship, to give me whatever penitence Their Lordships see fit. . . . Some day I shall be with Your Lordship, and I shall tell you things and give you living proof of them that will frighten you, that I am not in the habit of writing. For I have served a few kings and two pontiffs in this world, as Your Lordship knows, and I never wrote them without their deigning to answer me, and especially in matters that were in the service of Their Holinesses and Their Lordships. And for all the times I have written to the exalted Signoria and to

the gonfalonier [Piero Soderini], I have never had a reply, for the entire year and a half I have been with Their Lordships. But I believe that such is the custom of the country, so I am not surprised. I had promised not to write about this matter, but I was obliged to give justification for it to Your Lordship, since I know you love me and are fond of me. I would not have written of it to anyone in the world for anything. (Letter 147)

Don Micheletto is a bit player in this correspondence. Lest we assume that subtle reasoning and elegant diction characterize all the context in which Machiavelli lives and writes, however, we need look no further than the glimpse Don Micheletto provides of the workaday frustrations with which he also had to deal.

To alleviate these frustrations, Machiavelli could always rely on his nephew Giovanni Vernacci, a merchant whose letters to Machiavelli (Letters 253 and 268) are filled with commercial concerns. Machiavelli obviously took great comfort in his friendship, loyalty, and devotion, especially once his lively correspondence with Vettori was over. Yet Vernacci represents an enigma. His letters offer no clue as to why Machiavelli, during the gloom of his political disgrace, would choose to unburden his soul to him so completely and so regularly. In August 1515 Machiavelli writes, "[T]he times . . . have been—and still are—of such a sort that they have made me forget even myself" (Letter 248). Six months later, in February 1516, Machiavelli laments, "I have become useless to myself, to my family, and to my friends because my doleful fate has willed it to be so" (Letter 250). Finally, in June 1517, the self-doubt is explicit: "[S]ince the adversities that I have suffered, and still am suffering, have reduced me to living on my farm, I sometimes go for a month at a time without thinking about myself" (Letter 252).

To compensate for Machiavelli's feelings of disappointment, there was Francesco Soderini, Cardinal of Volterra, an active political figure and Gonfalonier Piero Soderini's brother. A recurrent theme throughout his letters is admiration for Machiavelli's mental agility. At least two of the letters, written four years apart, express his respect for Machiavelli's ideas. The cardinal, writing in Latin in September 1502 to thank Machiavelli for a "charming letter" (in which Machiavelli had evidently congratulated him on his brother's election as Florence's Gonfalonier for Life), comments: "We ourselves, in such a crisis of the republic, shall always be under such obligation that none of us would not most willingly offer his abilities and his own blood for the fatherland and for our citizens. And since you are second to none in ability and affection, you will not be only with us, but far dearer and more welcome" (Letter 31). The mutual esteem of Machiavelli and Soderini grew as they worked together on missions for Florence. The cardinal was an appreciative supporter of Machiavelli's idea that the best military defense Florence could have was a local militia, which he called "a God-given thing" (Letter 139). On 4 March 1506, in thanking Machiavelli for what we must assume was an informative letter, since it no longer exists, the cardinal expresses his gratitude, as he says, "because we learned clearly how your new military idea, which corresponds to our hope for the welfare and dignity of our country, is progressing." He continues, "You must get no small satisfaction from the fact that such a worthy thing should have been given its beginnings by your hands.... The things written by you are of such a kind that anyone of tempered judgment can read them. If you have not put all your efforts to this ... think of how outstanding the matters will be to which you put all the force of your intelligence and learning. We urge you to do so as much as is possible" (Letter 109).

The role of correspondents who were not charmed by Machiavelli, such as Filippo de' Nerli, should not be downplayed. Nerli was an aristocratic frequenter of the heady discussions at the Rucellai Gardens that led to Machiavelli's *Discourses on the First Ten Books of Titus Livius, The Art of War,* and *The Life of Castruccio Castracani of Lucca.* Writing from Rome on 17 November 1520, Nerli says that he eagerly anticipates receiving copies of the latter two works (Letter 265). Nerli's *Commentarii de' fatti civili occorsi nella città di Firenze dal 1215 al 1537* (Commentaries on the civil events that happened in the city of Florence from 1215 to 1537), not published until 1728, prove him to be a great admirer of Machiavelli. Some even consider Nerli the historian to be a disciple of Machiavelli. Nerli possessed an acid, often malicious, tongue. No evidence of these traits, however, could be deduced from a letter that he wrote from Modena, where he was governor. Nerli enthused:

> you and Fornaciaio have managed it so that the fame of your revelries has spread and continues to spread not only throughout all Tuscany but also throughout Lombardy. . . . The fame of your comedy [*Clizia*] has flown all over. You should not believe that I have heard these things from friends' letters, but rather I have heard it from wayfarers who go all about the roads preaching "the glorious celebrations and great spectacles" of Porta San Frediano. I am certain, just as the grandeur of such great revelries was not satisfied to remain within the boundaries of Tuscany but had to fly even farther, that it will also go beyond the mountains. . . . All in all, Niccolò, . . . I should like you to send me this comedy that you have recently had performed as soon as you can. (Letter 286)

This letter is signed, "[a]s a brother," a formulaic closing, but in this instance it is grating. Less than a week later, Nerli wrote Machiavelli's brother-in-law, Francesco del Nero, expressing an entirely different reaction to the reports he had heard about the opening night of *Clizia.* Reading these two letters together, one might describe the first one to Machiavelli as "smarmy." Yet despite the high-mindedness of the second one to del Nero, Nerli was titillated enough by what he had heard to want a personal copy of the play performed at Fornaciaio's house:

> Since Machia is a friend and relative of yours and a very good friend of mine, I cannot help saying, on this occasion that you have given me to write you, how aggrieved I am about what daily reaches my ears concerning him,

because recently and during this carnival period I have had so many complaints that I am no longer affected by all this city's wicked ways. . . . I am certain that people would talk about nothing else but him, given that a paterfamilias of such character is galloping off—I do not want to say with whom—and has written a comedy that, according to what I have heard, has some fine things in it. . . . And not later but sooner I beseech you that, without bringing me into it any further, you take whatever steps you can to put these matters right and for you to beg him on my behalf to be so kind as to answer a letter of mine, sending me as well the comedy that was put on in Fornaciaio's garden.[1]

Less ambivalent than Nerli about their relationships with Machiavelli are five people who are clearly his friends. First, there is the melancholic Filippo Casavecchia, one of Machiavelli's cronies but, like Biagio Buonaccorsi, not a major figure in histories of the times. His irony and wit pleased Machiavelli enough to make Casavecchia the comic butt of several homoerotic jokes. Their exchange encourages Filippo to vent his spleen, "since I find neither repose nor tranquillity in this indecent and pestilential abyss." What Machiavelli savors about his style can be seen in Casavecchia's continuation:

If I have well noted in particular what remedies are available for this, it seems to me that the only one is to let oneself be borne by wicked Fortune,[2] which I do not completely approve of, because, since she takes delight in new things, I should not like it a bit for her to lead me, by my bad luck, into the whorish and public place of that city. But if I knew which way to turn with my prayers, I would beseech that all the ills of this world should sooner come to me than the most pestilential, most pitiless, and putrid disease of melancholic humor, which I hear disturbs some of our most beloved friends, may nature rid them of it. (Letter 148)

Machiavelli savors his friend's clear notion of his accomplishments as well as his potential. After Florence's victory over Pisa in 1509, Filippo Casavecchia bursts out:

for truly it can be said that your person was cause of it to a very great extent. . . . Niccolò, this is a time when if ever one was wise it should be now. I do not believe your ideas will ever be accessible to fools, and there are not enough wise men to go around: you understand me, even if I am not putting it very well. Every day I discover you to be a greater prophet than the Hebrews or any other nation ever had. Niccolò, Niccolò, in truth I tell you that I cannot say what I would like. So be happy for that good friendship we have had together, and let it not seem like a burden to you to come and stay here with me for four days. Aside from our conversation, I am saving you a ditch full of trout and a wine like you have never drunk. (Letter 169)

Is it any wonder that four years later "Casa" was the first person to whom Machiavelli showed an early draft of *The Prince*?

The solicitous, conscientious Biagio Buonaccorsi's devotion is reflected in many personal letters to Machiavelli while the latter is out of Florence under orders from the Ten of War, the Florentine foreign office. Biagio's personal letters allude to "official" concerns, but they are distinct from the official variety. Buonaccorsi is not a name that turns up in many history books. Yet he was the fixed point around which much of Machiavelli's active political life turned because he resolutely kept Machiavelli abreast of the situation in Florence. His letters to Machiavelli are replete with expressions of friendship and admiration; in 1505 Biagio even made Machiavelli a godfather of his son Filippo. Machiavelli's failure to return Biagio's pleas for friendship, however, has remained a puzzle for which no satisfactory hypothesis exists. Nevertheless, in a letter dated 21 October 1502 Biagio allows us to glimpse a revealing image of Machiavelli, who seems to be obeying his own precept for successful leadership: foresight. Machiavelli was in Imola keeping tabs on Cesare Borgia because Florence was intent on learning Borgia's reactions both to recent overtures from Louis XII and to a threat to his power from among his supporters and most powerful condottieri, the "Assembly of Failures" (the *Dieta de' Falliti*): "We have tried to locate some *Lives* of Plutarch, and there are none for sale in Florence. Be patient, because we have to write to Venice; to tell you the truth, you can go to the devil for asking for so many things" (Letter 37). Behind some friendly banter lies an image of Machiavelli, stationed in Imola since 6 October, observing Borgia's stratagems. Four years after he formally entered political life, Machiavelli is ruminating about parallels between ancient and modern events and figures. Already he realizes that by probing Plutarch, he can fortify what he will later, in the Dedicatory Letter to *The Prince*, call his "resources," internal reserves as solid, useful, and basic as household utensils (*suppellettili*). This intuition, early in his career, empowers him to define these "resources" as "my knowledge of the deeds of great men, learned from wide experience of recent events and a constant reading of classical authors."[3] The choice of the word *suppellettile* in *The Prince* is felicitous; the letters prove that work on the foundations of his "knowledge" begins early in his political career. Hence, *The Prince* is not merely the fruit of enforced leisure later, during his exile from Florentine politics.

While Machiavelli carried out the Ten of War's commissions around Italy and in France and Germany, Biagio stayed home, keeping his superior posted about intrigues—both suspected and actual—in that body. Biagio's private letters consequently provide a first-hand view of what chancellery life was like on a day-to-day basis.[4] These two men provide us with a rare perspective: they enhance our appreciation of the competition that Machiavelli faced in expressing his ideas to his superiors.

They are complemented by a third voice, it too from the chancellery office—that of Agostino Vespucci. His typical day at the office sounds indeed distressing: "Poor me, I was the only one left, and sighing from the depths of my heart and panting, I take up my falling pen and scribble along, fearing that if I ventured a word, the same thing would happen to me here that they say happened to the man from Perugia in France, and since he is a colleague of our Signori, I swallowed a pill containing more bile than honey. I write three or four letters while he dictates." Finally, Vespucci in a plea to Machiavelli cries out, "So you see where that spirit of yours, so eager for riding, wandering, and roaming about, has gotten us. Blame yourself and not others if anything adverse happens. I wish that no one except you were standing by me and was my superior in the chancellery, although you attempt and dare all the things which that most poisonous viper attacks me, pursues me, and cuts me to bits for, about which that terrible man, worthless and contentious, gives me orders" (Letter 33).

Listening to the voices of Vettori and Machiavelli interact is a fascinating experience. The letters of these *compari* are vital to a full appreciation and understanding of the total correspondence. The give-and-take with Vettori is very much that of two "buddies," although Vettori is more partial to the term *compare* than is Machiavelli.[5] John M. Najemy defines the complex interplay of Machiavelli and Vettori with dexterity. He argues that *The Prince* is "addressed" to Francesco Vettori. Circumstantial evidence to support this argument exists. For example, the two men had a long-standing friendship. Machiavelli had joined Vettori on a mission to Germany for the Signoria in 1507 and 1508 and later appears to have asked Vettori to be godfather to one of his children. Vettori soon became Machiavelli's chief correspondent during his years *post res perditas.* In 1513 Vettori, whose relations with the Medici were as good as Machiavelli's were bad, was in Rome with Florence's mission to the new Medici Pope, Leo X. Vettori's letter to Machiavelli of 23 November 1513 (Letter 223) sets the scene for one of the most famous letters of the Renaissance. The best-known letter Machiavelli ever wrote, dated 10 December 1513 (Letter 224), it describes what he calls his "short study, *De principatibus.*"

Vettori's Letter 223 in and of itself does little more than detail his comings and goings in Rome. Accustomed as the two men were to dissecting current events, Vettori alludes to the relations between Louis XII and Pope Leo X by noting, "Even though the party is not over, still it seems to have quieted down somewhat; and I believe it is a good idea not to talk of it until it has started up again. . . . So in this letter I have decided to describe to you what my life in Rome is like." Vettori's usual practice is to establish topics and raise questions. Machiavelli's custom is to wield language and form not only to record his experience but also to knead it into shape. Thus, many of his letters read like essays—some personal, but mostly critical and analytical. Sometimes Machiavelli's reply takes its cue from Vettori; at other times, this lead is reversed. But his letter of 10 December parodies Vettori's letter of 23 November and matches it virtually point by point. He fills in Vettori's nonchalant outline with wit, prodding, one-upmanship, and joy in rising to an occasion.

Vettori's letter cannot be quickly dismissed, however. It supplies a significant link between the two men on a psychological level and offers dramatic clarification of why the form of these letters was of vital concern to Machiavelli. With the pretext of eliciting Machiavelli's comments on current affairs, so that he might possibly make sure they got into the hands of the Medici in Rome,

Vettori frequently writes analytical essays that deal with local and international politics. Machiavelli replies in kind. Yet, more often than not, he disagrees with Vettori's analyses. Rather than expressing discomfort with this disagreement, Vettori expresses dissatisfaction with his circle of friends in Rome:

> I want you to believe one thing, which I say without any flattery: although I have gone to no great trouble, nonetheless the throng is so great that one cannot help meeting a great number of people. In point of fact, few of them satisfy me, and I have not found any man of better judgment than you. . . . For when I speak at length to some, when I read their letters, I find myself astonished that they have attained any rank whatsoever, since they are nothing but ceremony, lies, and tales, and there are very few of them who are at all out of the ordinary. (Letter 223)

Machiavelli relished this kind of compliment, exiled as he was to his place in the country near Florence. But the remark also indicates the extent to which Machiavelli could rely on a friend for a sympathetic ear. Vettori was by no means a perfect correspondent; Machiavelli was keenly aware of his shortcomings. But Vettori frequently served to goad Machiavelli into thinking and writing more precisely. Their interchanges fostered an empathy, one that helped to shape a persona for Machiavelli the writer—whether of treatises or of letters. Because Machiavelli had such a thoroughgoing knowledge of Vettori as an audience of one, he eventually developed the freedom to construct for an audience of many not only two-sided arguments but also astutely drawn conclusions designed to win the day. It is as if in reacting to Vettori, Machiavelli burgeoned into a more potent thinker and writer.

Also fascinating is the interplay between Guicciardini and Machiavelli. Neither uses the word *compare* in addressing the other, but from Guicciardini's salutation "*Machiavello carissimo*" (Letter 269) to Machiavelli's "*Cazzus!*" (Letter 274), their "comradeship"—even their sense of being confederates and accomplices in practical jokes—is evident. Guicciardini at one point toys with the notion of the proper salutation between them. Simultaneously, he reminds us that if no man is a hero to his valet, he may be even less so to his buddy. Guicciardini, alert to irony, writes, "My very dear Machiavelli [*Machiavello carissimo*]. . . . I have to tell you that if you honor letters addressed to me with 'illustrious,' I shall honor yours with 'excellency,' and thus, with these reciprocal titles we shall renew each other's pleasure, but it will be turned into mourning when we all find ourselves, I say all of us, with our hands full of flies at the end. So make up your mind about titles, measuring mine against those you would enjoy having given to you" (Letter 293). The letter is signed, "[a]s a brother." Although this is a formulaic closing to a playful letter, it does not grate here; rather, it authenticates the notion of their mutual respect and friendship.

Aware of their difference in class, Machiavelli nevertheless was not intimidated by Guicciardini's offices (governor of Modena and Reggio and, in 1524, president of Romagna) or by his aristocratic connections. The two established their rapport because of mutual regard for each other's intellect. Guicciardini was a perceptive admirer of Machiavelli's *Mandragola*. It is not surprising, then, that their letters are marked by playful wit. When Machiavelli was on the outs with the Medici after the fall of the Florentine Republic in 1513, he certainly needed the company of such a roguish spirit. Unsure of where his next source of income might come from, and commissioned by the Medici to write a history in which their family would figure large in the narrative though small in his respect, Machiavelli was beset by tension and frustration. He must have been grateful for Guicciardini's intelligent and responsive understanding. This aspect of the relationship encouraged a type of empathy that was no less important than Vettori's to Machiavelli's development as a thinker and a writer. The equal measure of sport also fired Machiavelli's imagination.

An example of Guicciardini and Machiavelli's interplay illuminates their relationship. In the summer of 1525, at Guicciardini's request, Machiavelli examined a rural property that his friend had bought sight unseen. Machiavelli's "report" was not enthusiastic (Letter 292). Piqued at his apparent blunder, Guicciardini wrote back using the persona of the farmhouse. "She" writes that she is a solid, straightforward, blunt person: "since I was born and raised in these solitary mountains, I do not have so much eloquence that it might give me courage to cure you of this maliciousness." Machiavelli is evidently unable to appreciate her true qualities because he has become too accustomed of late to consorting with meretricious women such as the actress Barbera, "who strives, as does her kind, to please everyone and seeks rather to seem than to be." Instead, Machiavelli "ought to have remembered that it was rash of you to make a judgment in one moment and that things are to be judged not by their surface but by their substance" (Letter 294). In its own right, this is a clever letter. Machiavelli must have winced at seeing his relationship with Barbera described in this way. Despite the usual run of amorous apprehension, Machiavelli treated Barbera with laudable concern and compassion. Nevertheless, he surely took delight and not umbrage in having his own remark in the last paragraph of *The Prince* (chapter eighteen) and a phrase echoed by *Messer* Nicia in *La Mandragola* (V, 2) used against him.

THE SELF-CONSCIOUS MACHIAVELLI

A significant result of Machiavelli's successful vying with Vettori and Guicciardini is his conscious creation of a self that he gradually reveals to them and to us. For this self-conscious Machiavelli to emerge clearly, we must first be aware of his paramount concern for language. It is, after all, the vehicle through which he perfects his conception of himself and projects it to us. An examination of the letters Machiavelli wrote shows that he writes with a heavy hand. In this urgency is evident the imperative he feels both to express his ideas accurately and to convey their thinker deftly. Machiavelli's preoccupation with language began early in his political career, shortly over one year after he was in the Florentine chancellery. In Letter 11, written in early October 1499, he upbraids his counterpart in the chancellery of Lucca for not realizing that chancellery secretaries are mouthpieces (*la lingua Loro*) for their governments. Defining the nature of their careers in terms of language (*lingua*), Machiavelli reminds his fellow secretary that their statements must precisely reflect their governments' positions on every occasion. Machiavelli is clearly aware that one's use of language can manipulate another person's reaction to an idea: "since you are [the government's] interpreter [*lingua,* in other words, its 'language,' 'tongue,' 'mouthpiece'], people will always believe that the Signoria is satisfied with what you say." When a secretary is wrong or when states are misinformed, as Machiavelli believes is true in this particular instance, the writer creates hatred of the government "through no fault of" the government. Thrusting deeper, Machiavelli continues: "Among the many considerations that show what a man is, none is more important than seeing either how easily he swallows what he is told or how carefully he invents what he wants to convince others of, so that every time he swallows what he ought not or invents badly what he wants to convince people of, he can be termed both thoughtless and reckless." This blend of loyalty and discourse was to be a linguistic hallmark of his career as a political figure and as a theorist.

There are several other private letters that substantiate how crucial the issue of language was to Machiavelli. For example, while in Rome, on 21 November 1503 (Letter 85), he wrote a scathing letter to a member of the Florentine Signoria, Agnolo Tucci. The latter was furious that a prompt reply had not been made to the Signoria's requests for information on the direction papal policy might take concerning events in Romagna. Machiavelli dismisses Tucci's impatience by saying, "Although all these very same things have already been written in official correspondence to me and have been answered so extensively that you can consult what has been written, nevertheless, not again to fail in my duty to you, I shall reiterate these items. And I shall write in the vernacular [*parlerò in vulgare*], although I may have written in Latin [*in gramatica*] to the chancellery, even though I do not think I did." Machiavelli puts Tucci down in two ways. First, he promises to express in simpler vernacular language what he had already reported to the Signoria. Second, although he had not previously written the Signoria in Latin, he is insinuating that Tucci would never have understood any intelligence that he might have written in that language. Machiavelli is keenly aware of this letter's audience, one that stretches beyond Agnolo Tucci. Because a letter was often considered more an item of public property then than it is today, Machiavelli knew eyes other than the addressee's would read it; he may even secretly have wanted this. Hence, despite containing the quality of information Tucci sought, the letter was probably intended to be a humiliating one to receive. The letter is evidence to us that Machiavelli, even in the early stages of his career, was confident in his ability to handle language adroitly. He knew how to force a reader, even unwillingly, into being massaged by the message.[6]

This involvement of the reader as much in the expression of an idea as in its content is fundamental to our portrait of Machiavelli. It is a stylistic device that is deployed triumphantly in his ribald letter of 8 December 1509 (Letter 178) to Luigi Guicciardini, Francesco's oldest brother and author of *The Sack of Rome*, which describes the sad events just prior to Machiavelli's death in 1527. Containing one of several *novelle* embedded in this correspondence, this letter narrates an encounter with a whore while the forty-year-old Machiavelli was on a diplomatic mission in Verona. The old woman who washes his shirts lures him into a dark corner of her shop on the pretext of selling him a new shirt. She takes him by the hand and leads him over to a whore lurking in the shadows, saying, "[T]his is the shirt I wanted to sell you, but I'd like you to try it on [*la proviate*] first and pay for it afterwards." Machiavelli conflates the feminine genders of the whore and the shirt as antecedents for "it" (*la*) and gets some extra mileage out of the verb *provare,* which means "to test out" as well as "to try on." Machiavelli piles grotesquerie upon grotesquerie ("at the end of each eyebrow toward her eyes there was a nosegay of nits"), climaxing with the description, "I threw up all over her. Having thus repaid her in kind, I departed." This letter may be an account of an actual adventure; there are grounds, however, for taking it as a fabrication in the style and taste that produced "The Ugly Woman," painted by Machiavelli's Flemish contemporary Quentin Metsys. In iconographic terms, Machiavelli may even be toying with the notion of seizing opportunity by the forelock when he refers to her "tuft of hair, part white, part black . . . [on] the crown of her [bald] head." The literary antecedents for this short story range from verbal portraits in Jean de Meung's "La Vieille" to Chaucer's Alisoun, through Boccaccio, and on to Villon. Whatever its trappings, though, this letter exemplifies Machiavelli's use of language to delight and—perhaps—to instruct. Luigi Guicciardini was treated to a tour de force.

It is evident that for the letter-writing Machiavelli, whether or not his substance or its accoutrements are simple, the use of language shapes how he defines both himself and his career. He is assured, sometimes cocky, about his talent and proficiency. When he urges Giovanni Vernacci "to use a clear style with those whom you do business with so that whenever they get one of your letters they think, because your way of writing is so detailed, that you are there" (Letter 217), Machiavelli defines his fundamental conviction not only about how his nephew should write but also about how he seeks to write. We can measure the success of his desire by attention to a salient rhetorical strategy operative throughout his writing, regardless of its audience. The voice that Machiavelli draws on meticulously crafts a narrative shaped for the particular recipient. This ability is rooted in a procedure he defines in his mimetic response to Vettori's letter (Letter 223) describing the ambassador's routine in Rome. After Machiavelli reciprocally characterizes his typical day in San Casciano, he "get[s] the mold out of [his] brain and let[s] out the malice of [his] fate" and shifts into a sketch of his evening pursuits:

> When evening comes, I return home and enter my study; on the threshold I take off my workday clothes, covered with mud and dirt, and put on the garments of court and palace. Fitted out appropriately, I step inside the venerable

courts of the ancients, where, solicitously received by them, I nourish myself on that food that *alone* is mine and for which I was born; where I am unashamed to converse with them and to question them about the motives for their actions, and they, out of their human kindness, answer me. And for four hours at a time I feel no boredom, I forget all my troubles, I do not dread poverty, and I am not terrified by death. I absorb myself into them completely. (Letter 224)

Literally Machiavelli states, *"tutto mi trasferisco in loro,"* "I completely transfer myself into them." What he is saying seems clear, even if it is difficult to retain the resonances when rendering the Italian into English. He is giving himself over to the ancient writers; he is changing hands with them; he is transporting himself into them completely. In the previous paragraph Machiavelli has used the same verb *trasferire*—in the sense of "to go along," or "transportation"— specifically indicating the road to the inn nearby, so that he breaks his contact with ancient poets and initiates his interaction with those with whom he "slum[s] around." Thus, it is the active movement, the shift, the change that he is emphasizing: "I absorb myself into them completely." This process of incor- poration—literally, taking into his body—is an activity that defines Ma- chiavelli's unique ability as thinker and writer. Once he has absorbed the Other—the ancient writer, poet, statesman (or even petty despot)—Ma- chiavelli's own thinking and reflection can take over. As a writer, he must find the most acccurate means for converting thought or reflection into proper words. This procedure, enunciated in 1513, is reminiscent of the admonition concerning expression he made in 1499 to the chancellery secretary in Lucca.

This absorption process finds its way into much of what Machiavelli writes. Regardless of his content, he thinks as a creative writer would. For ex- ample, when the subject is clearly historical and political, he adheres to his practice of "absorption." In the midst of refining his thoughts about the Treaty of Orthez, agreed to in April 1513 by the French king Louis XII and the Spanish king Ferdinand the Catholic, Machiavelli writes to Vettori: "And be- cause I believe that the duty of a prudent man is constantly to consider what may harm him and to foresee problems in the distance—to aid the good and to thwart the evil in plenty of time—I have put myself in the pope's place and scrutinized in detail what I might now have to fear and what remedies I might use" (Letter 213). From the conceptual point of view, this passage is an important illustration of what Machiavelli means by a prudent leader with *virtù*. From the rhetorical point of view, this passage illustrates Machiavelli's tactic of impersonation. He dons the persona—he wears the actor's mask—so that he may more acutely feel and act as someone else might. It is the psycho- logical insight of this remark and its translation into practice that is a key to Machiavelli's effectiveness as a thinker and a writer.

Embedded in the topic sentences of the next two paragraphs of Letter 213 are the hypothetical clauses "were I the pope." These clauses are indicative of Machiavelli's systematic attempt to empathize with an opponent, to get inside that person's head so that he can "know," or be in a better position to predict, how that opponent may behave. Thus, Machiavelli believes that he can take counteracting measures. As far as the Treaty of Orthez is concerned, Machiavelli also wryly notes in the next paragraph, "[I]t could occur if France reached an agreement with England or with Spain—without me." This degree of empathy greatly sharpens Machiavelli's political analyses in these letters and in his major works.[7]

It is Machiavelli's talent for thinking as a creative writer that enables him to become absorbed completely into the Other, be it a historical personage, a mutual friend, or a literary character. On several occasions, he concocts narratives for the sheer delight of telling a story to Vettori or Guicciardini. Sometimes he is egged on by his correspondents. For example, on 18 January 1514 (Letter 228), Vettori recounts a visit paid him by a neighboring widow accompanied by her son and daughter. To Machiavelli, Vettori's straightforward account suggests the bare bones of a potentially vivid short story. Two cronies, Filippo Casavecchia and Giuliano Brancacci, are visiting Vettori, so he invites them all to stay for dinner. Because Vettori has "become almost a prisoner of this Costanza," his motives are transparent. In the broadest terms, Vettori describes an evening of widespread attempts at seduction: Vettori of the widow, Brancacci of her daughter, Costanza, and Casavecchia of her son. Machiavelli's imagination is piqued. He cannot resist an opportunity in his reply to spruce up Vettori's pedestrian account: "And when I meditate upon [your] story [*istoria*] . . . from beginning to end (which, had I not lost my notes, I would truly have included among the Annals of Modern Times), it seems to me as worthy a story for declaiming before a prince as anything I have heard about this year" (Letter 229). With gusto Machiavelli enthusiastically reshapes the *istoria* into a delightful, witty novella.

Stimulated by his success, three weeks later Machiavelli composes Letter 231, boldly proclaiming his form to be a novella. He begins: "I got a letter from you last week, and I have put off answering you until now because I wanted better to learn the truth about a yarn [*novella*] that I am about to tell you. . . . There has been some 'gentle' business, or rather, to call it by its proper name, some laughable metamorphosis—one worthy of being noted in the chronicles of old. And since I do not want anyone to take offense, I shall relate it to you in the guise of a fable." As he proceeds with his disguised story, his awareness of himself as narrator sharpens. He realizes that "the fable is inadequate, and this metaphor is no longer working." As if to draw back from this self-consciousness, he concludes his highly effective story, about a practical joke played in the context of a homosexual cruising incident, with the self-effacing aside to Vettori, "I expect that you have received this news from other hands, but I wanted to present it to you in fuller detail because it seemed to me I was honor-bound to do so." This statement is nonsense, since the "fuller detail" is motivated by a desire not to increase the number of precise details so as to churn out a more factual account but to parade his creative, narrative wares.

Practical jokes and narrative skill are also in play during an exchange of letters with Guicciardini, written while Machiavelli was at the Chapter General among the Minorite Friars at Carpi, affectionately known to these two anti-clerics as "the Republic of Clogs," in May 1521. Machiavelli relishes the joke because he enjoys the attempt to trick the friars. But this aspect is not nearly as important as the process of recreating the practical joke as narrative and then presenting it to Guicciardini for his delectation.

The correspondents with whom he exercises his narrative powers most regularly, Vettori and Guicciardini, are also those to whom he writes what often seems to us to be analogues of the position papers read in Washington at cabinet meetings during an international crisis. It is with them that he most frequently comments on the diplomatic options of popes, kings, and emperors. It is with them that he shares his political analysis and historical deductions. It cannot be emphasized too strongly that these essential characteristics are also rooted in Machiavelli's skill both at self-consciously absorbing and at translating what has been absorbed into effective language. A number of recurrent images, metaphors, and verbal echoes in the letters can be detected in the political writings (these are pointed out in the notes to this volume). In particular, Vettori and Guicciardini are correspondents against whom Machiavelli tested ideas. But his testing, different from what we might expect, was consistent with his need to "absorb." Machiavelli used Vettori and Guicciardini as sounding boards; they were good listeners. Rather than overtly dispute Machiavelli's points, they would phrase their reactions in the form of implied disagreement. Machiavelli, in turn, rather than modify his ideas because of their reactions, would absorb their viewpoint into his own and present it to the reader in a more representational form. Studying the publications of the last ten years of Machiavelli's life, Dionisotti draws attention to

> Machiavelli's passage from a personal discourse, in which the author is an actor or character on stage by himself, as in *The Prince* and *The Discourses*, to a representation of ideas and facts that the author promotes and directs from behind the scenes, participating only rarely, between one act and another, as in the proem to the individual books of the *Florentine Histories*. One can trace a dramatic development from monologue to dialogue, and from discourse to representation.[8]

When the letters to Vettori, in particular, are read as products of Machiavelli's absorption process, in which the writer's approach to his material has been transformed from "monologue" to "dialogue," it is clear that what Machiavelli learned was the ability to represent, rather than solely to present, thought. For example, Vettori's letter to Machiavelli of 12 July 1513 (Letter 216) exhibits some doubts about organizing "this world, and if not the world, at least this part here." The immediate "seems . . . very hard to organize in fancy," Vettori continues, "so that if it came to having to do it in fact I should think it was impossible." Such incredulity challenges Machiavelli's notion that he could absorb and digest ideas and then, thanks both to his "fancy" and to his ability with words, represent his conclusions for all to understand. Nevertheless, *The Prince, The Discourses, The Art of War,* and the *Florentine Histories* eloquently attest to Machiavelli's ability to meet that challenge.[9]

MACHIAVELLI IN CONTEXT

What a treasure these letters are! Their range is extraordinary. Not only are the subjects widely varied, but the language that the writers use to discuss these topics is also diverse. They provide a priceless, albeit unsystematic, first-hand account of a traumatic period in the history of both Italy and Western Europe. Our sense of history is immeasurably enhanced by having a listening post, as it were, on the intricate diplomatic maneuvers of condottieri (Cesare Borgia, Paolo Vitelli), popes (Alexander VI, Julius II, Leo X, Clement VII), and kings (Louis XII, Ferdinand the Catholic, Maximilian I, Charles V). As a commentary on this vast, busy, fascinating, passing scene, this correspondence is a valuable context in itself. Finally, these letters exist in another historical context, beyond the daily upheavals governed by people, places, and dates; they illuminate the broader context of upheavals in intellectual history. They offer the reader the opportunity to read between the lines and thereby to construct an intellectual, spiritual, and psychohistorical biography—almost an autobiography—of Machiavelli at least, if not of all the participants.

Taken together, these personal letters constitute a richly detailed and allusive body that introduces us to a valuable, highly charged intellectual milieu. They reflect the comments, thoughts, and considered opinions of people nurtured in humanistic disciplines. With hindsight, though, we see that the correspondents are approaching a turning point in western culture. Some isolated passages exhibit their sense of this significance, as well as their anxiety about it. In 1506 one of Machiavelli's correspondents bemoans the "ill fortune in these times" and compliments him for his chronicle poem *Decennale Primo,* because if Florentine readers "did not see this history, they would be compelled not to believe in what prosperity Italy was before, since it would seem impossible that in so few days our affairs should have fallen into such great ruin." He continues, "Although this causes me profound grief, yet the fear of worse afflicts me still more since it seems to me that the little that remains to us hastens toward that final ruin as toward a thing desired. Certainly, as far as human judgment can see, we cannot hope for anything but ill" (Letter 107). Machiavelli, too, is often pessimistic about his times: "I am aware that natural human shortcomings are at variance with my idea" (Letter 219). At the height of his despair he can see Florence as nothing more than "a magnet for all the world's pitchmen" (Letter 225). In fact, "there are nothing but crazies here; only a few are familiar with this world and are aware that whoever seeks to act according to others will accomplish nothing because no two men who think alike can be found" (Letter 227).

It might be helpful to think of these letters in terms of the figure-ground configuration that Gestalt psychology describes. These letters help us better to perceive the "figure" of humanists ambivalent about the "ground" of their cultural milieu. Machiavelli, despite his education and background, stands out from this humanist ground because of his perspicacity and the positions he takes. They are frequently at variance with those typically associated with his fellow humanists. For example, a member of the previous generation of humanists, Marsilio Ficino, can write to "his unique friend" Giovanni Cavalcanti as follows: "at present I do not really know what I want; it may be that I do not really want what I know and want that which I do not know."[10] Taken out of context, it might sound as if Ficino is prefiguring a mentality that some observers believe characterizes our era. But when Ficino closes his letter with the remark that "thanks should be given in all things to Him who, from His infinite goodness, converts all things to the good," we are less sure that these are the words of a twentieth-century writer.[11] Machiavelli, however, disputes such sanguine assumptions. Although the context is tinged with irony, the content is deadly serious when he writes to Guicciardini, "I was completely absorbed in imagining my style of preacher for Florence." He continues, "I am going to be as pigheaded about this idea as I am about my other ideas. . . . They would like a preacher who would teach them the way to paradise, and I should like to find one who would teach them the way to go to the Devil. Furthermore. . . . I believe that the following would be the true way to go to paradise: learn the way to Hell in order to steer clear of it" (Letter 270). A great rift in ethical theory has opened up during the forty-five years that have elapsed between the writing of these two letters. If God converts everything to the good, then there is hope in Ficino's world that evil can be eliminated from it. Machiavelli, in contrast, argues that no such eradication can exist in his world. In it we must know what evil is; only then can we find ways to live with it. Because evil will always be in mankind's heart, the good can only be achieved once the existence of evil is acknowledged.[12]

Machiavelli, then, is an imposing figure at the pivotal moment in our tradition when the gauntlet was first flung down to challenge the assumption that timeless truths existed, that they were discoverable, and that they could be implemented. As he enunciated his ideas on history, politics, literature, and society, however, he challenged the assumption that all measures of transcendent value are necessarily reconcilable. Familiarity with the context from which this correspondence emerges helps to demonstrate what prompted Machiavelli to overturn received, accepted opinion. Moreover, we are often in the midst of the "trial balloons" for his major political, historical, and literary writings. This context thereby furnishes us with an awareness of Machiavelli that significantly complements and qualifies his major published works. Because these are still open to interpretation, we have a valuable resource in this exchange of letters that permits us to consider the scope and range of ideas that fed into—and thus helped to mold—Machiavelli's thinking. A related benefit, of course, is our heightened sense of Machiavelli's human connections and their tonality.

In addition to supplementing our awareness of Machiavelli's intellectual milieu on the abstract and personal level, familiarity with this "trial balloon" context affords us a glimpse of the tactics he uses to confront the world of people and ideas. Insofar as Machiavelli thinks the way a creative writer would and is rightfully pleased with his narrative successes, it is because of his ability to absorb himself into the Other. We have seen how he utilizes this technique to absorb not only those writers whom he is reading but those people whose actions and thoughts he may be considering at any given moment. It matters not whether these are the princes or kings of an analytical text such as *The Prince* or *Discourses* or characters such as Ligurio and Friar Timoteo in *La Mandragola,* the result is a similar sense of heightened credibility. Once he is aware of how the Other thinks or feels, he creates a persona for the character so that he may think as does the character. The results of those thoughts then make their way from the persona into carefully crafted words. The aptness of this expression is the key to his eminence as a thinker and writer.

Machiavelli's expression is governed by what ostensibly is a kind of empathy. His empathic process is not, however, that of "putting yourself in another's place." As Elisabeth Young-Bruehl phrases the distinction, "Empathizing involves, rather, putting another person *in yourself,* becoming another person's habitat, without dissolving the person, without digesting the person. You are mentally pregnant, not with a potential life but with a person, indeed, a whole life, a person with her history. So the subject lives on in you and you can, as it were, hear her in this intimacy."[13]

Hence the value of Machiavelli's letters, particularly in the context of his friendships, is that they enable us to see the raw material for Machiavelli's process of becoming "mentally pregnant." In light of this revised understanding of empathy, or rather of his notion of "absorption," we see more clearly what Machiavelli is doing and we know him better. As he is able to absorb thinking, active figures and characters, so we can both read and "hear" the results of his absorption in the intimacy of having Machiavelli live on in us.

Machiavelli

AND HIS FRIENDS

LETTERS

1497-1498

Two men dominated Florentine life throughout 1497 and early 1498: Fra Girolamo Savonarola (1452–1498) and Charles VIII (1470–1498), the king of France. Savonarola, the Dominican reformer and preacher from Ferrara, had been recalled to Florence in 1490 by Lorenzo de' Medici because of his ability to preach rousing sermons; he became prior of San Marco in 1491. Savonarola devoted his career to simplifying religious practices, urging both clerics and the faithful to follow the moral rules in their daily activities and combating corruption within the Roman Catholic Church. In Charles VIII Savonarola saw someone with whom he might energize his adherents by playing on Florence's fear of France. Calling Charles a purifying *gladius Domini* (sword of God), Savonarola welcomed his 1494 expedition into Italy. The expedition soon led to the ousting of the Medici—Lorenzo's eldest son, Piero, had ruled the city since 1492—and the establishment of a new government in 1494 with a constitution inspired by Savonarola, one that was essentially operative throughout Machiavelli's career in Florentine politics. With the expulsion of Piero de' Medici, Savonarola's involvement in political issues increased. Because to most Florentines his dire predictions seemed to come true with the French invasion, his popular and political sway was extensive. The Florentines did not, however, cease the debauched practices he condemned.

During the Carnival season of February 1497, in response to the Florentines' excesses, Savonarola organized the first "Bonfire of Vanities." Savonarola's hymn-singing followers hurled into the fire the extravagances that they had gathered from the populace: dice, playing cards, cosmetics, hair switches, and pornographic pictures and books. The furor surrounding the friar was fed, during the remainder of 1497, by plague, famine, poverty, and a poor harvest.

The city, whether from expediency or conviction, seemed to divide itself into groups identified by their relation to Savonarola: the *Arrabbiati* (the "rabid" or "enraged" ones) were violently opposed to both the Medici and Savonarola and sought a republic along aristocratic lines; the *Bianchi* (the "whites") had no sympathy for Savonarola, but they advocated a popular form of government; the *Bigi* (the "greys") remained loyal to the Medici; the *Compagnacci* (the "naughty fellows") resisted Savonarola's interventions into their private lives; and the *Piagnoni* (the "mournful" or "wailing" fellows) formed Savonarola's party and regarded him as a prophet. The latter were also known as the *Frateschi* (the friar's fellows). Florence was in turmoil.

The papacy viewed the Florentine situation with deepening alarm. Rodrigo Borgia, Pope Alexander VI (c. 1431–1503), saw in Savonarola a double enemy: internally, he jeopardized Rome's control of the church; externally, his advocacy of French ascendancy in Italy threatened the pope's maneuvers to carve out his own power base by upsetting the balance of power that Lorenzo de' Medici had recently created. The pope tried to stifle Savonarola by summoning him to Rome—Savonarola spurned the order—and by forbidding him to preach—Savonarola found a fiery surrogate in Fra Domenico Bonvicini da Pescia. The pope also sought to join the congregation of Dominicans in Tuscany with the one in Lombardy, thereby robbing Savonarola of his independent status. Finally, in the early summer of 1497, Alexander VI issued a bull of excommunication.

Meanwhile, Florence, believing its interests needed more effective protection in Rome, sent Ricciardo Becchi as ambassador in March 1497. Since the Signoria still felt that local civil order could better be preserved by backing Savonarola, Becchi, who was also a member of the Papal Curia, was in an unenviable position. He was in Rome on behalf of the Signoria, yet he was obliged to support someone whom he considered detrimental to Florentine interests. Furthermore, during the same month, the Florentine Council of Ten thought it prudent to add its own secretary, Alessandro Bracci (Braccesi), to reinforce Becchi's pleading in Rome. In so doing, the Signoria was merely biding its time before the arrival of the appropriate moment for ridding the city of Savonarola. Thus, the point rapidly approached when the friar, instead of being prized as a prophet, would be scorned as a scapegoat. Florence was frustrated on two fronts. On the one hand, it could not readily obtain French support for its plans to solidify its control in Tuscany, plans centered on Charles VIII's return of Pisa, which Piero de' Medici had ceded to him to dissuade him from entering Florence in 1494. On the other hand, it could not resolve its domestic differences. Florence pinned these failures on Savonarola.

Opposition to Savonarola, crystallizing in the spring of 1498, soon contributed to Machiavelli's appointment to political office. Another "Bonfire of Vanities" occurred during the Lenten season. Then a new Signoria was elected on 1 March 1498, and Savonarola had good reason to suspect that it was against him, even though it was still writing to Rome on his behalf. When Savonarola began agitating for a general Church Council to investigate the pope's activities, the pope countered by ordering Florentine church officials to ban Savonarola from preaching in the Cathedral of Santa Reparata (known today as Santa Maria del Fiore—the Duomo). In a papal brief he threatened an interdict on all of Florence unless the Signoria sent the friar to Rome or detained him in a secure place. As a gesture of compliance, Savonarola ceased preaching in March, but he increased his efforts to persuade international leaders to intervene and to depose the pope. In Florence an ordeal by fire to establish the veracity of Savonarola's teachings and pronouncements was proposed; though clerical volunteers were readily found for both sides, the contest was canceled in early April. Several days later, a mob attacked the *Piagnoni* as they tried to enter the cathedral and stormed Savonarola's convent of San Marco. Savonarola and Fra Domenico were jailed, tortured, tried, hanged, and immolated on a pyre erected in the Piazza della Signoria on 23 May.

Machiavelli's ambivalence about Savonarola can be seen throughout his life. Although there is no evidence that Machiavelli supported the friar's ethical and religious teachings, it is clear that he admired his political acumen and reforms. Because Savonarola failed to add muscle to his prophecies, Machiavelli groups him with the "unarmed prophets" in the sixth chapter of *The Prince*: he "was destroyed together with his institutions when the mob ceased to believe in him and he did not have the means to be able to hold on firmly to those who had believed or to make the skeptics believe" (Atkinson, p. 151). In 1498, in the third letter we have from his hand, Machiavelli dismisses Savonarola because "he acts in accordance with the times and colors his lies accordingly," a judgment that Ridolfi decries as "unworthy" (*Life*, p. 9; *Vita 7*, p. 16).

Machiavelli remained constantly wary of the church's activities in Italy. Its worldliness diluted the exemplary character of an institution that he believed could foster the virtues that a state could utilize to bind a society together. Despite his wariness, the earliest documents in his hand that we have show Machiavelli's involvement in religious matters. Although the first two letters ascribed to Machiavelli, dating from December 1497, present some problems of attribution, they indicate that within his own family, at least, he was regarded as someone with persuasive rhetorical abilities. The extract from a draft, the first document dated 1 December, is in Latin and its object is special pleading. The addressee seems to be an ecclesiastic; some think it is a Spanish cardinal in Perugia, Giovanni Lopez, the addressee of the letter written the next day. Although this second document comes from the Machiavelli family as a group, handwriting analysis substantiates that it was written by the young Niccolò. The person who signed it, however, was not Niccolò Machiavelli but rather Niccolò di Bernardo di Jacopo Machiavelli, who was born in 1472 and worked in a bank in Rome (see Martelli, *L'altro Niccolò*, pp. 44–52, who also mentions a Piero di Francesco Machiavelli, the Piero of the signature block). The issue here clearly concerns support for the claims of the Machiavelli family against the powerful Pazzi family; the hard-pressed clan is trying to retain the benefice and endowment attached to the parish church of Santa Maria di Fagna, a town about twelve miles northeast of Florence in the

Mugello region. With the help of a letter from the Signoria to Cardinal Lopez, Machiavelli's kin successfully pleaded their case. This would seem to be the situation behind the first two documents. Ridolfi, however, disagrees with the idea that the first document is written to Cardinal Lopez; he argues that the tone and style are inappropriate for someone of that rank (*Life,* p. 262, n. 7; *Vita 7,* p. 434, n. 9). Ridolfi furthermore doubts that this draft concerns the living from the church in the Mugello. Gaeta offers another suggestion for the issue addressed in the first document (p. 63, n. 1). He wonders if it might not concern Francesco Machiavelli, the above-named Niccolò's brother. Francesco was studying for the clergy in Modena and was originally appointed to the parish church in Fagna before the Pazzi family contested his appointment.

Politics soon superseded these religious matters, this time through a set of circumstances related to Savonarola's waning career. Machiavelli heard two of the friar's sermons on 2 and 3 March 1498. By the end of May, with Savonarola now dead, Florence was in chaos. Machiavelli suddenly burst on the political scene within three weeks, amid riots throughout the city. Despite the fact that we know of no previous political experience on his part, the Great Council appointed Machiavelli Second Chancellor of the Republic of Florence on 19 June 1498. It may well be that his humanist training, in which he demonstrated great skill, impressed Marcello Virgilio Adriani, First Chancellor of Florence and a former professor of humanistic studies in Florence. Ironically, Machiavelli replaced the same Alessandro Bracci (Braccesi) who had been in Rome one year earlier arguing on Savonarola's behalf; Bracci's pro-Savonarola sympathies now led to his being ousted from the chancellery. Chancelleries were responsible for implementing, not formulating, decisions about domestic and foreign affairs; a rather permanent kind of civil service, they were run by six secretaries. On 14 July Machiavelli was also made the Secretary of the Ten of War (known sometimes as the *Dieci di Balìa* and sometimes as the *Dieci di Libertà e Pace*).

❖   LETTER 1

Extract from a Draft[1]

Florence, 1 December 1497

And with good reason: though I have received many letters from you, none [. . .][2] those who know might be able to infer that either our talent is very small or [. . .] unformed by nature or by talent, of which God and the truth is my witness, that the good deeds of friends and of those who have deser[. . .] well of me [. . .] For I know your zeal and effort in our behalf, without which our case and the others that remain [. . .] for which reasons you were not able to satisfy [. . .] character is closely examined, it will give satisfaction. Yet, beset by ill health, I did not have the strength to write back to you. Now, however, with my health recovered, I shall write nothing other than to encourage, beg, and pray that you do not cease until our efforts have a happy outcome. Toward this end I ask that you show your might, and use all your might; for if we, mere pygmies, are attacking giants, a much greater victory is in store for us than for them. For them, inasmuch as it is base to compete, so it will be a very base thing to give in; we, on the other hand, shall consider it not so ignominious a thing to be beaten, as it is honorable to have competed, especially having a competitor at whose nod everything is done immediately. Wherefore, whatever outcome Fortune may reserve for us, we shall not regret having failed in such endeavors. Farewell. Florence, December 1.

❖ LETTER 2
The Machiavellis to Cardinal Giovanni Lopez
Florence, 2 December 1497

As we know from experience, all the goods that mankind possesses in this world often, indeed always, proceed from two donors: first, from God, the just distributor of everything; second, either from our forebears through the laws of inheritance, or from our friends through gifts, or from possibilities of gain offered to us—as it is with merchants and their loyal agents. The worthier the donor, the more valuable the possessions. So, since Your Right Reverend Lordship has[1] by a pontifical annulment deprived us of our rights to a property in Fagna that we used to recognize as ours through our venerable ancestors,[2] now an opportunity presents itself both for Your Right Reverend Lordship to prove your human kindness and generosity—even more, your compassion—toward us, your most devoted sons, and for us to recognize our rights as stemming from a much worthier donor than were our forebears. And surely nothing is worthier of Your Right Revered Lordship than to give quite generously, when you could take away, especially to those who seek to preserve Your Lordship's honor and interest no less than their own, to those, furthermore, who in no wise deem themselves inferior—either in nobility, in mien, or in wealth—to those who contrive, or hope, or indeed assert without qualification that they have been named completely by Your Right Reverend Lordship as the proprietors. Whoever might wish to weigh our house with the house of the Pazzi on an accurate scale, if he determined the two to be equal in everything else, will determine ours far superior in generosity and *virtù* of spirit.

So, it is as suppliants that we pray Your Right Reverend Lordship not to permit us to see men less worthy than ourselves, men whom we may rightly consider to be our enemies, bedecked with our spoils and boasting ignominiously of such a victory. In this matter, be pleased, Our Most Reverend Lordship, with the same emolument that you expect of them, to allow our house to be as adorned with such honor as we judge your free concession of this property to us to be. And conversely, please do not mark us with such ignominy as to deprive us of what we have done our utmost through such enterprise to preserve until now. And truly, since unless your clemency[3] intervenes it will be

the greatest disgrace for us to lose it, we shall strive by every means available—to the prejudice of others—to recover it. But we trust in Your Right
Reverend Lordship's human kindness, as Your Reverence's good friend Messer
Francesco knows, we have always trusted; he is the person we have made our
petitioner in this matter and he is the person to whom we have given complete freedom to follow through in this cause. *May you continue in good health.
May you live forever. Florence, 4 December.*

> *Your Most Reverend Excellency's devoted sons.*
> *The Machiavelli family,*
> Pietro, Niccolò, and the entire family of Machiavelli,
> *Citizens of Florence*

❖ LETTER 3
Niccolò Machiavelli to Ricciardo Becchi
Florence, 9 March 1498[1]

In order to give you,[2] in accordance with your wishes, a full account of
matters here concerning the friar, you should know that once the two sermons (of which you have already received copies[3]) were given, he preached
on the Sunday of Carnival[4]; after speaking at length, he invited his entire audience to take communion on the Carnival day in San Marco, and he said he
would pray to God that if what he had predicted did not come from Him, He
might display a very clear sign of it. He did this, some say, in order to unite his
partisans and to strengthen their defense of him, fearing lest the new Signoria,
already chosen but not yet made public, might be against him. Once the
membership of the Signoria was made public last Monday, about whom you
must have been completely apprised, because he believed it was more than
two-thirds hostile to him, and the pope had sent a brief[5] that summoned him,
under pain of interdiction, and he feared that the Signoria would not actually
obey him, he decided—either because of his own choice or because of a
warning from others—to leave off preaching in Santa Reparata and go to San
Marco. Therefore, on the Thursday morning that the Signoria took office, he
said—still in Santa Reparata—that, in order to avoid strife and to preserve the
honor of God, he would withdraw and that the men should come and hear
him at San Marco and the women should go to Fra Domenico[6] at San
Lorenzo. Now that our friar was in his own house, if you had heard with what
boldness he began preaching and with how much he continued, it would be
an object of no little admiration. Because, fearing greatly for himself and believing that the new Signoria would not be reluctant to injure him—and having decided that quite a few citizens should be brought down with him—he
started in with great scenes of horror; with explanations that were quite effective to those not examining them closely, he pointed out that his adherents
were excellent people while his opponents were most villainous, and he drew

on every expression that might weaken his opponents' party and fortify his own. Because I was there, I shall briefly relate some of these matters.

The text of his first sermon at San Marco was this passage from Exodus[7]: "But the more they oppressed them, the more they were multiplied, and increased." Before he began explicating this passage, he showed why he had withdrawn and said, "When it comes to action, prudence is right-reason."[8] Then he said that all mankind had had and continues to have an end, but that it differs: for Christians, this end is Christ; for others, past and present, their end has been and continues to be something else, depending upon their religious sects. Since we who are Christians tend toward this end which is Christ, we ought to preserve His honor with the utmost prudence and regard for the times; and whenever the times call upon us to imperil our lives for Him, to do so; and whenever it is time for a man to go into hiding, to do so, as we read about Christ and about St. Paul. And so he added we ought to do, and so we have done; therefore, when it came time to rise up against violence, we have done so, as we did on Ascension Day,[9] because the honor of God and the times required it. Now when the honor of God demands that we give in to wrath, we have given in. After he had given this short address, he delineated two ranks: one which soldiered under God, that is, himself and his adherents; the other, under the Devil, that is, his adversaries. After he had spoken about this subject at length, he started in on an explanation of the passage from Exodus mentioned above and said that through suffering good people grow in two ways: in spirit and in number: in spirit, because people are more united when faced with adversity and become stronger by being near their activating power, in the same way that water heats up the closer it is to fire because it is closer to its activating power. They also grow in number because there are three types of human beings: namely, the good—they are those who follow me; the wicked and the obstinate—they are the adversaries; and there is another type of person, the intemperate—given to pleasure—neither obstinate about doing evil nor inclined toward doing good, because they cannot distinguish one from the other. But whenever some actual disagreement arises between the good and the wicked, people recognize the malice of the evil and the integrity of the good, *because opposites are more evident when placed near one another;* people frequent the former and shun the latter because everyone naturally shuns evil and willingly follows good. Therefore, during adversity the evil diminish and the good multiply; *and so the greater, . . . etc.* I am telling you about this briefly because the brevity of a letter does not call for a lengthy account. After he had digressed as is his wont, in order to weaken his adversaries further and to provide a bridge to his next sermon, he continued by pointing out that our dissension might cause a tyrant to rise up who would bring down our houses and lay waste to our land. This did not contradict what he had already said, that Florence should prosper and be dominant in Italy because it would soon come about that [the tyrant] would be driven out of Italy. And with this he finished his sermon.

The next morning, still expounding Exodus and coming to that passage where it says that Moses slew an Egyptian,[10] he said that the Egyptian represented evil-doers and Moses the preacher who slew them by exposing their vices. Then he said, "O Egyptian, I want to stab you." And it was your books, O priests, whose pages he leafed through, treating you in such a way that not even dogs would have eaten any of it. Then he added—and this is what he was driving at—that he wanted to give the Egyptian another stab wound, a big one. He said that God had told him that there was someone in Florence who sought to make himself a tyrant, and he was engaged in dealings and schemes in order to succeed, and that the desire to drive out the friar, to excommunicate the friar, and to persecute the friar meant nothing else than to seek to create a tyrant, and that the laws ought to be obeyed. And he made so much of this that later that day people speculated publicly about someone who is about as close to being a tyrant as you are to Heaven. Afterward, since the Signoria had written to the pope in his behalf[11] and he realized that he no longer needed to be afraid of his adversaries in Florence, instead of trying, as he once had, solely to unite his party through hatred of his adversaries and through frightening them with the word "tyrant," he has changed coats—now that he understands that he no longer needs to act in this way. So, he urges them to the union that was initiated, and he no longer mentions either the tyrant or the wickedness of the people; he seeks to set all of them at odds with the Supreme Pontiff and, turning toward him and his attacks, says of the pope what could be said of the wickedest person you might imagine. Thus, in my judgment, he acts in accordance with the times and colors his lies accordingly.

Now, as for what the common people are saying and what men hope or fear, I shall leave that up to you who are a judicious man to determine; you can determine these matters better than I can inasmuch as you are fully aware of our temperament, the nature of the times, and, because you are there [in Rome], the pontiff's state of mind. Only this I ask of you: if reading my letter has not been too much trouble for you, then do not consider it too much trouble to tell me in your reply what judgment you make about the condition of the times and the people's minds concerning our affairs. *Farewell.*

> *Dated Florence, 9 March 1497[8].*
> *Yours*
> Niccolò di M. Bernardo Machiavelli

L E T T E R S

1499

According to the surviving evidence, Machiavelli's work as chancellor and secretary to the Ten of War in the early part of 1499 was primarily centered on Pisa and its restoration to Florentine control. The documents indicate Machiavelli's attempts to keep the Florentine commissioner general, Pier Francesco Tosinghi, who was camped near Pisa, abreast of diplomatic maneuvers that might affect the outcome of the campaign against the city.

Pisa had been an important conquest: in 1406 Florence took it over, along with the sheltered harbor of Porto Pisano. Florence thus obtained a gateway to the sea for its foreign trade, but at a price. The delta area was subject to shoals and silting (farther south, Livorno, an attractive alternative for a port because it was not near the Arno's mouth, was purchased from Genoa in 1421). Yet the broad valley from Florence through Pisa to the Mediterranean considerably facilitated trade out of Florence. After Charles VIII entered Italy in 1494, he guaranteed Pisa's freedom in an effort to make Florence more dependent on him. Pisa promptly revolted against Florentine control in 1495. Because this conflict with Florence lasted until Pisa's unconditional surrender in 1509, it had long-term ramifications for both Florence and Machiavelli. The war was a severe drain on the Florentine treasury and its international prestige; furthermore, it placed the city squarely in France's orbit, thereby contributing to the ultimate downfall of the republican regime that Machiavelli was serving.

Florence's preoccupation with Pisa offered Machiavelli a chance both to write one of his earliest known works, *Discorso fatto al magistrato dei dieci sopra le cose di Pisa* (A discourse made to the magistracy of the Ten on the affairs of Pisa), in 1499, and to observe how undependable mercenaries were, an issue he espoused throughout his political career. Meanwhile, the letters continued. Letter 3 to Becchi and the next three to Pier Francesco Tosinghi make it clear that both of these highly placed political figures valued Machiavelli's analytical skills even at this early stage in his career. As a member of the Ten in 1497, Tosinghi had secretly worked to get the Duke of Milan, Ludovico "Il Moro" Sforza, on Florence's side against France and to support Florence's war with Pisa. Tosinghi had a long career of service to Florence: he became the gonfalonier of justice and ambassador to France in 1500, a commissioner in the continuing war against Pisa in 1503, a member of the Ten in 1502 and 1505, and ambassador to Rome in 1510.

Pisa was also a focal point for those who sought to maintain or to upset the delicate balance of power on the Italian peninsula. Ludovico Sforza favored Florence's efforts to regain Pisa because he feared that Venice, were it to gain a foothold in Tuscany from the military support it was providing Pisa, would be in a better position to challenge him. Early in April 1499, the Duke of Ferrara, Ercole d'Este (1431–1505), negotiated a peace that put Pisa under Florence's control but allowed the city to keep its fortresses, to trade freely, and to elect its own government. The Venetians agreed to withdraw their troops, and Florence agreed to pay Venice an indemnity.

By June, however, war had broken out again. In the previous June, Florence had hired Paolo Vitelli, a famous condottiere whose power base was Città di Castello, to lead the war against Pisa. Vitelli's reluctance to initiate a series of actions resulted in Florence's suspecting him of double-dealing. On 10 August his troops captured the Pisan stronghold, the Rocca di Stampace, and demoralized the Pisan forces. When he failed to send in support troops for an attack that everyone thought would have been victorious, Florence suspected treachery. The Florentine commissioners at Pisa imprisoned Vitelli; he was returned to Florence, tortured, tried, and beheaded on 1 October.

Machiavelli's earliest missions for Florence concerned negotiations with Jacopo d'Appiano, the ruler of Piombino, and Caterina Sforza (1462/3–1509), Countess of Imola and Forlì and the illegitimate niece of Ludovico Sforza, over disputes about the conduct of military affairs. These missions are alluded to in the letters from his faithful chancellery assistant, Biagio Buonaccorsi (1472–1525). He and Machiavelli were friends before they entered the Second Chancellery on the very same day. Throughout these letters Biagio demonstrates his concern for Machiavelli. Despite the fact that their careers are intimately linked, even to the point of their being dismissed from office simultaneously on the return of the Medici in November 1512, Biagio's feelings about Machiavelli remain ambivalent. On the one hand, we can note distinct envy; on the other, there is a steadfast effort, as late as the early 1520s, to defend Machiavelli from what Biagio deems to be unjust attacks aimed at his writings. Biagio is the typical worrywart. Because Machiavelli was so frequently out of Florence on diplomatic missions, Biagio set himself up as his protector at home. He prided himself on his practical knowledge of affairs and his awareness of petty power grabs, yet he also fancied himself a man of letters. For all his pride in his political observations, as Gaeta points out (p. 15), his political convictions, like those of the Vicar of Bray, followed those of his patron, Antonio della Valle, who got both Biagio and Machiavelli their jobs in the Second Chancellery in 1498.

In addition to della Valle, another significant figure in Machiavelli's career, one enmeshed in the complex web of personal and political relations in Florence, was the man whom Antonio della Valle assisted in the First Chancellery: Marcello Virgilio di Adriano Berti, more commonly known as Marcello Virgilio Adriani (1464–1521). Adriani was both a humanist, studying with Cristoforo Landino and Poliziano, and the head of the First Chancellery from 1498 until 1521. From 1497 until 1502 he taught at the university; it is possible that at some point Machiavelli may even have studied with him. Though he was responsible for Machiavelli's appointment to the Second Chancellery, he was temperamentally quite different from Machiavelli. According to Ridolfi, "The solemn and grave Adriani could not have been at his ease with his wild and womanizing young colleague, who lived and wrote in the vulgar tongue, to the great scandal of Adriani's academic gravity" (*Life*, p. 19; *Vita 7*, p. 32). It is not surprising, therefore, that the tone of Adriani's letters to Machiavelli is rather aloof.

✤ LETTER 4
Niccolò Machiavelli to Pier Francesco Tosinghi
Florence, 29 April 1499

To the Magnificent Pier Francesco,
Commissioner General in the Field at Pisa, with His Greatest Respect.
At the Bridge of Hera.
A copy of the dispatches in several letters from Milan,
received by way of the ambassador of Milan residing in Venice.
First, from a letter of the thirteenth:

That the Venetians have appointed as naval commander the procurator Messer Antonio Grimani,[1] who has offered to provide the Venetian Signoria[2] with twenty thousand of his own ducats, expecting thereby to become doge; that they proposed to commission forty to fifty light galleys, twenty-two heavy galleys, and eighteen fully rigged ships; that another rapid brig arrived from the Levant, making it known that the sultan of the Turks was pressing for their fleet to be commissioned, which would be one hundred and fifty ships, and that it will head for Syria; but, since it has to pass by Cyprus, the Venetian Signoria wanted to send its fleet there so that it would not be asked to provide ports; and that because of this trouble with the sultan [of the Turks],[3] the Venetians were not thinking at all about sending any money to the king of

France and that they had forgotten the affairs of Pisa.

That the doge, after the agreement with Pisa[4] was concluded, had kept showing a greater inclination toward the ambassador to the duke[5] of Milan; that it was incumbent upon everybody to try and preserve this peace and to keep the people from the other side of the Alps out of Italy; that the king of France was suffering badly from the gout, and those troops he planned to send into Italy were obliged to go in the direction of Burgundy because he heard that the archduke[6] wanted to support his father's wishes; and that, if the aforementioned does not go [into Italy], the Venetians will have an excuse not to hand one hundred thousand ducats over to him, especially since they need it themselves.

That people are talking about the pope[7] in a most insulting manner.

That King Frederick[8] has had a male child and everyone was delighted about it.

From a letter of the twenty-fifth:

That every day people notice an increase in the Venetians' willingness to comply with the arbitration.[9]

That fear of the sultan was also increasing, since they already have him at their borders, and that in addition to the fleet they are fortifying Cyprus, Corfu, and the cities they possess in Apulia[10]; and it is considered that, even if the sultan does not attack the Venetians, they are nonetheless obliged to keep on with their expenditures in order not to be at his mercy.

That the Venetians had ordered two ambassadors to France, not so much, as people assume, to replace those who are recalled as to justify, under the pretext of the sultan, their not paying the money and to convince His Majesty that at this point he must attend to matters other than Italian ones; and they believe that it is better to behave in this way than openly to deny him transit.

That a representative of the prefect[11] had arrived in Venice to arrange matters for him with its Signoria concerning three hundred men at arms and that this same man had said that the Venetian Signoria had promised in its pact with the king of France to supply fifteen hundred men at arms until the end of the war: namely, all those of Prefect Orsini; and that he had not yet received a reply.

That the duke of Milan has written to Genoa and other cities along the way that, if the Pisans turn up on their way to France, they should be sent there to him because he wants to stop them and to have them at his disposal.

That His Excellency is more keen than ever to benefit this city and that, if he now recalls his troops, he is doing so to comply with the arbitration, but that, should we need him, he would not fail us.

That the duke has been informed that the alliance between the king of France and the Swiss provides that the king is to give them eighty thousand ducats a year and artillery whenever they may so require and that he must come to their aid whenever they might be attacked; that the Swiss are committed to attacking his enemies, specifically the duke of Milan, whenever they may be requested.

Magnificent One, I send you these dispatches for the gratification of Your Magnificence, to whom I send my regards as always.

> *29 April '99*
> *Most Devoted to Your Magnificent Excellency*
> *Niccolò Machiavelli, Sec.*

❖ LETTER 5
Niccolò Machiavelli to Pier Francesco Tosinghi
Florence, 5 June 1499

To the Magnificent Pier Francesco Tosinghi,
Commissioner General in the Field at Pisa and with His Greatest Respect.

Magnificent One, etc. Several days ago the duke of Milan wrote to the Florentine Signoria that he wanted no longer to stay in the dark with you, and therefore he was willing to commit himself if you would too; he requested that you pledge that every time he needed your help, you would be obliged to supply him with three hundred men at arms and two thousand foot soldiers; and that you should let him know what you wanted from him for recapturing Pisa. After some consultation, your Signoria replied that once he had in fact made you freely master of Pisa, you would commit yourself to whatever he demanded; but since the matter stood in such a way that that was unlikely to happen, it was deemed both dangerous to clarify their position with respect to French matters and useless for His Lordship; therefore, they entrusted him with finding a means whereby His Excellency might make himself secure and our government might not be endangered. This response did not at all satisfy His Lordship and he answered our emissaries quite angrily. For this reason our Signoria thought it best to send a special envoy to His Excellency in order better to justify themselves to His Lordship; they sent Ser Antonio da Colle,[1] whom they recalled from Siena and who will depart the day after tomorrow.

That is all there is for now of any importance. Each day we get fresh news about the sultan and some believe that this time he is headed for Sicily; it is true that he has made such an effort both on land and on sea that everyone is staying on the alert. The duke of Milan fears the situation in France still more than anything else, and, since it has been quite a while since any dispatches from France have arrived, we are afraid that the duke of Milan may have intercepted them.

If I have not written you as regularly as I would have liked to, the reason has been my work load and also that nothing has come except the normal kind of dispatches. There is nothing left for me but to send my regards to Your Magnificence.

> *5 June 99*
> *Yours,*
> *Niccolò Machiavelli, Sec.*

❖ LETTER 6

Niccolò Machiavelli to Pier Francesco Tosinghi
Florence, 6 July 1499

To the Magnificent Commissioner Pier Francesco Tosinghi,
in the Military Camp against the Pisans, with His Greatest Respect.

Magnificent One. If I have put off writing to you, the reason has been my huge work load; you will please excuse me.

The state of your situation with respect to [the duke of] Milan is the following: Many days ago His Lordship requested that you declare yourselves his allies and pledge yourselves to supply him with 300 men at arms and 2,000 foot soldiers a month at any time that he might need them; in exchange, he would give you whatever was needed to recapture Pisa. Such a declaration did not seem prudent to the Signoria, yet it seemed dangerous to break off these negotiations *completely;* therefore, measures were taken to keep his hopes up and not to run any risk from France. For this reason Ser Antonio da Colle was sent to Milan. And so we remain still in this state of agitation. The duke is pressing you to declare yourselves; you avail yourselves of every opportunity to distance yourselves, since it appears dangerous for you.

The Signoria finds itself in the same difficulty concerning [the king of] France, because His Majesty urgently requests it to form an alliance with him under these terms: for as long as the Milanese campaign lasts, you would be obliged to supply him with five hundred lancers, and he would commit himself to supply you for a year with a thousand lancers for all your campaigns; he promises to get the Venetians and the pope committed to your defense. To which the usual reply was made, by pointing out that such a thing could not be done without there being manifest danger to us; thus we are temporizing with one and the other, making the best of our time.[1] If Pisa could be recovered in the meantime, God willing, then without endangering ourselves so much we might be able to declare ourselves, since we would not be so open to attack; or else, without having to fear being attacked, we could remain neutral and let others play for a while. People are convinced that, if the pope does not order this French fleet to interfere in our affairs in Pisa, there will be no obstacle to carrying out what we have desired.

These are the important matters that are going on right now and that are being negotiated by your ambassadors in France and Milan. In yesterday evening's public letter I wrote you about what dispatches there are from Venice.

I send you my regards.
From Florence, 6 July 1499
Yours,
Niccolò Machiavelli

❖ LETTER 7
Biagio Buonaccorsi[1] to Niccolò Machiavelli
Florence, 19 July 1499

To His Honored Niccolò Machiavelli,
Most Worthy Secretary of the Florentine Signoria.
In Forlì.

My very dear Niccolò. Although since your departure from here nothing has happened of much moment or that I consider worthy of your attention, *nevertheless* I do not want to fail to give you news of how things are going concerning our Pisa campaign. They have started to heat up so much that one can say without hesitation that they will come to the end that so just a campaign as this one deserves. For, as you know, Giovanni di Dino has returned from the camp; he had gone specifically to find out the courage and the intentions of Their Lordships: what they were planning, how much money they wanted, and the total quantity of foot soldiers and the number of artillery pieces and other things required for such expeditions. He returned fully informed and extremely confident; the things he requested on behalf of the commander and governor[2] have all been approved, because in truth they were so right and so proper that everyone felt completely satisfied. So that you may precisely understand the quantity of money, between the two of them they want right away—that is, prior to the capture of Pisa—twelve thousand gold ducats, which as you know is far better than anyone's expectations, since a much greater amount was expected. Well, that was the main item, and it has been settled. The other items are ordinary: they have already started to raise the foot soldiers and to get all the other necessary things ready; these the captain wants to get all together in camp by the 28th of this month, since he wants to be encamped without fail by the first day of August. If on the designated day, the 28th, things are not ready so that he can issue forth from camp on the day set by him, he says that he will not move then until the 15th of August: so that here we are making sure that everything is ready as promptly as possible by the above-mentioned 28th, etc.; which I judge they certainly will be, just as has been requested, please God.

Here the news is that the duke of Milan has called Monsignor Ascanio[3] back from Rome to come and stay in Milan, because he wants to ride to the border and be present in person in camp. Although we have not gotten any more letters from France, since they have been intercepted, etc., *nonetheless* by private mail we have learned that the king arrived on the 10th of this month in Lyons, with great ceremony; and the duke's going to camp in person is a sign that the matter is heating up quite a bit, as is *indeed* to be expected.

From Rome we hear that the agent of King Frederick residing there told the pope that His Holiness ought to think about healing the disorders of Italy, etc., and he answered that he had done so and would continue to do so, and the aforesaid agent replied that it was necessary to leave off generalities, and his king did not want to be caught napping, and it seemed as if His Holiness was seeking the ruin of Italy rather than its well-being, along with other more insulting words. He answered reproaching him for the lack of reverence he showed to His Holiness, and furthermore that if the king came into Italy, it would be to oppose the Turks and anyone else and to capture Milan, etc.

From Venice there is nothing else. If there should be, I shall let you know, etc.

While I was writing, some letters appeared from there, and indeed nothing else has been heard about the Turk except great raids and looting, since the other fleet, which they say is an enormous thing, has not yet arrived, etc.

I urge you to return as soon as you possibly can, since staying there does nothing in your favor, and here there is as great an overflow of things to do as ever there has been.

Between having to write on the run and being as busy as can be, I cannot do what I ought; nothing else occurs to me except to send you my regards, and to tell you again that the affairs of Pisa are being handled as quickly as possible, so that they may be ready by the 28th, etc. *Farewell.*

From the Palace, 19 July 1499
Your servant,
Biagio

❖ LETTER 8
Biagio Buonaccorsi to Niccolò Machiavelli
Florence, 19 July 1499

To His Honored Niccolò Machiavelli,
Most Worthy Secretary of the Florentine Signoria.
In Forlì.

That I am not angry, and that I always keep my promises, you will find fully confirmed by the announcements about both the Turks and the French that will be included in the public letter; for, although it was a bit difficult, still it seemed better for me to do it publicly rather than privately, even though I still am notifying you in private of a few minor things, and so I shall strive to do as long as you are there,[1] Niccolò, my friend. But I can assure you that, if there ever was business to take care of here, now it is overflowing, so that if my letters should not be written as they ought to be you will forgive me, and with your diligence and your intelligence you will derive as much benefit as possible from them. And when I have a moment's time I shall write you at greater length, more fully and in more detail, although I do not believe you will have to stay there very long, since there is need here for you to take care of your business.

And as for running off and going down there, if I had wanted to I would have come—I shouldn't have put it off until now; I would get Ser Antonio della Valle to put on such a face that it would look as if I had not understood what was going on. If you do as I advise, you will bring back a lot of rose water to soften him up, since here no one else but him can be heard. He has already made our magnificent directors bawl us out with damned good reason: I wish him bloody shit in his asshole. Still, that is how things stand, and a little massaging has settled everything. In fact, we all miss you, and your Biagio more than everyone else; he talks about you every hour, and every hour seems a year to him, unlike the way it seemed to you when he was away, which I believe ought to be comparable to his torments, etc.

I have no doubt at all that Her Excellency[2] is doing you as much honor, and is as happy to see you, as you write, especially for several reasons that I shall not repeat for the moment so as not to be tiresome, for I would quickly weary you.

In my judgment you have executed the commission entrusted to you with great honor to yourself up to now, and I have been greatly pleased by that, and continue to be so; thus let it be seen there is yet another person who, although he is not so experienced, is not inferior to Ser Antonio, etc., who puffed himself up so: so keep at it, for until now you have done us great honor.

I would like you to send me by return mail a portrait on a sheet of paper of Her Majesty's head, many of which have been done over there; and if you send it, roll it up so that the folds do not spoil it. I do not need anything else for the moment, except to send my regards and to offer myself to you, etc.

Farewell.
From the Palace, 19 July 1499
Your servant,
Biagio Buona. chancel.

❖ LETTER 9
Biagio Buonaccorsi to Niccolò Machiavelli
Florence, after 20 July 1499

To Messer Niccolò Machiavelli.

Copy of an item in a letter from Giovanbattista Ridolfi, ambassador to Venice, dated 20 July, to Their Excellencies of the Signoria—1499.

Yesterday there was an announcement from Corfu that the Turkish fleet issued forth from the straits on the 24th of last month, and it is expected to come and strike Napoli di Romania[1] or Corfu, if the weather should be favorable; and His Lordship with the land army is located around Salonika and will have to go where the fleet fights and then perhaps to Cattaro.[2] Thus I have learned that His Lordship had some small galleys transported by land from the Gulf of Morea[3] to the Gulf of Patras, which amounts to their being carried about six miles over land; it is thought that it was done because the weather on the sea was not proper for sailing in that direction, or in order to avoid the fleet of this Signoria,[4] which was located at Cavo Sant'Angelo[5] in the Peloponnesus, and to join forces with the galleys from Valona[6] and be used for those places from here toward Corfu and the gulf.[7]

This Illustrious Signoria continues to send boats and soldiers against them in Friuli,[8] by sea and by land, and they say that never has this state had a greater fleet than at present, and in fact it is very powerful, etc.

Copies of several items in letters from the ambassadors from the court[9] dated 17 July 1499, in Lyons.

That the French are keenly hastening the campaign and are not paying attention to anything else but that.

That the consignment of the lands of Picardy has been done, and that all the individuals delegated to that effect will be coming back.

That the king is willing for his fleet marshaled in Provence to join if need be with the Venetians'.

That they have sent about 70 cartloads of iron shot and other kinds of ammunition; and the infantry is beginning to cross over, but because they are coming from different places, it is not known exactly in what numbers.

That the fleet of Provence was being loaded up[10] to leave with the first favorable wind.

That Duke Valentino has stayed at Uson[11] in Berry up to now, and will be in Lyons shortly, and that he wishes to return to Rome; concerning which he is waiting for a reply from the pontiff, since he has sent him a message expressly to this end.

❖ LETTER 10
Biagio Buonaccorsi to Niccolò Machiavelli
Florence, 27 July 1499

To His Honored Niccolò Machiavelli,
Most Worthy Secretary of the Florentine Signoria, etc.
In Forlì.

Notable man and honored master, etc. By the hand of Messer Marcello[1] I was presented with a letter from you, which was for me, like all your other things, most exceedingly welcome, since they are from the one whom I love above all others, etc. So that you may learn just how we were bawled out by our chiefs, etc., in order that you may once again be informed of the news of the chancellery, hear them in brief. Ser Antonio,[2] as you know, busies himself with every slightest thing, and since we are not there so early in the morning, and do not stay until 9 o'clock[3] in the evening, he complained bitterly about it, so that in the morning, called on the carpet before the Signoria, we were given a serious admonishment, etc. To which first Alfano replied, then the great Ser Rafaello, as stupidly as possible, although he was allowed to explain it in his own way. He said, first of all, that Their Lordships had put in charge of that office one who had little to thank nature for and who did not know what was what; and that if they left things to him, he would do great things, greater than him; and so on, many other things and more insulting words, etc., such that his presumptuousness served him so well that he is constantly called by the masters, etc. And I am pushed around by Marcello and by everyone, and I keep on begging and praying for you to come back, for it is urgent. Finally I decided to gamble the remainder with my friend and told him I shall work with him until your return, and then I want to return to my place, that is, to writing alongside you. So I stick to my business, and if I am not spoken to, I do not talk with anyone, so my friend has already noticed that he has hurt me quite a bit: what he did was to keep me from seeing a certain letter and ordered that nothing at all be said to me; but that will be the last time, because he calls me six times before I answer. But I have my mind set and shall continue thus as long as I stay here. As for you, I urge you to hasten as swiftly as possible, since it does not do you any good to remain over there, as I shall inform you orally, as well as about many other things, and also about Marco, who has heard your letters being praised very highly and every day comes to sniff around and gossip; but you can take it for granted that I answered him in such a way that he does not talk to me about it any more, and will not speak to me about it in the future. So I think you will know in the end who Biagio was and is, and that is that. On your return we shall be back together, and we shall be able to discuss those things that are just our business, which it would take too long to write about, etc.

With Messer Marcello, concerning a swift reply to you, etc., I am no longer of any use to you, nor do I want to be. And so look for some other means, and whatever I can do, you know that I do not and never shall fail you, as you are someone to whom I am most deeply obligated.

Here the news is that the king has attacked Milan, and Messer Gianiacopo[4] has made a few forays, but not much damage, according to what we hear; and the more the king sees the duke[5] getting prepared, the more enthusiastic he becomes for the campaign.

The Swiss and the Germans have come to blows during the last few days, and as for who got the better of it, no one can know the truth, as you well realize; because whoever tells about it, if he is a friend, exaggerates it, and vice versa. But we believe that the Swiss have got the best of it in several encounters.

The Turkish fleet has issued forth from the strait, and it is thought it is going to strike Napoli di Romania; it is a great thing, according to what we have heard. And so that Signoria[6] has made great preparations to defend itself and in addition has begun to give money to the men at arms it wants to use in Lombardy, to attack Milan, since they say they want to keep their promises to the king, etc. God let it be for the best.

Our campaign in Pisa is going better and better, and Their Excellencies of the Signoria do not leave off day or night making the necessary provisions both of money and of everything else. They already have ready almost all the infantry, so that it is considered certain Pisa is almost in the power of Their Excellencies of the Signoria, although it still remains very obstinate, etc.

You know, of course, that Ser Filippo Radichi showed so many plans that he went as a commissioner to Lunigiana[7] to peck about,[8] and I can tell you he will do his best. Nothing else. I send my regards and offer myself to you, etc.

Florence, 27 July 1499
Your servant,
B. etc.

❖ LETTER 11

Niccolò Machiavelli to a Chancellery Secretary[1] in Lucca
Florence, early October[2] 1499

A letter addressed to Messer Jacopo Corbino, canon of Pisa, came into the hands of one of my friends, who brought it to me, and, in accordance with my duties, I opened it. I was amazed not so much at its subject as at its having been written by you because I was convinced that, for a man as serious as you are and holding a public position as you do, it was not to be expected that you would write something so incompatible with your profession. I shall let you judge whether it is appropriate for a secretary of your magnificent Signoria to mark so great a republic as ours with opprobrium[3]: because, more than anyone else, the members of your Signoria will feel the effects of whatever you say against any power at all in Italy. For, since you are their interpreter, people will always believe that the Signoria is satisfied with what you say, thereby creating hatred of them through no fault of theirs. I am motivated to write not so much to purge the calumnies with which you have marked our city as to warn you to be more judicious in the future; I feel obliged to do so because we are both in the same situation. Among the many considerations that show what a man is, none is more important than seeing either how easily he swallows what he is told or how carefully he invents what he wants to convince others of, so that every time he swallows what he ought not or invents badly what he wants to convince people of, he can be termed both thoughtless and reckless. I choose to ignore the maliciousness of your mind that your letter makes manifest and to expatiate solely on demonstrating to you how inept you were either in swallowing what was reported to you or in inventing whatever opprobrium you wanted to disseminate about this state. First, I thank you for congratulating the Pisan [Jacopo Corbino] about the glory that, in your judgment, they have won and the opprobrium that has redounded to us—attributing it all to the affection you bear us. Second, I ask you how can it be true both that this city has spent inestimable funds and that the Pisans can have defended themselves without any fraud on Paolo Vitelli's part—as you imply? Because, if you will kindly remember, the Florentine army—so well paid—approached Pisa so bravely and so swiftly, as was proved by M. Piero Gambacorti's flight[4] and your panic, that, had it not been for Vitelli's betrayal, neither would we lament the loss nor would you be rejoicing over it. Next, I ask what sound mind or what enlightened wit will swallow either that Paolo Vitelli would have lent us money or that the reason why he was imprisoned is in order not to pay him? Are you not aware, you poor man, that this completely exonerates our city and accuses Paolo? Because any time someone believes that Paolo lent us money, he necessarily believes that Paolo is a scoundrel, since he could not have laid money aside, as everyone knows, except either through graft given him so that he would do the wrong thing or through not keeping his troops together. Hence the result that either because he was unwilling, having taken graft, or because he was unable, not having his troops, countless troubles have befallen our campaign due to his culpability. Whether he committed one wrongdoing or the other or whether he committed them both, it deserves endless punishment. There is no need for me to answer the other parts of your letter, since they are based completely on these same two points, nor am I obliged to justify his seizure, either, because it is not something I am expected to do, and, *even* if it were expected of me to do so, it is not to you that I should do it. I shall *only* remind you not to rejoice much over the negotiations that you say are going on around us, especially since you are ignorant of the counternegotiations that are going on. And, in brotherly love, I admonish you that in the future, should you want in your evil nature to go on gratuitously insulting people, you should insult in such a way as to be considered more prudent.

L E T T E R S

1500

From Florence's point of view, France at the turn of the sixteenth century seemed to be the source of power that would help the city to regain control of Pisa. Firmly ensconced in Milan, with both Ludovico and Ascanio Sforza in French prisons, Louis XII appointed Georges d'Amboise (1460–1510), archbishop and soon-to-be cardinal of Rouen and powerful finance minister, as his governor in Milan. According to an agreement concluded in October 1499, the French would send Florence some of their troops in return for a cash settlement, which Florence could ill afford. In June 1500 Swiss and French troops marched on Pisa. Florence sent Machiavelli, along with two commissioners, Luca degli Albizzi and Giovambattista Ridolfi, to deal with the grumbling French army, which was dissatisfied because Florence was in arrears with its salary. When the French army mutinied and deserted, Louis XII, who by then had returned to French territory, feigned shock but did nothing. Florence sent Francesco della Casa, who had replaced Albizzi as a commissioner at Pisa, and Machiavelli, because of their familiarity with the Pisan situation, to France in mid-July to assuage Louis XII and to persuade him to honor his obligations with respect to Pisa. Della Casa had been an ambassador from Florence to the French court in 1493, so he was familiar with its diplomatic intricacies. He and Machiavelli reached the king at the end of August.

Within one month Cesare Borgia began his second campaign in Romagna with the aid of French troops; he conquered Pesaro and Rimini by the end of October. Because Florence knew that Cesare had the backing of his father, Pope Alexander VI, there was great consternation lest this aggrandizement entail a drive on Cesare's part to work toward restoration of Piero de' Medici and his family in Florence. Cesare is frequently referred to in this correspondence as "Duke Valentino" or "Valentino" because in 1498 the pope had worked out a deal with Louis XII whereby he would dissolve the king's marriage to Jeanne of France so that he could remarry Anne of Brittany if Louis would name Cesare duke of Valentinois and aid him in the conquest of Romagna.

❖ LETTER 12
Roberto Acciaiuoli[1] to Niccolò Machiavelli
Rome, 4 January 1500

To the Man of Wisdom, Niccolò Machiavelli,
Secretary of the Priors of Liberty.
In Florence.

Honored man, etc. I accept your excuses for the infrequency of your writing me, both because of your duties and because of the requirement of silence, for which you cannot be praised sufficiently, since that is what is demanded of a good secretary.

About the business of your friend, only this occurs to me. The pope is choosing governors for Bologna and all the other cities under his control, and has reserved for himself the power of choice. And, as usual, if those who have some friendly acquaintance and connection with him, or whose easy access has ingratiated them with him, intercede for anyone, the person and status of the intercessor are considered rather than those of the candidate, and, as happens generally all over, it is not hard to accomplish through mediators in favor and men conspicuous for their position. But I am afraid that your friend has reached the finish line too late. For our exalted Signori specially commissioned our ambassador a few days earlier to entreat His Holiness to choose Lord Peace Marvelous Light of L'Aquila as governor of Florence for the time being. That was freely granted to him, and his agents are merely waiting to complete and to expedite this promise. And so much for that.

I hear a good share of what you write to Giovanni Folchi,[2] thanks to his favor, *which I enjoy intimately;* and I receive all the news of our friends; I miss only Borsio, since I do not hear anything about him: I am afraid he has been transformed and transfigured into a Frenchman, *for so I had left him on our departure:* when you write to Giovanni give him a good tongue-lashing. I do not write to you about the jubilees,[3] since they have already become degraded and they are lavished on whoever wants them: so that this fellow[4] ought to be deeply commended, because in his time he will have revealed how much these things ought to be esteemed, and another man will not deceive us with such superstition. So as for myself, I am thankful to him for it, since he has enlightened me considerably and relieved me of a great concern, now that I have seen how these stories originate and what is at the bottom of them. But I am very happy if they cost me anything except for money. I shall be brief to make way for someone else. I send my regards to you, and to all our friends.

> *Farewell. 4 January 1499 [1500].*
> *Rob. Ac. in Rome*

❖ LETTER 13
Biagio Buonaccorsi and Andrea di Romolo to Niccolò Machiavelli
Florence, 23 August 1500

To the Notable Niccolò Machiavelli,
Florentine Envoy to His Most Christian Majesty, Honored Friend.
At Court.

My honored and dear Niccolò. If I must confess the truth to you, this let-ter of yours received this morning has made me swell and grow somewhat with pride, seeing that you still have a little more esteem for me among all the rank and file of the chancellery. In order not to descend from this opinion of mine, I decided not to see whether others had received letters from you. I de-rived very great pleasure from it, since I seemed to be talking directly and fa-miliarly with you, as we were wont to do. I had felt some degree of anger when I saw your letters the first time and there was no mention by you of me, fearing that the proverb that is generally said—out of sight, out of mind—might prove correct in you; but your letter has erased that. So I beg you to continue when you have time to spare; as for me, I shall never fail to do my duty toward you.

I do not want to fail to let you know how much satisfaction your letters give everyone; and you may believe me, Niccolò, since you know that adula-tion is not my forte, that when I found myself reading those earlier letters of yours to certain citizens, and some of the foremost, you were most highly commended by them, and I took extreme pleasure from it and strove adroitly to confirm that opinion with a few words, showing with what ease you did it. So wherever I see I can be of use, I do so, feeling as if I were doing it for my-self, as I most certainly am. Only this morning I was with Luca degli Albizzi,[1] whom your brother Totto[2] had already been to see, and did what was neces-sary; he did his duty as a friend, as he has always been wont to do. Thus Messer Marcello,[3] together with your Totto, does everything so that you get what you desire.[4] I believe as it happens that that will take effect before the sealing of this letter; and if you do not have it now, you will have it the next time. Write to Totto anyway, not to leave off trying, because this morning he said to me: If I do not do it today, I'll go off to the country, etc. A word to the wise is sufficient.

Our Messer Marcello gave me your letter, and with him was Totto, to whom he had given your other ones most faithfully. He had in this way sent those from Francesco[5] to his home by a special messenger, since I was not at the chancellery because I was not feeling well: the important thing is that they were delivered most expeditiously, as all the others will be. I have placed on one side all the pleasures that I have being here and on another all the others I would have if I were there, and certainly being together with you tips the scales. Still, one must have patience, since it is not possible; and if you go on writing to me, this absence of yours will be less hard to bear, so I entreat you as much as I can to do so.

I gave your message of excuse to Messer Cristofano.[6] He answered me that you should send word on your return to Rosso Buondelmonti[7] in Lyons, and you will be informed of everything by him, since he is an experienced man, etc.

Since your departure we have lost Libbrafratta and the bastion of La Ventura,[8] and for the time being the Pisans are masters of the field of battle.

Pistoia has been in great upheaval, and the chancellery faction has thrown out the Panciatica,[9] with much burning of houses and shops and the death of several men. But the faction that got the upper hand is showing itself very faithful and respectful to this illustrious Signoria. God help us, for there is need of it.

Niccolò, I beg you as a favor to me to spend a *scudo* for gloves and two cloth purses (the smallest you can find) and a few other trinkets, for which I shall pay you back through whomever you indicate. So I beg you to send me a rapier, but I want it as a gift, since I did not get the one you promised me on your departure. And give my very best regards to our Francesco della Casa, and tell him I am at his service for anything that he needs from here and that he thinks can be done by me. Nothing further. I send my very best regards to you, and I pray God to keep you from the hands of the Swiss.[10]

Florence, 23 August 1500.
Yours,
Blas. Bo. Chancellor

Post script. I was with Lorenzo Machiavelli,[11] and he promised me he would write to you and also have Brother Anfroi[12] and Casa[13] write to you: if they do, I shall send them to you with this letter, and also I shall urge them to do so. But answer me and act like the man of honor you are.

My Machiavelli, a thousand poxes upon you, for you keep us in great anxiety and things remain very hard for us in the 2nd Chancellery, so that these conditions, along with the rest of what goes on, etc., have us all in a tizzy. We are beginning to learn to deal with Ser Antonio,[14] and every day his stomach bothers him; I believe it is because he doesn't have his Madonna Agostanza here to warm him up or give him exercise on the seesaw. Anyway, we often laugh in the First Chancellery, and we also have a few little parties at Biagio's house, and M. Marcello lives next to Ser Gigliozzo and enjoys it, and these past days they have exchanged invitations with great festivity. I have done some things in that connection [. . .]. And so get ready, yourself, as soon as you arrive here, for she is awaiting you with open figs, and Biagio and I saw her several evenings ago at her window like a hawk, you know who I'm talking about, etc.: *i.e.,* along the Arno by the Grazie.[15]

Ser Raffaello[16] is on a legation to Bologna, but in 2 days he will start to serve under Gaddi,[17] who is going there as ambassador today. The Signoria writes to him, that is, to Ser Raffaello, that he should serve him in every possible way; you understand. For which reason Baccio[18] here is as mad as the devil, since he intended him to serve all his needs, etc.

To put my philosophy in tune with yours, I cannot help feeling resentment, Niccolò, at the trickery of Ser Traversa, for having found her in a brothel should be enough. The hornets will get angry with you, too, if you sting them in this way. But, in God's name, when you have come back we shall find other stings for you, at least if you haven't become too Frenchified. *Farewell.*

Yours, Andrea

❖ LETTER 14
Totto Machiavelli to Niccolò Machiavelli
Florence, 27 August 1500

To the Distinguished Niccolò di M. Bernardo Machiavelli,
Honored Envoy of the Florentine Signoria.
In France.
† In the name of God, 27 August 1500.

Honored brother, etc. This evening you have been granted parity[1] with Francesco della Casa by the *Signoria della Provisione,* following 15 straight days that I have been after them, both evening and morning. Most of them were set on going up to a sum of 30 gold florins[2] per month, saying that along with your regular stipend you would reach parity: I informed them several times in particular that it would not be just for them to make you spend your own salary, which when you are back here you can use to pay the commune and your other needs, and they would wrong you to make you spend it. Finally the affair has been settled as you wanted, and in the end everyone did it in good spirit and very willingly, especially Filippo Buondelmonti[3] and the Gonfalonier,[4] to both of whom we are obligated, and Antonio Giugni also gave us considerable help.

To, or for, Primavera[5] I have paid on your account 11 gold florins. In a letter of the 17th of this month I informed you, concerning the business of the money, that I had done everything you had requested me to; in it there was a letter of credit of the Nasi[6] to pay you 50 *scudi*. Roberto promised me to give you double notice of it, in case this letter did not arrive, so that you would be served by his people in Lyons one way or another.

And to the aforesaid Roberto I made a voluntary promise to pay them back to him within three months, as I wrote you in the other letter.

Nothing else. God keep you.

Yours,

Totto Machiavelli in Florence

❖ LETTER 15

Agostino Vespucci[1] to Niccolò Machiavelli

Florence, 20 September 1500

To His Magnificence Niccolò Machiavelli,
the Florentine Ambassador to His Most Christian Majesty.
At Court.

Your Magnificence, my honored master. Yesterday, which was a Saturday, the *Dieci di Libertà e Balía* were elected in the Great Council, and they are ten good men.[2] Since two of them were on the debtors' list,[3] there are 2 alternates, specifically Gualterotti, instead of Giovan Battista Ridolfi, and Clemente Sernigi, instead of Messer Antonio Malegonnelle. Since the others are not here so far, nothing else can be said. They are writing to Piero, who is in Bologna, as well as to the two commissioners in Pistoia, for them to come in the meanwhile, etc., and that the places will be filled. I wish you were here, my Niccolò, for reasons that you in your wisdom understand very well. The *Libertà e Balía* is exactly as before, except that among other things they are being somewhat restricted. The Turks have taken Modone, and Corfu is being talked about after it: they slaughtered everyone who was in it, however, since 20 thousand Turks died beforehand; they are also said to have been sent into Friuli,[4] in addition to those places and territory over there; also, that King Frederick[5] is advancing to recover his lands and ports and is being aided by the places themselves. The Ten[6] are in this situation. I write this hurriedly, for someone is leaving posthaste for those parts. It seems that everyone is rejoicing at this election of the Ten, except those very ones to whom the election has befallen. God willing, the hoped-for end will ensue. *Farewell.*

From Florence, 20 September 1500.

Agostino, your servant

❖ LETTER 16

Piero Soderini to Francesco della Casa and to Niccolò Machiavelli

Castrocento, 22 September 1500

To the Notable Francesco della Casa and Niccolò Machiavelli,
Envoys to His Most Christian Royal Majesty.

As dearest brothers, etc. It has pleased our most exalted Signoria on the present occasion and for the needs of the most illustrious prefect that I should of necessity travel here, as their ambassador to His Most Reverend Monsignor Cardinal[1] for a few days. Finding myself there at present, and having learned, not from His Most Reverend Lordship but from some other good sources, <that Pisan ambassadors have come to see His Most Christian Majesty, in order to conclude an agreement about their affairs with that king,[2]> I thought I should notify you[3] of it, so that you may talk with both the Most Christian King and the Most Reverend Monsignor of Rouen[4] concerning this matter, as you judge to be required by the city; <and it should be cause to cut off all contacts with them> until such time as the ambassador has left Florence for those parts, which should be shortly. Keep an eye on this, and use all your diligence and intelligence to prevent <such a conclusion from being brought about in any way while you are there.> And you will follow whatever is written to you in their letters by our exalted Signoria, despite the fact that they will not have this notice before tomorrow: but, in order to get a head start, I decided to notify you of it.

The bearer of this letter will be Messer Andrea Doria,[5] one of His Most Illustrious Prefect's men, who is a very good person; much account is made of him, and he is a very great friend of the affairs of the city. Give him fond greeting, and if you should want to make use of his efforts in any way, request it of him, for he has been asked to do so and will be glad to. *Nothing else. Farewell.*

From Castrocento, 22 September 1500.
Piero Soderini, Florentine ambassador, etc.

❖ LETTER 17
Luca degli Albizzi[1] to Niccolò Machiavelli
Florence, 24 September 1500

To the Notable Niccolò Machiavelli, Florentine Envoy.
At Court.

Dearest brother, etc. I have not answered your last letter before this, because I had not heard that you had first been written to officially via a safe route, and because it was not urgent. I thank you for your too high opinion of me: I am sorry that your judgment was not known to me earlier, because when your letter arrived I had already been chosen ambassador to His Majesty some time before and, citing my other responsibilities, had been excused. I would not, however, like this refusal of mine to create an unfavorable opinion of me there, since all that deterred me was the inconvenience and the expense. If it should be necessary, please make excuses for me insofar as required, although I am sure that little account will be taken of so minor a detail. We should consider everything to be for a good end and hope that whoever succeeds me will look after the needs of the city better. I do not think that Bernardo Rucellai, because of his ill health, and Giovanni Ridolfi, because of his indecorous family and many activities, will be coming. Four days from tomorrow, which is the deadline set for them, we shall make a definite decision about this. Someone else will have to be chosen again, particularly because everyone here desires that the ambassador there be prudent, esteemed, and acceptable to His Majesty. May God see to our needs. I shall not tell you about things here, since I expect that the public letters will make up for it. I remind you that I am yours and that I desire only to gratify you. Give my excuses to my friend Francesco della Casa if I do not write to him, which I refrain from doing so as not to tire him, having heard about his physical ailment, which distresses me as much as if it were in my very own person. Give him my greetings and my regards. May Christ keep you healthy.

Florence, 24 September 1500.

Yours,

Luca d'Antonio degli Albizzi

❖ LETTER 18

Agostino Vespucci to Niccolò Machiavelli
Florence, 20–29 October[1] 1500

To His Chief, the Noble Niccolò Machiavelli,
Secretary of the Eminent City of Florence,
Ambassador in France to His Most Christian Majesty.
At the Court of His Most Christian Majesty.

My patron, greetings, the recommendation having been sent well before this. Your let-
ter, which reached me three days ago, although in "Etruscan," was nevertheless very
welcome, for it came from Machiavelli and from Blois, a very distant region and, as the
poet says, almost from another world. You indeed will return to us, since today Pier
Francesco Tosinghi, as ambassador, and Bernardo Ricci, as envoy, have left for France or
Brittany to join you. Return as soon as you can, I beg; return posthaste, I pray; return
as swiftly as possible, I beseech. For a certain very noble citizen, who loves you particu-
larly, has implied that unless you are here you may lose your place in the palace alto-
gether. I just wanted to say this once, for that love with which I await and embrace you.
I read your entire letter to Signor Marcello,[2] two other chancellors, and Biagio,[3] who are
all seized by a marvelous desire to see you. For your amusing, witty, and pleasant con-
versation, while it echoes about our ears, relieves, cheers, and refreshes us, who are spent
and flagging from constant work. There are very many other things as well that urge
your return, but more face to face. Andrea and Giuliano[4] promise that they will write to
you whenever they get free from the stiffness of the joints from which they have long
been suffering. This ailment, though, results from frequent dicing and card-playing (they
say at ronfa[5]). Biagio, once a Protesilaus,[6] is not at all so sluggish but that he, too,
warms to dice and ronfa-playing, although Antonio della Valle keeps calling him his
own tender little dove. For this reason, and because he never throws Venus,[7] not out of
licentiousness, he has made a complete vow with this same Antonio not to play until
dawn. All your colleagues here are well; do not suspect nor divine, because you persuade

yourself, that while one of us there is sick, two of your friends here are likewise sick. The Aretine[8] says that indeed you will sicken and die just like your colleague there before any of the men themselves, since they fight more strenuously against any trouble, discomfort, or difficulty than we do.

But enough of pleasantries. Seriously, a matter that would not be out of place if you should return to Florence: make sure that the well-shod man himself can ride through mud, slime, and water with dry feet, with your help. Vespucci recalls that you brought him a hide for this very reason. Our distinguished Marcello has sworn that he will not have children by his wife within the next ten years; I do not know for what reason. I do know for certain that he loves you as his own brother, even though you do not baptize. Our Fedini,[9] the most impure[10] of two- or four-legged creatures, is at Pistoia with the commissioners. Ottaviano Ripa[11] alone is with the Ten, who will neither deliberate by vote nor send letters in their own name unless they see where they can ask for more money for military affairs. When in jest and to relax our minds we were speaking about you, how you so abounded in charm and drolleries, that we were so often forced to be delighted, to smile, even sometimes to laugh when you were present, Ripa added that there was no way you could stay in France, without grave danger, since sodomites and homosexuals are stringently prosecuted there. When we, who know your character is excellent and spotless, hesitated, and some asked what he meant, he muttered in reply that a horse had sodomized you and split your anus and buttocks (ah, what a crime!). Yet our Luca,[12] who especially has his hands full, what with the chancellery and his house, which he has built from the foundations, wretched on account of both these things, commends himself to you, for he is caught between a rock and a hard place and is miserably tortured: he cannot pay the treasury what he owes, and unless he pays up and frees himself from the debtor's list,[13] he cannot be ordained a scribe in place of Alfani[14] (as he has deserved by his virtues and as he hoped). This would not be difficult for him in any way but for the fact that he has no hope of being nominated in the council by the one who has the power. Nevertheless, he commends himself to Almighty God and to all his friends. You yourself know his trustworthiness and tact and how quickly and regularly he forms the shapes of letters in writing. There is no doubt that your return would aid him, and you would favor him with goods. I myself am as you left me and have no little labor.

As for public matters, I would have something to say but for the fact that several men are writing to you and to others there. Grain here is not expensive, the air is very healthy, and almost all are reasonably happy, except for those who suffer from the French or Neapolitan itch. For this sort of sickness gets worse every day and breaks out again. Thus you might learn that one man has lost his genitals or penis, you might perceive that another's nose has fallen off, another has gone blind in one eye, another has become very much like Vulcan.[15] I beg you, by your friendship, to take care and to return to us safe and sound. May you return happy and serene to your friends[16] Martelli, Casavecchia, Rafaello Girolami, B. Valori, Frate Ancroia, don Federico, and your many other friends who commend themselves to you. Duke Valentino is accomplishing great marvels by himself along the Via Flaminia,[17] and the rumor is spreading that when he has captured Faenza and Bologna, he will clear a path for Piero de'

*Medici to command such a great state as more than a citizen (a great crime). May God
keep all evils from us, of which evils for [six years] we have had a great share.*[18] *I await
your letter from Brittany. Farewell, write again, come home, cherish us in remembrance,
love us in return.*

20 October 1500. Held until the 29th.

Yours very truly, Agostino Vespucci, in the chancellery

❖ LETTER 19

Totto Machiavelli to Niccolò Machiavelli

Florence, 4 November 1500

To the Distinguished Niccolò Machiavelli.

In France.

Jesus. In the name of God, 4 November 1500.

Honored brother, etc. This is the year of our misfortunes. Since Primavera[1]
died, her son Giovanni has lain dying at death's door. Finally in fact [. . .] can
go. And since she did not make a will, and he was not yet [. . .] to be able to
make a will, the property was going to go to those people. However, at the
present time, the boy[2] is not likely to die of this illness and he will be able to
make a will [. . .] in this present month, on the condition that he reaches his
14th birthday, from which time forward he can legally make a will. I shall wait
for you, since you should be coming back; and before that time, nothing
would have been done; and therefore, during the time he was in such serious
condition, we did not see how we could have him make one. Let us know
your opinion in this matter.

We were not able to get any money out of the previous Signoria, nor your
discharge,[3] which I requested, because, not being able to get a cent or to see
any way to do it in the future, it seemed to me it was a game to make you endure hardship there, so I thought it would be much better for you to come
back here, where you could live honorably, than to live there in hardship.

Leonardo Guidotti,[4] who truly has shown himself to be your great friend
and who esteems you and is a member of the Ten, has done everything possible for you either to be furnished with money or to come home and several
times has requested the Signoria and his colleagues for you to come back, saying that the Ten need your presence: this has done you no little honor and
service, since he is a man who has a considerable reputation. Finally, you
should feel obligated to him for something else, of even greater importance,
which you will be informed of when you get here. We have not been able to
get the money, and we cannot, if they do not make provision for it; but your
discharge will be granted within a few days, I believe.

Nothing else. God keep you, for

Totto Machiavelli, in Florence

❖ LETTER 20

Francesco Machiavelli[1] to Niccolò Machiavelli

Florence, 5 November 1500

To the Magnificent Niccolò Machiavelli,
the Florentine Ambassador to His Most Christian Majesty.
Via Lyons, at the Court.
In the name of God, 5 November 1500.

   Your Magnificence Ambassador, etc. By the present letter I do not wish, my dear and honored Messer Niccolò, to renew in either you or me the sorrow of the losses[2] you and we have sustained, although ours was greater for having been in the more noble sex; we are saving it to be expressed orally, since I judge that will be within a short time, as we strongly desire it, and we know that you do the same. I inform you by the present letter that, although the late, beloved Giovan Battista is not in the house of Rinieri, in Lyons, everyone there is yours, and especially Maria, who must have arrived there by now with her husband Rinieri: her sons are there; there is such a residue of kindness and love in that house that all the relatives as well as the friends of the late beloved will always be greeted with love and good will, and every hospitality and favor will be given to them, and you can make yourself completely at home there. I know there is nothing new, and I thought I ought to write you this note, having in particular to send you your letters, which will be in this one.

   I understand a relative of Stiatta Ridolfi, your colleague[3] Francesco della Casa, is ill, and Stiatta has asked me several times about him, claiming not to have news from you as to how he is and expressing surprise. I feel you have done your duty in everything, since I know that is your nature: I wanted to tell you, if it should be appropriate, although I know Your Excellency has gone on to Nancy,[4] and he to Paris.

   I would desire, if you should have some opportunity (as I imagine you will), that you should inform His Lordship Messer Giulio[5] that I send him my regards and that I have promptly delivered every letter received from him. And because I know he will have a report from his friends as well as Niccolò as to the outcome of all his affairs, I shall refrain from wearying His Lordship and myself as well.

   When you see Ugolino Martelli,[6] be so kind as to give my regards to him and greet him a thousand times on my behalf.

   Today, Adovardo Buglione,[7] His Most Christian Majesty's steward, is leaving, bearing a dispatch from our Signoria for his return. To us a resolution seems to have been made that ought to be agreeable to His Majesty, as you will be notified by the public letter.

   And in this letter I shall say no more to you. I am yours and send you my regards. Christ be, etc.

Yours, Francesco Machiavelli, in Florence

❖ LETTER 21

Pier Francesco Tosinghi to Niccolò Machiavelli

Moulins, 22 November 1500

To the Noble and Distinguished Niccolò Machiavelli,
Envoy and Most Worthy Florentine Secretary, etc.

Noble and distinguished man, like a brother, etc. From Lyons I wrote you by the hand of Giovan Francesco Martelli, notifying you of my arrival there, and I answered a letter of yours I found here, of 27 October; and I told you how within a few days I would set out on my way to court. That is what I did, and, arriving there on the 12th, I departed on the 17th, and yesterday evening I came here to Moulins. Where, wishing to leave and to continue my voyage this morning, a rider from Lyons overtook me with the enclosed letters addressed to you and with orders for me to open them, as you will see. Having examined them carefully, and since it seemed to me that speed was *of the utmost importance,* and seeing that I could not myself hasten there, given the vehicles and the terrible road, I thought it best to dispatch to you Matteo del Vecchio, our horseman and the present bearer, with those letters, so that meanwhile you can act in accordance with the importance of their content and in accordance with our trust in you. In any case, I shall try my best to hasten my arrival as far as possible. If you see fit, after receiving the letters, to send the horseman back to me with notification of the place where one may encounter both the king and you, you may do so, as I believe it will be very helpful. And meanwhile I send my devoted regards to His Majesty, and farewell.

From Moulins, 22 November 1500, 16th hour.[1]
Yours, Pier Francesco Tosinghi, ambassador

L E T T E R S

1501

In *The Prince*, 20, Machiavelli quotes a piece of conventional wisdom in order to mock it: "Pistoia must be held by factions and Pisa by fortresses" (Atkinson, p. 321; he alludes to the adage again in *Discourses*, II, 24). During his early political career, both cities were a constant source of worry for Florence and, consequently, for Machiavelli. He was sent to Pistoia in February, in July, and twice in October. These experiences led Machiavelli to publish his *Ragguaglio delle cose fatte dalla repubblica fiorentina per quietare le parti in Pistoia* (Information about the things the Florentine Republic did to calm down the factions in Pistoia) in March 1502.

An increasing source of Florentine concern was Cesare Borgia, especially as his ambitions and those of his father, Pope Alexander VI, in Romagna would affect Florence. Many wondered whether, with Louis XII's help, Florence would be attacked next. Because Machiavelli thought that Cesare Borgia would call on Louis for aid, he was instrumental in convincing the Signoria to pay the wages, which Florence had previously agreed to, of the mercenaries France had employed against Pisa. He returned to Florence in the middle of January. By spring Cesare Borgia's second campaign was focused mainly on Romagna, and he captured Faenza at the end of April. He then shifted his attention to Florence; he considered seeking support from the Medici party by courting Piero de' Medici, but an attack on Naples diverted his attention. French and Spanish armies entered the Kingdom of Naples early in July and began an attack that they had agreed to under the Treaty of Granada, the provisions of which had been kept secret until late June. Before Borgia got to Naples, however, he began to press his attack on Piombino, a town on the west coast about sixty-five miles south of Pisa. The town was on his way to Naples, though he had to pass through Florentine territory to get there. As a means of placating him, the Signoria readily agreed to give him and his army the right to pass through its territory, and even paid him a levy of 36,000 ducats to delay any immediate confrontation.

Despite this upheaval in Naples, which was a source of conflict that was to upset the balance of power on the Italian peninsula for years to come, Machiavelli was able to establish some harmony in his personal life: he married Marietta Corsini in August.

❖ LETTER 22
Agostino Vespucci to Niccolò Machiavelli
Rome, 16 July 1501

To the Notable Niccolò di Messer Bernardo Machiavelli,
Second Chancellor of Florence, Honored Secretary.
In Florence.

Notable, honored man, etc. It is about noon, and I am gasping from the great heat here in Rome; since I cannot sleep, I am writing these few lines, prompted *as well* by Raffaello Pulci, who dallies with the muses. He often improvises verses in the vineyards of these great masters and merchants, and I understand he says them with one Ser Francesco da Puliga from up there; I do not know what he is doing in Rome. The latter in former days wrote a sonnet in reply to our Francesco Cei[1] that seems a bit too licentious to me. I have done all I could to get it in writing and have not been able to; this Ser Francesco has not given it to anyone but rather has read or, more exactly, recited it. If I can get it I shall send it to you. Pulci dallies and is always surrounded by 4 whores: we hear him solemnly, and it has been said to me that he is somewhat worried, because, since he has reputation and recognition as a poet and the Academy of Rome wants to crown him at his pleasure, he would not like to incur any risk *concerning sodomy,*[2] because Pacifico, Phaedrus, and some other poets are here *who, if they had not taken refuge in the sanctuary now of this, now of that cardinal, would already have been burned at the stake.*

As it happens, in these past few days a woman of considerable rank, a Venetian, was burned at the stake in Campo di Fiore for having sodomized a girl of 11 or 12 years, whom she kept in her house, and for doing other things to her that I shall not mention, since they were too licentious and similar to the things done by Nero the Roman. This confirms the above-mentioned Raffaello in his need to stay continually in the gardens among women, along with others like himself, where *they may tickle the reluctant muse* with their lyre, give themselves pleasure, and dally. But, *good Lord,* what meals they treat themselves to, according to what I hear, and *how much wine they guzzle,* since they have been poetized! Vitellius the Roman and, *among the foreigners,* Sardanapalus,[3] *if they were to come back to life,* would be nothing compared to them. They have players of various instruments, and with those damsels they dance and prance *in the manner of the Salii*[4] *or rather of the Bacchantes.*[5] I envy them for it, and I have to champ at the bit in my room, which is under the roof, hot, and oftentimes with a few tarantulas, and I am dying of the heat, *so that I can scarcely bear it.* If it were not for one consideration, which Biagio knows about, I would come back up there. I wish to beg you to reply to Raffaello or to me and draw this ill humor from our heads, as I know you will find a way to do.

The pope seems to me to have put on his thinking cap about this noise of the Turks, which has already become clamorous. He is beginning to say, with a sigh: *"O god! At this present moment, what land, what seas can take me in?"*[6] He has doubled the guards of the palace night and day, *he makes it hard for anyone to see him, and yet he behaves like Sulla*[7] *and proscribes more and more every day; for, in the sight of everyone,* he takes away the possessions of some, the life of others; some he sends into exile, others into forced labor on the galleys; he takes way the house of some and puts some renegade[8] in it: *and this for no cause or for some trifling one.* Aside from this, he allows these barons and friends of his to commit many abuses, and to steal property, and to empty warehouses, *and a thousand things of this kind.* Benefices are more for sale here than musk melons are up there, or buns and water down here. The Rota[9] no longer meets, because *might* (as well as those renegades) *makes right,* to the point that the Turks seem necessary, since the Christians do not bestir themselves to eradicate this blackguard from human society: *so everyone of good judgment says with one voice.*

It remained for me to say that it has been noted by some that, aside from the pope, who has his own illicit flock there at all times, every evening, from vespers to seven o'clock,[10] twenty-five or more women are brought into the palace riding pillion with some people, to the point where the entire palace has evidently become the brothel of every obscenity. I do not want to give you any other news from here for now, but if you answer me I shall give you even finer ones. Rejoice and farewell.

From Rome, 16 July 1501.
Yours, Agostino

❖ LETTER 23
Ugolino Martelli to Niccolò Machiavelli
Lyons, 17 July 1501

To the Notable Messer Niccolò Machiavelli,
Secretary of the Eminent Florentine Signoria.
Jesus, 17 July 1501.

My very dear Messer Niccolò. A few days ago I received a letter from you dated the fourth of this month, as cherished as you know you are yourself, and I beg you to write to me from time to time, as you will be giving me great pleasure, and I shall do the same.

I have seen the stipend that the eminent Signoria has arranged for me, for all of which the good Jesus be thanked. You know how much regard one can obtain in court, if one no longer can send dispatches. I have always done my duty toward our country, and I shall always do so, and you and the others can testify to what I have done; as long as things work out well, nothing else will trouble me, and you will recall when necessary that I have been wronged.

I have given your regards to our colleague, and he sends them back to you double.

The same with Messer Antonio di Bolonge, who has begun to write you a letter, which I imagine will be sent to you with this one or with the first next one; he is going off to the country. As usual, Frascone sends you his regards.

I beg you to give me a few items of news from time to time. Here I would not know what to tell you, for nothing is happening. Vittorio is going to Milan, and I also believe that your ambassadors must be about to go there: let it be something good, if possible, for once! If you send ambassadors here, make sure they are of the kind you are wont to send. The ambassadors of the archduke,[1] five of the most important ones, are coming here. So far there is nothing from Germany, and we do not expect it at all.

The Kingdom of Naples[2] must have been dispatched by this time. You can bear witness how many months ago I wrote to you that the campaign would be undertaken, and our general did not want to believe it.

Giovanni Martelli has come though there: make sure that the thirty-five *scudi* are collected.

Give my regards to everyone as needed, and make sure to bear me in mind for my affairs.

You did not answer me concerning either the Maréchal de Gié[3] or Robertet[4]: the latter was treated rather high-handedly,[5] and you know whether he has acted as a friend.

Nothing else for this letter. Yours,
Ugolino, in Lyons

❖ LETTER 24
Ugolino Martelli to Niccolò Machiavelli
Lyons, 12 August 1501

To the Notable Messer Niccolò Machiavelli,
Secretary of the Eminent Florentine Signoria.

My very dear Messer Niccolò. I have received a letter of yours dated the sixth of this month, many thanks. As for the news from Naples, as I wrote to you in a note of mine, we were the first[1]: for which I promise you the king commended and praised the Signoria very highly.

As for affairs in Milan, this delay has gone on too long, and I am very displeased by it; I cannot think, from the encounters I have had here, that things will work out well. It will only be as in the past, in my opinion, that is to say, to our disadvantage. I am waiting anxiously. I do my assignment, and I leave nothing to be desired. The king is happy to listen to me and is even glad to see me. I leave nothing to be desired. We shall see what happens. You do not have any friends here, and yet by the Lord you have scoffed at Robertet. I am no longer going to make him vain promises, for I receive injury and shame from them: let the worry be yours, in the end. Nothing has been left unremembered by me, and, in everything I could do, I have always helped.

I have given your regards to Messer Antonio and to Messer Frascone, and every one would like you to come here.

I have mentioned this to the ambassador,[2] but I do not know what to say, because he wants to be replaced, and if the king departs from here, I promise you he will not go back with him.

I am all yours, and keep me in mind wherever necessary. I shall do my duty, provided that I do not have to pay anything, for [?][3] money I cannot do anything worthwhile.

Our colleague sends his regards to you. Nothing else for this letter. Yours,

Ugolino Martelli, in Lyons,

12 August 1501

❖ LETTER 25

Agostino Vespucci to Niccolò Machiavelli

Rome, 25 August 1501

To the Notable, Most Honored Niccolò Machiavelli,
Secretary. With the Ten. In Florence.

Notable man, etc. My very beloved Niccolò Machiavelli. I have stripped down to an open cloak; I would be wearing a jacket, *if I did not fear the south wind, unhealthy for the body during the autumn days.* Since it is your expressed desire to hear *whether* the estate of the cardinal of Capua[1] was left to the pope or *he appointed other heirs,* in reply I shall tell you, *speaking seriously (for I shall perhaps conclude this otherwise than that),* that the pope does not permit any cardinal to make heirs, but *rather* he wants to look over the will very thoroughly. This is borne out by the case of the cardinal of Lisbon,[2] who in recent days, feeling ill and not being able to leave some money that he happened to possess, about 14 thousand,[3] to whomever he would have desired, decided rather to dispose of it while he was living than to let the pope, after his death, have it to enjoy. And calling all his family by bunches to his bed, he distributed it all[4] as gifts on sight to his household; and thus he truly renounced all his benefices, so that he has nothing in this world except the great gratitude not only of his family but of all Rome. He has regained his health since then, though he is old, and yesterday he spoke to the ambassador, in my presence, for an hour or more, always in Latin, *and he remained himself throughout.* Whereupon the pope gave the archbishopric of Capua, which is worth six thousand ducats a year, to the cardinal of Modena,[5] who, although he is or seems to be in the pope's good graces, paid out 15 thousand ducats for His Holiness; he gave another of his archbishoprics, which is in Spain, to Monreale,[6] on condition that he leave the bishopric of Ferrara to Cardinal d'Este.[7] Of the other benefices I shall say nothing except that the pope (*as I shall say with his leave*) has received, in currency, up to 25 thousand or more, because the appointment was a rich one. If you wanted to hear *what kind of death he died of,*[8] here *it is commonly held* to have been by poison, since he was not on very good terms with the Great Standard-bearer,[9] for one very often hears of such deaths in Rome: *and all things flow from the source, and not from the first stream.* There *you have, I think, more than you had asked for;* and so it remains for Ser Antonio, Biagio, Ser Luca, and Ser Ottaviano[10] to do what you wrote to me about.

Concerning Pulci, I shall find him and read him your letter: I believe we shall have some things to answer you, and pleasant ones: he is a nasty gadfly, he does more than he says, and he does not seem to be what he is.

Today, although it is the 25th, they are celebrating the feast of Saint Bartholomew[11] here, and it is said to be more to honor the feast of Saint Louis, King of France, which is on the same day. There is a little church of that saint in Rome, a humble one that never saw more than 50 people together; and this year, because an invitation was sent by the French ambassador to all the cardinals, ambassadors, prelates, and barons in Rome, this morning everyone was there—*namely,* 16 cardinals, all the ambassadors who happen to be in Rome, all the barons and other nobles—and all remained at the mass, which lasted 3 full hours. The pope's orchestra was there, and it is a wonderful thing; his pipers, who did their duty at the arrival of each cardinal; all his trumpeters; other exquisite instruments, that is to say, the papal band, which is a sweet-sounding and almost divine thing; I cannot for now name any of the six instruments by name, as I do not think Boethius[12] makes mention of them, *since they were from Spain.* There was also, halfway through the mass, a Latin oration recited by a most learned man, containing *in brief* the account of the life of Saint Louis, then *quite extensively (with along the way some mention of the kings of France)* of the grandeur, sublimity, and majesty of the present king, *in recounting whose virtues, namely, his physical and mental gifts, and how much he had trampled adverse fortune under his feet, and yet how well he had reined in, in prosperous times,* he took about a full hour. And in truth, Niccolò, my friend, this was the art of the orator, because he is base-born and has never been seen before or heard about around here, or very little; and nevertheless, because he was a Roman, he gave more pleasure than Phaedra or Marso or Sabellico or Lippi,[13] who *are considered excellent.* He showed, *first of all,* that he had a great memory, that he knew how to embellish well and to narrate clearly; he showed *how good his pronunciation was, how good his vocabulary and gestures, which harmonized together with both his voice itself and his thoughts, since the former served the latter at the same time; so that truly I venture to affirm* that, very often, *not only with his hands but also with his very nods* he would manifest his will to the audience. And I do not know how that man could ever have *spoken so felicitously,* unless he imitated Demosthenes, who was wont to compose a speech looking into a certain great mirror. And leaving aside his learning, his eloquence, the infinite shadings, many flourishes and cutting remarks with which his oration was strewed, he performed so well, by Hercules, that he won people over to himself, he persuaded, he moved, and finally he delighted. And at the end of his oration, he poured forth such a wave of eloquence, that everyone was astonished and amazed; because of which it came about that an almost theatrical applause was given to him by many, although it was in church. Many believe that, if he had been in the presence of the king, he would on the spot have made him a grandee in his council.

There remains only one other thing, that in the past few days, the pope having been in the heat of desire to go on vacation, and there being in the Parrot chamber a group of 5 or 6 learned men (for in truth there are many of them, although there are also scoundrels and ignoramuses), discussing poetry and astrology, etc., there was one of them who said there was only one man in Rome whom the pope trusted for astrology, and he was in ill health and living in misery and poverty for the great generosity of that prince. And Phaedra having told me that this man predicted to the pope, while he was still cardinal, that he would be pontiff, I persuaded them to make up some anonymous prediction and drop it on the floor, and so it was done. Before we departed from there, these 3 little verses were written, namely:

> I foretold that you would be pope, oh Ox,
> I now foretell you will die, you will go forth from here,
> And following the plowman will come the wheel.

The wheel is the insignia of Lisbon, he is the plowman. This effect of it was seen, that he never afterward talked of leaving, although people are saying if the wedding plans[14] with Ferrara are revealed, he will want to go there and travel about Romagna. We shall see what will ensue; and whether Duke Valentino comes back here, about which there are differing opinions, since many of his people are coming back one after the other; and he has also sent Vitellozzo[15] to do what he would normally want to be able to do in person by himself. And if His Beatitude the Pope should come down there, you and others who might want some dispensation, either to take or to leave your wives, will get it out of kindness of heart, provided that your hand is loaded with money. In the meantime, Camerino is afraid, Urbino is running off, because he is fearful of the relics of the House of Sforza, and I say nothing of Piombino.[16] Farewell, and please excuse me if I do not write you a long letter, because I have no time. Till the next time.

Rome, 25 August 1501.
Your most devoted Agostino

❖ LETTER 26
Biagio Buonaccorsi to Niccolò Machiavelli
Lomel,[1] 20 September 1501

To His Honored Friend,
the Notable Niccolò Machiavelli, Secretary of the Florentine People.
In the Florentine Palace.

My honored Niccolò. To tell you the truth, I was quite happy when I saw the address in your handwriting on the letter to Ser Luca,[2] and upon opening it I felt tricked; and so I shall not write you any of what I had planned: neither of the bishop's speech, which was a marvelous thing, although brief, because the cardinal[3] was busy; nor of Giamba; nor of the sordid lodgings in which we are living, etc.; and if ever you do your duty, I have a bunch of reports to give you on the discussions I have had with Their Excellencies the Ambassadors, both new and old. And so now it is up to you.

Farewell. From Lomel, 20 September 1501.
Biagio

I cannot help telling you that eloquence and performance, without making the slightest mistake, and knowing just how to enter into negotiations, are going to be of little use to us.

Although I am acting as if I am angry, I am not, because, since you wrote at such length to the ambassador, you should be excused.

❖ LETTER 27
Niccolò Valori[1] to Niccolò Machiavelli
Pistoia, 30 October 1501

To the Excellent Young Man Niccolò Machiavelli, Most Worthy Secretary.
In Florence.

Most cherished, as a brother. I get as much pleasure from a letter of yours as I could ever get from any other: I shall not take very long since I have nothing to tell you and I am worn out. You will talk with Lanfredini,[2] and although a city set on top of a hill[3] cannot be hidden, I have reiterated your good faith to him in more than one of my letters; and among other things do not pay attention to what I write him, for I judge it to be better to do thus, but to what you will tell him face-to-face, which are the things we discuss. In addition, here we must see to those soldiers, so that we are not reduced to 500. We have been organizing these things outside and inside the city; and since you left[4] we have hanged a few of them; and so all those strongholds have been straightened out. I have not been able to get any news to Antonio,[5] because he has ridden up into the mountains, but I shall do it right away, for I know it will be very gratifying to him, especially because of your affectionate letter.

And in truth, he is a good man. Give the enclosed letter to Bernardo[6] for me; it is important to me for a personal reason, and if you ever have any spare time write us a couple of lines. I send you my regards as usual. Christ keep you. I beg you to be so kind as to shake hands for me with our friend Giuliano Lapi. *Again* I am yours.

Niccolò Valori, in Pistoia
30 October 1501

❖ LETTER 28
Luca Antonio degli Albizzi[1] to Niccolò Machiavelli
Blois, 24 November 1501

To the Notable Niccolò Machiavelli, Florentine Secretary, His Dear Friend.

Notable man, etc. My last letter was dated the 8th of this month; since then your last letter, of the 9th, has been received; it calls for no other reply than that it gives pleasure that the city is arranging for the money, since there will be no little need of it. I am all the more delighted knowing that all our welfare is to originate from over there, and anyone who places his hopes in someone else will end up disappointed, because everywhere they are building on air.

Concerning the peace of which you give notice, here it has not been discussed, and those who are wont to must say what is good for their purposes. I thank you and send you my regards.

From Blois, 24 November 1501.
Luca Antonio degli Albizzi,
Ambassador, etc.

Our Ugolino,[2] who is a totally good man, wishes to do whatever you please.

L E T T E R S

1502

Urged on by Vitellozzo Vitelli, one of Cesare Borgia's partisans, Arezzo rebelled against Florentine control in early June. Arezzo was a powerful Tuscan
city in the Val di Chiana, southeast of Florence near the border of Romagna,
so it was not suprising that other figures loyal to Cesare Borgia helped the revolt: Giampaolo Baglioni and Piero de' Medici. Vitelli soon controlled most of
the important cities in the Val di Chiana. Cesare Borgia, too, wasted no time.
He captured the important duchy of Urbino in one day, on 21 June, and
forced Guidobaldo da Montefeltro to flee for his life. Thus, Borgia was
enough of a threat to Florence for the Signoria to comply hastily when he
told the city to send him some qualified negotiators. It sent Francesco
Soderini, bishop of Volterra and the brother of Piero, to Cesare along with
Machiavelli, who wrote most of the reports sent back to the Signoria, though
they were signed by Soderini. Machiavelli was in Arezzo and Florence for
most of the summer.

Florence was not the only power wary of Cesare Borgia. Louis XII realized
the potential threat that Borgia represented, so he concluded in April a defense
agreement with Florence whereby he agreed to defend the city and supply six
thousand cavalry on demand if Florence would pay the French an indemnity
of forty thousand ducats for three years. In July Louis XII followed through; his
troops were at Arezzo's walls. By the end of August, Arezzo and most of the
cities in the Val die Chiana that Florence regarded as necessary for her security
were safely under her control. Cesare Borgia, though, was simultaneously
courting Louis XII so that by early September they were said to be reconciled.

September was a significant month for Machiavelli and Florence. Piero
Soderini was elected gonfalonier of justice for life, a position he would hold

until he was overthrown by the returning Medici in 1512. To a great extent Soderini was Machiavelli's political patron. He thought highly of Machiavelli's political and diplomatic acumen (see his remarks quoted at the end of Letter 33) and saw to it that the Signoria benefited from it. From early October until January 1503 Machiavelli was in Romagna and in virtual daily contact with Borgia. As Guicciardini puts it, "in the interim, so as to keep [Cesare Borgia] on our side with some sort of favorable actions, the Ten sent Niccolò Machiavelli, chancellor of the Ten, to [Borgia] in Imola" (Guicciardini, *Storia d'Italia,* p. 198; *Storie Fiorentine,* p. 252; Domandi, p. 230). The Signoria insisted upon having someone on the spot to keep a sharp eye on Borgia and to anticipate devious policy moves. When its pressure on Machiavelli became oppressive, he lashed back, "I implore your lordships to forgive me and to bear in mind that such matters cannot be conjectured about and to understand that here we are dealing with a man who makes all his own decisions. Whoever is not to write down speculations and far-fetched ideas must check the facts—checking them requires time" (*Leg.,* I, p. 427).

While Machiavelli was with Borgia, a conspiracy was hatched at the castle of Magione near Perugia. The agreement was announced on 9 October by some of Borgia's supporters and most powerful condottieri: Giampaolo and Gentile Baglioni, Ermete Bentivoglio, Oliverotto da Fermo, Ottaviano Fregoso, Francesco Orsini (Duke of Gravina), Franciotto Orsini, Cardinal Giambattista Orsini, Paolo Orsini, Antonio da Venafro (sent by Pandolfo Petrucci, prince of Siena, who probably masterminded the conspiracy and soon arrived on his own), and Vitellozzo Vitelli. These men realized that Louis XII, now a firm supporter of Florence, might hold them responsible for threatening Florence and that Cesare Borgia, if necessary, would not hesitate to double-cross them. This group has gone down in history, however, as the *dieta de falliti* (the assembly of failures). They had little mutual trust and hence could not act jointly, although they did gain control of Urbino and some other towns in Romagna and the Marches. (It was after their victory at one of these towns, Fossombrone, that Machiavelli was able to obtain a safe-conduct for a Florentine merchant to get to ports on the Adriatic.) With French troops moving toward the territory, the conspirators sought an agreement with Cesare Borgia. Biding his time, Borgia finally summoned the conspirators to Senigallia late in December to wreak revenge. Machiavelli's *Descrizione del modo tenuto dal Duca Valentino nello ammazzare Vitellozzo Vitelli, Oliverotto da Fermo, il Signor Pagolo e il Duca di Gravina Orsini* (Description of the method used by Duke Valentino in the murder of Vitellozzo Vitelli, Oliverotto da Fermo, Lord Paolo Orsini, and Orsini, Duke of Gravina) is a factual account, in the form of a literary narrative, of this brutal attack.

❖ LETTER 29
Francesco Soderini to Niccolò Machiavelli
Empoli, 10 August 1502

To the Notable Niccolò Machiavelli,
Chancellor of the Eminent Florentine Republic, Very Dear Friend.
In Florence.

Dearest Messer Niccolò. You know that when our Signoria sent me to Urbino,[1] in order that the voyage could be made in goodly stages, they had some mares given to me by the post, among which were two belonging to Antonio da Sestri. They were kept by me until my return; one of them, a dark mare, I left with the captain of Bagno for him to have it looked after, because it was found to be exhausted, and I understand that it returned last night. The other one, which was a bay mare, I brought back with me and it was returned on the 22nd of July, with a sore forefoot, when I came back: but Antonio said it was lamed and needed good care. I cannot say what condition these mounts are in, but I can testify that they seemed fine and good, and they served me excellently until the day that I returned: therefore, since the beasts suffered as much as can be seen, it seems to me you ought to inform Their Lordships of the Ten, so that Antonio may be indemnified both for his trouble and for his loss insofar as it is fitting, for it seems to me the service he did for us deserves it: and you may bear witness to a good share of it. Farewell and give my regards to M. Marcello.

> *Empoli, 10 August 1502.*
> *F. Soderini—Bishop of Volterra*
> *Referendary of His Holiness the Pope*

❖ LETTER 30
Lorenzo di Niccolò Machiavelli[1] to Niccolò Machiavelli
Florence, 7 September 1502

To My Very Dear Messer Niccolò Machiavelli,
My Great Friend, Most Worthy Envoy to Duke Valentino.
In the name of God, 7 September 1502.

My very dear Niccolò. There will arrive with this letter Marco di Piero the driver, who is the master of some mules that were seized by Valentino's troops[2] along with many others and many other goods, which through the intermediary of His Lordship were all recovered, exactly how you will be able to learn from the mouth of the man himself. Anyway, the above-mentioned Marco is a workman for Martino dello Scarfa,[3] for whom I wish to do every service and favor that I possibly can. Using all those means that I can to do him service, I beg you with all my might and for all the love that has ever been between us that, in any way you can assist the above-mentioned Marco, you do it with all diligence. I shall also tell you that, if it should be necessary to spend up to the sum of 25 or 30 ducats in the recovery of the above-mentioned goods, or more particularly mules, we shall be quite happy. And also, concerning this, we wish to ask you to [...] not to worry about 10 ducats, if you should judge it was necessary [...] if the above-mentioned Marco should need in this case to make use of you, either for money or for credit, I beg you to do so, promising to make up to you any loss you might incur, up to the sum of a hundred gold ducats. If it should seem to you that I am taking you too much for granted, it is the great trust I have in you and the very great wish I have to serve Martino, who requests this thing of me with all diligence. Because I know you will understand me right away, I do not want to waste any more words, except that I appreciate this matter as much as I possibly can, and remind you that, insofar as you can salvage it, you should do so however possible. And if I can return the favor either in this or in another case, I am always ready at your command. Christ keep you from harm and give you good fortune in all your ventures.

Yours, Lorenzo di Niccolò Machiavelli, in Florence

❖ LETTER 31
Francesco Soderini to Niccolò Machiavelli
Volterra, 29 September 1502

To the Notable Messer Niccolò Machiavelli,
Chancellor of the Eminent Florentine Republic.
In Florence.

Greetings, my dearest Niccolò. It would take more than one hour, and more than my skill, to answer your very charming letter.[1] Therefore for the present I shall only welcome your affection for the fatherland and for my family, and give you undying thanks, and I will humbly ask God, along with you, to consent to stand by his election and the judgment of the Florentine people, for the sake of our common salvation and dignity. We ourselves, in such a crisis of the republic, shall always be under such obligation that none of us would not most willingly offer his abilities and his own blood for the fatherland and for our citizens. And since you are second to none in ability[2] and affection, you will not be only with us, but far dearer and more welcome. For as far as I am concerned, may I be found worthy of the many bounties with which divine beneficence has so far endowed me. But if anything should have accrued either by chance or through error, it will all be willingly offered to my country and friends. Farewell, and love me as you do.

Volterra, Sept. 29, 1502
Yours, Francesco Soderini
Bishop of Volterra
Referendary of Our Most Holy Pope

❖ LETTER 32
Niccolò Valori to Niccolò Machiavelli
Florence, 11 October 1502

To the Distinguished Niccolò Machiavelli, Most Worthy Secretary,
with the Most Illustrious Duke Valentino.

My very dear Niccolò. Although I know that you are very well informed
by the public letters, and I am happy with these, I cannot however help sending you a couple of lines for my own satisfaction. Your essay[1] and the description could not have been more appreciated, and people recognize what I in
particular have always recognized in you: a clear, exact, and sincere account,
upon which one can rely completely. And I, in truth, discussing it with Piero
Soderini, gave it its due as generously as one can possibly state it, giving you
this particular and personal praise. It seems that since His Lordship there is
etc., he ought to be more forthright[2]; and for those who have judgment of it,
it seems best to wait for him, and discussion ought to be accompanied by
some honorable offer and conditions. Your judgment is desired here about affairs over there, and your description of the French ones, and the hopes the
duke has about them. Because you promised us to describe both the present
forces of that prince, as well as those he hopes to get, both Italian and French,
it is not necessary to tell us anything else about it, except that the better they
can be understood, the more easily and the better we shall be able to come to
a decision here. If anything else is needed, I am as much yours as anyone you
have in this city, and let that suffice, just for your good qualities and the affection you have. I send you my regards. Christ keep you.

11 October 1502.
Niccolò Valori, in Florence

❖ LETTER 33
Agostino Vespucci to Niccolò Machiavelli
Florence, 14 October 1502

To the Notable Niccolò Machiavelli, Honored Florentine Secretary and Envoy.
In the Court of the Illustrious Duke of Romagna.

*Niccolò, greetings. I do not know whether to write or not. If not, I shall be accused of
negligence, but if I do write, I fear I shall be called a slanderer, especially against Marcello and Ricci.[1] Marcello, the negligent one in the matter (that is, of your duty), has refused the burden of writing. Meanwhile, lo! Ricci, who is always on the lookout for duties of that sort, since he was with the Council of Eighty yesterday evening, officiously
calls for Marcello, who just at that moment happened to be out of the palace. He rises
forthwith, descends the stairs, bursts into the chancellery, and cries out, somewhat threat-
eningly, "Hey, hey, write!" Immediately Biagio, as if guessing what has occurred, took*

flight in order not to write with Ricci dictating. Poor me, I was the only one left, and sighing from the depths of my heart and panting, I take up my falling pen and scribble along, fearing that if I ventured a word, the same thing would happen to me here that they say happened to the man from Perugia in France, and since he is a colleague of our Signori, I swallowed a pill containing more bile than honey. I write three or four letters while he dictates. That man returns whence he had come with the book and reads, and what he recited was approved. And so, whether for this reason or another, the Signori have ordered that it be sent by the long way to the king of the French. So you see where that spirit of yours,[2] so eager for riding, wandering, and roaming about, has gotten us. Blame yourself and not others if anything adverse happens. I wish that no one except you were standing by me and was my superior in the chancellery, although you attempt and dare all the things which that most poisonous viper attacks me, pursues me, and cuts me to bits for, about which that terrible man, worthless and contentious, gives me orders. But that is all water under the bridge. Biagio likewise, besides hating you on account of such things, blabbers on, reviles you with insults, damning and cursing you, says and cares for nothing, reckoning all things worthless.

I am sure, by God, that you are held in great honor there, you whom the duke himself and all the courtiers favor, so that they heap praise on you as a prudent man, surround and flatter you. That is a pleasure, since I love you dearly. Nevertheless, I would not wish you to neglect what may soon keep you from completing your work. My Niccolò, even if those things now creep and slink about, they must soon come out into the open. You know the nature of men, their deceptions and secrecy, their rivalries and hatreds, you know what they are like, upon whom a man depends entirely at this time. Therefore, since you are prudent, you look out for yourself and for us, plan for our common advantage. Rouse Marcello with your letters, urge him on, force him, press him, and goad him to consent doing your duty, for some days, to undertake the burden of dictating letters, not to resist it, not to shut his eyes and yet, as he does, despise it. Since you left, I think he worships the Goddess of Sloth, so slothful, that is, lazy and lacking in energy, has he become.

Your wife has received those two aurei, *the work of your friend and relation Leonardo.[3]*

Yesterday morning, while I was reciting a letter just written to Piero Soderini, and he grumbled at it countless times during the reading, he finally said: "The writer who wrote this in his own hand has much talent, is endowed with much judgment, and also no little wisdom." For the record. Farewell.

From the Chancellery. October 13, 1502, hastily and tumultuously.

Your coadjutor, Agostino

❖ LETTER 34
Niccolò Antinori to Niccolò Machiavelli
Florence, 17 October 1502

To the Notable Niccolò Machiavelli, Most Worthy Florentine Secretary and
Envoy to the Illustrious Duke of Romagna.

Distinguished, etc. I have learned what you write to M. Marcello about the
safe-conduct,[1] and to that end I am writing to M. Alessandro,[2] so that he may
have it sent and may forward it to me. Since you say that he will have to be
given something, I am writing him the enclosed and telling him that, as soon
as I have it, I shall send him an authorization for 30 ducats for that shipment. I
give you notice of this only for your information. I shall be grateful if you do
not show you know anything about this. *Farewell.*

From our audience, Florence, 17 October 1502.
N. Antinori

❖ LETTER 35
Biagio Buonaccorsi to Niccolò Machiavelli
Florence, 15–18 October 1502

To Niccolò Machiavelli, Most Honored Florentine Secretary.
In Imola.

Balls, Niccolò, my friend, I am in such favor with this Signoria that when
the rider sent by you arrived last night around midnight,[1] and they saw there
were letters for me, they sent them home to me right away: and I also managed to get my allowance the way I managed to chatter, and it took three
more times, so that, because Ser Antonio della Valle was afraid that I would
faint at the third one, he gave me a recipe for an enema that worked so well
for me that my Madonna Lessandra[2] is overjoyed, and Madonna Gostanza[3] is
in despair lest Ser Antonio publish his recipes; but I think I can console her,
because when they had to send to Leghorn for someone to teach them how
to grow new feathers on sparrows,[4] I put her forward and said that she grows
feathers so well that she knocked Ser Antonio right out of bed with one
refeathering. She has taken to this practice, and if Ser Snail[5] does not break it
off, I think she will sing my praises, and she, having heard of it, urges me to
keep it coming. Bust my balls, you have had your chance to rob the hen
house; since your expenses have been paid and you have been quartered so
honorably, try and carry out the errand I gave you, otherwise I won't commend you as Madonna Gostanza does Ser Tightass,[6] and if you do it I shall
urge you to continue: you will be doing the thing most cherished to my
heart: if you let me in on anything, I shall keep silent, otherwise I shall imitate
Fedini,[7] who still strings you along.

Niccolò, I am not angry,[8] nor am I judging your feelings toward me from these stories—because in truth it is nothing but bother for me, and I also am busy since you have been away—but rather from innumerable other things, which would compel me if I thought about them not to bear you all the affection that I have for you. I do not want you to be grateful to me for that, because even if I wanted not to love you and not to be yours entirely, I could not do it, so driven as I say by nature that compels me to do so, although in truth little account should be taken of it, since I cannot harm, or even less help, you. And if I saw or had seen that you were the same with all your other friends as you are with me, I would not have let it make such an impression within myself. But I see that I have to complain about my ill fortune and bad choices, and not about you, since I find no reciprocation whatever in those whom I love as much as myself, and whom I have chosen as my chiefs and masters—of this you can be an excellent judge, particularly for yourself, as well as for some others who are as well-known to you as to me. But let us not speak of this any more, for I wish nothing but what you wish, and enough said.

I sent all your letters this morning immediately and faithfully. I am waiting for the velvet from Lorenzo[9] and the doublet from Madonna Marietta, and, as soon as I get them, I shall send everything to you, and if you need anything else, just write.

As I was writing, Lorenzo sent me the velvet, and so by the present bearer, who will be Baccino, I am sending it to you and with it the doublet; but you really are a rascal, since in place of a yard of damask you want to wear a greasy and torn thing: go and throw up, and you will be doing us a great honor.

Madonna Marietta wrote to me via her brother to ask when you will be back; she says she does not want to write, and she is making a big fuss, and she is hurt because you promised her you would stay 8 days and no more. So come back, in the name of the devil, so the womb doesn't suffer, otherwise we shall be bothered along with Brother Lanciolino.

About <the selection of Bernardo de' Ricci to go to France,[10]> I would have a lot of things to tell you, one finer than the other, as well as <a lot of stories about our Ser Antonio da Colle, who went secretly to Siena with some of his wild notions, and nothing came of it;> but I think I shall do it better, and more safely, face to face. <Ricci> has not left yet, and I do not know whether he will go, although he has <gotten the commission and everything, except for the money;> and because those who were sending him were afraid <that the credentials would not be approved, they directed him to the ambassador[11] in order to be sure that he go, and they wanted him to present him to the king, and then for the commission to be carried out; and in fact he was not carrying anything, but it was done to have him rustle up[12]> a hundred ducats or so, since <that territory was taken, and similarly that of Milan. He has not left yet, and I do not know whether he will go, because the family of the ambassador complained, since it appeared he would not go there without expense to him. Your Leonardo[13] does not want to give him money if they do not allocate it, and that would never be approved, especially once the business is revealed.>

I go 4 or 6 times every day to the new gonfalonier, and he is completely ours, and his brother the monsignor asked me today about you when I was with him, and he appears to love you particularly. I performed my duty as a friend concerning your situation: I wish you would do the same for me, and I would not desire anything else from you.

If you do not mind, write a note to Guidotti in my favor so that, now that I have my appropriation, he gets me out of the general; do it if you see fit or if you have the opportunity.

Niccolò, I would like to know when Fracassa[14] gets there; and when he does I would like you to help a friend of mine by giving him a letter and saying a few words to him in conformity with what I shall say hereafter. The cashier of the Signoria here, when he was here, lent him 20 ducats and has never gotten them back. I would appreciate your saying a word to him about it, because in truth he is behaving badly, having been done a favor when he was in such need as he found himself in then. If he is willing to pay it back, as he has promised several times, we shall write you a letter for him to pay it to you. Do not answer concerning the code[15] above, or use the style that I have, that is, write in code. *Farewell.*

Florence, 15 October 1502.

Niccolò, I was wrong in wanting my friend to be done a favor, to show him I desired it, because nothing will come of it: and if this is the remedy, I do not care about it.

Yours, B. B.

It is the 17th and <our friend[16] has not yet gone, and I do not believe he will go, since they cannot give him money without an appropriation,> which he will never be able to get. Last night, <when he sought this favor, an appropriation for Luigi della Stufa turned up only 7 votes favorable to him.>

I had forgotten to tell you that Ser Antonio da Colle, when he was before <Pandolfo[17] and speaking with him, fell down from that illness and had to be carried away,> and the same happened to him <on horseback on his way there.>

Concerning public matters, I have nothing to tell you except what is written to you in the public letters: when there is anything, I shall not need reminding.

It is the 18th, <and I believe our friend, that is to say, Ricci, will go, so strong is his passion, and yet he has not yet gotten the money;> but since a way has been found <to get the letter approved for his passage from among the Signoria alone, for otherwise it would never be obtained, a way will be found to do the rest, but your Leonardo> will be mistaken <to give him any.>

Salvestro, that is to say, Ricci, sends you his regards once again. Nothing else.

Florence, 18 October 1502.
B. Bo.

Postscript.[18] Niccolò, my friend, both because Biagio is taking care of the public letters, and *also* because I do not have time, I shall not say anything else.

I shall be grateful if you write a couple of lines in reply to my Giovanni,[19] whether that M. Taddeo is there or not. And I beg you to write and ask me, if anything at all should be necessary, because no one will serve you more faithfully; you will find others more boastful and wishing more advancement. Because you know me, I shall say no more, since you have me especially at your command, body and soul. And what I wrote you in Latin[20] these past few days *I did on request,* and do not go to any trouble because nothing is lacking here, and nothing is ever desired by the Ten, and M. Marcello is as hard-working as ever in the palace. Campriano[21] would have liked to rustle up a ducat; and since you did not write about it I could not collect anything but 2 ducats that went to your wife, who sent one of your coats here and some velvet, which are being sent to you by the hand of Biagio. There is nothing new here, and by my faith everyone here is in good spirits; and the best local wine costs no more than 12 soldi a barrel, and there is an abundance of everything else. *Farewell.*

From Florence, 18 October 1502.
Your servant,
Agostino, in the chancellery

❖ LETTER 36
Piero Guicciardini[1] to Niccolò Machiavelli
Florence, 20 October 1502

To the Notable, Very Dear Man, Niccolò Machiavelli.
In Imola.

My very dear, etc. I received a letter from you a few days ago, and I treated it as it seemed proper to me. I did not answer you, since it did not seem necessary: and concerning the affairs down there, I have nothing else to tell you except for you to continue as you have done up to now, since it seems to me you are giving satisfaction to everyone. Here a favorable disposition is to be seen in everyone toward friendship with His Lordship there, because of the enemies' nature and out of belief that the king[2] will thus be pleased; an answer concerning this is awaited any time now: and in addition because such a friendship, if proper advantage were taken of it, would serve one and the other party because of proximity and other respects.

The bearer of this will be Girolamo, my usual one, who is coming there to get to know the place, urged on strongly in this by a certain Grechetto,[3] who was here recruiting for the duke, as you will hear from him. I shall be grateful if you do him whatever favor you can: and he is a man to serve well and who will do honor to you. I do not need anything else.

In Florence, 20 October 1502.
Piero Guicciardini

❖ LETTER 37
Biagio Buonaccorsi to Niccolò Machiavelli
Florence, 21 October 1502

To Niccolò Machiavelli, His Most Honored Florentine Secretary.
In Imola.

Niccolò. Because it was a holiday yesterday when I received your letter, I could not have the mantle made for you; but early this morning I went to see Leonardo Guidotti and got the cloth, letting myself be guided by him, as you wrote me; and it was cut according to a pattern that he had, which seems fine to me; and it took 7 1/2 *braccia* of cloth, which, from what I could see, will cost you 4 1/2 ducats or less per *canna*.[1] I had it cut to my measurements, and concerning the collar and the other things I did as you asked me to, and the best I could. I shall be happy for you to be well-served; if not, go scratch your ass.

We have tried to locate some *Lives* of Plutarch, and there are none for sale in Florence. Be patient, because we have to write to Venice; to tell you the truth, you can go to the devil for asking for so many things.

I expect you have written to Guidotti and not treated me as usual.

I am grieved not to have done everything for you, because your Madonna Marietta learned of this mantle and is making a big fuss. And if you had not married off her girl as well as you did, she would be unhappy; but she would like to hear the details of the dowry: the nuptial gift[2] and other things are in order, and all the old crows of Sardigna[3] will come to honor her and accompany her with honor.

I do not know whether I shall have the mantle this evening; if I do, I shall send it; if not, I shall not fail to by the first messenger. And you will inform me of the receipt of the velvet, whose price Lorenzo refused to ask Marietta for, but he says he will add it on to another account you have with him. And if that blind man Guidotti had been willing to give me my money, with cash everything else could have been done better. Be patient, since I have to be even more so.

I have nothing new to write to you, and so be patient; and if anything comes, I shall treat you as a friend.

Ser Antonio della Valle is going mad; a few days ago, when he and Ser Andrea di Romolo were arguing over a game of backgammon, Ser Andrea hauled off with a kick that broke his behind. The poor man is wearing saddle padding over it, not knowing how or being able to bandage himself more suitably, and there is no way for him to get rid of it. They are both going around armed—I do not know if you understand me: Ser Andrea with carping talk, and Ser Antonio with enemas; and each of them sticks to his story. I think that we shall fix the matter up if a way can be found to heal Ser Antonio's behind.

Niccolò, I am in a predicament, because Ser Antonio has lost his little brazier and blames me for it, and he wants me to pay him back damages and interest: I do not know how to set this matter straight, and yet I should like to satisfy him: so do not fail to give me your opinion.

The present bearer, who will be Jacopino, is bringing you the mantle, and it looks good to me. It is sewn up in front, because I have seen mantles worn that way: if you should not like it, it will not be much work to unstitch it. Indeed, I have done the best I could: just be sure that the first time it is fitted on you, it takes on the right shape.

I remind you of Madonna Dora's business with Ricci, which I am very anxious about. Leonardo has paid 5 lire for the sewing and cutting of the cloak, so you are in his debt for that amount, and you are in my debt for a few rustlings.

I have not spoken about your leave, because you do not care about it and I know it. For me it is enough to shit blood for you and for me, and for you <to go rustling about.[4]>

Niccolò, I have to tell you that our colleagues are making a big fuss about my appropriation,[5] and they say that if it is not revoked they will not do anything, because they do not want us to have two salaries; so that, whenever you come to the end of the amount you have earned and the money you got, arrange things so as not to have to ask for an appropriation, and I also do not think you will ever get it, so as to be able then to cancel the debit, where the money you got will appear. Act as best you see fit.

Ser Antonio da Colle <came back here, and he has gone back to Siena to take care of some business that looks like nonsense to me, because it will not have any success, and yet His Lordship[6] had siphoned off something from it.>

Ricci is still here, <although he got 150 ducats to go: I do not know what will come of it.>

Lorenzo di Giacomino tells me that tomorrow morning he will send the wine and that he has served you like a good man; by the time it gets there, it will cost you just under 5 ducats; so that you are going to be ruined by it. In addition, he has requested of me that, if His Lordship[7] should want to set up a post service here, he would like you to work it out with your friends there for him to have the post stage here in Florence. Because you know how fond I am of him, I recommend him to you as much as I can.

Florence, 21 October 1502.
Bi. Bo.

❖ LETTER 38
Lorenzo di Giacomino[1] to Niccolò Machiavelli
Florence, 21 October 1502

To Niccolò Machiavelli, Florentine Secretary, His Master.
21 October 1502.

Dear Niccolò. I am informing you that tomorrow morning I shall send you the wine. I had to buy the baskets and the cords and the straw; and when

I had everything set, the carter insisted on making an agreement with me whereby you have to promise him 12 lire per *libbra*.[2] He was not willing to come down. It is a drink you will like. I shall keep you informed of everything by my letters, etc.

I am informing you that I would like you to work it out with your friends over there, who are setting up the post stages from Rome to over there. They have set them up from Rome to here by word of mouth, and someone has come to set them up one by one. So, if you want to make use of the one you know, you have to act quickly. I think you will have to do there with the one who dispatched the courier. I gave you notice that I sent it on the run. I send you my regards. Act as quickly as you can.

Yours, Lorenzo di Giacomino, Florence

❖ LETTER 39
Salvestro di Salvestro Agostino to Niccolò Machiavelli
Florence, 21 October 1502

To the Excellent Messer Niccolò Machiavelli,
Florentine Envoy and Secretary, His Very Good Friend.
Imola.

Your Magnificence Niccolò, my very dear friend. I shall never fail to be your devoted servant, with all my heart, even if my election[1] should not come to fruition; because once more I again appreciate your efforts on my behalf. I put my hope in God and in my master Messer Marcello and in my Niccolò Machiavelli, in whom is all my trust, reminding you that I know I am the slave of your good will alone, and I do not know many who will do this for me, except that deeds will bear witness to my words.

I remind you that promptness is needed.

Aside from confirming my election, a letter is required to the commune of Orvieto that after the present *podestà* I should be the first. If I am presumptuous, it is your work and that of my master Messer Marcello that are the cause.

I send my regards to Your Excellency.
21 October 1502.
Salvestro di Salvestro d'Agostino,
Florence

❖ LETTER 40
Piero Soderini to Niccolò Machiavelli
Florence, 22 October 1502

To the Notable Niccolò Machiavelli, Florentine Secretary,
Envoy to the Illustrious Duke of Romagna, Friend, etc.
In Imola.

Notable man, very dear friend. Since I was designated by our people to the
rank[1] that you[2] know of in our city, I have not written to anyone, either a noble or a personal friend of mine, judging it to be fitting to wait until I am inaugurated and in the palace: and so I have not written even to that Most Illustrious Prince.[3] And therefore I shall write to you on behalf of some people
from whom six mules were taken during the past months at Castel Durante
by some of His Excellency's men[4]; about which it seems in the past few days
he was similarly written by our magistrate of the Ten. I would like you to be
so kind as to speak in my name to His Most Illustrious Lordship; first of all,
you will offer my respects to him; thereafter you will come with His Excellency to the specific case of the 6 mules that were taken, which may it please
him to have returned, for my sake, to Marco and Iacopo Brinciassi, our
carters; you will beseech him for this *over and over again:* and I, as I have said,
shall postpone writing to His Most Illustrious Lordship until I am in the
palace, in such a way as I shall judge proper for my private and public figure.
Meanwhile you will recommend me to his good favor, the which may God
increase for his happiness. *Farewell.*

From Florence, 22 October 1502.
Piero Soderini

❖ LETTER 41
Bartolomeo Ruffini to Niccolò Machiavelli
Florence, 23 October 1502

To the Excellent Messer Niccolò Machiavelli,
Envoy and Florentine Secretary, Chief and Honored Benefactor.
In Imola.

Niccolò, honored chief, etc. I hear from Biagio that you are about to marry
off my girl,[1] and that, if you can, you will give her a good capital, which would
give me great satisfaction. I beseech you heartily, if you have the opportunity,
to work it out with the court clerk or other administrators of yours for her
contract to be signed before you leave there, because I can no longer provide
for her expenses and I have great need of the money. The value, if you do not
know it, is known by the clerk, and I am writing him the enclosed letter to let
him know of my desire, and for everything to be done for the girl's good name
and your honor to have her offered in such a way as not to lose her good

name, but rather to increase it, as you will know how to arrange.

Your letters to Biagio and the others are most welcome to all, and the jokes and witticisms you write in them make everyone split their sides laughing and give great pleasure. This All Saints' Day you will be remembered to the director about that business we usually get,[2] and it will be sent to you at home. Your lady is well and is waiting for you and often sends here for news of you and your return. Nothing else comes to mind. I send you my regards. *Farewell.*

> *Florence, 23 October 1502.*
> *Yours, Bartolomeo Ruffini*
> *In the Chancellery*

I wrote you several days ago in recommendation of someone called Cianchera,[3] a Florentine and my relative, and he was supposed to bring you the letter: I would appreciate knowing what came of it, and I pray that it not be any trouble for you to send me a word about it. *Farewell.*

❖ LETTER 42
Niccolò Valori to Niccolò Machiavelli
Florence, 23 October 1502

To the Excellent Niccolò Machiavelli, Most Worthy Florentine Secretary.
With Duke Valentino.

My very dear, like a brother. I have a letter from you dated the 20th, which was most precious to me, as everything from you will always be. Truly, your reports and discussions could not be better, or more appreciated. Would to God that every man acted as you do, then fewer mistakes would be made. We here, since the news comes from over there, have not much to tell you. We are sending Ser Alessandro[1] to Rome, which should be welcome to His Highness there, and you can take great honor from it. The troops called up have not been sent to the border, because they would do nothing but harm; but you can tell His Excellency that several of the best constables[2] have been sent, capable of seeing action in Borgo[3] and elsewhere. Meanwhile we are thinking of making some show that will do honor to His Excellency and give security to us. Concerning our personal business, God is witness that I love and esteem you more than a brother. And since I know that you would like to be here for the inauguration of the new gonfalonier, I shall see what I can do, but it will not work out because he himself is not much in agreement. In all conscience, this is enough, people were not lacking to speak on your behalf to him and to tell the truth. And, upon the trust between the two of us, I in particular spoke twice with him about it at length, so that, from being your friend, I believe he has become your great friend. What you desire[4] in the second place ought not to be denied you; but these colleagues of ours are so testy, none of us has ever been able to get them to do anything; we shall not leave off getting them to help you and the others. Nothing else, for lack of time, except that I am always at your service. Christ keep you.

> 23 October 1502.
> Niccolò Valori, in the palace

❖ LETTER 43
Jacopo Salviati[1] to Niccolò Machiavelli
Florence, 27 October 1502

To the Magnificent Messer Niccolò Machiavelli,
with the Most Illustrious Duke Valentino.
In Imola.
Jesus. 27 October 1502.

Magnificent man, etc. I have your letter of the 23rd, by which I have been informed how much you have been assessed for the loan[2] and the desire you have to recover it, in order to provide for your affairs. At the start of the coming month, a few days from thence, the eighth will be drawn, then the subsequent payments that remain as the times require. Because I want to gratify you and so that you can provide for your needs, I am ready to let you have up to the amount mentioned from my funds, not as a cut from the above-mentioned appropriation but as a loan. If you should so need, let me know, and I shall pay it to whomever you ask, if it so pleases you. For this letter, there is nothing else to say. I am at your service. Christ keep you.

As for the news, I accept the judgment you made of it, and I recommend that.

> Jacopo Salviati, in Florence

❖ LETTER 44
Biagio Buonaccorsi to Niccolò Machiavelli
Florence, 28 October 1502

To His Most Honored Niccolò Machiavelli.
In Imola.

Niccolò. Even though you are wise and cautious, and it is presumptuous on my part to want to remind you of how you should write, and especially about those things that you see with your own eyes all the time, nevertheless I shall tell you briefly what I need to, notwithstanding the fact that I have done my duty here in all those places and with all those people who would have wanted to find fault with you. First of all, I must remind you to write more often, because the passage of 8 days at a time between the arrival of your letters does not bring you honor, nor much satisfaction to those who sent you. You were criticized about this by the Signoria and the others, because, since these things are of such great importance, people here are very anxious to hear often how matters stand. And notwithstanding the fact that you have written at length about the troops there with His Highness, and the reinforcements he hopes for, and the readiness of his courage to defend himself; and that you indicated very well both his own forces and those of his enemies, and set them before people's eyes, nevertheless you draw <too bold a conclusion[1]> when you write that <his enemies can no longer do much harm to His Lordship;> and it seems to me not that you have drawn criticism for this, as far as I know, but that you cannot make so absolute a judgment because, logically and according to what you have written, neither the progress of the enemy nor what forces they have must be made public there precisely enough to give rise to your judgment. <From a variety of authorities people here have heard that the league's forces[2] are quite powerful, and people do not have a very favorable judgment of the forces of His Lordship;> so that since you have done and you have judiciously discussed things, particularly everything you describe, <leave the judgment to others;> and stick yourself in the ass. And do not send me any answer at all to this.

The letter to Salviati was delivered, and he is answering you.[3] Since you write me that, if I get the money, I should send the hat to you, not having gotten any, I do not believe you want it; if you want it anyway, let me know and I shall buy it with my own money, and as cheap as I can. Your other letters to Niccolò and Albertaccio[4] were also delivered; and I performed my duty as your friend to Piero Soderini face-to-face, reading him your letter, because, at the end, where you ask for leave[5] or etc., he laughed, and I went on to say that you wrote me that, if you were not provided for, you would come back, because you have heard that appropriations were provided only for those chosen by the Eighty, and you did not want to waste your own funds. Laughing, he answered me, saying: "He is right, but he writes too infrequently." And so ended our conversation. I urge you not to go to sleep, because you would never get paid for your service: act now as best you see fit.

Your appropriation has been set, but I do not believe it will be anything much, God bless you and make you grow.

Things will be settled between Ser Antonio and Ser Andrea,[6] and Ser Andrea has calmed down quite a bit, now that he has understood the way to protect himself against Ser Antonio's getting into his business, for if he tries to hang something on him, by God, he will not stick his nose in again. A bow is not fast enough for him: he thought he was more like lightning. More power to him.

You will see by the enclosed letter from Jacopo Salviati what he replies about, etc. Let me know what I have to do, and it will be done.

Lord Niccolò Valori had me write two letters in your name, one to Lord Luigi Venturi, and the other to Lord Giannozzo, begging them to provide for you: and indeed they have promised me they will do so. I am working at it just as hard as I can, and I believe I shall dig so many holes, I shall send it to you. *Nothing else.*

Florence, 28 October 1502.

Biagio

❖ LETTER 45
Niccolò Valori to Niccolò Machiavelli
Florence, 28 October 1502

To the Excellent Niccolò Machiavelli, Most Worthy Secretary.
With Duke Valentino.

My very dear Niccolò. We are so busy that I have treated you badly: and *what is worse,* I do not know whether I can treat you better with deeds; you can be quite sure that I shall not fail for lack of effort. The notices coming from you could not be more appreciated; but to speak as we are wont, they would like you to write more often, even though they think it is not without some reason. We have word here from Rome that the pope is in close negoti-ations[1] for agreement with all those leagued together, and last night there was some verification and notice from Cortona[2] of marshaling and gatherings of troops, and they will cut across our territory: so that we would like to get to the bottom of this matter, as far as you possibly can, and inform our gon-falonier, who is completely devoted to you; do not answer me because I shall be away from here and I do not want to take care of state business. If possible, the ducats for you will be paid to Biagio: because I am being called, I shall not say anything else to you except that I am yours, as you know. May God keep you in good health.

28 October 1502.
Niccolò Valori, in the palace

❖ LETTER 46
Niccolò Valori to Niccolò Machiavelli
Florence, 31 October 1502

To the Excellent Niccolò Machiavelli, Most Worthy Secretary.
In Imola.

Very dear, as a brother. We have given Biagio 40 ducats on your account, which is the best we were able to do, for two reasons: one, because of the shortage and penury in which we find ourselves, the other I shall keep inside my pen. If I have failed to satisfy you with the ducats, God is my witness I have worked both in public and in private to make your accomplishments known, *for although they are evident enough in themselves,* it is not inappropriate to reveal them; and indeed with the new members of both the Signoria and the Ten I was pleased with what I did. Truly, these last two letters you have sent us had so much strength in them and show your judgment to be so good that they could not have been more appreciated.

In particular, I talked at length about them with Piero Soderini, who does not feel that you can be moved from there on any account, and I did not fail to inform him of what had to be done; and you will see that you find him very favorable to your demands. I urge you to be patient and to do as you are wont, for your accomplishments will have to be better known than they have been up to now. If I can do anything at all for you, since I have no brothers, I consider that I have you and you have me in no other stead than that of a brother. Let this letter take the place of a contract for you. Christ keep you. 31 October 1502. I shall not go into the news, since I do not want any from you either.

Yours, N.V., in the palace

❖ LETTER 47
Biagio Buonaccorsi to Niccolò Machiavelli
Florence, 1 November 1502

To His Most Honored Niccolò Machiavelli, in Imola.
Imola.

My Niccolò. I shall not answer your letter of the 27th at length, for lack of time. I shall only tell you that I have set my own interests aside for you and have been so importunate and so insistent with Lord Niccolò Valori that yesterday I rustled up[1] thirty gold ducats[2] for you, and I have them in my hand; and the only reason I am not sending them is that I do not know how they can get there safely as regards those French troops[3]: I am waiting for your directions as to what you want me to do, and if you want me to send them at your risk by the first messenger, I shall do so. Write me at length and clearly, in such a way that if there should be a mishap, I shall not be responsible for it. I can tell you truly that I do not know how we can get the appropriation approved; but you will have money soon: let it suffice that I have it in hand and you can spend it; and I have done what no one expected, to show you how a person can be of service.

The velvet was taken from Zerino at the gate; I shall see if I can get it back. My Madonna Alessandra will do what is needed, if she can, because she wants to be godmother and I want you as godfather, and you will not spend anything, by the ass's balls.

Find out whether Messer Alessandro[4] there will accept a letter from the Salviatis to pay you 30 ducats, and I shall give them to them here, and I shall have a letter of exchange made for it; but if it can come safely in cash, it will be a better idea.

Our friend[5] did not go to France, and Piero[6] is in the palace, and you would be better off here: excuse me, for it is affection that makes me speak.

I am sending this rider to Madonna Marietta to find out if she wants anything, and I send you my regards. In Florence, 1 November 1502.

The safe conduct is not being sent to you this evening because Ser Andrea has been playing backgammon all day long; but it has been authorized and will come by the first messenger.

Biagio

❖ LETTER 48
Biagio Buonaccorsi to Niccolò Machiavelli
Florence, 3 November 1502

To His Most Honored Niccolò Machiavelli, etc.

Niccolò. I wrote you briefly by the rider Carlo, since I did not have time, and in that letter I gave you notice that through the agency of Lord Niccolò Valori and my insistence we had gotten 30 ducats from the chamberlain in charge of loans; and I have them in my hands at your disposal, but I did not send them with Carlo, since I did not know whether they would arrive safely. In this letter I am telling you the same thing, and I shall not send them if I do not have your express request: so give me a clear answer about this, etc.

I got the velvet back and sent it to your house.

The gonfalonier is writing you the enclosed letter: see to it that he is obliged and that you honor his requests, and find a way to come back.

Nothing else. I send you my regards.

> *Florence, 3 November 1502.*
> *Brother Biagio*

The Signoria: Antonio Canigiani, Niccolò Capponi, Zanobi Carnesecchi, Ugo della Stufa, Piero di Brunetto, Antonio Benozzi, Tommaso Girardi, Tinoro Bellacci, Piero Soderini as gonfalonier.

❖ LETTER 49
Biagio Buonaccorsi to Niccolò Machiavelli
Florence, 3 November 1502

To His Honored Niccolò Machiavelli.
Imola.

My Niccolò. In order for a man not to arrive there without a letter from me, I write you these few lines, having written to you today along with a letter from the gonfalonier, who, since he has entered the palace, seems to have begun to take charge of everything. He has already inaugurated a policy of wanting all business to be done early, because everyone is showing up[1] at twelve o'-clock in the morning and at 9 o'clock in the evening. This evening he made his brother, Bishop Soderini, ambassador to France, with such favor that it was an amazing thing. And he spoke, when that was done, to the Eighty, saying that, although this must be a difficult matter for the bishop, nonetheless he will do everything in his power to see that he goes. And he is certain to go, and Alessandro Nasi with him. Today the sessions of the Ten began to be organized in the manner that you know of; and our chancellery will serve the Ten for now, and the hall[2] will accommodate us: let this suffice, you rheumy prick.

I wrote you that I have the 30 ducats but do not want to send them without your request: and so let me know, and I shall do so. The captain who paid the soldier withheld the 30 soldi: I shall have them given back to me, if he is willing; if not, I shall be patient; and you will get a good accounting of everything.

Alessandra did not go to see Marietta, because she does not go out of Piero del Nero's[3] house, and Alessandra did not know the house; I shall send her there as soon as I can.

I shall send you the velvet hat, unless you write to the contrary.

Nothing else.

Florence, 3 November 1502.

Biagio

Carlino Bonciani, the handsome one, was killed, and I do not know by whom. Giovambattista Soderini[4] sends you his regards.

❖ LETTER 50
Biagio Buonaccorsi to Niccolò Machiavelli
Florence, 5 November 1502

To His Most Honored Niccolò Machiavelli.

My Niccolò. Those who judge things too quickly often have to change their minds, as has just happened to me. <The new gonfalonier is beginning to reorganize the city, because he wants to reduce the salaries of the chancellery workers,> and he arranged to have a list of all the regular workers and their salaries, so that if this thing happens, it will have two bad effects: one, the decrease, the other, that he will not be able to get anyone. I had written wonderful things[1] to you, since the beginning seemed good to me: I shall not make that mistake any more, because I shall be guided from day to day, and even that will seem like a long time to me, and I shall do it rather from hour to hour. You yourself know the importance of the matter, and what a bad effect such rumors have, so I shall not write you at length about it any further. With Ser Antonio Vespucci, I wrote a statement, or it would be better to say I tried to, which it seemed to me would be very useful to us; it was that they should put into the list the salary we received precisely per month, so that they could see what the hundreds came to and so they didn't repeat anything: I do not believe even this will be done. And so everyone is upset, <and the gonfalonier> is doing it without our knowledge; but because I told you I no longer want to judge so quickly, I shall do the same for this, so as not to have to change my mind, because it could be that just as he wanted a list of beds and riders and everything else, he wanted this for the same purpose—that is, to see and to know once and for all how many administrators he has. I would be glad if it was for this end, although the rumor is to the contrary, and they are saying what I told you above. We shall wait and see, and pray God to help us.

The time of reconfirmation is coming closer, and I shall not take the trouble for you now to go and talk about trees and fruit, and about mules and shit, because I shall not do it for me, and also I would not do any good. Think about this, because it is important.

While writing, I received your letter of the 3rd, and although I am busy and, therefore, my Niccolò, wretched, since I am under pressure to go to France with these ambassadors, namely, Bishop Soderini and Alessandro, as I wrote you,[2] nevertheless I have let it be, or, to put it better, I shall let it be and do what you tell me; and I shall let myself be hanged before I go to France.

I shall arrange the cloth so that it will not be damaged, and I shall notify the rider as you recommend.

You have heard what Salviati wrote you about the loan,[3] and he has since confirmed the same to me, telling me that he will help you out with his own funds, but not on that appropriation; if you want, because the matter cannot be drawn, as for the salary and what you have to be reimbursed for now, I shall tell it to Guidotti, and I shall do what he tells me.

I got the velvet back and went to your house.

I gave 29 ducats to Lorenzo, and he will send me the cloth, and he will write you, according to what he has promised me, about the cost and everything else; so I am leaving that to him.

While I was writing, Lorenzo came to see me and tells me that, because he does not have black satin in his shop that is suitable for your purposes, he has to buy it, and because it is late and bad weather, in order to serve you well, he has to put it off to Monday. And I, who would like you to be happy and treated with honor, did not mind that.

The ambassadors are going off tomorrow, and I think I shall definitely get out of it, and they are bearing with them letters of exchange for 10 thousand scudi for the pay, etc. If our friend was alive, he would disavow God, because monsignor, as soon as he accepted, said he was raring to go,[4] and he urged Alessandro on, so with God's help they will go. Nothing else occurs to me right now.

I sent the letter to Marietta right away, and I shall send the other one to Andrea the same way.

Florence, 5 November 1502.
Brother Biagio

❖ LETTER 51
Marcello Virgilio di Adriano Berti to Niccolò Machiavelli
Florence, 7 November 1502

To the Notable Niccolò Machiavelli, Secretary and
Florentine Envoy to the Most Illustrious Duke of Romagna, as a Brother.
In Imola.

Notable man, etc. The gonfalonier told me this morning that it does not seem right in any way to him that you[1] should depart, since he does not feel it is time, and leave that place devoid of any representative of our city; since he would have to send someone else there, he does not know who could be more suitable, in respect to many things. Therefore he has told me to write you thus and advise you not to leave; the Lord knows whether I do so willingly, since I find myself with my business, yours, and my teaching on my hands. Whether you have to follow the duke or not when he goes to Rimini, you will be told more precisely by the public letter. *Farewell.*

From the Florentine palace, 7 November 1502.
Yours, Marcello Virgilio

❖ LETTER 52
Biagio Buonaccorsi to Niccolò Machiavelli
Florence, 12 November 1502

To His Honored Superior, Niccolò Machiavelli.

Honored Niccolò. I wrote you last night by the rider Carlo, and I was not able to send you that money, which made me very unhappy for your sake, and the same with the hat, which, although I had it packed in the post-box,[1] I forgot about. Then this morning Lorenzo[2] stopped by to see me, and he brought me the 29 ducats that I had given him, and so by the present rider, who must be an asshole, I send them to you and with them the hat, which costs you a ducat, since because it is of several colors I was not able to do better. Never mind.

I gave the bill to Leonardo,[3] so he can get those 2 florins coming to you now from the loan[4]; when I have them, I shall send them to Madonna Marietta or I shall have them recorded by him in your account, as well as the 30 soldi, which I have not yet got but are in a safe place; if you should want it otherwise, let me know, and I shall be glad to do anything.

Nothing more has been heard about what I wrote you concerning the reduction,[5] etc.; but there are some who say that it is necessary not to do it just with salaries but also with men. God make it turn out for the best. I think you must be fed up with it, and there is no need to bother yourself; you ought to keep on insisting on returning, as you have done up to now. I would have several <crazy> things to write you about, that our <Ricci did in this council position of his,> but I shall do it face-to-face, since I do not believe you will have to stay there much longer. I do not want to forget to tell you that of those 150[6] he has <ten left in his hands,> and he would like <them to be left to him because of his expenses; but it will not work.>

Florence, 12 November 1502.
Brother Biagio

❖ LETTER 53
Francesco Cei[1] to Niccolò Machiavelli
Florence, 12 November 1502

To the Notable Messer Niccolò Machiavelli, His Special Friend.
In Imola.

My dear honored one, as a brother, etc. Even though I know that you are very busy, I shall nonetheless give you a bit of trouble with the enclosed letter to my dear, beloved Agostino,[2] which I should like you to have given into his hands; and, if he should give you a reply, I should like you to send it to me by a safe means, offering you as a reward all the gossip that is or can be known by me upon your return, as we have greater abundance of it now than ever. I shall not say anything else, except that Pulci[3] claims to have been restored to life: a great sign for our faith! You can imagine if there is any lack of grounds for it. And since this pen does not do me justice, I send you my regards. Goodbye.

From Florence, 12 November 1502.
Yours, Francesco Cei

❖ LETTER 54
Piero Soderini to Niccolò Machiavelli
Florence, 14 November 1502

To the Notable Niccolò Machiavelli, as a Very Dear Brother,
Florentine Envoy to the Most Illustrious Duke of Romagna.
In Imola.

My very dear Niccolò. I received two letters from you[1] recently, which I did not answer earlier because of my work in the palace, which has been very busy. I was pleased to hear what you have written officially and in private: keep on writing frequently and diligently this way, because we are very desirous of hearing that His Most Illustrious Lordship will soon be ready to encounter his enemies. You will indicate to us what foot and horse troops he has and send us a list[2] of them. We have found the city very disorganized in respect to money, allotments, and many other things, as must be very well known to you: we are seeing to the way to reorganize everything, and already payment has been made to His Most Christian Majesty[3] in Lyons, and money has been given to all our cavalry troops and part of the infantry. Now we are seeing to the way to make payment to Milan. For the Swiss's pay, which runs until the 20th of this month, the allotments were used up months ago: we are seeing to a way to get new funds, but the problems are very great. Nonetheless, we are losing no time, and we hope very soon to work out something suitable, in order to be able to benefit both ourselves and others: up to now it has been the contrary. The entire city is well disposed toward His Excellency there, and I in particular shall certainly not fail to do all those things that may be useful to this republic and gratifying to His Excellency; soon I think we shall be able to inform him that we are ready to do more than talk. Monsignor of Volterra[4] has gone as ambassador to His Most Christian Majesty with instructions not to act otherwise on behalf of His Excellency[5] than of our republic. Although His Excellency has no need of favors with His Majesty, because he is [not][6] likely to favor anyone else, nevertheless, in order not to fail in anything at all that is possible for us, it [the Florentine republic] is ready to spend in public and private, just as soon as it hears from His Excellency that he wants it so, and you should offer my services to him *over and over again.*

A certain Jacopo Brinciassi from Legnaia, who had 6, or rather 5, mules taken from him in Urbino or thereabouts,[7] has been recommended to me by Martino dello Scarfa. Talk about that and make recommendations, I pray you.

I shall not say anything else in this letter. I remind you of what my Tommaso[8] wrote you about his business in Rome, which is very important to him; I want him to be satisfied.

14 November 1502.
Piero Soderini
Perpetual Gonfalonier of the Florentine Republic

❖ LETTER 55
Biagio Buonaccorsi to Niccolò Machiavelli
Florence, 15 November 1502

To His Most Honored Niccolò Machiavelli.

Honored Niccolò. Since I had written the accompanying letter, yours of the 10th appeared, and then one of the 8th[1] that came by a wagoner (may you shit blood), and, as I was writing, yours of the 13th. Concerning what you inquire about in the said letter of the tenth, to learn whether I went to France[2] and how I got out of it, first I shall answer you that I believe I am in Florence. It is just possible that I am wrong about that, since, considering the pressure that was put upon me, I still feel as if I am on uncertain ground. Nothing got me out of such a trip except tireless efforts put in by my friends and my making my feelings clear to the bishop.[3] The latter, although he and Alessandro[4] tried to warm me up to it, when he saw that I was ready to undergo any punishment rather than go, however, promised to help me out with it, and he did so.

The reason that prompted Monsignor to go so soon was to no other purpose than for the sake of his brother, and because of his certain belief that he could do some real good there, so the city would be in the good graces of His Majesty the King, who would have such assurances about the new gonfalonier that he will not be given any cause to alter them, since not one day will be missed in the payments due; and now they have brought with them the ten thousand ducats. All the good that will come to the city and all the honor that his brother will receive is going to depend on His Majesty the King, wherefore he has gone willingly to do both of these things and with the feeling that they are going to succeed, according to what he said to me on his departure. Having gotten to know him, I feel very good about him. He was prompted by urgency as well, because it seemed to him they had waited too long before sending ambassadors there, as it appeared to you, too, when you were here; and he is a determined man. He did not speak about the raise,[5] but Alessandro did, and he was satisfied by authority of the gonfalonier, although the gonfalonier promised, in recommending it to the council, that for the future it would not be spoken of anymore.

Concerning what I wrote to you about cutting us back, etc., nothing further has been said about it, and I do not believe that they are going to say anything. As for the transfer, I feel very good about it, because the disposition is generally favorable; but appetites differ. You would be better off here than over there; I believe you want to come back, but you see what the gonfalonier has had written to you: act in whatever way you believe will achieve your aims but also not displease him. The present bearer will bring you the hat and the money; it will be Carlo, and they are coming at your risk. I shall be glad if they arrive safely, please God and the thieves. I sent your letter to Marietta, and I gave your regards and your messages to everyone, and also gave your regards to Giovambattista Soderini, whom I speak to every morning at the office. Come back, for God's sake, because I cannot satisfy Piero Guicciardini, although I have almost caught on now. I manage as best I can and I work too hard, but you will pay me, etc.

The Signoria felt that you were taking too long to write, because a letter attached by you on the 5th never showed up, and perhaps you did not write it. That asshole Totti[6] took 8 full days getting here, and now Carlo has served very well.

Guidotti has the ticket for those 2 ducats; if he has not gotten them, I shall sure as hell remind him of it.

I shall not write to Ser Ottaviano, and he can go and shit blood before I do. Ask me to do something else.

How things are being arranged with the gonfalonier I have written you at length, and I have nothing else to tell you about him, except that his reputation is growing day by day, and he will know how to keep it up.

Niccolò, you are going to be let down, because you thought <you were going to conclude something over there that would please His Lordship[7],> and this answer muddies things up, <and you are an asshole if you believed that we want to buy everything cash on the line.>

I am sending you in a package 29 ducats, 25 singles and 2 doubloons,[8] and the hat. Let me know when you receive it, and don't look too closely if they should not be such fine gold, for I had a world of trouble to get them at all. I should like you to write to Niccolò Valori and thank him for what he has done for you, because he is a man who is drawn by nature to help out his friends. *Farewell.*

Florence, 15 November 1502.
Brother Biagio

❖ LETTER 56
Francesco Machiavelli to Niccolò Machiavelli
Florence, 15 November 1502

To the Notable Niccolò di Messer Bernardo Machiavelli,
Florentine Envoy to His Lordship the Duke of Valence.
In the name of God, 15 November 1502.

Notable and most honored man, etc. Since you have been with His Lordship, I have not written to you because I had no occasion to, though I would have done as at present with loyalty and affection. The reason for this present letter is that the Mariscottis from Marradi have always been very loyal to this city, and good servants both in public and in private. I therefore, for this reason and for the friendship I hold toward some of them, am compelled not to disappoint their just requests and to intercede for them where I feel I can be of use to them. They had a dispute, about 3 years ago, with some men of the Brisighella area[1] who are called the Zacherinis, one of whom was killed, quite innocently and against the will of the said Mariscottis. Since they have gotten into this dispute, these Mariscottis have never come to any agreement with them, except by way of the captain of Brisighella.[2] I would like it if, for my sake, you obtained from the duke a letter to the said captain of Brisighella so that he might make, if not full peace between them, at least an agreement for a few years. You will be accomplishing several good things, and these Mariscottis will always remain obligated to you for it. In the past His Lordship the Duke wrote from Rome about it, and the matter was broken off. Now I hope, if you set your hand to it, you will bring it to pass one way or another, which will be a very honorable thing. There are a number of these Mariscottis over there in the duke's camp, I believe in Sant'Arcangelo.[3] I do not want to trouble you any further, except to recommend the above-mentioned action to you once again. I shall not tell you any news about your affairs, since I am sure that you receive news of them every day, and everyone is well. I send you my regards as always. May Christ, etc.

Yours, Francesco Machiavelli, in Florence

❖ LETTER 57
Biagio Buonaccorsi to Niccolò Machiavelli
Florence, 18 November 1502

To His Honored Niccolò Machiavelli.
Imola.

I really have to get angry with you now, because you write me in your letter of the 14th as if putting off sending the money came from me, and not from you, who have such resoluteness that you cannot manage to stay with one idea for more than an hour. You know that I had given the money to Lorenzo and then, since you had changed your mind, I had to wait for Lorenzo, who was in the country, until I could send it to you. If I put it off for a while, it was because of my desire to do what you wanted. And when I offered you some of my own, and I reaffirm it once more, I had not yet gotten hold of yours. Just a sign will be enough whenever you want it, since I am not like you; I hope you shit blood 40 thousand times, you are so afraid you will have to spend 20 soldi, since I asked you to be my *compare,* that I couldn't have written you anything worse, and it is unbecoming to me to have had as master someone who was prince of the misers: you can go retch. Your wish now to know so precisely about the indemnity is all the more revealing to me since you ought not to be thinking about such petty things. So you got it, may God give you bad luck; for I did not manage to get for you here, during your absence, what you wanted, as you did during mine; and the *provveditore* is not here in Florence, but in Arezzo.[1] If you don't want us to write you on the feast of the Magi, we'll write you on the feast of the Ass, and that way we'll make you happy. Stick it up your asshole, you and the old wives.

Nothing is being said about the Ten for now, and I have written enough to you about everything else.

Leonardo Guidotti got those two ducats from the loan, and he put them into your account, as you asked me to do. If you should need anything else, write.

Your letters have been delivered.
Florence, 18 November 1502.
Brother Biagio

❖ LETTER 58
Biagio Buonaccorsi to Niccolò Machiavelli
Florence, 26 November 1502

To Niccolò Machiavelli.
In Imola.

Niccolò. It would be your turn to complain, this time, if it were not for me: because your appropriation was brought up last night, and it was not passed; the same with those of Francesco della Casa and Ser Alessandro Bracci; you have so much good favor, that all three of you can go shit blood. If it is brought up again, I shall go and cry for you, if need be, but I don't think it will do any good. So you have to go and rustle something up now however you can; and if you want me to be able to cry, try and supply me with a hundred of those onions[1] of yours, because, God help me, two colleagues asked me this morning to write you by the first messenger for you to send a few of them. If you do that, I shall present them to them on your behalf. I am telling you this without joking, and you will be doing a favor to more than one of your friends.

Tomorrow the Ten will be selected, and I shall send you their names as soon as possible; the same if anything else comes up.

The engagement of Giovambattista Soderini's two sisters has been revealed, one to Giovanni Manelli, the other to Lodovico de' Nobili. Right in your face.

Madonna Marietta is angry[2] and does not want to write to you. I cannot do anything else.

Florence, 26 November 1502.
Brother Biagio

❖ LETTER 59
Piero Soderini to Niccolò Machiavelli
Florence, 28 November 1502

To Niccolò Machiavelli, Florentine Secretary.

Notable man, etc. Niccolò, I have received several letters from you[1] these past few days that have not been answered by me because of the many activities I have been and still am involved in, as you can imagine. I just want to tell you by this letter not to leave, because, when the time comes for your discharge, I shall have you in mind. So be so kind as to stay there.

Meanwhile, you will write often, describing as much of the things there as you possibly can, as you have done up to now. I, along with the rest of the Signoria, consider myself quite satisfied with that. If you should need anything at all, you will let me know. *Farewell.*

From the palace, 28 November 1502.
Piero Soderini,
Gonfalonier of Justice

❖ LETTER 60
Piero Soderini to Niccolò Machiavelli
Florence, 4 December 1502

To Niccolò Machiavelli, Envoy [. . .] to His Excellency the Duke, etc.
In Imola.

Notable man, etc. Since I wrote you,[1] I have received two letters from you, very welcome as usual. In answer, I need nothing else but to commend and to urge you while you remain over there to continue to keep me informed of any developments as needed, in addition to what you write to the Ten. In addition, do not cease to keep me in the favor of His Illustrious Lordship,[2] and I shall make every effort for you to be able to come back quickly. *Farewell.*

From the Florentine palace, 4 December 1502.
Piero Soderini, Perpetual Gonfalonier of Justice of
the Florentine people

❖ LETTER 61
Totto Machiavelli to Niccolò Machiavelli
Rome, 5 December 1502

To the Distinguished Niccolò Machiavelli,
Florentine Envoy to His Excellency Duke Valentino.
Jesus. In the name of God, 5 December 1502.

Honored brother, etc. This letter is to let you know that I was here yesterday [. . .]ay[1] and things went completely well, and I believe without any [. . .], so that not only shall we have no loss, but we shall end up [. . .] with a profit of more than 100 gold ducats, and very soon, for according to what Filippo[2] writes us he should be here with the withdrawals before the middle of January. And so I would like you to notify me, landing our goods in Rimini or Pesaro if they are likely to come safely from there by this route, which of those places you judge safer for bringing them here.

I would also like you to obtain from His Excellency the Duke a safe-conduct for goods of Piero del Nero and company and of Filippo Rucellai and company, with an attestation that the said Filippo, who will be accompanying those goods, will be treated with honor and respect wherever he presents it in the towns and localities of His Lordship. Send it to me just as soon as you can, because I think Filippo is in Ragusa right now, and he has instructions from me to stay there until such time as I send him this attestation I am asking you for. Get a copy of it also in the hand of his chancellor.

I had our nephew take orders in Venice, as we decided should be done in Bologna, and I have a genuine episcopal certificate for it. All that remains now, if there is enough time to do him some good, is to do it. Since you are in a place where it would be easy for you to be of use to him, I am reminding you of it, as long as little is spent beyond the stamps.[3] If it should be necessary to spend anything, let us know about it, how much and for what, as long as, by way of spending, he has something that seems like a good idea to him. But, from what I have heard, you have Alessandro Spannochi[4] there, who is very devoted to you and has a lot of influence with the duke. For this reason, we hope that by means of him you can do something worthwhile on this occasion.

Andrea di Mariotto di Parigino will be the bearer of the present letter. I recommend him to you as much as I can, because he is a friend of mine. He will inform you face-to-face of his own case. I pray you [. . .] as much as for my own affairs. Nothing else. God keep you.

Yours, Totto Machiavelli, in Rome

❖ LETTER 62
Piero Soderini to Niccolò Machiavelli
Florence, 7 December 1502

To the Notable Niccolò Machiavelli,
Florentine Envoy to His Excellency the Duke of Romagna.
In Imola.

My very dear Niccolò. This evening I received a letter of yours[1] from the 11th, and I take note of what you write me. I am very happy to hear of His Lordship's good disposition. As for me, I never doubted it, since I know very well how much good will His Excellency has always had toward our republic, as well as how much he has been loved by all men of this city who wish to live well. I hope in any case that an alliance may come about between us of such a nature that each of the parties will derive benefit from it, since our mutual friendship cannot be more timely. Although we are somewhat reduced in our state, and still disorganized and greatly burdened by the excess expenses borne for 9 years running, nevertheless we hope (by the intervention of divine grace and the efforts we shall make to reorganize ourselves) that soon not only shall we be in such a position as to be good and useful for our own affairs but we shall also be able to carry on those that will give comfort and service to others.

The bishop of Urbino[2] has pressed us a great deal both in public and in private to be granted permission to be able to reside in our territory: we have declined to do so and shall continue to, both to him and to others of that state of higher rank, until we have heard the opinion of His Excellency[3] there, because this republic is wont, when it turns its face in a given direction, to proceed with sincerity of mind and with true benevolence in each of its actions of importance. And in truth, it will never be found, since I have risen to power in this palace, that anything of a different flavor or tenor has been said or done than what has been stated above: and that is the truth: and that is what you can assert *in my name* to His Illustrious Lordship there.

Concerning the business that you wrote us about, I shall answer you by another letter, *when I have more leisure.*

I shall write you a letter in favor of Paolo Rucellai of Rome, concerning some alum. Although it will be very enthusiastic, you will not go beyond suitable bounds, and you will make sure not to irritate His Excellency there. Your return will come soon, as you desire.

Farewell.
From the Florentine palace, 7 December 1502.
Piero Soderini, Perpetual Gonfalonier of Justice of
the Florentine people

❖ LETTER 63
Buonaccorso Rinuccini to Niccolò Machiavelli
Florence, 15 December 1502

† 15 December 1502.

To my very dear *compare.* Good health, etc. Since you left I have asked several times about your benevolence, as Messers Marcello and Biagio, and everyone, knows. It is very true that I have not written, since I had no occasion to; now I have occasion by this letter to ask you both with insistence and the need for an answer right away. That is, my dear *compare,*[1] that the Mariscottis from Marradi have always been very loyal to this city, and good servants both in public and in private. I therefore, for this reason and for the friendship I hold toward some of them, am compelled not to disappoint their just requests and to intercede for them where I feel I can be of use to them. They had a dispute, about 3 years ago, with the men of the Brisighella area[2] who are called the Zacherinis, one of whom was killed, quite innocently and against the will of the said Mariscottis. Since they have gotten into this dispute, these Mariscottis have never come to any agreement with them, except by way of the captain of Brisighella. I would like it if, for my sake, you obtained from the duke a letter to the said captain of Brisighella so that he might make, if not full peace between them, at least an agreement for a few years. You will be accomplishing several good things, and these Mariscottis will always remain obligated to you for it. In the past His Lordship the Duke wrote from Rome about it, and the matter was broken off. Now I hope, if you set your hand to it, you will bring it to pass one way or another, which will be a very honorable thing. There are a number of these Mariscottis over there in the duke's camp, I believe in Sant'Arcangelo. And so, my dear *compare,* as above, I beg you once again, as hard as I know how to and can, that you help me out in this matter, for I have hopes that His Excellency the Duke, if you request such a thing of him, will do what you want. I hope therefore I shall be gratified in this.

I have nothing else for this letter except to tell you that your godson is well and will come to see you on your return. I send you my regards; and do not forget me, as I do not forget you. God keep you from harm, for your *compare,*

Buonaccorso Rinuccini

❖ LETTER 64
Piero Soderini to Niccolò Machiavelli
Florence, 21 December 1502

To the Notable Niccolò Machiavelli,
Florentine Envoy to the Illustrious Duke of Romagna, etc.

Notable man, etc. I have received two letters from you,[1] which I shall answer briefly. Because it seems to me it is more necessary to provide for you than anything else, I have for now ordered that the sum of money you will see should be sent to you; you will continue in your duties to keep a good watch on affairs over there and write often. When the direction taken by those troops there can be seen, you will not fail to be discharged, and someone will be designated to come and take your place there, since it has been decided to keep a representative of ours there with His Illustrious Lordship. Meanwhile, do not fail to continue with your efforts as you have been accustomed until now.

From the palace, 21 December 1502.
Piero Soderini
Gonfalonier of Justice

❖ LETTER 65
Biagio Buonaccorsi to Niccolò Machiavelli
Florence, 21 December 1502

To His Most Honored Niccolò Machiavelli.

I should like to write you a whole mess of things, but if I did so, I would get you upset. So I shall refrain from it easily, and Totto will inform you of the actions I have taken with the gonfalonier so you would be provided for. As to whether it turned out right, the provision will show you; as for your discharge, you will see by the accompanying letter whatever our Most Illustrious Gonfalonier writes you. Suffice it to say that I have had good luck with your affairs, although I do not know how I have done with my own. But I am afraid that your indemnity is going to the dogs, because here the cry among these chancellors is that you are a cold fish[1] and you never acted pleasantly toward them. I, who want to cleanse you of any infamy that might befall you, will carry it out with them at your expense and right in your face. So go and retch if you are not satisfied, that is the way it has to be. Since Ser Antonio's prayer, etc., has had such good effect, I am very happy about it. If you had not written to me that it had worked so well for you, I would have sent you mine. But for fear that you'll shit your heart out, I shall not do it, because it would be an easy thing once that one has set you in motion,[2] if the other one caught up with it, for it to play you a bad trick, so even if I have to apply it, I do not want to get off the case.

Messer Federico Folchi has died, never mind, and Carlo Bonciani died. If you write condolence letters down here, you will get them in return over there, because someone has seen to it. I wrote it to you with tears in my eyes. But put these cares behind you, and let someone else worry about them, and I shall go along taking care of you as the need arises.

Ser Antonio della Valle is annoyed because his Madonna Gostanza is pregnant and his children say it is not his, and he is getting desperate about it. They have put her with the friars of San Felice, and both parties have resolved to accept their judgment. The abbot insisted on touching the body, and up to now things are going very well. You will hear of the outcome.

Totto stayed 4 hours with me today, chattering incessantly, so that I almost did the same as Ser Rafaello when he is talking with Luca.[3] But I managed things in such a way as to talk about my ideas as much as he did. But the next time I shall get prepared so as to make him shit blood. He spoke to me about Venice, and I about France, and for this time it turned out well. But I beat him when it came to the business of <Lucca,> and I can tell you I kept him bewildered for an hour.

From court, that is, from Monsignor,[4] there have been no letters so far except for a brief little letter from Lyons. However, there is a letter in private today from the court itself; they give news of his arrival there and say that he was shown very great honor and made to seem as welcome as any man that ever went there: you will hear what ensues. But I was waiting for you in these beautiful rooms, to give you a warm welcome; and perhaps before you come back, some will be transferred here and some there. God help us. I am managing this office[5] as well as I can, at your command, and so I go wallowing about and I am waiting for you, by God, very anxiously, and I just can't wait. Madonna Marietta is cursing God,[6] and she feels she has thrown away both her body and her possessions. For your own sake, arrange for her to have her dowry like other women, otherwise we won't hear the end of it.

I have written you sufficiently about the marriages that have been arranged recently, and your Albertaccio Corsini is a member of the new Eight.

I have gone in your place when the Ten have had some nice little dinners, and Ser Antonio is annoyed, the same to him. I remind you of the onions[7] that, now that they are on the fire, I was reminded by those <two colleagues,> are beginning to heat up in part. You do it, <and go and retch and stick it up your ass.>

Florence, 21 December 1502.
Brother Biagio

You must have heard that a few days ago the Savellis took back some fortresses that had been seized from them by the Orsinis when they lost power, and the pope is promising the Orsinis troops and every other assistance. But so far nothing has taken shape, and they have gained possession. <It is feared that the affair will have consequences.> We'll see what happens.

❖ LETTER 66
Biagio Buonaccorsi to Niccolò Machiavelli
Florence, 22 December 1502

To Niccolò Machiavelli, His Honored Brother.

Stick it up your ass, because we are sending you money and cloth and what you ask for, and Madonna Marietta is desperate, and I have spent 44 soldi in silver from your indemnity as tax on a letter for your Totto to Prospero Colonna. That's how things go, and I send you my regards, and the gonfalonier tells me again this evening that he will soon give you your discharge. Nothing else.

Florence, 22 December 1502.
Brother Biagio

But you will rustle up a doublet made out of this cloth, nasty scoundrel that you are.

❖ LETTER 67
Alamanno Salviati to Niccolò Machiavelli
Florence, 23 December 1502

My very dear Niccolò. I have received your letter, and I am delighted, with the list[1] that I was happy to get; and it truly is an army worthy of a man of His Lordship's quality, may it please God to enlighten him according to the needs of His Excellency and of our city. These needs, according to my poor judgment, are easily recognized because what is good for His Excellency is good for this city, and what is good for us is good for His Excellency, so it is all the easier to have one be of service to the other.

With this bearer I believe you will receive a few ducats, and yet it is very little compared to what you know about; that's how things go. Also, we are sending you the damask[2] for the chancellery. Make it serve your needs.

Concerning your discharge,[3] I do not believe you will be gratified for the present. You understand the reason very well, for the Signoria is not about to leave His Lordship without a man of its own; and I do not believe your being absent is going to reduce your chances for reconfirmation, especially since your activities are well known and are of such a nature that you are the one to be begged, rather than to be begging others; all the more since you are abroad on public business, and in a place of no little importance. I am very happy about it for the reason I have stated, and we should do everything necessary and make every effort, and I in particular, who could not desire your entire welfare any more than if it affected myself.

I have nothing else to tell you, except that I am your devoted friend, and I hope God keeps you healthy and in his grace.

In Florence, 23 December 1502.
Yours, Alamanno Salviati

❖ LETTER 68

Pier Francesco di Corbizzo[1] to Niccolò Machiavelli
Castrocaro, 23 December 1502

To the Magnificent Messer Niccolò Machiavelli,
Most Worthy Secretary of My Master His Excellency [. . .] Florentine in Cesena,
My Most Extraordinary Master.

Your Magnificence, most extraordinary Messer Niccolò. I have had an answer from Your Excellency, and from that I learn how much you have accomplished for our Salvestro di Bossi[2] and his dearest wishes with His Excellency the Duke, and that with the Bossis coming to an agreement with the Naldis, you will get him released from captivity right away. In reply to Your Excellency's letter, I am sending this with Ser Bartolomeo Mazuolo from Bertinoro, a relative of the Bossis, the bearer of the present letter. He will inform you face-to-face of what has happened, for the Bossis have not been and will not be found wanting, and of what would be necessary to take care of this business. I pray you give him that unequivocal trust that you would give me myself, praying with all my strength, if ever I should have favor, that you be so kind as to use all your influence so that such an agreement may be reached, that poor Salvestro should be released from this misfortune, since he is very badly off as a result of the bitter cold; so I shall consider it all done for me myself and I could not receive a greater favor, and I cannot beg you more strongly. If it should seem to you we had to make some arrangement more than some other, let us know, and it will be done. So I send you my enduring regards.

In Castrocaro, 23 December 1502.
Yours, Pier Francesco di Corbizzo

L E T T E R S

1503

Machiavelli returned to Florence on 23 January to resume his duties in the chancellery office. Florence, meanwhile, had to decide what action to take given the machinations of the Borgias, Cesare and Pope Alexander VI, plus those of Louis XII, as well as those of Spain, especially with respect to the Kingdom of Naples. Each rival power saw in Florence a useful ally in its policies of aggrandizement. Furthermore, Florence had its own expansionist aims: pursuing its war against Pisa and regaining control of Montepulciano. To do so required a stronger army. Yet to raise a militia required both money and a decision about where to obtain the troops. Concerning the latter topic, Machiavelli had firm convictions. One of his dominant notions during the next decade was that of a citizen militia. About the former topic, it is probable that in late March, when it came time to persuade the Great Council to impose new taxes, Machiavelli wrote his *Parole da dirle sopra la provvisione del denaio* (Remarks to be given about the money bill), a fervent speech designed for the person speaking in behalf of the proposed fiscal legislation. In it he urges the citizens of Florence to defend their freedom themselves because, he writes, "you cannot always lay your hands on another man's sword; therefore, it is a good thing to have one at your own side and to put it on when the enemy is still at a distance, because later another's sword will be too late and you will have no remedy" (Machiavelli, *Arte della guerra,* p. 60, and *Altre opere storiche e politiche,* p. 86; *AG,* III, p. 1442; for the question of dating, see Rubenstein, "World of Florentine Politics," pp. 11–13).

In addition to local military and fiscal matters, Machiavelli was involved in several diplomatic missions in 1503. In late April he was sent to Siena to discuss a proposed alliance of Florence, the pope, and Cesare Borgia with

Pandolfo Petrucci, who, from Machiavelli's point of view, "governed his state more with men whom he had once distrusted than with other citizens" (*Prince,* 20; Atkinson, p. 323). His most important mission, however, was to the papal court in Rome. He was scheduled to leave Florence in early September, after the death of Alexander VI in August, so that he could observe the election of the future Pius III on 22 September, but his appointment was canceled. When the new pope died shortly thereafter, on 18 October, Florence considered it extremely important to have a trusted representative on the spot, because Cesare Borgia stood either to increase his power, since he was being courted by France or Spain, or to be reduced to nothing, depending upon how the new pope chose to deal with him. Machiavelli's dispatches from Rome during the period from late October to mid-December contain a fascinating chronicle of the behind-the-scenes scuffle for power and of Borgia's fate. On 31 October the cardinal of San Pietro in Vincula, Giuliano della Rovere, was elected and assumed the name of Julius II. He was no friend of Cesare Borgia's; indeed, he had opposed policies instituted by both father and son.

The new pope's interest in self-aggrandizement, however, was no less than Alexander VI's. He aimed at restoring control over both the papal states and the Roman barons. He accomplished the former objective primarily by blocking Venetian inroads into the power vacuum left in Romagna by Cesare Borgia's waning influence there. (Thus, once Julius II had fulfilled his goals, the papal states remained under papal control until the mid-nineteenth century.) Venice had moved quickly into Romagna, taking Rimini, and moved northwest to Faenza on 5 November. Florence, aware that Venice was now more of a threat than Cesare Borgia, urged Machiavelli to persuade the new pope to thwart Venetian aims as well as to keep Borgia at bay. For its own part, Florence hired Gian Paolo Baglioni as its condottiere in Romagna and persuaded Louis XII to foot the bill. Another reason for Machiavelli's presence in Rome was to obtain a modification that Florence sought: namely, to get Baglioni to fight on its behalf, and not solely for France, in Romagna.

❖ LETTER 69
Biagio Buonaccorsi to Niccolò Machiavelli
Florence, 9 January 1503

To His Most Honored Niccolò Machiavelli.

Niccolò. I do not know which has been greater, the blame you get for our not getting letters from you or the delight we then had seeing from these letters of yours that you are alive. For we were not without misgivings here, seeing that for the eight days since the event[1] occurred, there were no letters from you, although from every direction and from everyone else reports kept pouring in to us. Yesterday your letter from the end of December arrived, written upon the capture of those men; it was given in the Urbino mail to a wayfarer, and the messenger you dispatched was robbed and never showed up here. The letter turned up in Borgo at Giovanni Ridolfi's, who for all his letters was counting on you for the details. Seeing such a brief letter, he figured out what in fact was the case, that is, that you had not been at all lacking in your efforts, writing those formal words, for he had nothing but affectionate feelings toward you. Your other letters, of the first and the second,[2] arrived today, which is the 9th, so we have had bad luck with your reports about this matter, although we have kept on receiving details, and very correct ones, from very many places. You should be able to send them more easily now, having several places in our neighboring cities where connections can be made, and not have any more lost; for, since that letter of the last day and these two, no other letters have reached us.

As soon as that first letter arrived yesterday, I sent a runner to Marietta so that she was not kept in suspense any longer. Today I went to see Messer Domenico Stradi, who acts as depositary, and he promised me he would reimburse me for the 5 ducats, which I shall send right away to your Marietta.

I wrote you several times in the last few days and gave you a lot of reports as well as a lot of gossip. I shall be glad to learn whether you have gotten the letters. *Farewell.*

In Florence, 9 January 1502[3].

Brother Biagio

❖ LETTER 70

Niccolò Machiavelli to Totto Machiavelli

Florence, after 23 January 1503[1]

Dearest brother. Saturday made it eight days since I wrote to you informing you how we thought you should think about getting San Pietro in Mercato[2] in litigation, since it was obtained by Messer Baldassarre through simony because the old parish priest refused to give it up unless he got a hundred ducats from Piero. Concerning this point there are so many witnesses—both authentic and willing to attest to it—that if someone were given an interest in this matter, the prior has extremely high hopes for it and believes that there is someone there who will attend to it. Messer Piero Accolti or the cardinal of San Pietro in Vincula or Messer Ferrando Puccietti were put forward.

It seems to me that you are striving to get rid of a man who is likely not only to support our cause but also to spend his own money and who will not incur expenditure on our part; it is better to come to terms with him generously on the condition that the titles survive once and for all. Concerning the other matters [. . .] arrange them as you see fit so that the cost gets taken off our backs and the others [. . .] with favors, with zeal, and with money. On our side, you can show definite simony, satisfaction of two-thirds of the proprietors, easy taking of vows, proofs of real and genuine simony, all of which are items to make one of those courtiers run to us—they whose wont it is to take care of nothing other than ventures like these whenever they can latch onto one. You know that there are many people who get—and quite a few have lost—disputed benefices by means of sodomy, which are more unjust grounds. Messer Giovanni degli Albizzi, who is a man of spirit, is here: you will see if he is someone whom you might make use of in some matter. Our Niccolò[3] will do us all these favors that are possible; he can hardly wait to see the smoke from this fire. The other letters were forwarded through the ambassador, and you must have received the code with which I am now writing you. Once more, I remind you to assign a man to this venture who will spend money and may himself have favor. *Farewell.*

❖ LETTER 71
Lodovico di Niccolò Buonaccorsi to Niccolò Machiavelli
Florence, 30 October 1503

To the Notable *Messer Niccolò* di Messer Bernardo Machiavelli,
My Very Dear Friend.
In Rome.
Jesus, 30 October 1503.

Notable man, etc. I have not had occasion to write you since your departure from here, and the reason for this letter, as you will learn from the letter from Our Lordships of the Ten, is that my brother[1] Guglielmo di Niccolò Buonaccorsi, formerly an accountant of His Lordship the Duke[2] and whom you know from times past, has been captured by the Orsini family there and, from what I have heard, is in the hands of Lord Giulio. For this reason I wish to pray you, for the friendship you have for me, to work together with your friends as well as with Our Most Reverend Cardinals and other friends of ours who are down there, to whom we have several letters of introduction that are included with this letter to you, praying you to make use of them and of your accustomed wisdom and to bring it about that we obtain the release of the said Guglielmo. For this both he and all the rest of us brothers shall remain eternally grateful and always ready to serve you. Without making any further proffers, I send you my regards. It will be no trouble to you to notify me of the opinion you have concerning this, addressing your letters to the Ten; proper use will be made of it. Christ keep you from harm. Yours,

Lodovico di Niccolò Buonaccorsi,
in Florence

❖ LETTER 72

Biagio Buonaccorsi to Niccolò Machiavelli

Florence, 2 November 1503

To His Most Highly Honored Niccolò Machiavelli,
Florentine Secretary, in Rome.
In the House of the Most Reverend Cardinal Soderini.[1]

Notable man, etc. This morning I received your letter of the 30th by the
hand of Niccolò del Bene, from whom we received a report on the new election of the pontiff, please God that it should be in accordance not only with
our desire and need, which you so well know, but also with those of all Italy. I
was glad to learn of your receipt of my two letters. Since you express a desire
to hear what happened in the <Godi> matter, although I am afraid you will
treat me as in that of the straw when it was in San Miniato, I shall go ahead
and tell you. <He was taken prisoner with great show and kept for several
days in the captain's room, and two days ago he was set free without any harm
whatsoever. The affair could not have aroused more bad feeling in everyone
there, and there was a great noise> about it, such that <our friend fled the
uprisings, but he did not> get <any benefit from it, and perhaps he is sorry
about the matter.> For now the thing has come to its end and, as far as could
be judged, a good one.

I gave your letters attached to mine to Niccolò,[2] who asked me to read
him your letter, and they have been very well received. You have set your
sights on that little bit of money for the safe-conducts: so be it, in God's
name, you will be satisfied and the others will go scratch their asses. Your
good luck conquers all difficulties.

I am filling in for everything having to do with our jurisdiction,[3] <and our
friend gets along easily without it,> so up to now the matter is going along
very quietly and smoothly. Those who manage the office declare themselves
satisfied up to now; do not write me anything about this.

Marietta has not yet given birth,[4] and if it were not for the fact that my
boy has been very ill and has not yet raised his head from the pillow, I would
have sent my wife to her. She will go as soon as she can, and you will be informed of everything.

Since you have been written to abundantly about everything necessary, I
shall not tell you anything else in the present letter. I send you my regards and
I beg you, as strongly as I know how and am able, to give my regards to my
most reverend chief. I remind you of this so that you do not do what you
usually do. Let my desire, about which I have spoken to you several times, remain in your mind. Do not forget your friends.

Florence, 2 November 1503.
As a brother, Biagio

❖ LETTER 73
Angelo Tucci[1] to Niccolò Machiavelli
Florence, 8 November 1503

To the Notable Niccolò Machiavelli,
Secretary and Florentine Envoy to Rome, etc.
In Rome.

Notable man, etc. With this letter will be one addressed to the Most Reverend Cardinal Soderini at the request of Brother Raffaello di Francesco Tucci, a Friar Observant of Saint Francis. In it we are seeking to have His Lordship act as intermediary for having the said Brother Raffaello given episcopal authority by His Holiness the Pope. As we are writing the aforesaid Most Reverend Cardinal, we believe it would be sufficient just to have an oral agreement, without going to any other expense. So I shall be grateful if you remind His Lordship of this matter and see to it that if it can be gotten without expense, it be so done, and you will also be doing something for which His Excellency our Gonfalonier will be grateful. I shall await your reply as soon as it is possible. *Nothing else. Farewell.*

8 November 1503.
Angelo Tucci,
a member of the Signoria

❖ LETTER 74
Battista Machiavelli[1] to Niccolò Machiavelli
Florence, 9 November 1503

To the Distinguished Niccolò Machiavelli,
Honored Ambassador of the Florentine Republic.
In Rome.

Distinguished ambassador, etc., my honored *compare.* You have had a fine, bouncing boy, who was baptized with honor today, as your standing requires. May God keep him in sound mind and body for us. I have very little to say in this letter. I know that Totto[2] recently gave you information about two abbeys: one named San Zeno, which is in Pisa and belongs to the bishop of Pistoia and is in the order of the Camaldoli monks, produces a hundred gold florins a year; the other is named San Giusto, also in the Camaldoli order, the diocese of Volterra, and belongs to the same bishop of Pistoia. When I gave this report to Totto, I did not tell him to notify you that you should be aware that San Giusto belonged to Cardinal de' Medici[3] and that I believed that the cardinal, when he gave it to them, had reserved for himself the right of repossession, and I do so believe. This information is being given to you because he is 64 years old. In fact, San Paolo in Florence is also his: it produces 120 gold florins; I believe the aforementioned cardinal has the right of repossession. In another letter, I gave you notice of Sant'Apollinaris here in Florence, which belongs to Messer Isaac, the son of the Greek Argiropulo: he was a familiar of San Clemente.[4] I know he was trying to make up his mind about it; I repeat it, if you should not have received the letter.

Today I got information about a parish called San Pietro in Sillano, the diocese of Volterra, which produces more than 100 florins. The priest is sixty-eight years old or more. The friars of the Badìa are its patrons, and it is easy to get it from the monks. The rector's name is Don Andrea. For now I have nothing else to tell you concerning this. Give my regards to Minerbetti.[5] I would like you to inform me whether it is true that our archbishop[6] has made up his mind about the archbishopric or is about to do so, and for whom.

9 *November* 1503.
Your relative,
Battista in Florence

❖ LETTER 75
Luca Ugolini to Niccolò Machiavelli
Florence, 11 November 1503

To the Notable Niccolò Machiavelli,
Florentine Secretary and Envoy.
In Rome.
Jesus, 11 November 1503.

My very dear *compare*. Congratulations! Truly your Madonna Marietta did not deceive you, for he is your spitting image. Leonardo da Vinci would not have done a better portrait.

Compare, my letters must have borne little fruit, or perhaps they remained in the carrying case. I am afraid that your tenderness toward my *comare* made them disappear from your memory. All in all, I have had replies neither from you, nor from Monsignor Pucci, nor from Messer Giorgio. I pray you to send me back just a line about how they are doing and whether you visited Messer Lorenzo Pucci[1] and so whether you have seen Messer Giorgio.[2] If you do not do it, I shall say that you are a *compare* either of straw or a prick, as you will, and we shall get the same done to your affairs by the gangs here as well, and your letters and everything else will go awry. You ought to set aside for a hundredth of an hour all the quibbles and the maneuvers and devote yourself to your friends, especially those who have kept the faith for those who needed it.

I have written to my Messer Giorgio that, when he writes, he should give you the letters so they will arrive safely, and it will be clear that they are not to go to the chancellery. You, too, when you see him, remind him to do good and to write often. If he should need your services, treat him as a friend.

This damp weather[3] has swelled the beans and tightened the holes, in such a way that here we have set up pulleys from the waist down with a suitable diameter. You have passed up a great opportunity by being down there.

Compare, I send you my regards. Be so kind as to accept them. Very truly yours,

Luca Ugolini, Captain

❖ LETTER 76

Biagio Buonaccorsi to Niccolò Machiavelli
Florence, 15 November 1503

To His Honored Niccolò Machiavelli, Florentine Secretary.
In Rome.

Niccolò. Your reply[1] to our letter of the 8th appeared this morning, sent specifically about the business in Romagna, and you discuss that business in it at great length, especially what we can hope for over there, but in fact these are plans likely to bear little fruit. Here everything possible has been done, and it seems to everyone that the city here, in addition to its own interest, has acted to the benefit of the Holy See there, so that we ought to receive some gratitude for it. We shall soon see that the Venetians are not doing this out of hatred for the duke but because of their unbridled greed and ambition, etc.

I do not want to fail to inform you in private again, although you will have been able to see it by our letter of yesterday,[2] that <here the mere name of that duke is so despised that every time it is mentioned in a letter it seems as if there could not be a more agreeable thing. I wish to give you the following example of this matter: when it was proposed yesterday, by way of an opinion among the Eighty and a good number of citizens, whether the safe-conduct[3] should be given or not, those who were opposed numbered about ninety, and those in favor about twenty.> It is strongly felt <here> that <the pope wants to get rid of him quickly and to this end talks of sending him into Romagna, and for no other reason, and that you on the whole are mistaken> to be writing now <about his being strong.[4] There are even some who think that you are again trying to get some indemnity but that it will not succeed,> because here you cannot <talk of anything> but what would <be likely to harm him.> I wanted to let you know about this for your information.

Your son and Marietta are well, as well as all of yours, and they wish you were here. I pray you that if you should get your hands on a plasma[5]—but I should like it to be a small one—you pick it up on my behalf, and I shall pay back whomever you designate. I am writing this not so that you should have to exert the slightest effort but because I am not sure yet about what you are up to, and I am crazy.

Florence, 15 November 1503.
Brother Biagio

We shall strive to see that your sprout is such that you will be proud of him, do not worry. But he looks like a little crow, he is so dark.

❖ LETTER 77
Piero di Francesco del Nero to Niccolò Machiavelli
Florence, 16 November 1503

To the Distinguished Niccolò Machiavelli,
Florentine Secretary and Envoy to the Supreme Pontiff in Rome.
In Rome.

As a very dear son. I am extremely sorry about your unhappiness, but little less or much more about the cause of it. To reassure you, I shall tell you that I, who have never left my mother's apron strings (and it is 4 years since she died), all those times I have spoken, eaten, slept with infected people,[1] should have died 20 times. I would be tempted to say that you are not Niccolò, if you are so overwhelmed and lose heart so over a thing that happens to every man 100 times in his life. In cases like this, those who are most careful take a few suitable purges and then think about it only as much as is needed. For your benefit, I wish that Totto had not shown me your letter and that you had not wanted him to. But he did his duty in this wisely, so that I might be able to admonish you as was proper, for you have had a son, and I do not think anything could happen to me this year, unless it was of great importance, that could disturb me, for there was never a finer little youngster, or a more lively one. I am teasing you, because you need it. Do not make me tell you, as Caesar did to Dolabella[2]: we shall have a fine consul indeed, etc. Try to be a man. Marietta is feeling fine, and she lacks and will lack nothing. Nothing else for this letter. God keep you.

In Florence, 16 November 1503.
Yours, Piero Francesco del Nero

❖ LETTER 78
Totto Machiavelli to Niccolò Machiavelli
Florence, 17 November 1503

To the Distinguished Niccolò Machiavelli,
Florentine Secretary and Envoy to the Supreme Pontiff.
In Rome.
Jesus. In the name of God, 17 November 1503.

Honored brother, etc. I received a letter from you last night, by which I learned from you the danger in which you have been, and indeed it cannot be said that it was not a great one. Nevertheless, these are situations that, in our dealings with other men, happen a few times every year to those who go about. If it has not happened to you more often, you have been very fortunate.

But let me tell you that last year, in Venice, there were several times people together in the same boat with me who died of plague within 3 or 4 days afterward. And what is more, our young men, who are in the land of the Levant, take the same boats all the time, from Pera[1] to Constantinople, that ferry those who have died of disease. When all is said and done, a few people do catch it and die, but in the past 10 years just one of our merchants has died of it, and during all that time they have taken the boat several thousand times, therefore they do not pay any attention to it. But I am not saying in this case that it is not a good idea to be careful, but just not to become upset about something that happens, as it has happened to you, but to remain in good spirits and keep in mind that there is no way you are going to be ill. Anyone who acts this way and is careful has no reason to think that he will be at all ill. So keep your spirits up, because losing heart is something for children or women.

> Nothing else. God keep you.
> Yours, Totto, in Florence

❖ LETTER 79
Piero Soderini to Niccolò Machiavelli
Florence, 17 November 1503

To the Notable Niccolò Machiavelli,
Florentine Secretary, with the Supreme Pontiff.

   Notable man, etc. I shall not make any other reply to your[1] last letter, except that you should continue day by day, as I told you in another letter, and I shall be exceptionally grateful for that, and in as much detail as you can concerning matters of the kingdom [of Naples],[2] and be assured that I shall do you honor here. *Farewell.*

> *From the Florentine palace, 17 November 1503.*
> *Piero Soderini*
> *Gonfalonier of Justice of the Florentine people*

❖ LETTER 80
Biagio Buonaccorsi to Niccolò Machiavelli
Florence, 17 November 1503

To His Honored Niccolò Machiavelli,
Florentine Secretary in Rome.
In Rome.

   This morning I received your letter of the 11th, with the postscript of the 13th, and you must have remembered me precisely when you went to the latrine, since you found it there among the notebooks, looking for something as a comparison, as usual. Enough said.

You should be certain that in affairs that are of importance to you, I have never taken them to heart otherwise than I do my own. And so, if I wrote you about your male child, I wrote you the truth. In addition, I shall tell you that Marietta has put him to nurse here in Florence. Both he and she are fine, thank God. It is true that she lives in great distress about this absence of yours. But there is no remedy for it. When Alessandra[1] can go there, she will not fail to; only last Sunday she was there. She and I think constantly of doing your service. If only you thought thus of me.

I wrote you recently, I cannot remember the exact date, about everything that I needed, and there was something for you to be happy about in it. If you have done as you usually do, you probably did not read it. Too bad for you. And I do not write you in any different spirit. On my part, you will never fail to receive your due, even though at times I get angry, and with reason.

I shall be happy if you added to my letter to the cardinal[2] what you said, which I doubt. I have no doubt, however, about its receipt, since I have had an answer from him. You know what I want. So when you get things for yourself, remember that I am here in the greatest possible exhaustion and bondage, with the wages that you well know.

The ambassadors[3] are getting ready to go down there, and have been assigned the date of the 25th of this month. Niccolò Valori will soon go off again to France.

It had slipped my mind to answer your question about the other godfathers, who were Messer Battista Machiavelli, Messer Marcello, Lodovico,[4] Captain Domenico, and me, a fine gang, and we all have given you a lot of news. *Farewell.*

Florence, 17 November 1503.
As a brother, Bi.

❖ LETTER 81
Totto Machiavelli to Niccolò Machiavelli
Florence, 21 November 1503

To the Distinguished Niccolò Machiavelli,
Florentine Secretary and Envoy to the Supreme Pontiff.
In the name of God, 21 November 1503.

Honored brother, etc. I have not had any letters from you since I got yours of the 13th, and I have not yet learned whether you wrote care of others. So I am waiting anxiously for notification from you, and as I told you in another letter, if you want me to come down there, let me know, and I shall not worry about disease or anything else, and I shall always be at your disposal.

You must have been written that Piero del Nero has been named to the Ten, which is something very much in your interest, and he was also drawn for the 6 of Trade. It has been two months and no more since he got off the debtors' list,[1] so you see that he managed to do what you predicted if he got off it.

In other letters, concerning the benefices where reservations were to be made,[2] we told you quite a bit concerning what we could notify you about up to now. Messer Battista[3] says it would be an excellent thing to have a promissory note for the sum of 500 or 600 florins in those two bishoprics, that is, Florence and Fiesole.

We have also heard that Messer Simone Rucellai got the bishopric of Pesaro, and therefore his canonicate has become vacant because it is one of the pope's. You can find out whether the pontiff has reserved it for himself and see if you think it is worth giving it a try.

Nothing else. God keep you.

Yours,

Totto Machiavelli in Florence

❖   LETTER 82
Agnolo Tucci[1] to Niccolò Machiavelli
Florence, 21 November 1503

[. . .] Machiavelli, Florentine Envoy.
In Rome.

My Niccolò. You[2] will learn via the public mail what affairs in Romagna have come down to, and from the example of Faenza judgment can easily be made about the other things, so every other place[3] will put up less resistance than Faenza did. We have paid more than our share for it, both in favoring them and in keeping them alive and protecting them. Those who ought to and could have taken greater care of them did not do it, and one may believe that they are not going to do differently with the remainder, so that we shall no doubt be wiser in the future, and learn from others, and act rather so as to gain some benefit from those who become great than to make opposition all by ourselves, etc. What result may yet come of it will be judged by the outcome.

We cannot believe that these things happen without the knowledge and the consent of the pontiff, both because we do not in fact see him suffer in any way and because we cannot believe that the Venetians would act so openly and completely undisguisedly to occupy what belongs to the Church. So it is a good idea to try and reveal this faction,[4] and not to hesitate to make it evident and manifest that we, not seeing other preparations being made, shall do our best not to be the last to gain benefit from these developments, since we have no other recourse.

We are anxiously waiting to hear of the development of the affairs of the French. Even though they also will probably want to do something one day about these disorders, they will not be able to. They will see how they are going to manage the affairs of Lombardy if Romagna is in the hands of the Venetians, and they will learn from experience what they were unwilling to learn from our words, for not only were they unwilling to do something about it but, so that we could not prevent it by ourselves, they took our armed troops[5] away from there; and if they had been in that area, undoubtedly much of the trouble would not have come about. In sum, this Italy of ours is wasted away at will, etc., and we have paid the price of it in every way, and we cannot hold up the heavens on our shoulders. Make[6] this known wherever necessary and especially that other recourse will be needed for this matter, that we shall do, because the Venetians will sooner be masters of all Romagna, and in less time, than the French took to cross the Garigliano. You are wise, etc. *Farewell.*[7]

Florence, 21 November 1503.

❖ LETTER 83
Marietta Corsini[1] to Niccolò Machiavelli
Florence, 24 November 1503

To the Notable Niccolò di Messer Bernardo Machiavelli.
In Rome.
In the name of God, the 24th.

My dearest Niccolò. You[2] make fun of me, but you are not right to, for I would be flourishing more if you were here. You know very well how happy I am when you are not down there; and all the more so now that I have been told that there is so much disease down there, just think how glad I must be, for I find no rest either day or night. That is the happiness I get from the baby. So I pray you to send me letters a little more often than you do, for I have had only three of them. Do not be surprised if I have not written you, because I have not been able to, since I had a fever up to now; I am not angry. For now the baby is well, he looks like you: he is white as snow, but his head looks like black velvet, and he is hairy like you. Since he looks like you, he seems beautiful to me. And he is so lively he seems to have been in the world for a year; he opened his eyes when he was scarcely born and filled the whole house with noise. But our daughter[3] is not feeling well. Remember to come back home. Nothing else. God be with you, and keep you.

I am sending you a doublet and two shirts and two kerchiefs and a towel, which I am sewing for you.

Yours, Marietta, in Florence

❖ LETTER 84
Biagio Buonaccorsi to Niccolò Machiavelli
Florence, 4 December 1503

To Niccolò Machiavelli,
Florentine Envoy and Secretary, as an Honored Brother.
In Rome.

Honored *compare*. This morning I received two letters of yours of the 29th and 30th, and I am surprised you have not received my letters from the 21st on, since I did write you two or 3 times, most recently by the hand of Bolognini, who came down there with the king's money. I shall be grateful to learn that you received that one, since for your sake I want to have a reply to it, in order to calm Messer Agnolo Tucci, who, as you will have seen by that letter, was very, very angry with you, because you never answered him, and he says he had you written about this by the gonfalonier and by as many chancellors as there are in this palace. I wrote you a few of the words that he had said against you in the presence of the entire Signoria, which were indeed of a bad nature. <All the other *Signori* stayed to hear him, and some people because of one ill feeling and others because of another did not take it badly. Upon your return I shall bring you up to date about things I do not judge proper to write you. Suffice it to say that there are malicious minds here, and some do not like your writing well about Volterra,[1] and others something else. And so people can work hard and put themselves out, and get little gratitude for it.> If you had been present at the reply, you would have judged that I love you more than myself. I shall not attempt now to persuade you otherwise, because one day you will have so many proofs of this that you will believe it, and perhaps you will act toward me in terms other than those you have used up to now. Wherever I can do honor to you, either in words or in deeds, I do so any way I can. And I am not ever going to change my mind about this, as long as I can do you the least good.

Those who write you saying you should find another post do not love you, because I see no danger in our situation other than the usual one. Vespucci took advantage of the opportunity once, more power to him, and he will do the same to us if it works. I think you have spent a lot and will keep on spending. I do not yet know how you can be satisfied[2] about that here. Once the ambassadors arrive, in 4 or 5 days, you will have your discharge right away. I do not yet know anything about my own arrival, and they are not thinking about that here. They will come fitted out most honorably, especially Girolami and Matteo Strozzi,[3] who are having clothes and other very luxurious things made for themselves. I believe we shall receive honor, so if you felt like going there, I believe it will cost you something, though I am not informing you of a certain report that came to my ears <because I understand the gonfalonier is thinking of sending you with Rouen[4] to Germany to be there at their parliament.> If it suits you, *that is fine;* if not, prepare your defenses; <but let this be confidential, for you could do me a lot of harm.>

Marietta has not been able to write until now because of her confinement. I think she will do it in the future, and only yesterday Alessandra went to see her. Good Lord, there is no way to get her to calm down and take comfort.

I am very sorry about your troubles, and Lodovico Morelli will carry your message. Whatever Tucci wants for his brother[5] will be in a voucher in this letter, and he says that if you spend anything, he will pay you back. I pray you to write just a word back about that. *Farewell.*

Florence, 4 December 1503.
Brother Biagio

Your Niccolò[6] says he is not writing you in order not to bother you, since he has informed your Totto, so he does not remind you of his situation.

❖ LETTER 85
Niccolò Machiavelli to Agnolo Tucci
Rome, November–December 1503

Magnificent man,[1] *etc.* I have received your letter of the twenty-first, even though I do not understand the signature,[2] but I think I recognize you by the handwriting and the wording; however, even if I were mistaken, it will not be out of place or inopportune for me to reply to you. You point out the danger involved for the rest of Romagna now that Faenza has been lost[3]; you indicate that you need to attend to your own needs because otherwise none of those who can make, or should be making, those provisions is doing so; you are afraid that the pope is favorable to this; you are afraid about the outcome of affairs in France; you remind me to be mindful and diligent, etc. Although all these very same things have already been written in official correspondence to me and have been answered so extensively that you can consult what has been written, nevertheless, not again to fail in my duty to you, I shall reiterate these items. And I shall write in the vernacular, although I may have written in Latin to the chancellery, even though I do not think I did.

You would like the pope and Rouen to remedy the situation in Romagna once and for all with something other than talk, being of the opinion that talk is inadequate for what the Venetians are doing and have done, and you have entreated both of them through the means that you know. I have already written you about the results of all that: the pope hopes the Venetians are going to fall in with his whims; Rouen trusts that, with either peace, truce, or victory, he will be in time to reform things. Both of them[4] are so fixed in these opinions that they are unwilling to listen to anyone who reminds them of anything else. Therefore, you may draw this conclusion: you should expect not troops or money from this quarter but only a few briefs, letters, or admonitory messages; these will be more or less vigorous as whatever fears the pope or the king of France may have are more or less potent. How potent they can or should be you can judge perfectly well by looking squarely at

Italy and considering your chances once you have seen and studied what can be done by others for your security and understood what can be expected from this quarter; as for what can be expected at present, it is useless to go over it again, because I have already spoken to that point. I shall add only this: should some other people seek either your troops or the enlisting of Gian-paolo[5] from Rouen, you need to show that you want them either to defend your state (and this latter point cannot be discussed with him because he becomes as angry as the devil, taking God and men as witnesses that he will don his own armor were anyone to touch a hair on your head) or to keep Romagna from being endangered—which, as was said, he thinks he is in time to do. Such is in substance what can be written to you about matters in this quarter; I do not believe anything else can be written to you by someone who is supposed to be writing you the truth.

L E T T E R S

1504-1505

At the beginning of 1504, Florence's two main foreign policy concerns were Venice's encroachments in Romagna and Spain's intentions in northern Italy. Having soundly defeated the French at the Battle of Garigliano, Gonzalo Fernández de Córdoba was now thought to be headed toward Lombardy to take on the French there. Florence's interests, however, were closely linked to those of France. The Signoria, aware that increased taxation, even for military purposes, was not politically feasible, relied on French military might. Nevertheless, military expenditures for the troops in Romagna and especially for increased operations in the ongoing war with Pisa were great. Florence hoped that it would continue to receive French aid, but the city feared a loss of resolve if it turned out that Spain was about to engage its troops in a frontal attack.

Early in January, the Ten sent Niccolò Valori to Louis XII. So concerned were they that by 19 January Machiavelli was also dispatched to the French court in Lyons. Evidently the Ten had doubts about Valori's discernment, because they sent Machiavelli to his good friend, as they wrote to him, "to note the preparations [the French] were making, to communicate them directly, and to append your own inferences and judgments" (*Leg.*, II, p. 751). Machiavelli remained in France until the beginning of March, although France and Spain signed a truce in Lyons on 11 February that temporarily eased the situation and provided Florence with reassurances of French friendship and protection.

Upon his return to Florence, Machiavelli was sent in April to Piombino to dissuade Jacopo d'Appiano from helping Pisa to fight Florence. One expensive (7,000-plus ducats) and ultimately fruitless project was devised during the year to insure victory against Pisa; it involved an attempt to divert the Arno River around the city toward Leghorn so as to deprive Pisa of access to supply lines from the sea and to leave it surrounded by a swamp. Florence was quite proud of its imaginative plan: Leonardo da Vinci created designs for it—though his sketches were not those finally used—Piero Soderini endorsed it, Machiavelli supervised it, and Biagio Buonaccorsi wrote at length about it. Concerning this project, initiated during the autumn, Guicciardini comments that "this undertaking, begun with the greatest of expectations and pursued with even greater expenses, turned out to be in vain because, as so frequently happens in such ventures, even though the surveys are based on virtually manifest proof, experience will prove them to be failures (the truest of examples of the distance that exists between plan and action)" (Guicciardini, *Storia d'Italia*, VI, p. 11; Alexander, p. 186; *Storie Fiorentine*, p. 628).

Machiavelli's experience in observing military leaders such as Cesare Borgia, petty princes such as Jacopo d'Appiano in Piombino, and Florence's own condottieri, as well as his study of ancient history, convinced him of the need to abandon the use of mercenary troops. The urgency to establish a citizen militia and to unite Italy informs his *Decennale Primo*, a 550-line chronicle in terza rima that he wrote in the fall of 1504, although it was not published until 1506. The poem depicts historical and political events in Florence from the invasion of Charles VIII in 1494 to the end of 1504.

The Signoria continued to regard Machiavelli as a useful person to send on diplomatic missions. Niccolò Valori, languishing at the French court, longed to return to Florence and argued that Machiavelli should be his replacement. Instead, the Signoria kept Machiavelli occupied during 1505 with Pisan affairs. When these complications were not uppermost on his mind, his brother Totto's search for ecclesiastical benefices was.

A focus on discovering and then hiring a strong military commander dominated the Signoria's policy in its war with Pisa. This search determined most of Machiavelli's diplomatic missions in 1505. Giampaolo Baglioni, lord of Perugia, at first agreed to serve as one of Florence's condottieri; Antonio Giacomini was to be commissioner general. But then Baglioni reversed himself and rejected the offer on the grounds that he had his own territory to protect. Machiavelli, sent on a mission to him after Pisa defeated the Florentines under Luca Savelli at Ponte Cappellese, on 27 March 1505, soon discovered the real reason for Baglioni's refusal of the Florentine commision: he was in league with the Vitelli, the Orsini, Jacopo d'Appiano, and Pandolfo Petrucci. Furthermore, the Signoria had reason at this point to believe that Bartolomeo d'Alviano, a respected mercenary leader with his own eyes on Florentine territory, was preparing an attack. To regroup and combat these combined forces, Florence's need for a *capitano generale* was becoming desperate. Medici partisans in the Signoria boldly proposed hiring Alviano, while Soderini's faction backed Muzio and Marcantonio Colonna. Other potential leaders included Iacopo and Luca Savelli. The Signoria finally compromised on Gianfrancesco II Gonzaga, Marquess of Mantua, and sent Machiavelli to settle the matter early in May. The Marquess, too, eventually turned them down. Florence, meanwhile, feared that Gonzalo Fernández de Córdoba was about to enter the fray on

Pisa's side and reinforce Bartolomeo d'Alviano, who had helped Gonzalo so greatly in his Naples campaign in 1504. "In order to have one of his intimate friends there," Soderini wanted to persuade the Ten to send Machiavelli, "in whom he had great trust," to Naples so that he could negotiatate with Gonzalo, but Machiavelli lost out to Roberto Acciaiuoli (Guicciardini, *Storie Fiorentine*, p. 277; Domandi, p. 253). Amid these feverish negotiations, Pandolfo Petrucci tried to gain time by proposing to shift his allegiance from the confederates and to help Florence recover Pisa. In mid-July Machiavelli was ordered to Siena to determine the good faith of this proposal. Toward the end of July, Alviano joined the confederates near Piombino and Campiglia and prepared to reinforce Pisa from the south, but Florence, under the leadership of Captain General Ercole Bentivoglio, turned them back at a battle near Torre di San Vincenzo, northwest of Campiglia, in mid-August. Elated by their victory, Bentivoglio and commissioner Antonio Giacomini prepared an all-out attack on Pisa. Toward the end of August, Machiavelli joined the Florentine army before Pisa with instructions from home, but he left before a week-long seige that ended in Giacomini's withdrawing his forces in disgrace in mid-September.

❖ LETTER 86
Francesco Soderini to Niccolò Machiavelli
Rome, 27 January 1504

Francesco Soderini,
Priest of Santa Susanna and Cardinal of Volterra,
to the Notable Messer Niccolò Machiavelli,
Our Very Dear Compare.[1]

Notable man, our very dear friend. We have received your letters,[2] which were very welcome, and we thank you for your reports, urging you to continue, since you could not give us any greater pleasure. We like the plan[3] that you have sent us very much. *Farewell.*

In Rome, the 27th, 1504.

We do not have time to answer the items: *more when we have more time. Farewell and give my greetings to Marcello.*

Compare Francesco Soderini,
Cardinal of Volterra

❖ LETTER 87
Francesco Soderini to Niccolò Machiavelli
Rome, 24 March 1504[1]

To the Notable Niccolò Machiavelli,
Florentine Secretary and Our Very Dear Compare.
F. Soderini, Priest of Santa Susanna and Cardinal of Volterra.

Our very dear, notable man. Ser Mariano Mori has been here, and we did not attempt to do anything at all in any way about his situation, on your account and with due respect to you, since we wanted to live up to the trust you have in us and to give satisfaction to your entire house and family, of which we are fond. We do say to you that *if there is corruption in anything at all, it is common,* and for this reason we urge you to exhort your prior *to keep his promises and to maintain the pledge he has given,* and to see to it that the matter and the dispute can be brought to an agreement without dragging it out or straining it otherwise. But, as we have told you, we are not going to do anything at all against your prior, and always, when we hear that you have some interest in matters that are our responsibility, we are going to have such respect for it in our deliberations as the trust you have in us deserves.

Farewell.
In Rome, 23 March 1503[4].

❖ LETTER 88
Giorgio dell'Antella to Niccolò Machiavelli
Rome, 20 April 1504

To Messer Niccolò di Messer Bernardo Machiavelli.
In Florence.
20 April 1504.

Dearest Niccolò. I have your letter of the 13th of this month, and another from the archdeacon and our Messer Battista Machiavelli, all dealing with the same matter, and with them one from your house to the Most Reverend Monsignor,[1] to whom I was not able to give it before this morning, because His Lordship has been on leave these past few days. I presented it to him, as I say, and he, on seeing it, answered me that he was very happy to do what you all desired and that up to now he has taken no decision on the benefice,[2] since he was keeping it available for your house ever since it has been in his power to dispose of it. We agreed that we shall have the request and all the rest made next week, according to the information that Messer Francesco Minerbetti gave us about it. I shall take care of it willingly and diligently, and when it has been entirely taken care of, I shall send it on to you. In whatever else I can do, I am ready to be at your service, and you will not mind telling

Messer Battista that I shall not answer his letter otherwise, since I have nothing else to tell him than what is contained in this letter. I send my regards to you and to him. God keep you.

Yours, Giorgio dell'Antella, in Rome

❖ LETTER 89
V. to Niccolò Machiavelli
Rome, 24 April 1504

To the Honored, Distinguished Messer Niccolò Machiavelli, etc.
Jesus, 24 April 1504.

My dear Niccolò. I have to respond to your two letters of the 13th and 20th, and I shall be brief for now, since, as this soldier is leaving for Lyons, I thought I should drop you a line and I do not have much time left.

Your letter of the 13th, in which you told me to speak with Bartolini,[1] did not arrive on time, since I found it in Rome on Friday, coming from Bracciano. That day I met Leonardo not far from Rome, riding back in that direction, so we did not speak of it, etc. If, in a similar matter, I can do anything else, let me know.

The letters to the cardinal of Volterra were given today into the hand of Messer Raimondo.[2]

I was pleased by those verses[3] you say that you wrote. If it were not that writing is tiresome and, for you, because of your constant activities, difficult, and especially amid all the chattering, I would judge that you had done well to send them to me without music. We shall save them for when we can sing them and accompany them on the rebec.

I have given your regards to Serristori,[4] and he is completely devoted to you: ever so, for I keep my distance, and especially in litigious arguments. Give my regards to all our friends. God keep you, for

Yours, V., in Rome

❖ LETTER 90
Francesco Soderini to Niccolò Machiavelli
Rome, 29 May 1504

To the Notable Niccolò Machiavelli, Our Very Dear Compare.
F. Soderini, Priest of Santa Susanna and Cardinal of Volterra.

Very dear compare. We were very pleased to see your letter of the 24th, and it is not necessary for you to say anything to us about my being your *compare*, since we shall want to show our love of you in other ways, and we hope to be able to do it some day.

Do not use others as your excuse for not writing us. But you know how welcome your letters are to us, especially in these times when precise and truthful reports are desired.

The argument against the militia[1] is not good *in a thing so necessary and so sound: and they cannot be suspicious*[2] *of the force, which will not be raised for private, but for public,* convenience. Do not leave off, for perhaps the favor that is not given one day will be given another.

You must have there Aloys d'Ars,[3] who is returning to France. Warm him up, because those matters are needful of it, especially if the preparations that are being threatened should go forward. Give him to understand clearly that those who wish to get to the furthest point must learn to clean up all the road between[4]; and if they consider carefully, they will find that the hostility is not with you, but with the others.

Although many things are being said and threatened, nevertheless they are believed to be rather a diversion than anything else, and it is believed you are not going to have such obstacles that, if you are willing to do quickly what is required, you cannot take Pisa by force, since it is reduced to the state it is in. Just be sure not to fail your own interests.

The behavior of our neighbors does not need seers to interpret it: it seems to be necessary to be patient so as not to bring pressure, but to remember it at the right time. Certainly, in states and in republics, too much patience gives courage to villains, wherever they may be found and whoever they may be.

Farewell, and be aware that you are loved *especially by us.*

In Rome, 29 May 1504.

❖ LETTER 91
Niccolò Machiavelli to Giovanni Ridolfi
Florence, 1 June 1504

To the Magnificent Commissioner General Giovanni Ridolfi,
in Romagna, His Patron.
Castrocaro.

Magnificent man. I shall put off writing you until there is something of importance and that you could not be advised of through official means. Here the news is that Bartolomeo d'Alviano[1] left Naples on the twenty-fifth of last month with two hundred fifty men at arms and three thousand infantrymen and is heading with them immediately toward Rome in order to move on Tuscany and to attack Florence; it is said that it is on Gonzalo's orders so as to overthrow our government and to bring Tuscany under Spain's control. It is thought that the people of Siena and Lucca will back this affair and are contributing their money to it; unquestionable signs can be seen that this is so.

People assess this situation in a variety of ways. Some think it is meant to strike fear; others think it is real. Nevertheless, it keeps the city on edge, and the Pisan campaign is not being discussed as it would be were there not this hesitation. But even if Bartolomeo were finally to get here, and if we here did not lose our heads, these are not troops that can do harm, especially if, as Niccolò Valori has written,[2] French troops keep coming to Lombardy all this month.

The campaign against Libbrafratta[3] turned out favorably, and Antonio Giacomini promises certain victory if we go forward. I believe that you will grow numb either from being too fearful or from being exhausted. *Farewell.*

> *Florence, the first of June 1504.*
> *Yours,*
> *Niccolò Machiavelli, Sec.*

❖ LETTER 92
Bartolomeo Vespucci[1] to Niccolò Machiavelli
Padua, 4 June 1504

To the Distinguished Messer Niccolò Machiavelli,
Chancellor of the Florentine People, as a Highly Honored Man.
In Florence.

Bartolomeo Vespucci greets Niccolò Machiavelli. I can scarcely express with my tongue or inscribe with my pen the great joy I conceived in my mind just now when I received your utterly delightful letter.[2] For your culture, well known to all, shone in it brighter than the sun; neither adornment, nor charm, nor wit was wanting, so that when, after reading it through, I wished to make some response, my tongue began to stammer, my pen to weaken, and my hand to become sluggish. The praises you lavished on me were so many and so great that if I recognized even the least of them in myself, it would seem hard to exchange my life with the greatest king's. However, I presume that you have attributed these things to me not because it is so but in accordance with the proverb that virtue increases when it is praised, so that my mind might be more keenly inspired to the good arts. I give you countless thanks for having applied such a spur. For knowing that I am praised by a man like you, I shall exert all my strength toward becoming such a man as will correspond to your opinion in some part. It is better that I pass over the praises of astronomy, and what utility it has for humankind, with dry feet rather than be drowned in the deepest whirlpool. Suffice it that your opinion must be called absolutely correct, since all the ancients proclaimed with one voice that the wise man himself is able to alter the influences of the stars—although of the stars' influences themselves no change can happen throughout eternity. But that statement is understood with reference to changing one's own step, now one way and now another.[3] But lest my discourse wander on farther than is proper, I shall answer your request. Yet, since I am burdened by continual lectures, and difficult ones as well, until the eighteenth of August (since, as the saying goes, the poison is always in the tail), after that time I shall therefore be entirely at your service. This alone pains me: that you show you do not trust me, since you have had my father send me a letter concerning the same matter, though I should have been utterly ready to obey your own slightest command, you whom I should not hesitate to consider as a second parent in all matters. In the future, therefore, you will request my help more boldly, and you will learn that Bartolomeo is the same toward you as you believe he is to his father. Farewell.

June 4, 1504, Padua.

❖ LETTER 93

Totto Machiavelli to Niccolò Machiavelli

Rome, 26–28 September 1504

† Jesus. In the name of God, 26 September 1504.

Honored brother, etc. Ever since I have taken to raising up a dead man—that is, keeping a rich merchant from being ruined, one who is going to be useful not only to himself and his friends but to the entire city in general, and he wants to be ruined at whatever cost, which suffices for the shame and harm of the city—he loaded the oven last week, without kneading more loaves every day.

Try to have Marco della Palla come see you at Piero del Nero's house; and both you and Piero make him understand that when someone is crazy enough to make a bad decision, he has to be wise enough to get out of it with as little harm as possible. Let him take care the next time not to make decisions like that, and keep in mind that the profit he may have derived from such a business is this—to be more careful the next time about testing men's honesty; when you have made him cautious, let him not start breaking in colts, if there is one that is wayward, as this one would be toward him, and likely to break any good rider's neck.

Marco thinks that since he has paid out his money to make the purchase with Giovanni, it is not possible for him to lose it. He does not yet know that those who lend money to other men have always done the same as he has. I have no doubt whatever that those who had promissory notes with Battista Dini,[1] and are his creditors of account, would not get 15 soldi on the lira for a period of two years with a good guarantor. Giovanni de' Nobili, who was so strict, is said to have got 12 soldi on the lira, when the Capponi were revealed to have gone under. In the same way, all the others who have invested their property badly have willingly settled for a part of it without trying to sue. If he thinks well about this, Marco has invested his money worse than someone who has lent money to a bankrupt man, because the creditor of a bankrupt can lose only the amount he has lent him, or get back a small part of that; but he who has his money in the hands of someone who has cosigned an obligation to buy can lose not only what he has placed in his hands but also what the contract for the purchase obliged him to give him, and in addition the expenses he is likely to make in undertaking such a suit, and a good part of Marco's furnishings, even if he had more than he does, will not be enough. So urge him to take advantage of all the efforts and skill I have used for his sake, to keep Giovanni ready to believe that he will complete this purchase for him by means of a discount agreement. Let Marco understand this well: that I have nothing left to hang on to in order to restrain this man, if either Marco or he runs around any further. So he has to be cautious and make up his mind right away, because this fellow is beginning to hedge on me, and by his words I can see that dragging the money from him that he has to give to Marco is like dragging the soul from his body.

He also tells me: "Don't you see that I am left with very little money after my expenses here, if I make an agreement with Marco, so that if the matter goes any further it will be just as possible to extract anything at all from him by way of an agreement as it would be to extract an eye from him by an agreement."

If Marco should say, "Since I am more powerful than he is, I shall wear him down through the lawsuit," let him not think so, because Giovanni has so many resources in this court that for every ducat that Giovanni spends, Marco will have to spend six. Finally, *in times like these,* even if he should get all the decisions in his favor, he would be a creditor to someone who would be neither able nor willing to pay him. In this city, there are people every day who deliberately lose face, and anyone who wants to do that never pays here. I do not know whether it is Marco's misfortune that he did not believe, the two times I wrote openly to Piero that he should make him understand who he was dealing with and what danger he was getting into, or whether he imagines that I do not have a good enough understanding of such things. But since I do not want to refuse to do anything at all in carrying out my duty as a friend, I want to validate my judgment with the judgment of two men in whom confidence can be given for greater and more important things than this one: one, His Excellency the Florentine Ambassador[2] Giovanni Acciaiuoli; the other, Giovanni di Simone Folchi; the two of them will sign at the bottom of the present letter in their own hand.

But, for the reason that both of them, and I in particular, do not want it to be said at any time in public[3] that we talk or write more loosely about others than is proper, we want you, Niccolò, to keep the present letter on your person, and not to leave it for Marco or allow anyone else to make a copy of it, because we do not wish in any way, in doing good for others, which is what our good nature moves us to do, along with the desire to sustain a friend, that it should be learned publicly that we write things that are improper for us. If, however, Marco is determined that he wants to knock his head against the wall in any case, let him do as he pleases: let him do as he thinks best without claiming to have had any advice from us; in particular, let Piero keep this and the other advice that I have sent him to himself, without giving any copies of it, as I have said of the present letter.

Now it is the 28th and, although until today I have gone ahead with as much energy as I could to keep Giovanni to the agreement, I have not been able to convince him, and he has become so emboldened that I see his mind set in everything not to let go of a *grosso* that he has gotten his hands on: he is all the more ready to find a way to have the rest of the body, since Marco is held to it by contract. Therefore, since Marco did not take the good advice given him by me and at the same time by the hand of Piero, tell him to take this one, if he does not want to wear himself out in this case—and that is: he had better hire the shrewdest attorneys there are here[4] (and also one or two of the foremost legal scholars) and show them the rules and ordinances of the Municipality of Florence, and have them turn up whatever law works in his favor in order to get the hearing of his case resolved or concluded in Florence, no matter how much these judges and lawyers may cost, even if they were to cost hundreds of florins, just so that this result comes about: that the case should be heard there. Because, if it were to be tried here, in time he would spend thousands, and in the end he would be buried under it, because here the rights would never be on his side, even if he were more right than he is. So urge him to take whatever recourse is at hand, and not stay and split hairs, because a hundred ducats that he spends over there in arranging it rapidly and having the trial of the case there will be worth more than a thousand that he might spend in a short space of time if he came and had his case tried here. Let him take this good advice and not quote us, because that would do no good for his case and would do us a disservice.

When I wrote on the 26th, I thought I could bring Giovanni to some agreement. Since then I went to see him to see what result it had, and finally I do not see any way at all. So Marco will have to prepare himself the way I have said, because once they have combed the wool very well, if Marco wanted me to take care of it for some time, with me being suspect, I could not help him or speak of it to any effect at all.

Nothing else. God keep you.

If I had been able to manage the business of the agreement, I would have had the letter signed by His Excellency the Ambassador to shut Marco's ears up tight, so he would not make a fuss about such a little matter but would be wise and take this thing the right way. If it is not enough to hire two legal scholars, let him hire three of the foremost of the city, as long as the case is heard there. If you write me again about this matter, put it in with a letter to the ambassador, and say the same thing to Marco and Piero, or Piero and Marco, because it would not be a good thing if Giovanni saw it.

Yours, Totto, in Rome[5]

❖ LETTER 94
Francesco Soderini to Niccolò Machiavelli
Rome, 26 October 1504

To the Notable Messer Niccolò Machiavelli, Our Very Dear Compare.
Francesco Soderini, Priest of Santa Susanna and Cardinal of Volterra.

Notable man and very dear compare. It gave us great pain that so great an error should have been made in those waters[1] that it seems impossible to us that it should not have been through the fault of those engineers, who went so far wrong. Perhaps it also pleases God thus, for some better end unknown to us.

If the agreement with France goes ahead, it must give rise to great results, although men's negligence is such as has been experienced several times. For anyone who considers divine justice will be able to believe that He wishes to use this instrument to bring about His results.

We shall be happy to hear about matters over there. However, we are very satisfied with the good, that God may be pleased to increase, for it seems to us to be very much to the point.

Concerning recruitment,[2] we are of the same opinion, but we are afraid that the person[3] whose enthusiasm you say has cooled off has done so to take away the opportunity from those who want to speak and do ill and to interpret the public good as if it were private good.

We have heard about your son, and we are glad our request was carried out. God keep him for you and give you other consolations as you yourself desire. *Farewell.*

In Rome, 26 October 1504.

❖ LETTER 95
Niccolò Valori to Niccolò Machiavelli
Paris, 22 January 1505

To the Most Wise and Learned Niccolò Machiavelli,
Most Worthy Secretary of Their Magnificences the Ten, Honored Compare.
In Florence.

Messer Marcello, in his absence open this letter and send the enclosed.

Honored *compare.* It seems to me as if we had turned our relationship as *compari* into enmity,[1] so I thought that in our interests I should add *whatever could be added. But speaking seriously,* I think that you have been absent and that is the reason you have not answered several letters from me. Whatever it may be, it will be enough for me to know that you are well and that you are managing things there so I may come back. I would not be averse to having a man of brains and of few words here for a few months, rather than one who was new to this place and had to stay here as befits an ambassador, and I have written about it to Giacomini[2] and to the gonfalonier. Since it was enough for me to have given them the reasons that would prompt me, it is not necessary to repeat them for you. I did go so far as to remind them that you are able to show the matters vividly to them and to defend our justifications. I do not know what decision they will make, but I do know that I should like it if, as you came here upon my arrival, you should come back here upon my return. Perhaps it would not be a bad thing if they showed themselves to have better taste there than we have shown ourselves to have up to now. They are wise and I do not think I can be wrong, especially in private as I have done, to have written what I happened to write. When you have any news at all over there, let us know about it, for it has been an entire month since we have had a letter from you. So send this by a trusted person, since it is important. Give my regards to our friends, and if you need anything at all, be aware that I am entirely devoted to you. Christ keep you.

In Paris, 22 January 1504[5].
Niccolò Valori, Ambassador

I have changed my mind and have written a word about this opinion of mine to Their Lordships of the Ten. Please let me know if I have been held responsible for it, since I know what we are like. *Farewell again.*

❖ LETTER 96
Totto Machiavelli to Niccolò Machiavelli
Rome, 15 March 1505

To the Distinguished Niccolò Machiavelli, Florentine Secretary.
In Florence.
† In the name of God, 15 March 1504[5].

Honored brother, etc. I got your letter of the 12th and the two letters enclosed on behalf of Messer Battista. I have looked after him in everything as you requested.

About the matter that you urged me to act upon in the other letter, I wrote you what I had arranged. Once what is necessary has been obtained, I shall let you know about it and send you a copy of it. Be of good cheer, for others will not eat, and not only will they not eat *but they will not cry out in their gluttony, if we go along gradually.*

I notified you that I needed some source of revenue, and thus I repeat it to you; so do what I advised you to do, which will be more profitable than a canonicate and of greater honor. But meanwhile I am keeping in touch with Ser Latino,[1] who told me that he wanted to write to the archdeacon this week.

Nothing else for this letter. God keep you.
Yours, Totto Machiavelli, in Rome

❖ LETTER 97
Francesco Soderini to Niccolò Machiavelli[1]
Rome, 24 March 1505

To the Notable Niccolò Machiavelli,
Florentine Secretary and Our Very Dear Compare.
Francesco Soderini, Priest of Santa Susanna and Cardinal of Volterra.

Our very dear, notable man. Ser Mariano Mori has been here, and we did not attempt to do anything at all in any way about his situation, on your account and with due respect to you, since we wanted to live up to the trust you have in us and to give satisfaction to your entire house and family, of which we are fond. We do say to you that *if there is corruption in anything at all, it is common,* and for this reason we urge you to exhort your prior *to keep his promises and to maintain the pledge he has given,* and to see to it that the matter and the dispute can be brought to an agreement without dragging it out or straining it otherwise. But, as we have told you, we are not going to do anything at all against your prior, and always, when we hear that you have some interest in matters that are our responsibility, we are going to have such respect for it in our deliberations as the trust you have in us deserves. *Farewell.*

In Rome, 24 March 1504[5].

❖ LETTER 98

Totto Machiavelli to Niccolò Machiavelli
Rome, 29 March 1505

To the Distinguished Niccolò Machiavelli, Florentine Secretary.
In Florence.
Jesus. In the name of God, 29 March 1505.

Honored brother, etc. The bearer of this letter is one Brother Cherubino, who will give information upon your order concerning the terms of the provostship of Santa Maria in Cigoli. According to what we have been told, it has fields for eleven pairs of oxen, in addition to many scattered lands. Because it belongs to a Lombard courtier who has never been to the place except in passing and since he is a foreigner, the peasants have gotten up the courage to oppose him, which is why they are consuming half of it or more. But the friar who is the present bearer says that if it were exploited as much as he expects, 300 gold ducats would be drawn from it per year. That is why I want you to send a man with this friar to find out the properties of the said provostship. It should be an honest man, who would go with the said friar under the pretext of wanting to bring them (that is, the farmers) to an agreement with the said friar, who in the past was the steward in the said place. I should judge it to be good for Filippo Rucellai to go there, and I am writing him a note about it. Since he is knowledgeable, he is sure to make such a report politely. But warn him to do it on some good pretext, that is, as one who has been asked by the ambassador who is here to make an effort in behalf of Messer Girolamo for the present possessor so as to bring the said peasants to an agreement with the said Brother Cherubino. Talk about it with Messer Battista and bring about this result: that is, you should answer me what the terms of the said provostship are, because I have fixed it for our friend, that is, that if we like his terms, it will be exchanged with him. If we could learn them without having to send over there, it would be best, and less obvious. Let me know about it, the faster the better, and do [. . .].

Nothing else for this letter. God keep you.

Yours, Totto Machiavelli, in Rome

The ambassador is very happy for his name to be used, in order to be of service to us and also because he is a friend of Messer Girolamo, the landlord of the said place.

If the matter seems suitable to you, send the said Brother Cherubino back here on horseback, as a means to such an end.

You will hear his needs from him directly in relation to this matter, and you will arrange for him to be taken care of.

❖ LETTER 99
Totto Machiavelli to Niccolò Machiavelli
Rome, April 1505

To the Distinguished Niccolò Machiavelli, Florentine Secretary.
In Florence. Into his own hands.
Jesus, 1505.

Honored brother, etc. I have your letter of the 5th of this month. I learn that you have sent Filippo,[1] which I am pleased at. I am awaiting a reply, and I shall do whatever you recommend about it, as long as the matter is as the friar claimed. If it should not be just so, the same landlord has some other little benefice, I have been told. Ask the friar about it, and find out from him or someone else in a deft way what its terms are, but deftly, because I hear that there is some fellow-citizen or other of ours in it as a renter or something like that, as I have been informed. This friar is a good intermediary with that man, that is, the landlord. And so by his hands we shall make a deal on either just one or both of them in any case.

Arrange for up to two hundred ducats in any case, and if Giovanni M. should not come up with that sum for you, he will come up with 50 or 60 ducats in any case.

Nothing else for this letter. God keep you.
Yours, Totto Machiavelli, in Rome

❖ LETTER 100
Totto Machiavelli to Niccolò Machiavelli
Rome, 12 April 1505

To the Distinguished Niccolò Machiavelli, Florentine Secretary.
In Florence.
Jesus. In the name of God, 12 April 1505.

Honored brother, etc. In another letter I wrote you sufficiently in reply to your letter of the 4th, concerning Filippo and Brother Cherubino's trip. That is fine, and we shall see what Filippo has learned. Remember to arrange for up to 200 ducats in any case.

As for the friars of Santa Croce, they must have from us 3 sealed florins[1] a year, which is approximately two gold ducats a year. Give them one of them and tell them you will give them the other on my return. If, however, you pay them both of them, make sure you get a receipt signed by their warden and by Giovan Maria, their auditor.

Nothing else for this letter. God keep you.

Yours, Totto Machiavelli, in Rome

Since writing you I received your letter of the 9th, from which I learn that you like the aforesaid business and you have not given the order. Give it right away if you have not yet done so, in any case, because it is too important; if someone else is there with the matter in hand, it will be increased from two hundred ducats. So, as soon as you have received this letter, don't delay in providing for the 200 ducats. I have nothing else from Filippo except for the information, but if it should be necessary, I know he will be useful to us for something. Make sure right away that these funds are not lacking, and even if this deal should not be concluded (but it will be concluded in any case), we shall make some other good deal. So, when you have read the present letter, arrange for the 200 ducats for me in any case when you read the present letter.

This office, which that man wants, is worth 1,150 ducats. So find out about that other little benefice that he has there, so that someone else can come to an agreement with him, because, for this one, such an office would be too much to give him in exchange. However, one way or another, we shall work out an agreement with him. If there should be no agreement with him, there will be one with someone else. But I shall not let this negotiation be broken off in any way.

❖ LETTER 101

Totto Machiavelli to Niccolò Machiavelli
Rome, 3 June 1505

To the Distinguished Niccolò di Messer Bernardo Machiavelli.
In Florence. Given at the Shop of Piero del Nero.
Jesus. In the name of God, 3 June 1505.

Honored brother, etc. Via Brother Cherubino I wrote you to work it out so that the friar would have a *tavolaccino*[1] of the Signoria to seize the harvest and to keep it at the disposal of the Signoria. I have since spoken of this with the cardinal of Volterra[2]: he says that this is a good method and that we should make the Signoria understand that the church as well as what is in it is in ruins; and with these arguments it will be easily kept from possession; and when it is done in this way he will think it a favor to come to an agreement with us; and, for the damage that he has done to us, it seems to him it would be fitting if he lost it completely. With these arguments and with others, whichever Messer Battista and you judge best, work it out so that possession is kept for the Signoria of Florence and so that he is kept once and for all from possession. The friar

is his proxy and can do a good deal against the interests of this Messer Girolamo, and he has promised me to make every effort for us. And so, in one way
or another, we can if we wish harm him and get confirmation of possession
beyond his reach.

The cardinal will write of this to the gonfalonier, so that he lends us all his
influence. Then, when the property is beyond his reach, I shall work it out so
that he has me informed and I shall obtain it. In this way the cardinal says that
he will come to good terms with him and he will have him do what is right.

We shall get for ourselves here an attestation from the ambassador, from the
cardinal, from Messer Lorenzo Pucci and Messer Raffaello Calvo, and 6 men of
honor of this court, known up there, of the damage and injury done to us by
the said Messer Girolamo, and that will always serve us with the Signoria there
and give us justification that if we have attacked him, he gave us cause for it.

He still has a suit pending that we have arranged to have quashed if the
matter should turn out for us. Now he is not looking after it. I shall gather information about such a suit, which he had with a friar of Ognissanti there
who has died.

Nothing else for this letter. God keep you. This will perhaps be (and the
cardinal believes it for certain) the way to get into it, rather than otherwise
with him.

Yours, Totto Machiavelli, in Rome

❖ LETTER 102
Biagio Buonaccorsi to Niccolò Machiavelli
Florence, 24 July 1505

To His Honored Niccolò Machiavelli, as a Brother.
In Siena.

Dearest *compare*. Work has not been so great or of such a nature that I
could not have written you by any courier. But two things kept me from it:
one is that in such duty as a friend I have few obligations toward you; the
other because I did not know how secure the letters were, and I still don't
know. But, *however it may be,* I shall write you these few lines to inform you
that here we have begun actively to make preparations of such a nature as to
make someone else[1] think again about his own situation. And perhaps those
who seek to light a fire could find it burning so strongly that they won't have
time to put it out. We here find ourselves at present, without counting those
that have been called up, with such forces and so much money that we should
not suffer much, if nothing else turns up. Anyone who thinks he can bring us
around to his desires by necessity is greatly mistaken, because such methods
have now become so tiresome that we would sooner consent to lose Florence
than to give in. A good portion of the advance[2] has been sent to the Marchese,[3] and it must be there by now, and he will come right away along with

his troops, because he has the French company that he got from the king under contract for us.

Chaumont[4] has been asked for a few units of lancers, and they will be en route within just a few days, and yesterday 500 infantrymen were hired under those chiefs who you know have been here for a while. Meanwhile, others are being gathered. Thus we shall not fail to organize the other matters in such a way as to be able to show our teeth and to bite again, if need be, those who would like to bite us. I have gone to obtain for you from His Excellency the Gonfalonier both your leave[5] and your money, and so I have four ducats of yours in hand, which I shall send if someone trustworthy should be going over there, otherwise no. *Farewell.*

In Florence, 24 July 1505.
Yours, Biagio.

❖ Letter 103
Niccolò Machiavelli to Antonio Tebalducci[1]
Florence, 27 August 1505

To the Magnificent Antonio Tebalducci,
Commissioner General in Camp, His Patron.
In the Field.

Magnificent man. Keep what I am writing you a secret. The consultative meeting this morning decided upon conferring the [marshal's] baton to Messer Ercole,[2] but they want to put off announcing it for a day or two in order to see what they have to do to placate Marco Antonio,[3] fearing that he may raise the devil. It would be a good idea to do two things: first, for Signor Iacopo[4] and Messer Annibale[5] to send someone here to let people know that the glory for the rout is not all Ercole's because he sent word several days ago seeking to have his prowess proclaimed; two, for you to write to some authoritative friend here and point out that Marcantonio is not going to share the camp nor will he be followed by Signors Luca[6] and Iacopo—as they assume—because such an assumption has delayed the decision in favor of Messer Ercole. In short, the honesty of Signor Iacopo and Messer Annibale has made this third man too insolent and has given him too much prestige. You can remedy the situation. Tear up this letter.

The twenty-seventh of August 1505.
Your servant, Niccolò Machiavelli, Secretary

❖ LETTER 104

Niccolò Machiavelli to Antonio Tebalducci
Florence, 23 September 1505

To the Magnificent Commissioner General,
Antonio Tebalducci, His Patron. Into His Hands.
In Cascina.

Magnificent man. For the love of God I beg you to be satisfied to stay the way you are for this entire month, as the Ten have ordered you; I give you my word that you will not stay there an hour more, because Piero Bartolini will be dispatched immediately; and on this I pledge you my word. Once more I beseech you not to depart just now, unless you are authorized,[1] so as not to provide a pretext to those traitors, those envious people, who are many, and not to give them any reason to start howling anew. It will just be a few days; in a republic, having such patience will bring it about that the good people who are worthwhile will open everybody's eyes. I commend myself to you.

The twenty-third of September 1505.
Yours,
Niccolò Machiavelli

L E T T E R S

1506

The ignominious defeat of the Florentine army at Pisa confirmed Machiavelli's notion that a citizen militia was absolutely necessary. Actualizing this conviction, despite the proof that these fresh defeats represented, required most of his energy during 1506. Authorized by the Ten, but without the authority of the Great Council, Machiavelli left Florence early in January and headed north and east into the rural, hilly districts of Mugello and Casentino to recruit and then to train a levy of men between the ages of fifteen and forty. The planners restricted their conscripts to men chosen from these remote areas because it was considered unwise to arouse the troops' loyalty to individual cities and to defeat thereby the primary purpose of an army devoted to the larger Florentine entity, Tuscany. In April the Ten urged the Council of Eighty to appoint the notorious Don Micheletto (Miguel de Corella, Michele Coreglia) to lead this army. He was a Spanish lieutenant whom Cesare Borgia had employed several years earlier to make soldiers out of peasants in Romagna; Machiavelli was fully aware of Don Micheletto's ruthless measures there, especially in his capacity as Cesare's henchman in the carnage of Senigallia in 1502.

The results of Machiavelli's efforts in the outlying districts were soon paraded before the Florentine citizenry. Landucci offers a description of Machiavelli's recruits during the Carnival season:

> there was a muster in the Piazza [della Signoria] of 400 recruits whom the *Gonfaloniere* had assembled, Florentine peasants, and he gave them each a white waistcoat, a pair of stockings half red and half white, a white cap, shoes, and an iron breastplate, and lances, and to some of

them muskets. These were called battalions; and they were given a constable who would lead them, and teach them how to use their arms. They were soldiers, but stopped at their own houses, being obliged to appear when needed; and it was ordered that many thousand should be made in this way all through the country, so that we should not need to have foreigners. This was thought the finest thing that had ever been arranged for Florence. (Landucci, p. 218)

This kind of display and training in public helped to overcome opposition within the Signoria to a citizen militia. Some members believed that there would always be the potential for such an army to turn against its employers; some *ottimati*, those in the aristocratic faction of the Signoria, believed that Soderini wanted these conscripts so that he could crush his adversaries and establish a tyranny. One of Machiavelli's contributions to the effort to sway opinion to the militia's side was his *Discorso dell'ordinare lo stato di Firenze alle armi* (Discourse on the organization of the Florentine state for arms). Instead of a speech, this work may actually be a persuasive letter that circulated among those actively seeking to institute a citizen militia. Convinced not only by Machiavelli but also by his brother, Cardinal Francesco Soderini, Piero Soderini shrewdly maneuvered the necessary legislation into existence through the Great Council. These efforts culminated in early December in the creation of a new magistracy, the *nove ufficiali dell'ordinanza e milizia fiorentina* (nine officers of the Florentine ordinance and militia), responsible for overseeing military affairs. Machiavelli wrote *Provvisione prima per le fanterie, del 6 dicembre 1506,* the order for the "first provision for infantry of December 6, 1506," and became the first secretary of the Nine in January 1507. He also retained his positions as chancellor of the Second Chancellery and secretary to the Ten.

Even the diplomatic events involving Machiavelli proved to be significant for his militia. At the end of August, the Ten sent him to deal with Julius II because the pope had requested Florentine aid in his attack on the recalcitrant cities and territories of Perugia and of Bologna; Giampaolo Baglioni led the forces of the former, and Giovanni Bentivoglio led those of the latter. To negotiate a response, Machiavelli traveled with the militant pope as the latter made his way northeast from Rome. The broad policy outline that Julius had in mind was to force the hand of the French into sending him aid. Specifically, Julius sought to accomplish this goal by annexing these two territories, by returning them to the papal states, and by luring Marcantonio Colonna, a condottiere whom Florence employed, into helping him carry the day. Florence wanted Colonna for her campaign against Pisa and ordered Machiavelli to temporize with Julius: this was a dangerous game, but Machiavelli was successful. Hence, Piero Soderini was even more impressed with Machiavelli's loyalty and skill.

It was during this legation that Machiavelli wrote Giovan Battista Soderini, Piero's nephew, Letter 121, known as the *Ghiribizzi* (Fantasies or Speculations) letter. Composed while Machiavelli was with the pope in Perugia during the second week of September, this is an essential document for understanding both the way in which Machiavelli's mind worked and the germination of ideas that blossomed forth in *The Prince* seven years later and eventually in *The Discourses*. Since Machiavelli's *Capitolo di Fortuna* is also dedicated to Giovan Battista Soderini and since it contains reminiscences of the *Ghiribizzi* letter, it has recently been argued that the poem also dates from this period.

❖ LETTER 105
Marcello Virgilio di Adriano Berti to Niccolò Machiavelli
Florence, 6 February 1506

To the Notable Niccolò Machiavelli, Florentine Secretary, as a Brother.
In Pontassieve.

My very dear man. His Lordship the Gonfalonier has asked me to inform you[1] in reply to a letter from you to His Excellency that neither all nor a part of the infantry[2] of Mugello has been sent into Romagna, and they would not be sent there in order to not test them out in such a lowly matter. He is sorry about the difficulty that you describe concerning those of Dicomano.[3] He nevertheless praises your decision, and it seems like a goodly number to him in any case, for if those of Scarperia and Barberino[4] go to that extent, it will not be an unuseful band. He urges you to make every effort, because here the idea is being considered more favorably every day. I inform you that Bastiano was here for three days and was so acclaimed that the companies from Borgo and Vicchio[5] will wear the uniform of hat, coat, hose, and shoes. Simone Banchi[6] was here, too, but he did not work very hard. Bastiano[7] has promised us to display them during this carnival, and says it will be a fine thing to see. Ser Antonio della Valle remained completely under cover, and this Carnival[8] you hear nothing but moans about the taxes; you must have borne your share of it, too. They have left me high and dry. The rest is as usual here. *Farewell.*

In Florence, 6 February 1505[6].
Yours, Marcello Virgilio

❖ LETTER 106
Leonardo Bartolini to Niccolò Machiavelli
Rome, 21 February 1506

To the Notable Messer Niccolò Machiavelli, as an Honored Brother.
In Florence.

Honored *compare.* A letter of yours, received two days ago, gave me so much pleasure that I shall feel good as a result all of this year, especially since I learned of the arrival there in safety of our Filippo,[1] added to the praises that were undeservedly given me by him. It seems to me, judging by what you wrote, that they are of such a nature that they will redound to him, because my experience tells me that I shall never approach such a mark by a long shot. But however that may be, while Filippo was here, we had a very good time, and I am very sad that he should have had to leave right in the midst of the festivities. I was very sorry about that because he deprived both himself and me of a remarkable amusement. However, I am sure that some day we shall so refresh ourselves with a certain plan we have made that we shall live happily ever thereafter, as you will be informed at the proper time and place.

Concerning the new militia, I am very glad that it is turning out as well as you indicated to me in the past. If it is helped along as is its due, I judge that it will turn out to be a wonderful thing and I shall be very happy when I see it completed, both for the good of the public and also because it is your invention. I am glad that, besides the foot soldiers, you have also thought of the constables, who are of no less importance than the infantry. So I shall speed up my arrival, for many reasons, as you write me to.

Here there is nothing of importance, except that Consalvo[2] apparently is getting ready to go to Spain within a few days. However, there are some who consider that he will do nothing of the sort. We shall soon be enlightened as to this. The pope keeps on amassing as much money as he can and has great plans in hand for building as well as those constituted by nature, and he uses it in various ways; and finally nothing comes of it, since there is little to be hoped and less to be feared from him.

If you keep your promise, I shall be very grateful—I mean about coming out to meet me as far as Panzano,[3] where there is that good wine. So that you can do it at your convenience, I shall inform Father Filippo what day I shall be there. I send you my regards; and to Giovan Battista Soderini and Folchi[4] as well. *Farewell.*

In Rome, 21 February 1505[6].
Yours, Leonardo Bartolini

❖ LETTER 107
Ercole Bentivoglio[1] to Niccolò Machiavelli
Cascina, 25 February 1506

To the Notable Man, My Friend, and as a Very Dear Brother,
Niccolò Machiavelli, Secretary of the Eminent Florentine Republic.

Notable man, very dear friend. A few days ago I received, along with your letter, your poem,[2] a brief history of the past ten years. Seeing with how much elegance you have discussed in it all the things that have occurred in that time, I cannot help but admire and praise profoundly what you have accomplished. In it, aside from the other things deserving of praise, one sees so great a number of effects that a very long history could have expressed with difficulty, which are so condensed in very few verses, that a very long matter has become quite brief, without history having, from its brevity, suffered any omission. And so he who reads neither desires nor needs anything at all to be added for his satisfaction. I thank you profoundly for sending me such a thing, which has profoundly delighted me; but I am far more obliged to you for having judged me such that you should desire to hear my judgment of it. I urge you to continue, because if indeed these times have been and are so unhappy that remembering them renews and increases in us other sorrows that are far from small, it is nonetheless most gratifying to us that these things, written truthfully, should be passed on to those who come after us: both because, knowing of our ill fortune in these times, they should not blame us entirely for being bad defenders of Italic honor and reputation and also so that they may weep together with us over our and their misfortune, knowing from what a very happy state we fell within a brief time into such distress. For if they did not see this history, they would be compelled not to believe in what prosperity Italy was before, since it would seem impossible that in so few days our affairs should have fallen into such great ruin. Although this causes me profound grief, yet the fear of worse afflicts me still more since it seems to me that the little that remains to us hastens toward that final ruin as toward a thing desired. Certainly, as far as human judgment can see, we cannot hope for anything but ill, if He that saved the people of Israel from the hands of Pharaoh[3] does not open up for us in the midst of this tossing sea an unexpected road to salvation, as that one once was. *Nothing more.*

I send you regards and my offer of service.

At Cascina, 25 February 1506.
Ercole Bentivoglio, Captain General of the army
of the sublime Florentine Republic

❖ LETTER 108
Battista Machiavelli[1] to Niccolò Machiavelli
Florence, 2 March 1506

To the Magnificent Niccolò Machiavelli, Honored Secretary and Commissioner.

Honored brother, etc. I spoke with your Battista, and concerning the woods in common with you and with Piero del Rosso he says that he has not made a decision and will not until you are there. Then I told him to make certain with the landlord about everything that he was in debt to you for, and he also said for the future he would do what he could. As far as I could draw out of him, he does not see any way, and he says he did not get anything but nine lire of rent; and he even did worse because he says he gave him 14 bushels of grain, and he cannot get the money back for it. So he also thinks that he should make certain if he can. I told him to get what he has in the house written down and attached. I don't know if he will do it; I shall remind him of it again.

Francesco del Nero has a letter from Totto from the 12th of last month, saying: "I am leaving Valona tomorrow by way of Ancona."[2] So he might arrive anytime now.

Filippo Machiavelli has been made *podestà* of Pistoia.

The bearer of this letter is Brunaccino of [. . .] from Romena,[3] who is my very great friend, and a man of spirit as well as of intelligence, and of good family; I know he has a reasonable reputation. He would like to get the command of the company[4] if you should not yet have given it. I believe he is capable of this and of anything else. You will also hear from over there about his capacities. But if you should have given the command already, do him as much honor as you can for my sake and act in such a way that he knows you are fond of me, because any favor you do for him I shall consider to have received myself. If you need him to accompany you up and down, or here and there, he will be ready for any of your orders. I know it is not necessary for me to recommend my interests to you. Concerning the way to get infantrymen from there, he suggested a way to me that I rather like. He will speak of it with you, and you will do what you think is most expedient. If you get to Pratovecchio, visit my wife on my behalf, as well as my niece, and put yourself at my wife's disposal for whatever you can, and let me know if I can do anything for you. God keep you.

2 March 1505[6].
Yours, Battista Machiavelli.
In Florence

✢ LETTER 109
Cardinal Francesco Soderini to Niccolò Machiavelli
Rome, 4 March 1506[1]

To the Notable Messer Niccolò Machiavelli, His Very Dear Compare.
Francesco Soderini, Priest of Santa Susanna and Cardinal of Volterra.

Notable man and our very beloved compare, greetings. Your letter[2] gave us all the more pleasure for its being lengthy, because we learned clearly how your new military idea, which corresponds to our hope *for the welfare and dignity of our country,* is progressing. It should not be thought that other nations in these times are superior to our foot soldiers, except because they have kept discipline, which has been banished for a long time now from Italy. You must get no small satisfaction from the fact that such a worthy thing should have been given its beginnings by your hands. Please persevere and bring it to the desired end.

You write wisely that this idea requires justice[3] above all, both in the city and in the countryside. Although His Lordship the Gonfalonier understands public necessity and is exerting every effort to that end, nevertheless, stimulated by your writing, we recall at present and shall not cease to recall in the future what you write about it, which we still judge to be necessary.

The things written[4] by you are of such a kind that anyone of tempered judgment can read them. If you have not put all your efforts to this, as you say and we believe, think of how outstanding the matters will be to which you put all the force of your intelligence and learning. We urge you to do so as much as is possible. And we pray that you will give us the benefit of your cogitations day by day. *Farewell.*

In Rome, 4 March 1505[6].

❖ LETTER 110
Agostino Vespucci to Niccolò Machiavelli
Florence, 14 March 1506

To the Notable Niccolò Machiavelli, His Florentine Secretary and Officer.
In Poppi.[1]

My dear master, Niccolò. Your most joyous letters in part entertained me and in part gave me courage for the task that I was taking care of in any case: *for I was at the door of the Eight of Security [Otto di Guardia] when your letter was brought to me, around the first hour of the night; I was occupied on your behalf, although the matter concerns us, too.* That was last night and not the night before, since I could not get free before then. *Now for the matter at hand.*

Having discovered with great difficulty that one Andrea da Pistoia had had your *Compendium*[2] reprinted, *rapidly and in haste* I went to the place *where it had been printed,* taking along with me also commander Tommaso Balducci. I did not leave that place until we had a copy, and I shall not bother to tell you what a dreadful thing it is: everything done fraudulently, without spacing; teeny, tiny little signatures,[3] without any blank page before or after; worn, and in many places incorrect, type, as I shall place a little list in this letter, with all the errors in it noted down. I went to see the Eight and made a great fuss, *in both my and your name, on various grounds:* for me, for the damage from reprinting it within 20 days of my edition, though I did not value this very highly because it was not my original objective to make money; but concerning you I insisted a great deal *and complained, perhaps too boldly, yet maintaining my dignity,* showing *simultaneously* this miserable thing as it was reprinted, noting one by one the errors in it. They concluded that an affront and a great injury had been done to you, *as if your very son had been cut and maimed.* I commended you strongly and *heartily* to them and said that the honorable thing was to help those who are authors and to give them encouragement, and to punish evil and wicked men, as is clearly seen in this matter. I was answered favorably by the provost, and it was decreed that the above-mentioned Andrea should be subpoenaed. He could not be found; but here I used my skill and got a fine of two *grossi*[4] set, with the result that he appeared at precisely 8 o'clock.[5] We were admitted: I expounded everything *in the presence of the man,* and since there was no reply to that, the Eight ordered him not to release this printing for anything in the world without their authorization and your return. If you should give permission for them to be sold, they would do so as well. Since that man cited a certain Ser Antonio Tubini, chaplain at the Misericordia, as his equal partner, early yesterday morning I went to the vicar. No sooner had I spoken than he had him appear there, and he gave him such a rebuke and ordered him to bring into his room his entire share[6] under penalty of 50 ducats; and they will not be removed from there without your consent. This is where the matter stands. Rest assured that none of them will be sold, for the vicar told me to keep some spies in order to be able to tell him for certain if any are sold, because he would like to punish this priest and make him acknowledge other vices of his as well. Messer Donato,[7] the vicar, is a friend of mine, and I know he would not fool me. I shall keep my eyes open, but I have no fear whatsoever about it.

I do not want to forget to tell you that your Giandomenico had some part in this printing, miserable man that he is. With the copy I have, I showed him the errors that are in it and recalled how we judged that in my edition there were only one or two *A*'s that were badly done. He was formerly with the Eight and the vicar.

What I would need is for you to write a few lines, in the style you know, either to the Eight or, in particular, to Lattanzio Tedaldi, *who did mighty good work in this matter,* or thank him however you see fit. Only yesterday evening I read to them[8] what you wrote me concerning that, and it was very much to the point. They asked to see your handwriting and the date. They told me that I ought to be fond of you in any case, indicating to me that some of them had not yet seen this cock-and-bull story[9] of yours. I am going out at this moment—it is six in the morning[10]—taking ten *Decennali* with me. I shall have them tidied up and bound elegantly, and I want to present them to all of them, as well as to Ser Alfonso and Ser Francesco.[11] I shall put all this, that is, these ten copies along with the two *grossi* to get that Andrea, on your account in my book, and this morning I shall send the stationer a message to sell the little works at two silver quattrini each. I do not do as the friend who is in Rome does, to cast in such a way, etc., so that, if you do not find verification of what I write you, *I may be a liar to you.* I shall go to your house before I go to the chancellery, and before closing this letter I shall tell you what is happening with your little troop.

I shall do what is necessary for Biagio, in the first letter I write him. I sent you a letter of his two days ago, along with one from the Most Reverend Soderini.[12] I got the rest of what is due you, and I have kept it all up to now in my house.

I have just come back from your house, and I took care of everything that you ask me to in your letter. They are all well, very well. Marietta was anxious for me to give you her and the children's regards. All of them, *as above,* are well: only Bernardo is a little bit cranky, but he has no fever or other illness.

On the Ponte Vecchio I met that Ser Antonio who does printing, and he told me he had such a person write you, and in such a way, that you are going to give him permission to do everything he sees fit, with both the printed matter and the others that he says he wants to do over again: just for your information. Be careful: speak clearly in a matter like this and make sure you are understood. I do not know of anything else to tell you except that I have presented those ten *Decennali,* as I said. They were grateful for them. *Farewell* and be happy.

In Florence, 14 March 1505[6].

Give my regards to Ser Giovanni Rilli, if he is there, and if not, to his father, Niccolò, if you see him.

Yours, Agostino

Some more substantive errors, for the little ones are numerous:

> Desiderosi fuggir tanta *pena*
> Qui la lega di nuovo *s'incaviglia*
> *La differenza che venne fra loro*
> Al cavallo *sfregiato* ruppe el freno
> La parte hispana fè *el sangue* adverso
> La Puglia, etc.

I do not say here what it should say, since you know it.[13]

❖ LETTER III
Totto Machiavelli to Niccolò Machiavelli
25 May 1506

To the Distinguished Niccolò Machiavelli, Florentine Secretary.
In Florence.[1]
Jesus. In the name of God, 25 May 1506.

Honored brother, etc. I wrote you all that was happening from Ronciglione, and I reminded you of Girolamo Gaddi's business. Now once again I urge you to it as strongly as I can, so that he can stop here during these suits or disagreements of his with his brother. For the inconvenience could doubtless not be greater for him. So it is better if neither you nor Piero neglects doing anything to leave it completely resolved.

Girolamo Gaddi was written to by Giuliano Parigi, who is in the Eight, that if his acquittal had been requested, he would have had it. So do not let the time pass by, every time you see an opportunity to get the result that is desired by us.

I spoke with Girolamo of that matter of Riacino, and I left him the bill; I also gave him the bill for all the matters of Valdifina. For this reason we thought it would be good to see about getting, along with this Riacino, that other property called Machiesti, especially if it can be used at present.

He says this Machiesti has 4,000 bushels' worth in three sections: hill, level land, small pastures. From the hill they got 200 sacks of grain and 40 lire, from the pastures 35 gold ducats. The level land was let out to sharecroppers and produced 400 sacks of grain at 4 denari each.

If this property were exploited, we estimate it would be a good idea to take it together with Riacino, in order that an evaluation would be set between the two of you and a minimal fief of 20 lire per year should not have to be shared.

Keep Girolamo informed regularly either of this place of Machiesti or of any other place in the archbishopric that might be near this Riacino.

Nothing else for this letter. God keep you.

Yours, Totto Machiavelli, in Florence

Give the enclosed contract to Messer Battista and tell him I have not done what he wanted because there was no authority to act for him.

I was with Messer Lorenzo, who does not approve this matter, as I shall write him at length in the meanwhile.

Tell Messer Battista that Girolamo will make an effort on his behalf with Stiattese.

❖ LETTER 112

Niccolò Machiavelli to Giovanni Ridolfi[1]

Florence, 12 June 1506

To the Magnificent Giovanni Ridolfi,
Commissioner General against the Pisans, Patron, and Special Benefactor.

Signor commissioner. If I have not previously written you any news, let this letter and the next make amends to you.

There are some letters from France from the fifteenth to the thirtieth of last month: they include news that the emperor and the king of Hungary[2] are in agreement and that the emperor cares for nothing else but hastening his arrival in Italy; that his entire army—nine thousand foot soldiers and four thousand cavalrymen—are also anxious for it; that he has sent to Trent a good part of the artillery he wants to bring with him; furthermore, he is getting ready to send four thousand foot soldiers to Gonsalvo.[3]

The archduke is in agreement with the king of Aragon[4] because they got together in Galicia; they are seen as being quite closely united, which goes contrary to the expectations of the French, who are evidently unhappy about it.

The king of England[5] is in agreement with the archduke because during his trip to Spain he provided him with money and two thousand infantrymen.

The barons from the Kingdom of Naples who are in Spain (that is, the exiled barons)—believing that their states would be restored in keeping with the pact between France and Spain and not having had them restored—have sent one of their men to the king of France for new support. And Duke Valentino, a prisoner in Spain,[6] has also sent to France for support; the king has sent one of his emissaries there with an order for him to favor both the duke and the barons.

The pope seeks to recruit the Swiss soldiers[7] and asks the king of France for men at arms and says he wants to campaign against Bologna and Perugia; the French—if he recruits few Swiss and if he wants to leave Bologna alone—are promising him support for Perugia because they would also like to take their revenge on Pandolfo Petrucci; but if the pope should want to recruit a large number of Swiss, the French are going to block him as much as they can, because they believe that that is something different from Bologna and Perugia and they are afraid he wants those men in order to back the emperor.

The king of France has sent—or is about to send—to the Swiss an envoy, who is called the chief justice of Provence, with orders that he go from there to Venice and from there to Hungary in order to keep the Swiss from accepting money from anyone other than the king, to keep the Venetians firm in their support, and to disturb the peace between the king of Hungary and the emperor.

The bailiff of Dijon[8] has returned to court, where he is in high favor and, it is said, because he knows German affairs quite well.

He is sending Monseigneur d'Argenton[9] with four gentlemen to the German border to take certain German alliances away from him so that they will furnish the emperor with neither men nor money.

The king of France is not observing the conditions of the recent agreement[10] that Rouen made with the emperor, because an envoy who a short while ago came to court to seek the stipulated men and troops was given neither the one nor the other but was dismissed and was told his emissaries will be sent to the emperor to let him know, etc.

The king of France[11] has given his daughter as a bride to Monseigneur d'Angoulême and made all the lords of the realm swear allegiance to the said Angoulême should there be no male heirs after his death. As a dowry he gave him the district of Blois and one hundred thousand ducats; the queen gave him one hundred thousand ducats and the duchy of Brittany should she die without male heirs.

There has been no new agreement made between the Venetians and the king, but people are smiling on one another and abiding by the former one.

The king of France has given orders to Monseigneur de Cisteron,[12] who was an envoy from the pope and is returning to Italy to visit Ferrara, Mantua, Bologna, and Florence, to promise them the moon on his part and to keep them well disposed to him during this incursion by the emperor, if indeed there should be one.

These dispatches are insufficient unless I communicate to you the commentary our fellow-citizens—the wisest ones—make on them; and, although you are wise and could comment on them as well as they can, I know their discussion will be welcome to you.

If these dispatches keep up, it seems to them more likely than not that the king of the Romans [13] will make an incursion into Italy, and this is how their reasoning goes. Whenever one wants to decide whether or not someone is going to do something, one has to see first if that person wants to do it and then what advantages and disadvantages that person has to do it. Whether or not the emperor wants to make an incursion into Italy, all the reasons are for it. One is the desire he reasonably must have to be crowned for his own honor and to pass this dignity on to his son. The other is to avenge the outrages he has received from the Italians and to regain the honor his coming into Tuscany [14] lost him. People therefore conclude that he does want this incursion. Now, as for seeing who may check or support him, one must consider who are his dependents and who are his allies. We do not have very much information here about his dependents [15]; it is believed, however, that he is more powerful now than he was, having gotten the Count Palatine [16] under control and having assessed the cities and the lords for what they are to supply him for his Italian incursion. [17] His allies are the archduke, the king of France, and the king of England. In Italy, where he wants to come, his allies are the pope, Venice, Spain, the Florentines, and other minor states.

If these dispatches are true, it can be seen that the archduke, the king of Spain, and the king of England are in agreement; and since they are in agreement together, it is necessary that they concur with the emperor—since the archduke is his son and we are dealing with interests in common. The pope, albeit in discussions with the king of France to get his troops, is seen to be leaning more to the emperor's side—that is how reason would have it, because the king's fortune is weary, especially in Italy, as a result of what has happened, and the emperor's fortune will be fresh; this pope must be intending to do with him what Alexander [18] did with France. There is no need to discuss the minor states in Italy once the others are agreed among themselves. Among the major powers, only the French and Venetians remain disgruntled at this incursion of his. Together these two could oppose him, but each of them will be wary and distrustful of the other. People also think that the French and Venetians could oppose the emperor with force or craft, and they believe that these two will not fail to use all their craft and diligence to thwart him, as, according to the dispatches received, the king of France is seen to be doing; but people do not think that this craft is sufficient and, should it come to having to resort to force, that the French and Venetians are unwilling to do so because people do not believe that the king of France is about to start a war with the emperor against the wishes of the king of England, the archduke, and the king of Spain; and people do not think the Venetians, having to fight a war in their own territory, are going to want to do so because they would always fear that the French might leave them in the lurch. People therefore believe that, since it is useless for them to try to restrain the emperor with their skill, they will decide to let him come and to guard their own affairs closely; and if they have to join in the fray with him, they will do so only after his incursion has begun—as the duke of Milan and the Venetians did with King Charles.

For his part, the emperor will be satisfied with being allowed unopposed entry because it is more advantageous to him to make war later than sooner. The reason for this is that two things cause him to come to Italy: he wants the crown, and he wants revenge for insults to him. If he declared war before he was crowned and lost, he could never again hope for the crown. But if he declares war after he is crowned, even if he should lose, they would be unable to take the crown away from him and he might always return home with less dishonor. It makes little difference to him whether he fights in this sector or that, since he has the pope as an ally—and all the others that, with his authority, he may have dragged along behind him.

I know that I have bored you—forgive me; I am yours to command; and if you do not want any more of these sermons,[19] let me know.

12 June 1506
Niccolò Machiavelli, Secretary

❖ LETTER 113
Biagio Buonaccorsi to Niccolò Machiavelli
Florence, 1 September 1506

To His Most Honored Niccolò Machiavelli,
Florentine Secretary, with the Supreme Pontiff, etc.
In Court.[1]

Honored Niccolò. I have received your letter of the 30th and sent the keys to Marietta,[2] informing her of what you asked me to. I shall do the same tomorrow with the money for the courier,[3] although I do not see any way to send it to you safely. I would therefore prefer for you to secure it there, either from the Most Reverend Monsignor[4] or from someone else, and have it drawn to me here, where I would pay for it right away. I shall await a reply to this: then I shall do whatever you request me to do.

Matters are going the way you want with the foot soldiers; thus I had them pay those 4 constables for whom you left me a bill. As if I did not have enough to do, this springs up again: you had not been gone two days when I was going around the palace with three of them tagging along. This morning I sent off Tedesco,[5] who decided to go to the region of Pisa to see the countryside. Rest assured about this, because those very notices that you write about the passage of the emperor having been confirmed here; among the first things said about such an event—as a most advantageous and important thing in every respect—was that the militia should be kept ready. I do not want to neglect to tell you that when they put Bastiano da Castiglione,[6] the head of the troops of lower Valdarno, in charge of the task, with the result that you are aware of, and he was asked how he had organized the men, he answered: "I shall give you 700 in 4 hours, and all men from every faction." They were amazed at these words, and savored them as something of great moment. And so everything that he wanted was provided for right away. I wanted to tell you these few words about this matter for your satisfaction, since I judged they would be welcome to you. Everything else is going as planned.

If I told you I did not envy you, I would not be confessing the truth to you; by my faith, if for nothing else than for the continual association that you will have with our Most Reverend Monsignor, which I am sure will turn out far better than I had portrayed it to you. Give him my regards, I pray you, when you find it convenient. With the other things, may God give you better luck than he gave us, because I believe those activities that arouse men and change their nature will be of great help to you.

I do not know what else to write you. Messer Giustiniano sends you his regards, and I do likewise. Goodbye.

In Florence, 1 September 1506.
Yours, Biagio[7]

❖ LETTER 114
Francesco del Nero to Niccolò Machiavelli
Florence, 2 September 1506

To the Distinguished Niccolò Machiavelli,
Florentine Secretary, with the Supreme Pontiff.
In the name of God, 2 September 1506.

As an honored father. I arrived here safe and sound on the 30th of last month, and I gave news of you to your Marietta, who was glad to hear that you were well. She is likewise, as is all the family, thank God. I also presented the letter from the great captain[1] to His Excellency the Gonfalonier, and I am sending you a copy of it at the end of this letter.

"Eminent lord. Having learned what your lordship wrote me in your letter of the end of last month concerning the violence wrought by the two Venetian galleys[2] against Francesco del Nero, who was sent from Valona to Lecce by Totto Machiavelli, a Florentine citizen, in the port of the tower of San Cataldo, I have taken great offense at it, certainly not otherwise than if the damage had been done to the person of whatsoever good subject of My Lord His Catholic Highness.[3] On learning of Your Lordship's desire, I wrote in no uncertain terms to the Most Illustrious Signory of Venice, for it to see to their complete restitution. If, on my part, I should need to provide anything else for this, I shall do so willingly, as if I were doing it at the suggestion of His Majesty above-named and as if Your Lordship himself were doing it, out of the desire I have to be of service to you because of the friendship you have with His Majesty above-mentioned. If I can be of use to you in anything else, I shall do it willingly, and I continue to offer my services to you. Naples, 20 August 1506."

As you see, I have sent you a copy of it so that if you should need to use influence in recovering the lost goods, you may know what the above-mentioned Great Captain has written to His Excellency the Gonfalonier. He says the same, with the same offers, in the letter to Niccolò del Nero.

There is nothing else I have to tell you in this letter, except that if I can do anything at all for you, I am at your command. I am your servant. God keep you.

Francesco del Nero, in Florence

❖ LETTER 115
Biagio Buonaccorsi to Niccolò Machiavelli
Florence, 6 September 1506

To His Most Honored Niccolò Machiavelli,
Florentine Secretary, with the Supreme Pontiff.
In Court, at the Home of the Most Reverend Monsignor of Volterra.

Honored Niccolò. I have written to you several times these past few days. I told you of my receipt of the keys and that they had been sent to Madonna Marietta, and of the precise origin of the disorder in the Casentino, and whatever other news there was, in addition to what people were thinking. But because I judge that you have received them by now, I shall not otherwise repeat it, since even if I wanted to I could not, because I do not remember what I did two hours ago. In addition, you must have received, by the hand of the sculptor Michelangelo,[1] the money for the courier,[2] about which I expect to hear something in your next letter.

Then yesterday the latest letters of the 2nd and 3rd were presented to me, and I have no need to say anything about them, because I have heard no one grumbling or your being criticized in any way at all. About the other matters, you know that I am of the same opinion as you, since on my return from that court[3] I had explained very well to you the style of life and the quality and condition of everyone. I shall give your message to Alessandro, and I shall not have much to do about those others, because I do not know too many of them. And you will do your duty as a friend for me, too, with the Most Reverend Monsignor of Volterra.

Today a certain fellow-citizen of ours, Jacopo Doffi, a sensible and most intelligent man who returned from Germany 3 days ago, was at the office of the Ten. He reports what I shall tell you hereafter concerning the emperor's affairs. First of all, that he left him about 5 days' journey this side of Innsbruck, but in the direction of the Friuli, where he was busy feasting and hunting. All his troops were in quarters, and (when he had them together) they were less than 4 thousand, including foot soldiers and cavalry. Little was being said there about his passage, even though he has ordered all those cities that are supposed to give him aid to be ready with it. In fact, there has been little preparation for his passage,[4] especially for money, since he says he does not have a cent. His council was in Innsbruck, along with a good number of artillery, but no movement at all was seen there. He[5] has heard nothing about his passage, until he was in the territory of the Venetians, who were talking quite a lot about it and were also sending some troops, though not many, toward that border. He had found at times 50, at times 100, foot soldiers, but no other preparations. 3 of his ambassadors were in Venice, and they did not have 12 horses among the three of them. What their demands were was not revealed. And so, having heard this man, a sensible person, I believe that this news of his passage has not been spread by the Venetians for any other purpose than what you write.[6]

I have nothing else to tell you this evening, except that His Catholic Majesty[7] is expected in Piombino any hour now. Here no ambassadors have been named to anywhere.

With this letter there will be one from Sisteron[8] to the pope; have it delivered right away. Nothing else.

In Florence, 6 September 1506.
Brother Bi.

❖ LETTER 116
Bartolomeo Ugolini to Niccolò Machiavelli
Florence, 7 September 1506

To His Notable, Most Honored Lordship, Messer Niccolò Machiavelli.
In Court.
Jesus. 7 September 1506.

Honored Messer Niccolò. Francesco del Nero has gotten here, and as for the goods that were taken,[1] he had nothing else but letters from the great captain to the signory of Venice and to the doge, which he left in Rome with Girolamo Gaddi, and one here to His Excellency Our Gonfalonier, in response to the one that he had had written for himself, as you know. The latter is as welcome as can possibly be told, containing in brief this purport: that the case displeases him as much as if it were done to His Catholic Majesty's own subjects, and that he has written of it to the signory of Venice in no uncertain terms, and that if anything else should be needed he should be so informed. So it seems to me that he appreciates the matter and desires to be of service to us. I told the Gonfalonier that it seemed best to me, if it seemed so to His Lordship, for him to write another letter thanking him for what had been done and begging him to be so kind as to continue until the end. He answered that we should do as we please, and it was his pleasure, too. It will be done today, and it will be sent Saturday, if not earlier.

Afterward I shall write again to Girolamo Gaddi and to Salvatore Billi[2] in Naples whatever I deem necessary for this business; and if in the beginning a man had been sent by post to Venice by the great captain, I should think that by this time the release would have been obtained, for the most important thing is that there should be someone in Venice to expedite the matter. I did not fail to remind Gaddi of it, and I shall not, although if the great captain tells it truly, since the ambassador of Venice is in Naples, he will be able to do this very thing himself with that ambassador. But, in my opinion, a man such as I describe would have been better in Venice, because he would be right on the spot and not have to shoot letters off here and there, from which, before things get settled, people's minds change a thousand times. Now I shall not fail, as I say, to recall everywhere what seems to me to be appropriate, and so I urge you, too. If you can give any service or aid, do not fail to, even if it should be unnecessary, since it is up to you more than it is to us. But according to what Francesco says, everyone will receive some harm, so that thus it will be more bearable to each one. All in all, let each one do whatever good he can.

Nothing else for this letter. If you should do anything at all concerning this, let us know. God keep you. Yours,

Bartolomeo Ugolini, in Florence

❖ LETTER 117
Biagio Buonaccorsi to Niccolò Machiavelli
Florence, 9 September 1506

To Niccolò Machiavelli, Florentine Secretary,
as an Honored Brother, with the Supreme Pontiff.

My very dear Niccolò, two hours ago you were written to by way of Cortona, and because I was busy, I could not drop you a line as I should have desired. However, I do not know whether that matters to you; but I shall endeavor not to let anyone get there without letters from me, since I think that will please you.

I got your letter of the 6th already opened, and I shall do what you request of me with Giustiniano, although I had done it before and always on your behalf; but now that <I see that this matter is of burning importance to you,> I shall do it all the more diligently; <you must not have found it so much better this way:> seek, and you shall find.

News of the emperor is updated here every day, and I wrote you personally of the latest ones there were, through that Jacopo Doffi, who had come from there, in my last letter, which Canon Serristori[1] brought, along with many others both public and private: look them up. Meanwhile, because the matter is important, as you know, and having to base ourselves on uncertain and confused notices is dangerous, Bernardo de' Ricci[2] is being sent there with a salary of two gold florins per day; and he was given 150 ducats in hand. He will have to do better than you; <and those who proposed him did it to resurrect him and to give you a counterweight and someone who knows how to adapt better than you.> God give him good fortune, and let Him not forget the others, if it please Him, because we need it, and urgently. His mission is to present himself to that prince and in the name of this Signoria to offer him their full services, like good children, with broad and general words. But the aim of the assignment is to have definite news of this passage, in order to be able better to decide on what should be done, etc.

Ambassadors will be named today to Naples, to honor His Catholic Majesty.[3] If he lands at Piombino, Messers Giovanvittorio, Alamanno, Gualterotti,[4] and Niccolò del Nero will be sent there to welcome him and to honor him again in that place. They are men of great worth, who will know how to do that; and His Majesty ought to be very satisfied by it.

I have nothing else to tell you about the militia, except that Bastiano da Castiglione,[5] who is staying in San Miniato, 8 days ago assembled the general battalion in the presence of the lord of Piombino,[6] who was on his way back from the baths and at whose behest it was done, and many others of those from Cascina. It gave great satisfaction, according to what Bastiano writes me. But that talk of money being given in Bologna and in Romagna has caused some of those of the vicariate of Firenzuola to go there. It was taken care of in such a way that no one will have to leave his house.

Your family is well: I wish mine were, too, for I have to move around in any case, so that I am hard-pressed. Let me know if you got that money from Michelangelo.[7]

I thank you for the offer you made, since although I am extremely needy I know that you do not have much left over there, and you would need a lot more. Nothing else.

In Florence, 9 September 1506.
Brother B.

Bernardo Nasi is in the Ten, in place of Guicciardini.[8]

❖ LETTER 118
Biagio Buonaccorsi to Niccolò Machiavelli
Florence, 11 September 1506

To His Magnificence the Florentine Ambassador Niccolò Machiavelli,
with the Supreme Pontiff.

My very dear Niccolò. I have written you several times in the past few days, along with public letters, and since you do not acknowledge any of them in this last letter of yours of the 9th, they must have gone astray somewhere. You will find them little by little.

Just when I thought that Michelangelo had given you that money, it was brought back to me by one of his men, who told me that he had turned back for good reason: I see that I can find no way of sending it safely to you, unless some trusted person comes along. Let me know what you want me to do since I do not know how dire your need of it is.

The ambassadors for Piombino[1] have left here today, very well appointed and with authority to honor His Majesty.

In Florence, 11 September.
Brother Biagio

❖ LETTER 119
Giovan Battista Soderini[1] to Niccolò Machiavelli
12 September 1506

To Niccolò Machiavelli, Florentine Secretary, as a Brother, with the Supreme Pontiff. In Perugia, or Wherever He May Be.[2]

Notable, most honorable one. If the affection that I bear you did not lead me to do many other inconsidered things with you, I would make excuses to you for writing to you, or I would seize on some pretext of excuse. I have nothing to tell you, and I do not want you to write me any answer. I could have sent the enclosed along with other letters or sent my regards to you by way of Biagio; all in all, as it befell me, I could have done without writing you for now. But I wanted to continue the practice of doing innumerable things aimlessly. I could not tell you how much Filippo di Banco[3] and I would like to go as far as Piombino.[4] But if one has a star, the other has the sun.[5] And so more people are going there than to Siena, and I doubt we shall. If you wait until January to return, we shall see your flash and hear your thunder at the same time.[6] And yet they would like to go about it step by step by step. We are in good health, and Filippo is expecting a decision[7] against him any time now. We shall see what happens. I send you my regards.

12 September 1506.
Giov. B.

❖ LETTER 120
Biagio Buonaccorsi to Niccolò Machiavelli
Florence, 19 September 1506

To His Honored Niccolò Machiavelli.

Niccolò. I cannot write you as I should wish, since it is late and I am very busy. I gave your letter to Bernardo Nasi, I added something else to it, and he was very pleased by it. He is doing his duty concerning the militia, and nothing less was needed, as we get so many objections every day.

I managed to get Tedesco[1] to settle for 15 ducats, and even for that it took quite a bit of effort.

I shall send you the money at the first opportunity, since it is still wrapped up as it was.

Your family is well, and the public letter gives you any news there may be.

Yours, Biagio
In Florence, 19 September 1506.

❖ LETTER 121

Niccolò Machiavelli to Giovan Battista Soderini

Perugia, 13–21 September[1] 1506

A letter came to me from you wearing a mask; yet, after ten words, I recognized it[2] and can well believe in the crowds at Piombino, since I know you;
and I am certain of the obstacles you and Filippo encountered, because I
know one of you is impeded by too little "light"[3]—the other by too much. I
do not find January a nuisance,[4] as long as I can count on holding onto
February's support. I am sorry about Filippo's apprehension[5] and await the
outcome in suspense. Your letter was short, but rereading it I made it longer.
{He who does not know how to fence can entangle one who does.[6]} I was
grateful for it because it gave me an opportunity[7] to do what I was hesitating
about doing and what you remind me not to do[8]—the only part of your letter that I admit is to no purpose.[9] This would surprise me if it were not for
the fact that my fate has shown me so many and such varied things that I am
forced rarely to be surprised or to admit that I have not savored[10]—either
through reading or through experience—the actions of men and their ways of
doing things. I know you and the compass of your navigation[11]; even if it
could be blamed, which it cannot be, I should not, since I see what ports it
has guided you to[12] and what hopes it may foster in you. (Hence I think not
according to your perspective, wherein nothing but prudence is visible, but to
the perspective of the many, which must see the ends, not the means, of
things.) And I see that steering along a variety of routes can bring about the
same thing and that acting in different ways can bring about the same
end[13]—whatever this conviction may have lacked has been filled in by this
pope's actions and their outcomes.[14] {In fine, advise no one and accept advice
from no one, except for a general suggestion that each man must do what his
mind prompts him to—and do it with daring.} Take Hannibal and Scipio: in
addition to their military training, in which they were equally preeminent, the
former kept his armies in Italy united through cruelty, treachery, and impiety
and made himself admired by the populace, who, in order to follow him, rebelled against the Romans {men tire of the good and complain about the
bad; bitter things irritate the taste, sweet things cloy it[15]}; the latter achieved
the identical result among the populace in Spain with compassion, loyalty, and
piety: both achieved victory upon victory.[16] {To try Fortune, who is the
friend of youth,[17] and to change according to the times. But it is impossible
both to have fortresses[18] and not to have them; it is impossible to be both
cruel and compassionate, etc.} But, because it is not customary to bring in the
Romans as evidence, Lorenzo de' Medici disarmed the populace to hold on
to Florence, Messer Giovanni Bentivoglio armed them to hold on to
Bologna; the Vitelli in Città di Castello and the current duke of Urbino in his
territory tore down fortresses in order to hold on to those territories, Count
Francesco in Milan and many others constructed fortresses in their territories
in order to secure them for themselves. Emperor Titus[19] believed that he

would lose his realm on any day that he did not do good to someone; another person might believe that he would lose his on any day when he did do good to someone. Many people [do not] succeed in their plans because they calculate and deliberate everything. {When Fortune slacks off it follows that a man, a family, and a city crumbles; each person's fortune is based upon his way of doing things, and each person's fortune slacks off; when it is slack, it must be regained by some other means.[20]} This pope, who has no scales or measuring stick in his house, obtains through chance—and disarmed[21]—what ought to be difficult to attain even with organization and with weapons. We have seen, and continue to see, in all the examples mentioned above—and in countless other examples that could be brought in as evidence in analogous instances—that kingdoms are conquered, or are subdued, or have fallen, as unforeseen events would have it. Sometimes the way of doing things that was praised when it led to conquest is vilified when it leads to defeat, and sometimes when defeat comes after long prosperity {the comparison of the horse and bit concerning fortresses}, people do not blame anything of their own but rather indict heaven and the will of the Fates.[22] But the reason why different actions are sometimes equally useful and sometimes equally detrimental I do not know—yet I should very much like to; so, in order to learn your view, I shall be presumptuous enough to give you mine. I believe that just as Nature has created men with different faces, so she has created them with different intellects and imaginations. As a result, each man behaves according to his own intellect and imagination. And, on the other hand, because times change and the pattern of events differs, one man's hopes may turn out as he prayed they would. The man who matches his way of doing things with the conditions of the times is successful; the man whose actions are at odds with the times and the pattern of events is unsuccessful. Hence, it can well be that two men can achieve the same goal by acting differently: because each one of them matches his actions to what he encounters and because there are as many patterns of events as there are regions and governments. But because times and affairs often change—both in general and in particular—and because men change neither their imaginations nor their ways of doing things accordingly, it turns out that a man has good fortune at one time and bad fortune at another. And truly, anyone wise enough to adapt to and understand the times and the pattern of events would always have good fortune or would always keep himself from bad fortune; and it would come to be true that the wise man[23] could control the stars and the Fates. But such wise men do not exist: in the first place, men are shortsighted; in the second place, they are unable to master their own natures; thus it follows that Fortune is fickle, controlling men and keeping them under her yoke.[24] I want the examples mentioned above to suffice as proof of this view; I have based it on them and so I should like the one to support the other. Cruelty, treachery, and impiety are effective in providing a new ruler with prestige in that region where human kindness, loyalty, and piety have long been common practice, just as human kindness, loyalty, and piety are effective where cruelty, treachery, and impiety reigned for a while;

for just as bitter things irritate the taste and sweet things cloy it, so men become impatient with the good and complain about the bad. These causes, among others, opened Italy up to Hannibal and Spain to Scipio,[25] and thus each one made time and affairs consistent with his pattern of doing things. In those days a Scipio would have made less progress in Italy and a Hannibal would have made less progress in Spain than each did in his own area.

❖ LETTER 122
Biagio Buonaccorsi to Niccolò Machiavelli
Florence, 21 September 1506

To Niccolò Machiavelli, Florentine Secretary,
as an Honored Brother, with the Supreme Pontiff.

Honored Niccolò. Two days ago I wrote you briefly and I told you of receiving your letter by the hands of Tedesco,[1] and that I had worked it out, both with His Excellency the Gonfalonier and with Their Lordships of the Ten, so that his position will be set at 13 ducats a month with the obligation you recalled about it. I do not have anything else to tell you about this. I do promise you this: that I am not going to take this matter into my hands now like you, and make it my shield, because we get a dozen objections per hour, which in fact have no value whatsoever; <and these groups make a lot of noise about them as if they really mattered to them,> but I can indeed tell you that <Bernardo Nasi is behaving> straightforwardly and much better than he promised you, for he truly is a man of honor and he loves you quite a bit. If you think highly of him, you will be doing the right thing and something that will be useful to you.

Here there is nothing new either about the emperor or about the king of Aragon. The ambassadors are in Bibbona[2] with the necessary furnishings to honor him: it is a convenient place from which to get to both Leghorn and Piombino, whereas it is not known for sure at which of these two places he is going to land. Jacopo Salviati and Gualterotti were elected as ambassadors to Naples. It is felt that they will be disposed to go: for the moment it is not being talked about.

Two days[3] ago about twelve foot soldiers, from among those of lower Valdarno, came here to Florence. When they went to a tavern that evening, they made some affront for which one of them was taken by the office of the Ten, and early the next morning, before anyone knew it, he received 4 pulls of the cord. In addition to this, he was interned in Leghorn; but it was worked out so that his internment was not put into effect. There have also been several disputes these past few days by Bastiano da Castiglione, the one who is staying in San Miniato. So it was necessary to have him come here and to give him a dressing-down, etc.

Three days ago, funding was voted for 18 months, so that unless new events arise the city is set for that period of time, God be praised. Meanwhile we shall think of something good; and we shall not have to have this obstacle for the re-engagements, which is a pretty good bit of luck.

The duke of Ferrara[4] had Count Albertino's head cut off on the 14th, as well as that of the said count's son-in-law and of another servant of Don Ferrante, who is being detained in his castle, as is Don Giulio, who was turned over by the marchioness of Mantua, where he had fled.

I have done and continue to do my duty as a friend in your name with Messer Giustiniano. Nothing else. Your family is well, as your worker told me 3 days ago, when he came to me to get news of you. I gave your message to Ser Agostino: if he does not send you those *Decennali,* I shall send them to you.

In Florence, 21 September 1506.
Yours, Bi.

❖ LETTER 123
Giovan Battista Soderini to Niccolò Machiavelli
26 September 1506

To the Notable Niccolò Machiavelli, *My Honored Friend.*

Notable, most honored man. I wrote you some days ago,[1] and because several letters went astray at that time, I think that mine may have been among them. If you got it, I am very glad; if not, please excuse me. When you write to Biagio or to Filippo,[2] I hope you will not mind letting them know whether it was a nice trip over there, because there are some who are thinking about it in order to see the countryside, to do their duty toward their family, and to pass the time pleasantly. So it might perhaps not be a good idea to fool around too much. I have no other need than to remind you on behalf of Filippo that the air is very thin there: dry your head well, because in any case you shall come back quickly if duties are of the same value during one's absence. No one understands this enigma except him, who is worried about it and thinks that because of the noise you cannot stay in the fire. Here it is said by us that Consalvo[3] was to get to Piombino by the 24th; the other news is deeper than I can fish. The battalions are going well, especially those of Scarperia, because the vicar pays them many compliments, and, when a foreigner happens by, to honor him, he unwinds a length of it on the field. We are well, and a big bunch of us send our regards to you. May God keep you from harm.

The 26th.
Giov. Battista

❖ LETTER 124

Biagio Buonaccorsi to Niccolò Machiavelli

Florence, 30 September 1506

To His Most Honored Niccolò Machiavelli, Florentine Secretary, with the Pontiff.
In Court.

Honored Niccolò. I am afraid I am becoming a little negligent with my
friends, like you. I tell you this, because it seems like a year to me since I last
wrote you, and it has happened only because of laziness, to call it by its right
name. Two days ago I received your letter, I believe of the 26th, with the enclosed letter to Francesco,[1] which was sent on faithfully. To answer your inquiry,
I believe you can ask with confidence for money from the public treasury because <none of the chosen ambassadors[2] will come, and no one is thinking
about it any more for now,> and so I believe the matter will remain for a few
days more, unless the wind shifts; and you should not take it ill because your responsibilities are not killing you. I do tell you this, though: your two letters[3] of
the 25th and 26th arrived at the right time, because <there were some who said
they wanted Gianiacopo to be brought back, since he is not doing anything,
along with other words of his, which were rebutted by your friend Bernardo
Nasi.> So write more often, if you see fit. I have read to Soderini what you
wrote to me. I believe we shall write again, and you will do as you see fit.

The two ambassadors will go to Naples, that is, Messer Francesco Gualterotti and Jacopo Salviati. It will be a fine legation, both for the quality of the
personages and for the company of young people who are said to be going
with them. It will all be appropriate because His Catholic Majesty, who was
in Savona two days ago, is coming with such pomp in his trappings and everything else that anyone who goes there well-appointed will need them if he
is to make a good showing. Consalvo was in Leghorn on the 27th, on his way
to meet his king, and he was visited and greeted by our representative in that
place, so that he went off very satisfied, saying that Italy will receive many
benefits from the coming of his king, and Florence will have its share of them.
He excused himself about the matter of Pisa, saying that those times required
it, but in the future he will act in such a way that the city will know that he
thinks highly of it. He went to Piombino, where there were Pisan ambassadors; and despite their begging him to go to Pisa, he categorically refused.

Affairs in Genoa[4] are being made continually worse by the noblemen, who
are all in exile. They have already taken away all the lands that Messer Gian-
luigi held in the Riviera di Levante, or a good part of them, <and he accepts
them from whoever wins, in his usual manner.>

This morning, by private notices from Lyons of the 23rd, it was learned
that the man from Aix[5] had been there, coming from court, with a mission
from the king to Chaumont,[6] to give our lord all the lancers that he wants for
the Bologna campaign. So the campaign will go forward in any case, now that
the people there are going willingly.

Here there is nothing else new, and I do not know what more to tell you, except that your family is well, and the money for the courier is in this same packet, since I did not learn of Giuliano Lapi's[7] arrival. I think I shall use a ducat of it tomorrow, since I shall give it back to you in a few days, since I have taken assurance of it from your own words. Nothing more.

In Florence, 30 September, 10 o'clock at night, 1506.
You know who, B.

At least let me know you have received this.

❖ LETTER 125
Giustiniano and "Your Comrade"[1] to Niccolò Machiavelli
1 October 1506

[. . .] to the Generous Messer Niccolò, Honored Father.

Your servants Giustiniano and your comrade in Imola, formerly with the late venerable Zoan Lorenzo, *health and apostolic blessing.*[2] *First of October 1506.*

Our most remarkable, excellent master. Since we learn here[3] with the greatest satisfaction of the good and happy state of Your Excellency in so great honor, dignity, pleasurable intercourse with him who is and those who are appropriate to and in conformity with your nature, where there is no deprivation but rather fertile bounty, and that you are well considered, beloved, and flattered by them; thanks as well to your luxurious life on most refined viands, healthful and pure and digestible to your stomach (since you have taken or indeed are partaking of more than usual, be careful: you are not in this light air here, but in those there, very light and gentle to the touch, pleasant and sweet, as we have heard from your magnificent and honored chief associate); we could not help, on the one hand, congratulating you and being most highly pleased for your sake (not, however, without some envy, since we do not have any in conformity to your nature); on the other hand, we are afraid that, because of all of your partaking of this air and the delicious enjoyment and pleasant fruits, you may become so filled and satiated that you might forget about us, as you have done up to now, and about returning to your country, and, *worse still,* you may take priestly vows[4] and become a thoroughly modern curial ecclesiastic. May God be such as to make you prosper and to hold his hand on your head, and give you more and more satisfaction.

We are desirous of hearing any news that can be communicated from those parts, and which is the best dish there, whether milk-fed veal or alpine and mountain kids, raised domestically; and in that area one of us is desirous of knowing about affairs in Pesaro.

There is no other news from here, except that the Arno is running downhill as it did before.

Farewell. We send our regards to Your Excellency *for infinite world without end. Amen.*

❖ LETTER 126

Pier Francesco Tosinghi to Niccolò Machiavelli
Castrocaro,[1] 4 October 1506

To His Very Dear Friend, the Notable Niccolò Machiavelli,
Envoy and Secretary of the Florentine Signoria, with the Supreme Pontiff.

Notable man, very dear friend, etc. Just now, that is, 12 noon,[2] I have received a letter of yours from yesterday, and with it a packet of letters bound for Florence, which were sent off right away. This morning we addressed a letter from the Ten to you, in Forlì, care of Bishop de' Pazzi,[3] judging that he would have the means to send it on. I have arranged with the present bearer that he mention it to him upon his return and if he has not sent it that it be given back to him. There is no need to make excuses to me for not having addressed the letters to me, because you know that I know how much affection you bear toward me.

I hear that we shall have the pontiff as a close neighbor and how brave he is in battle, and I am so anxious for him to do some remarkable deed that I find it hard to believe. I await your coming for a few days' rest here, and we shall have a fine time. I have no other need than to offer myself to you for any occasion that arises. God keep you from harm.

> *From Castrocaro, 4 October 1506.*
> *Pier Francesco Tosinghi,*
> *Commissioner General*

❖ LETTER 127

Biagio Buonaccorsi to Niccolò Machiavelli
Florence, 6 October 1506

To His Respected Niccolò Machiavelli, Florentine Secretary, with the Pontiff.
In Court.

Honored Niccolò. I have not given that money to Piero del Nero, and the reason was that I am so well off that I could not spare a florin to put back what I had taken from it. Since you do not want me to give him any, I shall not do it. Instead, I shall send it to Ruffini[1] by the first rider going to Castrocaro, with orders to follow your orders. There is nothing more to be said about this.

Their Lordships of the Ten, in answer to your request[2] for some money, said: That is quite right, we shall do it one way or another. The gonfalonier told me this morning that you wrote him about it in the letter I gave him and that I should talk to him about it today, and so I shall do. I believe I shall send you some funds without fail at the first opportunity. You can count on me; the request will not fail.

I shall read that article[3] to Giovambattista Soderini, as I did with the other.

But you always try to excuse yourself, either because of negligence or because of all you have to do. That is not enough for your friends, because they want to be recognized as such. I am so sick and tired of making excuses for you that if you were my father, more than once I would have said: Go and retch. Write once and for all whether you gave the letter from Alessandro to San Giorgio[4] or whether you ever saw him again after the first notice you gave me of it. If you knew what a good friend of yours he is, you would pay more attention to him. But you are a latrine cover, and anyone who wants you can pick you up with a stick.

I do not want to neglect to tell you, although I could put it off until your return, that, through someone who was present there, and more than one, <when Alamanno[5] was in Bibbona, dining with Ridolfi, where there were also a lot of young people, speaking of you, he said: "I never entrusted anything at all to that rascal since I have been one of the Ten,"> going on in this vein or better. Note this, if you were not really <totally clear about his opinion.> Make sure you are here before the reconfirmations. I could write you a lot of other things, *but more fully when we are face to face.*

This morning there was news at the Uguccioni's[6] about the death of the archduke[7] within 4 days, from taking chill when he was overheated. This is truly a thing of very great moment, because it is held to be definite, and the news must be there by now. It is not judged, however, that such news is going to turn back the king of Aragon,[8] who according to the latest news was expected in Genoa. For those barons of Castile have his little son[9] in their hands and will want to bring him up as they see fit, as the Flemish did with his father. They would not even trust him, since they have once and for all become enemies,[10] etc. Therefore, since His Majesty sees that the matter is uncertain and he is now near Naples, which is definitely his and not to be valued less than Castile, it is judged that he will go on. God will it, for the good of Italy. But if he should turn back, there will still be this good: that he has Consalvo[11] with him and he should not reasonably want him any more in the kingdom.

This matter is judged very much to the benefit of His Most Christian Majesty,[12] and the contrary for the Venetians, who will no longer be able to use the mask of the emperor, nor will he be able to pass into Italy; and the two above-mentioned kings, without concern, proceed to the acquisition of what they hold from them. Because if His Most Christian Majesty loses his fear of the passage of the king of the Romans, he will lose those concerns that made him court them. The pope will also have to look after his own interests more freely and more courageously. These are things that we have to wait and see how they turn out, if we do not want to be deceived.

By letters from France of the 25th, we hear the same thing that you write, about the generous and honorable settlement made to the pope for the troops; and, in addition, about an inordinate warmth of the legate[13] in favor of His Holiness. But Gian Paolo's contract[14] displeased him to the depths of his soul. Because, in speaking, His Lordship said: "The pope ought to help us punish that traitor, who did to us, etc. But before the game is over, we shall get revenge one way or another. Let him delay as long as he can, he will not get away with it." They are giving 550 lancers to the pope, and in addition Messer Mercurio[15] the Greek, with a hundred light cavalry, 8 big cannon, and many other artillery pieces, with Chaumont[16] in charge. They have arranged for Count Ludovico[17] della Mirandola to be dispossessed of his state and Count Giovan Francesco to be put there.

The king of England did not want the marriage of Madam Margaret[18] to be made public, because it appears that the duke of Savoy was dying of the French sickness and that she was suffering from it; it has been hung up on this suspicion. The French thought they would take advantage of that by holding discussions concerning giving him Mademoiselle d'Angoulême,[19] <not to come to a conclusion but to keep him hanging> and to make him hold back about coming to the aid of the archduke against Gelderland.[20]

His Most Christian Majesty has left Blois and is going toward Bourges. If the emperor does not pass, he will turn back with his mind made up to come to Italy in the spring. There was not yet news there of the death of the archduke. In addition, they have arranged to win the duke of Savoy[21] over by several concerns. I sent your letters to the shop of Piero del Nero. *Farewell.*

> *In Florence, 6 October 1506.*
> *You know who, B.*

Do not answer about the news I give you concerning those remarks <made in Bibbona.>

❖ LETTER 128
Piero di Francesco[1] del Nero to Niccolò Machiavelli
Florence, 6 October 1506

To Niccolò Machiavelli, Florentine Secretary.
At the Papal Court.

As a son. I wrote to you Saturday, and it must have arrived. From that letter you will learn that Francesco[2] has set out for Naples to recover the goods taken from us, since we think that we shall in fact get more justice there than in Venice, especially since we have been almost invited to do so by the great captain. And that is reasonable, because the injury was done to them, although the damage was done to us. The Venetians are supposed to be well disposed; nonetheless, we shall write to Alessandro de' Nerli instructing him to do what is necessary, so that he does not fail in this. Francesco should be in Naples within 2 days; when we have something, you will be told about it, and if we should need one man's favor more than another, beyond those we have there, we shall let you know. Totto, according to letters we have, might still be in Ancona. God protect him wherever he is. We have arranged for him to be paid the ten ducats for his room, and by now it must be done. The letter was sent to the painter.[3] The letter was sent to Marietta, who is well with the family in the country. Nothing else for this letter. God be with you.

In Florence, 6 October 1506.

You must have heard about the death of King Philip[4] of Spain, which is probably going to spoil some plans. Yours,

Piero di Francesco del Nero

❖ LETTER 129
Cardinal Francesco Soderini to Niccolò Machiavelli
Cesena, 6 October 1506

To the Notable Messer Niccolò Machiavelli, Florentine Secretary and
Our Dearest Compare, F. Soderini, Priest of Santa Susanna, Cardinal of Volterra.

Notable man and very dear compare. As you know, we were supposed to leave tomorrow morning for Forlì. Now the plans have been changed, and tomorrow will be a consistory, though we cannot see any matter of importance other than to examine the form of the censures[1] against the Bolognese.

The ambassador of the king of Castile has just now informed His Holiness that His Majesty died in Burgos of that fever that is called *mazuco*[2] in Italy. Since this death could cause either the return of King Ferdinand or other changes of importance and Your Lordships of the Signoria there might not get news of it so quickly, we thought it best to send you this posthaste, so that you let the Signoria know about it right away, since this death will reveal the judgment of the king of the Romans and many other matters.

His Holiness today hired Ramazzotti with 750 foot soldiers and Nanni Morattini[3] with 300 and arranged to have up to five or six thousand of them on his side; and the Feltri soldiers are a thousand; and the French will bring from 4 to five thousand with them.

These Bolognese have started some negotiations, and they are asking that two cardinals be sent to see and to reform them. But His Holiness is of the judgment in which you left him.

It is said we shall leave tomorrow after lunch, which seems difficult to us, but it will have to be the day after in any case. Let us know how you found things in Forlì and how you may find them over there. *Farewell.*

In Cesena, 6 October 1506.

❖ LETTER 130

Pier Francesco Tosinghi to Niccolò Machiavelli
Castrocaro, 10 October 1506

To the Very Dear, Notable Niccolò Machiavelli,
Secretary and Florentine Envoy to the Supreme Pontiff.
In Forlì.

Notable man, very dear friend, etc. Today I wrote you and I sent you via the
courier Mancini a sheaf of letters received from Florence. Since then, I have
your letter for the archpriest and, with it, one to the Ten, which I have sent,
and I believe it will be there by tomorrow evening. I have heard from the said
archpriest about the danger Our Reverend Monsignor underwent, which
gave me a fright.[1] However, by the grace of God, he was not harmed. I am
sending with this letter one of my servants, with a letter to the aforementioned monsignor; I pray you to direct him to His Most Reverend Lordship,
and please give him my regards and my offers of service. I have been to see
these men and convinced them in such a way that I think that Sunday, *unless I
am mistaken,* they will announce their debt. I would appreciate your bringing
the monsignor here, even though there is no way to honor him as His Most
Reverend Lordship would merit. *Once again,* I pray you to give him my regards. I need nothing else for now. Please keep us informed of the news you
have over there.

From Castrocaro, 10 October 1506.
Pier Francesco Tosinghi,
Commissioner, etc.

❖ LETTER 131

Pier Francesco Tosinghi to Niccolò Machiavelli
Castrocaro, 10 October 1506

To His Very Dear, Notable Niccolò Machiavelli,
Secretary and Florentine Envoy to the Supreme Pontiff.
In Forlì.

Notable man, etc. Niccolò, my friend, it is necessary for you to work it out
with the Most Reverend Cardinal of Volterra for me to obtain by means of
His Most Reverend Lordship a favor from His Holiness; but I would like it to
be gratis and without expense. It is that I have a son of mine, who will be 22
years old at the end of this month, who would like to receive a dispensation
so that he can hold ecclesiastical benefices, because Messer Niccolò, my
brother, would like to relinquish one of his to him, and I would not like to
have to spend anything. So I pray you speak of it with monsignor and assure
him that he will be doing this benefit for a man who would do anything for

him and for his house, and you know it. I would like in the same supplication for there to be also *a duobus incompetibilia.*[1] I have had this same supplication drawn up several times, but in order not to spend anything I never had it executed. I do not want to forget to tell you that when I came back from France,[2] I met His Holiness the Pope, who was a cardinal, in Asti, and he honored me and made me a great many proffers, etc. I believe when His Holiness hears that it is for me that such favor is to be done, he will accept more easily. I recommend this matter to you, and I pray you to do for me what I would do for you.

This municipality will announce its debt tomorrow, and I have also done some work with the municipality of Modigliana. If you have anything new that can be told, I pray you to let us know of it, and do not forget to come and see us again. Nothing else, except to offer my services to you. God keep you.

From Castrocaro, 10 October 1506.
Pier Francesco Tosinghi,
Commissioner, etc.

❖ LETTER 132
Biagio Buonaccorsi to Niccolò Machiavelli
Florence, 11 October 1506

To the Most Esteemed Niccolò Machiavelli,
Florentine Secretary, with the Supreme Pontiff.
In Forlì, or Wherever the Hell He Is.[1]

Honored *compare.* I would have a whole bunch of things to tell you, and because I do not know where to start, I shall keep it all for when I speak to you, even though, since you have not answered my latest letter yet—I believe it was of the 6th, at least that you received it—I could without any blame not bother to; but I do not want to do that, so I shall not be learning from your example, since you have done the same favor for me with a letter from Luigi della Stufa[2] that you did with those from Jacopo Ciachi[3] the other time you were in Rome, which was going to Gian Francesco Martelli.[4] If you were to say, "He is not here," I answer you that you ought to have sent it back here and not taken so little account of things as you do. I was given an admonition on account of it, but it will be the last one, because I shall never again accept letters that are given to me for me to send to you, the way you treat me. You do harm to yourself and to me as well, in addition to no small amount of unpleasantness. Let us not speak further of this, for if anyone should be blamed, it falls on me, since I know you, and yet I keep on sticking my neck out.

His Excellency the Gonfalonier told me last Saturday that I should ask Francesco Davanzati for money for you. I did not do it, because I was not able to, but I did do it this morning. This evening I shall get twenty ducats, and I shall send them to Pier Francesco Tosinghi in Castrocaro. If I can borrow that florin of yours that I spent, I shall also send you those; if not, I shall put it off until another time, judging that it will not be a hardship for you, since I am sending you the twenty ducats. If it should ever happen when I was sent abroad to keep the hangman company, at least do the same duty by me, if your nature allows it.

You added a little grease to the launchways in the matter of the foot soldiers by your letter of the 5th[5]; it was noted and acknowledged. You should know that Bernardo[6] had not been in office for six days when they made a decision in favor of the militia that will satisfy you. So the matter is proceeding with very good favor; but the objections every day are endless. However, it is making progress.

I believe Pepi[7] will arrive there soon if his allocation is voted, for they are giving him 3 ducats a day and, in addition, the 200 ducats, and they are lending him 300 for three years. You should come on back—because I desire it so much that I could not tell you—to get rid of this trouble and to stay in some corner where I can have fun.

You have not told me anything at all of the danger[8] that our monsignor of Volterra underwent. When I think about it, by God, I still tremble. That is what comes of following men at arms, and I would have that mule hanged in any case. Ruffini[9] wrote me about it, and it came at the right time, because there had been some news of it and the truth about the outcome was not known. Let him be careful, for God's sake, because we would be deprived of a very great hope.

This morning I stayed for two hours in San Giovanni with Antonio Giacomini. We talked about innumerable things, and last of all about you. He asked me to greet you and to send you his regards, and I do so. So go and retch. Your Marietta is in the country and is well, with all the family.

In Florence, 11 October 1506.
Yours, Bi.

❖ LETTER 133
Lattanzio Tedaldi[1] to Niccolò Machiavelli
Florence, 11 October 1506

To the Noble Man[2] Messer Niccolò Machiavelli,
Florentine Secretary, with the Pontiff.
Jesus Christ. 11 October 1506.

Enclosed with this letter will be one to Cardinal Soderini. I pray you[3] to give it on my behalf, and in time for him to read it well. Ask for an answer, and urge one, and send it to me, as I humbly pray you. Afterward, if it should be necessary (and it will be), you will inform him *what I heard from the Pontiff,* as I have spoken with you about it several times; *similarly, what I had said publicly about the comet in the council. Farewell, and give him my regards.*

Lattanzio Tedaldi, in Florence

❖ LETTER 134
Pier Francesco Tosinghi to Niccolò Machiavelli
Castrocaro, 12 October 1506

To My Very Dear Friend, the Notable Niccolò Machiavelli,
Secretary and Florentine Envoy to the Supreme Pontiff.
In Forlì.

Notable man, very dear friend. By your letter of yesterday I was informed and satisfied about the efforts and diligence you had exerted with the Most Reverend Cardinal of Volterra concerning what I wished to obtain.[1] I thank you for that, and I pray you, when you have the opportunity, to remind him of it and to give my regards to His Most Reverend Lordship. And you, when you have some news, share it with us as you promised me, for we have very scant news concerning matters of the court, and from Florence; ever since that summary, I have not had any news.

I am sending you a sheaf of your letters by the same man who brought them from Florence, with one for the Most Reverend Cardinal of Volterra: you will present it to him. I have no need of anything else, except again for you to give my regards to His Most Reverend Lordship. I am yours. Christ keep you.

From Castrocaro, 12 October 1506.
Pier Francesco Tosinghi,
Commissioner

❖ LETTER 135
Pier Francesco Tosinghi to Niccolò Machiavelli
Castrocaro, 14 October 1506

To My Very Dear Friend, the Notable Niccolò Machiavelli,
Secretary and Florentine Envoy to the Supreme Pontiff.
In Forlì.

Notable man, our very dear friend, etc. Niccolò, I have heard from the archpriest here that the cardinal of Volterra feels like coming to lunch with us tomorrow, which would be a very great favor for me. I pray you to encourage him to come. Although we shall not be able to honor him as His Most Reverend Lordship deserves, we shall not fail to offer him an excellent welcome. *Again,* I pray you to bring him here, and I shall set that beside the other obligations I have to you. Please answer concerning this by the present bearer.

Several letters are being sent to you in a sheaf to the above-mentioned cardinal and to His Lordship the Governor,[1] as you will see. You will present them and give notice thus of what news you have and when you judge the pope will leave.

Your letters to Florence were sent off right away, and, as you wrote, I wrote to Messer Francesco Gualterotti.[2] *Nothing else is necessary.* Christ with you.

From Castrocaro, 14 October 1506.
Pier Francesco Tosinghi,
Commissioner

❖ LETTER 136
Agostino Vespucci to Niccolò Machiavelli
Bologna, 12 November 1506

To the Notable Niccolò Machiavelli, Chancellor, etc.
In Florence.

My dear master Niccolò, etc. Yesterday evening Messer Francesco[1] requested me to write you *in his name,* and *first of all* he thanked you for the room he was given in Imola, where, beside the fact that it was very damp and there was danger of being crushed, as you know, it was told to him and he was able to feel for himself the day before he left there to come here to Bologna that where his head had been when he was lying in his cot he had above his head in the wall a yard of false earth in the courtyard behind the wall of the bedroom. It was seen by experience that that very wall of his room exuded a certain liquid, which he believes got into his body while he was sleeping and made him shit blood,[2] so that for 8 days continuously as of yesterday he lay in bed with the gout as well as a fever. The doctor who treated him asserted that, and therefore he wanted to make sure you were informed of everything, and you should want a room for him similar to the one you had found for yourself. That one, such as it was, cost him 40 lire for the 15 days that he lived there. Therefore, Niccolò, if you do not answer me, excusing yourself in the way I know you will know how, His Excellency is holding a bit of a grudge against you. Do as best you see fit: *certainly wit is not lacking.*

Baccio di Ruffino[3] went to Imola and, from what he told me, he would gladly go back there. I, who know from a man of Modigliana by the name of Ser Zoanni Antonio that he did his business well in those places and that he exceeds 20 ducats of extra pay, do not believe him. But you, if you need him, write me and let me know of his desire, and you or Biagio or Ser Luca[4] will not have to shit blood.[5] I do not know what else to say in this letter, except that I shall write you in another letter of this great pontifical entrance[6] into Bologna. I am yours; give my regards to Messer Marcello and to Biagio, to Ser Luca, to the director, and to those under him. *Farewell.*

In Bologna, 12 November 1506.

Agostino, etc.

❖ LETTER 137

Giovanni da Empoli[1] to Niccolò Machiavelli
Bologna, 16 November 1506

To the Most Honored, Distinguished Man,
Messer Niccolò Machiavelli, Florentine Secretary, etc.

Distinguished, most honored man, etc. I thank you for giving me these tasks every day, of giving letters into the hands of people, etc., as I did with this one: but anything to be of use to you.

Messer Raimondo[2] thinks that you are delaying too long in carrying out his godfathership; if, however, you are going to delay much longer, he would like to know whom he has to complain about. I pray you not to wrong him. We shall be able to do without your pages and your saliva, and all in all we do not need such learned people. Therefore you do not want to go back there very often. The power of attorney will come as we have decided, but we are still up in the air and shall have to stay here now for a while. I send you my regards.

In Bologna, 16 November 1506.

Yours, Gio. da Emp.,

Valet of the Cardinal of Volterra

❖ LETTER 138

Carlo Albizzi[1] to Niccolò Machiavelli
Bologna, 25 November 1506

To His Magnificence, Most Honored Messer Niccolò Machiavelli,
Most Worthy Chancellor of the Florentine Republic.
In Florence.

Your Magnificence and most honored man, greetings. In the past few days I have received a most welcome letter from Your Excellency, by which I learn that Our Reverend Archdeacon has confided in you about that affair he had also spoken of with Our Most Reverend Monsignor of Volterra, who had promised him to help him. I understand what Your Excellency informs me about my speaking to my Most Reverend Monsignor of Pavia,[2] and I shall do so. If you should hear anything at all from over there, I pray you to be so kind as to give notice of it, because it will get to me more quickly than to anyone else, and I shall always be very obliged to you for this. If it should happen that you give early notice about providing your son with some benefice, I shall make such effort that you will consider yourself satisfied by me.

Also, when your lady gets close to giving birth, you will be doing me an unusual favor if you let me know about it, so that, if I should not be there, I can arrange for someone in my place.[3] I pray you to do this, because, if you do not so write me, I should consider myself insulted by you. Nothing else. *To Your Excellency, my wishes that he be well.*

In Bologna, 25 November 1506.
Your Excellency's Servant, Carlo Albizzi

❖ LETTER 139
Cardinal Francesco Soderini to Niccolò Machiavelli
Bologna, 15 December 1506

To the Notable Messer Niccolò Machiavelli,
Florentine Secretary and Our Very Dear Compare.
Francesco Soderini, Priest of Santa Susanna and Cardinal of Volterra.

Notable man and very dear compare. In your letter of the 10th, you recommended the wagoner to us, and we have done and shall do everything possible for him. Their affairs would already have been well dispatched if they had not become entangled in Rome and fallen into the hands of scoundrels and enemies of that city.

It really seems to us that this militia is a *God-given thing,* because it grows every day, notwithstanding malice, etc. We have gotten remarkable satisfaction from the new magistracy,[1] and we pray God that the election will be such that a solid foundation will result from it, because we do not see that that city has done anything for a long time so honorable and certain as this, if it is used properly. The good people must put all their efforts to this and not let themselves be led by those who, for other purposes, do not love the welfare of that city as much as is fitting in this new freedom of hers, a divine and not human gift, *unless it is perverted by malice or ignorance.* And you who have played so great a role in it, do not fail in anything, *unless you want to make God and men angry.*

Farewell.
In Bologna, 15 December 1506.

❖ LETTER 140

Agostino Vespucci to Niccolò Machiavelli

Bologna, 28 December 1506

To the Honored, Notable Niccolò Machiavelli, Florentine Secretary.
In Florence.

My honored friend Niccolò. So that you may be able to satisfy that relative of yours who is a creditor of Giovan Marco,[1] a jeweler from what I have gathered about him, I am writing this for you. On Christmas eve, our ambassador got a letter from the said Gian Marco dated the 18th from Rimini, and he told him of certain of his private matters, in particular of a house that he rented to us. Whereas he had first promised that he would not have to be paid rent, etc., *he reconsidered the matter afterward,* and since the ambassador is not getting much satisfaction, he is *again* seeking another lodging, even though it is difficult to find any there.

I hear that Gian Marco has nothing in the way of real estate, and here in Bologna he had a house, and since it has already been entangled, he cannot get it back. He wanted to collect 2 thousand Bolognese lire[2] he said he was supposed to have from the account of the Bentivoglios, but nothing came of it. Not only did he not collect them, but he cannot stay in Bologna, for reasons that I do not yet understand well, although I have investigated it thoroughly. These two big cubs of his are going easy, like dumb birds; and Gian Marco's wife is staying in a convent, because she does not want to stay in a hovel they have rented. They live off some jewels or other that a Jew got from Gian Marco, which is not much. In sum, if we did not begin to bring suit and try to get into that house that is to be determined whether it is his or not, there is not, as far as I have heard, much profit to be gained here.

I hear, by information from a fond common friend of yours and mine, that the Nine[3] are to have one or more[4] coadjutors in addition to the chancellor. I pray you to give me a recommendation in such a case, and if you see that it suits my needs more securely than where I am, work it out so and in such a way that I may be one of those coadjutors, *since I hold it to be for certain that you will be the chancellor of those Nine unless you hold on to that position[5] which you now enjoy, God forbid.*

Abbot Basilio,[6] who has *recently* been made majordomo of our cardinal of Volterra, sends his regards to you and *congratulates you on the new militia,* etc. He says that I should offer you *in his name* a bed board[7] but that the deed cannot be brought to you there. He says this because of Pepi's telling him he wants to ask for leave and thinks he is going to get it, and you are to come here.

Here there is nothing new. As for the emperor, although the Venetians gabble about him, nevertheless he does not go out of the house of the German cardinal,[8] except that he is expected either to stay on the other side of the mountains or to come on over completely to the pope. Similarly, there is nothing new from Naples, since there is nobody from His Catholic Majesty here, for which His Beatitude is cursing God. From France there is nothing but sugar and honey; and His Christian Majesty is expected here on the calends of May.

This pope has not gained much from having given internment to a certain number of Bolognese, since, in addition to being citizens, they are henchmen and emissaries of Messer Giovanni.[9]

I shall not say anything else in this letter, except that I send you my *heartfelt* regards. Give my regards to Messer Marcello and to Biagio, and some greetings to Nobili, to Ser Luca,[10] and to everyone.

In Bologna, 28 December 1506.
Yours, Agostino
Chancellor

I am not writing to Biagio, since I wrote him yesterday. I do expect a couple of lines from you in reply to this letter, and I pray you to do so or have Biagio answer me *in case* you cannot do it yourself.

L E T T E R S

1507-1508

As he had begun the year 1506 conscripting soldiers for his citizen militia in Florence's outlying districts, Machiavelli was similarly engaged early in 1507. This time, however, his activities from the middle of March to the middle of April bore the cachet of his position as secretary of the Nine.

Machiavelli's nonmilitary duties were again diplomatic. France's entry into Genoa in April, without concomitant willingness to aid Florence in its campaign against Pisa, helped exacerbate relations between Louis XII and the Holy Roman Emperor, Maximilian I. Many in Italy feared that Maximilian would attempt to unite the empire and papacy and seek to be elected and crowned in Rome. This policy would have necessitated his entering Italy and driving Louis out of Lombardy, so Maximilian convened a diet in Constance late in April to gain the consent of the German princes to supply him with troops and money. As Guicciardini puts it,

> when [Florence] learned that the king of France deemed these movements significant and ordered major preparations be made and that the Pope and the Venetians had emissaries in Germany, many Florentines concluded that this was a matter of great moment and hence proposed that it would be good to send someone too. Through the intervention of [Piero Soderini], who wanted someone whom he could trust, Machiavelli was chosen. But just as he was preparing to depart, many well-thought-of men began clamoring that other people should be sent because there were many decent young men well-suited for going to Germany, and it would be good that they might become experienced. (*Storie Fiorentine,* p. 297; Domandi, p. 271)

The Ten selected Alamanno Salviati and Piero Guicciardini. Soderini believed they would sabotage Florence's traditional alliance with France. Although he had to give up his choice of Machiavelli, he agreed that Francesco di Piero Vettori should be sent. Vettori left Florence at the end of June. To counter the threat that they believed the Diet of Constance represented, Louis XII and Ferdinand the Catholic met in late June at Savona, a town about thirty miles west of Genoa, to reaffirm their friendship and to agree, after receiving a healthy payment in Florentine ducats, that Pisa should be returned to Florentine control.

Machiavelli's disappointment at being denied permission to go to the court of Maximilian was short-lived because he was soon sent on two other diplomatic missions. In early August, news spread throughout Italy that the Diet of Constance had agreed to Maximilian's plans. Florence sent Machiavelli to discuss the ramifications with Bernardino Carvajal, the cardinal of Santa Croce, who was on his way to Maximilian's court as the pope's legate. The two conferred in Siena during the second week of August. By the middle of December, Machiavelli was sent on a much more important assignment: he was finally allowed to join Francesco Vettori at the German court with an offer of 50,000 ducats if Maximilian guaranteed the safety of Florence and her territory. Acrimonious debate preceded this commission; a contemporary even referred to Machiavelli at this time as Soderini's *mannerino*, his "lackey" or "hatchetman" (Ridolfi, *Life*, p. 99; *Vita 7*, p. 158). Soderini thought it imperative to have someone in Germany "in whom he might have confidence and in whom he could believe, and probably attend to his own as well as to the town's interests. Suspecting that letters might be misunderstood, he proposed to the Ten that it would be better to send someone who might report in person. And, since there was no opposition, Soderini succeeded in having Machiavelli sent to Germany" (Guicciardini, *Storie Fiorentine*, p. 302; Domandi, p. 275). Machiavelli left Florence on 17 December.

Machiavelli was with Vettori at Maximilian's court until the middle of June 1508. The mission initiated their friendship, although Vettori always seems to have had the edge on Machiavelli in political terms. Their relationship began under conditions of hardship. Because the letter is written to the Signoria in code, we do not know whether it was Machiavelli or Vettori who wrote about "being here on a lost island," yet it is clear that they both felt isolated and forlorn during their long stay (*Leg.*, II, p. 1108). From Vettori's point of view, Machiavelli's continued presence at the German court was "necessary" (*Leg.*, II, p. 1101) both because he was acting as Vettori's secretary and cowriter of the dispatches sent to Florence and because, with his inveterate inquisitiveness, Machiavelli was a valuable agent for picking up useful information. What he gleaned led him to regard the emperor as a threat to Florentine interests. Machiavelli's remarks generally run counter to Soderini's desire to maintain Florence's traditionally strong ties with France. The day after a return to Florence, precipitated by an attack of gallstones, Machiavelli wrote the *Rapporto delle cose della Magna fatto questo dì 17 Giugno 1508* (Report on affairs in Germany written this day 17

June 1508) that became in 1512 the *Ritratto delle cose della Magna* (Portrayal of German affairs), a more polished version of the *Rapporto*.

Toward the end of Machiavelli's foreign service, the war with Pisa was pursued with new vigor on the part of the citizen militia, now under the leadership of Niccolò Capponi. In August, Machiavelli was dispatched as a commissioner to the camp at Pisa. He was temporarily alone there, the only one "to represent the public good" (Guicciardini, *Storia d'Italia*, p. 242; *Storie Fiorentine*, p. 333; Domandi, p. 304). Guicciardini notes that Machiavelli "was sent to Piombino to learn what [some representatives from Pisa] had to say" about a possible Pisan capitulation (*Storia d'Italia*, p. 243). Florence, meanwhile, had to contend with Louis XII, who despite his agreement with Ferdinand the Catholic at Savona saw the military build-up around Pisa as a potential threat. Negotiations between France and Florence dragged on until 1509, but with an about-face characteristic of the times, Maximilian and Louis XII reached an accord in late December: the League of Cambrai. This accord was also agreed to by Ferdinand the Catholic, the leaders of several important Italian towns, and, finally, in 1509, Julius II. According to the agreement, Venice was the object to be contained, and each signatory would get a piece of Italy in return for stripping Venice of her power on the mainland.

❖ LETTER 141
Giovanni Ridolfi[1] to Niccolò Machiavelli
Florence, 20 April 1507

To the Notable Niccolò Machiavelli, Florentine Secretary, as a Brother.

Notable man, etc. The bearer of this letter will be Antonio di Michele di Giusto from Castellina di Chianti, a friend of mine, whom it seems you have enrolled and put on your list together with his son, Michele. Since Antonio, because of his age, is not suited to armed service, and Michele, because he is a cobbler and the one who runs the shop, cannot leave it without very great inconvenience and harm, I therefore pray you to be so kind for my sake as to remove both of them from your list and leave them behind, so that they can take care of their business; you will be doing me an extraordinary service thereby. I offer myself most readily to do whatever you please. God keep you.

In Florence, 20 April 1507
Giovanni Ridolfi

❖ LETTER 142
Lorenzo Berardi[1] to Niccolò Machiavelli
Cigliano, 14 June 1507

To Messer Niccolò di Messer Bernardo Machiavelli.
In Florence.

My very dear Niccolò. From Ispratichino and others you have heard that Gaza[2] has packed up his belongings,[3] for which we should raise our hands to heaven, since the decision to leave had come from him. When we were with the priest in Sant'Andrea this evening, two or three workmen happened into our hands, and we decided to give it to the bearer of this letter: they are three brothers and they have a sister; two of them are 20 years old, and the other is there to guard the cattle; and they are good people and very well off, so that they will not give you any problem with their begging anything from you, and they will do us honor. Now the priest, hearing that a certain Vittorio, who is a tenant in San Casciano, had come over there to you, we do not feel he is what you need, because he is more likely to look after trade than his work, and it was decided I should write to you, so that you would not let yourself be fooled by anyone, and he said that he would write to you and that he would be there tomorrow morning. I shall come and see you, and perhaps the priest will come, too, and we shall leave this matter so that you hear a bit from the bearer what you need as far as what has to be done, and then we shall make up our minds.

The priest says for you not to worry about anything, because he has already had half a field marked off, and the rest he has more or less let, and everything will be fine, so there is no need at all for you to worry about this, because he is taking loving care of your affairs. I shall not say anything else. I shall be there tomorrow morning, and we shall see each other face-to-face. Christ keep you from harm.

14 June 1507.
Yours, Lorenzo Berardi, in Cigliano

❖ LETTER 143
Bartolomeo da Filicaia to Niccolò Machiavelli
Pescia, 15 June 1507

To the Notable Niccolò Machiavelli, Secretary of the Signoria.
In the name of God, 15 June 1507.

My very dear, etc. Yesterday evening at seven[1] I received your letter, in which you wish to learn whether Battista di Maestro Iacopo from Bologna, who is staying in Buggiano,[2] has arrived here, and also whether a young man of Casa, your worker and debtor for 200 lire, came with him. For your information:

we sent someone to do this reasonable favor, and to be brief, I have your said worker (who has a wife and two children in Buggiano) here in prison and shall follow your orders about this. So let me know. He says that he is a debtor but that he left as much as can be paid and that he departed because he could not pay the chamberlain and did not want to be stuck in prison. I have nothing else to say. I am yours. Christ keep you.

In Pescia, Bartolomeo da Filicaia,
Vicar and Commissioner

The Bolognese man is not in town, and according to a brother of his who has shown up here, he says he is in Bologna. For your information.

✣ LETTER 144
Filippo Casavecchia to Niccolò Machiavelli
Fivizzano, 30 July 1507

To the Notable Messer Niccolò Machiavelli, Most Worthy Secretary
with Their Lordships of the Military Nine of the Florentine Republic.

"If I grieved, now I grieve again,"[1] when I thought that there ought to be, in men of your quality, the crutches and the support of my life, and to resolve my doubts; and now I should hear you come out with things of such a sort that they seem to me like asking which came first, the system of the heavens or astrology, or which is denser, water or the terrestrial globe, or which are more perfect, triangulated figures or rounded circles. Now, do you not know that there have been very, very few friendships[2] that in the passage of time do not become their opposite? That, as man in his youth, or to put it better, his childhood, takes pleasure in gradually changing his clothes and in different colors, in the self-same way friendships change? And, to come now to more mature age, that some through the fault of pressure, others oppressed by a squalid and mean poverty—so also from social emulation and various forms of anger—all these things make men change from friends to great enemies with the passage of time? Now do you not know that the empire and grandeur of Rome was undone countless times on account of friendships? Who were greater friends than Collatinus and the son of Sextus Tarquinius?[3] Thanks to which came the downfall of the kings and of that family completely. Then if we come down to the time of Marius and Sulla,[4] whose alliance was never equaled, yet finally there resulted from it the destruction of that peaceful and popular government of that city. Are you not aware of the brotherhood and closeness of Julius Caesar and the great Pompey[5]? Is the same not true as well of the triumvirate, that is to say, Antony and Octavius and Lepidus,[6] who brought about the ruin not only of their own country but also of the entire circle of the earth? Were it not also for the lateness of the hour, I should fill up a ream of pages with Hebrew and Greek and Latin examples. But what need is there of seeking out ancient things, when in our modern times and with our own eyes we have, for similar causes, many and many a time seen our country in the greatest ruin and hardship? Where was there greater intimacy and friendship than between Dietisalvi and Piero di Cosimo,[7] and then also between Giuliano and Francesco de' Pazzi[8]? And you see what an evil end came of it. But right away I seem to hear one of you reading this letter sneering and saying:"Oh, these things did not come about while the friendship endured, but once they had become enemies." And I answer that all the effects are generated by their causes, and therefore it can justifiably be said that almost for the greater part all the downfalls of cities are caused and generated by close and daily friendships, which with time and particularly in great men generate such and similar effects, for the reasons cited above. Therefore, my very dear friends, I exhort and urge and even pray you to behave moderately and civilly among yourselves, first because I deem the friendships will last longer, and also in order to avoid all the suspicions and jealousies that are wont to arise in such a city.

But in order for this letter of mine not to become a cock and bull story,[9] I shall bring my sermon to an end, reminding you only of one thing: that is, never mind about the German triumph, and those who take the credit for having prevented it[10] have not and will not thereby triumph over Asia; you had nothing to regret in these matters except what you will not want. Nothing else.

From Fivizzano, 30 July 1507.

I pray you to be so kind as to give my regards to His Excellency the Gonfalonier when you run into him. But this word would have to be sent by a mortar that could reach that far and could just make it. But I am clear on one thing: that you will get yourself completely excluded one day; enough said. You inform me that you are all waiting on pins and needles for Gigi Manelli[11] to come: if you have to soil him, soil him in Masino del Tovaglia's hole. God be with you all, try to be happy, and give my regards to Paolo, to Giovan Battista, to Luigi, to Messer Francesco, to Tommaso del Bene, and enough said.

Yours, Filippo Casavecchia,
Commissioner

❖ Letter 145
Alessandro Nasi to Niccolò Machiavelli
Cascina, 30 July 1507

To the Notable Niccolò Machiavelli, Florentine Secretary, My Excellent Friend.
In Florence.

My good, and not unfortunate,[1] Machiavelli, now that you[2] are completely over it; you spoke in your letter of the 23rd in such a way that I am enlightened about many things, to which I do not want to reply, because there is not enough time and also the person writing has not brought along much stationery. I am glad that you have shat out the imperial commission, since you are entirely purged. I believe it is a very good thing, particularly for you, to be in Florence rather than in Germany,[3] as we shall discuss when we are together again.

Let things tighten up, and it will happen to many people as it does to children who are allowed for a time by their fathers and their mothers to fool around with things that make them very happy, and then that is the very means by which to take them away from them. Therefore those who are of good spirit, attentive to both God and the common good, we can reasonably judge, are likely to make better decisions in all occasions, whether they be rich or poor, of social standing[4] or not, as you like.

Our Neapolitan friend often interprets things so well in reverse that if he commented badly on this one it was not surprising. I am very glad, in order for you to know what men are like, that he should have interpreted it in that way and you should have found out about it. After it has rained and cooled off, I shall expect you in any case, that is to say, Alessandro, Biagio, and you. If by some chance you should write in the meantime, however, it would not be a mortal sin. If the battalion is not in any different shape than what you tell me, I can form a good and true judgment. Nothing else. My regards to you and to Zampa.

From Cascina, 30 July 1507.
Alessandro Nasi, General Commissioner

❖ LETTER 146
Miguel de Corella[1] to Niccolò Machiavelli
Firenzuola, 3 August 1507

To His Magnificence Messer Niccolò Machiavelli, Secretary of the Nine
[. . .] with the Militia of the Florentine Republic, with My Deepest Respects.
In Florence.

Your Excellency. Since the constable of Firenzuola[2] is coming over your way, I shall not write at great length. I only have to tell Your Excellency that I have seen all the battalions except those of Val d'Elsa. From what I have seen, there is nothing that has pleased me more than this one, and with a different organization than the others, so I swear to Your Excellency that men who have been in service for twenty years could not have better satisfied me, without disorder and with admirable discipline—as I would not have believed—since the troops are in the shape Your Excellency knows. Therefore, since the said constable is a very good friend of yours, it is not necessary for me to recommend him to you. Only, if there is anything that needs to be done, I pray you be willing to make use of him, because he is going to do honor to Your Excellency. I beg you to be so kind as to give my regards to the Most Illustrious

Gonfalonier and to Their Lordships of the Nine, who can get information about my activities from the directors of the various places. *Nothing else.*

From Firenzuola, 3 August 1507.
By the hand of Your Excellency's more than devoted
Don Miguel de Corella

❖ LETTER 147
Michele Corella[1] to Niccolò Machiavelli
Firenzuola, 15 September 1507

To My Honored Magnificence Messer Niccolò Machiavelli,
Secretary of Their Excellencies the Nine.
In Florence.

My dear Excellency Messer Niccolò. I have received a letter dated the 10th of September, which has made me the most worried man in the world, to think that it is said that I have become partisan. It is quite true that I am partisan to those who serve Your Most Exalted Lordship, and who are obedient.

As for the part[2] where Your Lordship writes me that he wishes to understand how I came to seize one of Del Bello's men, he will be happy to learn how the matter came about; the reason is this, that while I was seated in the palace of the gate of the captain of Castrocaro, a poor woman comes to me and says: "Sir, I should like to say a few words to you for God's sake." So I went off to one side with her to hear her out. When I was alone with her, she knelt down and began to weep, crying: "Mercy, justice, justice." I asked: "What is the matter, good woman? Get up, get up." She said: "Sir, there is a stranger, a workman who has taken one of my daughters from me by force, a virgin, and had his will with her; and now he is trying to carry another one off on me." I said to her: "Good woman, is that man in our town?" She said: "Yes sir. Give me two or three soldiers, and I shall point out who he is." So I gave her three soldiers, and this woman sent one of her relatives with those soldiers to point him out to us. Two of the soldiers took off along one street, after they were well informed what clothes the man was wearing, and the other went with the boy along another street. The one who went with the boy ran into this workman, and he had been instructed by me to take him and bring him to the palace, before the captain and me, who were waiting for him at the palace.

So he pushed him along with his pike to bring him here, and he began to resist, so that when they were near a house of one of those Del Bellos, or of Pier Francesco, for I have little to do with those houses, he went inside, with the soldier after him, both of them shouting. Hearing the noise, I got up from my seat and ran over there. I went into the house, and I found Achille del Bello there with a short spear in his hand, hanging on to that soldier of mine, saying that he would not take him away; he should go about his business, or else he would do and say this and that. While I stood there, the soldier said to me: "Sir, the workman is in this room." Then I said: "Achille, give him to me, or else I shall make a lot of trouble today." He told me I could go ahead, that he was not going to give him to me, and he did not want him to be removed from there. I then ordered him, insofar as he held the favor of Our Most Exalted Lordships[3] dear, to go to the palace. He told me that he did not want to go. So I grabbed him by the chest to lead him off. At that point the brother and more than forty armed men from Acugiano arrived. Seeing that, I went out then and got a buckler and had my company take arms, and went back to go inside, determined either to get my hands on that man or to die, so the captain of Castrocaro himself came there. And there was such a furor there, I never saw him, and he went back out and left. Then he came back for me, and they promised me they would bring that workman to the palace, and they would come along, too. So I went out of the house and went back to the palace together with the captain. A little while later they brought the culprit, and they also presented themselves before His Honor the captain and me.

When they were there, I said to the captain: "Here is the culprit," and to the others: "Now that I am before Your Lordship, I do not want to be bothered with it any more. It is enough that I have done what any good servant of the exalted Signoria should do." The captain and one Ser Bacio and one Ser Giovanni, who are friends of mine—and the others also are friends of mine, though at that moment I was more concerned about my shirt than my coat[4]—begged me that we make peace with one another and that I should not write about this matter to Florence or have it written about. And I promised to do so, saying I was not in the habit of writing or having others write about trifles of this sort. So they invited His Honor the captain and me to have lunch with them one morning, and we all had lunch together.

If it should seem to you that I have sinned by the Holy Spirit in this part, I pray Your Lordship to tell those people who have related this matter to you, along with Your Lordship, to give me whatever penitence Their Lordships see fit. If it seems to them that I have sinned by the Holy Spirit, as I have said above, that I ought to have done something else than what I did—for they are all very great servants of Marzocco,[5] in words, and with great flourishes of their hat, from Castrocaro and Modigliana and Marradi[6]—they would see where loyalty lies. Some day I shall be with Your Lordship, and I shall tell you things and give you living proof of them that will frighten you, that I am not in the habit of writing. For I have served a few kings and two pontiffs in this world, as Your Lordship knows, and I never wrote them without their deigning to answer me, and especially in matters that were in the service of Their Holinesses and Their Lordships. And for all the times I have written to the exalted Signoria and to the gonfalonier, I have never had a reply, for the entire year and a half I have been with Their Lordships. But I believe that such is the custom of the country, so I am not surprised. I had promised not to write about this matter, but I was obliged to give justification for it to Your Lordship, since I know you love me and are fond of me. I would not have written of it to anyone in the world for anything. The past captain of Castrocaro is better informed than I am, and he will be able to tell everything to Your Lordship. I believe they have not written about this matter to Florence, because I would open the pouch then if ever I believed they had written anything.

As for the part where you say that I have become partial toward the arch-priest, I do not want any other witness than the captain of Castrocaro that right from the first day I told him that it would be better for both the arch-priest and a few others to be removed from Romagna. I sent a list of them to the exalted Signoria by my chancellor Ser Apardo; and all the directors will agree with me that they should be removed from Romagna for a few years. There is one of them over there that should not be sent, and that is the arch-priest. Just see if I was being partial, you who say I go around with his follow-ers. Whoever said that to Your Lordship is lying falsely in his teeth, for I had no dealings with anyone except for an old man called Giorgio della Golfaia, so that he should pay for half of his things and remain in peace. And he lent me a bed so I could sleep in it.

As for the part about Matteo Facenda, I inform Your Lordship that he has told you the biggest lie in the world. Since I have been in Castrocaro, he has never set foot in the territory of the Florentines. They have pestered us, both the captain of Castrocaro and me, so we would trust him enough to come and talk with the two of us and tell us his side of things. We would never do so or hear it mentioned; and he was staying in Bagnacavallo[7] then. The cap-tain of Castrocaro will bear good witness to this. So that you may recognize the wickedness of those who want to stain the honor of a gentleman, even though I do not care at all about things like this, I shall stand and be judged before God, and not so much by the men of this world, for the proverb says: "Piss clear and vex a doctor." For I still have the instructions that Your Lord-ship gave me already a year and a half ago, and I have them in my heart and inside my head: that is, you told me that I should never ever eat in the house of the head of a party and I should never ever become friendly with banished men who had a ban on their heads and who were in revolt against the Signo-ria. It is true, of course, that during this time I have talked to two or three of them that I trusted, only when they came to talk to me, because they had promised me to let me get my hands on others. Of the three, one of them turned out well.

Moreover, the night I arrived at the fortress coming from Firenzuola, they learned about it right away in Castrocaro. Thereupon this Francesco del Bello went there and informed or had word sent to Matteo Facenda, who was stay-ing in the parish church of the archpriest, that I was in the town and that he should get going. Thereupon that man got on his horse and rode away. Where-upon the devil helped him, for at that time he ran into several horsemen of Bartolomeo Moratini, his enemy, who is staying in Forlì; and they gave chase to him as far as Bagnacavallo, and he escaped by a horse's hoof.[8] Matteo Facenda would not get it out of his head that this man had done it on pur-pose, and so the said Matteo Facenda is seeking to cause trouble for Francesco del Bello, believing he spied for Bartolomeo Moratini. How did you learn about all these things, Don Michele? I shall tell you. A poor man, a relative of Matteo Facenda, talking with me, told me this, about Matteo Facenda's having this grudge against that man. So I went off and told this business to the captain of Castrocaro, and he told me point by point that it was true, that he had also learned about it. So we decided that the said Francesco del Bello should be watched. These are the parts I take; let Your Lordship use your judgment whether you think they are parties.

As for the part where Your Lordship notifies me about a vineyard belonging to Antonio Corsini, I answer you that it is indeed true that one of my crossbowmen came to Ferragamo di Castrocaro, just he and his son, and asked him if he would let him go with him to harvest a vineyard, which belonged to Antonio Giacomini, because some bandits would not let them harvest it. So this crossbowman, who had been a servant of Antonio Giacomini, went with the said son of Ferragamo (how do you know this, Don Michele?[9]). They went off at the closing of the gates, and in the morning, as daylight came, a comrade of the said crossbowman came and said to me: "So and so has run away, he went off last night and he has not come back here." So I got out of bed in a rage, and a lot of people came with me, and I ran into Ferragamo. He said to me: "Why are you going like this, in a rage, Sir?" I said: "Every day some scoundrel plays a trick on me. One of my crossbowmen has run away. By God, if one of them should fall into my hands, I shall plunge this sword into his heart, so that it will be a lesson to the others." Ferragamo said to me: "Do not be disheartened, he went to harvest a vineyard of Antonio Giacomini's with my son, because some bandits did not want it to be harvested." Then I said: "What, going out of town at night without my permission? So be it, by God." When he got back, everyone knows the punishment that he got for this and of the other wicked things that he has done. How do you say I should try to resolve this matter? I am innocent of it. Ferragamo comes to Florence every day—have him seized and give satisfaction to Messer Antonio Corsini. Or let a letter come to me from the Signoria, and you will see whether I shall make him pay twice as much as the wine he took: because I am innocent in this matter, and I do not believe the exalted Signoria has a condottiere who is fonder of Messer Antonio Corsini than I am. If I had known it then, I would have dismissed him from my sight; but Ferragamo told me that he was from Antonio Giacomini. Have the slightest sign sent me from the Signoria, and you will see whether I give him satisfaction. I do not want to send the letter to anyone in the world until I am in Castrocaro, and I shall be there soon. I shall send for Don Nicola, and he will be with me; and I shall be with the captain of Castrocaro. We shall see this thing settled in such a way that it comes to a good end. But when Ferragamo comes to Florence, and he comes often, he should be seized and very well punished, so that he might serve as an example to the others that they should not go around murdering in this way. Whatever I write to Your Lordship, I bear witness before God and the men of the world that I am a gentleman and was born a gentleman, and I do not do anything that is not proper and clear. When Your Lordship learns anything about these matters, I pray Your Lordship to be so good as to write me and answer my letters that I send to Your Lordship, and I would write him about everything as long as I believed that Your Lordship would answer me.

Dated in Firenzuola, 15 September.
Your Lordship's more than servant,
Miguel de Orella,[10]
by his own hand.

Nothing else, except may Christ keep Your Lordship in that condition you yourself wish and that I should wish for my own life.

❖ LETTER 148
Filippo Casavecchia to Niccolò Machiavelli
Fivizzano, 22 September 1507

To the Notable Messer Niccolò Machiavelli, Most Worthy Secretary
of the Nine of the Militia of the Florentine Republic, as to an Honored Brother.

My very dear Niccolò. I have already answered[1] a little epistle of yours, which in truth seemed more admirable than comforting, because I have been left more downcast than ever by it. I understand especially that man is not happy in any condition, either temporal or spiritual.[2] So you should not have been nor should you now be surprised if at times my peevish words make their way to your ears, since I find neither repose nor tranquillity in this indecent and pestilential abyss. If I have well noted in particular what remedies are available for this, it seems to me that the only one is to let oneself be borne by wicked Fortune, which I do not completely approve of, because, since she takes delight in new things, I should not like it a bit for her to lead me, by my bad luck, into the whorish and public place of that city. But if I knew which way to turn with my prayers, I would beseech that all the ills of this world should sooner come to me than the most pestilential, most pitiless, and putrid disease of melancholic humor, which I hear disturbs some of our most beloved friends, may nature rid them of it. Nothing else.

From Fivizzano, 22 September 1507.

❖ LETTER 149

Alessandro Nasi to Niccolò Machiavelli

Cascina, 12 November 1507

To the Distinguished Man Niccolò Machiavelli,
Most Worthy Florentine Secretary, and His Compare.
In Florence.

Compare. Yesterday a letter from you was presented to me by Matteo da Caprigliola. I have promised him that he should remain alert, and when money is provided for infantry, we shall have him put in one of these companies. If he had come 4 days earlier, he would have entered the guard of Vico under Morello da Campo Giallo. I shall be happy to help him out, not so much for your sake as for the one who asked you for it, etc.

If you come along with Granico to stay here ten days, you will be doing the right thing, and then you will become the Redhead[1]: adapting to times and places is the nature of wise men, so it will not be unsuitable on your return to go back to the nature of Guicciardini.[2]

The emperor's trick is probably real,[3] but in the opposite way from what you mean. Let him come anyway, since in any case I hope for good from evil, and *it is necessary that scandals come, woe however to those men,*[4] etc.

You will tell His Excellency the Gonfalonier that fellow Rosaro from Rome died 4 days ago in Lucca, and he was a criminal and a great highwayman; therefore one could expect rather good than evil from relations with him. The friar also died, and it did not come at the right time. If it was not poison, it was fear. May his relations with Alfonso help His Excellency, because he is more likely to gain profit from him in this way that I hear talked about than from having him dead or, even if he should manage to stay alive, from keeping him in despair. Our *compare* has pursued me a great deal about this Count Lodovico, who must be a devil. I have written the truth for once; if it displeased anyone, too bad; for once I am in such a mood as to go along with reality for the benefit of the public, without any private respects, and I am not about to fall in love or to get married with any of those chiefs, or to raise up idols. So let whoever wants to talk, talk, and let them go and retch. Answer this letter, in any case.

In Cascina, 12 November 1507.
Alessandro Nasi, General Commissioner

Tell *compare* Biagio that from haste yesterday morning I forgot to tell him that on my departure I gave his letter and the orders of the Ten into the right hands, and it will be so: tomorrow, if not today, I shall leave. *Farewell again.*

❖ LETTER 150
Roberto Acciaiuoli to Niccolò Machiavelli
Rome, 4 December 1507

To His Very Dear Honored Secretary of the Eminent Signoria,
Niccolò Machiavelli.
In Florence.

Honored secretary. From your letter I have learned a part of your desire,[1] but in order for me to be able to explore something that will both hold up under pressure and be permanent, I have to have more specific notice of your intention and the plans of the office, because you know that *this title of* bargello[2] *is hated by active men, and they are all disgusted.* Because it seems to me that a difference should be made between a *bargello* and a discipliner for this job, and therefore you will give me a note as to what rank he is to hold, what authority, what term, what stipend, and what contract. *In the meanwhile* I shall go on searching for a man suitable for our purposes, and I shall keep you informed of everything. I am doing a bit of service for the Sophi[3] because I am beginning to feel a little bit more kindly toward him, because these rascally priests have brought me to the point where I would willingly arrange with him for my expenditures; so let him come when he wants, and I shall not refuse to go to him as ambassador. I know that you would come along with me no less willingly, *in the way that* Rinaldo said[4]: "Do you believe that I would go / Without taking my Dodone with me?" *Farewell, and when you have leisure and you write, I recommend our Zeffi[5] to you, if you can be of service to him, and greet Biagio and give Marcello my regards.*

In Rome, 4 December 1507.
Roberto Acciaiuoli, Ambassador

❖ LETTER 151
Niccolò Machiavelli to Piero Soderini
Bolzano[1], 17 February 1508

*To the Most Illustrious Messer Piero Soderini,
Gonfalonier of Justice for the People of Florence, Sole Leader.*

Most Illustrious leader. Your Lordship will see everything that is written about matters here, which is, after all, as much as can be said if one wants to put these matters before your eyes; whatever else might be said would need to enter into making a judgment, which is for someone who is down there rather than someone who is here to do. I shall say only this: many things make me believe and many things do not, so that I am completely up in the air; still, I lean more to the pro than to the con, persuaded more by the judgment of the many than by my own. I commend myself to Your Lordship and promise you that if ever there were a wretched journey, it was the one that I made, as that nasty devil will be able to report to you, and we will send him to you when we have anything else to tell you. I know that I need not implore you not to leave me here alone, because if you did so, you would worsen your condition here and you would be blamed for it there. I am quite happy if it should seem best to stay there for several days and make a mere chancellery secretary out of Francesco.[2] I shall write no more officially, but I shall do here what little good I can think of, even if my staying here is completely superfluous. I send you my regards.

From Bolzano, the 17th of February 1507[8].
Your Servant, Niccolò Machiavelli, Secretary

❖ LETTER 152
Cesare Mauro[1] to Niccolò Machiavelli
Cologne, June 1508

To the Most Honored Messer Niccolò Machiavelli.

Honored notable sir. I have such a wealth of topics and of amusing stories that I am altogether at a loss to know which to sing of first or which to sing of next. So I thought it better to keep silent than to say few things, not however neglecting that men who threaten great things often do them less, from whose mountains' laboring with mighty noise is born a ridiculous mouse.[2] Terrified by this, the man from Herculanum[3] fled to us, where he almost burst with laughter, although he pitied Venafro,[4] who, limping, will not be able to escape the enemy attack or repel violence, despite summoning Bartolo, Baldo, Cino, Giovanni Porcio, or De Belleperche[5] to arms, when the laws are utterly silent. There "woe to the wretched,"[6] unless he is favored by our Antimachus,[7] not at all despairing, while subsidies are provided in the customary way to ward off enemies who are snaring the nearest towns every day, while others hunt. But enough about these matters. The manuscripts about which you addressed me at your departure, though I have searched thoroughly, I have so far been able to find nowhere. I am rather amazed at this, since I have not failed to search among the book shops in some well-known cities where schools of literature flourish. If by chance I discover them somewhere, consider them yours, for I am not unmindful of you, to whom I have dedicated my mind and my body and my meager property. Meanwhile, farewell, and please commend me, greatly commended to you, to our magnificent Signor Francesco.[8] God keep him safe. The courier could not run back more swiftly to you about an honorable matter, as he himself will explain more fully face-to-face.

Cologne, June 1508.
Cesare Mauro, the Younger,
Chancell.

❖ LETTER 153
Roberto Acciaiuoli to Niccolò Machiavelli
Rome, 1 July 1508

To the Notable Niccolò Machiavelli,
Secretary of the Exalted Signoria, My Very Dear Friend.
In Florence.

Notable man, etc. Your letter, sent by post, was presented to me just now; what you inform us of in it will be carried according to your plan and your orders,[1] and it will not be spoken of until it is so instructed in another letter. I have not yet received news of the Rucellai's letter, but I am surmising some misspent funds. God willing, one day we should begin to distinguish the good people from the bad! About matters in Germany, I want us to wait until Santa Reparata[2] with Casa. I wish and hope that will be soon, since it seems to me to be really material for bench-sitting.[3] *Farewell.*

In Rome, 1 July, six o'clock[4] in the evening, 1508.
Roberto Acciaiuoli, Ambassador

❖ LETTER 154
Roberto Acciaiuoli to Niccolò Machiavelli
Rome, 5 July 1508

To His Honored Niccolò Machiavelli, Secretary of the Exalted *Signoria*.
In Florence.

Our very dear, etc. This morning the letter of our sublime Signoria appeared, with the order to Mariotto,[1] who had it delivered into his hand right away, as you will see by the Signoria's letter. I remind you to give your business a firm base, because he is boasting about both letters in Totto's hand and other guarantees. So you be careful and examine everything well. I made him an attestation, as I told you in another letter, that I had not offered to make payment to him for what he was supposed to get from Totto, but Totto was prepared to settle with him and to pay him if he had to get it from him. That does not cause much of a problem; and he thought that it was to his benefit since he would not have to come to Florence. He is still complaining about me, because I gave the questions to Lorenzo Machiavelli, because he says that I should have sent them sealed to the Signoria. But that does not cause much of a problem, because I do not think that anything but the truth should be employed in them. For his greater precaution and so that he can make no complaint, he also has a copy of it, and I kept it for myself as well so that, if he should come and complain of this outcome, you will know that he cannot cite you as a suspect.

I should like you to recommend to His Excellency Lord Gianfilippo Bartoli, both on your behalf and on mine, the suit of a sister of Messer Iacopo Salvestri, who is an honorable man and in matters pertaining to the city unlike many Florentines who are there. Because she has received all decisions in her favor in this suit, her opponents have turned to the Signoria on other occasions and have always been dismissed. Because Giovanni Buongirolami, an opposing attorney, is in the Signoria, he has started it up once again. Therefore I pray you to recommend it to them, so that it does not get overturned. Since there is nothing else to add, farewell. In the letter of the Signoria, you will see Mariotto's reply.

In Rome, 5 July 1508.
Roberto Acciaiuoli,
Ambassador

❖ LETTER 155
Roberto Acciaiuoli to Niccolò Machiavelli
Rome, 29 July 1508

To the Distinguished Man Messer Niccolò di Messer Bernardo Machiavelli,
Honored Secretary of the Signoria.
In Florence.

Honored, etc. I happened to be with Monsignor de' Pazzi when I received your letter. I told him what you wrote me, asking him if it was true that he had written, etc. He was very surprised by that and told me that it was not true and that, aside from everything else, he does not know Mariotto, and he knows nothing of this matter. When Messer Leonardo had been found again, I yelled at him about it and he took it quite badly. So give the Monsignor's excuses to those concerned, because he has not heard anything and Messer Leonardo did not know whom this matter [1] was turned against; because having been asked by Mariotto and not knowing, etc., he did not say no to him. Afterward, Mariotto came to see me and read me a letter from his brother, which informs of a certain argument made before the Signoria and where it appears that your family has alleged many things. He complains about me for that, and, among other things, for an attestation of the chancellor that he says weighs against him considerably, and for a letter that Lorenzo Machiavelli [2] received from me, in which he says I wrote him that I had offered Mariotto to pay him if he gave me the document. He complains about me and says that I never offered him payment, which is true, because I would not have done it. But if I did happen to write to Lorenzo, it was by mistake, but I am surprised at it because I believe that I only wrote him that I had offered to return the document to him and that if Totto had anything to give him, he was ready to call accounts even. He asked me for an attestation of that and I, in order for him not to think that I have any interest in this, gave him one. Therefore I pray you that anything that is to be shown about me should not go beyond reasonable and true limits. I shall be grateful if you send me by return mail a copy of that letter that I wrote to Lorenzo Machiavelli, because I want to see if I went beyond what the said Lorenzo instructed me to do. The letter in answer to the Signoria will be dealt with as you have written and will be with this one. But it will be a good idea to present it right away, because it is not good for it to remain in the hands of a party and you will be able to get it easily afterward. Let me know if Vettori has returned and what you are doing with so many ambassadors up there that the little people must be feeling vain and getting terribly cocky about it. *Farewell.*

In Rome, 29 July 1508.
Roberto Acciaiuoli, Ambassador

❖ LETTER 156
Cardinal Francesco Soderini to Niccolò Machiavelli
Rome, 3 August 1508

To the Notable Niccolò Machiavelli, Our Very Dear Compare, etc.
In Florence.
F. Soderini, Priest of Santa Susanna and Cardinal of Volterra.

Notable man, very dear compare. With your letter of the 22nd we have the summary[1] you sent us, which, because we received it today, we have not yet been able to go through. We are sure that it will be such as to give us great pleasure, as we shall indicate to you when we have looked at it. You may be certain that it will be used well by us.

Messer Ramondo must have been there. We shall be pleased if you have spoken together, for of the other appointments we do not wish to say anything. It indeed seems to us that not much interpretation is needed today, *since the actions speak for themselves.*

There is no need to thank us for the good will we have toward Totto: because we love him *not only on account of you and your family but also on account of himself since such are his merits.*

If you act in the future so as not to have to excuse your silence, we shall be glad, although we shall not accuse you in this, either.

Greet our Messer Marcello, about whom you have not kept your promise to me.

In Rome, 3 August 1508.

❖ LETTER 157
Piero Soderini to Niccolò Machiavelli
Florence, 26 August 1508

To Our Very Dear Friend, Niccolò Machiavelli, Florentine Secretary
and Officer in the Successful Florentine Army against the Pisans.[1]
In Camp.

My very dear Niccolò. To our group here it seems as if this laying waste[2] is going very slowly. Therefore we thought we ought to write you[3] the present letter and urge you to press for it to be finished, in such a way that the least possible fodder is left to the enemy and with the greatest possible swiftness, and you will be very highly praised for it over there. Here it has been said that the enemy had sowed it in such quantity that if they were permitted to bring it in, they would feel very little the waste we laid to their wheat. Therefore, make sure you do as much as possible, always with the understanding that you should not put yourself in a position where our troops there would run any risk. *Farewell.*

From the palace in Florence, 26 August 1508.
Piero Soderini
Perpetual Gonfalonier of Justice of the Florentine People

❖ LETTER 158
Giannessino da Sarzana to Niccolò Machiavelli
Castello San Niccolò, 4 September 1508

To My Honored Chief, Niccolò Machiavelli
In Florence.
Jesus.

Your Magnificence, honored Messer, etc. A few days ago I was in Florence and Your Excellency was in camp.[1] I was sorry not to see you. Nevertheless, my good will toward you is sufficient, etc. I was with Filippo di Banco[2] and told him that I have raised a bear in your name that at present is three feet tall and as tame as it can possibly be. Nevertheless, I could not bring it to Florence as you wanted. Now I inform you, if you have a way to have it brought, I shall make a present of it to you, and whether or not you accept it, I would be grateful to hear about it, so that it will not have to go to waste: it is sufficient, etc. I have received a letter from Their Lordships of the Nine on reviewing these companies, and each one separately. I trust in God that I shall receive honor because these men are happy with my work and I with theirs. It is indeed true that they have a lot of disputes among themselves: nevertheless I exert all my wit and effort to keep peace among them, etc. Also, I should be grateful to have a little powder or else saltpeter for these gunners, because I would teach them to make fine powder, and for training, but I should like to have it quickly because this coming Friday, the feast[3] of the Nativity of the Virgin, I shall begin to review a company, and so on every feast day another one until I have executed the will of Our Lordships of the Nine, etc. I need nothing else at present except to remind you that I am your servant, and I send my constant regards to Your Excellency. Again I pray you to give me a reply about the bear, so it does not go to waste, etc.

In Castello San Niccolò,[4] 4 September 1508.
Giannessino Sarzana, your servant

I pray you to give my regards to Filippo, and whenever Your Lordship pleases, the rooms are at your orders.

❖ LETTER 159
Francesco Miniati to Niccolò Machiavelli
Poggio Imperiale, 28 September 1508

To the Notable and Most Honored Man Messer Niccolò Machiavelli,
Secretary in the Palace of the *Signoria*.
In Florence.

   Notable and most honored man. Today I received a letter of yours from the
18th, by which I learn what you say concerning Giovan Paolo's wood. He has
been trying to sell me the said wood for several months; I have always put
him off, in order to get him to lower the price. Now that I learn what you
want, I am ready to make every effort. If I find another source of supply of
wood, I shall do it; and if I can do anything else for you, I am at your disposal.
Farewell.

In Poggio Imperiale, 28 September 1508.
Yours, Francesco Miniati

❖ LETTER 160
Andrea Carducci[1] to Niccolò Machiavelli
Bientina, 23 November 1508

To the Notable, Honored Man Niccolò Machiavelli, in Florence.
Jesus.

   My honored chief, etc. I am sending you with this letter an eagle weighing
5 pounds, which you will be pleased to eat for my sake. For the moment I
have need of nothing, except that I pray you to love me as your servant and
give me your orders. I remind you, when Lorenzo Nerli, my uncle and your
relation, was with the Signoria, he called you into his room and recommended me to you. And so I pray you to be recommended to you. God keep
you in happiness.

In Bientina, 23 November 1508.
Your servant, Andrea Carducci

❖ LETTER 161
Niccolò Serristori[1] to Niccolò Machiavelli
Rome, 7 December 1508

   My very dear and honored, etc. Last Sunday I received a letter from you
dated the 23rd of last month, and because I received it on Sunday, I have not
answered you before this. I am very sorry not to have been Jonah.[2] As for
your business, I have had people look around: I say that I had people look

around and not that I looked around, for the reason that I shall tell you below, God willing. It turns out that our friend has had two orders drawn up and had them collected by messengers, each of them addressed to the auditor of the chamber, but of these only one has happened to be presented, which a way was found to see and to read, even though that is an exceptional thing for anyone who does not have a letter of attorney; and it has nothing to do with you but is some suit on behalf of some woman and her dowry. I do not believe he has had the other one presented yet, since he is not as yet very well decided about his affairs. I shall continue to have the rest of this watched for, and I shall give you news and let you know my opinion, even though you have not asked me for it, because with Totto I do not have to keep such close track of my actions. I shall tell everything if I find anything else that turns up.

What I promised to tell you above is this fine business that you will hear: I was planning to tell it to you more or less in brief, but I have changed my mind and shall tell you the entire story, in order that, following my example, you may better confirm how very foolish it is to deal with asinine men and to talk with them, because anyone who is asinine is, after all, an ass in every way and turns everyone who stoops to look at him, much less anything else, into asses. Around three months ago, Piero del Bene and I were talking, seated on his bench, that is, outside, where people sit. Antonio Segni came walking by there: we invited him to sit down, I moved over, he accepted, we put him in the middle. So Piero del Bene takes out a coin struck by the new minters, for you must know that the Fuggers[3] have the mint and no longer Antonio Segni, and he praises it. Then, after Antonio has talked to both of us and we have asked him several things concerning the money profession, he makes a digression, saying that the popes, because of either too much saintliness or greater concerns, do not think of the welfare or the hardship of the people. And I said, "Maybe they do not want to think about their welfare, but they do think about the opposite," and he said that it was not the pope's doing, and I spoke in the third person, saying, "Others are of the opposite opinion," so he incites me to listen to the reasons by which I would see that such people were in error. I answered that I would listen willingly. He made his argument quite properly, and I praised him and gave him my reply. He answered, I again replied to his answer. He re-answers, I reply again, still speaking in the third person, that is, "They say, etc." Then he said, smiling, "The fact is that, if the reflection of such people is good, those are not things for lawbooks and judgments." I replied that lawbooks and judgments are a trade like the others, and that I was not speaking according to them but according to what I gathered from men who make a calling of such things and who know about them, and that I also had spoken on my part, and that I did not think that lawbooks took away men's brains. I said these things, too, with a smile, and he, also smiling, said, "As for what I said about talking on my part, etc., the primary thing is whether you can get yourself to understand it." On the subject of lawbooks and brains, I said that they take them away; rather, that I have known a dozen judges, lawyers, and attorneys who were fools. I said that I did not think that they were all like that, because I had known just as many merchants who had become brokers and yet that had not happened to all merchants. Then he said, but softly, "So you see, brokers know more than your kind do." I said, "Antonio, let us not become enemies over this: you know a lot about your trade, which you make your calling. Whatever I know about mine or I feel I know about it does not take away from you nor does it add. It suffices that what I tell you I am not basing on my trade." He answered me that he knew more about his trade and mine than I do. To cut the discussion short and not to seem to be leaving in anger, I said that I was speaking to him neither with his trade nor with mine but with my brains, and that everyone considers he has brains to spare, and that I felt that I had been born with as much of them as he had. So I acted as if I was thinking about something else, although I remained seated next to him. Staying that way for a while and looking toward the bridge, so that my back was turned toward him, I felt someone give me a punch in the cheek. I turned around, amazed, and saw that it had been Antonio, because he was still standing, and he wanted to show me that at least, since I had gotten together with an asinine man, I should give his asinine words their due with a slap, because he would have been satisfied at last and not want to consider: what will people say? Whereupon I got off the wall to send him to Kingdom Come.[4] So I reached for a bread knife of mine, a fairly big one. Seeing that, he ran into a shop next to the Beni's, where a beltmaker works, and he picked up a marble pressing-block to defend himself. I knocked it out of his hand, and finally, after he had run around into a corner of the shop, I took him by the chest to kill him, and just as I unleashed the blow and the blade was already at his coat, I was grabbed from behind on the arms by someone and pulled back, and someone else grabbed my knife hand, so that there was no way that I could make use of that. And so, fearing that Antonio might reach for his weapons, which I felt that he had (and at first he acted as if he wanted to draw it and could not because of the speed and force I used), or he might grab some other blade from the shop, I pulled Antonio along by the chest, so that, hanging on to him, I pressed him against the wall, and he flung his hands down on the knife out of fear, and they say he cut himself a little because the knife was not very sharp. Then, after we had remained hanging on tight to each other for a while, seeing that I was held too strongly by those two, I decided to make an effort to get loose, so that, between pushing and being pulled, held so tightly a prisoner as I was, I got out of the shop with my knife in my hand and he remained there. And so, out of fear that the court may hold me to more than I would want, I am not leaving sanctuary[5] until certain little matters are cleared up and I get back to Florence, where I want to stay for a while; if it were not for this business, I would have arrived two months ago. I send my regards to you, to Messer Niccolò, to the prior, and to our *cronies*,[6] although the term is faulty because with men of honor words change their significance or their manner of signifying.

In Rome, 7 December 1508.
Yours, Niccolò Serristori

L E T T E R S

1509

In the spring of 1509 the tide turned in favor of Florence in its war against Pisa. The campaign had lasted throughout the winter. Machiavelli joined the army early in February and was constantly checking on its readiness. On 10 March the Ten ordered him to Piombino because its prince, Jacopo d'Appiano, claimed that Pisa wanted to capitulate and had chosen him as its representative. The negotiations fell through, and Machiavelli returned briefly to Florence to inform the Signoria; then he rejoined his beloved forces at Pisa. An indication of his commitment and patriotism exists in his remark on learning in mid-April that the Ten wished him to join Capponi at the relatively safer camp at Cascina: "I know that encampment would be less dangerous and less strenuous, but had I not wanted danger and hard work, I would not have left Florence. So, may it please Your Lordships, let me stay here in these camps and work with the commissioners on the events that may occur: here I can be of some good use; there I should be of no good use at all and I would die of despair" (text in Machiavelli, *Legazioni e commissarie,* pp. 400–401; see Ridolfi, *Life,* p. 107; *Vita 7,* p. 171). The "good use" soon led to the successful completion of the Pisan campaign. By the end of May, Machiavelli was with the Florentine commissioners laying the groundwork for the peace agreement that was proclaimed in early June. Machiavelli entered Pisa with the triumphant army and was lauded for his role in letters from Vespucci and Casavecchia (Letters 167 and 169).

Machiavelli's other mission this year was to protect this victory over Pisa. Five months later, on 10 November, he was dispatched to Mantua with 10,000 ducats as a down payment to Maximilian I so he would not interfere with Florence's policy toward Pisa. Various delays and the court's movements kept

Machiavelli away from Florence until the beginning of January 1510.

Northern Italy was the center of most political interest on the Italian peninsula in 1509. The powers that had formed the League of Cambrai were pursuing their policy against Venice, although the ostensible aim of the league was a war against the Turks. On 14 May Louis XII attacked the Venetian forces at Vailà (or Agnadello) "where in one day's battle Venice lost what she had very laboriously acquired over the course of eight hundred years" (*Prince,* 12, ll. 143–146; the battle is also known as the Battle of Ghiaradadda, since the town is on the Adda River). The fact that no one in the League of Cambrai trusted anyone else meant, however, that all was not immediately lost for Venice.

Political affairs in northern Italy between Venice and the emperor played a role in Machiavelli's literary activity. Letter 178, a scurrilous correspondence to Luigi Guicciardini, may well be a literary effort, with a debt to Boccaccio's *Decameron* (the fourth story of the Eighth Day). Although it is believed that Machiavelli's *Decennale secondo,* a verse chronicle in terza rima that he left uncompleted, was actually composed around 1514, it starts with historical events in 1505 and stops abruptly at the Venetian recovery of Vicenza from Maximilian in mid-November 1509—that is, shortly after Machiavelli arrived in the north of Italy. During this same quest for the emperor, Machiavelli may also have whiled away some hours by writing a *capitolo,* a burlesque poem in terza rima, entitled *Dell'ambizione* (On ambition).

✤ LETTER 162
Biagio Buonaccorsi to Niccolò Machiavelli
Florence, 20 February 1509

To His Most Honored Niccolò Machiavelli, Florentine Secretary.

Your Magnificence the Captain General,[1] *etc.* I shall not write you any more letters if you do not at least tell me you received them, because, since you have 4 chancellors[2] over there, you really ought to do it. The pope[3] has sent for six thousand Swiss, and he is beginning to spend money, too, and he is weaving this mesh on all sides. The Venetians are doing the same and bolstering themselves with masses and Our Fathers, and they have sent troops over there, as you will have seen by the letters that were sent to you with Tarlatino and Romeo.[4] You see on what their hopes are founded. The emperor, as far as can be judged from these latest letters from France, does not seem to be going to pass into Italy this year. Still, we hear he is getting both troops and money ready. But it is not necessary to speak too much about this with you, since you know better than we do what he can do. The king of Spain, as I told you, is sending troops and artillery into Apulia for the siege of his towns[5]: we shall see what follows.

Here no one is thinking of anything but finishing up the business in Pisa, and no expense[6] whatever is being spared. The bridge[7] that Antonio da Sangallo had them send to him from here, with a lot of engineers for that purpose, will be in operation before 4 days have gone by. So they have cut down a lot of wood, and everything is flying around. Take care down there[8] that they do not try to enter under cover of a bad storm while the fleet is withdrawn, because all the water in the Arno would not wash you clean.

That wind that I told you had arisen and had not had enough strength began to blow once again and came to the same end, and so it will be unless something else comes up[9]; so let those chatter who will.

The commissioner of Cascina[10] writes that those poor musketeers, as badly led as they were by that treacherous, roguish drunkard, slaughtered 13 enemy horses and 5 men and wounded a lot of them, which shut the mouth of those who were acting like men of wisdom and showed them to be men like all the others. Here arrangements are being made to ransom them in any case and to give them some other benefits to encourage the others for the future.

Write to Niccolò Capponi, who is grumbling and complaining[11] that you have never written him, and tell that asshole Ser Battaglione to go easy and not to be so confident any more, because the excuse about his foot will not always work. Remind him first to get trust in his hand before he goes any further. Give my regards to Baldovino,[12] who is also a teeny, weeny asshole. I have not seen our friend for several days now because I have not been able to, and also all the things he has to do during this carnival do not permit us to give him very much trouble: we shall do it during the coming Lenten season. Let me know if you want me to do anything else. I talked to Fantone about what I wrote you yesterday: he told me that 4 other lawsuits had been brought against you and that you should not doubt there would be notification of them.

In Florence, Carnival day 1508[9].
You know who

❖ LETTER 163
Biagio Buonaccorsi to Niccolò Machiavelli
Florence, 21 February 1509

To His Most Honored Niccolò Machiavelli, Florentine Secretary.
In Camp.

My honored Niccolò. I am answering you with a few words about the part dealing with the case[1] of the commissioner against you, which did not at all please the office. But the more powerful always must be right, and one must show respect for them. So you have to get used to being patient and knowing how to behave on such occasions, even though this one is of little moment since you have to stay away. So if one or two letters are needed to make him happy, it will not take much effort. Our *superior*,[2] with whom I spoke of this at length yesterday evening, asked me to write this to you and to urge you for his sake to be patient, with other words that you should be glad about and value highly. The leave is not to be discussed for now, and that shows whether or not you are giving satisfaction. For only this morning, in the efforts that you are making to get hold of someone in Mutrone, some would have liked you to be transferred as far as Lucca to ask for that thing. However, the fear that they could not manage over there without you won the day, and they decided to try it in another way.

I want to remind you of one thing, and that is that when you write, you should tell every slightest event that happens, both over there and in Pisa, because these details give a good deal of satisfaction and fulfillment to the group, and it is those that will get you lauded to the skies. If it should seem otherwise to you, I leave it up to you. This evening, aside from your last one, all your letters will be read in the Eighty and the Eight of *Pratica,* and so it will continue to be done; so send us some of those you are wont to.

If you do not want to send back Ser Francesco,[3] answer that you need him, and what you want will be done with him. The bridge[4] is being hastened along in every way possible, and nothing more can be done than what has been done.

Write a few times more to the Nine, because everyone wants to be coddled and esteemed, so that is what someone who finds himself where you are has to do. A few kind words with a couple of notices will give satisfaction, and it will seem as if they have been given consideration. Do it, I pray you.

I have nothing at all new to tell you, because since I wrote you nothing new has happened. Yesterday I went to visit our friend; he was not at home, if I was told the truth, which I doubt. But being the day that it was, I am not surprised; I hope that now he will have more leisure. Here they say that Ser Battaglione got his ass busted and that Baldovino kicked the bucket. Let us know what is up, for we are very anxious to hear. Both their wives are making a big fuss. That crazy Ser Antonio della Valle has made a model of a bridge and wants to make a drawbridge over the Arno, and we cannot get it out of his head, so that I am afraid he will lose his mind over it. Try to fix it if you can.

In Florence, the first day of Lent[5] 1508[9].

You know who

I beg you, urge Messer Bandino to give back those animals without going any further because it is not something that will give him profit, and he will be doing a favor to more than one person.

Postscript. I have received your letter of the 20th, and concerning the musketeers I have done what was necessary, in this as in your other affairs. But you have to write how many of them were taken, how many killed, and how matters stand, because here people are agitated. The gratuity will go to your house tomorrow, and I shall do what is necessary with our friend, because I have not been able to up to now. That other business has not yet been judged; I do not know what will happen.

❖ Letter 164
Piero Soderini to Niccolò Machiavelli
Florence, 22 February 1509

To Our Friend Niccolò Machiavelli, Scribe and Florentine Secretary
[. . .] Also Serving in [. . .].

Dearest Niccolò. We have received two letters of yours,[1] which we shall answer briefly, reminding you that the way of this world is to receive great ingratitude for great and good operations, although not from everyone. Keep on doing as you have done up till now, and first our Lord God, then a few people, will help you. The money will be sent for the infantry troops, that is, Saturday or Sunday, so that it may be given at the proper time and not before, because you know they are supposed to have a third of their pay at a time and serve for thirty-six days, and thus it will be equalized for them when they are in camp [< . . . >].

Make sure that the Pisans are kept shut off and especially that food supplies do not enter either by water or by land. *Farewell.*

From the palace in Florence, 22 February 1508[9].
Piero Soderini, Perpetual Gonfalonier of Justice of the Florentine People

❖ Letter 165
Biagio Buonaccorsi to Niccolò Machiavelli
Florence, 1 March 1509

To His Honored Niccolò Machiavelli.
In Camp.

Niccolò. I shall write you just this note, since it is late and I am busy, and tomorrow I shall write at length. I shall tell you this, that the answers are here from France and you can consider matters arranged and settled for certain, since there is a difference of a couple of little words, which in fact are not of much importance and are accepted here, and instruction is given to sign and everything is arranged, by the grace of God. They are not talking about any news at all except that Consalvo and one of his nephews[1] have withdrawn to Portugal, and the king of that country has come to Burgos, and His Most Christian Majesty[2] is hastening his coming, so that he will be in Italy by Easter. Rucellai and Giuliano[3] thrashed about vainly in Mantua and Milan and are not paying attention to anything else. And Antonio Francesco degli Albizzi says he has gone to this diet of theirs and not to Rome, which is something to laugh about, and all the more now. I talked today with our *superior*[4]: I showed him that you had written to me about the loss of the money and you were very sorry about it, etc. He answered that you should remain of good cheer and that you have nothing to do with it, etc. The matter of Piombino[5] is not to be disdained, because it has great foundation. I am not able and I do not want to say anything further, since I have no way to write with security. Our friend is well and sends you a hundred thousand regards. Let me know when you receive this.

In Florence, the first of March 1508[9].
You know who

❖ LETTER 166
Lattanzio Tedaldi[1] to Niccolò Machiavelli
Florence, 5 June 1509

To the Notable Niccolò di Messer Bernardo Machiavelli.
In Camp.
Jesus, 5 June 1509.

Niccolò, my very dear brother, *greetings,* etc. I should like you[2] to tell the commissioners that, since they are to take possession[3] of Pisa on Thursday, they should on no account enter before six-thirty in the morning, but if it is possible they should enter very shortly after seven o'clock, which will be a very auspicious[4] hour for us. And if they were to take it not on Thursday but rather on Friday, similarly very shortly after seven o'clock and not before six-thirty[5]: the same on Saturday morning if it should not be taken on Friday. If it should not be possible to observe either the time or the hour, let it be done and be taken when it can be, *in the name of the Lord.* You will say this on my behalf to Antonio da Filicaia. I send you my regards. May Christ keep you from harm. *Farewell.*

Lattanzio Tedaldi, in Florence

❖ LETTER 167
Agostino Vespucci to Niccolò Machiavelli
Florence, 8 June 1509

To His Honor the Notable Niccolò Machiavelli, Florentine Secretary.
In Pisa.

Honored Niccolò. Either I am deceived or the letter that came by Zerino was from you. Here it is not possible to express how much delight, how much jubilation and joy, all the people here have taken in the news of the recovery of that city of Pisa: in some measure *every man* has gone mad with exultation; there are bonfires all over the city, although it is not yet three in the afternoon[1]; just think what they will do this evening after nightfall. I repeat to you once again that the only thing that might be lacking is for the heavens to show some delight as well, since it is not possible for men, both great and small, to show any more of it. *May it benefit you* to have been present at a glory of this nature, *and not the least portion of the ill.* If you should deign to send me back a few lines written by your hand in Pisa, nothing will be more pleasing and nothing more welcome. *Farewell.*

> *In Florence, 8 June 1509.*
> *Yours, if [you are] his, Agostino*

Postscript. If I did not think it would make you too proud, I should dare say that you with your battalions[2] *accomplished so much good work, in such a way that, not by delaying but by speeding up, you restored*[3] *the affairs of Florence.* I do not know what to say. I swear to God, so great is the exultation we are having that I would write a Ciceronian oration for you if I had time. *But it is completely lacking.*

❖ LETTER 168
Niccolò di Alessandro Machiavelli[1] to Niccolò Machiavelli
Florence, 9 June 1509

To the Honored Niccolò Machiavelli, Commissioner.
In Pisa.
† 9 June 1509.

Honored, etc. The bearer of this letter will be Alessandro di Dino, a man of honor and our friend, one to be made use of in any assignment. I pray you, if you can give him any help on his way at all, that it be done. If a word should need to be said about him to Alamanno[2] on my behalf, do so. Let whatever possible good be done for him, because he will give honor in any occasion; and I shall be singularly grateful for it. I have no other need.

> God keep you from harm. Yours.
> Niccolò Machiavelli, in Florence

❖ LETTER 169
Filippo Casavecchia to Niccolò Machiavelli
Barga,[1] 17 June 1509

To His Honor the Notable Niccolò Machiavelli,
Most Worthy Commissioner in Pisa.
In Pisa or Florence.

Your Magnificence, and honored as an elder brother, greetings, etc. I believe, my very dear friend, that I may have acquired a reputation with you as negligent or careless or some other nasty thing, with respect to your having written me several days ago, when things were doubtful, that, in truth, gave me very great pleasure. I answered you by two messengers: one never found you, the other says that he saw you at Pontedera[2] with Alamanno and the Pisan ambassadors, and he did not have enough courage to present my letter to you. Therefore I feel certain that these justifications must be sufficient in your eyes, and let that suffice.

I wish you a thousand benefits from the outstanding acquisition of that noble city,[3] for truly it can be said that your person was cause of it to a very
great extent, although I do not thereby blame any of those very noble commissioners concerning either their wisdom or indeed their efforts. Although I
have taken marvelous satisfaction from it, and wept and lurched about and
done all those things that dignified men do, etc., in imitation of old sheep,
nevertheless, my reason having afterward recovered its power, I remain extremely anxious about it, and I cannot think nor can I help in any way thinking that weighty things[4] run toward the center and lighter things toward the
surface. Niccolò, this is a time when if ever one was wise it should be now. I
do not believe your ideas[5] will ever be accessible to fools, and there are not
enough wise men to go around: you understand me, even if I am not putting
it very well. Every day I discover you to be a greater prophet than the Hebrews or any other nation ever had.[6] Niccolò, Niccolò, in truth I tell you that
I cannot say what I would like. So be happy for that good friendship we have
had together, and let it not seem like a burden to you to come and stay here
with me for four days. Aside from our conversation, I am saving you a ditch
full of trout and a wine like you have never drunk. This will be a pleasure for
me that will make me forget all the others. Please, Niccolò my friend, gratify
my wishes in this last, just for four days; let me inform you that, if you do not
come, you will be the cause of my living unhappily ever after. This is, however, not such a big thing that I should not deserve to be gratified. Whether I
deserve it or not, I place this price on your head. It will take you only a day,
because there are only 26 miles of level road, so let me know when, and get
ready to cheer me up, because, if you should not come, I would set out to
come and find you and that would be my undoing, because the laws do not
permit me to leave the province[7] under penalty of 500 florins, enough said: I
shall not say anything else to you. Give my regards to the angelic commissioner Niccolò Capponi and tell him that he has not done what I wrote him
but that he will be the first to be sorry for it, enough said. *Farewell.*

From Barga, 17 June 1509.
Filippo Casavecchia, Commissioner

❖ LETTER 170
Filippo Casavecchia to Niccolò Machiavelli
Barga, 2 July 1509

To His Honor the Notable Niccolò Machiavelli,
Most Worthy *Secretary* of the Nine of the Militia of the City.
In Florence, or Wherever He May Be.

My very dear Niccolò. I have sought you by letter through all this world
and the next. Now to find you I have sent to Pisa and to Florence, and finding you over there, I pray you, as has been written to you elsewhere, to be so

kind as not to mind coming to stay with me for 4 days, because I am sure you will not be sorry for it, with respect to my having ordered an entire furnaceful of mortar that contains 40 *moggia*,[1] with which we shall plaster the river, for we shall take at least 2,000 *libbre*[2] of fish and have a great time doing it. Let me inform you that during the past days Francesco Capponi, Giovanni Bartolini, Lorenzo Strozzi, and Lorenzo Segni have been here, and they did not go away in the least unhappy, both for the air and for the wines, which have been recognized to be the best there are in Tuscany. Indeed, Niccolò, if you do not come, I am going to do something very foolish, so that in fact you and all our other friends will be sorry about it. Whatever the devil may be, if you should come, I do not however believe you would lose your position. Let me inform you that, although I did not know where in creation you might be, the main reason for not sending you any fish was my desire for you to come here, and you will take back with you an entire packload of trout. The fishing party is arranged for the end of this month more or less whenever you come. Niccolò, may it please you to please me, and leave behind any rancor, if ever there was any, which I do not believe and shall never believe. Please, Niccolò, come quickly and send me or rather write me a couple of lines about when and where you are and whether you are going to stay put in that place; let me know all about it. I send you my regards. *Nothing else.*

> *From Barga, 2 July 1509.*
> *Filippo Casavecchia, Commissioner*

❖ LETTER 171
Pietro Corella[1] (Pedro) to Niccolò Machiavelli
Pisa, 17 July 1509

Jhs. My Lordship, Your Excellency. I was already full of many, many things, and yet I was waiting to see if anyone else was going to talk about it and also to do anything about it, as reason required, since I am a person little desirous of ill to any man. Now, forced to the point where I can no longer bear it, troubled by the abundance of opportunity, I thought it best to write to Your Lordship about the life of my flag bearer, and what he has done here recently just out of craving and rascality to go back home, but very ready to take money to make his glazes, as you will for jugs or tiles, but not to make himself a pair of hose for his own wear. Although it would be tiresome to give you a report on everything, I shall not expand too much on it except in a few little things, and you will be informed about everything more fully by my chancellor.

Your Lordship knows that I came to Florence, and I had not been gone from here for two days, leaving him in charge of the company, when he went to the commissioners and asked them for leave to go home to see his girlfriend, without any consideration for my departure or anything else, like the miserable ox that he is. So my commissioners told him off more rudely than you would an ass and threw him out; he found as an excuse that he had a quinsy of the throat, when even if he had been at death's door[2] he should have waited for me. And he stood there with his pants down, as I believe you will see he always goes around, and barefoot, like the very potter he is. I arrived here from Florence; as soon as I arrived, he asked me for leave because he wanted to go back home. So I answered him: he should serve first and then go on back. So he said to me that God could not make him not go home. So I kept quiet. Without saying anything else to me, he left and went off to Anziano[3] to his brother's kiln, and he stayed there three days and came back here laughing. When I saw him, I rebuked him, and he found some stupid excuse, and I passed it off lightly. Now today, when it is the sixteenth of the present month of July, when I was at home, this fellow came to my house in a rage, with another from Santa Maria Impruneta, and told me about how he had beaten up a Pistoian over some merchandise or other of tiles and jugs: so if you want to spare me, have someone tell you all about his idiocy and the cowardly and roguish things he did, as he himself accuses himself like a fool when he tells about it. He came to my house and bragged that he had sharpened the spit to hurt someone and he was accustomed to getting into arguments and fights, and that since he got his flag he had turned into a monk.[4] He asked me for advice about the rascality he had done. So I told him to go away and let me take care of it. The commissioners sent for me right away, and I answered Their Lordships with those words that were fitting; let Their Lordships hear one party and the other, and I only wanted what was right, and whoever was wrong should be punished. The poor man with his nose broken and his face all swollen is an honorable person. And so I left the commissioners, and I got them half calmed down, hoping I would bring everything to a good end.

My good flag bearer, without saying anything else to me, had gone off that evening and taken the flag, and he had arranged to come back in the morning with it, by God, and to leave me like a fool. He let me know he would stay in the house of Signor Bandino until the matter had passed. Now, as Your Lordship knows, there are those who always blame things for whatever happens. I was informed of everything; and right away I got the flag and brought it back to my house, since I am the one who is supposed to keep it near me and to have custody of it and to consider it an honor or a dishonor for me more than anyone else. The good man, learning of this, had to say that I had known better than he; and that he wanted to do the thing that day and not wait for the evening; and that the devil had tricked him; and that the flag was his, and he wanted to take it wherever he felt like without the permission of Christ or anyone else in the world; and that I was being a fool in this matter.

In conclusion, the next morning his friend Calcangio, without a by-your-leave or anything, as well as his comrade and he came over here. I felt I should give you warning of it so that, if he gets over there, Your Lordship is informed about everything. And if a more detailed report ought to be given to Your Lordship, as necessary I shall give it to that wretch and before my Signoria and whoever else may be necessary, without any stain whatever of ill will that I may have toward him but rather in truth, as you will always find in me and not otherwise, as the entire company knows openly; for there is not a man but who does not hate his guts and who does not wish him deathly ill. Stingy as a louse, so that when he was to enter Pisa he entered with a pair of torn, rotten hose. I rebuked him more than twenty times about the said hose, but he managed to enter with them on. When you speak with him, he has no respect for Christ. There is nothing he would not be capable of doing. He is neither for my Signoria nor for Christ. He has said so openly thirty times here and in camp.

He knows well, the scoundrel, that before taking pay, I told him and everyone that anyone who was not thinking of staying here should not draw pay. But out of a scoundrelly craving for the money of the entire pay that he got that seemed like a lot to him, he took it, and if we do not make him give some of it back, it will be very wrong, although Your Lordships are the boss. And so that Your Lordship may know my mind fully, I shall be grateful if my Signoria, if Your Lordship thinks it proper, hears the present letter and is informed of what I write: and I am making one for Their Lordships, so that, if my flag bearer should happen to arrive there, they will hear the whole thing from Your Lordship, since I am not writing at such length about it to Their Lordships so as not to be wordy. And so, if need be or if Your Lordship thinks it proper to give it to Their Lordships, Your Lordship will do so for my sake.

I pray Your Lordship to remember me, and any good that he may do for me will be for a good servant of his. I shall continue to have God prayed to for Your Lordship, by my people above all others. I tell you that there is a far better man and a more upright one who can carry this flag, when Their Lordships are willing. If trust cannot be put in me, you will find and see for yourself that what I say is the Gospel truth. You will see it and be informed in time when it has to come to this. It is not out of enmity but out of truth that I am talking: if not, may God not help me. Nothing else is needed. I am always prepared to obey Your Lordship as a good servant, and I pray God to keep you in good health.

In Pisa, 17 July. *By my own hand.*
Your Lordship's obedient servant
Pietro Liberio Corella, Constable.

❖ LETTER 172
Filippo Casavecchia to Niccolò Machiavelli
Barga, 25 July 1509

To the Most Honorable, Notable Messer Niccolò Machiavelli, Most Worthy Secretary of the Nine of Militia and the Florentine Republic, as a Brother.
In Florence.

Honored, notable man, as an elder brother. Having in days gone by somewhat consoled our spirit, and that not being sufficient, according to the blessed soul of Messer Cristofano da Casale, for it is still necessary that the frailty of the flesh have its share in part, therefore I send you these few trout so that the senses may be nourished and the spirit thereafter may be readier for the matters of this world: which in these times are so great that I take my nourishment from them. It remains for me only to learn by a letter from you in what state are the affairs of Gallia Cisalpina, or rather Transpadana,[1] since because I have heard confusedly of them here I have a greater desire to learn the truth about them, though not however by a discussion such as your last letter was, because I almost judge myself unworthy, but such as is fitting to one of the plebeian order, completely ignorant, remaining yours as always. I inform you that the friars do not say their offices otherwise, morning and evening, than I read your letter, and I believe I already know it completely by heart.

I shall say nothing else to you, except I send the trout to you on this condition, that my friend Nero da Diacceto should come to lunch or to dinner along with you, which will be the highest favor to me. I continue to offer myself and my regards to you and to him. *Farewell.*

From Barga, 25 July 1509.
Filippo Casavecchia, Commissioner

❖ LETTER 173
Alamanno Salviati to Niccolò Machiavelli
Pisa, 4 October 1509

To My Dear Niccolò Machiavelli.
In Florence.

Jesus. My dearest Niccolò. I have your letter,[1] which was very dear to me, especially since I see I am in your heart because you often remember me, for which I am most obliged[2] to you. By it I have seen what state Padua is in now, both within and without, and I liked that very much. Your discussion is quite beautiful, and I showed it to Their Lordships the Condottieri and the Consuls, *since all men desire to know,* and it was very highly praised by all. I can neither approve nor disapprove of it, because here we have been abandoned by father and mother and by all relatives and friends; because we learn nothing at all except from any stray people who may come to camp once in two weeks or a month. Therefore we can only judge things here poorly, since we do not hear some details as you sometimes do over there. I have indeed asked Their Lordships the Condottieri a few times what judgment they make about the assault and capture of Padua. They are in unanimous agreement that Padua cannot be lost by force, giving good reasons for that. And so, trusting in them, I would willingly incline to that opinion. But my being monkish makes me draw back from it somewhat, and I willingly adhere to such an opinion, especially when I see it turn out that way in great part.[3] We are constrained to it by seeing the times disposed totally against those Venetians, to such an extent that I believe it is more of a miracle than a natural thing. *However that may be,* I believe that our duty is rather to look to God and pray Him to let whatever is best befall rather than to hope to form some other judgment; although I do not know whether this conclusion is one that will satisfy you much, not because I believe that you are lacking in faith, but I am sure that you do not have much left.

I do remind you, make every possible effort to keep His Most Christian Highness, His Holiness, and His Catholic Majesty[4] together. And watch out lest one of them, out of desperation, be made to do one of those things from which would result the total ruin of Italy; so that the French army does not remain completely in the hands of others, because it would matter too much. I shall be pleased if I have satisfied you, and if I should have left anything out I shall let my teacher make up for it. Remember that I am yours and I send you my regards. God keep you.

> In Pisa, 4 October 1509.
> Yours, Alamanno Salviati, Captain

❖ LETTER 174
Biagio Buonaccorsi to Niccolò Machiavelli
Florence, 20 November 1509

To Niccolò Machiavelli, Florentine Secretary.
In Verona, or Wherever He May Be.[1]

Honored Niccolò. I received your letter of the 15th from Mantua and learn of the anxiety of your mind, etc. I am very surprised about it, since you have had other concerns of much greater importance in your hands and much more dangerous decisions to make than going as far as Verona.[2] If ever you were diligent in your reports, you need to be so now in order to <shut the mouths of the bench-sitters.[3] I took your message to the gonfalonier: he replied, "Let him make sure to write promptly."> Today I shall go and see our friend who has sent for me, and I shall do what is necessary. There is no news, for it is all coming from over there. The entire Nine have been constituted, both the five that were lacking and the other 4 who are supposed to take office in January. They have already discharged Francesco da Cortona, which was money well spent. Nothing else.

> *In Florence, 20 November 1509.*
> *You know who*

❖ LETTER 175
Francesco del Nero to Niccolò Machiavelli
Florence, 22 November 1509

In the name of God, 22 November 1509.

My very dear Niccolò. I have your letter of the 18th, and from it I learn what you say, and everything will be done in the manner that you write. I wrote to Totto Machiavelli precisely in the manner you advise. Messer Giovan Vittorio would not make up his mind, so I have had Messer Antonio write concerning the principal suit[1]; Messer Antonio wrote again on the incompetency, and Messer Giovan Vittorio[2] has promised me to sign it. Today I am to have the incompetency signed by Messer Giovan Vittorio and the principal suit by Messer Antonio. I shall get it signed right away by your other lawyers, and I shall send them off immediately to Messer Antonio, as you asked. I have not failed to hasten it along, so that I am blamed more for importunity than for negligence; for I go at least four times every day to the palace of the *podestà*. I do not hope for any agreement on it, because I have never heard anything at all. I went to His Excellency the Gonfalonier, reminding him of your suit and that I had a proxy, so that I could take care of you; if ever he learned anything at all, His Majesty should be so kind as to let me know of it. He told me that Francesco del Pugliese was to answer him and that he would send for me if ever he got anything. As I have told you, I am taking care of this suit of yours with all concern, diligence, and haste. Today I am sending Messer Francesco Nelli and Piero to the judge; and when the judge gets the principal suit, I shall send your relatives and friends and Ser Giuliano there. I wrote in your name and had Giovan Battista Soderini write to His Most Reverend Monsignor, and I gave one ducat to Ser Filippo del Morello, and as things go along I shall keep him satisfied. Giovanni Uguccioni told me your account was at par and he did not have money: therefore I had the money that I needed supplied to me by Lodovico Machiavelli. He seemed to be doing it willingly. I would not judge it to be out of place if you wrote him a note to thank him. In addition, because I do not know how much I shall have to spend, tell him to provide me with what I need: he has put you down as his debtor for it. If I can get it from Giovanni Uguccioni, it will not be necessary to bother him. As for the prior, what you write will be done; if I should have anything to tell you about the litigation, I shall always do so. I am at your orders.

Francesco del Nero, in Florence

❖ LETTER 176
Niccolò Machiavelli to Luigi Guicciardini[1]
Verona, 29 November 1509

To the Notable Luigi Guicciardini, as a Dearest Brother.
In Mantua. Written from the House of Giovanni Borromei.

Dearest Luigi. Today I received your letter of the twenty-sixth, which distressed me more than if I had lost the lawsuit,[2] since I learned that Jacopo[3] had again caught a bit of fever. Your common sense, Marco's diligence, the doctors' *virtù*, and Jacopo's patience and goodness, however, inspire me with confidence and make me believe that you will drive it out—like the stupid, shameless, disgusting slut that it is; from your next letter I expect to learn that, despite it, you all have merrily gone off toward Florence.

As are you, I am high and dry here because we know nothing about anything; still, in order to show signs of life, I dream up diatribes that I write to the Ten; I enclose their letter, unsealed, which, once you all have read it, you will give to Giovanni[4] for him to send with the first courier when Pandolfini[5] writes—or whatever seems best to him. Give him my regards and tell him that I am here with his Stefano and having a good time. I would have gone to court, but Lang[6]—to whom I have a letter of introduction—is not there; I have no letter to the emperor, so that I might be arrested as a spy. Furthermore, people are saying every day that he is on his way here and all those Mamelukes who are in his retinue are here.

I am glad you have sent those certificates to Florence; for this you deserve great praise to God and to men of the world. If you write your Messer Francesco,[7] tell him that I send the gang my regards. I am yours, very much yours; as for what I am writing,[8] I am still thinking about it. *Farewell.*

This day, the 29th of November 1509. *Verona.*
As a brother, Niccolò Machiavelli, Secretary, with the emperor

❖ LETTER 177
Biagio Buonaccorsi to Niccolò Machiavelli
Florence, 30 November 1509

To the Honored Niccolò Machiavelli, Florentine Secretary, as a Brother.
In Verona.

Honored Niccolò. I wrote to you briefly a few days ago because there was nothing at all new to inform you of, and there is less at present: so that, in this case, if I was brief then, now I shall be very brief. <Filippo Strozzi[1] would have greased wings to come to Florence.>

Although a lot of gossips have noised it about that he was <in Florence,> none of it is true; <rather he asked for it, and I do not know what result he obtained.> God will <it should turn out right.> I told you also that I had visited our friend and given him a ducat, which Francesco del Nero gave back to me because I was in need of it. I told him I had sent you a few odds and ends you had asked me for. I have since gone back there: when I found him, the illness[2] that he was afraid of was evident, and he wanted to go to his friend's house in Prato; he had had his hair cut. I do not know what will be done, for patience is required, and here there is none. The quicker you want to be cured of it, the longer it takes you to be cured. What has happened to him is what I have always expected. Try to write us a lot of news, and you will be doing us a favor. Nothing else. I send you my regards.

In Florence, 30 November 1509.
You know who

I shall get the book back today, and I'll give it back, etc.
The new Ten: Lanfredini,[3] † Giovanni Ridolfi, Antonio di Sasso, Miniato

Busini, Agnolo Miniati, Giovan Battista Bartolini, Scolaio Spini, Bartolo Tedaldi, Lorenzo degli Alessandri.

❖ LETTER 178
Niccolò Machiavelli to Luigi Guicciardini
Verona, 8 December 1509

To the Notable Man Luigi Guicciardini, as a Dearest Brother.
In Mantua.

Hell's Bells, Luigi,[1] see how Fortune hands out to mankind different results under similar circumstances. Why, you had hardly finished fucking your woman before you wanted another fuck, and you want to take another turn at it. But, as for me, why, I had been here three days, losing my discrimination because of conjugal famine, when I came upon an old woman who launders my shirts; the house she lives in is more than half underground—the only light you see in it enters through the door. One day, I was passing by when she recognized me and greeted me profusely; she asked me to be so kind as to enter her house for a moment, she wanted to show me some fine shirts that I might want to buy. So, naive prick that I am, I believed her and went in; once inside, I made out in the gloom a woman cowering in a corner affecting modesty with a towel half over her head and face. The old slut took me by the hand and led me over to her saying, "This is the shirt I wanted to sell you, but I'd like you to try it on first and pay for it afterwards." I, shy fellow that I am, was absolutely terrified; still, to make a long story short, alone there with her in the dark (because the old bawd promptly left the room and shut the door), I fucked her one. Although I found her thighs flabby and her cunt damp—and her breath stank a bit—nevertheless, hopelessly horny, I went to her with it. Once I had done it, and feeling like taking a look at the merchandise, I took a piece of burning wood from the hearth in the room and lit a lamp that was above it; but the light was hardly lit before it almost fell out of my hands. Ugh! I nearly dropped dead on the spot, that woman was so ugly. The first thing I noticed about her was a tuft of hair, part white, part black—in other words, sort of whitish; although the crown of her head was bald (thanks to the baldness one could make out a few lice promenading about), still a few, thin wisps of hair came down to her brow with their ends.[2] In the center of her tiny, wrinkled head she had a fiery scar that made her seem as if she had been branded at the marketplace; at the end of each eyebrow toward her eyes there was a nosegay of nits; one eye looked up, the other down—and one was larger than the other; her tear ducts were full of rheum and she had no eyelashes. She had a turned-up nose stuck low down on her head and one of her nostrils was sliced open and full of snot. Her mouth resembled Lorenzo de' Medici's, but it was twisted to one side, and from that side drool was oozing, because, since she was toothless, she could not hold back her saliva. Her upper lip sported a longish but skimpy moustache. She had a long, pointy chin that twisted upward a bit; a slightly hairy dewlap dangled down to her Adam's apple. As I stood there absolutely bewildered and stupefied staring at this monster, she became aware of it and tried to say, "What's the matter, sir?" but she could not get it out because she stuttered. As soon as she opened her mouth, she exuded such a stench on her breath that my eyes and nose—twin portals to the most delicate of the senses—felt assaulted by this stench and my stomach became so indignant that it was unable to tolerate this outrage; it started to rebel, then it did rebel—so that I threw up all over her. Having thus repaid her in kind, I departed. I shall stake my berth in heaven that as long as I am in Lombardy I'll be damned[3] if I think I shall get horny again. Therefore, you can thank God—trusting that you can again possess so much delight—while I can thank God—knowing that I no longer need fear experiencing so much disgust again.

I believe that I shall be able to put a little money aside after this trip, and once I return to Florence, I should like to put it into some small business. I thought about going in for raising chickens, but I need to find an agent to run it for me. I gather that Piero di Martino is capable in such matters; I should like to hear from him if he is interested and for you to let me know; for if he does not want to, I shall get hold of someone else.

Giovanni[4] will gratify you with all the news from here. Greetings to Jacopo and give him my regards—and do not forget Marco.

In Verona, *the seventh of December 1509.*

I am looking forward to Gualtieri's reply concerning my doggerel.[5]

Niccolò Machiavelli

❖ LETTER 179

Francesco del Nero to Niccolò Machiavelli

Florence, 9 December 1509

To the Notable Niccolò Machiavelli, Most Worthy Secretary, with Maximilian.

As a father, etc. I wrote you my last letter six days ago, and I have not had any from you since. This is to let you know that we have married off our Sandra, God be praised, to Giovan Luigi Arrigetti, a very honorable young man who sends you his regards. You must have heard, concerning our affairs, that the Six were judged competent judges, but the Pitti have not pursued the business otherwise for that: I believe that they have no faith in their scanty justifications. Messer Antonio Strozzi and Messer Antonio da Venafro[1] wrote, and very elegantly; and Messer Giovannetto has promised me to sign it, but he has not yet done so. I found the letter that I lost with the receipt for the two hundred ducats, and since no agreement ensued, I did what was necessary *face-to-face, since he is here.* No letter came from the cardinal.[2] Giovan Battista has told me he got a letter from his brother, as our lord wrote: it must have gone amiss. Your friends will take themselves to the judges as you notified us, *and we are awaiting judgment. Farewell.*

From Florence, 9 December 1509.

Francesco

❖ LETTER 180
Pigello Portinari[1] to Niccolò Machiavelli
Verona, 12 December 1509

To His Magnificence the Excellent Messer Niccolò Machiavelli,
Secretary and Commissioner of the Eminent Florentine Republic.
In Mantua.

   Your Magnificence, greetings. I have heard there are several letters to you from
Florence, which Stefano del Benino[2] is sending you. I shall be happy if you
take solace in it, and if any should be for me I pray you to send them to me. I
should be happy, and it seems to me it would be in the city's interest, if you
were here, since I hear that His Imperial Majesty is getting closer to here. I
believe at this moment he is in Trent; in any case, do as you see fit. If you
should need anything I can do, let me know. The Most Reverend Monsignor,[3]
the emperor's lieutenant, has asked me in the name of Caesar to remain here
in His Majesty's service; and believe me, I am not idle and I have no time for
amusement. With this letter there will be one for my brother. It will be a favor
to me if you send it by the first messenger you can. *Nothing else at present.*
Farewell.

From Verona, 12 December 1509.

   Do not forget to try to get for me what is due me, and it will be added to
the favors, etc.

Yours, Pigello, etc.

❖ LETTER 181
Biagio Buonaccorsi to Niccolò Machiavelli
Florence, 28 December 1509

To Niccolò Machiavelli, as an Honored Brother.
Wherever He May Be.

   Honored Niccolò. I have been stirred to write you the present letter because the matter[1] that will be narrated below is of such great importance that
it could not be greater. Do not make fun of it and do not neglect it, and do
not depart from what I shall tell you for anything in the world, because it will
be one of the most powerful remedies for avoiding your ruin and that of others. To that end I have stolen a march by making you ready to counter things.
   Tomorrow will be eight days since a masked man with two witnesses went
to the house of the notary of the conservators and in their presence gave him
a notification, protesting to him if he did not give it, etc. It stated that since
you were born of a father, etc. you can in no way exercise the office that you
hold, etc. Although the matter was taken care of in the past and the law is as
favorable as can be, nevertheless the nature of the times and a great number
who have arisen to gossip about this matter and to shout about it everywhere

and to threaten that if something is not done, etc., make it such that the matter is not going very well and needs a good deal of help and scrupulous care. From the time that our friends informed me of this until now, I have spared no effort night and day concerning this, so that I have softened up the minds of some people quite a bit. Where the law was being stretched in a thousand ways and given sinister interpretations by those seeking to act against you, etc., it has been laid to rest a bit. Nevertheless, your adversaries are numerous and will stop at nothing. The case is public everywhere, even <in the whorehouses,> so that it can be done openly and it is aggravated by infinite circumstances. Believe me, Niccolò, I am not telling you the half of the things that are going around, and before I pointed out the law, the matter was considered already judged.[2] I am helping it along by every means: so is Piero del Nero, whom I am keeping informed of everything hour by hour, because the same as what I am doing is being done by those who do not want to see the ruin of <both you and me.>

I have been urged at this point by someone who loves you, and is a person that you consider highly, to write you for you to stay where you are and not return here for anything, because the matter is quieting down and no doubt will come to a better end if you are not here than if you are, on a number of grounds. Also, I am doing some things that you would not do, which are nonetheless necessary; because all men want to be recognized and honored and esteemed, even though matters are clear, and it seems fitting that those who serve should be thanked and solicited and then solicited again: how well you might be fitted for this I let you yourself judge. In sum, one of the powerful remedies for this ill, which is so great that it would frighten you, is to stay away for a few days until the end is seen. That is why I am sending you the present letter, urged on to it by others, also private citizens, but of such quality that one can err less in doing thus than otherwise. Your other companions are ready for the defense, if it is useful; for in past days, in another similar case, <it was not helpful, which is what made this arise again.> If I told you that I have never slept since this happened, you can believe me, <because you have so few people here that want to help you, and I> do not know where that comes from.

Once again I tell you to do what you are advised to, and do not go off and assume that I am making the worst of things, as you are wont to say,[3] but that it is much more. <Since I have an interest in it, you should believe me, because it affects me more than you.> Nothing else.

28 December, eight in the evening,[4] 1509.
You know who

L E T T E R S

1510-1512

Machiavelli spent most of the first five months of 1510 outside Florence dealing with matters related to his militia. But Florence was soon to send him out of Italy because of the dilemma posed by the quarrel between Julius II and Louis XII. Once the League of Cambrai had helped the pope defeat Venice, thereby removing a powerful obstacle to papal aggrandizement, Julius changed his tune. His battle cry now was to free Italy from the barbarians: France, Spain, and Germany. Florence realized that it might soon be forced to choose sides. Temporizing both because of the pope's troops on his borders and because of his traditional alliance with France, Soderini sent Machiavelli to France late in June. Even though Louis XII had demanded that Florence clearly define its policy toward him, Machiavelli was charged with justifying Florence's wary fence-sitting; privately, though, he was to reassure Louis that both of the Soderinis, Piero in Florence and Francesco, the cardinal of Volterra, in Rome, were loyal to the French king. Soderini acknowledges in his instructions to Machiavelli that "although a Pope as a friend is not worth much, as an enemy he can do much harm" (*Leg.,* III, p. 1228).

This judgment may be one reason why Florence granted Marcantonio Colonna, a condottiere who had left Florence's service to take part in the pope's attack on Genoa in July, a safe conduct through Florentine territory. The ire of Louis XII meant that Machiavelli had some explaining to do, even though the pope, with Venice now as his ally, failed in his attempt to invade Genoa. They were foiled by the prompt intervention of French troops who kept the people of Genoa from rebelling and siding with the invaders. Florence, meanwhile, had recalled its ambassador to France, Alessandro Nasi, whom Machiavelli met on his way to the court. The new ambassador, Roberto Acciaiuoli, left Florence at the beginning of August and arrived in the middle of September. In this highly charged atmosphere, therefore, Machiavelli was effectively Florence's voice in France. His reports to the Signoria consistently warned that Florence would inevitably be dragged into the affair. In code he wrote on 13 August: "there is no way out—[the French] seek to entangle you in this war; hence you must give all the more thought to what I wrote about before [about being a mediator] and consider how we can prevail where we might expect to lose" (*Leg.*, III, p. 1294).

Upon his return to Florence, Machiavelli wrote his *Ritratto di cose di Francia* (Portrayal of French matters) (Machiavelli, *Altre opere storiche e politiche*, pp. 150–166). As part of his official functions, he set out to persuade the government that his precious infantry needed cavalry protection. He was authorized to levy several units, and he spent the better part of both November and December in the Valdichiana carrying out these orders.

Military matters pressed on Florence and Machiavelli at the beginning of 1511. In addition to organizing more cavalry units, Machiavelli was ordered on a series of missions to buttress Florentine security by checking the fortresses scattered throughout Tuscany. In May Machiavelli was sent, this time as an ambassador, on a month-long mission to Luciano Grimaldi in Monaco to discuss a navigation agreement between Florence and Monaco. Upon his return he resumed recruiting more cavalry in the Casentino, Val d'Arno, and Valdichiana in late August and early September.

Foreign policy considerations, however, recalled him to Florence. Four schismatic cardinals, at the instigation of Louis XII, determined that they would convene a general council at Pisa in order to depose Pope Julius II. Knowing that the pope would be angered by Florence's allowing such a meeting to occur in its territory (indeed, Julius placed Pisa and Florence under interdict), Machiavelli was sent to France to urge Louis XII to call the council off, or at least to delay it. Machiavelli eventually returned to Italy in early November, and after several general council meetings at Pisa, he persuaded the cardinals to continue the council in Milan, a city clearly identified with France.

Julius II, meanwhile, was lining up supporters for his side. Early in October he realigned his position by forming the Holy League with Venice and Ferdinand the Catholic, who in his turn feared Louis XII's expanding power base in Italy.

Florence sensed the inevitable in 1512. Pursuing her usual delaying tactics, she sent Francesco Guicciardini to Spain; although his orders were drafted by Soderini, Guicciardini received them personally from Machiavelli. But Machiavelli's primary duties were still in the outlying areas, recruiting for the infantry and cavalry and shoring up fortifications. On 19 February 1512 Landucci notes, with a civic pride that Machiavelli shared, "300 mounted bowmen and musketeers were levied here, all from our district. They were mustered in the Piazza [della Signoria]" (Landucci, p. 249). In March Machiavelli prepared the *Provvisione seconda per le milizie a cavallo* (The second provision for cavalry). Machiavelli's men, however, were virtually doomed after the Battle of Ravenna on 11 April. Although the French were victorious, their hold on Italian territory was endangered, especially after the Swiss joined the Holy League; eventually the French lost Milan and were driven out of Italy.

The jubilant Julius II was intransigent about making Florence rue its French alliance. In August there was a meeting in Mantua to discuss how the Italian states would be reconstituted now that the barbarians had finally been driven out. It was decided that Milan should be returned to the control of the Sforza family, that is, to Massimiliano Sforza, son of Ludovico, "Il Moro." A return of sorts was due Florence also. Giovan Vittorio Soderini, Piero's brother, represented Florence in Mantua, but it was clear that the Medici, represented by Giuliano de' Medici, had enough power behind them to be allowed to return from exile. It was also decided, especially since it was the pleasure of Julius II, that Spanish forces under Ramón de Cardona, Ferdinand the Catholic's emissary to the meeting at Mantua, should march on Tuscany with the aim of deposing Piero Soderini in Florence. Advancing from the north, he sacked Prato, about thirteen miles north of Florence, on 29 August. The menace was felt intensely by all in Florence. Machiavelli was no exception. Furthermore, he was mortified because 30 to 40 percent of those men routed at Prato were from his own hand-picked militia. Guiccciardini, never a militia partisan, says of the Florentine troops at Prato that they were "hastily levied from all the crafts and lower-class trades, very few of whom were experienced in warfare. . . . The Spaniards were astonished that such cowardice and lack of experience could flourish among unskilled men of low birth" (*Storia d'Italia*, XI, 3–4, pp. 1065, 1067–1068; this material is also in Gaeta).

This blow to Machiavelli's self-esteem was soon followed by personal defeat. On 31 August the pro-Medici party forced Piero Soderini to resign; he fled for his life to Siena. Giuliano de' Medici, who was the third son of Lorenzo the Magnificent and who was forced into exile at the court of Urbino when his brother Piero was exiled from Florence in 1494, entered Florence in triumph the next day. Soon the Medici faction rioted. Florence was obliged to institute governmental reforms vitiating the republican machinery that Soderini and his party had worked so hard to create. The new pro-Medici party moved swiftly to cashier Machiavelli as well as Biagio Buonaccorsi because of their unwavering support for Soderini. In early November Machiavelli was dismissed as Second Chancellor, relieved of his duties as secretary to the Ten, confined within Florentine territory for one year, forced to put up a bond of one thousand gold florins, and denied entrance to the Palazzo della Signoria for one year. He was permitted to break this last provision, however, because he had to account for his militia expenditures. As proof of his abiding interest in working for the Medici, it is thought that at this point he quickly wrote his *Ricordi ai palleschi* (Memorandum to Medici supporters), a rare venting of emotions on Machiavelli's part. Its vehemence against the aristocratic *ottimati* (party) and its advice that the Medici should beware of their potential for factional divisiveness may ultimately be what kept Machiavelli from active political service during the next several years. For passages from a letter Machiavelli wrote to Cardinal Giovanni de' Medici on 29 September 1512, see Appendix, Letter D. It is also believed that this was the moment when, mulling over his official papers, he wrote *"post res perditas,"* "after everything was ruined," on his personal copy of the *Discorso dell'ordinare lo stato di Firenze alle armi* (Discourse on the organization of the Florentine state for arms), which he had written in 1506.

❖ LETTER 182
Cardinal Francesco Soderini to Niccolò Machiavelli
Florence, 28 June 1510

To Our Very Dear Compare, the Notable Messer Niccolò Machiavelli,
with His Most Christian Majesty for the Eminent Florentine Republic.
At the Court.
Cardinal F. Soderini, Priest of the Basilica of the Twelve Apostles.

Notable man and very dear compare. In respect to both public and personal feelings, the decision to send you there was very pleasing to us, knowing your skill and prudence and how useful you can be in all matters. Be patient if it is not without some personal inconvenience to you.

Concerning public matters we have nothing to say, knowing you have good instruction[1] and are a wise man. We urge you, in addition to the duties you will perform for our country, to make every effort to keep that prince in good union with His Holiness the Pope. That will be of benefit not only to them but also to us and to all of Italy. We consider it necessary that they should not be divided from one another, even though disagreements sometimes may arise. You have in court as papal ambassador[2] the archbishop, a very prudent man and a most worthy one. We are certain that he will be happy to see you, so for our sake, because he is a very good friend, hold on to him, because he will be useful to you, and you will derive great benefit from him, and you will help one another for the common welfare.

We do not recommend our affairs to you, because we are certain that you consider them as your own. Giovanni Girolami[3] will be with you every day and will inform you of what is needed from day to day.

If we were in Rome we could help you in some matters. We shall not fail to do so from our country estate if it should be necessary.

In Florence, 28 June 1510.
Your compare, F. Cardinal of Volterra

❖ LETTER 183

Bartolomeo Panciatichi[1] to Niccolò Machiavelli

Lyons, 26 July 1510

To the Notable Messer *Lord* Niccolò Machiavelli, Florentine Secretary.

In Court.

Jesus, 26 July 1510.

Honored and dear Messer Niccolò. I send you my regards. I told you I had gotten your letters of the 18th and the 22nd, and that evening I immediately dispatched Targa, who was supposed to take the road via the region of Ferrara, passing by Barga to go to Florence. He is an experienced person, and I am satisfied that he must have known how to proceed properly. Afterward, as I said, came yours of the 21st, which are still here; they will leave by the first messenger. Just now your letter of the 22nd arrived with others for Florence, which I shall send off as well by the first messenger. At this very hour a soldier, that is to say, Piero Porco, has arrived from Rome, to many people's benefit; another soldier had left Rome earlier, on the 13th, who we hear from Piacenza was sent to Milan. It is believed he had letters of the pope, since he did not pick up letters of merchants. This detaining of him indicates he was bearing things of importance. This man who arrived today has brought your letter, enclosed, and Acciaiuoli's[2] letter for you, under a cover of mine from the Ten. They were opened in Piacenza and many other places, and the courier tells me that some of them that were in the packet from the Ten were kept in Piacenza. I believe it was the one in code, which, since they did not understand it, they probably became suspicious of and will send to Milan. I am surprised that they should touch letters of the Signoria; they should not be surprised if you do not give them reports. Perhaps it will be sent to you from Milan, if suspicion should not arise with our friends. In Bologna they say nothing to the couriers except at the passage of this one. It may be that they will do so in the future. I shall send these letters of yours by the best way I can. This soldier tells me orally that he saw the marquess of Mantua[3] in Bologna dining with the legate. I shall leave the commentary up to you. I am sending these by post: I think you will get better service for them than in Lombardy.

I pray you to give my regards to Giovanni Girolami and tell him I recommend to him that letter of naturalization. I send you a hundred thousand regards, thanking you for the news. I have given your regards, and I send them back to you in duplicate. Antonio Taddei took as his wife the daughter of Galeazzo Sassetti. God give you what you desire.

Bartolomeo Panciatichi, in Lyons

❖ LETTER 184

Francesco Vettori to Niccolò Machiavelli

Florence, 3 August 1510

To the Notable Niccolò Machiavelli, Florentine Secretary,
with the Most Christian King of France.

My dear *compare*. I have begged Roberto[1] to send you right back, so that at least, losing him, we may get you back again. For this reason, be so kind, once he has arrived, as to return here quickly, because Filippo[2] and I call out for you every day. Since you left, which was the feast of San Giovanni, if I have understood rightly, since I was not there, I have been continually ill and have believed I would inevitably pass into the other world. However, for the last two weeks I have recovered enough so that I feel well, but I hear about so many things at one time that they make my brain whirl, because while I was ill I was not able to hear about them day by day as others have done. First of all, that Marcantonio Colonna went with 150 cavalry and 500 infantrymen, by order of the pope, to overthrow Genoa,[3] and he got close to there, but, his hope failing, he was forced to board the fleet of the Venetians, which was sailing around in the vicinity for that very purpose, and he put some of his horses and a part of his company on it, leaving the rest willy-nilly. I considered Marcantonio, according to what many people told me, as a man of great judgment and good intelligence and very cautious in his undertakings. So I cannot figure what can have been a powerful enough cause to constrain him with so few troops to put his company and his honor, which he prized so highly, in jeopardy, along with his life, because if he fell into the hands of the French I do not believe they would have spared him. I shall let you think a bit about this, and we shall talk about it upon your return.

But let us get to the pontiff, of whom it cannot be said, since he has been in that rank, that he has governed like a madman and in what he has had to do seems to have acted very cautiously so far. Nevertheless he picks a war with the king of France, and it cannot be seen up to now that he has anyone on his side but the Venetians, half ruined and desperate, and he begins in such a way as to insult the king so that peace cannot come about very soon, because first he seizes Mons. d'Auch,[4] whom the king showed he esteemed highly, like a thief. Then he seeks with words and deeds to make Genoa rebel against him, and before sending a fleet or anything else he says in public that Genoa will revolt, which is as much as if he said to the king, "Guard it." Then, when he does not succeed the first time, he says that he wants to attempt a second time. He attacks the possessions of the duke of Ferrara[5] in Romagna, and because they are badly guarded, he seizes part of them. There remained the fortress of Lugo, which was being bombarded: perhaps 600 French cavalry issued forth from Ferrara, and at their mere cry all the pope's troops took to flight and left their artillery, and the French took back all the towns that they had already taken from Ferrara. In conclusion, I do not understand this pope.

How can it be possible that he alone with the Venetians should want to pick a war against France? Giovanni Canacci says that it seems to him that the pope has been acting like someone who is playing *flussi* or *primera*[6] and wants to throw out and indeed has done so, and that the king remains unsure of staying in, saying to himself: "If he did not have a good hand, he would not risk such high stakes." But if the king stays in, which we shall know when he begins to move boldly against Bologna,[7] then the pope will attempt to come to an agreement. I shall tell you the truth: I should like it if the king took Bologna, followed up his victory, threw the pope out of Rome, and we got out of this mess; and then come what may. It remains for us now to see whether the pope has the emperor and the king of Spain with him, as many judge. I might be wrong, but I think not: I do think that the emperor, if he had the treaties that he wanted from the pope, would turn against the king, because he has his mind set, as you know, on not stopping. But they would be such and so many that the pope would be left without any money, and he would be afraid of losing his war against the king, and if he won, of having to fear the emperor more than he now does the king. The king of Spain, without the emperor, would seem weak to him. With him he would be afraid, if he won, that he would lose not only the kingdom[8] but also Castile and Aragon, because of the claims his nephew[9] has on them.

Compare, I have acted as if I were talking with you, and I do not want to say anything about matters within, because Roberto will give you an account. Our friend is in the hands of the butcher, as he was at your departure. Nothing else. I send you my regards.

Francesco[10]
In Florence, 3 August 1510.

❖ LETTER 185
Francesco del Nero to Niccolò Machiavelli
Florence, 6 August 1510

To the Notable Niccolò Machiavelli, with His Most Christian Highness.
In the name of God, 6 August 1510.

Notable and most honored man. Yesterday I received your letter of the 25th of last month, and you inform me in it that I should notify you of Totto's confirmation. I would have done so myself if he had answered, but there are letters in the hand of the nephew of Prior Battista, who has come back overladen with certain oils that Totto sent to Ancona on the condition that the said oils be traded for bolts of cloth and sent to him there in Apulia. He does not write about the agreement, because he did not yet know anything; but since then I have talked to a wagoner who went to Lecce[1] eight days after the agreement was made and brought a proxy of mine to Totto. He has come back and says that Totto is well. But there is not a line from Totto. So now you can judge for yourself: if Totto confirms, I shall do whatever you order me to.

At the market the 200 ducats have not been confirmed, because at times I did not find Ponentino, and at other times it was a holiday. I shall do it as soon as they come out; even though Totto has no other creditor except Girolami, nevertheless, in any way possible, it will be done. My father, Piero, says that if you should happen to go to the house of Martino Martini in Lyons, where there is a son of Andrea Guidotti named Antonio, you should urge him to do well and to keep himself from ill and give his regards to the said Martinis as your brother-in-law, etc. Nothing else for this letter. I am yours,

Francesco del Nero, in Florence

❖ LETTER 186
A Friend [in the Chancellery] [1] to Niccolò Machiavelli
Florence, 17 August 1510

To the Notable Niccolò Machiavelli.

Notable man, etc. I told you three days ago what I had to; all the notices and news that there have been since are told in a small public letter. I have nothing else to tell you <except that it seems to us that Ferrara has begun to be left almost as plunder: whence that arises I do not know. If those people were to advance, I do not doubt that they would make others who are still afraid retreat. But it seems to us that the fear is shared, since an agreement is being sought. But the pope's forces are small, and yet he is feared. We shall see what ensues. The pope says he has an agreement in hand and does not want it, and he keeps on threatening.>

Our friend is well and in the favor of heaven and well-born souls. *Farewell.*

In Florence, 17 August 1510.
Your friend

❖ LETTER 187
Biagio Buonaccorsi to Niccolò Machiavelli
Florence, 22 August 1510

To His Most Honored Niccolò Machiavelli, Florentine Secretary.
In the Court of His Most Christian Majesty.

Niccolò, I wrote you a note today, under D. Marcello's [1] dictation, as you will see. If I have not written and shall not write you, do not be surprised, for all the troubles in which I find myself are making it slip my mind. As you know, my wife was ill at the time of your departure. Finally everyone has given her up for dead, and if God does not offer me his grace, you will not find her alive. I have been brought to such a pass that I desire death more than life, since I see no glimmer of hope for my well-being if I should lose her. [2] I spend little less than a florin every day; and so I shall be left abandoned, without company and without possessions. Nothing else. I send you my regards. Pray God to give you better fortune than he does me, who perhaps deserve it more than you.

In Florence, 22 August 1510.
Yours, Biagio

❖ LETTER 188
Antonio della Valle to Niccolò Machiavelli
Florence, 22 August 1510

To My Distinguished, Most Honored Chief, Niccolò Machiavelli,
Florentine Secretary and Emissary to His Most Christian Majesty.

Distinguished, most honored chief, etc. <By the public mail you are being written about the affairs of Modena and Ferrara,[1] which, because of the rapidity of the turn-around in Modena, are such as to make one doubt that the rest of it can be true. Seeing how that lord has been abandoned, everyone who might be in need of aid is frightened, and therefore it is necessary for you to talk in the style that the present times require and for us to think of everything that could happen in these present circumstances.[2]> *Farewell.*

From Florence, 22 August 1510.
Yours, Antonio della Valle,
Notary, etc.

❖ LETTER 189
Bartolomeo Panciatichi to Niccolò Machiavelli
Lyons, 24 August 1510

To Monsieur Niccolò Machiavelli, Secretary of the Signoria of Florence.
In Court.
Jesus, 24 August 1510.

My dear secretary. I send my usual regards. I got your letter of the 18th, and seeing no soldiers being sent off to Rome, or very few, I decided as you ordered to send it to ambassador Francesco Pandolfini in Milan. They must be there by now, and since then no one has left here for Italy. At this moment, while we are writing, a courier has arrived from Rome, who left there on the 12th and from Florence on the 14th; he did not bring any letters for you, as far as I know, except for one that will be with this one. It came under cover for me without signature. I hear that in Lombardy the letters of the Signoria are no longer touched as long as they are recognized, and I know this for sure by certain letters of the Signoria that came to me that, because of a lack of attention by the ones who were carrying them, who did not know enough to say that they were from the Signoria, they were opened and as soon as they were recognized by the commissioner, he did not read them but rather made all sorts of apologies and said that he had been instructed to let them pass. The others must also be treated this way. Here they are talking about Modena,[1] Carpi, and other houses having gone over to the pope: the truth about this will be learned from there. Tomorrow at lunch, which will be Sunday, the new ambassador is expected. God bring him to safety.

It is necessary for you to send us authorization to collect, pay, and change, because the merchants are more fearful than necessary, and especially of a few officers who have sticky fingers, because there is no reason to be afraid of insolence from those over there: the ones here frighten us, and I am certain that they do not take things in a strict way, nor in the way that some people interpret it. For them it is enough for money not to go from here to the Swiss,[2] since it would not go or be done for our people, so that it turns against the crown and so would be against us. By your faith, see to it that we have authorization, and if they want to except Rome from the exchange, let them do so and let them remember that if we do not collect, we shall not pay them, for I have to collect those that I have to give for the Signoria, etc. Be so kind as to do it, and as soon as you can. *Farewell.* Girolami[3] has managed to get to Florence, God be praised.

Yours, Bartolomeo Panciatichi, in Lyons

❖ LETTER 190
Giuliano della Valle to Niccolò Machiavelli
Florence, 25 August 1510

To His Very Dear Friend, the Notable Niccolò Machiavelli,
Florentine Emissary to His Most Christian Majesty.

Most esteemed emissary. Since Ser Antonio[1] is not here, I shall fill in for him with these few lines: if you want to answer Ser Antonio, you will also be answering me. I have seen your letter of the 13th, and you know that I like the profit; but I am troubled by the expense and more by the risks that are run getting into such trade in these times, which are very great, to the point that anyone who manages to keep what he has, let alone tries to make a profit, will be doing quite a bit. We see this pontiff becoming more and more eager[2] for war every day, and he has assembled a very large fleet at Civitavecchia and has hired three or four thousand infantrymen. He is convinced, according to what he says, that he must pursue the campaign. The city here, however, has become very fearful about Piombino,[3] our Maremma, Vada,[4] Leghorn, and Pisa; and our Signoria has sent all its armed cavalry into those areas of the Maremma and a great number of infantry. So they have incurred a very great deal of expense. In addition, a good number of infantrymen have been sent to Volterra, Poggio Imperiale, and Arezzo, for the reason that those who have gone out from Arezzo have retreated to

Castello, and Lord Marcantonio is now between Chiusi and Sarteano,[5] Giovan Capoccia is in Montepulciano, and they are paying money and hiring as many cavalry and infantrymen as they can get. Gianpaolo Baglioni is in Perugia, and he is carrying on discussions continually on our territory, so that our Signoria is very fearful and unhappy and has incurred very great expense, as I have said, much greater than was the case with Pisa: God will that this should not be a bad war.

From elsewhere we learn the Swiss are at Saint Bernard Pass and are planning to descend in any case. The pope is having his great galley[6] laden with wheat in Civitavecchia, along with many other ships, so that it can be seen that he wants to use the said wheat for the feeding of these Swiss. It is thought that if his fleet gets more powerful, it will go on up to Savona, or to Villefranche or Nice,[7] or to some port above Savona. Details of the Genoan fleet really have not yet been learned.

We also learn that the Venetians' troops have recaptured all of the Polesine[8]; and if the army at Legnago[9] is not very large, it will cross the Po opposite Carpi or Mirandola.[10] If two or three thousand light cavalry come with a fair number of infantry, they will come with the Rossi into the territory of Parma. They have gotten the war off their backs and their homes, and now they will take it into Lombardy, if they do not find large and strong opposition. May our Lord God take care of everything, and especially help this exalted Signoria of ours, which is in great travail. Out of haste I shall say nothing more. Your family is well, *and farewell to you.*

From Florence, 25 August 1510.
Yours, Ser *Giuliano della Valle*

❖ LETTER 191
[?] to Niccolò Machiavelli
Florence, 29 August 1510

To the Notable Niccolò Machiavelli, etc.

My very dear Niccolò. These fellows in the chancellery are not afraid of a pen, but they would be of an oar. If they have not informed you[1] of the state that all your affairs are in, it has been because no one wants to do what does not concern him. Your wife is here, and she is alive; your children are getting along, each in his own way; the end [?][2] of your house has not been seen, and there will be a meager harvest at Percussina.[3] This is where you stand now. I have sent for your nephew twice today. He has not yet come here: he must perhaps be out in the country. Tomorrow I shall make sure I see him, and I shall tell him what is necessary. The holiday and the suddenness of this mailing have made it impossible to send you the 50 ducats: I shall take charge of it myself. I think that in the first letter that is written to Lyons, what is needed will be written to you there.

<Your letters have made everyone over here yawn: people think and think again, and then nothing is done. You can see us from all the way over there, what is being done and being said. In sum, we are men, and heat melts us and cold shrinks us. In sum, it will befall us as it did those of whom Quinctius said: "Without favor, without honor, we shall be the prize of the victor."[4] This search for troops takes us into places where one cannot perhaps yet see clearly. As for me, I see it as making us take a step toward another obligation, with great ill-fortune on our part because we lack what is needed and shall perhaps have to patch it up with more cloth than the entire garment would have taken. That is what happens to people who do not have foresight. It would be good if those who were the cause of Marcantonio's departure[5] should now look after this disorder, which has arisen with many others from that abandonment. But it is a benefit for him, or to put it better, a lesser ill, because if these things go forward, we shall make a mess of everything. As for me, I think that in any case it will happen with the pope and the Church as it happened with Venice, which pushed so hard that it got in. I do not know what else to tell you.> *Farewell.*

In Florence, 29 August 1510.
Your compare[6]

<Do not talk with others about these fantasies of mine.>

❖ LETTER 192
Francesco Pandolfini to Niccolò Machiavelli
Gallarate,[1] 30 August 1510

To His Magnificence Niccolò Machiavelli,
Secretary and Emissary of the Florentine Republic to His Most Christian Majesty.
In Blois.
Jesus.

As a brother, etc. Last night I received your letter, enclosed in mail with a courier coming from Florence, which was sent to me opened so that I might read it and, after resealing it, send it on to you thereafter. I do so. You do not take as much account as is fitting <of Ferrara,> and that arises because <you are running from the Swiss. The duke[2]> seems to have <retreated inside with all his troops in Ferrara, which remains without danger> if nothing else is done, <and this movement of the Swiss prevents it from being done. The pope will get the 300 lancers from the king of Spain,> and in time this beginning will be the cause <that produces mistrust and enmity between the king of France and the king of Spain. The king wants our 300 lancers in any case, and the request> must <arise from there.>

I sent you your letters yesterday, with letters of Panciatichi,[3] under cover of the Ten, however. Nothing else occurs to me at present. If Roberto[4] should have appeared by now, I would say that I send him greetings on my part. The world is getting entangled, and the friar will append his signature, so God may give you back your belief.

In Gallarate, 30 August 1510.

When you see monsieur Robertet, give His Lordship my everlasting regards.

Francesco Pandolfini, Ambassador [5]

❖ LETTER 193
Bartolomeo Panciatichi to Niccolò Machiavelli
Lyons, 1 September 1510

To My Honored *Messer* Niccolò Machiavelli,
Emissary of the Florentine Signoria to His Most Christian Majesty.
In Court.

My dear secretary. I wrote my last letter to you by way of Giovanni Girolami. This morning I received yours of the 27th of last month, and the one for Florence to the office of the Ten will be sent. Since there is no other means, it will be done by means of the post as far as Milan, addressed to ambassador Pandolfini, from whom the present communication has just been received at this moment, with strong recommendation. Ambassador Acciaiuoli having left this morning, they are being sent to you as the instructions state. Notify us of their receipt. Before the departure of the ambassador this day, as mentioned, I reported to him what you wrote, and you will be together over there soon. God be with him everywhere, because in truth his quality deserves praise. Please God his coming may be to his benefit and that of our country, and may those neighbors of ours in Pisa be recommended to you.

I thank you for the news you gave us, and I reported right away to those of our colony about the matter of the exchanges, for which authorization has been received. This turmoil and these actions of My Lord the Pope hurt and oppress all the merchants and will cause the ruin of the Roman court. God provide what is needed. Nothing else for this letter. I send you my regards, praying God to keep you from harm.

In Lyons, 1 September 1510.

I recommend Luigi Cei [1] to your good graces; I have written to Raffaello Milanesi concerning the matter, according to instructions.

Yours, Bartolomeo Panciatichi

❖ LETTER 194
Francesco del Nero to Niccolò Machiavelli
Florence, 12 September 1510

To the Notable Niccolò Machiavelli, Most Worthy Secretary.
In Blois.
In the name of God, 12 September 1510.

Notable man. This morning there are letters from Totto, by which it seems to me that he confirms what was done by you. He has sent a contract for it to Prior Battista, with letters and instructions, all of which, since Prior Battista is in Montespertoli, I have given to Messer Giovan Pietro[1] and told him to send to the said Messer Battista, so that the deeds of confirmation can be made in time. One can see that Totto had a bit of a struggle, because he writes and says to me that, in good part, my arguments were the reason for having had it confirmed. There are no letters for you, but he says to tell you that he is in good health; he did not write to you because he knows you are not here.

Your family is all well.

Francesco del Nero, in Florence

❖ LETTER 195
Giovanni Girolami[1] to Niccolò Machiavelli
Tours, 21 September 1510

To the Notable Messer Niccolò Machiavelli.
In Lyons.

To my most honored, notable chief. I send you all my most heartfelt regards. Anyone who believes he can derive any profit whatsoever from this nation[2] must be very audacious if he thinks he understands it. They want what is theirs for themselves and what is others' in common. After many requests for your letter in passage, it was given to me by one of its consignees, who charged me two *deniers* for his trouble in writing and for his parchment. I was going to leave it; however, I took it and I still have not given him anything. If it were not for the fact that I shall have to deal with them, I would show him my ass. If I can get out of it, I shall do so; if not, I shall tell Niccolò Alamanni[3] to take care of him. When I had got it, I went to Monsieur de la Trémoïlle[4] to have it sealed, because he holds the private seal. He dropped everything and came and took care of me right away without reading or seeing what it was, and he used these precise words: "I love all the Florentines so much, and you in particular, that it will never be any trouble for me to do anything that may please you." I thanked him as much as was fitting.

With this will be both the letter of the ambassador to the Ten and Lorenzo Martelli and the letter in passage and a copy of the articles[5] given to the council by His Majesty. I have nothing else new to tell you. The conclusion will take place Monday; when I hear of it and if I judge I can notify you, I shall do so. Very, very hot buns⁶: the ambassador's neighbor is a good piece of baggage; I know Jeanne⁷ in Lyons is devoted to you, and therefore you will leave her a letter if you like for her to give me the first time I get there.

Nothing else occurs to me. I pray you, when you are in Florence, to give my regards to you know whom, and be fond of me, for I am entirely devoted to you.

In Tours, 21 September 1510.
Yours totally, Giovanni Girolami

❖ LETTER 196
Roberto Acciaiuoli to Niccolò Machiavelli
Blois, 7 October 1510

To My Very Dear Compare, the Notable Niccolò Machiavelli, Florentine Secretary. In Florence.

Notable compare. I got your last letter from Lyons and have put off answering it to await your arrival in Florence, where I think that, by grace first of God and then of Jeanne,¹ you have arrived safely, and on your arrival there you will perhaps have seen La Riccia² again. The treasurer Robertet's letter I think was paid at the first request by the man of the 500. If these were not very certain,³ I am quite certain myself that he is a good go-between to sell us every time you might find a buyer. I do not know if he will put yours into the account of the 500; I think not, in order not to spoil the number. Monseigneur de Quatrefoys is busy discovering lands and making forays; and because I have staked my reputation on that Gian di Ponte, I have dragged him here from the coast to give him a longer run. The ambassador⁴ from Mantua bought some big fish from a beautiful girl these past mornings with his own hand, in your very teeth, and he says he did it to spite you. When I see anyone selling, I approve it as well done and I go buy some there too, on the first Friday. But do not tell Lorenzo about it, because he would yell like a madman and think that I was having a fine time. You will hear how our dealings⁵ turned out on your arrival. Since Pigello came for advice, you can see how little our friend⁶ has to do, and how can he ever do anything, since he goes to someone who never makes up his mind for advice: for this thing could not be more fitting than that a man who never had any effect should take council with someone who never has any; concerning which, it seems to me that we have treated him according to his nature and ours.

I seem to see Casa and Francesco and Luigi⁷ coming to drag you from your house after your arrival and taking you to a sunny place or to Santa Maria del Fiore to consecrate you⁸ and to hear about everything over here. I remind you that the more you keep up your credit, the more they will esteem you, and so give it to them in dribs and drabs. Give them my regards from time to time, and tell my *compare* Casa he should send me his regards in this desert; if not, I shall not remember him if we go back over the mountains, and I shall have that run-down shack of his put to sack. I shall say nothing else of matters here, since you have access to the public letters. I send you my regards. *Farewell.*

From Blois. 7 October 1510.

Monsieur de Quatrefoys says for you to make good a ducat that he paid for your letter, which he made good to the grenadier.

Compare Roberto Acciaiuoli,
Ambassador

❖ LETTER 197
Roberto Acciaiuoli to Niccolò Machiavelli
Blois, 10 October 1510

To My Very Dear Compare, the Notable Niccolò Machiavelli,
Secretary of the Exalted Florentine People.
In Florence.

My very dear *compare.* I wrote you six days ago. Since then, as you see by the public letters, the favor[1] that was asked <of the king, to have a condottiere, is put off until renewal because, urged by some people here, he wants Messer Teodoro[2] to be chosen. And you, now that you are no longer afraid, do not remember what was requested of the king, namely, that we be allowed with his approval to choose a condottiere from Lombardy. He gave it to you and you leave him up in the air. So do not be surprised if you are not employed[3] for anything. You would like one who was dependent neither on France nor on the pope or Spain or the Venetians or the emperor. Send to the Sofi or the Turk for a pasha, or for Tamerlane.[4] May you get—as Monseigneur de Quatrefoys says—the plague.[5]> So I remind you, Messer Hercules, that doing and not doing cannot go together. To want advice and favor from here, and to ask for it and not accept it, do not go together. I tell you that if <you do not take someone in Lombardy, you will fall into ill favor, because I know that the king has indicated his intent to have you choose Messer Teodoro.> Let anyone you want know, and leave off these discussions, since it does not seem that anything can be done without ill favor and displeasure to everyone.[6]

Since nothing else is needed, give my regards to His Excellency the Gonfalonier and our friends. *Farewell.*

From Blois, 10 October 1510.
You recognize the hand

❖ LETTER 198
Roberto Acciaiuoli to Niccolò Machiavelli
Blois, 21 October 1510

To My Very Dear Compare, the Notable Secretary
of the Eminent Florentine Republic, Niccolò Machiavelli.
In Florence.

Notable compare. I wrote you another letter these past days, which I believe you must have received on your arrival. Since then there has occurred what you must have heard via the public letters concerning <the condottiere's contract, that the arrival of Lord Gian Giacomo[1] will give a boost to all those here who feared the prince of Melfi.[2]> You[3] have been the cause of this with all your delays. What stirs our friend,[4] if we are willing to tell the truth, is not without reason, since he was asked for an Italian condottiere, because it seems to him that you[5] are insulting him by not taking the one whom he has suggested and whom he advises you to take. Although you did not ask for one man more than another, you did ask him for an Italian. His preference not having been honored, I believe he feels he has been mocked, especially because he wrote about it to the interested persons who, having been deferred to others, are unhappy, as they feel their honor is at stake, having been requested and then rejected. I am afraid that, since they had instructed me in the letter of August 29th[6] as to what was to be sought of the king, it seemed to them as if they had been too frightened and had instructed us to make a request that afterward seemed too great to them.

I see that they were so afraid of the pope in those days that they judged they had no other recourse than to throw themselves in this direction for a quick solution. And a little while later, when their fear had gone away, they did not remember what had been instructed over here. Which was that, seeing so many dangers and threats, and seeing themselves unarmed, we should take council with the king and then we should seek to have him fix us up with an Italian condottiere who could be in our service within a month, and we should seek him out insistently. It does not say we should ask about one, but rather we should arrange for one and employ him[7]; and it insists on the fact that he should be employed within a month. These circumstances show that you wanted one of those who were in his hire and had their company ready. So he, to be helpful to you, has satisfied our friend, and now that the news is out, you do not honor his choice, and I think that you will incur bad will from both of them.

Therefore, if you should adroitly indicate this disorder and error to someone up there, as if it came from you, it would not be amiss, because I cannot and must not give them advice. I think they keep an eye on everything. *However,* I shall leave this worry to you, and I have nothing else to do but stay in the background a little. But I do not like it that we never do anything without acquiring some enemies. May God inspire you to do the right thing. Give my regards to Vettori[8] and *to the other friends* in the square.[9] *Farewell.*

> *In Blois. 21 October 1510.*
> *Roberto Acciaiuoli, Ambassador*

I had breakfast recently with Finale,[10] and he asked me about Valori.[11] If you had been there, we would have made a league for his revenge. Your loss, because I do not want to be alone in those profits.

❖ LETTER 199
The Seigneur de Quatrefoys to Niccolò Machiavelli
Blois, 22 November 1510

To My Very Dear Friend, the Notable Niccolò Machiavelli,
Secretary of the Florentine Republic.
In Florence.

My most honored Messer Niccolò. I send you my most heartfelt regards. If I have not written you since your departure, the causes have been many: with your prudence you will understand them all, discreetly, and let that suffice.

I have gone to Lorraine to conclude some business for My Most Reverend Master. I have done what I went for, and I believe that His Most Reverend Lordship will be happy with me as to that part. I have already been back fifteen days and I have heard a lot of things, and few of them have pleased me. Because I cannot do anything about them and can find no other way than patience, I go along with them and keep my ears open.

Messer Niccolò, I have long heard it said that the devil takes those who make promises and do not keep their word, and all those who fail to keep their word are tormented: I believe that it is by the great crosses they bear, and those protect them; but with those persons who, because of their weakness, can only bear a cross of straw, the wind can carry it away, and he finds himself in the mouth of the ogre. But it is indeed true that when a person has been ill for a long time, if he then begins to feel a little better, it seems to him because of the long illness he has had that this slight improvement is for him the strength of a giant, and he wishes to exert the same efforts as a body strong and free of illness does; it is not surprising if he falls ill again, and if he dies of it everyone laughs about it, etc.

Here many things are being spoken about, but since it is not my profession to think about matters of state, I shall let it drop, especially since all the important news comes from over there. Wait to have a good time until the arrival of your friends, which will certainly come, and of this you may be sure, and meanwhile see about ridding yourself of these fancies, which are really fitting for a Sienese mind.

Nothing else occurs to me. I am completely yours, whether you like it or not. I pray God to keep you from harm.

In Blois, 22 November 1510
Your servant and friend,
the Seigneur de Quatrefoys

❖ LETTER 200
Alessandro Nasi to Niccolò Machiavelli
Pisa, 30 April 1511

To My *Compare* Niccolò Machiavelli, Secretary of Our Exalted Signoria.
In Florence.

Machiavelli. I did not feel I should write to the gonfalonier during the holy days or during the Easter holidays either, because you[1] were not in Florence. I think that you have come back for the sake of the ordinary and extraordinary maneuvers.[2] Therefore I have written a good letter to the gonfalonier about that matter, and I have also written one addressed to Piero Guicciardini and to Francesco d'Antonio di Taddeo.[3] Keep your ears open and help out, then notify me how it has been taken, although nothing more can be done for me in this. If you feel like it (and I pray you concerning this), you will send me a discussion of the matters abroad, making a résumé of them all. Similarly, you will add your judgment to it, discussing the present and the future. *Nothing else comes to mind.* I send my regards to you and to God.

From Pisa, 30 April 1511, by
Alessandro Nasi, etc.

With this letter there will be one of mine to the gonfalonier and another of mine to Piero Guicciardini that is to be shared with Francesco d'Antonio di Taddeo. The bearer will be a footman of Lord Jacopo,[4] and you will have them given, especially the one for Piero Guicciardini, by other hands than your own to Piero Guicciardini. Help, and answer. Tell this bearer where Roberto Nasi lives and where Andrea Tedaldi lives and where Bernardo Corsellini lives, that is, the soul of Janus.[5]

❖ LETTER 201
Giovanni Negroni to Niccolò Machiavelli
Genoa, 12 June 1511

To the Noted Man, as an Honored Brother, Messer Niccolò Machiavelli,
Most Worthy Chancellor of the Eminent Florentine Republic.
In Florence.

My dear messer Niccolò, as an honored brother. Alessandro Salvaigo has gone to France with our illustrious governor[1] but has left a few letters addressed to you that I am sending you. *In addition,* I am certain that you must have taken good care of my business with that exalted republic and with the illustrious gonfalonier, and I shall appreciate being informed by you of what you have done and of what hope I can entertain about it, and I so pray you. Our above-mentioned governor, who has left today, told me he was surprised not to have had an answer yet to his letters and in my presence left instructions to his lieutenant that if he gets the answer, he should give me news of it so that I may know everything. *Furthermore,* he promised me when he gets to court to take proper steps with your ambassador, who will *also* write about it to Florence. Therefore be so kind as to see to it that your esteemed municipality and the gonfalonier answer the above-mentioned governor, addressing the letter here because that is the instruction. I am hoping that the business must have been taken care of, and I shall be most obligated to you in part and make myself always most ready to serve you. You will *also* be so kind as to notify me of the time when the election will take place, because it will be very helpful to me to know it.

Captain della Scala, who *also* has gone with the above-mentioned governor, left me a message saying he wishes to write you that if you want him to do anything in court for you, you should write him of it and address the letter to your ambassador, with whom he expects to feast, since he considers himself completely Florentine. I tell you so on his behalf. I shall be grateful, if you should happen to write him, for you to let him know that I have done my duty by writing you what he asked me to.

There is nothing else to say in this letter, except that I send you my regards and offer my service, while awaiting your reply. *Farewell.*

In Genoa, 12 June 1511
Yours, Giovanni Negroni,
Y[our] D[evoted] S[ervant]

❖ LETTER 202
Biagio Buonaccorsi to Niccolò Machiavelli
Florence, 27 August 1512

To His Master Niccolò Machiavelli, Florentine Secretary.
In Camp.[1]

Honored Niccolò. You know who[2] wants me to inform you to make haste there in working out some arrangement, because he does not at all like this enemy camp coming to Campi this evening to lodge there, and he is surprised at it. *Farewell.* Do what good you can so that time is not wasted in discussions.

In the palace, 27 August 1512, four o'clock.[3]
Brother Biagio[4]

❖ LETTER 203

Niccolò Machiavelli to a Noblewoman[1]

Florence, after 16 September 1512

Most Illustrious Lady. Since Your Ladyship, my Most Illustrious Lady, wishes[2] to know about these changes of ours in Tuscany, which lately occurred, I shall gladly tell you about them both to please you and because the successes of these changes have honored the friends of Your Most Illustrious Ladyship and my patrons; these two reasons cancel out all the inconveniences experienced, as Your Ladyship will understand from the way in which the material is set forth.

When it was decided at the meeting in Mantua[3] to restore the Medici in Florence, and when the viceroy[4] left to return to Modena, people in Florence greatly feared that the Spanish army would come into Tuscany. Nevertheless, since no one could be sure on this score, because matters had been handled in secret during the meeting, and since many people were unwilling to believe that the pope would permit the Spanish army to stir that region up—particularly since it was learned from letters from Rome that there was not much trust between the Spaniards and the pope—we waited with our minds irresolute, without making any other kinds of preparations until certainty about it all might come from Bologna. Since enemy troops were already only a day's march from our borders, the entire city was instantly terror-stricken by this sudden and virtually unexpected attack. And, having consulted about what should be done, we decided—since we were unable to defend the mountain passes in time—to send two thousand foot soldiers as rapidly as possible to Firenzuola, a stronghold on the border between Florence and Bologna, so that the Spaniards—in order not to leave such a large detachment behind them—would opt for besieging that town and would give us time to reinforce our troops and to oppose their attacks with more forces. We decided not to deploy these troops in the open field, because we did not deem them strong enough to stand up to the enemy, but instead to have them entrenched at Prato, a large stronghold located ten miles[5] away from Florence in the plain at the base of the mountains that come down from Mugello. We deemed it capable of withstanding their army and secure for ours, and since it was near Florence, we could come to its aid at any time if the Spaniards were ever to head over there. Once this decision was made, we moved the entire army so it would go to the designated spots. But the viceroy, whose intention it was not to attack the towns but to come to Florence in order to effect a change in the government—hoping to be able to do so easily with the aid of the [Medici] party—left Firenzuola behind him; crossing the Apennines, he came down to Barberino di Mugello, a stronghold eighteen miles[6] away from Florence.[7] Every stronghold there in that region, since all their garrisons had deserted them, accepted his orders without opposition and supplied his army with provisions as best they could. Meanwhile, a good part of our soldiers were led into Florence; the commanders of the men at arms met and sought their advice about the defense against this attack. They recommended that the troops entrench themselves not at Prato but at Florence, because they deemed themselves unable to withstand the enemy were they to be shut up in that stronghold. Although the commanders did not yet know the enemy's strength, they could believe that, since he entered this region so boldly, it was such that their army could not stand up to his. Therefore, they thought it was safer to recall them to Florence, where with the aid of the populace there were enough to defend the city and with this arrangement they could try to retain Prato by leaving a garrison of three thousand soldiers there. This decision was agreeable, especially to the gonfalonier, since he thought he was more secure and stronger against the [Medici] party when he was surrounded by more forces. Since matters were in this state, the viceroy sent to Florence his envoys, who declared to the Signoria that they did not enter this region as enemies and that they had no desire to alter the city's freedom or its constitution; they only wanted to make sure that she would withdraw from the French cause and join the League, which did not believe that while Piero Soderini was gonfalonier it could be sure of Florence or of what it was promised, since they had known he was a French supporter. Therefore, they wanted him to relinquish that position and the Florentine populace to name someone else who would be more to their liking. To this the gonfalonier replied that he had not come into that office through either fraud or force but that he had been put there by the people. Therefore, even if all the kings in the world heaped together should order him to relinquish it, he would never do so; but if the people of Florence wanted him to leave it, he would willingly—just as he willingly took it when it was granted him without any ambition on his part. As soon as the envoy departed, in order to test everyone's intention, he assembled the entire council and notified them of the proposal that had been made; he volunteered, should it please the people and should they deem his departure might bring about peace, to return home. Everyone unanimously rejected this; they all offered even to offer up their lives in his defense.[8]

In the meantime, it came about that the Spanish army had appeared before Prato and attacked it vigorously. Since they were unable to take it by storm, His Excellency began negotiating an agreement with the Florentine ambassador; he sent him to Florence with one of his own men, offering to be satisfied with a certain amount of money. As for the Medici, their case would be handed over to His Catholic Majesty, so he might request—and not force—the Florentines to accept them. When the ambassadors arrived with this proposal, reported on the weakened condition of the Spaniards, and asserted that they might die of hunger and that Prato was going to hold out, the gonfalonier and the scores of people with whom he was consulting were inspired with such great confidence that despite the advice from the wise for peace on that basis, the gonfalonier kept on postponing[9] matters, until two days later news of Prato's capture arrived and of how the Spaniards, having broken through some of the walls, began to force the defenders[10] back and to terrify them. So that, after slight resistance, they all fled and the Spaniards took possession of the city, put it to sack, and massacred the city's population in a pitiable spectacle of calamity. In order to spare Your Ladyship cause for worry in your spirit, I shall not report on the details. I shall merely say that better than four thousand died; the remainder were captured and, through various means, were obliged to pay ransom. Nor did they spare the virgins cloistered in holy sites, which were all filled with acts of rape and pillage.

This news caused the city great consternation; nevertheless, the gonfalonier, relying on some chimeras[11] of his own, did not take fright. He was intending to hold onto Florence and to reach an agreement with the Spaniards by lavishing money on them, provided that the Medici were kept out. But once his envoys[12] left and returned with the answer that it was necessary for him to accept the Medici or to expect war, everyone started to fear a sack because of the cowardice[13] our soldiers displayed at Prato. This fear began to be intensified by all the nobility who sought to change the government, so that Monday evening, 30 August, at eight o'clock at night, our ambassadors were ordered—come what may—to reach an agreement with the viceroy. And everyone's fear intensifed so much that the palace and its customary guard provided by the government's men were abandoned and left totally defenseless; the Signoria was compelled to release many citizens who, since they were thought to be suspect and friendly to the Medici, had been detained for several days in the Palazzo under a heavy guard.[14] These people, together with many other of the city's most noble citizens, who sought to recoup their prestige, took heart. Consequently, on Tuesday morning they came armed to the Palazzo, and after they seized every site in order to force the gonfalonier to depart, several citizens persuaded them to do no violence but to let him leave as agreed. And so, accompanied by these same citizens, the gonfalonier returned home; with the Signoria's consent and with a large escort, he went off to Siena when night fell.[15]

Once they heard what happened, Their Excellencies the Medici did not think that they should come to Florence until they had settled the city's affairs with the viceroy, with whom they reached an agreement after some difficulties; they entered Florence and were greeted by the entire population with very great honor.

Meanwhile, certain new governmental regulations[16] had been instituted in Florence that the viceroy did not consider provided security for either the house of the Medici or the League; he informed the Signoria that it was necessary to bring the regime back to the condition it was in during Lorenzo the Magnificent's lifetime. The noble citizens were willing to comply, but they were afraid a majority of the people would not support it; while they were debating about how to handle these matters, the legate[17] entered Florence—and a large number of soldiers, mainly Italian ones, arrived with His Lordship. On the sixteenth of this month the Signoria assembled many citizens at the Palazzo, and with them was the Magnificent Giuliano, and they were discussing governmental reform when there chanced to be an uproar heard in the Piazza, so that Ramazzotti[18] with his soldiers and some other men seized the Palazzo shouting, *"Palle, palle."* [19] The entire city was suddenly up in arms, and that name was echoing everywhere throughout the city, so that the Signoria were compelled to summon the populace to an assembly, which we call a parliament, where a law was proclaimed that reinstated [20] the Magnificent Medici in all the honors and dignities of their ancestors. The city is quite peaceful and hopes, with the help of these Medici, to live no less honored than it did in times past, when their father Lorenzo the Magnificent, of most happy memory, governed. [21]

There, Most Illustrious Lady, you have a detailed account of our events, into which I did not want to interpolate any of those matters that might offend you as being lamentable and redundant. I have expatiated on the other matters as much as the limits of a letter permit. If I have satisfied you, I shall be quite content; if not, I pray Your Most Illustrious Ladyship to forgive me. *Long and prosperously may you live.*

L E T T E R S

1513

Medici power was fully established in Florence during the winter months between 1512 and 1513. It was well on its way to being entrenched in Rome, too, because on 20 February Julius II died, and Cardinal Giovanni de' Medici was soon elected as Pope Leo X. (For these festivities, Machiavelli wrote one of his *Canti Carnascialeschi* [*Carnival Songs*], "Degli Spiriti Beati" ["On the Blessed Spirits"].) Upon his election, Leo X is said to have commented, "Let us enjoy the papacy since God has given it to us." In Florence, however, the Medici party's power did not go unchallenged. Pietro Paolo Boscoli, aided by his friend Agostino di Luca Capponi, organized an anti-Medici conspiracy. Because the former was inept enough to write down the names of those whom he considered to be opposed to the Medici (Machiavelli's among them), once the list was discovered by Medici sympathizers, Machiavelli was imprisoned, tortured, and finally freed in early March, after twenty-two days behind the high windowless walls of the *Stinche*. Two playful yet pleading tailed sonnets date from this period. These "Prison Sonnets," addressed to Giuliano de' Medici, the family's nominal representative in Florence, were designed to show off Machiavelli's wit, to suggest that he was more a literary artist than a political writer (for example, he writes that the "set of fetters" on his legs bears witness "to the way poets are treated"), and to win his release. Once he had his freedom, Machiavelli sent Giuliano another sonnet in gratitude. Because there is evidence that at this point, with his career in shambles, Machiavelli was trying to curry favor with the Medici so that they would employ him and because no solid proof has yet been adduced to link him to the plot, it is thought unlikely that he ever really was a conspirator. The desperation that he felt at the possibility of being permanently ousted from Florentine political life is voiced in his famous remark in Letter 208, "I have to talk about politics." Furthermore, as evidenced in Letter 214, he steadfastly maintained his innocence. As a result of this experience, however, he retired to his farm at Sant'Andrea in Percussina near San Casciano, about ten miles southwest of Florence. His life there is poignantly delineated in Letter 224, written to his friend Francesco Vettori, dated 10 December 1513, the most famous one he wrote.

Meanwhile, as Machiavelli's fortunes waned, those of his friend Vettori seemed to wax. On 30 December 1512 Vettori was appointed to join Matteo Strozzi and Jacopo Salviati in Rome for a two-month stint as Florence's ambassadors to Pope Julius II. Vettori faced the beginning of his duties firm in the belief that he was a redundant, and hence somewhat powerless, figure (see Letter 207). With the accession of Leo X, Vettori's assignment stretched on until May 1515. Machiavelli viewed this as an enviable position, one that might be used to secure a job with the Medici for him, though Machiavelli always thought he stood a better chance with Giuliano de' Medici, who Leo X had seen to it was made governor of Florence. Machiavelli also counted on Francesco's brother Paolo, an early Medici supporter, an adviser to Giuliano, and a person highly regarded in the Medici circle. Perhaps Machiavelli's optimism was exaggerated, because the only patronage Francesco Vettori could procure for his brother was as the registrar for tithes due Rome from the Florentine clergy.

As the fortunes of Vettori were rising, so were those of a Florence momentarily jubilant at the return of the Medici. Again, however, matters were not what they seemed. As one historian puts it, "Florence virtually ceased to be an independent entity pursuing her own separate political destiny, but found herself drawn into an extensive web of papal and ecclesiastical interests" (Bullard, *Strozzi and the Medici*, p. 73). Some commentators have blamed Vettori for not successfully achieving some sort of preferment for Machiavelli; but they have lost sight both of the city's new fiscal responsibilities to back Rome's military policies and of Francesco's heartfelt disappointment and frustration, expressed in his apology, "I am sorry to be able to offer you so little" (Letter 207).

Meanwhile, Rome became a powerful political focal point. Leo X was in the spotlight because of his attempts to consolidate the Medici's fortunes throughout Italy by juggling positions of power among three of them: his nephew, the future duke of Urbino, Lorenzo II (1492–1519); his first cousin Giulio; and his brother Giuliano. By mid-August Leo saw to it that Lorenzo became governor of Florence. Giulio de' Medici (1478–1534) had been made archbishop of Florence in May 1513 and became cardinal in September. (Giulio significantly affected Machiavelli's later career: in 1519 he became ruler of Florence and provided Machiavelli with several commissions, most notably in 1520 to write *The Florentine Histories* [1525]; finally, in 1523, he became the hapless Pope Clement VII.) Giuliano de' Medici (1479–1516), the youngest son of Lorenzo the Magnificent, is also frequently referred to as the duke of Nemours. Part of Leo's policy to balance power among the Medici necessitated his placating Giuliano in May by making him a patrician of Rome and captain of the ecclesiastical military forces. Because Giuliano had been one of the Ten in Florence, many still considered him to be the city's representative in Rome. Nevertheless, his portrait as duke of Nemours, one of the interlocuters in Castiglione's *Courtier*, is a true one: he was temperamentally better suited to being a private citizen remote from the flurry of political intrigue.

With the locus of power now in central Italy, because of this consolidation of Medici power, Louis XII of France was obliged to rethink his Italian foreign policy. Despite his record of duplicity with Venice, he began to court that republic. He signed an agreement at Blois in late March and inveigled Venice to withdraw from the Holy League. Meanwhile, he arranged a one-year truce with Ferdinand the Catholic: the Treaty of Orthez, which was signed on 1 April. Although it ostensibly concerned non-Italian matters (compare Vettori's *di là da' monti*, "beyond the mountains," in Letter 216), Italians were deeply interested in its implications for them. Ferdinand neglected, however, to keep Henry VIII of England apprised of his conciliatory plans, and Henry, expecting his participation, was preparing an attack on France. On 5 April a treaty in the name of Ferdinand the Catholic, Henry VIII, Leo X, and Maximilian I was drawn up at Mechlin (Mechelen, in north Belgium). But Ferdinand, much to the bemusement of Machiavelli and Vettori, decided to stick by the terms of the earlier Treaty of Orthez with Louis XII. His choice yields passages of extended, closely reasoned, and acute political analysis, especially on Machiavelli's part. Indeed, the intense excitement palpable in Machiavelli's letters to Vettori foreshadows his analysis of examples from the recent past in *The Prince*.

The Treaty of Orthez left France in a dilemma and Henry VIII out in the cold. Nevertheless, Henry continued his preparations for a French attack, this time with the lukewarm support of Maximilian I. Ferdinand, of course, was freed to strengthen his control of Navarre, which had been annexed during the summer of 1512. Furthermore, Louis XII thought he saw a power vacuum in northern Italy and cajoled Venice into joining his attack on Milan, led by Gian Giacomo Trivulzio and Louis de La Trémoïlle (known as the *Chevalier sans reproche*). With the defeat of these forces at the Battle of Novara on 6 June, Louis was obliged to forgo his designs on Italy. It was not long before he met with another defeat. Henry VIII and Maximilian I entered northeastern France in early July and won both the siege of Thérouanne in Picardy in July and the "Battle of the Spurs," so designated because of the French army's hasty flight, at Guinegate (today known as Enguinegatie in the Pas-de-Calais) on 16 August.

❖ LETTER 204
Niccolò Machiavelli to Francesco[1] Vettori
Florence, 13 March 1513

To the Magnificent Francesco Vettori,
Most Worthy Florentine Ambassador to the Supreme Pontiff.
In Rome.

Magnificent One. As you must have learned from Paolo Vettori, I got out of prison, amid this city's universal rejoicing,[2] despite the fact that I had hoped for it because of action by Paolo and you—for which I thank you. I shall not repeat the long story of my disgrace to you but shall merely say that Fate has done everything to cause me this abuse. Anyhow, thanks be to God, it is over. I hope not to come up against it any more both because I shall be more wary and because the times will be more liberal and not so suspicious.[3]

You are aware of the condition in which our friend Messer Totto[4] exists. I implore both your favor and Paolo's together for him. He seeks, he and I, only this one thing: that he may be appointed and enrolled among the pope's household and be certified for it—we ask for your help in these matters.

If it is possible, remind Our Lordship about me in order that, if it should be possible, either he or his family might start engaging my services in some way or other, because I believe I shall do honor to you and do something useful for me.

13 March 1512[3].

Yours,

Niccolò Machiavelli, in Florence[5]

❖ LETTER 205
Francesco Vettori to Niccolò Machiavelli
Rome, 15 March 1513

To My Dear *Compare* Niccolò di Messer Bernardo Machiavelli.
In Florence.

My dear *compare.* For the past eight months I have had the greatest sorrows that I have ever had in all my life, including some you do not know about. Nevertheless, I have never had a greater one than when I heard that you had been imprisoned, because I immediately judged that, without fault or cause, you would be subjected to torture,[1] as indeed it turned out. It grieves me not to have been able to help you, as the faith you had in me deserved, and it gave me great sadness when your Totto sent me the messenger and I could not help you in any way. I did so when the pope was elected,[2] and I asked him for no other favor than your liberation, which, I am happy, had already taken place. Now, my *compare,* what I have to tell in this letter is that you should take heart against this persecution, as you have done with the others that have been done to you, and you should hope that, now that things have settled down and the fortunes of those people[3] exceed any fancy and discussion, you will not always have to stay down. Now that you are freed from all confinement, if I should have to stay here, which I do not know, I want you to come and stay here at your pleasure for as long as you want. I shall write you when my mind is more settled whether I have to stay here, which I doubt, because I believe there will be men of a different standing[4] than I who will want to stay here, and I shall make the best of everything.

Our Filippo[5] got here today, taking post-stages from Poggibonsi[6] in four days, exhausted, worn out, broke, and this evening it was not possible for him to go and see the pope, because Messer Giovanni Cavalcanti[7] did not let him. I have nothing else to say except to send you my regards.

Francesco
In Rome, 15 March 1512[3].

❖ LETTER 206
Niccolò Machiavelli to Francesco Vettori
Florence, 18 March 1513

To the Magnificent Francesco Vettori,
Florentine Ambassador to the Supreme Pontiff.
In Rome.

Magnificent ambassador. Your very kind letter has made me forget all my past suffering; and although I was more than certain of the love that you bear me, this letter has been most welcome to me. I thank you as much as I can and pray God that to your advantage and benefit He will give me the power to be able to give you satisfaction for it, because I can say that all that is left to me of my life I owe to the Magnificent Giuliano and your Paolo.[1] As for turning my face toward *Fortuna,* I should like you to get this pleasure from these troubles of mine, that I have borne them so straightforwardly that I am proud of myself for it and consider myself more of a man than I believed I was. And if these new masters of ours see fit not to leave me lying on the ground,[2] I shall be happy and believe that I shall act in such a way that they too will have reason to be proud of me. And if they should not, I shall get on as I did when I came here[3]: I was born in poverty and at an early age learned how to scrimp rather than to thrive.[4] If you stay there, I shall come and spend some time with you when you tell me that it is all right. And, to cut this short, I send you and Paolo my regards; I am not writing to him because I do not know what else to say.

I related the passage about Filippo[5] to some of our mutual friends, who were delighted that he had arrived there safely. They were quite sorry that Messer Giovanni Cavalcanti has such little respect or regard for them. While they were thinking about how this situation might have developed, they real-

ized that little Brancacci[6] told Messer Giovanni that Filippo's brother had instructed him to recommend Ser Antonio's son Giovanni[7] to His Holiness the
Pope and that this was the reason Giovanni Cavalcanti did not wish to give
him an audience. They attach a great deal of blame to Giuliano Brancacci for
prompting this scandal, if it turns out to be false; and if it turns out to be true,
they blame Filippo for taking desperate measures—so warn him to be more
careful next time. Tell Filippo that Niccolò degli Agli is slandering him all
over Florence, for what reason I know not; but he accuses him openly and
unrelentingly—to such an extent that there is not a man who is not surprised
by it. So, if he knows the reason for this hostility, warn Filippo to remedy it in
some way. Just yesterday Niccolò came to me with a list in hand, and every
gossip-monger[8] in Florence checked off on it; he told me that, in order to get
revenge on Filippo, he went around signing them up to malign him. I wanted
to inform you about this matter so that you can warn him about it; send him
my regards.

The whole gang sends you regards, beginning with Tommaso del Bene and
going as far as our Donato.[9] Every day we visit the house of some girl to recover our vigor; just yesterday[10] we were at Sandra di Pero's house to watch
the procession pass. And so we go on marking time during these general festivities, enjoying the remainder of this life, so that it seems to me I am dream-
ing it all up. *Farewell.*

Florence, 18 March 1512[3].
Niccolò Machiavelli

❖ LETTER 207
Francesco Vettori to Niccolò Machiavelli
Rome, 30 March 1513

My dear *compare.* Since this new pontiff was elected, I have received two
letters from you and two from your Messer Totto, who requests of me what
you had sought from me in your first letter: for me to manage to get him enrolled in the household of the pope. I had obtained that from His Holiness; but
because of the great number of those he[1] had taken, neither he nor innumerable others were approved by the *Camera,* because the clerics say that the offices are being wasted, since such a great number of household members who
can all dispatch benefices without payment makes it so that the offices are not
profitable.[2] Nonetheless, once this turmoil that arises in the beginning is past, I
shall try once again and I shall make every effort that I can. I am certain, *compare,* that you will say in your own heart that I struggled a good deal, finding
myself by chance the ambassador at the election of a Florentine pope, and did
not have enough warmth to get someone enrolled in the household. I shall
confess that that is true and comes in great part from me, since I do not know
how to be bold enough to be of use to myself and to others.[3] This ambas-
sadorship of mine began having bad luck at the gates, where you were present.

On the road I constantly felt apprehension that Pope Julius would die and I would be taken prisoner and robbed. I arrived here and found him in such a state that I could not speak to him, because he did not want to. He died; Pope Leo was elected, something that should have been honorable and useful for the city [4] publicly and individually for its citizens. Nonetheless, it will certainly be an expense to me, and I believe that just when I am about to make it back, another man will take my place. Thus I shall have invested honor in it and 500 ducats of capital. Nonetheless, as you know, I adapt to everything and I shall always strive to do good to every man, and then come what may. Even though I did not learn to know want as a youth,[5] as an old man I shall adjust to whatever I can. I am one of those who, although I urged you to turn your face toward *Fortuna,* nonetheless am better able to convince others than myself, because in prosperous Fortune I do not become proud, but in adverse fortune I lose heart and I am fearful about everything; and if I were to talk to you I think I could make you able to fear with good reason. It seems to me that from this papacy the city has derived this: that it should remain secure within and without. So I have gotten this fancy into my head, and as I have told you on some other occasions, I do not want to go on any longer discussing things rationally, because I have often found myself to be wrong, and now more than ever in the election of this pope of ours, in which I went along discussing who ought to get it, cardinal by cardinal, and I found so few of them, some on one account and some on another, that it seemed impossible to me to think who could succeed. In addition to this, it seemed to me that the king of Spain, young, poor, with many relatives, with a state in his hands that could make him formidable, would want a weaker pope; the same for the emperor. I considered that Julius had been elected for money, even though he was abject and with few relations; that Siena [6] had not wanted it at that time, because of old age; nor Naples,[7] although he was old, because he had too many relatives. Nonetheless, all these discussions and reasons of mine missed the mark. He was elected pope with the consensus of all the cardinals; with the approval of the imperial, Spanish, and Venetian ambassadors, who were seen to rejoice heartily; with general rejoicing of the entire Roman populace; with the union and good favor of the Orsinis and Colonnas; and four days after the election, to make his happiness more complete, he gets his hands on Santa Croce and San Severino, the heads of the council [8]; and in addition to this it has been learned from a letter from Roberto [9] that His Most Christian Majesty [10] was greatly pleased by it and said that since this good pope had been elected, he would do his best to quiet things down, and he would not fail in anything for his part. And so, my Niccolò, you see what good luck does, and he who lacks it, as I do, had better undertake few things or, to put it better, none. I have made a habit of following that rule; but sometimes I am forced by others to do what I would avoid on my own. I hope it will not be long before I see you, and I am thinking of spending the rest of the time that remains to me in the country, toward which I have been averse in the past; but now I have arranged to do the opposite. Wherever I am, whether in the country or in Florence or here, I shall be, as I have been, always at your disposal. I am sorry to be able to offer you so little, because I cannot and never thought I should be able to do much. I shall pay you for your horse on my return, which I believe all the time will be soon.

Give my regards to all our friends, and especially to Giovanni Machiavelli and to Donato.[11] Nothing else for this letter. I send you my regards.

Rome, 30 March 1513.
Francesco, Ambassador

❖ LETTER 208
Niccolò Machiavelli to Francesco Vettori
Florence, 9 April 1513

To the Magnificent Ambassador Francesco Vettori, with the Supreme Pontiff.
In Rome.
Magnificent Lord Ambassador:

> And I, noting his change of color,
> Said, "How shall *I* come if *thou* art afraid,
> Thou who art wont to strengthen me against doubt?"[1]

Your letter terrified me more than the rope,[2] and I regret any thought you might have that I may be angry—not on my own behalf, because I have resigned myself to desiring passionately nothing further, but[3] on your behalf. I implore you to follow the example of the others who make a place for themselves through importunity and cunning rather than intellect and judiciousness. As for that tale about Totto, to the extent that you are annoyed by it, I am too. Otherwise I am not going to bother about it: if he cannot be enrolled, let him be unscrolled.[4] Once and for all, I am telling you not to go to any trouble concerning the things I ask from you, because if I do not get them, I shall not suffer for it.

If you find that commenting upon matters bores you because you realize that they frequently turn out differently from the opinions and ideas we have, you are right—because the same thing has happened to me. All the same, if I could talk to you, I could not help but fill your head with castles in air, because Fortune has seen to it that since I do not know how to talk about either the silk or the wool trade, or profits or losses, I have to talk about politics.[5] I need either to take a vow of silence or to discuss this. If I could disentangle myself from Florentine territory,[6] I, too, would certainly go down there to see if the pope is at home; but, among so many requests for pardon, mine fell to the floor because of my negligence. I shall wait until September.

I hear that Cardinal Soderini is busying himself a lot with the pontiff.[7] I should like you to advise me whether or not you think it would be appropriate for me to write him a letter requesting a recommendation to His Holiness.

Or would it be better for you to speak on my behalf directly with the cardinal? Or if neither should be done, perhaps you could give me a brief reply to this matter.

As for the horse, your reminding me about it makes me laugh, because you shall pay me for it when I remember it—and not before.

By this time our archbishop[8] must have died; may God receive his soul and the souls of all his family. *Farewell.*

In Florence, 9 April 1513
Niccolò Machiavelli, *former* Secretary

❖ LETTER 209
Francesco Vettori to Niccolò Machiavelli
Rome, 9 April[1] 1513

To the Notable Niccolò Machiavelli.

Niccolò, dear *compare.* In eight days I have gotten two letters from you, and even though I had told you I no longer wanted to chatter or to discuss rationally, nonetheless these new events had made me change my mind; but I cannot do it at this time because I am in a hurry, since this soldier wants to leave; so I shall save it for another letter. I shall tell you only this: that if the truce[2] between France and Spain is real, it must of necessity be concluded that His Catholic Majesty[3] is not the man he is reputed to be, in shrewdness and prudence, or else that there is a snake in the grass and that what has been said many times has gotten into these princes' brains, and that the king of Spain, the king of France, and the emperor are planning to divide this poor Italy up among themselves. If someone who closely analyzes things said that this could not be, I should not believe him, and I should rather align myself with someone who measures it more broadly, because in our days that measurement has been seen several times to turn out right.

If I were not thinking of your problems, I should not be thinking of my own, and I want you to be convinced of this: that if ever I should see your honor and profit increased, I should take no less account of it than if such benefit came to myself. I have ruminated at length whether it is good to speak of you to the cardinal of Volterra, and I have decided not to, because, although he is very busy and is in good credit with the pope as far as what can be seen outwardly, he still has many Florentines opposed to him, and if he put you forward, I do not think it would be suitable. And also I do not know whether he would do it willingly, because you know how cautiously he proceeds. In addition to this, I do not know whether I should be a suitable channel between you and him, because he has given me some show of affection, but not as I should have expected; and he seems to me to have gained ill favor with one party from this defense of Piero Soderini and little gratitude from the other one. Nonetheless, it is enough for me to have satisfied the city and the friendship I had with him, as well as myself.

If I am going to stay here, Paolo will be among the Eight[4]: you will be able to get permission to come here, and we shall see if we can swing it so that we manage to make something of it for ourselves; if we do not, we shall not fail to get a girl whom I have near my house and spend some time with her. That seems to me the way that we ought to choose, and we shall be certain about that very soon.

Francesco Vettori, Ambassador in Rome

9 April 1513.

❖ LETTER 210

Niccolò Machiavelli to Francesco Vettori

Florence, 16 April 1513

To the Magnificent Francesco Vettori, His Patron and Benefactor,
the Florentine Ambassador to the Supreme Pontiff.
In Rome.

Magnificent Ambassador. Last Saturday I wrote you, and even though I have nothing to tell you or write you about, I did not want this Saturday to go by without writing you.

The gang, which you know all about, seems to be in confusion, for there is no dovecote around to contain us—all their minds have been in a ferment. Tommaso[1] has become eccentric, churlish, irritating, shabby—to such a degree that, when you return, he will seem to you to be a different person. I want to tell you what happened to me. Last week he bought seven pounds of veal and sent it to Marione's house. Then, because he thought he had spent too much, he tried to find someone to share the expense with him, so he went around begging people to eat with him. So, inspired by pity, I went along with two others whom I had scrounged up for him. We had dinner, and when the bill arrived it came to fourteen *soldi* each. I had only ten on me, so I owed him four; every day he demands them from me—just last night he dunned me for them on the Ponte Vecchio. I do not know whether you may think he is wrong about this, but, compared with the other things he does, it is a trifle.

Girolamo del Guanto's wife died, and for three or four days he was like a fish out of water.[2] Then he revived and is anxious to take another wife; every night we have been lounging around on the Capponi's bench[3] discussing this marriage. Once again "Count Orlando" is smitten, with a young boy from Ragusa, and we no longer see hide nor hair of him. Donato has opened another shop at the sign of the horn[4] where they sell doves, and like a dolt he goes all day long from the old one to the new one; at one time he goes with Vincenzio, at another time it is with Piero, sometimes with one of his shop boys, sometimes with another—nevertheless, I have never seen him have a falling out with Riccio.[5] I do not know the cause of it all—some people think that it has more to do with him, others think that it has to do with fate; for my part, I am completely baffled by it. Filippo di Bastiano has returned to Florence and complains bitterly of Brancaccino,[6] but in general terms; so far, he has not come up with any details. If he goes to Rome, I shall let you know so that you can caution him.

> Therefore, if at times I laugh or sing,
> I do so because I have no other way than this
> To give vent to my bitter tears.[7]

If it is true that Jacopo Salviati and Matteo Strozzi[8] have been sacked, then you will stay there in your official capacity; and since Jacopo is not staying there, I do not see anyone—given those who will be coming—who can stay there and send *you* away. Thus I take it for granted that you will continue in Rome for as long as you want. His Magnificence Giuliano will be coming there, and you will find him naturally disposed to please me[9]; the same is true of the cardinal of Volterra.[10] So if my case is managed with some skill, I cannot believe that I shall not succeed in being put to some use, if not on Florence's behalf, at least on behalf of Rome and the papacy; in which case I should be less mistrusted. And since I know that you are staying there and that you are in favor of my coming—for otherwise I am not going to move from here—and if I can come without risking any prejudice here, I shall proceed there to Rome. I cannot believe that if only His Holiness began to put me to work, I would not help myself and bring utility and honor to all my friends.

I write you this not because I want things so much or because I want you, for my sake, to get entangled in any blame, hardship, expense, or anxiety about anything but so that you should be aware of what my inclination is; if you can help me, you should know that my entire welfare resides in you and your family, to which I am grateful for whatever remains to me.

16 April 1513
Niccolò Machiavelli, in Florence.

❖ LETTER 211
Francesco Vettori to Niccolò Machiavelli
Rome, 21 April 1513

To the Notable Niccolò Machiavelli.

I woke up early this morning and immediately began to think that four florins imposed as a tax assessment on me and my brothers and four others on our Bernardo[1] were too much, especially considering how low the taxes are on greater fortunes. Examining my situation, I am perplexed in this matter. I carry on no trade of any kind, I have so little revenue that I can scarcely live on it, I have daughters who need dowries, I have never derived any gain from my activity for the state, I show no luxury either in my garments or in other visible things but rather a certain shabbiness; it cannot be said, either, that I am so miserly that in this way I might accumulate money, because if I have to pay someone, I do not want him to have to ask me for payment; if I buy anything, I always pay more for it than others do. It might be said to me that they have assessed it upon the opinion that Bernardo is rich and without children and upon the business they see my brothers carry on. This certainly should not have harmed me, and indeed if they had that fancy, they should have divided up the taxes. I never offended anyone either in deeds or in words, either in public or in private, and I had so much confidence in these officials especially that I would have relied on their judgment in everything. I draw the following conclusion: that Paolo's having, with good results, gone to the trouble of getting the gonfalonier out of the palace and mine of saving him as far as I could are doing us a good deal of harm, because all those who were friends of that government[2] hold it against Paolo, for which they are wrong if they really knew the truth; all those who are friends of this one[3] hold it against me, since they think that if Piero Soderini had died he would not be able to give them any trouble. Thinking this way, it was evident to me, in both taxation and other matters, that I would be badly treated, so that I stopped worrying about this. And I started thinking about these great entanglements and treaties and truces that have occurred recently, and I could not get them straight in my brain, on the basis of the following two ideas: the first, that the Venetians should have agreed with the king of France to be ready by the middle of May with 1,000 lancers and 1,200 light cavalry and ten thousand infantrymen, and for the king to be going to send to Italy at that time 1,000 lancers and ten thousand infantrymen, to make war on the state of Milan, which once it is taken would belong to France, and the Venetians would have Brescia, Crema, and Bergamo, and, in exchange for Cremona, Mantua; the other one, that a truce[4] should have been declared between the kings of France and Spain for a year only on the other side of the mountains, with a promise made by Spain that the king of England and the emperor will ratify it within two months.

If the convention and the truce hold firm and true, I should like it if we could walk together from the Ponte Vecchio through Via de' Bardi as far as Cestello[5] and discuss what the king of Spain's fancy might be, because I see almost everything concluded for the benefit of the king of France; the same for the Venetians as well, since they are reduced to the condition they are in; and although it could be said that the king of France will either win or lose in this campaign against the duchy of Milan, if he loses, the Venetians will lose with him; if he wins, he will remain very powerful, and, not having kept his promise to them in the past, he will do the same this time. To which it is answered that if he loses, they will withdraw to defend Padua and Treviso as they are accustomed, and they presume it will turn out well for them. If he wins, he will perhaps keep his promise to them; and if he does not keep it, in the same way they will defend Padua and Treviso against him. In addition to this, they are exhausting themselves and, as we say, dying of consumption. He who is used to being great has a difficult time remaining lowly, and he puts himself in danger in order to return to his rank. In this way it will be an easy thing for them to regain both their lost states and their honor and renown in just a few days. If they remain in this fever, as they have already been doing for the past three years,[6] they are going to their death. If the king is so powerful as not to care whether he keeps his promise to them, it is to be presumed that they will go down accompanied by the rest of Italy, and this common affliction will make theirs more bearable.

But let us get to the king of Spain, who has taken the entire Kingdom of Navarre, defended Pamplona,[7] and shown himself rather to be superior to the French than the contrary; made war against them in Italy[8] outside of the confederation, for fear, as he said, that the king of France would occupy the Kingdom of Naples and after that all of Italy. And, nevertheless, he then makes a treaty that brings nothing but ill to him, and yet he is considered an expert and shrewd man. Since we do not really know because of the infrequent letters and uncertain reports that come to us whether he is weak or strong at present, it can be said that if he is strong, he is not acting rationally to let his enemy grow strong when he has reduced him to the point where he can dictate his own conditions; if he is weak, he cannot carry on war, and if the king of England and the emperor do not uphold him, he ought to have agreed with him in everything and given him the state of Milan, which, because of the army he has in that place, can be said to be in his hands; and the king of France would have received it from him as a favor, and it was not necessary for him to make a treaty with the Venetians, nor was he obliged to send an army into Lombardy to frighten the rest of Italy, and he did not have to go to such expense if he promised not to go any farther. But this way he[9] brings an army into Italy, he takes the state by force, he becomes insolent by his victory, he has no obligation to him, he remembers the insults, he has not made him any promises, he will end the truce, and he will be able to offend him with reason, avenge himself, deprive him of the Kingdom of Naples, and afterward of that of Castile.[10]

Some will say: in this war the king of Spain has acquired the Kingdom of Navarre, something that he greatly desired and that protects all of Spain for him; and whereas before he was always afraid that the French, with that alliance,[11] would easily jump on him, now the French must fear that he can attack France at his will. Considering that he[12] is not powerful enough to bear the expenses of one army in France and another in Italy, he wanted to free himself with this truce from war at home, and everything that he had to spend in two places he will spend in one, and so his army in Italy will be strong. In addition to this, the duke of Milan, the Swiss, the pope with his allies, considering the risk they run if the king of France is victorious in Lombardy, will all help his army with both money and troops, so that the king of France will be left with shame, and he will meanwhile have consolidated the Kingdom of Navarre, and then he will come to some compromise.

If His Catholic Majesty was thinking in this fashion, I confess to you that I would not judge him to be as prudent as I have considered him up to now, because he can very well have learned by the experience of last year [13] that his army is not able to do battle with the French, especially if they have hired a quantity of German soldiers, as they have. He can also know that the state of Milan has been overrun, laid waste, burned, and pillaged by both the Swiss and his army. He can presume that the men are very unhappy there and are anxious for a change. He can believe that in that state there is very little money for the above-mentioned reasons, and what little there is the duke [14] cannot have because he is young and still new and weak in his position. The Swiss will not move if they do not get money. The pope and others in league with him, learning of this truce and not knowing for what cause it was made, will remain undecided and will have little faith in His Majesty, and will rather seek a treaty with the king of France. The Venetians will attack that state from their side; the good strongholds are held by the king of France; Genoa is discontented; and so it can be judged that when the king of France turns his face toward Italy, immediately at the report the Spanish army is going to leave, and all the cities of Lombardy are going to revolt, and the new duke is going to take flight. Nor can he count on the emperor's holding off the Venetians, because he has given such evident signs of himself that not only the king of Spain, considered so wise, but any man of common sense ought to be certain as to what His Majesty can do. Therefore, my *compare,* there must be something else beneath this that is not understood. I stayed in bed for two hours longer than usual, to examine what it might be, and I could not come to any firm conclusion. I got up and wrote so that when you find it convenient you may tell me what you think was the fancy of the king of Spain in this truce. I shall agree with your judgment because, to tell you the truth without flattery,[15] I have found it more sound in these matters than that of any other man that I have spoken with. I send you my regards.

> *Francesco Vettori, Ambassador in Rome*
> *21 April 1513.*

[*P.S.]*[16] I have not copied this letter in order to save trouble; I know you read so well that you will understand it.

❖ LETTER 212
Niccolò Machiavelli to Francesco Vettori [1]
Florence, 29 April 1513

Magnificent Ambassador, whom I honor greatly, etc. According to your letter of the 21st,[2] you would like to know what I think has prompted Spain to make this truce with France, since it seems to you [3] to contain nothing in any way for Spain. So, on the one hand, considering that the king is wise and, on the other hand, since it seems to you that he has made a mistake, you are compelled to think that beneath it all lies some major condition that, for the moment, neither you nor anyone else understands. Surely your commentary could not be more detailed or more judicious; I think nothing more can be said on this topic. Still, to give a sign of life and to pay you heed, I shall tell you what comes to mind. It seems to me that your hesitation is primarily based on the question of [4] the king of Spain's common sense. My response is that it is undeniable that this king is wise; nevertheless, he has seemed to me to be more cunning and fortunate than wise.[5] I do not want to go over his other deeds, but I shall go [6] into this campaign that he has lately undertaken against France in Italy, before the king of England would reveal his intentions.[7] I once thought, and still do, that despite the fact that it achieved the opposite result, in this venture the king of Spain unnecessarily endangered all his territories—always a reckless course of action for any man.[8] I use the word "unnecessarily" because, thanks to indications during the previous year,[9] after all the wrongs the pope [10] had done to France (attacking his allies and seeking to get Genoa to revolt against him) and thus after all the provocations the king of Spain himself had given France (by sending his troops along with those of the Church to the detriment of France's dependents), Spain had nevertheless realized—once France was victorious (having chased the pope out and stripped him of his entire army) and was capable of hounding the pope out of Rome and Spain out of Naples—that France did not wish to do anything to him and turned his attention to the treaty.[11] Hence, Spain had nothing to fear from France. And there can be [12] no wisdom in the reason that people might allege for him, that he did it to secure his hold on the kingdom [of Naples], since France had not turned his attention there because he was exhausted and riddled with doubts. France was always going to have these doubts because the pope was always going to be against Naples reverting to France, and France was always going to be hesitant with the pope and afraid of the other powers uniting—which was always going to keep him in check.[13]

If anyone were to say that Spain feared that if he did not join the pope in declaring war on France, then the pope, out of anger, might join France in declaring war on him, since the pope was as irascible and demonic as he was—and so was obliged to make such a decision—I would counter [14]: if at that point he had been able to reach an accord with either one, France would have always preferred to reach an accord with Spain rather than with the pope. This was so both because victory was more certain, since France would not have had to resort to arms, and because at that point France thought the pope—not Spain—had wronged him to the utmost degree.[15] In order to be revenged for this wrong and to satisfy the Church with a council, he could always have deserted the pope. So it seems to me that at that point Spain could have been either the mediator of a stable peace or the architect of a sound accord for himself. Nevertheless, he rejected all those alternatives and chose war, even though he might fear that in one decisive battle his entire territory might go, as he feared when he lost at Ravenna; immediately after the news of that defeat, he ordered Gonsalvo [16] to be sent to Naples, since the kingdom [of Naples] was all but lost and the government of Castile was tottering under him. He should never have thought that the Swiss might avenge him, secure his safety, and restore his lost prestige to him—as it turned out. So if you reflect on all this [17] and on how these matters were handled, you will realize that the king of Spain is a man of cunning and good fortune rather than of wisdom and common sense. Whenever it is clear that a great man has committed such a mistake, it is to be assumed that he will commit a thousand.[18] And I shall never believe that behind this decision that he has made there lurks anything unseen because I do not think the moon is made of green cheese [19] and in these matters I do not want to be prompted by any authority but reason. Hence I conclude [20] that the king of Spain may have made a mistake, however true your commentary may be, and that he may have understood matters badly and brought them to a worse conclusion.

But let us set aside this idea, see him as a wise man, and discuss this decision as if a wise man made it. It seems to me that if I wanted to argue such a premise and honestly discover [21] the truth of the matter, I should need to know whether this truce was made after the pontiff's death and the succession of the new pope—or before—since it might possibly make some difference. But since I do not know, I shall assume [22] it was made before. If I should then ask you what you think the king of Spain ought to have done, given the expedients available, your reply would be what you wrote: namely, he could have done everything to make peace with France, returning Lombardy to him, thereby both obligating the king to him and taking away from him any reason for bringing armies into Italy and thus securing the situation for himself. My answer to this is that to discuss this matter properly, it needs to be observed that Spain [23] mounted his campaign against France confident of defeating him—counting [24] on the pope, the king of England, and the emperor more than he ought to have, given the outcome, because he assumed he could extract large sums of money from the pope. He believed that the emperor would mount [25] a vigorous offensive against Burgundy, and he believed that the king of England—since he was young and rich and, in all likelihood, glory-hungry—would, whenever he got under sail, enter in with all his might—to such a degree that France would be forced to accept his conditions both in Italy and at home. Not one of these events turned out for him. From the pope he received money in dribs and drabs, at the outset; more recently, not only would the pope not give him any money but he also sought to destroy him daily and carried on negotiations against him. From the emperor nothing resulted except the visit from the bishop of Gurk,[26] malicious gossip, and wrath. From England, there was nothing but debilitated troops that could not be united with his own men. Thus, had it not been for the conquest of Navarre, before France entered the war, both of those armies would have been disgraced—albeit they gained nothing but shame from it—because one never got out of [27] the forests of Fuenterrabía [28] and the other retreated to Pamplona and had a hard time defending it. Thus, the king of Spain found himself enfeebled amid his muddled allies, from whom he could expect nothing better; in fact, he could daily expect worse because each one of them was holding daily negotiations for a treaty with France. Realizing that, on the other hand, France was meeting its expenses, pursuant to the agreement with

Venice, and counting on the Swiss, Spain deemed it better to forestall the king [of France] however he could rather than continue in such great uncertainty and muddle and lay out an intolerable sum of money. For I have learned from a well-placed person[29] that someone in Spain reports that their exchequer is bare and there are no means for replenishing it and that the king's army consisted only of conscripts who, moreover, were starting to disobey him. I believe that with this truce, once pledged to its ratification, his design has been either to make his allies realize their mistake and make them keener for warfare, etc., or to remove[30] the war from his own backyard and from such great expenditures and danger[31]; for if Pamplona had yielded[32] during the spring offensive, he would lose Castile in any event.[33] As for the situation in Italy, Spain[34] might perhaps be counting on his own army more than he reasonably should, but I do not for a moment believe that he is counting on either the Swiss, the pope, or the emperor more than he should, and [I do not believe] he thinks that one thing may lead to another[35] for the emperor and the rest of the Italians. I believe that he did not make a more binding agreement with France to give him the dukedom [of Milan], etc., both[36] because he had not found France on his side and because he did not deem it a useful decision on his part. I am therefore afraid that France made such an agreement, distrusting both him and his army,[37] because he would have believed that Spain acted not in order to reach an agreement with him but rather in order to spoil France's treaties with others.[38]

As for Spain, I see no advantage to him, for the moment, in peace,[39] because in any case France, in whatever way he got into Lombardy,[40] would become influential in Italy. And if Spanish weaponry had been adequate to win it, to retain it France would have had to send in his own troops—and large numbers of them—who might arouse the same fear among the Italians and the Spanish king as might those troops arriving to win it by force. No one these days has any regard for promises or commitments. So Spain, for this reason, did not see any security in it[41] and on the other hand saw this loss, for he would make this peace with France either with his allies' assent or without it: seeking to make it with their assent, he would deem it to be impossible, since he would be unable to reconcile the pope, France, the Venetians, and the emperor.[42] Therefore, since he would be obliged to make peace counter to his allies' assent, he saw an obvious loss for himself because he would be bound to a king—whose influence he would be increasing—who, each time he had an opportunity to do so, must remember more about old wrongs than recent favors.[43] Spain would have inflamed every powerful person inside and outside Italy against himself because, having himself been the only person to instigate all of them against France and having then abandoned them, it would have been too great an outrage to them. Hence if this peace were made as you would have had it made, Spain would see the king of France's prestige emerge as certain, his allies' wrath for him emerge as certain, and France's promise emerge as doubtful; in this promise alone he would have had to trust because, having made France powerful and the others irate, he would have had to side with France. Except out of necessity, wise men never put themselves at the mercy of others.[44] Hence I conclude that he has decided that making a truce is a safer decision, because with it he proves to his allies their mistake and makes it so they cannot complain, since he gives them time to ratify it[45]; he removes the war from his own backyard; and once more he brings wrangling and turmoil into Italian affairs—where material for destruction and bones to chew on are manifest to him. As I mentioned above, he hopes that one thing leads to another. He is obliged both to believe that neither the pope, the emperor, nor the Swiss will like the prestige of Venice and France in Italy and, if they are insufficient to keep them[46] from seizing Lombardy, to deem that—with his help—they at least will be enough to keep France[47] from going any farther. Thus he believes that the pope will have to fall into his lap,[48] since he can presume that the pope will not come to terms with the Venetians or their partisans concerning the situation in Romagna. So, given this treaty, the king of Spain considers a French victory dubious; he realizes that he neither has to trust France nor needs to fear his allies' estrangement because the emperor and England will either ratify it or they will not. If they do, they will think that this treaty is going to benefit them both; if they do not, they ought to become keener on war and attack[49] France with armies greater than last year's.[50] In either case, Spain achieves his purpose. Therefore, I repeat that the aim of the king [of Spain] has been this: either to[51] compel the emperor and England to declare war in earnest or to settle affairs to his advantage, given the influence of those two, with means other than arms. He saw dangers in any other alternative—either pursuing the war or making peace[52]—and therefore he chose a middle way,[53] one that might result in either war or peace.

If you have observed His Catholic Highness's scheming and progress,[54] this truce will not surprise you in the least. As you know, this king has risen to these heights from a low and poor fortune; he has always had new states and equivocal subjects to contend with. One method for holding on to new territories and for either stabilizing equivocal minds or keeping them hanging and irresolute is to arouse great expectations of oneself, always keeping men's minds busy with trying to figure out the aim of one's decisions and one's new ventures. This king has recognized the need for this and has employed it to advantage; hence his attacks in Africa, the partition of the kingdom [of Naples],[55] and all his other various campaigns. He has not tried to foresee the outcome: for his aim is not so much this, that, or the other victory, as to win prestige among his various peoples and to keep them hanging with his multifarious activities.[56] Therefore, he always started things off ardently,[57] later giving them that end which chance places before him or which necessity teaches him; up until now no one has been able to complain about either his luck or his courage. Proof for my conviction lies in the partition he made with France of the Kingdom of Naples, about which he must have been sure that war between France and him was going to break out, a war whose outcome he was a thousand miles from divining; he could not have thought he was going to beat France in Apulia and Calabria, or on the Garigliano. But to achieve this prestige, it has sufficed for him to get started, hoping to go forward thanks either to Fortune or to artifice.[58] And always, as long as he lives, he will go from one labor to the next, without otherwise giving any thought to the outcome.[59]

All the preceding points I have written about presupposed Julius alive.[60] But if [Ferdinand] had learned of his death and the other's election,[61] I believe that he would have acted in the same way, because if he were unable to have faith in Julius because he was capricious, violent, impetuous, and stingy, he would be unable to count particularly on this one because of his wisdom. If Spain has any common sense,[62] he is not going to be prompted by any obligations incurred during [Leo's] *younger days,*[63] because then he obeyed, now he commands; then he was gambling with what belonged to others, now he is gambling with what belongs to himself; then war[64] was to his advantage, now he makes peace.[65] Spain has to believe that His Holiness the Pope does not wish, *unless compelled,* to stir matters up among the Christians with either his money or his armies; I believe that everyone will hesitate to force his hand.

I know this letter is going to seem higgledy-piggledy[66] to you, not of the consistency you might have expected. Excuse me for being alien in spirit to all these political discussions, removed from any human face and ignorant of matters going on around me, as my being restricted[67] to my farm bears witness. Thus I am obliged to discuss in the dark; I have based everything on the information you have given me. Therefore I implore you to consider me excused. Give my regards to everybody there, especially to your Paolo, if he has not yet left.

Florence, 29 April 1513
Your compare,
N. M.

❖ LETTER 213
Niccolò Machiavelli to Francesco Vettori
Florence, 20 June 1513

To the Magnificent Ambassador Francesco Vettori, with the Supreme Pontiff.

Magnificent Ambassador. Several weeks ago I wrote you in reply to a discussion of yours concerning the truce drawn up between France and Spain. Since then I have not had any letters from you, and I have not written to you because, since I heard that you were about to return, I waited to speak to you personally. But now that I hear your return has been delayed and that by chance you may remain there for several days, I have decided to pay you a return visit with this letter and to discuss with you in it all those matters we would discuss were you to be here. Even though it is necessary for me to skim the surface,[1] since I am at a remove from confidential matters and activities, nevertheless I do not believe that any thoughts that I may have about events will do any harm either to me, divulging them to you, or to you, hearing them from me.

You have seen what outcome, for the moment, France's campaign[2] in Italy has had. It has been, for the most part, contrary to everything that was believed or feared by most people; such a result can be included among the other great blessings that His Holiness the Pope and that magnificent House[3] have had. And because I believe[4] that the duty of a prudent man is constantly to consider what may harm him and to foresee problems in the distance—to aid the good and to thwart the evil in plenty of time—I have put myself in the pope's place and scrutinized in detail what I might now have to fear and what remedies I might use. Referring to the commentaries of those who, because they are better informed, can produce better ones than I can, I shall write you about these matters.

It would seem best to me, were I the pope, to rely completely on *Fortuna,* until an agreement could be drawn up providing for a total or almost complete cease-fire. And I should feel sure of neither the Spaniards, unless they had more to fear in Italy than they have now, nor the Swiss, unless they had more to fear from France and Spain; I should not feel sure of any others who might be too powerful in Italy. So, on the other hand, I should not be afraid of France as long as he stayed on the other side of the mountains or else he came back into Lombardy in agreement with me. Considering the current state of affairs, I should be as afraid of a new treaty as of a new war. As for a war that might make me go back to those apprehensions we had a few days ago, there is now no fear other than that France might win a great victory over the English.[5] As to the treaty, it could occur if France reached an agreement with England or with Spain—without me. And when I think about whether it might be easy or hard to reach an agreement with England, as well as with Spain, I am of the opinion that if a treaty with England is hard, one with Spain is both possible and reasonable; if we are not on the lookout, I am very much afraid that it might come upon someone unexpectedly, as did the truce between them. These are the reasons that influence me. I have always believed and still believe that it would please Spain—and still does—to see the king of France out of Italy, provided that he was able to hound him out of Italy with his own army and his own prestige. I have never believed, and still do not, that the victory the Swiss won over France last year[6] tasted altogether good to him. My opinion is rooted in the reasonable, because the pope and the Swiss are too powerful in Italy, and in some analyses from which I have learned that Spain still complains about the pope since he thinks the latter has given too much power to the Swiss; I believe that this might be among the reasons that caused him to make a truce with France. Now, if this first victory annoyed Spain before, the second that the Swiss won will, I believe, annoy him more because he realizes that he is alone in Italy, that the Swiss enjoy great prestige here, and that the pope is young, rich, and rightly eager for glory—and that the pope, aware of his brothers' and nephews' lack of territory,[7] is unwilling to give any less account of himself than did his predecessors. Spain, therefore, quite rightly ought to be afraid of having his possessions taken from him by the pope, because if he supports the Swiss, Spain's possessions could be taken away and because, should the pope decide to act, Spain realizes there are not many impediments to those actions. And Spain could not make a more secure arrangement than reaching an agreement with France, through which he would easily acquire Navarre and would deliver to France a territory difficult to defend because of the proximity of the Swiss; he could deprive the Swiss of their access to an easy passage into Italy; and he could deprive the pope of the opportunity to avail himself of them. Given the position France is in, such an agreement would be something the pope would not reject but rather would seek from France.

Therefore, were I the pope, and assuming this situation could happen, I should want either to thwart it or to be on top of it; it seems to me that conditions are such that it would be easy to conclude a peace treaty between France and Spain, the pope and the Venetians. I include neither the Swiss nor the emperor nor England because I think England is going to let itself be led by Spain; I do not see how the emperor can be in agreement with the Venetians or how France can come to terms with the Swiss. Therefore, I let them be and choose those for whom an agreement is more tolerable. It would seem to me that such an agreement would do a great deal for all four of them: it ought to suffice for the Venetians to possess Verona, Vicenza, Padua, and Treviso; for the king of France to possess Lombardy; for the pope to possess his own territory; for Spain to possess the Kingdom of Naples. To effect this situation would harm only an ephemeral duke of Milan, the Swiss, and the emperor, who would all be left to attack France. For him to protect himself against them, he would always have to wear his cuirass; this would make all the rest safe from him, and they could keep an eye on one another. Consequently, I see a great deal of security and ease in this agreement because there would be a fear of the Germans common to all; it would be the adhesive that would make them stick to one another, and there would be no reason for them to argue—except for the Venetians, who would have to go along with it.

But, taking it from the other side, I see no security in it because I am of the opinion—and I do not believe that I am mistaken about it—that once the king of France dies, the next one will consider a campaign in Lombardy and this will always be a reason for him to keep his weapons at hand. Otherwise, I believe Spain will play a dirty trick on the others, come what may; if the first victory for the Swiss got him a truce, this second one will get him to make peace. I value neither the negotiations he holds nor the things he says nor the promises he makes. Such a peace, were he to make it, would be extremely dangerous if it were concluded without the participation of the rest. *Farewell.*

Florence, 20 June 1513
Niccolò Machiavelli

❖ LETTER 214
Niccolò Machiavelli to Giovanni Vernacci
Florence, 26 June 1513

To Messer Giovanni di Francesco Vernacci.
In Constantinople.

My very dear Giovanni.[1] I have received several letters from you, most recently one from last April in which, among other things, you complain that you have not received any letters from me. My answer is that since your departure I have had so much trouble that it is no wonder I have not written to you. In fact, if anything, it is a miracle that I am alive, because my post was taken from me and I was about to lose my life, which God and my innocence[2] have preserved for me. I have had to endure all sorts of other evils, both prison and other kinds. But, by the grace of God, I am well and I manage to live as I can—and so I shall strive to do, until the heavens show themselves to be more kind.

You have written me several times that I should see to it that the taxes on your farm are settled. I shall tell you that for this matter, you must be here; and for what has to be done, you will not be too late because there is no deadline for doing it. Marietta and all of us are well; try to stay well so that you can succeed in a few things. Lorenzo Machiavelli[3] has a bone to pick with you. He says that you do not write him plainly because, concerning the half bolt of cloth that you have remaining on hand, you write that you have sold it on credit to I do not know whom and you do not tell him at what price; the man to whom you write that you have given it on credit is, he says, not a good risk. Consequently, I implore you to write plainly about these matters: in your explanation exaggerate with too many words rather than too few, so that he has no reason to pick a bone with you.

Greet the consul[4] on my behalf, tell him that I got his letter and that I am alive and well. I have nothing else that is worth saying. Christ keep watch over you.

26 June 1513.
Niccolò Machiavelli, in Florence

❖ LETTER 215
Francesco Vettori to Niccolò Machiavelli
Rome, 27 June 1513

To the Notable Niccolò Machiavelli.

My very dear *compare*. I have not answered a letter of yours I received about a month and a half ago because I was hoping to leave from week to week and to be able to talk with you upon my return both of that and of many other matters that I wanted to. I am still in this uncertainty, and you will know I was not fooled by what I wrote you about when this pope was first elected. I have thought about you several times, when we spoke of a friend of ours whom you urged me not to trust in and to steer clear of as much as I could, and perhaps it would have been to my advantage to have done so. Nonetheless, as you know and have experienced in yourself, it is difficult to change one's nature: it would be impossible for me to harm anyone, so come what may.

I shall stay down here as long as the pope wishes: and whenever he wishes, I shall go back more willingly. As long as Jacopo[1] did not say that he wanted to leave, not a week went by that I did not ask the pope for his leave to depart. Now that he says that he does not want to stay (nonetheless he does not leave), the way is cut off for me to ask for it any longer, so that I stay on without any activity, and Brancacci[2] and I go about doing as I did in Trent,[3] and I am only sorry that you are not here, because this good time would not be taken away from us; so let either the French or the Swiss win as they will; and if that is not enough, let the Turks come with all of Asia and all the prophecies be fulfilled at one stroke, because to tell you the truth I would like what is to be to be quickly, and in addition to what I have seen I would be glad to see farther.

But to return once again to your old letter and then to this new one, I confess that in the former you hit it right and I was wrong; because I was convinced that the king of Spain had not made such a simple truce but that there was something beneath it, and yet it was not true, as experience has shown in accordance with what you said. Therefore I liked your letter then, and I like it much more now, and I agree with it. I recognize also that you discuss things very well in this last letter, and I would agree completely with your opinion if I did not have as much respect for the Swiss as I do: they have impressed me so much in this last battle[4] that I do not know what army could oppose them. I know what you say is true, that the treaty between Spain and France will now be easier, because since the king of France has an unbelievable thirst for Lombardy and the king of Spain a very great fear of losing the kingdom [of Naples], and since it seems to them that the Swiss have become too powerful and they fear the pope's strength joined with them, there is no covenant that they will not conclude between themselves. But when you put together the pope, the king of France, the king of Spain, and the Venetians, to the Venetians rather the pope seems fearful of having to trust in the king of France and to abandon the Swiss than that they, angry with him, whom they think of as obligated to them, should throw themselves completely to the king of France; and he, not caring about his promises as do the French, would think of acquiring by means of them not only Lombardy but also all of Italy. But let us assume promises do not have to be worried about: does it not seem necessary to you to remove the duke[5] from that state? Armies are not needed for this, and as the Swiss understand that, they come down and they will defend him from everyone. I also add that even if the treaty between the kings of France and Spain comes about, I do not see the one with the king of England as so easy, and I am not convinced that the king of Spain has him so much at his disposal.[6] And the one between the emperor and the Venetians would not come about so quickly, because he is there amid those mountains, and since he is not afraid for himself, he always threatens others and is little concerned about his agreements. If you were to ask me: "What would you want the pope to do now?" I would answer you: "Just the opposite of what he is doing," because he has not stopped spending, and I would not want him to stop gathering by every means and on every side; I would want him to keep the Swiss well satisfied in fact and the others in words, because I would want to keep on as good terms and speak as good words as possible to all; if I were afraid of a treaty between the kings of France and Spain, I would strive to break it off; and finally, I would not want to take part in any treaty unless it was universal, and I do not think this would be very difficult because, given that the king of France cannot be happy without Lombardy, as I am quite sure, it could be conceded to him so he should give a pension to the Swiss, because you can imagine that once they have begun to draw tribute from that state, they will not be willing to do without getting it. They will not think that the king of France will be so great as not to observe it, even though he has promised, because they have gained so much courage and they are so confident in their strength that they think they can defeat any sort of man whatsoever and every prince, and experience of that has been seen to such an extent that I would never advise the pope to make a treaty without them.

However, my dear *compare,* we are going along quibbling among the Christians and we are leaving out the Turk, who is someone who, while these princes are discussing treaties, will do something that few now are thinking of. He has to be a man of war and a captain *par excellence:* it can be seen that he has set his sights on ruling, fortune is favorable to him, he has soldiers attached to him on duty, he has a lot of money, he has a very large territory, he has no obstacle whatever, he has an alliance with the Tartars, so that I would not be at all surprised if he should strike a great cudgel blow against this Italy of ours before a year has passed by and make these priests fall out of step; but I do not want to say any more concerning that for now.

I have hopes that we shall be able to talk together about this and many other matters before fifteen days go by; and since you and I shall have nothing to do, I think we shall [not]⁷ mind talking about it.

Francesco Vettori, Ambassador in Rome

27 June 1513.

❖ LETTER 216

Francesco Vettori to Niccolò Machiavelli

Rome, 12 July 1513

To the Notable Niccolò Machiavelli.

My dear *compare.* Although, as I have written you, it often appears to me that things do not proceed reasonably, and because of this I judge it to be superfluous to speak of them, to discuss them, and to argue about them, nonetheless someone who has grown accustomed to one way until the age of forty finds it hard to give up and to get used to other habits, to other ways of talking and thinking. Therefore, for every reason, and especially for this one, I wish I could be with you and see whether we could organize this world, and if not the world, at least this part here, which seems to me very hard to organize in fancy, so that if it came to having to do it in fact I should think it was impossible.

We must consider that each of these princes of ours has an aim, and because it is impossible for us to know their inner thoughts, we have to judge it from their words, from their actions, and some part of it we imagine. Beginning with the pope, we shall say that his aim is to maintain the respect for the Church as he found it, not to want its states to be diminished, unless what is diminished should be handed over to his own, namely, to Giuliano and Lorenzo, to whom he is thinking of giving states in any case. This judgment, that he wants to maintain the Church in its states and its preeminence, I make on the basis of the words I have heard him speak and also on the actions he has taken; because, since Julius occupied Parma and Piacenza [1] without any just title and the duke of Milan took them back when the pontificate was vacant, the pope thought at first of nothing else than getting them back. According to my judgment, he was going to his ruin, as I told him several times, and he seemed to me to think it over carefully, because since these cities were occupied when the See was vacant, there had not been any shame to him; but it would bring shame on him to take them back and then, either by force or by covenant, to have to give them back, as was likely to happen. And I told him: "Either the truce between the kings of France and Spain is limited to beyond the mountains, as we have heard, or else it is a treaty and a covenant concerning everything. If it is a covenant, it cannot be otherwise than for the king of France to regain the duchy of Milan; and if the king of Spain has granted him this without your participation, it is likely that he has also granted him Parma and Piacenza; and for this, coming to the French, you will have to give it up either by force or willingly, because the king of Spain will want it so. If the truce is limited, when the French come the Spaniards will want to defend Milan and will oppose them. In opposing them, either they will lose or they will win; if they win, they will want those cities back in any case, and they will consider themselves ill-satisfied with you, saying that when the duke was about to choke you put your foot on his throat and wanted those cities back and took away his reputation with the people. If they lose, the king will want to get them back. If you give them back willingly, it is a disgrace; if you want to defend them, you get into a war with the king of France, whom it is to be thought you will not be able to withstand."

He heard these reasons; and yet he went ahead with his plans. That he wants to give a state to his relatives is shown by the fact that the past popes,[2] Calixtus, Pius, Sixtus, Innocent, Alexander, and Julius, have done so; if any did not do so it was because they were not able to. In addition to this, it can be seen that his relatives in Florence do not think much, which is a sign that they fancy states that are solid and where they do not have to think continually of flattering men. I do not want to get into consideration of what state he intends, because in this he will change his plans according to the occasion.

After the pope we shall come to the emperor, who although he has never shown himself to have great power nonetheless has remained respected by all the princes, so that in this case I have to give my brain a ground for judging him as the others do. I shall therefore say that his fancy and his aim have been to make trouble[3] and to start one war after another, and today to have a treaty with one man and tomorrow with another; to favor the council, to take his favor away from it, so that, by some way or other he has not yet determined, he may arrive at his plan of possessing Rome and all that the Church possesses, as true and legitimate emperor. I judge this from his words, which he has spoken in my presence and also to others, and from his actions as well, for it can be seen that he has tested the king of France several times about this; from his having favored the council and then, fearing that the king of France might make a pope after his own fashion, changed his mind, drawing closer to Pope Julius. And so it seems to me that a definite judgment can be made of this aim of his.

As to what aim the king of Spain has, I believe that few can be mistaken about it: because he thinks of keeping himself at the head of Castile, he thinks of making sure that the Kingdom of Naples cannot be taken from him, and because neither of these things can be done without money he thinks of being so esteemed and feared in Italy that he can draw money from all the potentates in it, to make use of it for this aim of his.

Of the king of England, as well, I shall say that the aim that has induced him to make war on the king of France is his fear lest he become too great: and since he has already offended him once, he would like to diminish him so much that he would not have to be afraid of him at any time, and if it were possible he would like to detach Normandy from him.

The Swiss, whom I esteem above all the kings, have as their aim to be able to come into Italy as they like, for the duke of Milan to stay more or less with them, and to get a large tribute from him every year; they do not want neighbors that they have to fear, but they would rather be feared themselves by their neighbors; respect and glory move them greatly. I shall not go to any length to show the reasons that prompt me to believe that the kings of Spain and England and the Swiss have the intention I speak of above, because it is so clear a matter that it would be superfluous to speak of it.

The Venetians, Ferrara, Mantua, the Florentines, the Sienese, the Luccans, and so on have a more or less well-known aim: to hold on to what they have and to regain what they have lost; but in fact they can do very little.

Now, my *compare*, all these things being so, I should like you to organize peace terms for me with your pen. I know very well that if each of these princes wished to remain firm in what I say above, nobody but God could conclude a treaty among them. But if one should relent on one side and someone else on another, perhaps some means could be found that I am unable to decide on. That is why I ask you for your idea. And since it might be that you presume the aims of these princes differently than I do, I would appreciate your stating your opinion about it. If it should seem tiresome for you to answer all at one time, answer in two or three, for I shall always be glad to see your letters, and with them I shall pass the time; because you should realize that the greatest activity I have is just staying, because I have grown tired of reading, having, since I have been here, read all the books that quite a big bookdealer had, who lent them to me one at a time.

Normally there will be little activity here for an ambassador, because there used to be many cardinals to talk with and now it will no longer be necessary, because the pope will let you know what he wants to tell you. Aside from this, there have been so many ambassadors, and there still are, that it has fallen to me, since I am the youngest, to see what is going on; and you know that I normally avoid ceremonies as much as I can.

Francesco Vettori, Ambassador

12 July 1513.

❖ LETTER 217
Niccolò Machiavelli to Giovanni Vernacci
Florence, 4 August 1513

To Messer Giovanni di Francesco Vernacci.
In the Levant.

My very Dear Giovanni. About a month ago I wrote you[1] and told you what was going on with me; in particular, the reasons why I had not written you before then. I think you must have received it, so I shall not go over them further.

Since then, I have gotten your letter of 26 May, to which I have nothing more to say than that we all are well; Marietta gave birth to a baby girl, who died after three days. Marietta is well.

I wrote you, in addition, that Lorenzo Machiavelli[2] was unhappy with you, and especially with your reports, because he said you informed him so rarely and hesitatingly that he can obtain nothing specific from your letters. Therefore, I urge you to use a clear style with those whom you do business with so that whenever they get one of your letters they think, because your way of writing is so detailed, that you are there. As for sending you anything else, he has told me that if he does not expedite this deal completely and come out ahead, he is not willing to embark upon another one.

A certain Neri del Benino,[3] Giovanni Machiavelli's brother-in-law and someone to whom he gave some cloth, has arrived over there, so there is no reason for you to deal with anybody else. And Filippo wants to sell it to him for cash.

Try to stay healthy and pay attention to business matters because I know that if you stay healthy and do your duty, you will want for nothing. Physically I feel well, but ill in every other respect.[4] And no other hope remains for me but that God may help me, and, until now, He has not in fact abandoned me.

Remember me a thousand times to consul Giuliano Lapi and tell him I am alive. There is nothing else to say. Christ keep watch over you.

4 August 1513
Niccolò Machiavelli, in Florence.

✤ LETTER 218
Francesco Vettori to Niccolò Machiavelli
Rome, 5 August 1513

To the Notable Niccolò Machiavelli.

If I kept a copy of the letters I write, my dear *compare,* as soon as I received yours[1] I would have run to look at the copy and would have been amazed to have been so absentminded as to have failed to write the main thing I should have. I remember having clarified in my mind the aims of all these Christian princes who are raising trouble and having given the king of France the same as you and worked out the reason why, when he could have occupied all of Italy at his pleasure several times, he had not done so. What this resulted from, whether through his ill fortune, or through my lack of diligence, or through scatter-brainedness, I believe I did not write it to you. We are in agreement that his aim is to regain Lombardy and then to rest. In truth, your discussions are as organized and as prudent as they could be. The treaty you speak of would please me greatly, and I believe it could be concluded between the pope, the kings of France and Spain, and the Venetians as well. But I see a great problem with the king of England, and I cannot believe that a young, courageous, rich king would have undertaken so great an endeavor, brought so many troops to this side of the sea,[2] spent such a sum of money on infantry and ships, and then through the pope's and the king of Spain's inducement should withdraw to his shame with some tribute. I should indeed think that if ever the king of Spain let him know this to be the truth, showing him that if he did not withdraw he would have him as an enemy, then he would yield. But I do not think the king of Spain is going to do this because, since so many serious hostilities have arisen between Spain and France, His Catholic Highness will never want to detach himself completely from the king of England, because he will not trust the king of France, nor will he count on the pope's power and authority being so great as to be able to defend him from the power of the king of France, especially when you add that some fear might enter his mind that the pope was aspiring to royal power and judged he could achieve it with the favor of the king of France. Going forward with consideration of this matter, I cannot find anyone who is going to make the English withdraw—since they have the means to campaign this year, next year, and the following one—except the Swiss, and I believe they would show themselves in favor of the king of France if ever he was willing to leave Lombardy. It is not in their interest completely to destroy a kingdom of France from which they have derived so many benefits and will continue to. Even if the pope, the kings of France and Spain, and the Swiss were in agreement, the king of Spain would find himself less against the king of England, because the Swiss alone would suffice. Also, if he were in company with the Swiss, it would seem to him he was surer of the king of France and also the pope, because it would seem that the Swiss should be a moderator between them for someone who did not want to stick to his agreements. Also the Venetians, if they regained Brescia and Bergamo, would be more than satisfied. Verona would remain to the emperor, and since he would remain alone and have nowhere else to turn he would have to be satisfied. The duke of Milan would regain all his territory along with Piacenza and Parma, and so would the duke of Ferrara. And it would not be necessary to fear for the Swiss, who would have on one side the French, on the other all of Italy and any Spaniards who were there, because His Catholic Highness is obliged to keep a good number of them there always, thanks to the changeableness of the people of the kingdom [of Naples]. And what Casa[3] writes me, that it is your notion that the Swiss may join with the rest of the Germans, is not to be feared, because even if we leave out the enmity that exists between them and set aside the offenses they have done against the House of Austria, they have enough brains to recognize very well the emperor's strength and they will never consent to make him stronger; nor is it to be feared that they are going to establish colonies, because they are not numerous enough, as you know, to do so. They are satisfied with raking up booty, getting paid money, and going back home. If you said to me, "We might change emperors, and the Swiss might learn at others' expense," I would admit it to you; but the affairs of this world are quite unstable, and I would like to imagine a peace for a few years, not a long one, because it would never come about. Now you will tell me what I think, that the king of France is not going to leave Milan; to which I reply that the English are not going to let him rest, nor are the Swiss, and the king of Spain will work under cover as well, and the pope, who will make use of whatever helps him, will have no way to do anything about it. In conclusion, if His Most Christian Highness[4] were willing to leave Lombardy, I see all Italy at peace, and on the death of His Catholic Highness the kingdom [of Naples] would return to a son of King Federigo[5] and Italy would return to its original terms. Without this happening, I can find no suitable way without France and Italy suffering greatly. I am afraid that God wants to punish us poor Christians, and while our princes are all irritated against each other and no way can be seen to bring them together, that this new Turkish ruler[6] will attack us by land and by sea and make these priests give up their simpering[7] and the other men their pleasures. The sooner it happens the better, because you would not believe how hard I find it to adjust to the nauseating ways of these priests—I am not talking of the pope, who if he were not a priest would be a great prince.

I do not want to say anything else to you in this letter except to send you my regards and pray you to write me. Every slightest bit of news from you will please me. May the Lord help you.

Francesco Vettori, Ambassador in Rome
5 August 1513.

❖ LETTER 219

Niccolò Machiavelli to Francesco Vettori

S. Andrea[1] in Percussina, 10 August 1513

To the Magnificent Ambassador Francesco Vettori,
His Patron, with the Supreme Pontiff.

My lord ambassador. You do not want this poor king of France to get
Lombardy back again and I do. I suspect that your not wanting it and my
wanting it have the same basis—a natural feeling or temperament that causes
you to say "no" and me to say "yes." You justify your "no" by pointing out that
were the king to regain Lombardy, there would be more difficulty in achieving peace; to justify my "yes," I have pointed out that this is not true—furthermore, peace gotten by my method will be more secure and more stable.

Once again getting down to brass tacks, and to reply to your letter of the
fifth, I am with you concerning the king of England: it will always seem pecu-
liar that he entered France with so much display and had to withdraw; it must
be, therefore, that his withdrawal is based on some necessity. I thought that a
great enough necessity would be what Spain and the pope forced upon him. I
have thought and continue to think that should England, on the one hand,
find that the venture is difficult and, on the other, realize the willpower of
these two, it then would be easy to influence him. And if he should be disgruntled, that would seem to me to be germane, because the more the king of
France is or would come to be weak, since he stands between the hostile and
dangerous English and Swiss, the less he could think about appropriating other
people's property; in fact, he would have to think about getting others to help
him hold onto his own. In this instance the king of Spain would have
achieved his purpose, because I believe that, in addition to making himself secure within in his own territory, he thought about how his armies might continue being the cock of the walk in Italy—and in this way they could. Since
France cannot send a lot of troops into Lombardy because of England's doubts
and Germany's hostility, he must, in any case, engage the services of the Spanish armies. I do not understand why only the Swiss could force the English to
yield, because I do not believe they are able, or want, to serve France except as
mercenaries; because the Swiss are poor and the country does not border on
England, France must pay them handsomely; he can also hire lansquenets[2] and
derive the same benefit—England would be just as afraid of them. And if you
were to tell me that England can get the Swiss to attack France in Burgundy,
my response is that this measure hurts France; if they want to make England
submit, they need to find a measure that hurts England. I do not for a moment
think that Spain and the pope will send in their armed forces against them;
rather, on the one hand, I think they are going to abandon him and, on the
other, they are going to pretend their reason for attacking France was their regard for the Church. Now that the king of France has ceased attacking the
Church,[3] they are not out to attack him. I am absolutely convinced that without stronger medicine England would withdraw—especially since, as I have

said so often, he has discovered, and is discovering, that the French campaign is risky. England has to consider that if he comes to a decisive battle and he loses it, then it could mean that, just as with the king of France, he too could lose his kingdom. Were you to tell me that he will send the Germans quantities of money and have France attacked on another front, my response is the belief I have always held that, out of pride and glory, he will want to spend his money on his own army—besides, whatever he might send the emperor would be squandered and the Swiss would want too much. I further believe that trust between Spain and France can easily develop because it does Spain no good to destroy the king of France in this way; France has experienced proof of this because Spain laid down its arms right in the middle of the gravest dangers. The king of France would have all the more trust in him if through his efforts he were restored to Lombardy—new favors usually cause old injuries to be forgotten.[4] On the other hand, Spain would not have to fear an old, exhausted, sickly king[5] stuck between the English and the Germans—the one dangerous, the other hostile; he would not need to have only the pope's authority to protect him because cultivating that hostility would be sufficient. In seeking to bring about this peace through the line of argument I have been writing you about, therefore, I see no greater difficulties than through the one you have been writing me about; in fact, if there is an advantage, I see that advantage in mine. On the other hand, I see no safety in your plan, whereas some can be seen in mine—though of the type that can be had in these times.

Whoever wants to find out whether or not a peace treaty is permanent or secure must among other matters figure out what parties are disgruntled with it and what the ramifications of their discontent may be. Consequently, reflecting upon your idea about the peace, I see England, France, and the emperor as the disgruntled parties because none of them has realized his aim. The disgruntled parties in my idea about the peace are England, the Swiss, and the emperor. Your disgruntled ones can readily cause Italy's and Spain's destruction because, immediately upon the conclusion of this peace—despite France's approval and England's not having rejected it—both of these kings will alter their aim and notion; whereas France sought to enter Italy and England sought to control France, they will opt for reprisal against Italy and against Spain. Reason requires that they reach a second agreement among themselves in which they will encounter no obstacles to whatever they want to accomplish—if France is willing to come out into the open, because the next day the emperor, with England's and France's support, will leap on Castile, enter Italy at will, and make France go there again. And so, very quickly, together these three can stir up and demolish everything. Neither the Spanish and Swiss armies nor papal money is enough to stem this tide because those three would have too much money and too many soldiers. It is reasonable for Spain to realize these dangers and seek to avoid them at all costs because under your peace France has no reason to like him and every opportunity to attack him; there is no way France would be likely to let such an opportunity slip by. Hence if Spain has any eye for seeing things at a distance,[6] he will not agree to it or follow it because it would turn out to be a peace that would provoke an even greater and more dangerous war. But if a peace treaty similar to the one I wrote you about were drawn up, in which the disgruntled parties would be England, the emperor, and the Swiss, these malcontents—either together or alone—could not easily attack the other allies because France would persist as an obstacle both on this side and on the far side of the Alps. With the support of the other two, France would create such opposition that the allies would be safe; the others, realizing the problems, would not set out upon any campaign. There would be nothing any one ally had to fear from any of the others because, as I have often written you, each would have achieved his purpose and their enemies would be so powerful and dangerous that they would be kept chained together.

There is another extremely serious danger to Italy in your peace treaty: every time a weak duke is left in Milan, Lombardy will belong not to that duke but to the Swiss. Even if those three disgruntled parties in your treaty fail a thousand times to make a move, I think this proximity of the Swiss is very important and deserves more consideration than it receives. I do not believe, as you do, that the Swiss will fail to make a move because they would be afraid of France, they would have the remainder of Italy against them, and they would be satisfied with ransacking Italy and withdrawing. First of all, as I mentioned above, France will want to be avenged and, having been insulted by all of Italy, will be delighted at seeing the country ruined; he will sooner give them money under the table and ignite this fire than do otherwise. As for the rest of the Italians uniting, you make me laugh: first, there will never be any union in Italy that will do any good; even if all the leaders were united, that would be inadequate because the armies here are not worth a red cent—except for the Spaniards', and because there are so few of them, it is insufficient. Second, the tails are cut off from the heads: no sooner will that Swiss race take a step, for whatever unforeseen event may arise, than everyone will vie to become their ally.

As for their being satisfied with doing a mopping up operation and then withdrawing from Italy, I urge you not to lull yourself or to encourage others to lull themselves with such a view. I beg you to reflect upon human affairs as they should be given credence to and upon the powers of the world—and particularly of republics—how they develop: you will realize how at first men are satisfied with being able to defend themselves and with not being dominated by others; from this point they move on to attacking others physically and seeking to dominate them.[7] At first the Swiss were satisfied with defending themselves against the dukes of Austria; this defense began to make them appreciated at home. Then they were satisfied to defend themselves against Duke Charles,[8] which gave them a renown beyond their homeland. Finally, then, they were satisfied with taking their pay from other people so that they could keep their youth ready for warfare and do them honor. This process has given them more renown and, for having observed and become familiar with more and more regions and people, made them more audacious; it has also instilled in their minds an aspiring spirit and a will for soldiering on their own. And Pellegrino Lorini[9] once told me that when the Swiss came to Pisa with Beaumont, they frequently discussed the *virtù* of their military organization with him—how it was similar to the Romans' and what reason might prevent them from one day doing as the Romans had done. They bragged about having given France every one of his victories up until then, and they did not know why they might not one day fight for themselves. This opportunity has now arrived, and they have seized it; they have gone into Lombardy under the pretext of restoring the current duke. Actually, they themselves are the duke. At the first oportunity, they will make themselves the complete masters of Milan, liquidating the duke's line and every one of that government's nobility; at the next opportunity, they will overrun all of Italy, producing the same result. Hence I conclude that they will not be satisfied with ransacking Italy and withdrawing; on the contrary, we have to be prodigiously afraid of them.

I am aware that natural human shortcomings are at variance with my idea: first, wanting to live from day to day; second, not believing that what has not been can be; third, always sizing people up in the same way. For this reason there will be no one who might advise us to consider getting the Swiss out of Lombardy in order to put the French back in because they are unwilling to incur the immediate dangers that would be incurred in trying to do so, they will not believe in evils to come, and they will be unable to conceive of relying on France. *Compare,* this German river is so high that we need a huge dike to hold it back. Even if France had never been to Italy and you had not recently experienced the arrogance, greed, and extortion of the French—things that have interfered with this mutual deliberation—you would already have run to France begging him to come to Lombardy because the remedies against this flood must be taken now before the Swiss take root in this land and start savoring the sweetness of domination. And if they graft[10] themselves onto Italy, she is completely leveled because all the disgruntled parties will befriend the Swiss and erect a ladder for their prestige—and the destruction of the others. And I am afraid of them alone, not of them plus the emperor, as Casa[11] has written you, even though it would be an easy matter for them to unite. Because, just as it has pleased the emperor that they ravage Lombardy and become lords of Milan, which in no way seemed reasonable for the exact reasons you wrote to me about, so—those reasons to the contrary—the Swiss might be satisfied for him to make some progress in Italy.

My lord ambassador, it is more to gratify you that I write than because I am certain of what I am saying. So, therefore, if you want me to be able to discuss these weighty matters with you knowledgeably, I beseech you to let me know in your next letter how it is with this world, what is being done, what is being hoped for, and what is feared. If you do not, you will pick up the legacy of an ass[12]—or some similar sort of thing—à la Brancacci.[13] My regards to you.

The tenth day of August 1513.
Niccolò Machiavelli, in the country

❖ LETTER 220

Francesco Vettori to Niccolò Machiavelli

Rome, 20 August 1513

To the Notable Niccolò Machiavelli.

My dear *compare*. Although I shall always take pleasure in any subject that you write to me about, whether it may be serious or comic, nonetheless, to satisfy you, I shall begin by answering the last part of your letter, in which you request me to write to you what this place is like, what is being talked about, or what is hoped and feared. I shall tell you how matters stand at present, although if you go to San Casciano once in a while, now that you are in the country, you must hear about it there. I shall tell you again as much as I know is being talked about; I shall leave out what is hoped or feared, because I fear or hope one thing, you another, Filippo[1] another, and so I believe do the princes, and a definite judgment of this cannot be given.

We shall therefore begin with the pope, and we shall say what he is doing and talking about. His task is not to get entangled in wars but to get in their way, and to reconcile and to calm those that have arisen between the princes; and he has done this from the beginning, since his election until now. If the king of France had been willing to do in words what he has done in deeds, the pope, if nothing else, would have gone ahead with censure against anyone who wished to offend him. But the king of France has sent here for the dispatch of benefices[2]; on the other hand, he has never sought absolution or said that he is willing to renounce the Pisan Council and come over to the Lateran.[3] And so every time that the pope has tried to talk of him, all these cardinals, all these ambassadors have always cried out and said that since the king is schismatic, it is not proper for anything to be carried out in his favor and that they have taken the defense of the Church and deserve to be helped, in order to give an example whereby it may find, when necessary, people willing to defend it. The pope was not able to reply to this, and now he is doing nothing with this ambassador who is here except to urge him that this end be brought about, in order to keep these negotiations from being upset. He has also striven and continues to strive for the Venetians to make a truce with the emperor, so that arms may be laid down in Italy and the duke of Milan, being safe for now from the French and not fearing the Venetians because of the truce, could let the Spaniards return to the kingdom [of Naples]; but he has not yet succeeded in this end, and he has made no league or agreement except that, seeing the Swiss so powerful, he continues to give them twenty thousand ducats a year as Pope Julius did.

The king of Spain, after making a truce with the king of France, on the one hand was afraid that France might become strong again in Italy; on the other hand that the king of England and the Swiss might make a truce in France and, having abandoned them at his insistence, that he would not be safe from them. For these reasons he did not remove the Spaniards from Lombardy when the French army was coming, and he has always said he wants to break with the king of France because the truce is not lasting, France having been the first to break it.[4] If matters go badly for the French, it is possible that he will start some small matter in order to return to his promise, particularly with the king of England.

The king of France is faced with an army of forty thousand Englishmen who are besieging Thérouanne, and he has no way to come to its aid because he does not have all told a third of the English troops and he does not want to risk a kingdom to Fortune, so he is counting on time. On the other hand, the Swiss, on the 20th of this month, are setting off in the number of twenty thousand to attack either toward Burgundy or toward Lyons; they have a good deal of artillery and a thousand cavalry from the emperor. The king of France is discussing a treaty with them, promising the strongholds of Milan, and for now they will not listen to anything. He is counting on letting them overrun the fields and letting the towns defend themselves, since he has no troops to oppose them. The money with which they are paid comes from the emperor, who this year has gotten from the king of England, in a league[5] they made, one hundred thirty-five thousand ducats in order to defeat the king of France.

The king of England is sparing neither expense nor effort; he is at Thérouanne[6] in person, and he talks of nothing except wanting to destroy the king of France.

The Swiss have decapitated perhaps fourteen who took the part of the king of France, and perhaps thirty have fled and their houses have been burned and their property confiscated. It can be seen that as they took Italy they also want to take part of France. They have a regular tribute of sixty thousand ducats from Milan and twenty thousand from the pope.

The emperor is doing as usual, one war after the other, and one negotiation after the other. Right now he wants to retake Burgundy, and he is sending his troops against the king of France. He also wanted to capture Padua, where, as you know, the bishop of Gurk[7] and the viceroy[8] stayed for a few days to make camp. Seeing the difficulty, they did not do it and perhaps it will cost them dearly: they are leaving and they intend to stop for a while in Vicenza.[9] He is nonetheless negotiating an agreement with the king of France and with the Venetians; as I have said to you, it is his habit to make a war and to start negotiations for an agreement and friendship with his enemy.

The duke of Milan, if he has any brains at all, I think must feel like those "kings for a day" of our feast days who realize that in the evening they are going to turn back into the men they were before. However, he lets this fortune of his carry him bouncing along and he waits for what the others will do. He now thinks that the pope will give him back Parma and Piacenza. The duke of Ferrara thinks he will get Reggio back from the pope; the Florentines, Pietrasanta from the Luccans: and about these things every man labors, argues, and racks his brains. This is all I know, and if I have left anything out, let your cleverness make up for it, since I am sure that you have asked me about this not because you do not know the same thing but to see whether it matches up.

After this, *compare*, I want to answer the first part of your letter, in which you appear to fear that a natural penchant or emotion might lead either you or me astray. To which I answer you that I have no penchant at all for the side opposed to France, nor any emotion that influences me. You know that before the Council of Pisa was talked about, I always upheld the French side because I believed that Italy had more to gain from it and our city would have repose, which I have always placed above every other thing because I am a man of peace in my pleasures and my fancies, and among the other pleasures that I take, this is the greatest: to see our city well off. I love without exception all its men, its laws, its customs, its walls, its houses, its streets, its churches, and its countryside, and I can have no greater displeasure than to think that it would suffer and that those things I talk of above would go to ruin. And yet, when I saw then how badly we behaved in that matter of the council[10] and how dissatisfied the French went off, I began to fear that their victory would be our ruination and that they were thinking of treating us like a Brescia[11]; Monseigneur de Foix, who was young and cruel, frightened me more, and therefore I changed my mind. Nonetheless, I always agreed, and urged, that we should discuss treaties with them, because it seemed to me that we were protecting ourselves from that danger. Then things happened as you know; and I could show you a report I wrote to Pope Leo a few days after he was elected, in which I concluded that the greatest security Italy could have, and the surest peace, was to let the French recapture the state of Milan, and I urged him to do everything he could to that end. And so my opinion is not based on emotions, and I do not believe that yours is either, because I have always seen you not remaining obstinate but yielding to Fortune, yielding to reason. If you said to me: "If you had one opinion four months ago, why have you changed since?" I would say to you that then I had not seen the Swiss wanting to defend that state in any way possible, I had not seen the king of England move against the king of France with such an army and such expense as he has done, and thus many other things have come about; and I did not think Italy could be bound together, but I saw in that alternative a lesser ill; thus I still do not believe now that I could succeed in arranging these affairs of ours completely with my peace plan, but I think I could bind them together a little.

To come to your arguments, you say that you would think that the king of England ought to yield to the authority of the pope and the king of Spain, if they showed him that such was proper. I would grant you this if the war he is making on the king of France were aided by either of them; but since he is making it on his own, why should you expect their authority to stop him from his undertaking? A prince who is waging a war can be made to give it up in two ways: first, when his allies abandon him; second, when they not only leave him but furthermore turn against him and want to be in his enemy's favor. The king of England does not have as allies in this war the king of Spain or the pope, but he does have the emperor and the Swiss; therefore if the Swiss left him, his undertaking would become difficult, and for this he could be turned from it, and if they not only left him but also were against him, he would be forced to withdraw to the island. The king of France would gain more advantage by this from the Swiss than from lansquenets, because in addition to having them as soldiers he would be taking allies away from his enemy. I do not admit, however, that he can have as many Germans as you believe, because the emperor forbids it, so that the lords of Germany and the free cities as well are careful not to let their men go there. The proof of this is that, for all the fears and deeds that the king of France has had and everything that you believe he has spent, he has not been able to assemble more than ten thousand infantrymen, and there are very few Germans among those, and those few are from the lowlands and do not have the same organization or the same strength as the lansquenets. And you may believe that this young king,[12] who thinks he is starting a just war, will not withdraw from this undertaking for words, when he has become so eager that in the past days, when he came from Calais to join with his army at Thérouanne, having along with him eight thousand infantry and nineteen hundred cavalry, he passed only three miles away from the French army, which had ten thousand infantry and fifteen hundred lancers, and he sent them an invitation to battle and they refused. Because, as you know, it is a big thing to have war at home, and every slight movement makes you lose courage and disheartens you, as experience shows every day. Even though, as you say, a pitched battle could make him run the risk of losing his kingdom, he judges that one could also to a great extent let him acquire that of France. Although he is perhaps wrong in this, nevertheless it can be seen that he is stubbornly convinced of it, and he does not spare his money for it, and he makes it a point of pride to spend his own by himself for his own troops and offers after these to give others to the Swiss. And it does not seem to me that the king of Spain can in any way trust in the king of France and just count on saying: "I have given him favors such that past injuries must have been forgotten"[13]; if he could give favors without offending others, I would agree with you, because he would have both him and the others as friends; but giving offense to the king of England, the Swiss, and the emperor by putting him back in Lombardy, I see no way for him to have any security. And even if the king of France did not offend him, he would not care if he was offended by others and he would like him to be weakened in order to take back Naples, which you think grieves him, and he would not take it ill, either, if he were to have disorder in Castile.

I am of the same opinion as you, that whoever wants to see whether a peace is durable and secure must first of all examine who is left dissatisfied by it and consider what can result from that dissatisfaction. It seems to me that in the peace that I drew up they could remain less dissatisfied than in yours and they could make fewer alterations because, although the king of England would not have completely gained his ends, nevertheless he got them in part; and a young man who greatly appreciates glory in his first expedition would have found it a splendid thing for it to have been said that he had forced the king of France to give up Lombardy, which he seemed to have his heart set on as much as Paris. For this reason I am convinced that he could never have come to an agreement with the king of France, because aside from not being dissatisfied, even if it were true, it is not in his interest because, being located over there out of this world, he well knows that joining with the king of France would do nothing else than make him strong, and he could gain no benefit from it; and even if he were willing, it would not be acceptable to his subjects because of the natural enmity between the two peoples. We saw a year ago [14] that they would not get along with the Spaniards, for whom they do not have such enmity. From this we can imagine how they would get along with the French.

So the only ones who are left dissatisfied with this peace of mine are the king of France and the emperor: the king, if he is not old, is infirm and disheartened by adverse fortune; the emperor is unstable, without money, and very little respected, and although he has this fancy for the temporal power of the Church, nonetheless that is not so likely to happen for him that it should be much feared, even if the king of France wanted to help him; it must be remembered that he has spent so much that he would have a hard time providing the money the emperor needs for this campaign. There would then be the Swiss, the Spaniards, these remaining Italians who, even though they have at times given a bad account of themselves, could still give a good one, because these things do not remain unchanging and we have seen the French troops in Italy, so bold and invincible, nonetheless in this last rout [15] run away without fighting and afraid now of the English, who have not had a war for twenty-five years, and they have been in arms for twenty years. There now are [. . .] Ferrara, Mantua, Bartolomeo d'Alviano, these Colonnas [. . .] these Italians are not completely to be set aside as scrap metal. [. . .] to consider greatly the matter of the Swiss, [. . .] the duchy of Milan, granted that they left some of it to him (which in my judgment will never be) for this, would be protected from being overrun by them. But considering and seeing the French so negligent, such ill treaters of the people, even though [. . .] in their greater strength, they have been chased out of that state by twenty thousand Swiss without money.

I am among those who fear the Swiss greatly, but I do not much believe they can become the next Romans, as they said with Pellegrino, [16] because if you study the *Politics* [17] well and the republics that have existed, you will not find that a republic divided like this one [18] can make its way. It seems to me that an example of this has been given by them, because when they could easily have taken all of Lombardy they did not do it, because they say it was not in their interest because, as you can see with those they have taken up till now, they have made them allies and not subjects. They do not want any more allies, because they do not want to have to divide their tribute into more shares; it is not in their interest to keep subjects, because they would disagree about governing them, and in addition to this they would have to look after them at their own expense, and for this reason they would rather have tribute. Disunity can also be seen to have started among them, as I have written above. Nonetheless, *compare,* it is not for this reason that I have said I do not fear them greatly, because things do not always turn out for me according to reason, but I cannot yet see any remedy, if time does not bring one along with it; and it happens many times that when a republic is small it is united, and when it has grown, then it is not the same.

To conclude, everything I write you I am doing so you will have a reason to answer me. I am sorry not to be able to talk of it face-to-face as I should like. I have nothing else to say except to send you my regards.

20 August 1513.
Francesco Vettori, Ambassador

❖ LETTER 221
Niccolò Machiavelli to Francesco Vettori
Florence, 25 August 1513

To the Magnificent Ambassador Francesco Vettori,
His Patron, with the Supreme Pontiff.

Magnificent Ambassador. Because I know how much you love our Donato del Corno,[1] and he is aware of it too, together we have unhesitatingly decided to give you some trouble in order to see whether through Signor Giuliano[2] as intermediary we can give him some satisfaction by putting Donato's name in the bag,[3] which needs to be done for the scrutiny.[4] You are aware of how much goodwill Donato was entitled to from the said Signor Giuliano in what was needed for him to be able to be eligible—which, to a certain degree, surprised everyone: it must have resulted from the great affection Giuliano bears him or from his very praiseworthy qualities. I know something about these qualities; they are such that you or anyone else could advocate his cause before His Lordship with absolute confidence. And because nothing can be done unless there is an order that his name be put in the bag and then recognized,[5] we think we should inquire into Donato's name being put into the bag now because the *accoppiatori* are in the process of putting people's names in bags. Consequently, Donato writes the enclosed to His Lordship simply reminding him of his opinion—entrusting you with its utterance. So we beseech you to be so good as to hand the enclosed letter over to His Lordship personally and then to beg him to draft an order to one or two of the *accoppiatori* that Donato's name be among the first put in the bag. I specify two so that his will is more clearly understood; but, however he writes them, the letter must be explicitly imperative that he wants it so, because you know how finicky those people there are. And if his letter is not enthusiastic, we shall encounter objections and Donato would experience shame and harm. And because Donato trusts Messer Francesco Pepi,[6] you might arrange for one of the two men to whom he writes to be Messer Francesco; you may send Donato the letter so that he may use it to his greatest advantage.

Were I ignorant of your solicitousness and devotion for your friends, I would find it hard to ask you for help, and so would Donato. May it suffice that Donato says he acknowledges that for the most part this good turn comes from you. I am yours to command.

August 25, 1513.

Yours, Niccolò Machiavelli, in Florence

❖ LETTER 222
Niccolò Machiavelli to Francesco Vettori
Florence, 26 August 1513

To the Magnificent Francesco Vettori, Ambassador in Rome to the Supreme Pontiff.

My Lord Ambassador. Your letter of the twentieth dismayed me: its organization, its countless lines of reasoning, and all its other merits entangled me in such a way that at first I was bewildered and confused; had I not been able to collect my wits somewhat by rereading it, I would have given up the game and would have answered you by going on to something else. But as I became more familiar with it, the same thing happened to me as it did to the fox when he saw the lion[1]: the first time he almost died of fright; the second, he halted behind a clump of bushes to take a look; the third, he chatted with him. And so I, having collected my wits by becoming more familiar with your letter, shall answer you.

As for the state of affairs in the world, I derive this conclusion from them. The sort of princes who govern us possess, whether by nature or by chance, the following qualities: we have a wise pope, and therefore a serious and scrupulous one; an unstable and capricious emperor; a haughty, timorous king of France; a niggardly and avaricious king of Spain[2]; a rich, impetuous, and glory-hungry king of England; the brutish, victorious, and insolent Swiss; and we Italians—poverty stricken, aspiring, and cowardly. I know nothing about the rest of the kings. Hence, considering these qualities in connection with matters currently going on, I agree with the friar[3] who said, "Peace, peace, there will never be peace!" I grant you that every peace treaty has its problems—yours as well as mine. And if you see more problems with mine, that is fine with me; but I should like you to listen patiently to the points where I both am afraid and feel certain that you are mistaken. A point where I am afraid that you are mistaken and where it seems certain that you are mistaken is, first, that you too quickly make a trifle out of this king of France and too great a thing out of this king of England. It seems unreasonable to me to think that France has no more than ten thousand foot soldiers; even if he should not have any Germans, he can get a lot from his own country—if these are not as experienced as the Germans, they are as experienced as the English. What leads me to believe this is I realize that this king of England—with all his passion, with all his army, and with all his lust to "eradicate" it, as the Sienese put it—has yet to take Thérouanne,[4] a stronghold like Empoli, during his initial attack; and at a time when his troops are acting in such a frenzy, this fact alone is enough for me not to be so afraid of England and not to underestimate France so much. And I think that France's caution results from choice, not fear, because, since England is not gaining a foothold in that country and winter is coming on, France hopes that England will be compelled either to go back to his island or to stay in France at his peril. I hear those regions are treeless marshes, so the English must already have suffered a lot. Therefore, I did not think it would take much for the pope and Spain to influence England. Furthermore, France's decision not to give up on the council convinces me of the idea mentioned above because were he to be so vexed he would need all of them and would want to be on good terms with each one of them.

Concerning the money that England has sent the Swiss, I believe it; but I am amazed that he did so through the emperor's hands because I should have thought the emperor would rather have spent it on his own troops, not on those from the Swiss. And I am unable to get it through my head how this emperor is so careless and the rest of Germany so negligent as to stand for the Swiss acquiring such prestige. And when I realize that this is in fact so, I hesitate to express an opinion about anything because this one goes contrary to any judgment a person might make. I also cannot understand how it can be that the Swiss could have taken Milan's stronghold and not have wanted to do it because it seems to me that once they got it they would have achieved their objective[5]—they ought rather to have done this than to take over Burgundy for the emperor.

Where I think you are completely mistaken concerns the Swiss, whether or not to fear them, because I believe that we have a very great deal to fear from them. And Casa[6]—as well as many of the friends with whom I am wont to discuss these matters—knows that I once had a low opinion of the Venetians, even at the height of their greatness, because I always thought it a much greater miracle that they acquired and retained their dominion rather than lost it. But their collapse occurred too honorably, because what a king of France accomplished could have been done by a Duke Valentino or by any respected commander who turned up in Italy at the head of fifteen thousand men. What prompted me were the Venetian procedures while they were without their own commanders or soldiers. Now those reasons that caused me not to fear them do make me afraid of the Swiss. I do not know what Aristotle says about confederated republics,[7] but I certainly can say what might reasonably exist, what exists, and what has existed; I recall having read that the Etruscans[8] held all Italy as far as the Alps until the Gauls drove them out of Lombardy. The reason why the Aetolians and Achaeans did not advance had more to do with the times than with themselves because they constantly had an extremely powerful Macedonian king on their backs who would not let them escape from the nest—and after the Macedonians came the Romans. So, rather than their constitution, it was foreign military power that prevented them from expanding. Now the Swiss do not want to create subject nations because they do not see any advantage in it for them; that is what they say now because they do not see any now. But, as I said to you in the other letter, matters move along step by step; necessity often persuades men to do things they did not intend to: a people customarily goes slowly. Given how things are, the Swiss already have a duke of Milan and a pope as their Italian dependents; the Swiss have added the tribute these two pay to their revenue and will not want to lose it; when the time comes that one of them does miss it, the Swiss will consider it sedition and resort to their lancers. Once they have won the contest, they will think about making themselves secure; to do so, they will tighten the screws on those whom they have conquered. Thus, they will gradually subjugate everything.

Put absolutely no trust in those armed forces that you say will one day produce some fruit in Italy because that is impossible. First, as regards these troops, there would be many leaders and those would be divided; I do not see it being possible to furnish them with a leader who might keep them united. Second, as regards the Swiss, you need to be aware of this fact: the best armies[9] are composed of an armed populace; only a similarly constituted army can hold out against them. Recall to mind some armies of renown: you will find those of the Romans, Lacedemonians, Athenians, Aetolians, Achaeans, and those swarms from beyond the Alps; you will find that the ones who have accomplished great feats have armed their own populace—as Ninus did with the Assyrians, Cyrus with the Persians, and Alexander with the Macedonians. I find only Hannibal and Pyrrhus as examples of men who have done great deeds with mixed armies[10]—a result of their leaders' extreme *virtù*, which was so very influential that it inspired their mixed armies with the same spirit and discipline as exist in armies composed of an armed populace. And if you reflect upon France's defeats and victories, you will realize that he was victorious as long as he fought against Italians and Spaniards, whose armies were similar to his own; but now that he has to fight against an armed populace, as the Swiss and English are, he has been defeated—and risks more defeats. Knowledgeable people have consistently forecast such a defeat for him, inferring it from a lack of his own infantry and from his having disarmed his subjects—something that went counter to every action and precept of those reputed to be prudent and great. But this was not a shortcoming of the early kings, but of King Louis[11] and his successors. So, do not rely on Italian armies either unless they are uniform like the Swiss or, if they are mixed, unless they form one unit the way the Swiss do.

And, as for the divisions or disunions that you mention, do not think that they will produce any effect as long as their laws are observed—and they are going to be observed for a while because in our country heads with tails cannot exist or even arise; tailless heads soon destroy themselves and produce little effect. And those whom the Swiss have killed probably, as magistrates or in some other capacity, were those who sought to favor the French faction through irregular measures and have been found out and murdered; they are of no greater import to their government than a number whom ours hangs as thieves. I certainly do not think that they will create an empire like the

Romans, but I do think they can become masters of Italy thanks to their proximity and thanks to our disarray and bad situation. And because these things appall me, I should like to remedy them; if France is not adequate, I see no other remedy—and now I am ready to start weeping with you over our collapse and our servitude that, if it does not come today or tomorrow, will come in our lifetime. This will be what Italy owes to Pope Julius[12] and all those who do not come up with a remedy for us—if a remedy can now be found. *Farewell.*

26 August 1513, in Florence.
Niccolò Machiavelli

❖ LETTER 223
Francesco Vettori to Niccolò Machiavelli
Rome, 23 November 1513

To the Notable Niccolò di Messer Bernardo Machiavelli.
In Florence.

My dear *compare.* As Cristofano Sernigi[1] says, I have treated you so sparingly with my pen that I cannot recollect where I was. I do seem to recall that the last letter I had from you began with the story of the lion and the fox; I have looked around for it among my letters, and not finding it right away, I decided not to search any more. For in truth I did not reply back then because I was afraid that what has sometimes happened to me and Panzano[2] would happen to you and me: we would begin playing with dirty old cards and send for new ones, and when the messenger came back with them, one of the two of us had already lost money. And so we were talking about bringing the princes together, and they went right on playing, so I was afraid that while we were wasting our letters bringing them together, some of them would have lost money. And since we last wrote, several events[3] have occurred. Even though the party is not over, still it seems to have quieted down somewhat; and I believe it is a good idea not to talk of it until it has started up again.

So in this letter I have decided to describe to you what my life in Rome is like. It seems fitting for me to let you know, first of all, where I am living, since I have moved and I am no longer near as many courtesans as I was last summer. My residence is called San Michele in Borgo,[4] and it is quite near the palace and Saint Peter's square; but it is in a somewhat secluded place, because it is toward the hill the ancients called the Janiculum.[5] The house is very nice and has many rooms, though small ones; and it faces toward the north wind, so that the air is just right.

From the house you enter the church, which, what with my being as religious as you know, comes in very handy for me. It is true that the church is used more for walking in than it is for anything else, since neither mass nor any other holy service is ever said there, except once in an entire year. From the church you enter a garden, which formerly was clean and pretty but is now largely abandoned; still, it gets tidied up regularly. From the garden you go up the Janiculum, where you can walk at leisure through lanes and vineyards without being seen by anyone; according to the ancients, this was the site of Nero's gardens, vestiges of which are still visible. I am staying in this house with nine servants and, in addition to them, Brancacci,[6] a chaplain, a scribe, and seven horses; I easily spend all the salary I get. When I first came here, I began by trying to live lavishly and elegantly, inviting out-of-town guests, serving three or four courses, eating out of silver dishes, and so forth. Then I realized that I was spending too much and that I was not at all better off for it; so I decided to stop inviting people and to live at a good, normal level. I returned the silver plates to those who had lent them to me, both so that I would not have to watch over them and also because they would often request me to speak to O[ur] L[ordship][7] about some need of theirs. I would do it and they would not be helped; so I determined to rid myself of this chore and not to annoy or to burden anyone else, so that I would not be annoyed or burdened by them.

Mornings, these days, I get up at ten o'clock, and after dressing, I go over to the palace; not every morning, however, but once out of every two or three. There, on occasion, I speak twenty words with the pope, ten with Cardinal de' Medici,[8] six with Giuliano the Magnificent[9]; and if I cannot speak with him, I speak with Piero Ardinghelli,[10] then with whatever ambassadors happen to be in those chambers; and I hear a thing or two, though little of any moment. Having done that, I go back home; except that sometimes I dine with Cardinal de' Medici. When I get home, I eat with my household and sometimes a guest or two who come to see them, such as Ser Sano and that Ser Tommaso who was in Trent, Giovanni Rucellai, or Giovanni Girolami.[11] After eating, I would play cards if I had someone to do it with; but since I do not, I walk through the church and the garden. Then, when the weather is fine, I go for a short horseback ride outside of Rome. At nightfall I return home; and I have arranged to get quite a few histories, especially of the Romans: for instance, Livy with the epitome of Lucius Florus, Sallust, Plutarch, Appianus Alexandrinus, Cornelius Tacitus, Suetonius, Lampridius, and Spartianus, and those others who write about the emperors—Herodian, Ammianus Marcellinus, and Procopius.[12] And with them I pass the time; and I consider the emperors that this poor Rome, which once made the world tremble, has put up with, and so it is no wonder if it has also put up with two pontiffs[13] of the kind that the last have been. Once every four days, I write a letter to Their Lordships of the Ten, and I relate some tired and irrelevant news, since I have nothing else to write for reasons that you yourself can understand. Then I go off to sleep, after I have had supper and exchanged some bits of news with Brancacci and with M. Giovan Battista Nasi, who often stays with me. On holidays I hear mass; I do not do as you, who sometimes do not bother. If you asked me whether or not I have any courtesans, I would tell you that when I first came here I did have a few, as I wrote you; then, frightened by the summer air, I abstained. Nevertheless, I had accustomed one so that she often comes here on her own; she is reasonably pretty and pleasant in speech. Even though this place is secluded, I also have a neighbor whom you would not find unattractive; and although she is of noble family, she does carry on some business.

Niccolò my friend, this is the life I invite you to; and if you come, you will give me pleasure, and then we shall go back up there together. Here you will have no other business than seeing the sights and then coming back home to joke and to laugh. And I do not want you to think that I live like an ambassador, because I have always insisted on being free. Sometimes I dress up, and sometimes I do not; I go riding by myself, with my servants on foot, and sometimes with them on horseback. I never go to the cardinals', because I have no one to visit except Medici and sometimes Bibbiena,[14] when he is well. And let anyone say what he will, if I do not satisfy them, let them recall me.[15] For in conclusion, I intend to go home at the end of a year and to have held on to my capital, once my clothes and horses have been sold off; I would prefer not to be out of pocket if I can help it. I want you to believe one thing, which I say without any flattery: although I have gone to no great trouble, nonetheless the throng is so great that one cannot help meeting a great number of people. In point of fact, few of them satisfy me, and I have not found any man of better judgment than you. *Sed fatis trahimur.*[16] For when I speak at length to some, when I read their letters, I find myself astonished that they have attained any rank whatsoever, since they are nothing but ceremony, lies, and tales, and there are very few of them who are at all out of the ordinary. Bernardo da Bibbiena, who is now a cardinal, has a well-bred mind, in truth, and he is a witty and discerning man and has done his share of labor in his day. Nonetheless, he is ill now, and he has been so for three months; I do not know if he will ever again be as he was wont to be. And thus we often labor to find rest, and it does not turn out. So let us be merry, come what may. And remember that I am at your service and that I send my regards to you, to Filippo and Giovanni Machiavelli, to Donato, and to Messer Ciaio. Nothing more. Christ watch over you.

Francesco Vettori, ambassador
23 November 1513, in Rome.

❖ LETTER 224
Niccolò Machiavelli to Francesco Vettori
Florence, 10 December 1513

To the Magnificent Franceso Vettori, His Patron and Benefactor,
Florentine Ambassador to the Supreme Pontiff.
In Rome.

Magnificent Ambassador. "Divine favors were never late."[1] I say this because it seemed to me that I had lost—no, rather, strayed from—your favor; it has been a long time since you wrote me, and I was unclear about what the reason might be. And I paid little attention to all those reasons that came to mind except for one: I was afraid that you might have ceased writing to me because someone had written you that I was not a good steward[2] of your letters. I knew that, except for Filippo and Paolo,[3] no one else had seen them through my doing. I am reassured by your recent letter of the 23rd of last month, from which I am extremely pleased to see how methodically and calmly you fulfill your public duties. I exhort you to continue in this manner, because whoever forgoes his own interests for those of others sacrifices his own and gets no gratitude from them. And since Fortune is eager to shape everything, she wants people to let her do so, to be still, not to trouble her, and to await the moment when she will let men do something. That will be the moment for you to persevere more unfailingly, to be more alert about matters, and for me to leave my farm and announce, "Here I am." Since I want to repay you in the same coin, therefore, I can tell you nothing else in this letter except what my life is like. If you decide you would like to swap it for yours, I shall be happy to make the exchange.

I am living on my farm, and since my latest disasters, I have not spent a total of twenty days in Florence. Until now, I have been catching thrushes with my own hands. I would get up before daybreak, prepare the birdlime, and go out with such a bundle of birdcages on my back that I looked like Geta when he came back from the harbor with Amphitryon's books.[4] I would catch at least two, at most six, thrushes. And thus I passed the entire month of November.[5] Eventually this diversion, albeit contemptible and foreign to me, petered out—to my regret. I shall tell you about my life. I get up in the morning with the sun and go into one of my woods that I am having cut down; there I spend a couple of hours inspecting the work of the previous day and kill some time with the woodsmen who always have some dispute on their hands either among themselves or with their neighbors. I could tell you a thousand good stories about these woods and my experiences with them, and about Frosino da Panzano and other men who wanted some of this firewood. In particular, Frosino sent for some loads of wood without saying a word to me; when it came time to settle, he wanted to withhold ten lire that he said he had won off me four years ago when he had beaten me at *cricca*[6] at Antonio Guicciardini's house. I started to raise hell; I was going to call the wagoner who had come for the wood a thief, but Giovanni Machiavelli *eventually* stepped in and got us to agree.[7] Once the north wind started blowing,[8] Battista Guicciardini, Filippo Ginori, Tommaso del Bene, and some other citizens all ordered a load from me. I promised some to each one; I sent Tommaso a load, which turned into half a load in Florence because he, his wife, his children, and the servants were all there to stack it—they looked like Gaburra on Thursdays when he and his crew flay an ox.[9] Consequently, once I realized who was profiting, I told the others that I had no more wood; all of them were angry about it, especially Battista, who includes this among the other calamities of Prato.[10]

Upon leaving the woods, I go to a spring; from there, to one of the places where I hang my birdnets. I have a book under my arm: Dante, Petrarch, or one of the minor poets like Tibullus, Ovid, or some such. I read about their amorous passions and their loves, remember my own, and these reflections make me happy for a while. Then I make my way [11] along the road toward the inn, I chat with passersby, I ask news of their regions, I learn about various matters, I observe mankind: the variety of its tastes, the diversity of its fancies. By then it is time to eat; with my household I eat what food this poor farm and my minuscule patrimony yield. When I have finished eating, I return to the inn, where there usually are the innkeeper, a butcher, a miller, and a couple of kilnworkers. I slum around [12] with them for the rest of the day playing *cricca* and backgammon: these games lead to thousands of squabbles and endless abuses and vituperations. More often than not we are wrangling over a penny; be that as it may, people can hear us yelling even in San Casciano. Thus, having been cooped up among these lice, I get the mold out of my brain and let out the malice of my fate, content to be ridden over roughshod in this fashion if only to discover whether or not my fate is ashamed of treating me so.

When evening comes, I return home and enter my study; on the threshold I take off my workday clothes, covered with mud and dirt, and put on the garments of court and palace. Fitted out appropriately, I step inside the venerable courts of the ancients, where, solicitously received by them, I nourish myself on that food that *alone* is mine and for which I was born; where I am unashamed to converse with them and to question them about the motives for their actions, and they, out of their human kindness, answer me. And for four hours at a time I feel no boredom, I forget all my troubles, I do not dread poverty, and I am not terrified by death. I absorb myself into them completely. [13] And because Dante says that no one understands anything unless he retains what he has understood, [14] I have jotted down what I have profited from in their conversation and composed a short study, *De principatibus,* in which I delve as deeply as I can into the ideas concerning this topic, discussing the definition of a princedom, the categories of princedoms, how they are acquired, how they are retained, and why they are lost. And if ever any whimsy of mine has given you pleasure, this one should not displease you. It ought to be welcomed by a prince, and especially by a new prince; therefore I am dedicating it to His Magnificence Giuliano. [15] Filippo da Casavecchia has seen it. He will be able to give you some account of both the work itself and the discussions I have had with him about it, although I am continually fattening and currying it. [16]

Magnificent Ambassador, you would like me to abandon this life and come and enjoy yours with you. I shall do so in any case, but I am kept here by certain commitments that I shall attend to within six weeks. What makes me hesitate is that those Soderinis [17] are in Rome; were I to come there, I would be obliged to visit and to talk with them. I am afraid upon my return that I might not count on dismounting at home but rather that I should dismount at the Bargello.[18] For although this regime[19] has extremely strong foundations and great security, it is still new and, consequently, suspicious. There are plenty of rogues like Paolo Bertini who, in order to be impressive, would order a meal for others and leave the tab for me to pick up. I beg you to make this fear evaporate, and then, come what may, I shall come and see you in any case at the time mentioned.

I have discussed this little study of mine with Filippo and whether or not it would be a good idea to present it [to Giuliano], and if it were a good idea, whether I should take it myself or should send it to you.[20] Against presenting it would be my suspicion that he might not even read it and that that person Ardinghelli[21] might take the credit for this most recent of my endeavors. In favor of presenting it would be the necessity that hounds me, because I am wasting away and cannot continue on like this much longer without becoming contemptible because of my poverty.[22] Besides, there is my desire that these Medici princes should begin to engage my services, even if they should start out by having me roll along a stone.[23] For then, if I could not win them over, I should have only myself to blame. And through this study of mine, were it to be read, it would be evident that during the fifteen years I have been studying the art of the state I have neither slept nor fooled around, and anybody ought to be happy to utilize someone who has had so much experience at the expense of others. There should be no doubt about my word; for, since I have always kept it, I should not start learning how to break it now. Whoever has been honest and faithful for forty-three years,[24] as I have, is unable to change his nature; my poverty is a witness to my loyalty and honesty.

So I should like you, too, to write me what your opinion is about all this. I commend myself to you. *Be happy.*

10 December 1513.
Niccolò Machiavelli, in Florence.

❖ LETTER 225
Niccolò Machiavelli to Francesco Vettori
Florence, 19 December 1513

To His Magnificence, Francesco Vettori,
Ambassador of the Republic of Florence to the Supreme Pontiff.

Magnificent Ambassador. In response to yours of the twenty-third of last month, I wrote you eight or ten days ago and told you what made me uncertain about my going there. I am waiting for your opinion and then I shall do whatever you advise.

I am writing you this letter on behalf of our Donato del Corno.[1] You are aware of how his affairs stand and of the letter that, at the beginning, he obtained from His Magnificence Giuliano to the Magnificent Lorenzo. Then Messer Francesco Pepi, who had taken up his affair, died, so Donato was left almost without hope. Still, not giving up, we—Donato and I—went to see

Jacopo Gianfigliazzi,[2] who actively promised us not to leave anything undone. Two days ago, as well, with the letter that you wrote to him, we talked
to him again about this matter, and Jacopo made better promises than he had
the first time; he convinced us not to consider the matter from now until
mid-January because the other names had to be put in the bag first. To our
query as to whether or not he thought we should obtain other letters from
Giuliano, he replied that it could only be to the good but that we ought to
wait until the last moment so that it could be received at the right time, because should it be received now, it would be out-of-date when the moment
did arrive and things would have to be started over from the beginning.
Consequently, we shall need to act so that the letter will be ready on time.
And if by chance you have not obtained what you recently wrote Donato
about, you can forget about the matter. If you should obtain it, we shall need
to consider what should be done when the moment arrives.

Based on our knowledge of what happened previously, it seems to us that
unless there is someone who keeps the letter in mind, a letter is cold comfort.[3] Hence we deemed it necessary that something be done there, whenever
it might be possible, so that Messer Niccolò Michelozzi[4] might have these instructions from Giuliano here and might remind Lorenzo of it either through
a letter that Giuliano might write him or through a letter Piero Ardinghelli[5]
might write him in Giuliano's name and so that whatever excuse Niccolò
might have he would be made to remember the matter at the right moment.
And because we think it would be easy for Piero Ardinghelli to carry this
business out, we suggest that you work him over, promising whatever you
judge to be the best to offer him—and Donato will meet his obligations to
you. And Piero will not overlook ways to get this job done, because he is
aware how His Magnificence Giuliano has done favors for Maestro Manente
and a few others whom Giuliano wants taken care of—this is how Donato's
favors need to be launched. If Piero is willing, I believe we can have everything. Therefore, we think Piero's medicine ought to be made use of and that
all the support that is to come ought to arrive between the eighth and fifteenth of January because Piero, for the reasons given, will be in the right
place. And in order that you may be aware of everything and may gauge
whether or not Donato deserves to be numbered among the devoted retain-
ers of the Most Illustrious Medici Family, you should know that about a day
after the Medici returned to Florence, Donato took five hundred ducats
(which were lent him gratis[6] and without being asked for) to His Magnificence Giuliano. He remains Giuliano's creditor for them still. You are being
told this not so that you may repeat it to anyone but so that, being aware of it,
you can take this venture up with greater heart.

Donato and I are not trying to exhaust you and then exhaust you again
about this business, since, knowing what an obliging friend you are, we believe we are giving you pleasure by asking this of you; on that account, Donato simultaneously both implores a favor of you and apologizes for
it—should that indeed be required. What we write we offer you as our opin-

ion, but we shall always accept every measure you adopt as being the most prudent.

We recited from memory to Giovanni Machiavelli those four verses about Riccio[7] that you wrote at the beginning of Donato's letter. We replaced Machiavelli and Pera by inserting "Giovanni Machiavelli." He acted surprised about it and said he could not figure out where you found out about whom he is seeing; at any rate, he is going to write you about it. Filippo and I got a huge kick out of it for a while.

In this city of ours—a magnet for all the world's pitchmen[8]—there is a friar[9] of Saint Francis who is half hermit and who, to increase his standing as a preacher, professes to be a prophet; and yesterday morning in Santa Croce, where he preaches, he said *"many things great and wonderful"*: that before much time elapses, so that whoever is ninety years of age will be able to see it, there will be an unjust pope created against a just pope, and he will have false prophets with him, he will create cardinals, and he will divide the Church. *Item,* that the king of France was to be crushed and someone from the House of Aragon was to be master of Italy. Our city would go up in flames and be sacked, the churches would be abandoned and would crumble, the priests dispersed, and we would have to do without divine services for three years. There would be pestilence and widespread famine; in the city, not ten men would remain; on farms, not two would remain. That for eighteen years there has been a devil in a human body—and he has said mass. That well over two million devils were unleashed in order to supervise the above-mentioned activities. That they would enter into many dying bodies and not allow those bodies to putrefy so that false prophets and clerics might resuscitate the dead and be believed. These activities demoralized me so much yesterday that I was supposed to go this morning to see La Riccia,[10] but I did not go; I am not at all sure whether, had I been supposed to go see Riccio, I would have been concerned. I myself did not hear the sermon, for I do not observe such practices, but I have heard it told about in this manner throughout all of Florence.

I send you my regards; would you please greet Casa for me and tell him that if he does not behave otherwise than he did here, he will lose his standing with the crew there just as he has lost it with the crew here? *Farewell.*

19 December 1513.
Niccolò Machiavelli, in Florence

❖ LETTER 226
Francesco Vettori to Niccolò Machiavelli
Rome, 24 December 1513

To the Notable Niccolò di Messer Bernardo Machiavelli.
In Florence.
† 24 December 1513.

My dear *compare*. If I have not answered a letter of yours of the 10th right away, and perhaps my answer now is not very much to the point, the cause of it is Casavecchia and Brancacci, who disturb my mind every day by reminding me of the dignity of the city and that which is fitting to my office. You know that I take a bit of pleasure in women,[1] more to stay and chat with them than for any other reason, because I am now so far gone that there is little else I can do than talk. You also know how averse Filippo's disposition is to them. Before he came here, because my residence is somewhat out of the way, some courtesans often came to visit me, to see the church and the garden attached to the house where I am living. I did not think, when Filippo arrived, to send them a message not to be so bold about showing up here, so that two days after his arrival, just at dinner time, one showed up in my room, and as usual, she was allowed by my servants to come in freely, and when she got there she sat down as if she was in her own house, so that I did not know how to dismiss her or to cover the matter up with Filippo, who stared at her with a pair of wondering and disdainful eyes. We sat down at the table, and she in her place. We dined, we talked, and after eating, she went off as usual for a stroll through the garden. Filippo and I remained, and he tried to start making me a speech according to all the rules, and he opened his mouth in this vein: "You will not take it ill, magnificent ambassador, since I have been, from childhood . . . ," but I, knowing that the speech would be a long one and seeing what he wanted to say, interrupted him, saying that I had understood his intention from those few words and that I did not want to justify myself or to hear his reproof, because I had lived free and without any regards up till now, and I wished to do so for the remaining time I had left to live. So that, although unwillingly, he agreed to let women come here as they please.

But I want to tell you now of the disturbance that Brancacci has given me. I think you are aware how good a friend of mine Jacopo Gianfigliazzi is, and in many respects I have reason not only to love him but also to honor him. When he was ambassador here, he entrusted a certain suit of his to me that it is not necessary to tell you about. Perhaps imagining that I had more to do than I have, he asked Ser Sano[2] to remind me of it. He, for this reason, has come almost every week to speak with me about this matter, and sometimes to dine with me. Giuliano, when he saw him come once, and twice, and three times, began to tell me that Ser Sano is a depraved man, and that in via dei Banchi[3] he was asked by some merchants of good reputation what relations I have with him, and that I ought to avoid having relations of that sort; so that to excuse myself I was forced to tell him in detail about the entire connection between Jacopo Gianfigliazzi and him. And so, my *compare*, you see what a situation I am in and how I have to give account of what I say and of every man who comes to talk with me. I would like you to tell me your opinion: which one seems to have more reason to reprove me, Filippo or Giuliano, both of whom I nevertheless am fond of. With all their admonitions and reproofs, I shall still not fail to do what seems fitting.

You write me, and Filippo also has told me, that you have written a certain work about states. I shall be grateful if you send it to me; and although I am not an authority, I judge it proper that I should judge your thing; so far as knowledge and judgment are lacking, affection and trust will make up for them. When I have seen it,[4] I shall tell you my opinion about presenting it or not to the Magnificent Giuliano, as it may seem to me.

The concern that you have about coming here seems to me easy to resolve, because if you go and see Cardinal Soderini once, you will not be given any trouble. Piero[5] has made up his mind, and I do not think he would be happy to be visited, and especially by you, and if you did not visit him I do not think it would be attributed to ingratitude on your part; because I have studied the question, and I do not find that he or his people have done you so much benefit that you should have any obligations toward them except the normal ones. You did not receive your office from them; you began to be employed three years before he was gonfalonier; in what he employed you for afterward you served him faithfully, and you did not receive any other reward for that except the normal one. And therefore, if you should be going to come here, I do not want any such concern to hold you back, because you will not be blamed for a single visit, and if you should abstain from it you will not be considered ungrateful by anyone.[6]

From your letter and from Filippo I learn that you, being accustomed to working and earning money, find it difficult to stay there and use up what little income you have, because you still have some remaining desires, as I do. We have studied the question, and here in Rome we do not find anything suitable for you. There has been some talk that Cardinal de' Medici is going to be named legate to France, and I have thought about speaking of that, if it should be done, since you have been there and have some experience of that court and information about their customs. If it turns out, so be it; if it does not, we shall not have lost anything.

When you have sent me that treatise, I shall tell you if I think you should come and present it.

Now let us get to Donato, whom I very much want to see satisfied, and I do not think I shall have any difficulty convincing you and him of this. As I wrote him, I asked Giuliano for an extraordinary letter for him, and he promised it to me generously; and because Piero[7] is not very quick to write, because of all the things that he has to do, I got hold of someone who stayed there long enough to write it; and because he was dispatching a courier I had a cover made in my name to Donato and asked that it be left for Piero to send. I am surprised it has not arrived; I shall speak of it again to Giuliano, and I shall go into it with Piero as you told me; but I would not like to add injury to injury for Donato, that is, that I should have to give and it should not turn out well for him, because I do not know what way we shall have to make sure that he will be reimbursed.

Give me news about how Master Manente's business went, so that I can ask Giuliano and Piero in the same way, and be assured that I shall not hesitate to do anything if I can be of use to him.

Give my regards to Filippo, to Giovanni Machiavelli, and give him my excuses if at times, to arrange a verse, we depart somewhat from the truth; I did not think it would get back to his hearing, and if I have offended him, I ask him to forgive me.

Casa is in his element here, and I think he will make some profit both for his purse and for his body, because with three farthings[8] he will do some good business. He and Brancacci often have differences, and I have to get between them to make peace.

I have nothing to answer you about the hermit,[9] because, as you say, Florence was founded under such a sign that men like him run to it and are listened to willingly there. I have nothing else to tell you in this letter except to send you my regards. Christ watch over you.

Francesco Vettori, Ambassador

L E T T E R S

1514

M achiavelli spent most of 1514 as an observer of local and international affairs. What happened locally is readily apparent in the context of the letters. But political machinations on an international scale were a bit more complicated. Milan was the bone of contention between Louis XII and the Swiss, who sought to hold the king to an agreement signed late in 1513 at Dijon, under the terms of which France renounced all claims to Milan. To circumvent this treaty, Louis XII considered offering his four-year old daughter Renée (Renée of France [1510–1575]) in marriage to one of the grandchildren of Ferdinand the Catholic: either to Archduke Charles of Hapsburg (1500–1558), the future Holy Roman Emperor Charles V (1519–1556) and king of Spain as Charles I (1516–1556), or to Archduke Ferdinand of Hapsburg (1503–1564), the future Ferdinand I, Holy Roman Emperor from 1556–1564. Because Louis sought to regain control of Milan, he would have had to make sure that Renée's dowry included his rights to Milan and Genoa as part of the deal. The offer never materialized; nevertheless, its terms were bruited about. They prompted Pope Leo X to action because he realized the dangerous potential for Italy of the alliance between France, Spain, and Germany that such a proposal might create. Through his agent Ludovico of Canossa, bishop of Tircárico and later Bayeux, Leo X persuaded both Louis XII, with whom he was now on better terms, and Henry VIII to sign a treaty in August; Thomas Wolsey, then archbishop of York, was also instrumental in the signing. Its ratification came in the form of the marriage on 9 October between Henry's sister, Mary (Mary Tudor, Mary of France [1496–1533]), and Louis XII (Louis's second wife, Anne of Brittany, died in January). The marriage's effects were short-lived, however; Louis died on 1 January 1515.

Leo X, meanwhile, could concentrate his efforts on securing a locus of power in northern Italy for his brother Giuliano. The pope purchased the towns of Modena and Reggio from Maximilian I. Two other northern cities were also part of the pope's plans for Giuliano. At Julius II's death, in February 1513, Ramón de Cardona had returned Parma and Piacenza to Massimiliano Sforza, the duke of Milan, who had then turned them over to Leo. As part of his family aggrandizement plans, Pope Leo X was prepared to go to great lengths to help Giuliano de' Medici, but the objections from Massimiliano Sforza, from the Swiss, and soon from the belligerent new French king, Francis I, were too strong; Leo dared not risk their ire.

❖ LETTER 227
Niccolò Machiavelli to Francesco Vettori
Florence, 5 January 1514

To the Magnificent Florentine Ambassador Francesco Vettori,
His Most Regarded Benefactor.

Magnificent Ambassador. Surely it is a great wonder to contemplate how blind human beings are in matters that involve their sins and what implacable persecutors they are of the vices that they do not possess. I could cite Greek, Latin, Hebraic, and Chaldean instances and go as far as the lands of the Safi and of Prester John[1] to produce them for you—if domestic and recent examples did not suffice. I believe that Ser Sano[2] would have been able to appear at your house from one Jubilee to the next,[3] and Filippo would never have thought that it would result in any accusation against you. On the contrary, he would have thought that you were picturing yourself in association with him and that it was indeed an arrangement suitable for an ambassador who, since he is forced into countless constraints, must of necessity have some pleasure and diversion; he would have thought that Ser Sano fit in precisely—he would have praised your common sense to everyone and lauded your choice to the skies. On the other hand, I believe that if the entire bordello of Valencia[4] had paraded through your house, it would have been impossible for Brancacci to have reproached you for it; on the contrary, he would have commended you more for this than if he had heard you hold forth before the pope better than a Demosthenes.

And if you had wanted to examine the evidence for this reasoning, without either one having been aware of the other's admonitions, you would have had to feign belief in them and a willingness to comply with their precepts. And had you locked the door against the sluts and driven Ser Sano away, and had you withdrawn into the serious life and immersed yourself into the thoughtful life, not four days would have gone by before Filippo would have started saying, "What has become of Ser Sano? What does it mean that we do not see him any more? It is a shame he does not come around here, he seemed like an upright person to me; I do not know what that gang is blabbering about, but it seems to me that he understands full well the context of the papal court and that he is a useful contact to have. Mr. Ambassador, you ought to send for him." I do not need to tell you whether or not Brancacci would have regretted, or been surprised at, the absence of women, and if he had not told you so while keeping his ass turned to the fire—as Filippo would have done—he would have said so when he was alone with you in your room. To put it more clearly, given your puritanical predisposition, if I—who handle and care about women—had chanced to enter the room, as soon as I had gotten the drift of the situation, I would have said: "Ambassador, you are going to be ill; I don't think you're allowing yourself any diversion; there aren't any boys here, there aren't any girls here; what kind of a fucking house is this anyway?"

Magnificent Ambassador, there are nothing but crazies here; only a few are familiar with this world and are aware that whoever seeks to act according to others will accomplish nothing because no two men who think alike can be found. These people are unaware that whoever is considered wise by day will not be considered crazy by night[5] and that whoever is deemed a decent, able man will occasion honor, not blame, whatever he does to refresh his spirit and live happily; instead of being called a sodomite or a lecher, people will say he is well-rounded, easy-going, and a boon companion.[6] They are also unaware that he gives of himself and takes nothing from others and that he acts as the must does when it boils: it imparts its own pungency to dishes that reek of mold without taking on the mold from the dishes.

Therefore, Mr. Ambassador, do not be afraid of Ser Sano's mold or of Mona Smeria's[7] rotten mess, and stick with your natural dispositions and let Brancacci talk; he does not realize that he is like one of those little wrens that is the first to squawk and to scold and, once the owl arrives, is the first to be caught. And our Filippo is like a vulture who, when there is no carrion in a rural district, soars a hundred miles to find some; and when his gullet is full, he sits on a pine and mocks the eagles, hawks, falcons, and their ilk who spend half the year ravenous because they feed upon dainty foods. So, Magnificent Ambassador, let the one squawk and the other fill its crop, while you attend to your affairs as you see fit.

In Florence, 5 January 1513[4].
Niccolò Machiavelli

❖ LETTER 228
Francesco Vettori to Niccolò Machiavelli
Rome, 18 January 1514

To the Notable Niccolò Machiavelli.
In Florence.

My very dear *compare*. I have always praised your wit and approved your judgment in both small matters and great. But the discussion concerning Filippo and Brancacci that you send me in this last letter turned out in fact for me within just a few days, because, as you have known me, I believe in others more than in myself, and I always want to please anyone else before myself. For this reason, prompted by the arguments that they gave me, as I wrote to you in the other letter, I decided to believe them and I informed Messer Sano in a good way that if ever Jacopo Gianfigliazzi wrote me anything else I would send for him and that he should not go to the trouble of coming to see me. And so he, who is quite shrewd about these matters, realized very well what I meant. Thus I asked the two women[1] who were used to coming here often not to come unless I called for them, because a relative of mine had come for whom I had respect and whom I did not want to see them.

I kept to this way for about eight days, so nobody stopped by here except a few people on their business and one Donato Bossi,[2] who is a grammarian by profession, with an austere and odd face. He never speaks of anything else except whence a word is derived and whence a name is formed and whether the verb should be placed at the beginning of a clause or at the end, and similar things of little importance that give considerable boredom to those who hear them. I did nothing else but ask him about these trifles so that he might be able to speak about them more freely; and even though this life displeased me, I bore it as well as I could, so that Filippo and Giuliano might realize their mistake. That came about quickly, because one evening, when we were standing by the fire, Giuliano began to say that I ought to invite a certain neighbor woman I have here and that not inviting her for dinner one evening was a sign of unsociableness, which is interpreted badly by many people, and men who live so stingily are considered odd and unsociable.

But it is necessary for me to tell you about the quality of this lady, so that you can consider to what end each of them was urging me to invite her. As I have already written you, my lodging, although it is very close to the palace, is a little out-of-the-way and in a street that has few passers-by and with neighbors of a base sort. However, next door to it, in a very proper house, there lives a Roman widow lady of good family, who used to and still does play around a bit,[3] and although she is past her prime, she has a daughter of around twenty who is supremely beautiful and who has in the past and still does carry on some business. She also has a son fourteen years old, courteous and well-bred but of good morals and virtuous, as is proper at that age. Because the houses are close together and the gardens open onto one another, it has been impossible not have some contact with that lady, if only outside. She has often come to ask my assistance with the pope or the governor, and I have helped as far as I could because we are obliged to help widows and orphans. So Giuliano recommended that I invite this widow to dinner; and Filippo supported him concerning that young boy, citing the example of Alessandro Nasi, whom he often visited when he was in Rome on another occasion and whom he always found on winter evenings accompanied by some neighbor, along with several other arguments as you know he is wont to do. Both he and Giuliano managed to say so much to me that I consented to their doing as they saw fit.

When we had this discussion together, it was about eight o'clock at night, so I did not think that they would invite these neighbors that evening; so when they left me, I sat down to write a letter to Their Lordships of the Ten. It was my notion to arrange it in such a way as not to reveal to them, however, all the plans of O[ur] L[ordship],[4] because I did not know whether he wanted it, and yet I did not want it to be so curt that they would judge either that I had not been very diligent or very smart or else that I was not taking as much account of them as was proper, especially since they are in every capacity the first men of our city. While I was absorbed in that fancy, the neighbor arrived with her daughter and her son, and in addition a brother of hers who came almost as a chaperon for this family. When I saw her, I greeted her with that most pleasing manner that nature grants me, since you must have noticed that such merry greetings and flattering words do not come easily to me. However, I made an effort and brought the letter to a swift conclusion, saying that it was necessary if they wished to come to a judgment for them to await the resolution of the Swiss at the Diet of Epiphany.

So Giuliano started to chat with the daughter, and Filippo with the son, and I, in order to make it easier for them, called the widow and her brother over to one side and started to ask them about a certain suit they have pending, so that, with them occupied in this conversation, they would give some time to the others until it came time for dinner. I could not, however, help listening in from time to time on what Giuliano was saying to Costanza, for that is her name, and they were the sweetest words you ever heard, praising her for her nobility, her beauty, her speech, and every part of a lady that can be praised. Filippo also, with the son, did not stop at certain little expressions suited to the occasion, asking him whether he was a student, whether he had a tutor, and to go into it further, he questioned him as to whether he slept with him, so that the bashful boy would often lower his eyes without answering him. Dinnertime came, and we dined merrily. Afterward we sat by the fire, where we spent the time exchanging gossip, asking questions, saying tongue-twisters or what you will.[5] But you would have laughed, because a little before dinner, to break, I shall not say into ours, but into their calm, who should show up but Piero del Bene, who I would rather had not come into the room. But I cannot be disagreeable or simulate, and so he came in; but seeing that he was given a cold welcome by Filippo and Giuliano, he did not stay long before leaving. We spent the evening pleasantly, and around midnight the neighbors left and we, remaining, went off to sleep.

But Niccolò, I cannot help complaining to you that out of a desire to make my friends happy I have become almost a prisoner of this Costanza. Before, sometimes one woman[6] and sometimes another one would come, and I did not offer them any sentiment; nonetheless, I would indulge my fancy with them. This one came along, and I shall be so bold as to say that you never set eyes on a more beautiful woman, nor a more seductive one. I had indeed seen her before, but from a distance, but once she came closer I liked her so much that I can think of no one else but her. And because I have seen you in love a few times and heard how much suffering you have borne, I am putting up as much resistance as I can at the outset now; I do not know whether I shall be strong enough, and I fear I shall not, and I shall write you what ensues in this matter.

I have seen the chapters of your work,[7] and I like them immeasurably. But since I do not have the entire work, I do not want to make a definitive judgment.

I wrote to Donato as much as I could about his case last week. Nonetheless, if he needs anything else, I shall not fail to do it. It is indeed true that the case of Master Manente is easier, because he won in the balloting and that is certain.

Filippo does not approve your saying he throws himself away on "bitches," because he says that he has always wanted perfect things and that you are the one who offers himself everything without distinction.

I had intended to make this letter longer, but out of haste I have scribbled it, because I read your letters with such pleasure that it seems as if it is taking me forever to answer you, so as to have one from you. I send you my regards. Christ watch over you.

Francesco Vettori, Ambassador in Rome

18 January 1513[4].

❖ LETTER 229
Niccolò Machiavelli to Francesco Vettori
Florence, 4 February 1514

To the Magnificent Florentine Ambassador Franceso Vettori,
His Benefactor, with the Supreme Pontiff.

Magnificent Ambassador. Yesterday I returned from my farm and your Paolo gave me your letter of the twenty-third[1] of last month in answer to one of mine from I know not when. I took great pleasure in it, as I realized with what solicitude Fortune has dealt with you and has arranged matters so well that thanks to you Filippo and Brancacci have become one soul in two bodies, or rather, to be correct, two souls in one body. And when I meditate upon their story and yours from beginning to end (which, had I not lost my notes,[2] I would truly have included among the Annals of Modern Times), it seems to me as worthy a story for declaiming before a prince as anything I have heard about this year. I can imagine seeing Brancacci concentrating, sitting low in a chair the better to gaze upon Costanza's face, and with words and gestures, with poses and pleasant expressions, with fidgeting movements of mouth and eye, drooling, totally infused with and consumed by—hanging on to—Costanza's words, sighs, glances, scent, delicate manners, and receptive feminine ways.

> Turning to the right I saw our Casa,
> Who now was nearer that boy as his target,
> A bit reserved, and with a shaven pate.

I see him gesticulating, shifting first to one side and then to the other; I see him nodding his head now and then at the boy's hesitant and shy answers. I see him talking with the boy, playing the role now of father, now of tutor, now of lover—and that poor young boy is doubtful as to just what Casa has in mind: first he fears for his virtue, then he trusts in the dignity of the man's years, and then he defers to his elegant air of mature authority. I see you, Mr. Ambassador, attentive to that widow and her brother, one eye (the right one, for that matter) on the young man and the other one on that young girl—with one ear for the widow's words and the other for those of Casa and Brancacci. I see you answering them in generalities, and like Echo to their most recent words; at last you cut the conversation short and rush to the fireplace, with rapid, inch-long steps, stooping over a bit. Upon your arrival I see Filippo, Brancacci, the youth, and the girl all rise; you say, "Sit down, stay seated, do not trouble yourselves, continue your conversations." After quite a few formalities, of a somewhat homey and smarmy type, each one sits down again and starts up some pleasant topic of conversation. But I especially imagine that I see Filippo when Piero del Bene arrives. If I knew how to paint, I should capture him on canvas because some of his typical gestures, some of his sidelong glances, and some of his superior posturing can in no way be rendered in prose. I see you all at table—the bread, the glasses, and the table with its trestles brought in—and everyone happy, or rather, exuding happiness; eventually everybody is drowned in a flood of good cheer. Finally, I see Jove before the chariot in chains[3]: I see you inspired by love. Just as fire is more powerful when it spreads to green wood, so your internal flame is more ardent because it has come upon stronger resistance. At this point I should be allowed to cry out with that character in Terence, *"O heaven, O earth, O seas of Neptune."*[4] I see you struggling with yourself, and because *"majesty and love do not go well together, or share the same abode,"*[5] now you would like to turn into a swan so you could lay an egg in her lap, now turn into gold[6] so she could carry you in her pocket, now into one animal, and now another—as long as you are not separated from her.

And since my own precedent causes you dismay, remembering what Love's arrows have done to me, I am obliged to tell you how I have handled myself with him. As a matter of fact, I have let him do as he pleases and I have followed him through hill and dale, woods and plains; I have discovered that he has granted me more charms than if I had tormented him. So then, take off the saddlepacks, remove the bridle, close your eyes, and say, "Go ahead, Love, be my guide, my leader; if things turn out well, may the praise be yours, if they turn out badly, may the blame be yours—I am your slave. You have nothing more to gain by tormenting me; rather, you will be losing out because you will be tormenting what is yours." And with such words as these, fit to pierce a hole in a wall, you can make him show compassion. So, master, be happy, do not be dismayed, face Fortune squarely, and follow whatever course both the revolving heavens and the conditions sent you by the times and by mankind lay at your doorstep; never doubt that you will snap every snare and overcome every obstacle. And should you want to serenade her, I shall volunteer to come there with a beautiful composition that will make her fall in love.

That is all I have to say in response to your letter. There is nothing to tell you about from these parts except prophecies and proclamations of calamities; if the prophets are telling lies, may God annihilate them; if they are telling the truth, may He convert it into good. When I am in Florence, I divide my time between Donato del Corno's shop and La Riccia; I think I am getting on both their nerves because he calls me "Shop Pest" and she calls me "House Pest." Yet both of them value me as an adviser, and so far this reputation has stood me in such good stead that Donato has let me warm myself by his fire and she sometimes lets me kiss her on the sly. I believe this good will not last long since I have given both of them some tidbits of advice that have never panned out; just today La Riccia said to me in a certain conversation she feigned to be having with her maid, "Wise men, oh these wise men, I don't know what they have upstairs; it seems to me they turn everything topsy-turvy."

Magnificent Ambassador, you can see where the hell I am. I want to keep them as friends, yet there seems to be no remedy for the situation. If anything occurs to you, or to Filippo, or to Brancacci, I should be glad if you would write me about it. *Farewell.*

4 February 1513[4]
Niccolò Machiavelli, in Florence

❖ LETTER 230
Francesco Vettori to Niccolò Machiavelli
Rome, 9 February 1514

To the Notable Niccolò Machiavelli, etc.
† 9 February 1513[4].

My dear *compare*. I shall not reply right away to the last letter I have from you, but I shall continue where I left off, which I think was concerning my resisting love as much as I could. Do not imagine I thought that dignity and love[1] do not go well together, because I feel I have greater dignity when I am Francesco in Florence than now that I am here as ambassador. But I took into consideration that I am forty, I have a wife,[2] I have married and marriageable daughters; therefore I do not have anything to throw away, but it would be reasonable for me to keep everything that I can save for my daughters; and what a base thing it is to let oneself be overcome by sensuality, and that she[3] lived nearby, and that I would spend money on her, and every day I would get a thousand annoyances from it; in addition to this, since she is beautiful, young, and graceful, I had to realize that since I liked her, others, of a different rank than I am, would also like her, so that I would not be able to enjoy her much and I would be subject to constant jealousy. And so, turning these ideas over and over in my head, I decided to get her completely out of my mind. I stuck to this notion for two days, and I already felt as if it was secure enough not to be dislodged from my judgment. It happened that on the third day her mother came to talk to me in the evening, and she brought her daughter with her; "and I, who would have sworn / to defend myself from a man covered with armor, / was bound up by words and by gestures."[4] The mother spoke of her business, then went out of the room and left me alone with her by the fire. I could not help but talk with her, and touch her hands and her neck. She seemed so beautiful and so delightful to me that all the resolutions I had made went right out of my head, and I decided to offer myself as prey to her and that she should rule and guide me as she saw fit. I do not wish to tell you what happened then: suffice it to say that it happened to me and I no longer thought about annoyances and jealousy. The expense has in fact been minor up to now, but my mind has remained in constant distress. The more I talk to her, the more I would like to talk to her, and the more I see her, the more I would like to see her. But it happened to me by good luck that Piero,[5] my nephew, came here: because she used to come to dinner at my house when she felt like it, and now she comes no longer; and the fire might still go out, however, for I do not think that it has been set in such a way that this water should not extinguish it. But Niccolò, my friend, you have never set your eyes on a more beautiful thing: tall, well proportioned, rather plump than thin, white, with a bright complexion, a face that I do not know whether it is sharp or rounded—suffice it to say that I like it. Graceful, pleasant, bantering, she is always laughing, she pays little attention to her person, without waters or lotions on her face: I do not want to talk about the other parts, because I have not experienced them as much as I should desire.

Do not think, however, that I have not had some reproofs about this, or let us say affectionate admonitions, from Filippo and Giuliano. I have answered them what I felt was true: that no one is ever to be reproved if you know that he realizes he is doing wrong; because this does nothing but increase his suffering, but he does not withdraw or leave off from his error for that. It just so happens that Filippo has become involved in what he reproved me for; but his is the employee of a goldsmith, whose equal, according to him, has never been seen; but he has been marked by the host, that is to say, by the master of the shop. However, Filippo has tried to get around the pitfalls and has attempted the crossing. And I, who know what these Romans are like, have striven to pull him back before he takes many steps in that direction, but I was not able, and now the master has threatened him and would have harmed him except that he, taking fright, not only no longer looks at the boy but also scarcely walks through via dei Banchi, where his shop is. He will have to lay siege to a more vulnerable fortress, one that is less well-guarded. For this reason he is continually dealing with Ser Sano, so that Giuliano, who is disgusted by this business, avoids going around Rome with him. Whenever they are in the house, they argue together and choose as their judge a secretary of mine as tall as Piero Ardinghelli but who is not very familiar with such discussions, because he has paid more attention to exercising his handwriting, which is the first thing one looks for in a scribe, than to anything else.

Anyone who lives has diverse things happen to him; therefore I am not surprised if La Riccia in anger has blamed the advice of wise men.[6] But I do not think for this reason that she does not bear love toward you and that she will not open her door to you when you want; because I would consider her ungrateful, whereas up to now I have judged her to be humane and kind. I am sure that Antonio Francesco[7] has not made her haughty; he sent a friar of his here for a benefice, who told me that he[8] no longer sleeps in his house, but in a garden near Bernardo Rucellai that is called La Riccia, and he does so in order to have greater convenience for studying. But even if La Riccia should shut the door in your face, stick to Riccio di Donato, who does not change with fortune, but has sinew and backbone, and stays with friends more when they are down than when they are up.

And speaking about Riccio, I do not want to forget Donato. I have always been more sparing of others' money than of my own, and therefore I have not used what he sent. I would like Donato to hear from Jacopo Gianfigliazzi, if he thinks that Lorenzo will get him put back on the list as he promised me. If he thinks so, let us not go and spend more than what has been spent up to now; if he does not think so, we shall make use of those remedies that he wrote to me. When he is put back in the bag, we shall think about getting him recognized[9]; I believe this will work out for us, and so think about whether you like this means, because I shall do as you want. I have nothing else to tell you in this letter. Christ watch over you.

Francesco Vettori, Ambassador in Rome

❖ LETTER 231
Niccolò Machiavelli to Francesco Vettori
Florence, 25 February 1514

To the Magnificent Florentine Ambassador to the Supreme Pontiff,
Francesco Vettori, His Most Regarded Benefactor.
In Rome.

Magnificent Ambassador. I got a letter from you last week, and I have put off answering you until now because I wanted better to learn the truth about a yarn[1] that I am about to tell you; then I shall appropriately respond to the various parts of your letter. There has been some "gentle" business, or rather, to call it by its proper name, some laughable metamorphosis—one worthy of being noted in the chronicles of old. And since I do not want anyone to take offense, I shall relate it to you in the guise of a fable.

One recent evening, after the *Ave Maria* rang, someone, let us say[2] Giuliano Brancacci, was eager to go into the woods.[3] Realizing that it was becoming overcast, the wind was picking up, and it was raining lightly—each an indication to expect the birds to be about—he returned home, pulled a pair of stout boots onto his feet, strapped on a game pouch, took a lantern for fowling, a little hand bell, and a wicker paddle. He crossed the Ponte alla Carraia and took the Via del Canto de' Mozzi[4] to Santa Trinita, went into Borgo Santo Apostolo, and meandered around in the alleys that run through its center. Unable to come across any birds on the lookout for him, he turned by your goldsmith's and, near the Parte Guelfa, crossed the market, going by Calimala Francesca, and took refuge under the Tetto de' Pisani, where, scouring every nook and cranny one by one, he landed upon a young thrush. And, with his paddle, lantern, and bell, he caught it and skillfully led it down into the depths of the thicket near Panzano's cave. After a lingering conversation with it and realizing its disposition was generous and kissing it repeatedly, he ministered to several of its hind feathers and ended up, as most people would have it, by placing it in the game pouch he had behind him.

But since the thunderstorm obliges me to come out from under my shelter, the fable is inadequate, and this metaphor is no longer working, Brancacci tried to find out who it was. He replied, let us say, "Michele," the nephew of Consiglio Costi. At this, Brancacci answered, "That's fine, you are the son of a man of probity; if you are sensible, you'll have it made. Know that I am Filippo da Casavecchia and I own a shop in such and such a place; since I don't have any money on me, come to my shop tomorrow, or send someone else, and I'll give you satisfaction." When morning came, Michele—who was more sly than stupid—sent an agent with a note calling in his debt and reminding him of his promise. To this Filippo pulled a long face and exclaimed, "Who is this person? What does he want? I have nothing to do with him; tell him to come and see me himself." So when the agent went back to Michele and told him what had happened, the young man was not in the least flummoxed but boldly dashed off to find Filippo, berated him for the favors he had received, and ended up saying that if Filippo had no scruples about cheating him, he would have none about denouncing Filippo. Since Filippo saw this as an embarrassing situation, he drew Michele into his shop and said, "Michele, you've been tricked. I'm a man of upstanding character and don't get involved in seamy matters such as these. You'd do better to consider how to get to the bottom of this trick, to find out who has had his pleasure with you, and to get your money back, than to bark up this tree and denounce me without any profit in it for you. So, do as I say: go on home, come back here tomorrow, and I'll tell you what I've devised." The boy went off completely mixed up; however, since he was to return, he continued to be patient. And Filippo, when he was alone, became distressed at the strangeness of the situation and, since he saw no escape from it, tossed and turned like the sea at Pisa whenever a gale out of the southwest blows into its estuary. So he said to himself, "If I remain silent and appease Michele with a florin, I become his goose with the golden egg, I'm in his debt, and I admit my sin—instead of being innocent, I become guilty. If I deny it without discovering the truth of the matter, it'll be my word against a boy's, and I'll have to vindicate myself both to him and to others—the wrongdoing will all appear to be mine. If I try to discover the truth, I'm going to have to accuse somebody and I could be off target; I'd thereby create an enemy, and for all that, I'd still not have vindicated myself."

While in this state of anxiety, he decided upon the latter course as the lesser evil; Fortune was so good to him that he hit the bull's-eye with his first shot: he thought it might be Brancacci—who liked doing things on the sly—who had done this piece of dirty work; on other occasions, Brancacci had tricked him, as when he had made a vow at the Servi. So he went to look up, let us say, Alberto Lotti and told him what happened and what he thought about it and asked him if he would go get Michele, a relative of his, to see if this matter could be checked out. Alberto, a man of experience and intelligence, thought Filippo quite perceptive; he promised him his full cooperation, sent for Michele, and after sounding him out a bit, came to this conclusion, "If you heard the man who claimed to be Filippo talk, would you be sure of recognizing his voice?" When the boy said "yes," Alberto took him to Santo Ilario[5] with him because he knew that Brancacci hung out there; when he saw Brancacci sitting down, spinning yarns to a bunch of his cronies—and keeping Michele hidden behind him—Alberto managed to get Michele near enough to hear Brancacci's voice. Turning around and spotting Michele, Brancacci, completely flummoxed, got out of there immediately. Everybody thus clearly saw the situation so that Filippo was completely exonerated and Brancacci denounced. And during this carnival season you hear nothing in Florence except, "Are you Brancacci or are you Casa?"

The story was talked about quite a bit all over heaven.[6]

I expect that you have received this news from other hands, but I wanted to present it to you in fuller detail because it seemed to me I was honor-bound to do so.

I have no response to your letter, except that you should give your love full rein and that whatever pleasure you seize today may not be there for you to seize tomorrow; if things still stand as they did when you wrote, I envy you more than the king of England. I beg you to follow your star; do not let things slide—not even an iota—for anything in the world, because I believe now, I have always believed, and I shall continue to believe that what Boccaccio says is true: it is better to act and to regret it than not to act and to regret it.[7]

25 February 1513[4]

Niccolò Machiavelli, in Florence

❖ LETTER 232
Niccolò Machiavelli to Francesco Vettori
Florence, February–March[1] 1514

I do not want to fail to give you news of the way Lorenzo the Magnificent[2] is acting, which until now has been of such a sort that he has filled the entire city with high hopes; and it seems that everyone is beginning to recognize in him the beloved memory of his grandfather[3] because His Magnificence is diligent in his work, generous and agreeable during an audience, deliberate and serious in his replies. His way of conversing is so different from the others[4] that people attribute no pride to it; nor does he mingle too familiarly so that he generates too low a reputation for himself. His manner toward the young men of his class is such that he neither alienates them nor encourages them to indulge in any youthful, cheeky remarks. In sum, he makes himself both loved and revered rather than feared; the more difficult this is to achieve, the more praiseworthy in him it is.

In his palace there is great magnificence and liberality, yet he does not stray from decent living. So that in all his activities, those inside and outside his palace, nobody is aware of anything offensive or reprehensible—everyone appears to be extremely satisfied with them. And although I know that you will hear all this from many people, I thought I should write you about it so that you can have the same pleasure from my account of it that we who continually experience it have; and when you have opportunity, you can attest to it on my part to His Holiness Our Lord.

❖ LETTER 233
Niccolò Machiavelli to Francesco Vettori
Florence, 16 April[1] 1514

To the Magnificent Ambassador Francesco Vettori, etc.

After a thousand years, will it then seem reprehensible for me to write to you about something other than trivial matters? I trust not. Hence, putting all irrational considerations aside, I think I should ask you to untangle one of my mental knots.

I realize that the king of Spain, who has always been the prime mover[2] of all the disorders in Christendom, ever since he came into Italy, has been lately plunked down in the midst of many difficulties. First of all, it seems to me that there is no advantage to him for Italy to maintain its current appearance and that he cannot tolerate both the Church and the Swiss having so much power here. It would appear that he has more to fear from the state of Naples now than when the French were there, since then the pope was a buffer between Milan and Naples and the pope did not want to allow the French to become masters of the Kingdom of Naples because he would then be left in the middle. But at this point, between the pope, the Swiss, and the king of

Spain, there is absolutely no middle position. Moreover, it seems to me that there is no advantage to him for there to be warfare on the other side of the Alps, because warfare does not always have to end up in a stalemate, as it has done in the year past.[3] And in the long run, the king of France would have either to win or to lose[4]; neither instance means security for Spain. So unless a third situation crops up in which they all destroy one another, each one might turn against the cause of all their evil, because we must believe that his snares are well-known and that they have begun generating repugnance and loathing in the minds of his friends as well as his enemies.

So I conclude that since there is no advantage to him in the current situation, he must figure out ways to change it. If he wants to change the Italian situation so that his own security is greatest, he must get the Swiss out of Milan without installing the French there. He has two problems in doing so: first, without the French, how can he get the Swiss out; second, whom does he have to install there? Because, reflecting upon the first instance, I do not believe the king of France will ever agree to enter Lombardy with his entire army unless it be to remain there as master.[5] Were there to be treaties—either that the king of France should come or that he should hand Milan over either to King Philip's second son,[6] who is Louis's son-in-law, or to someone else—it is not clear to me how Louis could comply with them, since, if he were not always such a dolt,[7] his armies are the more powerful. It is also unclear how Spain can trust such a promise. I believe that everybody will shout "no!" to the possibility of the Swiss being gotten out without the king of France's aid because, given who they are, where they are, how many they are—and the courage they have attained—everyone will deem it impossible to drag them out of there without the king of France's army. As to the second problem, that of handing Milan over to someone, I do not believe he will turn it[8] over to the Church or, much less, to the Venetians; he himself cannot seize it. As people say, he might hand it over to his grandson—that is more rational—but in so doing there is absolutely no security for him because it is tantamount to turning it over to the emperor[9]; were the emperor to see himself as the ruler of Milan, he would quickly get the idea of becoming emperor of Italy and he would start with Naples, to which the Germans have greater claim than the Spaniards.[10]

I imagine, therefore, that should Milan be seized for the archduke contrary to the will of the Swiss, retaining it would be a problem, particularly without the French army, because if the Swiss cannot withstand the flood when it hits them, they will let it pass by and reclaim Milan once the flood has passed and because they know that unless a duke constantly keeps twenty thousand infantry and at least six thousand cavalry there he will never be safe from them—and neither Spain nor the emperor has adequate resources to keep this number there. Hence it turns out that the Swiss, despite learning about the current negotiations for handing the dukedom over to the archduke, are holding firm against the French; they are insouciant about these negotiations because they reckon that no other country but France can hold onto that dukedom against its wishes; therefore, they oppose the French and ridicule the rest.

Consequently, Mr. Ambassador, I should like you to tell me whether or not my conjectures seem valid to you; if they do, tell me what your solution is, and should you like to hear mine, I shall very willingly write you about it at length.

Lorenzo the Magnificent, Lorenzo Strozzi, Lorenzo Pitti, Ruberto de' Ricci, and Mattio Cini are the current officials of the *Monte*.[11] The officials for sales have not been appointed; the composition is being left up to the *Monte* officials. I am obliged to appear before them with nine florins of tithe and four and a half florins of judgment; during the year I spend forty florins and my income is ninety florins or less.[12] I do the best I can to make ends meet. If you could see your way clear to write[13] to one of these officials, attesting to my impossible state, I would put myself in your hands. There is no need to write the Magnificent because he does not attend to these matters—writing to one or two of the others would suffice.

16 April 1514
Niccolò Machiavelli, in Florence

❖ LETTER 234
Niccolò Machiavelli to Giovanni Vernacci
Florence, 20 April 1514

To Messer Giovanni di Francesco Vernacci.
In Pera.[1]

Dearest Giovanni. I have your two letters from last month in which you instruct me to see about withdrawing that nun's money from the *Monte;* I shall attend to it at the first opportunity; I cannot get to it until after Easter Week because people cannot go to the convents. I shall take care of it then and let you know the results.

I shall see Lorenzo[2] and others about sending some business your way; if I can, you shall hear about it.

There is an extremely rich craftsman who has a daughter—she is lame but otherwise beautiful, good, and bright; according to the other craftsmen, he is of good family because he is eligible to hold office. I have been thinking that if he were to give you two thousand *fiorini di suggello*[3] in cash, to promise to open a shop for you in the wool trade, and to make you partner and manager, then perhaps it would be in your interest to marry the daughter; for I believe that I could advance you fifteen hundred florins, and with them and your father-in-law's help, you might get yourself some distinction and profit. I have mentioned this matter in this way, in general terms, and decided to write to you so that you might mull it over; let me know what you think about it in your first letter and, should it seem all right to you, give me permission to act in your behalf.[4] Christ keep you.

Florence, 20 April 1514
Niccolò Machiavelli

If you should prefer to stay there for a while, it could be arranged for you to wait two or three years before marrying her.

❖ LETTER 235
Francesco Vettori to Niccolò Machiavelli
Rome, 16 May 1514

To the Notable Niccolò Machiavelli, etc.
† 16 May 1514.[1]

I approve completely of a few of the conjectures[2] that you make, and a few of them differ a little from my notions. I approve of the first: that the king of Spain, ever since he came into Italy, has been the cause of its remaining constantly at war and that he has done so because, feeling he held the Kingdom of Naples very precariously, since he saw someone there stronger than himself,[3] he has been afraid that he might take that state away from him and he has made others afraid, in order to have company in lowering the one that he saw as strong. It does not seem to me, though, that he should have that same or greater fear of the pope and the Swiss at present than he had of the French, because the French were strongly armed, and always remained so; they had a share in the kingdom; he had usurped it from them by fraud and ruses, and he could know that they were continually thinking about getting it back, although the pope was between them and it was not in his interest to have the Kingdom of Naples and the duchy of Milan in the hands of the same person. It could be conjectured that the pope was desirous of acquiring empire for the Church; the signs of that were seen in such a way that an agreement could easily arise between the French and the pope for them to help him take that kingdom, and the hatred the French had for the Spaniards was such as to believe they were going to listen to him. Now the pope cannot drive the Spaniards from the kingdom by himself, but he needs the Swiss, who want a lot of money. He has to bring them from the border of Italy to the ends of it, and the preparations have to be seen; he has no claim on the kingdom; he is a man desirous of peace; he does not have weapons in his own hands, but he has to count on others, even though he has Giuliano the Magnificent. Up to now he has no experience; he has no soldiers of his own and he has to make use of hired soldiers: if they are Colonnas, they will never hold that state for him, because they will not want to; if they are Orsinis, the Colonnas who fight for their own faction will make so much resistance against him that it will be impossible for him to get anywhere. For this reason I conclude that the king of Spain was more afraid of the king of France when he was lord of Milan than he is at present of the pope with the Swiss.

I do come into agreement with you that war beyond the mountains between France and England is not in the king of Spain's interest and that he wants to stop it for the reasons you give, which satisfy me a great deal. I also believe that he would prefer the affairs of Italy to be different, especially those of Milan, and that he would like to remove the present duke from its government, which would be to remove the Swiss and not to put the king of France there. I think that he would not like to break off with the Swiss, nor would he like to come into possession with the aid of France, because he would be afraid of what you say: that France, becoming bold in taking that state, might keep it for himself. It is not to be believed that he wants this state to come into the hands of the Church or into the hands of the Venetians, or that he thinks he can take and keep it by himself: not that the will might be lacking, but he knows that he would have the Swiss, the emperor, and all the people against him. But he is counting on one thing, that the king will give his second daughter to his nephew, Ferdinand, with the claim to Milan as a dowry,[4] and that he will be obligated with so many troops to help him drive out the present duke; he thinks that the emperor is going to consent to this, and I think that will turn out for him. He is planning then that when this agreement is revealed the present duke will take fright, and that his governors, who are all partisans of the emperor, will persuade him to get an agreement, and that he, without waiting for war and without any troops coming from France, is going to hand over the strongholds to the said Ferdinand, and that the people are going to accept his troops, and thus without war he will become lord of that state. And he does become quite a bit if his grandson, who is ten years old, whom he has raised and had trained under Spanish men, takes it, and he thinks he is going to rule him, especially until he is twenty years old. I think that just as the present duke appeases the Swiss with money, he will also do the same and that this young man is going to have the Guelph party in his favor, since he has the claims of the king of France and his daughter as his wife, and the Ghibelline party, since he is the emperor's grandson. And although he knows the emperor's mind is set on war and unstable and he knows that if he ruled Milan he would then get an urge to take Naples, he does not believe that this can happen, because he thinks that he is going to rule over this boy, and since he has been brought up near him, it seems fitting that he should have Spanish ministers who, until he is able to rule by himself, will keep him in that opinion. He is not afraid of the Swiss, whom he will win over with money. In addition to this, that state will have in its favor France, which is a neighbor, and that part of Germany that the emperor holds. Now, my *compare,* if you were to ask me if these things that the king of Spain is convinced of are reasonable, I would say "no" to you; nonetheless, as you wrote me a year ago[5] and I remember it, for all the progress he has made I consider this Catholic Highness to be rather fortunate than wise. In order to see this better, we shall examine his public actions a bit and leave aside those he has carried on in Spain and against the Moors, because I do not have real information about these; we shall speak of what you and I remember.

In '94, in order to regain Perpignan, he made a treaty with King Charles,[6] he did not care about his family, he did not care about honor, for the House of Aragon to be losing a kingdom, he did not think that if he enhanced the king of France with a state as great as the Kingdom of Naples, it would be an easy matter for him to grow so bold as to be able to take Perpignan back from him, and other matters. He then realized the mistake that he had made; and not caring about his promise, now that the king of France had taken Naples, he made a treaty[7] with the emperor and the pope, with Milan and the Venetians, and he did not think of what happened, that these others would make a treaty and the war would remain on his back, as it turned out for him. But fortune aided him, for King Charles died. The present king succeeded him, he decided to come and take Milan, which was like taking a door to the kingdom: he did not stand in his way, he did not forbid it even with words. He took Milan, and he could easily have taken Italy; he was not troubled by anything, neither when the pope was tyrannizing over Rome nor when Duke Valentino was destroying and laying waste to Italy. The king of France got it into his head to take Naples, and he agreed to take half of it,[8] and he might have thought that since the French were so strong in Italy they were going to drive him out of that part that was supposed to be his. The bad rule of the French and the prudence of Gonzalo made the opposite turn out; and with cunning, deception, and promises he did to the king of France what he was not able to do to him. He then let him take Genoa,[9] at which time, if he had wanted to go on, he would have taken the kingdom and the rest of Italy. The treaty of the League of Cambrai[10] was signed, the king of Spain consented and could easily have understood that if the king of France won he could do as he wished; if the Venetians won, the same was true, and in either case it would hurt him. But once the king of France had won, he felt he was in danger, against all reason, because he had seen signs that he did not want to go beyond his borders. But he persisted in that idea of his and got the pope frightened and offered to be his partisan, and he began by helping him with only three hundred lancers: so he did not satisfy the pope and was acting against the king. The pope lost, and if Messer Gian Giacomo[11] had followed up on his victory, the Kingdom of Naples would have been lost. Once again he signed a treaty[12] with the pope, and the rout of Ravenna ensued, and then the kingdom had no way out: fortune and the discord that there was between Sanseverino[13] and Trivulzio were favorable to him. Nonetheless, not satisfied with this, with a mind rather to stay in his room than in an army camp, since he was a thousand miles away, he put the viceroy[14] back in charge, although he has twice already set that army out on the board so that, if it had been defeated, the loss of his states would have resulted, as when he came to Florence, where he ran a risk and it was not in the king's interest to put a cardinal[15] back in power, since he would be dependent on the pope; the other time, this year in Vicenza, when he got into a situation where nothing but Bartolomeo d'Alviano's lack of patience could have helped him. But last year, when he made the truce, did he not once again give Italy into the hands of the king of France? And he did not know how to be either his friend or his foe. So if one considers his actions well, one will judge him to be fortunate and that everything has turned out well for him; but no one of sound mind will be able to judge that he initiated them prudently.

My *compare*, I know that this king and these princes are men like you and me, and I know that we do many things by chance, many of them things that are of the greatest importance to us, and so it is to be thought they do, too. This king of Spain loves his grandson, Ferdinand, greatly, and he would like to give him a state in Italy, and his will carries him away in such a fashion that he does not see all the dangers he is getting into. In addition to this, a man who is accustomed to winning does not think he can ever lose. I have recalled another error of his. He did everything he could to get Pope Leo made pope, and he had given orders to his agents to this effect when he heard that Julius was ill; and he did not notice that he was making a pope of one of the most noble men who were in court, of the highest state and repute, and that the Kingdom of Naples had always been troubled by pontiffs, and he should have striven for the election of a pope of his own faction, but a weak one. When he had helped him to become pope, he made a truce with the king of France without even letting him hear a word about it, which meant nothing else than to begin to lose all the benefit that he had given him. And so if one should continue to examine the case well, one would find others[16] that do not come to my mind right now.

If I were to tell you what I think, I do not feel that making this match[17] is in Spain's interest. First of all, the king does not have the government in hand, whereas the present duke does; it is therefore necessary for him to make a treaty with the king of France for him to help him recapture it, because he is not capable of it by himself, as we have seen proof that the Swiss have defended it from a larger army than his; and he cannot hope for such aid from the emperor as to be able to hope that he is going to enter into possession of the state with it, because he does not have so many troops or so much money that he can hold off the Venetians, who are beaten and ruined, much less aid anyone else. If the king of France helps him, he has a share in the state and he will become lord of it; and, as you have said, if he is not a simpleton he will keep it for himself and he will not be bothered by what many say, that for security the king of Spain will want to have the girl in his hands,[18] because he knows very well that nothing but honors and flattery will be given to a girl of five years of age, and he will take revenge on Spain by the same means with which he has been several times offended by him. It is not in the king of Spain's interest, either, to have the rumor get out that he wants to make this match, with which he is frightening all of Italy, and if there should be no *virtù* in her, neither is she so lacking in armed troops or in money that by hiring six thousand Swiss, who would be ready, she could not defeat this Spanish army, which in fact has no more than three thousand infantry and six hundred lancers. And if the army were defeated, it would be easy to drive it out of the kingdom and he could not parry this quickly, and the king of France, who has troops organized, would stand by watching the game and would laugh about it. It can also be seen that the king of Spain has always greatly loved this viceroy of his, and he has not punished him for the mistakes he has made but rather has made him stronger, and one may think, as many say, that he is his son and that he has the notion of leaving him as king of Naples. If he puts this grandson of his in Milan, this other plan of his is shattered, because he will be so strong that it will be easy for him to take not just Naples, where he will have many claims, but all the rest of Italy. I do not want to say whether this match is in the king of France's interest or not, because he seems to me to be led by force, because he has had such expenses and so much bad luck for several years that I believe he cannot wait to get out of the war.

Francesco Vettori

❖   LETTER 236
Niccolò Machiavelli to Francesco Vettori
Florence, 10 June 1514

To the magnificent Florentine ambassador Francesco Vettori,
with the Supreme Pontiff.
In Rome.

Magnificent Ambassador. I have received two of your letters, which Donato sent on to me in Brancacci's behalf, while I was on the farm where I have been staying with my family. I answered them as seemed appropriate, concerning my own personal matters, your love affair, and other matters. But when I came to Florence two days ago, I forgot them,[1] so since I think it would be a tiresome effort to rewrite them, I shall send them on to you at some later date. And for now, I shall write you this letter so that you will know yours have arrived safely and to tell you briefly that I have not gone to Rome, held back by the very reasons you now clarify and that I had already understood on my own.

So I am going to stay just as I am amid my lice,[2] unable to find any man who recalls my service or believes I might be good for anything. But I cannot possibly go on like this for long, because I am rotting away and I can see that if God does not show a more favorable face to me, one day I shall be forced to leave home and to place myself as tutor or secretary to a governor, if I cannot do otherwise, or to stick myself in some deserted spot to teach reading to children and leave my family here to count me dead; they will do much better without me because I am causing them expenses, since I am used to spending and cannot do without spending. I am writing you this not because I want you to go to any trouble for me or to worry about me but simply to get it off my chest and not to write anymore about this matter, since it is as odious a subject as can be.

As for your love affair, let me remind you that Love tortures only those who attempt to clip his wings or to fetter him whenever he flies into their laps. Because he is a young, fickle boy, he gouges out the eyes, livers, and hearts of such people. But those who rejoice at his arrival and pamper him, and then let him go whenever he wants to, gladly welcoming his return visits—those he always reveres and cherishes: under his command they triumph. Consequently, my dear friend, do not try to control one who flies or clip someone that grows a thousand feathers for every one lost, and you will be happy.

10 June 1514
Niccolò Machiavelli, in Florence

❖ LETTER 237
Francesco Vettori to Niccolò Machiavelli
Rome, 27 July 1514

To the notable Niccolò Machiavelli, etc.
† 27 July 1514.

My *compare*. Do not be surprised if I have not answered a letter of yours of 10 June, because I was waiting for the one that you said you had left in the country, and I wanted to answer you then. In addition to this, you seemed to me excessively afflicted in it, and I could not console you as I should have desired and as I desire, because there would be no burden or trouble or nuisance that I would not take up for you. Even though I told you in my letter of the reason I had had for not calling you here, I shall tell you in this one that if you should think it was to your purpose, you should not pay any attention to that and you should come as freely as if you were coming to your own house. Because, although more fears beset my mind than any other man's, nonetheless I avoid offending anyone, and then come what may.

From your letter of the 22nd of this month, I learn what you write me about Donato. I therefore wish to reply to you all that I have done in this matter and why I asked for the letter with the hundred ducats. A year ago, Donato wrote me that he wanted to be put in the bag.[1] So I sought out Giuliano the Magnificent on his behalf, and he wrote about him to Lorenzo. I do not know what result the letter had, except that Donato asked me again about this same matter; so that, judging that Giuliano's letter did not bear fruit, I asked Cardinal de' Medici for one. He promised to write it; but meanwhile Lorenzo came here last December and I had the cardinal talk to him about it then, and I did, too, and he promised freely[2] to have him put on the list.

It then turned out that Donato and you as well thought it would be better to have something given, saying that in this matter you would spend a hundred ducats. Since I was not confident in a single letter from the cardinal, I conferred about it with that friend[3] you know about, saying to him: "If we are successful, we shall get a hundred ducats out of it." He said: "Get the cardinal to put it into my hands, and then let me take care of it." So I got it written not once but twice; and then I asked you in a letter when it was time for our gonfalonier to be chosen by the lesser arts.[4] The time was far off, as you know, and so nothing could be done at that time.

I began thereafter to remind Their Lordships, and I found our friend no longer in the same state of mind. I was afraid he was worried about the hundred [ducats], thinking that, since he was to get them from me, I would just act as guarantor. So I wrote to Donato, so he would ask for the money to be sent here. I did this not because, although I am poor, I do not have the means to spend a hundred ducats for a friend but only so as to be able to say to him: "Here is the letter of notification to such and such a bank, for it to pay the money into my hands." And it happened, in fact, that one morning, when our friend was dining with me, a letter came from Donato with one enclosed for Piero del Bene and company. He asked me what the letter was, and I told him about it. I sent someone right away to take the letter to the Benis and ask if they would pay it to me whenever I wanted. They answered that they would pay it any time but that they did not want to be obligated for two months, but it would be enough for them to be obligated for six days. This answer did not satisfy him; and although I told him: "I shall have the money given to me, and when the matter has been settled, you will get it," he did not like that, as if he did not want to be getting it from me. In fact, I was not going to get the money until the outcome had come about, because I do not want any man ever to think that I want to profit or to make anyone else profit on such an account. It was enough for me merely that the Benis had said that they would pay me the hundred ducats within six months if ever I should want them. I could have shown this to my friend and perhaps he would have been satisfied. But they wanted to give it to me in cash, which was not what was needed. Nevertheless, here the case stands. I shall pull this string again; and if he wants to write in the name of the cardinal, fine; if not, I shall get a letter from the cardinal to Lorenzo in any case, and I shall write one, and we shall see what result it has. I would not, however, blame Donato if he were to make some effort over there with Giuliano the Magnificent, which I think would be a good idea. Rest assured that I shall not fail to do what I can; and I am your devoted servant and his. Christ watch over you.

Francesco Vettori, Ambassador in Rome

❖ LETTER 238
Niccolò Machiavelli to Francesco Vettori
Florence, 3 August 1514

To Francesco Vettori in Rome.

You, *compare,* with several dispatches about your love affair in Rome, have kept me in good spirits and lifted countless burdens from my mind as I read and reflect on your pleasures and torments, because one cannot exist easily without the other. Fortune truly has brought me to where I may be justly able to requite you, for while in the country I have met a creature[1] so gracious, so refined, so noble—both in nature and in circumstance—that never could either my praise or my love for her be as much as she deserves. I ought to tell you, as you did me, how this love began, how Love ensnared me with his nets, where he spread them, and what they were like; you would realize that, spread among the flowers, these were nets of gold woven by Venus, so soft and gentle that even though an insensitive heart could have severed them, nevertheless I declined to do so. For a while I reveled within them, until their tender threads hardened and locked into untieable knots. And do not think Love employed ordinary means to capture me, because aware that they would be inadequate, he resorted to extraordinary ones about which I was ignorant and against which I declined to protect myself. Suffice it to say that although I am approaching my fiftieth year,[2] neither does the heat of the sun distress me, nor do rough roads wear me out, nor do the dark hours of the night terrify me. Everything seems easy to me: I adapt to her every whim, even to those that seem different from and contrary to what my own ought to be. And even though I may now seem to have entered into great travail, I nevertheless feel so great a sweetness in it, both because of the delight that rare and gentle countenance brings me and because I have laid aside all memory of my sorrows, that not for anything in the world would I desire my freedom—even if I could have it. I have renounced, then, thoughts about matters great and grave. No longer do I delight in reading about the deeds of the ancients or in discussing those of the moderns: everything has been transformed into tender thoughts,[3] for which I thank Venus and all of Cyprus.[4] Consequently, if you need to write anything about the lady, write, and discuss the other matters with those who appreciate them more and understand them better[5]; I have discovered nothing but harm in these other matters, but in matters of love there are always good things and pleasures.

From Florence, 3 August 1514.
Yours, Niccolò Machiavelli

❖ LETTER 239
Francesco Vettori to Niccolò Machiavelli
Rome, 3 December 1514

To the notable Niccolò di Messer Bernardo Machiavelli.
In Florence.
† 3 December 1514.

My dear *compare*, do not be surprised if, although you have *appeared enough, and have already been given your foil, I seek once again to include you in the old game,*[1] because I am doing it only to find out if I might be of use to you. You might say to me you have had a lot of talk from me for quite a while without corresponding results. For which I have an easy excuse, that since I have not been able to help myself, you cannot be justly surprised if I did not help you, and I think you are sure that it was not for lack of good will.

Now I want you to answer[2] what I am going to ask you. First, I put this conjecture to you: that the pope[3] wants to keep the Church in the same spiritual and temporal dignity that he found it in, and the same authority, or rather to increase it. Then I put this other one: that the king of France wants any way he can to strive to regain the state of Milan and that the Venetians are allied with him in the same way they were last year. I presuppose that the emperor, His Catholic Highness, and the Swiss are united to defend it. I inquire of you what the pope has to do according to your opinion. If he joins with the king of France, what he can hope for from him if he wins and what he can fear if he loses; what he can fear from his adversaries if he joins with him; if he joins with those others, what he can fear from France if he wins and what he can hope for or fear from his adversaries if they win; if he stays neutral, what he can fear from France if he wins or from those others if they should win. Also whether you think, if he clings to the emperor and His Catholic Highness, that it would be in their interest to deceive him and to make a treaty with the king of France; whether you would judge, finally, that if the Venetians were to abandon the king of France and make a treaty with these others, it would be in the pope's interest to join together with them to keep the king of France from coming into Italy.

I am sure that my question is difficult and that I have explained it rather confusedly than otherwise. With your prudence and intelligence and experience, you will be better able to understand what I have tried to say than I have been able to write it. I should like you to discuss this matter in such a way as if you thought your writing was going to be seen by the pope. Do not think that I want to do honor to myself with it, because I promise you I shall show it to him as yours if you should judge that proper. I have never taken pleasure in taking anyone else's honor or goods, especially yours, since I love you as myself. You are to understand concerning what I have said above that the truce between the kings of France and Spain ends at the beginning of April and that although the king of England has a marriage and peace[4] with the king of France, it can still be thought, although we have no certainty of this, that he will not like his strength in Italy. Examine everything, and I know you have such intelligence that although two years have gone by since you left the shop,[5] I do not think you have forgotten the craft.

Give my regards to Donato, and tell him that the *cavaliere* de' Vespucci has often recommended that business of his to me and that I intend to try again, and if it does not work out for me, he will excuse me. Christ watch over you. Answer, the sooner the better.

Francesco Vettori, Ambassador in Rome

✤ LETTER 240
Niccolò Machiavelli to Francesco Vettori
S. Andrea in Percussina, 4 December 1514

Francesco Vettori, Florentine ambassador with the Sprm. Pontiff.

Magnificent Ambassador. The person who presents this letter will be our friend Nic-colò Tafani.[1] *The reason for his journey is his sister, whom he entrusted in marriage to a certain Giovanni some time ago. He was even contracted to her through the bond of a ring; nevertheless, spurning all oaths and laws of matrimony, he betook himself to Rome, where he has lived for a long time and still lives, oblivious to both marriage and wife. So this friend of ours wants one of two things: either for Giovanni to join his wife here or, once he has restored the portion of the dowry he received, for him legally to di-vorce her; our friend is of the opinion that all such matters can easily be accomplished there where dwells the Vicar of Christ. In this matter we therefore implore your help and support and we request that you approach this unfaithful husband and, with all the authority you have at your command, compel him to give satisfaction to the two Niccolòs*[2] *who so urgently entreat it. We are prompted both by justice, which supports our cause, and by the zeal of this man himself and of his entire family—nothing here in our part of the country is more agreeable to me than they are.*

But enough about Tafani. As for what relates to me, if you are interested in knowing what I am doing, you can get an idea from this very Tafani about the full nature of my life; if you love me now as you once did, you will perceive—not without indigna-tion—how sordid and ignominious my life is. Yet my torment and anguish at this are the greater when I note that amid so many and so great felicities for the Magnificent Family [of the Medici] and for our city, [the spirit of] Troy remains alive for me alone.[3]

From Percussina, 4 December 1514.
Niccolò Machiavelli

✤ LETTER 241
Niccolò Machiavelli to Francesco Vettori
Florence, 10 December[1] 1514

To Francesco Vettori, ambassador in Rome. 20 December 1514,
according to the Florentine style.

If His Holiness Our Lord seeks to maintain the Church's influence at the level at which he found it, you ask me what decision he might make should France, with the support of England and the Venetians, want to regain the ter-ritory of Milan at all costs and if, on the other hand, the Swiss, Spain, and the emperor were united in defense of it. This question, as a matter of fact, is your most important one because all the others depend on it, and if you want to clarify it properly, you must clarify them. For the past twenty years I do not think there has been a more serious problem than this one; I know of nothing among those in the past that was so difficult to understand, so ambiguous to pass judgment on, or so hazardous to settle and follow through on. Still, since you oblige me to, I shall embark on a discussion of this matter—doing so in good faith, at least, if not with competency.

Whenever a prince seeks to find out what the outcome of two belligerents might be, he must first gauge the armed strength and the *virtù* of each. As for this question of France and England, their strength is the preparations those kings are said to have made for conquest: to attack the Swiss in Burgundy with twenty thousand men, to attack Milan with a greater number, and with an even greater number, to attack Navarre in order to stir up and to destabilize Spanish territory, and with a great naval armada, to attack Genoa or the Kingdom of Naples with a huge naval armada—or wherever it may be to their advantage. These preparations are, I submit, possible for these two kings and, if they want to be victorious, necessary; I therefore presume they are real. And even though among your latest questions is whether I might consider if England would break away from France—should he be annoyed at the latter's expansion in Italy—I want to discuss this issue now because if England should break away from France, all these questions would be resolved. I believe that the reason why England has clung to France was to avenge the insults[2] Spain inflicted upon him during the war with France. This indignation was justified and I see no issue that might so readily eliminate this indignation and destroy the loving relationship that has formed between these two monarchs; unlike many who are influenced by the inveterate hostility between the English and French, I am not, because the people want what their kings want, not the reverse. As for the English being offended by France's power in Italy, this would inevitably have to result from either envy or fear. Envy might exist if England too were unable to find a spot for acquiring honor and were obliged to remain idle; but if he too can achieve glory for himself in Spain, the cause of the envy is removed. As for fear, you must understand that frequently one acquires territory and not armed forces[3]; and if you think it through carefully you will realize that as far as the king of England is concerned, the king of France's acquisition of cities in Italy is one of territory, not armed forces, because with so great an army France could attack that island whether or not he had Italian territory. As for tactical diversions to Milan, France has more to fear because he has untrustworthy territories and because the Swiss, who can be prompted to act against him with money, have not been used up; once they were attacked by France, the Swiss would really be his enemy—the situation would be unlike the previous one. And because it might also turn out that England would overturn the regime in Castile[4] while France was seizing Milan, England—for the reasons given—might do more damage to France than France could do to him by attacking Milan. Consequently, I do not see why England would have to break away from France during this initial onset of the war; hence, I reaffirm those associations and preparations of armed forces mentioned above being both necessary and possible. There remain the Venetians. They are as important to the affairs of these two kings as the armed forces of the Milanese are to that other group: I consider the forces to be

weak and few in number; half of the troops stationed in Lombardy can keep
the Venetians in check. Now to consider the defenders of Milan: I think the
Swiss can field two armies that would be able to fight any French armies
coming into Burgundy or any coming toward Italy because, were all the Swiss
to unite in such a situation—with the Grisons and the Vaudois added to those
from the cantons—they could bring together more than twenty thousand
men for an army. As for the emperor, I do not want to go into what he might
do now because I have no way of ever knowing what he is going to do. I do
not think more than fifteen thousand soldiers could be raised by joining together the armies of Spain, the emperor, Milan, and Genoa; since Spain expects war at home, it is unable to provide any new forces. As for the sea, I believe that between them, if they have enough money, Genoa and Spain could
form a fleet to oppose their opponents' for quite some time. I therefore believe that these represent the strengths of these two[5] for anyone wishing to
gauge toward which the victory might currently tend. I submit that since the
two kings are well off, they are able to keep their armies together for a long
time and that since the others are not well off, they are unable to do so.
Hence, bearing in mind their armies, their discipline, and their finances, I believe it can be said that if they start fighting soon, the Italian side will be victorious; if war is delayed, victory will go to the other side. People maintain
and it seems reasonable that since the Swiss are aware of this problem and
they want to start fighting soon, they intend to fight the French in the mountains of Savoy so that the French, should they intend to cross, will be obliged
to fight or, if they do not want to fight, will be obliged to retreat because of
the narrow terrain and the dearth of provisions. To judge whether or not they
can succeed in this plan, one would have to have an expert knowledge of
both the topography and warfare; nevertheless, I shall maintain that I have
come across no one in ancient history who ever succeeded in holding onto
these passes,[6] but I have certainly come across many who have abandoned the
passes and lain in wait for the enemy in the plains since they deemed it easier
to defend themselves there and to test the fortunes of war there in less disarray. And although there might be reasons to show how this situation arises, I
shall ignore it since they are not necessary for the discussion of the current
topic. All things considered, then, I regard the only hope for the group in Italy
to be an early start to the battle—which also might end in their defeat. On
the French side, I regard them as capable of winning the contest, and should
they prolong it, they would be unable to lose it. As for those in Italy, I foresee
two obvious perils, among others, in their handling of the war: one, that the
French might come with their navy into the territory of Genoa or Tuscany
either by force or by means of a treaty; no sooner would they be there than
the entire region of Lombardy would belong to them.[7] Many people—some
because they are apprehensive, others because they are disgruntled—will run
to submit to them; hence the French, once they find out that they are being
welcomed, could keep the Swiss dangling and dawdle with them at will. The
other peril concerns those cantons on the border of Burgundy, upon which

the full burden of any war fought in that region will fall; if the war is pro-tracted, they might force the other cantons to come to an agreement with France. The example of Duke Charles [8] leads me to be very fearful of this pos-sibility: by dint of waging war and raiding those areas, he wore them down to such a degree that they raised the white flag; had he not been suddenly forced into battle, he would have disposed of them completely. And because many people are counting—or fearful—that the Swiss, because they are so deceit-ful, might reverse themselves and conclude a treaty with the king and aban-don the rest, I am not afraid of that because they are currently fighting out of their own ambition; unless one of the necessities discussed above arises now and obliges them to do otherwise, I believe they will be loyal during the war.

Now, then, should His Holiness the Pope be obliged to decide and should he choose the imperial and Spanish group,[9] I think victory is doubtful be-cause of the reasons given above and because his adherence is not a total guarantee for them. For, if he deprives the French of some of his interests and influence, that removal does not give the others enough armed forces to con-tain the French; for, since the king has a large naval force at sea and the Vene-tians can also raise one, the pope would have to protect such a stretch of coastline [10] from north to south that his troops plus yours [11] would hardly suf-fice. If people intend to make sure of him, it may well be that His Holiness escapes immediate danger and even realizes some immediate profit, since he is able to do his family honor immediately. Should His Holiness choose the di-rection of France, were he able to do so prudently and to keep the French waiting [12] without danger, I consider victory certain. For, since with his fleet he can place a large army in Tuscany along with his own, he would instanta-neously cause a huge disturbance in Lombardy in consort with the Venetian army there; the Swiss and Spaniards could not hold out against two different armies on two different flanks or defend themselves against the popular upris-ing that would occur at that moment. Hence, I do not see how it would be possible for the king to be robbed of victory.

Furthermore, you want to know which would be less dangerous for the pope—an alliance with France or the Swiss, were either one, with him as ally, able to prevail. My answer is that I believe that if the Swiss, their allies, and their friends were to win, they would—for the nonce—keep the promise they made and give him his territory. But, on the other hand, he would have to tolerate the victor's importunate conduct. Since I recognize only the Swiss as victorious, he would have to tolerate their abuses; these would be immedi-ately of two kinds: first, taking away his money; second, taking away his friends. For you can be sure the money that the Swiss maintain they do not want now while they are carrying on the war they will want as soon as the war is over; they will start off with some tribute, which will be steep, and they will not be refused both because he will want to appear to be honest and be-cause he will be afraid of provoking them during the first flush of their vic-tory. I think—rather, I am certain—that the duke of Ferrara,[13] the people of Lucca, and such will rush to make themselves their protégés. Once one of them is taken by the Swiss, *it will be all over for Italy's freedom,* because under various guises they will daily impose fines and plunder them, they will change governments, and what they cannot do now they will bide their time and do later. No one should count on them not to consider this plan because they have to be considering it; if they should not, the course of events will make them consider it: one success leads to another, one victory makes people thirsty for more. No one should be surprised that they have not seized Milan openly and have not proceeded farther than they have because just as their way of governing at home is different from others', so it is different abroad—and one comes across this throughout ancient history. For until now, if they have linked themselves with others, in the future they will create protégés and tributaries to whom they will give no heed about control or detailed management; they will be content solely if they stand by them during war and pay their annual tribute. The Swiss will preserve this situation with the prestige of their army at home and with punishment for any who might defect. In this way, and quickly if they win this victory, they will dictate the law to you [Florentines], to the pope, and to every other Italian prince; once you realize that they assume a protectorate, *"you know that summer is nigh."*[14] And were you to say, "There will be a remedy for this situation because we all shall join together against them," I reply that this would be a second mistake and a second deception, because a league of many leaders against one is hard to achieve and, once achieved, is hard to preserve. Take France, for example: everybody formed a league[15] against him, yet suddenly Spain concluded a treaty with him, the Venetians became his ally and the Swiss attacked him without enthusiasm, the emperor was never seen again, and finally England joined the league on his side. Because, if the man against whom a league is formed is of great enough *virtù* so that he does not immediately go up in smoke, as the Venetians did,[16] he will consistently find a remedy in the multiplicity of views—as France did, and as the Venetians would have found out had they been able to keep that war going for two months. But their weakness could not bide its time while the allies dissolved; the Swiss would not experience such a situation because they would always discover—whether with France, the emperor, Spain, or the powerful leaders of Italy—a means for preventing all of them from coming together, or if they did unite, a means for dividing them. I know many people will ridicule this idea, yet I am so convinced of it—and so afraid of it—that if the Swiss successfully stem this tide and if we both are still alive in six years, I count on reminding you of it.

Now then, since you want to know what I think the pope has to fear from the Swiss should they be victorious while he is their ally, I have come to the conclusion that he has to be afraid of some immediate taxes and within a short time his own bondage and that of all Italy—*without hope of redemption*—since theirs is a republic, one armed without parallel[17] among any prince or powerful leader. But were the pope an ally of France and should he be victorious, by the same token I believe France would fulfill his agreement if the terms were appropriate and if too much craving had not caused him to ask the pope for too much and to relinquish too much to the king. I believe he would tax not the Church but you Florentines and he would have to respect the Church because of his alliance with England and the Swiss—who would all be far from dead—and because of Spain, who, albeit driven out of Naples, is still alive and so would be of some importance.[18] Therefore, it would appear to be reasonable that [the king of France], for his part, would want the Church influential and friendly, and the Venetians, too. In short, whatever the outcome of these victories may be, I predict that the Church will be at the mercy of someone; so I deem it better for her to be at the mercy of those who will be more reasonable and with whom she is familiar from previous experience and not at the mercy of those with whom she is unfamiliar and I know not what their desires might be.

Should the group to which His Holiness Our Lord belongs lose, were I the pope, I would be afraid that I would be led into every extreme situation possible: flight, a council meeting, and everything popes can be afraid of. Hence, whenever one is obliged to choose one of two alternatives, one ought, among other things, to figure out where the bad fortune of either alternative might lead him and he ought to choose, all things being equal, the one whose outcome, should it be bad, will be the least galling. A loss with France as an ally would undoubtedly be less galling than one with the others as allies. Because if His Holiness has France for an ally and loses, there remains the territory of France,[19] which can uphold the honor of a pontiff; he dwells in wealth that because of the kingdom's power can be resurrected in a thousand ways and he remains in his own house where many popes have had their seat. If his alliance is with the others and he should lose, he would have to depart for Switzerland and starve, for Germany and be a laughingstock, or for Spain and be bled dry; so, there is no comparison between the evil resulting from the bad fortune of these two alternatives.

I do not believe that remaining neutral was ever useful to anyone confronted with these conditions: he is less powerful than those fighting and he has territory scattered among the belligerents'. And the first thing you must understand is that there is nothing more necessary for a prince when interacting with his subjects, his allies, or his neighbors than not to be hated or despised by them; if he must abandon one or the other, let him not value hatred but be on guard against contempt.[20] Pope Julius II[21] never gave any heed to being hated, provided that he was feared and respected; it was through this fear that he turned the world topsy-turvy and brought the Church to the position where it is now.[22] And I submit that it is necessary for whoever remains neutral[23] to be hated by the loser and despised by the winner; once people start discounting a neutral person, holding him to be neither a useful ally nor a formidable enemy, then he has to fear that all manner of abuse will be heaped upon him and all manner of ruin will be plotted against him. The winner never lacks justifications because, since the neutral person's territories are scattered about, he is forced to accept within his gates sometimes one group and sometimes another, and to accept them within his house as well as to help them with food and shelter; both sides will [always] [24] believe that they are being gulled and a host of things will occur that will [prod]uce a host of wrangling. And even if none of these things should come up while the war is being carried on—an impossible hypothesis—something will after a victory because those with little power, who are afraid of you, will immediately run under the victor's wing and provide [him] with reasons for attacking you. And to whoever might point out, "true it is that we can be robbed of one thing and given another," my reply would be that it is better to lose everything gallantly than to lose a part ignominiously, and a part cannot be lost without shaking the whole. Therefore, whoever reflects upon the territories of His Holiness Our Lord in their entirety—where they are located, the kind of lesser powers they contain, and whom they are fighting with—will deem that under no conditions can His Holiness remain [neutr]al. Were he to choose neutrality, he would be obliged to treat both the winner and the loser as enem[ies] [25]; each side would wish [him] harm: one because of a desire for revenge, the other because of a desire for profit.

You also ask me if, supposing the pope were to ally himself with the Swiss, the emperor, [26] and Spain, it would be in the interest of Spain and the emperor to betray him and to side with France. I believe that a treaty between Spain and France is impossible and that it cannot be reached without England's consent; England cannot make a treaty except against France. Hence, France cannot entertain the notion because, since the king of England is young and swaggers excessively about military matters, England has nowhere to go with his armies except toward France and toward Spain; just as peace with France would entail war with Spain, so peace with Spain would entail war with France. Consequently, so as not to lose England and not to have a war on his back and possessing thousands of reasons for hating Spain, the king of France is not going to lend an ear to peace; because if he wanted peace or were able to achieve it, he would do so: that king could have brought forward countless plans for ruining others. Hence, as far as Spain is concerned, I believe that the pope could reasonably expect to fear everything; as far as France is concerned, he can expect to be safe. As for the emperor, because he is unpredictable and capricious, any change is to be feared, whether or not it be in his interest, since he has consistently lived in and been nourished by such unpredictability. Should the Venetians side with our faction, it would be of great importance not so much because of the addition of their troops but because of this group's remaining more openly hostile to France; and should the pope side with them, the French would encounter numerous problems both in coming down into Italy and in establishing roots here. But I do not believe the Venetians will adopt this strategy, because I believe they have received better terms fr[om] France than they would get from the rest, and having followed the fortune of France when it had practically given up the ghost, it seems unreasonable for them to forsake it now that it is on the point of resurgence; I fear that they, as is their wont, are merely starting rumors to their own advantage.

To close this discourse, I therefore conclude that since there are more signs of victory for the French side than for the rest, since the pope's accession can provide a certain victory to France and not to the rest, since France as ally and victor is less formidable and more tolerable than the rest, since defeat is less bitter with France as an ally than it is with the rest, and since he is unable to remain neutral safely, His Holiness Our Lord ought either to side with France or, should the others side with Venice, surely to side with them, and not do otherwise.[27]

❖ LETTER 242
Francesco Vettori to Niccolò Machiavelli
Rome, 15 December 1514

To the notable Niccolò Machiavelli.
In Florence.
† 15 December 1514.

Dear *compare*. After a long silence, I have gotten three letters from you within the past two days: one[1] in which you ask me for blue woolen yarn for a pair of hose, which I shall send you tomorrow without inquiring for whom you want it, because I shall be satisfied with making you happy; another one,[2] in Latin, a certain friend of yours, Tafani, was supposed to bring me. Whatever may be the cause, he did not appear before me, but had it given to me by a shopkeeper who put it in one of my servants' hands. I am sorry not to have seen him, both to help him for your sake and to hear about how you are living, since you rely on him. I shall have him sought out, and if I find him, although I have but little authority, I shall show him that your letter will be of use to him. The other one,[3] which answers the questions I asked of you, I got yesterday. I have not yet shown it to Monsignor de' Medici,[4] who asked me to have you write it for him. I think he will be satisfied by it, because it satisfies me, too: when I have shown it to him I shall tell you what he says to me.

I have often spoken of you with my brother Paolo, who loves you very much. He will be back, as I hope, within the month, and you will be able to learn from him how much I esteem you and how much I think about you. But, believe me, we are driven by the Fates. In the past few days I have read the book of Pontano, De Fortuna, recently published,[5] which he himself sent to the great Gonzalo.[6] In this book he clearly shows that neither talent, nor foresight, nor fortitude, nor the other virtues avail at all when Fortune is absent. We see proof of this every day in Rome. For we know that some lowborn men, unlettered, without talent, are nevertheless in positions of the highest authority. Still, it must be accepted, and you especially, who are not ignorant of evils and have endured much worse, ought to do so. God will bring an end to these things, too.[7] I live and am well here, but not excessively. The swelling that I have on my neck, as you know, grows every day, and I do not know whether it should be cut off. I am in reasonable favor with the pope and the rest of our Medici, in my judgment; nevertheless, I ask nothing of them. From the salary granted to me according to the laws I make my ex-

penditures, and at the end of the month I have nothing left. I am free from love and have returned to favor with books and playing cards.

I have asked Lorenzo the Magnificent about Donato's business, so neither you nor he should think I might have forgotten it. He promised me to have him selected on his return, and up to now no one has been selected, and all those who are eligible or whose names are drawn[8] had a vote. But you and Donato made me go and promise that friend, who is expecting to get something out of it, in any case, however the matter turns out, even though he is not going to any trouble for it, because he may have written the letters but I asked for them; and I have made the effort myself with Lorenzo the Magnificent, as enthusiastically as I could. Nonetheless, he knows that I have that letter with the hundred *frati*[9] for Piero del Bene, because I showed it to him to get him to go along, and he knows that it is valid for only six months, which are near their end. I would not want him, thinking he is not going to do any better by it, to try to spoil it, as you know would be so easy. Therefore, if ever Donato should feel like having it done again, I leave it up to him, letting him understand always that not a penny of it will be paid until the result has been achieved. Even then we shall attempt to save money, if it is possible. But if you do not want it to be hindered, we have to be able to show the letter, as he reminded me not more than two days ago. Too bad for you that I could not get it all in time for you; you could still have accomplished something, and you let the bird get out of your hand. I have nothing else to tell you except that I send my regards to you and the other Machiavellis. Christ watch over you.

Francesco Vettori, Ambassador in Rome

❖ LETTER 243
Niccolò Machiavelli to Francesco Vettori
Florence, 20 December 1514

To the magnificent Florentine ambassador Francesco Vettori,
with the Supreme Pontiff.
In Rome.

Magnificent Ambassador. Now that you have stirred up my juices, if what I write bores you, then say, "It's all my fault because I wrote him first." I am afraid that you will think that I was too terse in that part both about neutrality in my reply to your questions and in my discussion of what was to be feared from the victor should the side the pope joined lose; both alternatives seemed to present many considerations.[1] Hence, I have tried my hand again at writing about the same material. And as for neutrality, a strategy it seems to me I am aware of many people approving, I cannot look favorably upon it because I can recall neither in what I have seen nor in what I have read that it has ever been a good thing; in fact, it has always been an extremely destructive policy because it is certain to lose. And even though you understand the reasons for this better than I do, still I would like to remind you of them.

You realize that the main duty of every prince is to keep himself from be-ing hated and despised, to avoid, in fact, *contempt and hatred*[2]; whenever he does so well, everything must turn out well. And he must carry out this policy both with his allies and with his subjects; whenever a prince *does not avoid con-tempt at least,* he is done for. I think taking a neutral stand between two bel-ligerents is nothing short of asking to be hated and despised, because there will always be one of them who believes that as a result either of the services he has rendered or of some long-standing alliance you have with the prince you are obliged to follow his fortune; if you do not side with him, he con-ceives a hatred for you. The other belligerent despises you because he views you as timid and uncertain and you immediately are taken to be an ineffective ally and an enemy not to be feared; consequently, whoever wins has no scru-ples about attacking you. And Livy expresses this opinion briefly when putting these words in the mouth of Titus Flaminius, when he said to the Achaeians, whom Antiochus had persuaded to remain neutral: "Nothing is farther from your interests; you will become the spoil of the victor without thanks, without dignity."[3] Furthermore, in the conduct of a war between two such belligerents, countless reasons for hatred of you will inevitably arise be-cause the third person is so situated that frequently he is able to help or to hinder one side or the other in numerous ways. And within a short time, starting on the day war breaks out, you will always come to the point where you are obliged to take the position secretly and to your disadvantage that you tried not to be obliged to state openly and to your advantage; even if you do not take such a position, there will still be some people who think you have. And even if Fortune were to be so propitious in the neutral person's behalf that during the conduct of the war no just cause for either belligerent to hate him arose, such causes must arise once the war is over because everyone whom the neutral person has harmed and all those who fear him rush to the victor's side; the latter thus has a reason to hate and to scorn the neutral per-son. And were someone to counter by saying that the pope, because of the veneration felt for his person and because of the Church's authority, is in an-other category and will always have a refuge where he may save himself, I should respond that this point merits some consideration and that one can find some grounds for it. Nevertheless, it is not something to be relied upon; on the contrary, I believe that should the pope wish to be well-advised, he should not consider it because such an expectation might cause him to make a bad decision. Because all things that have existed, I believe, can exist again[4]; and I know that we have seen pontiffs flee, be exiled, be tracked down, and suffer the supreme penalty, just as temporal lords have been—even during a period when in the spiritual realm the Church had more veneration than to-day. Therefore, if His Holiness Our Lord will consider where his territory is located, who the belligerents are, and who are the ones who might take refuge with the victor, I believe that His Holiness will be by no means able to lull himself into taking a neutral position and that he will realize he gains more advantage by taking sides, one way or the other. So, as for neutrality, to clarify my position on it more extensively than I did in the other letter, I have nothing further to say to you. And as for what he might have to fear from whoever might conquer and might get the better of whatever side he had joined, I shall say no more because I have said everything about it above.

I think that it will appear from the letter I wrote to you that I have tended toward France, and whoever might read it could suspect that, to a certain extent, emotion had brought me to a position. Such a suspicion would annoy me because I always strive to be unfaltering in my judgment, particularly about matters such as these, and not to let it be corrupted by a vain spirit of competition—as practiced by many other people. Because, though I may have tended a bit too much toward France, I do not think I have been deceived; I should like briefly to go into what prompts me again—it will be a kind of recapitulation of what I have already written. If someone wants to figure out which one of two belligerent powerful leaders must be victorious, one should—in addition to taking stock of each one's armed forces—gauge all the different ways each of them might prove to be victorious. I see nothing for the anti-French faction to do but to attack right away, whereas the French side has all the opportunities I already wrote to you about in great detail.[5] This is the first reason that leads me to believe more in France than in the others. Furthermore, if I have to declare myself the ally of one of the two groups—and I realize that by joining one group I am providing him with unquestionable victory and that by joining the other I am providing him with a questionable one—I believe that it will always be right to choose the unquestionable side; I should put to one side any commitment, any interest, any apprehension, and anything that I might find offensive. And I believe, were the pope to join with France, that there would be no argument about this position; but were he to join with the others, there would be plenty of argument, for the reasons about which I have already written you. Besides this, whenever wise men do not have to gamble with all their property, they are glad for the occasion; while providing for the worst that might happen, they figure out where, within the harm, lies the lesser of two evils.[6] And because all of Fortune's activities are uncertain, wise men willingly link themselves to the kind of Fortune that, doing the worst she knows how to do, will bring about the least galling result. His Holiness Our Lord has two squares[7]: one in Italy, the other in France. If he joins France, he gambles with one of them; if he joins the others, he gambles with them both. If he is France's enemy and France wins, he is obliged to follow the fortune of the others: to go to Switzerland and starve, to Germany and live in despair, or to Spain and be swindled and betrayed. If he joins France and loses, France still remains his, as does his house; he is with a kingdom at his command that equals a papacy and he is with a prince who can arise again in a thousand ways, thanks either to a treaty or a war. *Farewell.* I send you my regards a thousand times.

20 December 1514

Niccolò Machiavelli, in Florence

❖ Letter 244

Niccolò Machiavelli to Francesco Vettori

Florence, 20 December 1514

To the magnificent Francesco Vettori, etc.

Magnificent Ambassador. After I had written the enclosed,[1] I received yours of the fifteenth[2]; I shall deal only with the part concerning Donato, to whom I read the passage. He was so filled with joy that he is jumping out of his shirt. Because he has decided that he will spare nothing in order to obtain this favor, he had the letter to the Beni rewritten; pursuant to it, there will be one hundred ducats payable to you within six months. And should you need any more in addition to this sum, he told me that no economy should be made and no expense should be spared. The letters will be included with this one; as is customary with such letters, make use of them at the right time. As to whether or not to save it, Donato did not want me to write you anything about it; yet I am bringing the matter to your attention—especially since I think our friend's business has no more need in any way, because, since there is no further reason to write about this matter, it seemed to me it could do neither harm nor good. If only Donato can finally extricate himself from his plebeian status, he does not want this to be worried about or any avenue overlooked.

Again, thank you for all the effort and all the thoughtful attention you have paid out of love for me. I cannot promise you anything in return because I do not think I shall ever be able to do any good for either myself or others. And had Fortune intended that the Medici might once have employed me, whether for affairs in Florence or abroad, whether for their private concerns or their public ones, I would be content. I do not, however, lose complete hope in myself yet. And if that were to happen and I should not know how to bear up, I would have a bone to pick with myself alone; but let be what must be. Each day I realize that what you say Pontano writes is true: when Fortune wishes to hound us, she places in our way an immediate advantage, an immediate peril, or both at the same time; I believe these two possibilities to be the greatest enemies there are to the position that I upheld in my letters.[3] *Farewell.*

20 December 1514

Niccolò Machiavelli, in Florence

❖ LETTER 245
Francesco Vettori to Niccolò Machiavelli
Rome, 30 December 1514

To the notable Niccolò Machiavelli, in Florence.
† 30 December 1514.

> *See, desire again begins a violent war against me,*
> Compare; *see, a new fire again racks me!* [1]

Truly, Ovid spoke well when he said that love proceeded from idleness. I, who have nothing to do, would like to do as Mino da Siena,[2] and I am so busy with this that I do not write back to you, as would be my duty. Both your letters concerning the questions I asked you have been seen by the pope and Cardinals[3] Bibbiena and de' Medici, and all were astonished at their wit and praised their judgment. And although nothing else has been gotten from them but words, both because of ill luck and because I am not a man who knows how to help his friends, nonetheless being in the good opinion of great men might be of use to you sometime. I wanted to contradict some of your arguments, to pass the time and to give you matter to write about; but being busy, as I have said above, I have put aside the writing that I had begun. Perhaps I shall finish it another time and send it to you.

I do not know whether you got the cloth for the hose, which I sent by the post rider, and I asked him to leave it at the house of Simon the horseman, and then Filippo del Benino should let you know; and I do not have an answer from him, either, so that I am afraid you did not get it. So go and recover it, because I would not want to fail you for anything, in anything that you have asked of me for the last hundred years.

I got your letter concerning the case of Donato, and his to the Beni, with Piero's request. Tell him that Lorenzo has promised me when he goes back to draw him and then have him chosen. Whether he does, experience will show. That was what he promised me, and before he leaves I shall remind him of it. Because you know me, you can assure him that if he had not promised it to me I would not say so, because it is not my custom to fill my friends with vain hopes. As for the money, we shall do the best we can with our friend because, even though he is not going to be of use, if he were deprived of hope he might try to hinder it. Therefore I shall keep him with some excuse that I think is suitable for that. I have nothing else to say in this letter. Christ watch over you.

Francesco Vettori, Ambassador in Rome

L E T T E R S

1515–1519

The precise dating of both *The Prince* and *The Discourses* presents several thorny problems, although it is clear that a lot of work was done on the latter during this period. By 31 January 1515, the day Machiavelli wrote Letter 247 to Vettori, *The Prince* was finished—except, perhaps, for its final chapter—and was circulating privately among his friends, though without a dedicatory letter. Although he had originally intended to dedicate it to Giuliano de' Medici, Machiavelli changed his mind, perhaps because Giuliano was never very interested in either Machiavelli or military theory, a topic fundamental to *The Prince*. Machiavelli was aware, however, that Pope Leo had appointed his brother, Giuliano, to be captain general of the Church on 10 January. He knew, too, that later in January, Giuliano married Filiberta of Savoy, a sister-german of Louise of Savoy, whose son Francis I had just succeeded to the throne of France on 1 January after the death of Louis XII. Aware, through observation, deduction, or perhaps even rumor, of the project to carve out a power center in northern Italy for Giuliano, Machiavelli found it easy to categorize Giuliano as a "new prince," someone for whom *The Prince* might have been written.

But Machiavelli's interest in Leo X's nephew, Lorenzo II de' Medici, was also keen (see Letter 232, written during the second or third month of 1514). By 1515, Lorenzo was the virtual ruler of Florence and he was elected the Florentine captain general in May. He understood the military; furthermore, he had a military aura about him that Machiavelli respected. At some point in the first half of 1515, Machiavelli wrote *Scritto sul modo di ricostituire l'ordinanza* (Document on the means of reestablishing conscription), sometimes referred to as the *Ghiribizzi d'ordinanza* (Speculations on conscription). This brief work was probably addressed to Paolo Vettori, who in 1515 was a firm supporter of Lorenzo. Machiavelli may have hoped through it somehow to receive a nod from Lorenzo, but neither this "document" nor *The Prince* ever impressed the latter. The hope that such a nod would come is apparent from Letter 247, written to Francesco Vettori late in January 1515. The evidence shows Machiavelli's hope turning to despair. Not only is he despondent in his letters to his nephew Giovanni Vernacci, but he also seems to have nothing to say to anyone else, either in letter or book form, for quite some time.

Francis I, however, impressed all of Italy and had a lot to say about Italian political affairs. He forced military considerations once more to a level of paramount concern, because he was determined to assert French claims to Milan. As proof, he signed treaties with England, Venice, and the Netherlands. Leo X countered, unfortunately, by joining with Spain, the Swiss, Milan, and Maximilian I. The French entered Italy in August and drove the Swiss out of Italy at the Battle of Marignano on 13 September. The French were thus able to control Milan, and the pope had to relinquish his hope to protect Milan from foreign domination. His armies, though on the losing side, had been kept from the fray by their new commander Lorenzo de' Medici—Leo X had given his nephew the title of *gonfaloniere di Santa Chiesa* in August—and by the Florentine commissioner, Francesco Vettori. (Vettori returned to Florence from Rome on 15 May; there are only eleven personal letters exchanged between Machiavelli and Vettori throughout the rest of Machiavelli's life.) Because he continued to pursue his career energetically, Lorenzo still attracted Machiavelli's admiration. Eventually, through papal investiture, Lorenzo became duke of Urbino in October 1516. We may never know the personal or theoretical reasons for the change in the dedicatee of *The Prince*, but we do know that Giuliano died on 17 March 1516. So we can assume that Machiavelli dedicated *The Prince* to Lorenzo at some point between March and September 1516.

The date when Machiavelli began work on *The Discourses* is also difficult to determine, but it is clear that he began his study during this period. A strong stimulus was provided by a Florentine group with a humanist bent that met at the *Orti Oricellari* (Rucellai Gardens) for literary, philosophical, and political discussions hosted by Cosimo Rucellai. Machiavelli may have started to participate in these intellectual discussions in 1514 or, more likely, in 1515; but he was one of the habitués by 1516, the fictive date for *The Art of War*. He first mentions the *Orti Oricellari* meetings, however, in Letter 254, dated 17 December 1517. Hurt at receiving no recognition from Lorenzo de' Medici, he gratefully and gracefully dedicated *The Discourses* to Cosimo Rucellai and Zanobi Buondelmonti. In so doing he drew a sharp distinction between people who "know how to govern" (those friends of his at the *Orti Oricellari*) and people who "without knowing how, do govern" (Lorenzo de' Medici).

The intellectual friendship in the Rucellai Gardens bore literary as well as political fruit. These were the years when Machiavelli wrote *Dell' asino [d'oro]*, an incomplete poem modeled on Apuleius and perhaps on Angelo Firenzuola dealing with the theme of metamorphosis, a *serenata, Salve, donna, tra le altre donne eletta* (Hail, lady, elect among other ladies), and a sonnet, *Se sanza a voi pensar solo un momento* (If I could help thinking of you for one moment). He also translated the *Andria,* a charming comedy by Terence. *Dialogo intorno alla nostra lingua* (Dialogue concerning our language), attributed to Machiavelli, also dates from this period. In it the persona of Machiavelli dares to debate Dante on the merits of the vernacular, an issue to which Machiavelli was firmly committed. His novella *Belfagor,* often referred to in English as "The Devil Who Took a Wife," is usually thought to have been written during these years, although it was first printed in 1549. His most remarkable literary work is *La Mandragola,* an excellent comedy that bitingly combines literature and politics. A manuscript version dates from 1519, and there was a production in Florence prior to April 1520, but we do not know exactly when Machiavelli wrote the work, one of the best comedies of the Italian Renaissance.

This productive period of writing allowed Machiavelli a brief opportunity to hone his political and negotiating skills. During Lent, in March 1518, a group of Florentine merchants (Mariotto de' Bardi, Jacopo di Bernardo Altoviti, Carlo di Niccolò Strozzi, and Antonio Martellini) employed Machiavelli to deal with their affairs in Genoa following the bankruptcy of Davide Lomellini. Although it was a minor commission, Machiavelli was glad to be active in the political arena once more.

❖ LETTER 246
Francesco Vettori to Niccolò Machiavelli
Rome, 16 January 1515

To the Notable Niccolò Machiavelli.
In Florence.
† 16 January 1514[5].

Dear *compare.* I get letters from no one that I read with more pleasure than yours. I wish I could write many things that I know cannot be entrusted to letters. Several months ago I understood quite well how much in love you were, and I was about to say to you, *"Ah, Corydon, Corydon, what madness has seized you?"*[1] Then, thinking to myself that this world is nothing other than love or, to speak more clearly, lust, I restrained myself. I considered how far men are in their hearts in these circumstances from what they say aloud. A father has a son whom he says he wants to raise virtuously; nonetheless he begins by giving him a master who stays all day with him, and who is free to do with him as he wishes, and lets him read things that would arouse a dead man. The mother cleans him, dresses him well, so that he may be more comely; when he starts to grow up, she gives him a room on the ground floor with a private entrance and all the other conveniences, so that he can wallow about as he wishes and bring and invite there anyone he feels like. And we all do thus, and those who are orderly do all the more wrong in this: it is not surprising therefore if our young men are as wanton as they are, because this results from their very bad upbringing. You and I, although we are old, retain to some degree the habits we learned in our youth, and there is nothing to do about it. I am sorry not to be over there, so that we could talk together about these and many other things.

But you tell me something that astonishes me: you have found so much faith and so much compassion in La Riccia[2] that, I swear to you, I was partial to her for your sake, but now I have become her slave, because most of the time women[3] are wont to love Fortune and not men, and when Fortune changes, to change as well. I am not surprised about Donato, because he is a man of faith, and in addition to this he continually experiences the same as you.

I wrote you that idleness made me fall in love and I reaffirm this to you, because I have practically nothing to do. I cannot read much, by reason of my eyesight, which has been diminished by age. I cannot go out and enjoy myself unless I am accompanied, and this cannot always be done: I do not have so much authority or such resources as to be sought out; if I spend my time in thought, most of them bring me melancholy, which I try my best to flee; of necessity one must endeavor to think of pleasant things, but I know of nothing that gives more delight to think about and to do than fucking. Every man may philosophize all he wants, but this is the utter truth, which many people understand this way but few will say. I am thinking of going to see you in the spring, if I am allowed to, and we shall speak together of this and many other things. Give my regards to Filippo,[4] Giovanni and Lorenzo Machiavelli,[5] and Donato.[6] Christ watch over you.

Francesco Vettori, Ambassador in Rome

❖ LETTER 247
Niccolò Machiavelli to Francesco Vettori
Florence, 31 January 1515

To Francesco Vettori, Ambassador.
In Rome.

> The youthful archer[1] many times had tried
> To wound me in the breast with his arrows;
> He takes his pleasure thus—spite for all
> And harm to everyone is his delight.
>
> Though no diamond exists that might withstand
> His arrowheads brutal and keen,
> Yet now they've struck an obstacle so strong
> It took little account of all their power.

So, full of rage and anger, in order
To demonstrate his consummate skill,
He made a change of quiver, bow, and shaft;

With such great force he let one fly,
That I feel its painful wound still; thus I
Confess and recognize his power.

I should not know how otherwise to reply to your last letter about lust with
words that seem to me more on target than with this sonnet;[2] from it you will
realize to what extent that little thief, Love, has gone in order to bind me with
his fetters. Those with which he has bound me are so strong that I am in absolute despair of my liberty and I am unable to conceive of any means of unfet-
tering myself; and even if fate or other human stratagem should open some
path for me to get out of them, perhaps I should not wish to go down it; so do
I find these fetters—now sweet, now light, now heavy—and they make such a
tangle that I believe I cannot live happily without this kind of life. And because
I am aware of what delight you take in such thoughts and in learning about
such ways of living, I regret that you are not here to laugh, sometimes at what
darkens my life and sometimes at what brightens it. And all this entertainment
that might be yours is now enjoyed by both our Donato and the woman about
whom I wrote you earlier, who are the sole havens and refuges for my skiff
bereft of rudder and sail because of the unending tempest.[3] And it was only
two nights ago that I found myself able to say, as Apollo did to Daphne:

O Nymph, daughter of Peneus, I entreat you, wait:
it is not as an enemy that I pursue—wait, Nymph.
Just as the lamb flees the wolf, the hind flees the lion,
and doves with quivering wings flee the eagle,
so does every creature flee its enemies.[4]

And just as this song was of little help to Apollo, so the same speech carried no
weight and availed not with her who was fleeing me.[5] Anyone who might see our
letters, honorable compare, and see their variety, would be greatly astonished,
because at first it would seem that we were serious men completely directed
toward weighty matters and that no thought could cascade through our heads
that did not have within it probity and magnitude. But later, upon turning the
page, it would seem to the reader that we—still the very same selves—were
petty, fickle, lascivious, and were directed toward chimerical matters. If to
some this behavior seems contemptible, to me it seems laudable because we
are imitating nature, which is changeable; whoever imitates nature cannot be
censured.[6] And even though we have grown accustomed to this multiplicity
over the course of several letters, this time I want to do an about-face in one
letter—as you will see if you read the next page. So hawk up some phlegm.

Your Paolo has been here with His Magnificence and, among other discussions he had with me about his prospects, he told me that His Lordship

promised to appoint him governor of one of those cities over which he is currently taking control.[7] And having understood—not from Paolo but from a rumor—that His Magnificence is to become lord of Parma, Piacenza, Modena, and Reggio, I think this is a rule that would be considerable and would be strong; it is such that, were it to be governed correctly from the outset, it can be held onto under any condition. And in order to govern it correctly, he needs to understand fully the nature of the subject. If these new states, taken over by a new ruler, are to be preserved, they present countless problems.[8] And if problems exist in preserving those states accustomed to being unfied as if they were one body—for example, the dukedom of Ferrara—many more problems exist in preserving those that are recently formed from diverse elements—as this state of Lord Giuliano's would be because one section of it is part of Milan and another of Ferrara.[9] Therefore, whoever becomes prince over such states must concentrate on unifying them into a single body and training them to think of themselves as one unified body as soon as possible. This can be accomplished in two ways: either by dwelling there in person or by appointing one of his lieutenants to rule them all; thus, those subjects, *even though* they are from different cities and turned in various directions, may begin to respect one person and to recognize him as their prince. And were His Lordship,[10] desirous of remaining in Rome for the time being, to appoint someone there who fully knows the nature of things and the circumstances of those regions, he would create a firm foundation for this new state of his. But were he to install in each city a leader of its own—and were His Lordship not to live in the region—that state will always be divided and devoid of prestige for him as well as unable to regard the prince with respect or fear. Since Duke Valentino, whose deeds I should imitate on all occasions[11] were I a new prince, was aware of this necessity, he appointed Messer Ramiro president in Romagna; this decision united those peoples and made them afraid of his authority, fond of his power, and trusting in it: all the love they felt for him, which was considerable, considering his unfamiliarity to them, resulted from this decision. I believe that this point, because it is true, could easily be proved; should this situation happen in your Paolo's case,[12] it would be a step toward making him known not merely to His Magnificence but also to all of Italy; along with profiting and honoring His Lordship, he would provide prestige for himself, for you, and for your family. I spoke to him about this idea; he liked it and will consider how to avail himself of it. I thought I ought to write you about it so that you may be aware of our discussions and, wherever necessary, you may pave the way for this matter.

> And in his fall the arrogant villain
> Still did not forget his Macone.[13]

Our Donato sends his regards.

31 January 1514[5]
Niccolò Machiavelli, in Florence

❖ LETTER 248
Niccolò Machiavelli to Giovanni Vernacci
Florence, 18 August 1515

To Messer Giovanni di Francesco Vernacci.
In Pera.[1]

   Dearest Giovanni. If I have not written to you[2] earlier, I do not want you
to blame either me or anyone else, but only the times; they have been—and
still are—of such a sort that they have made me forget even myself. Not on
this account, however, have I really forgotten you, because I shall always regard
you as my son; I and all that I have will always be at your disposal. Take care to
stay healthy and to do well, because to anyone who wishes you well nothing
but good can come from your well-being.

18 August 1515.
Niccolò Machiavelli, in Florence

❖ LETTER 249
Niccolò Machiavelli to Giovanni Vernacci
Florence, 19 November 1515

To Messer Giovanni di Francesco Vernacci.
In Pera.

   Dearest Giovanni. I have written to you[1] twice during the last four months,
and I am sorry that you have not received them, because it occurs to me that
you will think I do not write because I have forgotten all about you. That is
not true at all: Fortune has left me nothing but my family and my friends and I
make capital out of them—and particularly out of those who are closest to
me, as are you[2]; I trust that, should Fortune send some honorable business affairs your way, you will do unto my children as I have done unto you.

From Florence, 19 November 1515.
Niccolò Machiavelli, in Florence

❖ LETTER 250
Niccolò Machiavelli to Giovanni Vernacci
Florence, 15 February 1516

To Messer Giovanni di Francesco Vernacci.
In Pera.

   Dearest Giovanni. You[1] never write me that you have not received my letters without stabbing me with a knife, because I have written you six times
during the past year and handed the letters over to Marietta to be sent to Alberto. She says she has sent them; you say you have not received them: I am

saddened at this. So, the most recent one I wrote you two months ago I sent with Bartolomeo Federichi, who told me that he gave it to someone who was going there.

I have heard about you and your travails from several persons. I thank God that they have calmed down enough for you to remain alive and you need not be sad any more. And if their deaths have deprived you of several initiatives, you ought to get them back, since you have conducted yourself well. So do not lose heart, and stay in good spirits.

As for me, I have become useless to myself, to my family, and to my friends because my doleful fate has willed it to be so.[2] The best I can say is that all I have left is my own good health and that of all my family. I bide my time so that I may be ready to seize good Fortune should she come; should she not come, I am ready to be patient. And whatever may happen to me, I shall always hold you in that spot where I have kept you until now. I am yours. May Christ watch over you.

15 February 1515[6]
Niccolò Machiavelli, in Florence

❖ LETTER 251
Niccolò Machiavelli to Paolo Vettori
Leghorn, 10 October 1516

To the Magnificent Paolo Vettori, Most Worthy Captain of the Papal Galleys.[1]

Magnificent One. We arrived here in Leghorn today at four o'clock in the afternoon. We are informing you of this fact by Your Lordship's servant Antonio so that you may be aware of how we are and, should you need us to do something here before our arrival, you can let us know. No one knows anything about the Pasha's galleys. We have brought your Vicenzio here—he has double tertian fever; even though he has lost a pound of blood through his nose, the fevers continue nevertheless. If they should diminish a bit, I think it would be a good idea, while the nights are milder, to put him in a wicker litter and carry him there to you. Should you be obliged to put off your arrival, let us know what Your Lordship thinks of this. Everyone here sends you their warm regards.

10 October 1516
Niccolò Machiavelli, in Leghorn

❖ LETTER 252
Niccolò Machiavelli to Giovanni Vernacci
S. Andrea in Percussina, 8 June 1517

To Messer Giovanni di Francesco Vernacci.
In Pera.

Dearest Giovanni. As I wrote you[1] at another time, I do not want you to wonder if I do not write or if I have been slow about answering you, because the reason is not that I have forgotten you or that I have lost my habitual respect for you, because I respect you more. Men are respected according to their worth; since you have proved that you are a man of worth and ability, I must love you more than I used to and at least take pride in you, since I raised you and since the good that you have and are going to have began in my house. But since the adversities that I have suffered, and still am suffering, have reduced me to living on my farm, I sometimes go for a month at a time without thinking about myself—so it is not surprising if I neglect to answer you.

I have received all your letters and am pleased to learn that you have done well and continue to do well; nothing could please me more. And when you have dispatched your obligations and return, my house will always be at your disposal as it has been in the past, humble and wretched though it may be.

Bernardo and Lodovico[2] are growing up to be men, and I hope upon your return and with your assistance that I may find one of them some employment.

Marietta and all the family are well. When you come back, Marietta would like you to bring her a piece of tan-colored camlet and sewing needles of damascene steel—both coarse and fine ones. She says they must be polished because the ones you sent earlier were no good. May Christ watch over you.

8 June 1517
Niccolò Machiavelli, in the country

❖ LETTER 253
Giovanni Vernacci to Niccolò Machiavelli
Pera, 26 October 1517

To the Notable Messer Niccolò Machiavelli.
In Florence.
† Jesus. 26 October 1517.

Honored and dearest foster-father: after the due regards, endless greetings, etc. In the past I have received quite a few, and since then I have received no letters from you,[1] and by the grace of God and of my good conduct it has been more than a year since I have had a line from you, which truly displeases me because I can tell that you do not recall me as your dear nephew, and that makes me unhappy. But on the other hand, the great faith I have in you, more than a good son for his father, makes me hope that even if you no longer have pen and paper to write to me, you still keep the love that you have borne so long for me, not as your dear nephew but rather as a dear and good son. Please God that it be so, and then that he accord me the grace that you may address a few lines to me to give me some consolation, which I await with very great desire to learn of your well-being and that of all your family, may the Lord make us worthy of it.

These past few days a little caviar has been sent to Alberto Canigiani there, just as a present for parents and friends, whom I feel as if I have lost. You are being informed of this caviar because the said Alberto has been asked to send you twenty pounds of it. You will accept it and enjoy it for my sake during this Lent. Do not look at the nature of this humble present, but rather accept it as a gesture of the greater will and generosity that I should like to show toward you. Let this serve as notice to you.

At present I am carrying on as usual and I am not making much profit here. I yearn to come back there within a short time, which I judge will be soon if God accords me grace for it.

I do not know what else to tell you except that I send you countless regards, and then to your Madonna Marietta to whom I am not writing, so you will share this letter with her and give her countless greetings on my behalf, as well as to Bernardo and Lodovico and Guido and the others I do not know by name. May God keep them all from harm along with you.

Held until the first of November. Nothing else to add except to remind you and pray you once more to send me a few lines, which will give me pleasure. *Farewell.* Yours,

Giovanni Vernacci himself, in Pera

❖ LETTER 254
Niccolò Machiavelli to Ludovico Alamanni
Florence, 17 December 1517

To the Greatly Honored, Notable Ludovico Alamanni.
In Rome.

My honored Ludovico.[1] I know that I need not go to much trouble to convince you of how much I love Donato del Corno[2] and of how much I would like to do anything that may give him satisfaction. Consequently, I know you will not be surprised if I importune you for his sake; I shall do it with all the less scruple because I believe that I can do so with you and also because his cause is just and—*to a certain extent—virtuous.*

About a month after the Medici lords had returned to Florence, the aforesaid Donato, without being asked, took five hundred gold ducats to Lord Giuliano[3] and told him that he might use them and that he should return them whenever it suited his convenience; he was prompted to do so partly because of his obligation to Lord Giuliano and partly because of his own good nature. Since then, five years have gone by, and the aforesaid lords, despite all their good fortune, have not repaid him. Since Donato is currently in some need and he has learned that creditors such as himself have lately had their loans repaid, he has gathered his courage to request repayment and written to Domenico Buoninsegni[4] about this situation, sending him a copy of the receipt in Giuliano's own hand. But with a man such as Domenico, with his scores of tasks, inquiries such as this one are likely to die unless they have some private influence on their side to keep them alive, so I decided to gather my courage and write you about it; I pray that you will not think it tedious to speak to Domenico about it and that the two of you can figure out a way for that money to be restored to life. Out of love for me, please be so kind as to include this matter among your other activities because, in addition to being virtuous and just, it will not be to your disadvantage—I beg you to drop me a line in reply.

Lately I have been reading Ariosto's *Orlando Furioso*[5]; the entire poem is really fine and many passages are marvelous. If he is there with you, give him my regards and tell him that my only complaint is that in his mention of so many poets[6] he has left me out like some prick and that he has done to me in his *Orlando* what I shall not do to him in my *Ass*.[7]

I know that you find yourself there all day long together with[8] the Most Reverend de' Salviati, Filippo Nerli, Cosimo Rucellai, Cristofano Carnesecchi, and sometimes Antonio Francesco degli Albizzi, that you devote yourselves to eating heartily, and that you remember little of us poor wretches here—dying of cold and of lack of sleep. Nevertheless, so that we can appear to be alive, Zanobi Buondelmonti, Amerigo Morelli, Battista della Palla, and I sometimes get together and discuss that excursion to Flanders with so much energy that we dream we are already on the road—so that it seems we have already used up half of the pleasures we might have been able to have. In order that we may plan for it more systematically, we shall make a small trial run the last Thursday of Carnival by going as far as Venice; we cannot make up our minds, however, whether we should set off early and go down there for you or wait for you to come here so we can go straight to Venice. At any rate, I should like you to get together with Cosimo and write us about what would be better to do. I am at your disposal. May Christ watch over you.

Since I forgot to tell you to, give my regards to Messer Piero Ardinghelli. *Again, farewell to all.*

17 December 1517
With friendship and humanity for Y[our] E[xcellency]
Your Servant
Niccolò Machiavelli

❖ LETTER 255
Niccolò Machiavelli to Giovanni Vernacci
Florence, 5 January 1518

To Messer Giovanni di Francesco Vernacci.
In Pera.

Dearest Giovanni. I am surprised that you[1] inform me in your last letter you have received none of my letters, because I wrote you four months ago and also had Lodovico and Bernardo, who asked you about I know not what nonsense, write you; the letters were given to Alberto Canigiani.

As I told you in that letter, had you received it, you ought not to be surprised if I have seldom written to you because I have had numerous setbacks since you left; their nature is such that they have brought me to a point that I can do little good for others and less for myself. Yet, nevertheless, as I told you in that letter, my house and whatever I have left are at your disposal because, aside from my own children, there is no man I value more than you.

I believe your affairs have greatly improved during this stay that you have had out there; if they are in as good a state as I have heard tell, I would advise you to get married,[2] to marry a woman through whom you will strengthen your family connection with me—who is beautiful, has a good dowry, and is of good standing. Therefore, as long as you have to remain out there, I should like you either to write to me or to let me know through Alberto Canigiani what your thoughts are; should you be disposed to marry, give me some idea about your state of mind.

All of us are in good health and we send you our regards. Christ watch over you.

5 January 1517[8]
Niccolò Machiavelli, in Florence

❖ LETTER 256
Niccolò Machiavelli to Giovanni Vernacci
Florence, 25 January 1518

To Messer Giovanni di Francesco Vernacci.
In Pera.

Dearest Giovanni. Just about twenty days ago I wrote you[1] two letters saying the same thing and gave them to two people so that you might receive at least one of them. Since then I received yours dated the fourth of November.[2] It hurts me to the quick that you have received none of my letters because six months ago I wrote you and had each of my sons write you a letter too; so that you can have one of them, I shall also make a copy of this one.

As I have said in many of my letters, Fate has done the worst she can to me since you left; so, I am reduced to a condition where I can do little good for myself and less for others. If I am careless about answering your letters, I have become careless about other matters as well; still, however I may be, I and my house are at your disposal—as they have always been.

Many thanks for the caviar.[3] And Marietta says that you should bring her a piece of tan-colored camlet[4] upon your return.

I wrote you in another letter that if your affairs should improve—to the degree that I have heard about and am convinced is so—I would urge you to marry; should you decide to do so, there are currently some objects at hand whom you could not do better than—so that I would be glad if you would give me some sort of answer to this question.

All of us are in good health, and I am yours.

25 January 1517[8].
Yours, Niccolò Machiavelli, in Florence

❖ LETTER 257
Francesco . . . to Niccolò Machiavelli
Florence, 15 April 1518

To Messer Niccolò Machiavelli.
In Genoa.[1]
Jesus, 15 April 1518.

My very dear Niccolò. I[2] got your[3] letter today, and concerning the business of Davide I am afraid I have thrown away a goodly sum to his benefit and that of his affairs. And I shall not be remiss in this, either. May God let what is best for us ensue, and you shall pursue whatever his agents tell you.

You received twenty-five ducats from Salvago,[4] and you are in debt for them.

I have been to see Messere[5] and I showed him your letter. He is doing Dioscorides[6] and living from day to day, like a worthy man.

You like Casano, and so do we. He is a man of business, like a good friar and an excellent secular cleric, and he swings his staff in such a way as to profit every type of person and give a good example. Give him my regards.

The letter was given to Mazzingo and the other letters to the heirs of the Ugolini.

Give my regards to our friends, and go see that Simone della Mandorla when you have free time. I am your devoted servant. *Farewell.*

Francesco de [. . .] in Florence

❖ LETTER 258
Niccolò Machiavelli to Giovanni Vernacci
Florence, 9 October 1519

To Messer Giovanni di Francesco Vernacci.
In Pera.

Dearest Giovanni. I have not written you[1] for several months now because you have written in all your letters that you are about to leave—so I
have been waiting for your return. Now, realizing that you are not returning, I do not want to fail to write to you and tell you that you must leave as
soon as you receive my letter, that you are to leave immediately and to leave
everything behind because, in addition to the suit that Piero Venturi has
filed against you, as you ought to have heard by now, it turns out that Alberto Canigiani has died. Two months ago he went to Naples and got there
on the sixteenth of last month—he suddenly became ill, and died two days
ago; we got word of it here yesterday. Now since he is dead and there is no
longer anyone here who can either handle or carry out your business activities or answer for you in any matter, you must return and, once and for all,
show yourself to those who have done business with you; you must look
into your affairs squarely and put them in order. If you do not, harm and
disgrace will ensue. So do come back. May God give you safe conduct.
Farewell.

9 October 1519
Yours, Niccolò Machiavelli, in Florence

L E T T E R S

1520

After the death of Lorenzo II on 4 May 1519, Leo X sent Cardinal Giulio de' Medici to safeguard the family's interests in Florence. His aim was to calm down the *ottimati* who resented the dictatorial policies that Lorenzo had followed once he became duke of Urbino in 1516. In early March 1520, Lorenzo Strozzi and some other friends from the *Orti Oricellari* introduced Machiavelli to Giulio de' Medici, when the latter was in Florence. Concerning this visit, Lorenzo received the following from his brother, Filippo Strozzi: "I am quite pleased that you introduced Machiavelli to the Medici because, should he gain the confidence of the masters, he is a person on the rise" (Ridolfi, *Vita 7*, p. 277; see *Life*, p. 177).

Giulio sought to ease the restrictions on political life in Florence, and discussions on constitutional reform in the *Orti Oricellari* played into this general policy shift. This is also the period when Machiavelli wrote his *Discursus florentinarum rerum post mortem iunioris Laurentii Medices* (A commentary on Florentine affairs after the death of the Lorenzo de' Medici the younger [Lorenzo II]). It is believed that Giulio asked him to write it so it could be shown to the pope, because Florence was now in the hands of the pope and the cardinal, two ecclesiastics without legitimate heirs.

From July to September, perhaps because of his earlier experience in Genoa, Machiavelli was in Lucca representing the interests of some Florentine merchants in another bankruptcy case, a significant one that involved Michele Guinigi. Again, it was not a major commission, but among these merchants were the Salviati, related to Pope Leo X, so Machiavelli was eager to serve and to keep his name before the Medici. While there he wrote *Sommario delle cose della città di Lucca* (A summary of matters in the city of Lucca), and *La Vita di*

Castruccio Castracani di Lucca (The life of Castruccio Castracani of Lucca), modeled on Diodorus Siculus and the *Lives of the Philosophers* by Diogenes Laertius. Rather than a true biography, it is a literary essay written in a historical style about someone who had been one of Florence's worst enemies in the early fourteenth century. Machiavelli sent it off to his "noontime friends" as a model of the kind of writing that he hoped would show off his abilities and win him a commission from the Medici—a goal his *Orti Oricellari* comrades hoped he would achieve.

These comrades were also cognizant of his efforts to finish his *Arte della guerra* (Art of war), a dialogue set in 1516. The fiction depicts Cosimo Rucellai presiding over a conversation of his guest of honor, Fabrizio Colonna, a first-rate soldier who was then the papal captain and visiting Florence after being recalled to Rome from the fighting in Lombardy, with Cosimo's other guests: Zanobi Buondelmonti, Battista della Palla, and Luigi Alamanni. In addition to paying tribute to Cosimo Rucellai, who died in 1519, the preface was addressed to Lorenzo di Filippo Strozzi, in gratitude for a recent kindness about which we know little. Nevertheless, Lorenzo did Machiavelli the favor of getting him in Giulio de' Medici's good graces. *Arte della guerra,* published in 1521, is an important work for understanding Machiavelli's thought: it synthesizes the thinking, reading, and experience of a lifetime's devotion to a citizen army.

Machiavelli's patience and perseverance finally paid off. By the end of the year, Giulio de' Medici hired him to write the *Florentine Histories;* Machiavelli even wrote the conditions for his own employment (see Letter 264). This work was to take him four years to complete and was his most significant writing of the last ten years of his life. The irony of a partisan of a Soderini-style republican form of government now yoked to the Medici was not lost on him: see the remark at the end of the penultimate paragraph of Letter 270.

❖ LETTER 259
Niccolò Machiavelli to Giovanni Vernacci
Florence, 15 April 1520

To Messer Giovanni Francesco Vernacci.
In Pera.
† In the name of God. 15 April 1520.

Dearest, etc. Since I wrote you [1] about Alberto Canigiani's death, I have not received any letters from you and I have also not written because I believed that you would return any day now; but, realizing that you are not returning, I have been prompted to write you these few lines so that I may fulfill my duty to you—seeing that your affairs here are falling into ruin. You are aware that Piero Venturi has filed suit against you, according to which you were obliged to remit his balance here and now, so that you have incurred sixty florins worth of damages—or so Piero Corsali tells me. Furthermore, Giovan Luigi Arrigetti, Giorgio Bartoli, and many others want to sue you; they all have judgments against you, since there is no one here who is able to, or knows how to, answer them. For my part, I am no good in this matter because I would do you harm and not good, as a result of the conditions under which I exist. Your uncles and your paternal cousins have refused to speak up, if nothing else, to one of the Six[2]; none of your friends here has been able to take up this fight. So if you do not return, you will lose your property and your honor here. Piero Corsali has made his excuses about it to me and tells me he has written you about it. Consequently, my Giovanni, consider very carefully what it is best for you to do, because should you stay out there another year, you will lose everything that you own here and be at the mercy of those who have commissioned you. I am writing this letter in order to fulfill my duty to you and so that you cannot say these matters have not been written about to you. Christ watch over you.

Yours, Niccolò Machiavelli, in Florence

❖ LETTER 260
Battista della Palla to Niccolò Machiavelli
Rome, 26 April 1520

To the Notable, Most Honored Niccolò Machiavelli.
In Florence.

I have not answered your letter of the 17th of last month before this because I did not have anything new to say. For the last several days, during which I have been bothered so much by a cold and catarrh, I have not been able to do anything at all with myself, much less write. I want to inform you that in an agreement I have discussed with the pope, I offered him in addition the five hundred ducats to be paid to Donato, telling him concerning that matter a lot of things that people were saying, prompted by the respect that I have for the honor of His Holiness and for the good memory of Giuliano[1] and of the entire house, as their good servant. He answered me that I was telling the truth, and because he knew exactly what is what he had already given the order for it to be paid, and that it would be done without fail. When I tried to ask him in what manner he had given that order, so that that portion that you have designated as coming to you should not be omitted, he twice took me so far astray with his words, between asking me and telling me, that it was not possible for me to get back to the subject; but I think that he has planned to add these five hundred ducats that I have offered to pay Donato to a sum that I am supposed to pay on his account, which comes in very handy for him. And so when we get down to brass tacks, which I hope will be within three days, he will find me arguing hard and I shall strive to get to the bottom of how he gave this order for Donato to be paid. If I cannot do anything else, I shall get authorization from His Holiness to whoever I understand was given the order to pay, for them to send it off swiftly and to see to it that he is among the first paid, etc. You, on the other hand, let me know once again whether Raffaello de' Medici has been asked for this, as you wrote to me before, and let me know right away so that even if he refuses to let me pay him, as he has begun, when I have more news about the affair I can carry it out according to our desires. But as I have said to you, write immediately, because I am not thinking about anything else but arranging my leave, so as to come back there within a few days.

We have great hopes about the affairs of our company,[2] as you will hear in part from Zanobi, for I have written to him about it, and in full, orally, on my arrival.

I have spoken of your affairs in detail with the pope, and in truth, as far as can be seen, I have found him very well disposed toward you, so much so that I was quite tempted when I spoke of Donato's business to tell him of the part of it that was supposed to come to you, trusting that in these circumstances he would do it much more willingly. However, I kept silent about it. I have been asked to tell Cardinal de' Medici on behalf of His Holiness, when I am there, that he will be very pleased if the good will that His Reverend Lordship has toward your desires should henceforth be put into effect. I think I can say that to him with such effectiveness and be believed to such an extent that it will not have been in vain. This concerns commissioning you to do some writing or something else,[3] as was discussed several days ago; I spoke at length about it with the pope, and on the basis of this I got the above-mentioned authorization. I have also spoken of you with His Holiness in connection with the matter of our company, telling him that we are sure we shall derive great profit from your intelligence and judgment, etc. In addition, I spoke of your comedy,[4] telling him that it is all ready, learned in entirety by its players, and that I think it is going to give great pleasure, etc. I have this to tell you, good for you and for something, that everyone esteems it[5] much more than anything that has been brought to Rome by my hands, but not having had the ability to be of help, I was apprehensive of risking to do harm, although up to now, sometimes as many as four or more, I have been given the opportunity to speak by the benevolence of the patron, etc.

I gave the message about his Calandro to Santa Maria in Portico[6] from your Messer Nicia; his answers were courtly, as is his wont. I thanked Salviati[7] for the letter; he is angry that you should stand on ceremony with him. I gave the message about the poles to Carnesecchi[8]; I do not know whether, because he is a priest, he wanted to make use of some of them, but they would be ten years too tender. I am your devoted servant. God keep you.

In Rome, 26 April 1520.

B. d. P.

❖   LETTER 261
Bernardo Machiavelli to Niccolò Machiavelli
Florence, 30 July 1520

To Messer Niccolò di Messer Bernardo Machiavelli.
In Lucca.[1]
† Jesus. 30 July 1520.

Dearest father, greetings, regards, etc. This letter is to tell you that we are well, and we hope you are, too.

We have not written you before, because the weather has not permitted us to do the harvesting. The wine you wrote to tell us to sell we have allocated to yield wine for wine.

Maddalena has had a daughter and has given her the name Oretta. She sends you a hundred greetings. Madonna Marietta[2] reminds you to come back soon, and to bring her something. The same for me and Lodovico and the others at home.

There is nothing else to tell you. Christ keep you from harm. Written hastily, by lantern-light. I had a pen that did not work for me.

Yours, Bernardo Machiavelli, in Florence

❖   LETTER 262
Filippo de' Nerli to Niccolò Machiavelli
Florence, 1 August 1520

To the Notable Niccolò Machiavelli, as a Very Dear Brother, in Lucca.
In Lucca.

My very dear Niccolò. I have gotten a letter from you that, first of all, tells lies: because you say you will be brief, and then it is two full pages of writing from edge to edge.[1]

The reason why it was not answered earlier was because the letter came while I was out of this city. I came with Lorenzo's wife only three miles from Lucca, intending to come and see you there. Then I thought, when I was at Bagni di Lucca, that if I wanted to return from Lucca to go back to Florence the way was lengthened by a good sixteen miles, which makes more than twenty for the return. So I judged that seeing you was not worth going to so much discomfort. When I got back here, I found your letter with the one enclosed for Sibilia. Because, as has been said, he stayed over here because of my absence, he will really think that he got it by dispatch-rider. I shared your letter with Zanobi, and we made the same judgment of it as we always make of your affairs, because you always make a stupid mess of these affairs. He and I were of a mind today to answer you in common; but he has had a son and for this reason I did not want to bother him. When you write here you can congratulate him, because he was extremely pleased by it; because the more sons are born, the more protection we shall have against the Turks. You do not think of these things; they are more important than you believe: remember that, and notify those gentlemen of Lucca there that they should make sure and screw a good deal, to make infantry, which will be of as much use to them as their *torrone*[2] is.

I have gone over everything you tell us with Gherardo. I believe that this stay of yours over there is going to be your last plunge. You know how little favor you used to have; and now that the coast has been left clear for your competitors and rivals, I let you be the judge. And if you try to do something in time to cure it, the remedies will be harder to find than the disease is. Go ahead, go ahead.

With the poets and the muses we talked of language for quite a while: we thought, in order to straighten out your taste when you come home, of giving you some good preceptors. We had thought of Sernigi[3]; but since he is not here, they are thinking of having you frequent Gualtieri Panciatichi on your return. As your lesson, you should make a habit of reading twice each day his epistle on the entrance of the pontiff into the fatherland. They think they will straighten out your ears that way.

Filippo, Giovanni, Guidetti, and our noon-time friends[4] all send you their regards, and there is nothing else to tell you on their part. It is true that Giro-lamo would like you to give his regards to that peasant who you say was such a comfort to you over there, since it was to his harm; he was so generous that he asked me to write you that he would give a hundred ducats to whoever gave him into the hands of one of the rectors of our Signoria. If ever this should seem an honorable step to you, and one that was in your interest, the choice of whether to take it is up to you.

You must have heard that Francesco Vettori has gone to San Leo and Mon-tefeltro[5] to take possession of those provinces for our Signoria.

You must understand that people here are thinking about jokes. We shall seem more beautiful than ever to you on your return.

I remind you for your return trip that I have provided you with a residence in Pistoia, because Roberto[6] will not be there, since today he has finished his dictatorship in that city. When you are at the gates, ask for the house of Zinzi, or, if you want to call him by his right name, Bastiano di Possente. You will be greeted very affectionately by him for the sake of La Riccia and myself and for your own good qualities. Do not fail him.

Donato del Corno complains greatly about you. I am afraid, when you come back, that I shall have to be a referee between you, in any case, because I know what I know, and I feel what I feel, and he does what is done, and it is going as badly as it can.

I have found, during the time I was away, that one can do a few little things with one's hand a bit more freely, if one is taken before the magistrates, both outdoors and indoors. I find that women can be whores more freely. If one feels like it, any man who might want either to read the Trojan[7] or to do any-thing else can do it even more. Anyone who might want not to believe or to

wear one kind of clothing more unusual than another, *and so on,* can do it all
with greater safety. Because God has taken unto himself Piero degli Alberti,
who went off in Santa Croce with so much water that it really seemed as if he
wanted to get his revenge,[8] dead as he was, by giving so much discomfort to
those who accompanied him; it was Saint James's eve.[9] I have nothing else for
now except to send you my regards. No more. *Farewell.*

From Florence, 1 August 1520.
Yours, Filippo de' Nerli

❖ LETTER 263
Zanobi Buondelmonti to Niccolò Machiavelli
Florence, 6 September 1520

To My Very Honored *Compare* Niccolò Machiavelli, Secretary.
In Lucca.

My honored *compare.* We received your letter of the 18th of last month,
along with the *Life of Castruccio Castracani* written by you. The latter was as
dear to us as anything in the world, both because it is a good work and also
because we know that you remember your friends everywhere you are. We
read it and considered it thus together a while, Luigi, Guidetti, Diaceto, Antonio Francesco,[1] and I. We all decided that it was a good thing, and well written. Of course, certain places were noted that, even though they are quite
good, could nonetheless be improved: for instance, that last part with the
apothegms[2] and the witty and sharp sayings of said Castruccio, which would
only turn out better if it was shortened, because in addition to these sayings
or witticisms of his being too numerous, there are some of them that are attributed to other sages, both ancient and modern; another part does not have
the liveliness or the grandeur that would be expected of such a man. But
there remain so many good sayings that can be attributed to him that his life
still remains quite rich. The other notations are rather concerning words than
other considerations: but we shall save all these things for when we speak
face-to-face, with much greater pleasure. Jacopo Nardi and Battista della Palla,
who is here and is well and greatly desires your presence, have seen it and read
it, and they praise it highly. Pierfrancesco Portinari and Alessandro also, with
whom I was out in the country when it was brought to me, have universally
commended it; as to what each of them hesitated or doubted about, concerning both language and the story and the explanation of your meaning and
concetti, as I have said, we shall talk about that face-to-face.

It seems to everyone that you ought to set yourself to writing this history[3]
with all diligence. I desire it above all others because, even if I do not understand as well as each of the aforementioned people and I cannot give that discussion of it that would be fitting, I feel that this model of a history of yours
delights me not otherwise than do those things that are considered good by
men of good judgment. Above all else, it seems to me that you are strong in

that prayer.[4] I believe it is because you rise higher in your style there than you do elsewhere, just as the material requires. I have nothing else to tell you concerning this item in my letter, because it would be too long. I do not have anything else to write you about, except to pray you to hasten your departure from there and to return here among your friends, who always long greatly for you and even more so since, because of Battista's arrival, it is necessary for us to speak with you about that notion of ours that you know about[5]; so for your part make sure you lose no time answering our prayers, as long as it is not a matter of your profit or your honor there, both of which things we long to accomplish for you with our own. We send you our regards as always. *Farewell.*

> 6 September 1520, in Florence.
> Your *compare,*
> Zanobi Buondelmonti

P.S. I have heard that a message has been sent from here asking you to return home, which gives me pleasure.

❖ LETTER 264
Niccolò Machiavelli to Francesco del Nero
Florence, 10 September–7 November 1520

Honored Brother-in-Law Francesco del Nero.

Honored Sir. The substance[1] of the contract should be as follows.

He is to be hired for _____ years at a salary of _____ per year with the condition that he must be, and is to be, held to write the annals or else the history of the things done by the state and city of Florence, from whatever time may seem to him most appropriate, and in whatever language—either Latin or Tuscan—may seem best to him.

> Nic. Machiavelli

❖ LETTER 265
Filippo de' Nerli to Niccolò Machiavelli
Rome, 17 November 1520

To the Notable Niccolò di Messer Bernardo Machiavelli.
In Florence.

My honored Niccolò, etc. I have not written you since I left, because I had no reason to. Whether I had the *Life of Castruccio* made no difference; and of the book *De re militari,*[1] *the same.* You should know that I read Justin[2] and Quintus Curtius's[3] *De rebus gestis Alexandri* in the evening to Madonna Lucrezia.[4] There was some new ass[5] who gave her a treatise on the life of Alexander, and although I have not read it, I do not like it. She asked me to send it to you so that you might rearrange it, adding certain parts of her doing as you saw fit. Now I did not do it or say I would do it, but I laughed about it, saying, "We shall see," with the intention of writing you about it first to see if you had a mind to do this job. If you should answer me yes, I shall send it to you and tell her that I have done it, although I believe it would be better to discuss what you know about the life of Alexander, according to Plutarch, rather than see anything else written by this animal. I shall do as you advise me, and as I have said, until you answer me that you are happy to, I shall never say that I have written about it. I should rather be negligent than for you to have to refuse it, if you do not want to undertake this effort. So answer me right away about it.

Tell Zanobi Buondelmonti that I send him my regards and that he should remember his promise to come. I also wrote him the other day before I went off to court, where I have remained for ten days, between Corneto and Montalto[6] and along the way. The tenor of my writing to him was concerning the book *De re militari,* which, since he had told me to send it, will get me taken for a liar by His Most Reverend Monsignor[7] if I do not send it. So make sure between you and him that I do not fail to get it.

Give my endless regards to Donato del Corno and all his bunch that he has in his shop at night, and give greetings on my behalf to everyone. For now I shall say no more. I send my best to you endlessly and exorbitantly, etc.

From Rome, 17 November 1520.
Filippo de' Nerli

L E T T E R S

1521

On the international scene, Charles V had attained the Spanish throne in 1516, upon the death of Ferdinand the Catholic, and become the Holy Roman Emperor in 1519, at the death of Maximilian I. An intense rivalry was looming between Francis I, the king of France, and Charles V, the Holy Roman Emperor, which would break out in a series of Hapsburg-Valois wars in 1522. Italy was a significant pawn in these concerns. According to Pope Leo X's ruinous policy, it was to his advantage to foster enmity between the two rulers so that he could play the peacemaker. On the one hand, he concluded an agreement with Francis I to divide Naples between them once it was conquered; on the other hand, he formed a league with Charles V to force the French out of Milan. This agreement provided the basis for the emperor's growing influence in Italy. Consequently, Machiavelli and all Italians concerned with political developments followed the movements of Charles V with keen interest.

Machiavelli's political career, after the fallow years, was growing more active. Piero Soderini, the Signoria, and the Florentine Wool Guild (*Arte della Lana*) each provided him with opportunities. In a letter that has been lost, Soderini, the former gonfalonier of the republican government in Florence, now living as an exile in Rome under the protection of Leo X, was in a position to offer Machiavelli the post of secretary to the Republic of Ragusa. This was an area around the modern port of Dubrovnik on the Adriatic, then an important commercial and shipbuilding center, that had offered Soderini refuge when he fled Florence in 1512. When Machiavelli turned that offer down, Soderini tried to negotiate a well-paid position for Machiavelli as secretary to Prospero Colonna (1452–1523), a member of a powerful Roman family and the cousin of Fabrizio Colonna, to whom Machiavelli had recently dedicated the *Art of War*. Ridolfi believes that Machiavelli thought matters were going so well for him in Florence that he would never consent to subject himself to "a foreign master," whether that be a person living in Italy or in Ragusa (*Life*, p. 185; *Vita 7*, p. 290). Machiavelli was reaffirming his commitment to Florence and perforce asserting his loyalty to the Medici family.

Early in May, at the behest both of the Signoria, specifically the *Otto di Pratica* (the Eight of Affairs), and of Cardinal Giulio de' Medici, who was the real power in Florence, Machiavelli was sent to the chapter general meeting of the Minorite Friars, held at their convent in Carpi. His mission was to urge the chapter general to sever connections between the Minorite convents within the Florentine domain and the convents in the rest of Tuscany. The Florentine officials believed that if the Franciscans living in their territory were in a separate congregation, they could keep a closer eye on them and thus be in a better position to control them. Since Machiavelli was eager to be useful to the Medici, he was quite content to travel north, even for this rather demeaning work.

Because of a letter that Francesco Guicciardini, the papal governor of Mantua and Reggio, wrote to Machiavelli on 17 May (Letter 269), it is believed that Machiavelli stopped at Modena to talk with him; Carpi lies about ten miles north of Modena. Machiavelli also wrote to Guicciardini on 17 May, thus cementing a friendship that was to blossom during the six remaining years of Machiavelli's life. In addition to the letters between the two, betokening a friendship that virtually replaced that with Vettori, these letters afford many significant glimpses into the kinds of issues with which Machiavelli was dealing.

Shortly after this correspondence began, on 14 May, the officers of the Florentine Wool Guild asked Machiavelli to do his best while he was in Carpi to get the friars to send one of their most famous preachers, Fra Giovanni Gualberto da Firenze, known as "il Rovaio," to Florence to preach the Lenten service at the Duomo. Again, this may not have been a task worthy of Machiavelli's talents, but it was indicative of his being once more given consideration by powerful people in Florence.

While Machiavelli was in Carpi he stayed with Sigismondo Santi, the chancellor of Count Teodoro Pio, a bishop who was the lord of the city. It did not take long for Machiavelli to think of playing a trick on both his host and the friars by getting Guicciardini to send him messengers at frequent intervals, so that the Carpians would think Machiavelli was an important figure and give him more respect and better food.

There are two significant personal events that occurred in 1521. Machiavelli was trying to clear up some financial problems for his nephew, Giovanni Vernacci, who was still in Pera. More importantly, on 16 August 1521 a Florentine publisher, Giunta, brought out Machiavelli's *Arte della guerra* (Art of war), the only one of his works that Machiavelli personally saw to print. He immediately sent a copy to Cardinal Giovanni Salviati (1490–1533), who was

proud to be "the first in Rome to see such a fine work." The cardinal was a
well-connected Florentine: his father, Jacopo Salviati, was a well-known Florentine patriot and statesman (see Letters 43 and 326); his mother was Lucrezia
de' Medici, the daughter of Lorenzo the Magnificent.

❖ Letter 266
Niccolò Machiavelli to Giovanni Vernacci
Florence, 15 February 1521

Dearest Giovanni, I have been a little lax about answering your two letters
because you write me all the time that you will be leaving in a month. Now,
since I realize that you are not coming back, I shall write you about what is
happening. I received your two letters with the proxy. Though I wanted to
change the amount so that you might have the entire sum, I could not because the proxy you sent me was useless for this business of the *Monte*.[1] So I
am sending you a form for a proxy as it ought to be; have it completed. Then
I shall carry out the transfer from the *Monte* according to your written instructions.

What I know about the concerns of Madonna Vaggia that should come to
you are as follows: two hundred sixty-six florins[2] at seven percent free and
sixty-three and one-third florins. These are deposited in the *Badìa*[3] in your
account. And I have let them remain there for you, awaiting your return; if
you do not return, I shall take them out and invest them at seven percent.
There remains to get some money from the Tempi, and recently thirty-six of
those ducats were paid out; I paid thirty-two ducats to some servants for
Madonna Vaggia's legacy that they were supposed to get. These others, which
are cashed, will be made equal to your share. There are still some household
effects, and your share is in the hands of the will's executors. I am trying to do
my best to keep Piero Venturi satisfied so he takes the farm's revenues, although he is yelling about wanting to be paid. I have handed over this year's
revenues to him, except for all the income from the osiers.

The seventy-five pounds of caviar arrived; I paid nine lire, seven *soldi* for it
and distributed it as you instructed in your letter.

We are all in good health and await your arrival; come back, for God's sake,
as quickly as you can. Christ watch over you.

15 February 1520[1].
Niccolò Machiavelli, in Florence

❖ LETTER 267
Piero Soderini to Niccolò Machiavelli
Rome, 13 April 1521

To My Very Dear Niccolò Machiavelli.
In Florence.

My very dear Niccolò. Because the affair of Ragusa was not satisfactory to you, since Lord Prospero has asked me to recommend a man capable of managing his affairs and I know your trustworthiness and your ability, I proposed you to him. You are very satisfactory to him because he has information about you. He has authorized me to ask you about it. The stipend will be two hundred gold ducats and expenses. Think it over, and if it is satisfactory to you I would urge you, without discussing it,[1] to get here before your departure is known about there. I know of no better prospect at present, and I judge it much better than to stay there and write histories for *fiorini di suggello.*[2] *Farewell.*

In Rome, 13 April 1521.
Yours, Piero Soderini

❖ LETTER 268
Giovanni Vernacci to Niccolò Machiavelli
Pera, 8 May 1521

To the Notable Messer Niccolò Machiavelli.
In Florence.
† Jesus. 8 May 1521.

Honored foster father, regards and endless greetings, etc. My last letter was on 4 February 1520[1]. Since then I have got your letter of 15 February, which I read with pleasure. Answer follows.

It was learned that you received the proxy, but you said it was not valid for the money in the *Monte.*[1] The form in which such a proxy must be made out was received in your said letter, and the said proxy has been made formally as you indicated, by the hand of our clerk. It is being sent to you with this letter so that you can transfer the said money from the *Monte* to whomever you want, in order that the whole of the payment can be made. So make use of it as if it were your own property, may God send his blessing.

About the inheritance from Madonna Vaggia, you say I get two hundred sixty-six florins, thirteen and four, money at seven percent free, and sixty-three and a half florins that are deposited in the *Badìa*[2] at my disposal. You also say there still remains some money to get from the Tempi, and you do not say how much. I also learn that a certain share of mine is in the hands of the executors of the will: I would like you on receipt of this letter to get hold of it all, the money that is in the *Badìa* along with the rest, and do with it as if it were your own, for I shall consider everything as having been done very well. As for Piero Venturi, it is agreed that you will satisfy him by giving him the revenue from the farm. You said you got it all except the osiers, so you did well. Go on doing thus until my return. At that time I have hopes of getting possession of it all.

I learned that you received the caviar.[3] Claim as much of it as was allotted to you and that will be fine. There is nothing else to say to you in this letter, except that I shall have a decision between Biliotti and me in fifteen days and I shall come back as soon as it is settled, may God grant me grace. Enough said. I send you my regards as always. Please excuse me if my letter is brief, for the reason is that I took some medicine yesterday that has upset me. God keep you and us always from harm.

For your Giovanni di Francesco Vernacci, in Pera

❖ LETTER 269
Francesco Guicciardini to Niccolò Machiavelli
Modena, 17 May 1521

To His Magnificence Messer Niccolò Machiavelli, Florentine Nuncio.
In Carpi.

My very dear Machiavelli. It was certainly good judgment on the part of our reverend consuls of the Wool Guild to have entrusted you with the duty of selecting a preacher, not otherwise than if the task had been given to Pachierotto, while he was alive, or to Ser Sano[1] to find a beautiful and graceful wife for a friend. I believe you will serve them according to the expectations they have of you and as is required by your honor, which would be stained if at this age you started to think about your soul, because, since you have always lived in a contrary belief, it would be attributed rather to senility than to goodness. I remind you to take care of this matter as swiftly as possible, because in staying there long you run two risks: one, that those holy friars might pass some of their hypocrisy on to you; the other, that the air of Carpi might make you become a liar, because that has been its influence not only in the present age but also for centuries gone by. If by ill chance you were to be lodged in the house of some Carpian, your case would be without remedy.

If you have visited that governing bishop,[2] you have seen a fine specimen of a man, someone you could learn a thousand fine tricks from. I send you my regards.

From Modena, 17 May 1521.
Yours, Francesco Guicciardini

❖ LETTER 270
Niccolò Machiavelli to Francesco Guicciardini
Carpi, 17 May 1521

To the Magnificent Lord Francesco Guicciardini, J. V.D.,
Governor of Mantua and Reggio, Most Worthy and Much Honored.

Magnificent One, my most respected superior. I was sitting on the toilet when
your messenger arrived, and just at that moment I was mulling over the ab-
surdities of this world; I was completely absorbed in imagining my style of
preacher for Florence: he should be just what would please me, because I am
going to be as pigheaded about this idea as I am about my other ideas. And
because never did I disappoint that republic whenever I was able to help her
out[1]—if not with deeds, then with words; if not with words, then with
signs—I have no intention of disappointing her now. In truth, I know that I
am at variance with the ideas of her citizens, as I am in many other matters.
They would like a preacher who would teach them the way to paradise, and
I should like to find one who would teach them the way to go to the Devil.
Furthermore, they would like their man to be prudent, honest, and genuine,
and I should like to find one who would be madder than Ponzo,[2] wilier than
Fra Girolamo,[3] and more hypocritical than Frate Alberto,[4] because I think it
would be a fine thing—something worthy of the goodness of these
times—should everything we have experienced in many friars be experienced in one of them. For I believe that the following would be the true
way to go to Paradise: learn the way to Hell in order to steer clear of it.[5]
Moreover, since I am aware how much belief there is in an evil man who
hides under the cloak of religion, I can readily conjure up how much belief
there would be in a good man who walks in truth, and not in pretense,
tramping through the muddy footprints of Saint Francis. So, since my imaginative creation strikes me as a good one, I intend to choose Rovaio,[6] and I
think if he is like his brothers and sisters he will be just the right man. The
next time you write I would appreciate it if you would tell me what you
think of all this.

Here I languish because I cannot execute my mission until the general
and the assessors are chosen, and in my mind I am turning over some way in
which I might stir up such strife among them—either here or somewhere
else—that they might start going after one another with their wooden clogs;
if I keep my wits about me, I think I shall be successful. I believe that Your
Excellency's help and advice would be of great service. In fact, it would not
be a bad idea if you were to come here under the pretext of going on an excursion, or at least to write me suggesting some master stroke; because if every day you were to send me a servant for this express purpose, as you did
today, you would accomplish several good things: first, you would shed some
appropriate light on a few matters, and second, you would cause my reputa-

tion to rise among those friars in this house, once they saw the dispatches arriving thick and fast.[7] I must tell you that when the crossbowman arrived with your letter and said, bowing down to the ground, that he had been sent expressly—and in all haste—everyone sprang up with such bowings and such a hubbub that everything was turned topsy-turvy and several people asked me what the news was. And I, in order to heighten my prestige, said that the emperor was expected at Trent, that the Swiss had convened fresh assemblies, that the king of France wanted to go and confer with that king, but his counselors were advising him against going—so that they all stood around with their mouths hanging open and with their caps in hand. And even as I am writing this, I have a circle of them about me; to see me write at length, they marvel and gaze at me as at one inspired; and I, to make them marvel even more, sometimes pause writing and breathe deeply; then they absolutely begin drooling—if they knew what I am writing you, they would marvel all the more! Your Lordship knows how these friars say that when one is confirmed as being in a state of grace, the Devil no longer has any power to tempt him. Well, I have no need to fear that these friars will infect me with their hypocrisy because I believe that I have been adequately confirmed.

As for the lies of these citizens of Carpi, I can beat all of them out, because it has been a while since I have become a doctor of this art—and good enough not to require Francesco Martelli[8] as an errand boy; so, for some time now I have never said what I believe or never believed what I said; and if indeed I do sometimes tell the truth, I hide it behind so many lies that it is hard to find.[9]

I have not talked to the governor; since I have found lodgings,[10] it seemed superfluous to talk to him. It is quite true that this very morning in church I peered at him a bit while he stood looking at some paintings. To me he appeared to be an example of a man properly formed, and I think the whole corresponds to the parts and he is what he seems to be—his hump does not lie[11]; so, had I had your letter with me, I would have made a good try at drawing a bucketful[12] out of him. So no harm has been done; tomorrow I expect some advice from you about my affairs and that you will send one of your crossbowmen; let him gallop and get here covered in sweat so that this gang will be dumbfounded. By so doing you will bring me honor and at the same time give that crossbowman of yours some exercise—and it is quite healthy for the horses on these spring days. Were I willing to overwork my imagination, I would write you about some other matters now, but I want to hold it in reserve so that I can have it fresh tomorrow. I send Your Lordship my regards, *may you ever prosper as you desire.*

Carpi, 17 May 1521.

Most resp[ectfully] yours, Niccolò Machiavelli, Ambassador to the Minorite Friars

❖ LETTER 271
Francesco Guicciardini to Niccolò Machiavelli
Modena, 18 May 1521

To His Magnificence M. Niccolò Machiavelli, Florentine Nuncio, etc.
In Carpi.

My very dear Machiavelli, although I have neither the time nor the wit to give you advice[1] and am not in the habit of performing any such service without pay, I do not wish to fail to be of help to you, so that at least you can carry out your arduous undertakings with honor. Therefore I am sending you posthaste the present crossbowman, whom I have ordered to come with the greatest dispatch, since this is a most important matter, so that he has come with his shirt flying behind his hips. I do not doubt that, between his racing and what will be said by him to those present, it will be believed by everyone that you are an important personage and that your business has to do with more than just friars. In order for the thickness of the packet to give witness to your host, I put into it some notices that came from Zurich that you can make use of either by showing them or by holding them in your hand, accordingly as you may judge more expedient.

I wrote to M. Gismondo[2] yesterday that you were a very exceptional person. He answered me, begging me to inform him as to what this exceptionalness of yours consisted of. I did not feel I should answer him, so that he may be kept in suspense and have reason to show you full respect. Make good use of this repute while it lasts: *for you shall not always have the poor among you.*[3] Let me know when you will be freed from those friars; if you sowed discord among whom, or at least left a seed that might take root later on, it would be the most outstanding deed that you ever accomplished. But I do not judge that to be very difficult, given their ambition and ill will. Let me know and, when you can, come here.

In Modena, 18 May 1521.
Yours, Franc. Guicciardini
Governor

❖ LETTER 272
Francesco Guicciardini to Niccolò Machiavelli
Modena, 18 May 1521

To His Magnificence M. Niccolò Machiavelli, Florentine Nuncio.
In Carpi.

My very dear Machiavelli. When I read your titles as ambassador of the republic and of friars, and I consider how many kings, dukes, and princes you have negotiated with in the past, I am reminded of Lysander,[1] to whom, after so many victories and trophies, was given the task of distributing meat to those very same soldiers whom he had so gloriously commanded; and I say: You see that, with only the faces of the men and the extrinsic colors changed, all the very same things return; and we do not see any incident that has not been seen in other times. But changing the names and forms of things means that only the prudent recognize them; therefore history is good and useful, because it sets before you and makes you recognize and see again what you had never known or seen. There follows from this a brotherly[2] syllogism: that he who gave you the task of writing annals is greatly to be commended; and you are to be exhorted to carry out the charge given to you with diligence. I believe this legation will not be completely useless for that, because in these three days' idleness you will have imbibed the entire Republic of Clogs[3] and you will make use of that model for some purpose, comparing it or measuring it against some of those forms of yours.

It did not seem to me to your benefit to waste time or to abandon Fortune while it shows itself to be favorable. Therefore I have continued the fashion of sending you the messenger: if he serves no other purpose, he ought to get you to pick up one more pie tomorrow evening. I remind you nevertheless that M. Gismondo is nasty and accustomed to gossip or, in Lombard, to japes; therefore it is important to go cautiously, so that we are not turned from shepherds into plowmen.[4] I have written him with this letter that I am not informing him of the truth, because I am confident in the penetration of his intelligence, and that he must have recognized you. That way he will remain in suspense, and if you keep him in doubt by not talking about your ancestors,[5] he will conclude that you are a rare bird. Anything is to be tolerated, as long as meals continue to be kept up.

I am not surprised about Rovaio because I believe, or rather I have understood, that he is not fond of your wine. I do not praise your selection, since it does not seem in conformity with either your judgment or that of others, all the more so because, since you have always been considered exceedingly extravagant in your opinions by most people, and the inventor of new and outlandish things, I think that those lord consuls[6] and everyone who is informed of your commission will expect that you will bring back some friar, one of those, as the man said, who are not to be found. But it is better to resolve both this and the joke of the separation than to put off any longer your return here, where you are awaited with the greatest desire. I send you my regards.

From Modena, 18 May 1521.
Yours, Francesco Guicciardini
Governor

❖ LETTER 273

Niccolò Machiavelli to Francesco Guicciardini
Carpi, 18 May[1] 1521

To the Magnificent Lord Francesco Guicciardini, etc.
In Modena.

I can tell you that the smoke rose right up to the sky,[2] for between the breathlessness of the messenger and the huge bundle of letters, there is not a person in this house—or in this neighborhood—who is not excited; and so as not to appear ungrateful to Messer Gismondo, I showed him those passages about the Swiss and the king.[3] He thought they were quite significant. I told him about the emperor's illness and about the states he wanted to buy in France, so that he was left drooling by them. But I really think that, despite all this, he wonders whether we are not pulling his leg, because he is lost in thought and cannot understand why such Bible-length letters need to be written to these Arabian deserts where there are nothing but friars; because I remain here in the house or I sleep or I read or I keep quiet, I do not think I appear to him to be quite the extraordinary man you have written to him about—so I think he perceives that you are out to mock us both. Still, he keeps on probing, and I reply with a few ill-chosen words, and I fall back on the deluge that is to come, or the Turk who is bound to invade, or the advisability of having a crusade during these times, and similar barstool gossip. So I think he cannot wait to speak to you personally so that he can get better information or bring up his questions directly, since it is you who have gotten him into all this trouble, for I interfere with his house and keep him busy here. Nevertheless, I believe he feels confident that the game is not going to last long, and so he keeps on maintaining a welcoming appearance and serving up immense meals, and I gobble up enough for six dogs and three wolves; at dinner time I say, "This morning I'm saving two *giulios*"[4]; and at supper, "Tonight, I'm saving four." Still, I am nevertheless in your debt and his; if he ever comes to Florence, I shall make it up to him—meanwhile, you find some [kind] words for him.

That traitor Rovaio needs coaxing; he goes on procrastinating and saying he doubts if he can come because he has no idea what preaching methods he might adopt and he is afraid of being sent to the galleys like Pope Angelico.[5] He says that he is no longer shown the proper respect by affairs in Florence, that after he preached there last a law was passed requiring whores to wear yellow veils when appearing in public, and that now his sister writes him that they appear as they please and wiggle their tails more than ever—he complained bitterly about this situation. However, I kept on comforting him by pointing out that he ought not to be surprised at this news because it was customary for great cities not to stand by a decision for any great length of time and to do one thing today and to undo it tomorrow; I brought up Rome and Athens so that he was quite comforted and almost promised me. In my next letter I shall tell you the outcome.

This morning these friars elected their minister general: it is Soncino,[6] who was, to begin with, a humane and good man, and following that a friar. This evening I must go before their friarhoods, and tomorrow I count on being entirely finished, so every minute seems an hour; then I shall spend one day with Your Lordship, *may he live and reign forever and ever.*

18 May 1521
Niccolò Machiavelli
Ambassador from the Florentine Republic to the Minorite Friars

❖ LETTER 274
Niccolò Machiavelli to Francesco Guicciardini
Carpi, 19 May 1521

To the Magnificent Lrd. Francesco Guicciardini, etc.

Shittus![1] We are going to have to go carefully with this fellow,[2] for he is as crafty as thirty thousand devils.[3] I think he has realized that you are toying with him, because when the messenger arrived, he said, "Look here, there must be something big going on; the messengers are coming thick and fast." Then, after he had read your letter, he said, "I think the governor is scoffing at you and me." I acted like the Albanian[4] who became a *Messere* and said that I had left some dealings in Florence up in the air that had to do with you and me, that I had requested you to keep me informed about them whenever you learned anything about them from over there, and that this request was the major reason for the correspondence. Consequently, I am scared shitless[5]: I live in constant fear that he will take a broom and pack me off to the inn. So, I beg you tomorrow to take the day off, so that this joke does not turn harmful and that the good it has done me is not yanked out from under me: solid meals, splendid beds, and the like in which I have been recovering my strength for three days now.

This morning I made a start on the matter of partition,[6] and I shall be busy with it all day today; tomorrow I hope to finish it.

As for the preacher, I do not expect any honor from this affair because the fellow is on the fence. The Father in charge says that he is pledged to others, so I think I am going to return in disgrace; I am not at all happy about all this because I do not know how I shall show up before Francesco Vettori and Filippo Strozzi, who wrote me privately about this matter, begging me to do my utmost so that during this Lenten season they might dine on some spiritual food that would be to their advantage. And they will be sure to point out that everything I do for them is cast in the same mold: one Saturday evening last winter I was with them at Giovan Francesco Ridolfi's house in the country, and they assigned me the task of locating the priest for the next morning's mass. Sure enough, it turned out that that blessed priest arrived after they had eaten so that the entire household was turned topsy-turvy and I experienced everyone's ill will because of it. If now in this second commission I set up another disaster, imagine what crazy faces they will make at me. So I am counting on you to write them a couple of lines and to get me out of this mess as best you can.

As for the *Histories*[7] and the Republic of the Wooden Clogs, I do not think I have lost anything by coming here, because I have found out about many of their regulations and their organizational arrangements, which have good things in them, and so at some point I think I may make use of them—especially in comparisons, because whenever I have to discuss silence, I shall be able to say, "They are quieter than friars eating." So it will be with a good many other things that I shall be able to bring in thanks to what I have learned from this little experience.

19 May 1521.
Yours, Niccolò Machiavelli

❖ LETTER 275
Cardinal Giovanni Salviati to Niccolò Machiavelli
Rome, 6 September 1521

To the Notable Messer Niccolò Machiavelli, My Very Dear Friend.
In Florence.

My dear Messer Niccolò. I did not want to answer your letter, which came together with your book on military art,[1] without first having read the book and considered it well, to tell you about how [. . .] my opinion, and not to do like many who, although they are wiser than I am, I nonetheless do not approve of in this: who follow the opinion of the majority in praising a thing and not their own. And so, since the majority of men are ignorant, many times, judging according to them, they judge badly. I therefore, following my custom, have looked diligently at your book, and the more I have considered it, the more I like it, for it seems to me that you have coupled to the most perfect manner of warfare in antiquity everything that is good in modern warfare and compounded an invincible army. To this opinion of mine has been added some small experience from those wars that there are at present, since I have seen that all the disorders that have arisen or arise today in the French armies or in those of the emperor or of the Church or of the Turk come about for no other reason than for the lack of the organization that is described in your book.

I therefore thank you deeply for having published this book for the common welfare of all Italians, which, during the times to come will at least, if it has no other effect, give good testimony that in Italy in our time there has not been lacking someone who knew what is the true way of waging war. I have no little obligation to you for having sent it to me right away, so as to be the first in Rome to see such a fine work, truly in the image and worthy of your intelligence, experience, and prudence, and I urge you to continue thinking and writing things, and to adorn our country with your talents. Stay well and remember that among the things I most desire is to do whatever is pleasing to you.[2]

In Rome, 6 September 1521.

I, *Cardinal Salviati*

❖ LETTER 276
Niccolò Machiavelli to Francesco Vettori
Sant'Andrea in Percussina, 26 December 1521

To the Magnificent Messer Francesco Vettori, Most Worthy Gonfalonier of Justice.

Signor Gonfaloniere.[1] Parigino, the present agent, is a great friend of mine and says that when Your Lordship was at home, he was saddled with a certain proposal so that he would waive some litigation or other. If it is at all possible, he would appreciate being freed from it, and he has had recourse to me so that I might recommend him to you: I do it with all my heart. You will hear the merits of the case from him, and should the matter seem reasonable to you, I beg you to help him. I always send my regards to you with whom I have so many obligations that may God grant that some day I may be able to repay them with your health and interest. *Farewell.*

26 December 1521

Your most obliged Niccolò Machiavelli,

in the country

If the personal correspondence is any indication, the years between 1522 and 1524 were fairly quiet ones for Machiavelli. Letters written in 1525 indicate that in 1524 Machiavelli began an extended affair, which he conducted with sympathetic tenderness, with an actress whom his contemporaries knew as Barbara Fiorentina and history knows as Barbera Raffacani Salutati. Until then, he presumably devoted most of his attention to the *Florentine Histories*. He may well have chosen to spend a good deal of time in the country to work on this book, as well as to avoid the plague, because in September 1523 he offers to give his brother-in-law's "regards to the chickens" (Letter 283). Yet a brief letter to Guicciardini (Letter 285, dated 30 August 1524) is evidence that rural tranquillity could not dispel the doubt that pursued him as he was composing these *Histories* at the behest of a Medici. Furthermore, even if he had been content in his pastoral life, the political scene surrounding him was anything but restful.

Locally, Florence was a center of activity. The Medici pope Leo X died on 1 December 1521. Although Cardinal Giulio de' Medici was a candidate for the papacy, he lost out to Adrien Boyers of Utrecht, cardinal of Tortosa, who was the regent in Spain for Charles V and the emperor's former tutor. He became Pope Adrian VI early in January 1522. To forestall any efforts on the part of the Soderini—Francesco, the cardinal of Volterra, and his brother Piero—to return to Florence and to reassert their influence, Giulio was obliged to concentrate his efforts on maintaining calm and his control in Florence. A draft of some suggested political reforms for Florence exists in Machiavelli's hand, though he must have felt some ambivalence at distancing himself from his former political allies in the Soderini camp. In fact, several of Machiavelli's own "noontime friends," including Zanobi Buondelmonti and Luigi Alamanni, organized a conspiracy against Giulio de' Medici at the end of May. Their efforts were thwarted, but the incident probably caused Machiavelli some bad moments. In the fall of 1522, Machiavelli's *Memoriale a Raffaello Girolamo, Quando ai 23 d'Ottobre Partì per Spagna all'Imperatore* (Memorandum to Raffaello Girolami when he departed for the emperor in Spain on 23 October) indicates that Florence still valued his opinion on diplomatic matters. Within a year Florence had other political factors to consider. In mid-November 1523, Giulio de' Medici, after a bitter papal conclave, succeeded Adrian VI and became Pope Clement VII.

International politics were no less active during these years. Lombardy was the center of campaigns and counterattacks as Spain and France fought for control in the region. Neither pope, however, was particularly astute in dealing with the political intricacies fomenting in northern Italy. Rome botched efforts to deal effectively with the whole Italian peninsula. Because of the waffling policies of Clement VII in northern Italy, these attempts to operate successfully in Italy eventually led to Rome's being sacked a few short weeks before Machiavelli's death in 1527. Meanwhile, the steps leading up to this debacle were hesitant, oscillating, and disastrous. At first, papal policy, whether directed by Leo X or by Adrian VI, sided with Charles V and Henry VIII against France. That seemed to be a wise course, because during 1522 France lost a lot of ground in northern Italy: Milan, Genoa, Parma, and Piacenza. In October 1524, however, Francis I crossed the Alps with a huge army and recaptured Milan. Clement VII, alarmed at the widening power of Emperor Charles V, chose a poor moment to side with Francis I; but he did so and also put Florence under French protection.

Meanwhile, the politics of the other Italian states were no less chaotic. In 1521 and 1522, for example, Urbino was stirred up by Francesco Maria della Rovere's recovery of his duchy. Florence feared that the duke of Urbino's designs on Perugia and Siena would not stop with those cities and that he might make a move against Tuscan territory.

❖ LETTER 277
Roberto Pucci to Niccolò Machiavelli
Florence, 8 June 1522

To My Honorable Niccolò Machiavelli, as a Brother.
At Home.

My honored Niccolò. Because of our Messer Totto's affliction,[1] I am beside myself, since there are not two other men for whom I more desire life and welfare than for him. But it will be necessary to accept the will of the Lord, who does everything for a good end. I urge you as a prudent man to the same effect, praying God for his grace that He may keep him in any way, and may it be for the best. It will be necessary, however, if God should destine it so, that the love I had for him and you, I should have for you alone, and thus vice versa. As for the benefices, if you should grant them to my son, they will be as if in your person and that of your son in all and for all, I promise you. I send you my regards as always, and I pray God again to watch over Messer Totto for us.

From the palace, 8 June 1522.

Inform me by Giovanni's boy. If I were my own master,[2] I would never leave the sight of your Messer Totto. You and he must excuse me.

Brother R. Pucci, Gonfalonier

❖ LETTER 278
Ser Vincenzo to Niccolò Machiavelli
Sant'Antonio alle Sodora, 30 July 1522

Given to Niccolò di Messer Bernardo Machiavelli.
In Florence.
In God's name, 30 July 1522.

My honored master, etc. I have received a letter from you through Ser Sansone, telling me to sell two *mog[g]ia*[1] of grain,[2] and I got ten ducats for them. I shall do exactly as you have instructed me to; I shall try to do the best I can. The workers in San Quirico have threshed fifty-four *staia*[3] of grain up to now, and nothing else; the one in San Vito has threshed six *mog[g]ia*[4] and twenty *staia*,[5] twenty-seven *staia*[6] of seed grain, ten *staia*[7] of grape seed. I cannot leave because I want to take care of your affairs as they should be, and it is necessary to keep one's eyes peeled. Concerning this, an odd thing has happened to me. You know I told you that I am supposed to give some money to the friars of Sant'Antonio; the other day I was sent a request from the bishop's palace, asking for seven ducats, as when I came there in the beginning. They kept it for me there for a month and no more, and after those Orsinis came there, Messer Totto had it given back to me by those Orsinis. They do not give anything, except to go begging. I promised them I would give them a load of grain; I have not been able to send it so soon, and he sent an excommunication up here; they had me excommunicated; I send them a load of grain out of my kindness, not that he can show any document that I am supposed to give any to him: you can be sure of it; if not, I want you to give me thus and so. Messer Totto said several times: "You have to drag it out, give him something," otherwise I let him take care of it. I want to pray you, not by commandment, but for God's sake, to take the trouble on my behalf to go with my priest to talk to the brother of the vicar, who knows well that he said he would let me do the harvest on this condition: I should send him a load of grain and let him come into the bishop's palace to the notary and have abso-

lution sent me by my priest, and, if necessary, he should talk a little on my behalf with whoever may be there. Do for me as I do for you, because I want to
be able to say mass, and if I do not have letters about how much he wants me
to pay him, he still cannot show any document that I am to give him anything, except as I have said above. Excuse me if I am giving you too much
trouble: give me a load and I shall bear it for your sake. Nothing else for now.
God keep you from ill and preserve you for a long time in good health.

Yours, Ser Vincenzo,
in Sant'Antonio alle Sodora

❖ LETTER 279
Niccolò Machiavelli to Francesco del Nero
S. Andrea in Percussina, 14 October 1522

To the Notable Francesco del Nero, Honored Brother-in-Law.
In Florence.

Notable man, greatly honored. You will hear from Grazia how brutally one of
Raffaello Girolami's servants has wounded one of her brothers. Raffaello was
not there, but I know he will not be happy about the incident. My only wish
in the matter is that it might stop here so my people might be able to attend
to their work. My idea would be that, out of his human feeling, Raffaello
would call upon one of my people and, speaking a few kind words to him,
would indicate that the incident made him unhappy; then he would require
that servant of his not to show up for eight or ten months. I beg you, when
you find Raffaello, to talk to him about this idea and to advise Grazia about
what you think she should do. I shall come over there tomorrow or the next
day; I would still like to bring in thirty thrushes, but I doubt that I shall succeed. I am always at your command.

14 October 1522
Niccolò Machiavelli, in the country

❖ LETTER 280
Ser Vincenzo to Niccolò Machiavelli
San Quirico alle Sodora,[1] 23 October 1522

To the Notable Niccolò di Messer Bernardo Machiavelli.
In Florence.
In God's name, 23 October 1522.

My honored master, etc. I inform you that I have stayed to see if you were
coming up here. I see now that you have not come. I would appreciate now if
you were to look at my accounts, because I would appreciate your sending
me some money, because you know I am paid up to the account that we

made for all of August. I should now have the payment for two months, that is, September and October. If I were not in need, I would not send to ask you for them. You know you told me in San Casciano that once we had taken care of the account we had together and I was in need, you would always pay me my salary for a month or two in advance. It is of course true you said you could not keep spare money as Messer Totto did; but for a ducat you would always pay me in advance. I officiate the churches in such a way that neither you nor the peasants have anything to complain about. About what you requested of me, I said one Sunday per month in Ortimino, I have obeyed you about this, and so for this reason I pray you as much as I know how and can strictly do that you send me what is coming to me for this aforementioned time, because we are almost at All Saints. You know that all the masters pay their servants and their people. I would appreciate, if it is possible, if you paid me in addition to this the salary for the next month or two to come. It makes no difference to you whether it is sooner or later, since you are paid as you go along, because I have to take care of more than one thing for myself this All Saints, as is proper for our kind. Rather, once again have me paid one month as a present and I am very satisfied. It is also normally the custom on the morning of All Saints or All Souls day to renew two candles on the altar, just as is required. Now, you do so, to be able to say vespers on All Souls and what is fitting for the churches. I shall not go on at any greater length. If I can do anything for you, let me know, and I shall do whatever it is. *Farewell.* Yours,

Ser Vincenzo, Chaplain in
San Quirico alle Sodora

[At the bottom of the page, in Machiavelli's hand:] For Giovanni di Simone from San Miniato, his servant, one crown *di sole*.

[On the back, in Machiavelli's hand:] . . . who writes to ask me for money for his pay, so I paid him one crown.

❖ LETTER 281
Francesco Vettori to Niccolò Machiavelli
Florence, 16 April[1] 1523

I understand from your letter that you are most afraid that the new tax collectors, who are to be appointed very soon, will be too vigorous in exacting tribute, especially with necessity pressing, and you ask that I put in a good word for you with them so that you will not be obliged to pay more than twelve aurei,[2] *the sum that you were obliged to pay last year with the greatest difficulty. To tell the truth, I do not know if those tax collectors will be appointed very soon. The cardinal* [3] *is leaving tomorrow for Rome, and perhaps this appointment will be put off until his return, which will be within a month. But rest assured that whenever they are appointed I shall not fail you. I have heard that Lorenzo Acciaiuoli, the brother of our Roberto, will be one of them. I know nothing about the others. But more about these later.*

You fear that the jests of Francesco del Nero [4] *may harm you, and rightly so. Why*

should they not harm you, when in the past days they have harmed even the man himself? In Via San Gallo, near the gate, there is a nuns' convent called San Clemente.[5] *Francesco, since he is a religious man, had a very great friendship with them. Because the plague had infested some houses nearby, he told the nuns at some point that he had an estate in the country (I do not know whether it is called Paterno or Villamagna) to which the nuns could comfortably relocate themselves to avoid the neighboring contagion. The plague grew until about fifteen of the nuns, remembering his promise, left the convent and went to Francesco's farm. They got the keys from the farmer, occupied their rooms, sent grain to the mill, and treated the house and all its furnishings as their own. The farmer, after he gave the keys to the nuns, went to Florence, met Francesco, and tells him what the nuns had done. Francesco was walking with me in the Piazza della Signoria, and when he heard the farmer, you might have seen a man crying out, running through the piazza with his cloak thrown back over his shoulder and calling loudly for his brother, Agostino. When he caught him, he tells him to hitch six horses to the carriage, go to his estate, get the nuns out of his house, even if they are unwilling, put them on horses, and send them back to the nunnery. His brother obeyed and ejected the unwilling nuns from his house, and* the story was well known, to all the heavens.[6] *Why, then, should I be surprised about your son, Lodovico?*

What is so surprising, then, since Francesco had nuns in the country, if Lodovico,[7] *your sister's son, wants to have a confessor with him in the country? Since, I might say, not his father, Aeneas, but his uncle, Hector, has inspired him to these things.*[8] *But as we grow old, we become too morose and, so to speak, finicky, and we do not remember what we did when we were young. Your son Lodovico has a boy with him; he plays with him, sports with him, walks about with him, whispers in his ear; they sleep in the same bed. What about it? Perhaps even beneath these things there is nothing wrong,*[9] *but we sometimes accuse nature herself, as a stepmother, when we ought rather to blame our parents or ourselves. You would never have married if you had really known yourself; my father, if he had known my ways and my character, would never have tied me down to a wife, since nature had meant me for games and sport, not sighing after profit, scarcely concerned for family matters. But a wife and daughters have forced me to change, which cannot turn out happily for anyone.*

❖ LETTER 282

Niccolò Machiavelli to Francesco del Nero

S. Andrea in Percussina, 31 August 1523

Honored brother-in-law, here are the game birds that, had you come, we would have enjoyed tonight; since you did not come, I am sending them to you so you might enjoy them this morning. Lodovico brings them to you; and, in his new capacity, I recommend him to you. May Christ, in truth, protect you.

31 August 1523

Niccolò Machiavelli, in the country

❖ LETTER 283
Niccolò Machiavelli to Francesco del Nero
S. Andrea in Percussina, 26 September 1523

To His Magnificence, the Honored Brother-in-Law Francesco del Nero.
In Florence.

Honored brother-in-law. I am sorry about all the trouble[1] I am causing you. As you will see from the enclosed, the churches have been placed under an interdict, and, because of the study, I beg you to send me the release with Bolognino, whom I am sending to you for that purpose; otherwise, I shall have that chimney bricked up again. I shall give your regards to the chickens. I am yours.

26 September 1523
Niccolò Machiavelli, in the country

❖ LETTER 284
Ser Piero to Niccolò Machiavelli
Sant'Antonio a Orbana, 6 August 1524

To Messer Niccolò Machiavelli, in Sant'Andrea.
In Percussina.
Jesus, 6 August 1524

Honored Niccolò, greetings, etc. This letter is to notify you how much grain you have received in San Quirico for your share: five *moggia*[1] and sixteen and a half *staia*[2] of grain were received for your share, and because twenty-three and a third *staia*[3] were held out from your share for seed, that leaves four *moggia*[4] and sixteen and a half *staia*[5]: you can pick this up, and the sooner the better, because it really is very hot. In addition: we got from the workers, of the grain they had gotten from the cooper, thirteen *staia*[6] from the small holdings, of which one *staio*[7] was given as a tithe to the priest: that leaves twelve and a half *staia*,[8] which makes in all five *moggia*,[9] four and a half *staia*.[10] As I have told you, hurry up and get it into the troughs.

I made a contract with you in July, I do not remember what date, that on the first of August I was supposed to start officiating in your churches,[11] and I have done so. It so happens that the chaplain, that is, Ser Michelangelo, says he is supposed to officiate for all of August and to draw the salary for that month. I am very surprised at this; I do not know the reason, and he has locked me out: I cannot get either chalice or vestments, and he is more or less threatening me. I should like to have you give me an answer whether you prefer me to officiate or not by the present bearer, because I want to have peace and quiet. If you should have changed your mind, I shall try and do something else; whether any wrong may have been done to me, I shall leave it up to you to decide.

In recent days I went to a service in Orbana, and he had me informed that he did not want me to say mass, so I went away for better or worse and that caused me to lose those alms; and he gave the whole gang something to say, so for that reason I pray you to take care of this matter so that no scandal may come of it, because so much injury has never been done to me. I have borne it and continue to while awaiting your arrival or your letter, or have us come and settle our case in your presence so that everyone may know what he is supposed to do; or at least, as I told you, write. Nothing else. God be with you and keep you healthy. Yours.

Ser Piero,
in Sant'Antonio a Orbana

❖ LETTER 285
Niccolò Machiavelli to Francesco Guicciardini
S. Andrea in Percussina, 30 August 1524

To Messer Francesco Guicciardini, Commissioner in Romagna.

[. . .] Here in the country I have been applying myself, and continue to do so, to writing the history,[1] and I would pay ten soldi—but no more—to have you by my side so that I might show you where I am, because, since I am about to come to certain details, I would need to learn from you whether or not I am being too offensive in my exaggerating or understating of the facts. Nevertheless, I shall continue to seek advice from myself, and I shall try to do my best to arrange it so that—still telling the truth—no one will have anything to complain about.

30 August 1524
Niccolò Machiavelli

LETTERS

1525

To fulfill a promise to his mistress, the actress Barbera Raffacani Salutati, Machiavelli wrote a comedy, *Clizia.* Inspired by Plautus's *Casina,* it had its first performance on 13 January at a private house in Santa Maria in Verzaia beyond the San Frediano gate where a rich, though not aristocratic, patron, Jacopo di Filippo Falconetti, lived. Falconetti, a former member of the councils of the Signoria who had been dismissed and exiled to this house, was known as *Il Fornaciaio,* "the brickmaker" or "kiln-operator." He organized this gala performance, designed to outdo a private production of *La Mandragola* (The Mandrake) that had occurred in Florence in 1524, so that he might celebrate his release from banishment. Philippe Verdelot composed intermezzos for the production, and Bastiano (also known as Aristotele) da San Gallo designed the stage set, which, according to Vasari, pleased all who attended.

Meanwhile, Machiavelli's major project, still the *Florentine Histories,* was coming along so well that since he had covered the period up to the death of Lorenzo the Magnificent in 1492, he wanted to go to Rome and present what he had finished to Pope Clement VII. Vettori, however, counseled against making the trip at that point because the political situation was "opposed to reading and to gifts" (Letter 287, dated 8 March from Rome). Clement VII, having switched his allegiance to France, was preoccupied with matters in Lombardy. Francis I, after a four-month siege, lost the Battle of Pavia to an advancing imperial army of twelve thousand troops led by Charles III de Bourbon (1490–1527), Constable of France, who had defected to Charles V in 1523, and Ferrante d'Avalos, Marquess of Pescara, one of Charles V's most trusted generals. Furthermore, Francis I, to his disgrace, was captured and imprisoned in Madrid until January 1526. The vacillating pope reexamined his options and decided in April to cast his lot once more with

Charles V. Although the pope was operating under misguided assumptions about restoring a balance of power to the Italian peninsula, he had little choice but to accept whatever crumbs Charles granted him. The emperor was quicker to ratify the military provisions of the agreement than to accede to the pope's political concerns for the Italian states. The pope decided to further his cause by sending his nephew, Cardinal Giovanni Salviati, to Madrid. At one point in early May it looked as if Machiavelli might accompany Giovanni, especially since the cardinal's father, Jacopo Salviati, was advocating it. The possibility came to naught.

While the pope's military affairs were in disarray, Machiavelli arrived in Rome during late May to present the completed manuscipt of his *Florentine Histories.* During an interview, Clement must have alluded to his military concerns, because Machiavelli immediately began advocating a national citizen's militia as an answer to the pope's dilemma. Machiavelli's commitment to this idea so impressed Clement and his advisers, Jacopo Salviati and Jacopo Sadoletto, that they sent him to Faenza in Romagna to try to bring Francesco Guicciardini around to the idea. Romagna was thought to be a good place to try out the plan, but Guicciardini, who had been named "President" of Romagna in 1524, had indicated some reservations about conscripting a citizen's militia there when his opinion on the question was solicited by the pope.

Although he was disquieted by his friend's cool reception and his practical reservations about the militia, Machiavelli was gratified by his visit with Guicciardini. Despite the chill on the theoretical level, their friendship grew considerably warmer. Guicciardini, upon Machiavelli's departure at the end of July, could twit him about an amour in Faenza, and Machiavelli, taking no offense, could heartily accept a commission concerning some property of Guicciardini that produced a captivating exchange of letters (Letters 292 and 294).

In mid-August Machiavelli had another opportunity to visit Guicciardini, because he was once more on a brief commercial mission. The Florentine superintendents of affairs in the Levant *(Provveditore del Levante)* sent him to Venice to lodge a complaint with officials there about a Venetian shipowner who had seized a ship on the Adriatic carrying goods belonging to several Florentine merchants. Conversation in Venice with Ludovico Canossa, the papal nuncio, kindled Machiavelli's interest in politics, all the more since about this time his name was once again put on the list of Florence's eligible officeholders.

Letters to Guicciardini in the latter part of the year are full of information about Machiavelli's life and thought. He treats us to explications of *La Mandragola,* and we abruptly learn of his despair over affairs in Italy. Girolamo Morone, the secretary of Francesco II Sforza, duke of Milan, was an active supporter of a league against Emperor Charles V to drive Spain out of Italy. Morone attempted to involve the marquess of Pescara in the plans. So he could become king of Naples, the marquess pretended to play along with Morone, but he betrayed both Morone and the plan to the emperor. Morone was imprisoned in mid-October. With Milan lost, at some point after 21 October

Machiavelli wrote to Guicciardini, commenting on the affair, and with poignant self-awareness signed his letter: "Niccolò Machiavelli, Historian, Comic Author, and Tragic Author."

❖ LETTER 286
Filippo de' Nerli to Niccolò Machiavelli
Modena, 22 February 1525

To the Notable Niccolò Machiavelli, etc.

My very dear Niccolò, like an honored brother, etc. Fornaciaio[1] and you, you and Fornaciaio have managed things so that the fame of your revelries has spread and continues to spread not only throughout all Tuscany but also throughout Lombardy. So go on and do not lose hope. I know about the garden leveled off to make it into a stage for your comedy. I know about the invitations not only to the first and most noble patricians[2] of the city but also to the middle class and after them to the plebeians. These are things that are usually done only for princes. The fame of your comedy has flown all over. You should not believe that I have heard these things from friends' letters, but rather I have heard it from wayfarers who go all about the roads preaching "the glorious celebrations and great spectacles[3]" of Porta San Frediano. I am certain, just as the grandeur of such great revelries was not satisfied to remain within the boundaries of Tuscany but had to fly even farther, that it will also go beyond the mountains, if it is not held back by these armies, which will have their mind on other things than festivities and so will not feel like fooling around.[4] All in all, Niccolò, to say things as briefly as possible and to call a spade a spade[5] and to abbreviate this matter, I should like you to send me this comedy that you have recently had performed as soon as you can. Make sure that you do not fail me for anything, insofar as you esteem the favor of the king of Tunisia, and give my regards to all the dotards.[6]

From Modena, 22 February 1525.[7]
As a brother, Filippo de' Nerli,
Governor

❖ LETTER 287
Francesco Vettori to Niccolò Machiavelli
Rome, 8 March 1525

To My Dear *Compare* Niccolò di Messer Bernardo Machiavelli.
In Florence.

My dear *compare.* I could not advise you as to whether you should come with the book[1] or not, because the times are opposed[2] to reading and to gifts.

On the other hand, the pope, on the first evening I arrived, after I had talked to him of something I had to, asked me about you on his own and inquired of me whether you had finished the *Historia* and whether I had seen it. When I said that I had seen a part of it and that you had completed up to the death of Lorenzo, and that it was something that would give satisfaction, and that you wanted to come and bring it to him but I had dissuaded you from it on account of the times, he said to me: "He ought to come, and I feel for certain that his books are going to give pleasure and be read willingly." These are the very words he said to me; but I would not want you to put your trust in them for coming and then find yourself left with empty hands. And that is what could happen to you, given the state of mind in which the pope seems to be now; but I did not want to fail to write you what he said to me.

Give my regards to Francesco del Nero and tell him that I would like him to write to his friend Berlinghieri here, for him not only to pay me money for his account but also to oblige me in everything else I should ask him for. And give my regards to Donato del Corno, too. God keep you.

In Rome, 8 March 1524[5].
Francesco Vettori

❖ LETTER 288
Agostino del Nero to Niccolò Machiavelli
Florence, 26 June 1525

To His Honor the Notable Messer Niccolò Machiavelli.
In Romagna.[1]
Jesus. In the name of God, 26 June 1525.

Honored foster father. This letter is in reply to one of yours of 9 June, which I shall answer as far as possible. With that letter you sent me one from Piero del Bene addressed to Domenico Giugni and company, for them to pay me sixty-three gold *scudi di sole,* which have been paid and the receipt drawn up.[2]

I also learn from that letter how you wanted me to distribute them, and I have done so completely with as much diligence as I knew how or could, as you will be told here on your return. For Baccina's dowry,[3] as of that time you wrote me, fifty-two florins and five lire, with twelve soldi in change, have been spent; and for the taxes on four registers, thirty-seven lire, three and four, which I arranged to pay as advantageously as was possible; the rest I gave to your Madonna Marietta, that is to say, twenty-one lire, fourteen soldi, since that was what I had left.

I am very surprised that you should make excuses to me for giving me any trouble, since you know how obligated I am toward you and your house. And so, if you should need anything at all here and you know I am capable of doing it, do not ask anyone else than me: you might well commit your affairs to someone who would handle them more prudently, but not so willingly.

From the Levant there comes news by several merchants this morning that the janissaries have tried to assassinate the sultan[4] and have put to sack three or four houses of the chief pashas. Many houses and shops of Jews in Adrianople[5] were also put to sack, and our colony has received some harm. So this does not seem to me like good news for your Lodovico, who really is unlucky because nothing like this has ever been heard of. When there are letters from him, I shall send them to you.

Nothing else. I send you my regards as always. God keep you healthy and put you in a happy state of mind, so that anyone who wishes you ill should burst.   .

Your almost son
Agostino del Nero, in Florence

❖ LETTER 289
Jacopo Sadoletto to Niccolò Machiavelli
Rome, 6 July 1525

To the Notable Niccolò Machiavelli, as a Brother.

Notable man, as a brother. I got your letter of the 29th of last month, and after reading it I showed it to O[ur] L[ordship][1]; His Holiness looked with favor on everything that is discussed in it and in the one from His Lordship the President[2]; but he did not answer me then or since because of much other business, telling me that he wanted to think a little more about it and that I should write you to postpone any action. When I asked him again if His Beatitude had made up his mind yet, he answered me that he wants to think about it some more and that you should hold on. You will therefore wait, and meanwhile, if anything else should happen worthy of notification, you will write me about it so that I can show it to His Holiness and he can deliberate better. I have nothing else to write you except that I love you as always and I am happy to do your pleasure. And so I offer myself and send my regards.

From Rome, 6 July 1525.
Your good brother.
Jacopo Sadoletto, Secr[etary]
to O[ur] L[ordship]

❖ LETTER 290
Francesco del Nero to Niccolò Machiavelli
Florence, 27 July 1525

To His Honor, the Notable Niccolò Machiavelli.
In Faenza.

Notable man and brother-in-law, greetings. I received a letter from you from Rome, to which I replied. Since then I have received another letter from Faenza, concerning the great knowledge of the friar,[1] which Francesco Vettori did not believe. And he would never have believed it if he had not been shown a letter from His Excellency the President[2] that reported the same thing. The count has taken note of it, etc. Filippo Strozzi writes me that he has spoken to His Holiness concerning the raising of your stipend[3] and finds him very well disposed. Therefore he reminds us that as soon as you get to Florence, you should write him a note reminding him of your business; and Filippo will show the item to His Beatitude and will make sure that the commission comes here from him. Thus your fortunes are multiplying. I am also keeping a pigeon[4] for you that is worth two hundred gold ducats per year. So if you should go back to Rome, I should like to know when you are thinking of departing from there[5] and in what direction, so that the vain world may turn under you. Donato is waiting to bring you chickens; but because he is one of those gossips from the Ponte Vecchio, he cannot help showing your letters, so that one of them fell into the count's hands, and it is that honorable letter you wrote him a month ago, that is, the second one from Faenza, etc. Nothing else. I send you my regards.

In Florence, 27 July 1525.
Yours, Francesco del Nero

❖ LETTER 291
Francesco Guicciardini to Niccolò Machiavelli
Faenza, 29 July 1525

To the Notable Niccolò Machiavelli.
In Florence.

Notable man. Having to send back to you the enclosed letter,[1] which came with a cover to me, has given me the opportunity to write you, as I would not otherwise have done since I have nothing to say. I await letters from you eagerly; and once again I have nothing that is worth writing about. But I do not want to leave out that I understand that after your departure Mariscotta[2] spoke of you very flatteringly and greatly praised your manners and conversation. That warms my heart because I desire everything that makes you happy; and I assure you that if you come back here you will be most welcome, and perhaps even more caressed. I wrote as was necessary to Rome, but I have not received anything else in the way of materiel from there. If I should hear anything at all, I shall inform you. I send you my regards.

From Faenza, 29 July 1525.
As a brother, Francesco Guicciardini

❖ LETTER 292
Niccolò Machiavelli to Francesco Guicciardini
Florence, 3 August 1525

To the Magnificent Lrd. Francesco Guicciardini, etc.

Signor President. Because I was unable to go and look at the property of
Colombaia[1] before today, I have put off writing until now; I trust Your Lordship will excuse this delay.

I shall begin telling everything with Finocchieto.[2] And the first thing I have to
tell you is this: for three miles around, you can see nothing that is pleasing—Arabia Petraea[3] is no different. The house cannot be called bad, but I
will never call it good, because it lacks the comforts people require: the rooms
are small, the windows are high—a dungeon is no different. There is a stunted
little meadow in front; every exit gives onto a slope except for one, which is
flat for perhaps a hundred yards; and, given all this, it is so buried in the hills
that the longest view is not more than half a mile. As for the farms, Your
Lordship is aware of what they bring in, but they run the risk of bringing in
less each year because there are many fields that are washed out by water in
such a way that unless assiduous care is used in order to hold the soil back
with ditches, there will soon be nothing there but the bones. All this requires
the master's presence, and you are too far away. I understand that the Bartolini
have bought up many farms in that district but that they do not have a manor
house; if you could unload the farm on them, I would advise you to get rid of
it because it would be a good deal for them and it ought to get you out of
harm. If they should not come under your thumb, and whether you want to
hold onto it or to sell it, I would advise you to spend a hundred ducats on it
with which you could tidy up the little meadow, plant vineyards all around
the knoll on which the house perches, dig eight or ten ditches in those fields
that lie between your house and those of your first farm—those fields are
known as *La Chiusa*. I would plant winter fruit and figs in these ditches; and I
would build a fountain where there is a fine spring—the only fine thing
there—in the middle of those fields at the foot of a couple of rows of
grapevines. These improvements will be useful for either of two things: first, if
you want to sell, anyone who comes to see it will see something to his liking,
and perhaps that may bring him to discuss its purchase; for if you keep it in its
present state and the Bartolini do not buy it, I do not think you will ever sell
it except to someone who, like yourself, has not seen it. If you should decide
to hold onto it, these improvements will enable you to get more wine from it,
which is good here, and not to die of grief when you to go to inspect it.
Enough about Finocchieto.

As far as I can observe, I agree with what Iacopo has written you and Girolamo[4] has told you about Colombaia. The farm has a good location: it has
roads and ditches around it and a southeastern exposure. The soil appears to be
good, because all the fruit trees, old and young, have a lot of vigor and life in
them. It has all the advantages that a farm near Florence could have—church,

butcher, roads, mail service. There is a large number of fruit trees; nevertheless, there is room to double them. The house is set up in this way: you enter a courtyard whose sides are about twenty yards long; in front, facing the gate, there is a loggia with a balcony above it as long as the courtyard and about fourteen yards wide. This loggia, looking at it head on, has a room and an anteroom on the right-hand side; on the left, there is a hall with a bedroom and an antechamber. All these rooms, along with the loggia, are habitable and not shabby; off the courtyard are a kitchen, a stable, a vat room, and a smaller courtyard for chickens and housecleaning materials. Underneath it there are two roomy wine cellars, and above there are quite a few rooms, three of which could be fixed up for ten ducats and used to accommodate people of rank. The roofs are neither bad nor good. In short, my conclusion is this: with an expenditure of one hundred fifty ducats, you could live comfortably, agreeably, and not at all indecorously. You would need to spend these one hundred fifty ducats on redoing the gates, relaying the stones in the courtyard, redoing the low walls, replacing a beam, repairing a stairway, redoing the eaves of the roof, mending the kitchen and putting in a new window, and similar kinds of small repairs that would make the house pretty to look at and give it charm; thus, with this kind of expenditure you could live until you saw fit to enter into a great sea [of expenditures].

As for the rents, I have yet to check them out to my satisfaction, since I was unable to talk to someone I wanted to. I shall give Your Lordship a detailed report in another letter.

This morning I received your letter,[5] in which you tell me in what good grace I am with Maliscotta; I glory more in this than in anything I have in this world. I shall be pleased if you would give her my regards.

As for the affairs of kings, emperors, and popes, I have nothing to write; perhaps I shall have something, and I shall write them to you in another letter.

I pray Your Lordship to tell your lady[6] that I passed on her greetings to all her friends, both male and female, and especially to Averardo[7]; all of them send their regards to Your Lordship and to her. And I send Your Lordship my regards and dedication a thousand times over.

3 August 1525
Yours, Niccolò Machiavelli, in Florence

❖ LETTER 293
Francesco Guicciardini to Niccolò Machiavelli
Faenza, 7 August 1525

To the Notable Niccolò Machiavelli.
In Florence.

My very dear Machiavelli. I have gotten your letter of the third,[1] and principally I have to tell you that if you honor letters addressed to me with "illustrious," I shall honor yours with "excellency," and thus, with these reciprocal titles we shall renew each other's pleasure, but it will be turned into mourning when we all find ourselves, I say all of us, with our hands full of flies at the end. So make up your mind about titles, measuring mine against those you would enjoy having given to you [. . .].

Once again I have heard nothing that has any consequence, and I believe that we are all walking in the shadows, but with our hands tied behind our backs, so that we cannot avoid bumps.

From Faenza, 7 August 1525.
As a brother, Francesco Guicciardini

❖ LETTER 294
Francesco Guicciardini to Niccolò Machiavelli
Faenza, 7 August 1525

Milady Property of Finocchieto,[1]
who wishes health and clarified judgment to Machiavelli.

If I believed that what you[2] wrote about me to my lord and master had been written by you maliciously, I would not go to the trouble of contradicting you because, since I was born and raised in these solitary mountains, I do not have so much eloquence that it might give me courage to cure you of this maliciousness, and because I deem that it is a better vengeance to let the malicious man remain confirmed and stubborn in his maliciousness than to make him blush by making the truth known. But since I am convinced that everything has been caused by error, which if it is not praiseworthy is at least excusable, I think it is the duty of kindness and courtesy, which is stronger in me than this place requires and my appearance suggests, to make you aware of the truth. I do it all the more willingly because, being a woman, though I cannot detest the origin of your error that also springs from a woman, and even though she has been brought up with indecent manners that displease me, she is still a woman; and the similarity of our sex does not permit there to be no spark of good will between us. You are used to your Barbera[3] who strives, as does her kind, to please everyone and seeks rather to seem than to be. Therefore your eyes, accustomed to that sort of meretricious company, are not satisfied so much by what is as by what seems to be; and as long as there is a little beauty in it, they do not consider anything beyond appearances. But you, who have read and written so many histories and seen so much of the world, ought really to know that a different adornment, a different beauty, a different manner of making oneself up and of appearing is sought in a woman who lives with everyone and loves no one than in those who, full of chaste thoughts, have no other concern than to please only the one to whom they have been honorably and legitimately given. If, however, through long experience with such women, and I have heard that you have never lived otherwise, you have gotten into such bad habits that their corrupt manners seem good to you and worthy of such as us, you still ought to have remembered that it was rash of you to make a judgment in one moment and that things are to be judged not by their surface but by their substance; and that under the rigidity and harshness that were apparent in me at first glance so many good aspects might be hidden that I deserved to be praised, not insultingly blamed, in that way. If no one else, your Barbera certainly ought to have made you aware of this since, although her name denotes complete cruelty and ferociousness, she has concentrated in herself, according to what I am willing to believe from your words, such gentleness and such mercy[4] that she would season[5] an entire city for you.

But I want to tell you of my qualities with the idea, if you realize the truth and take back what you wrote of me, not only of pardoning the injury you have done to me but also of being satisfied that a good share of the fruits of which all my fields are full may be given to your Barbera every year: I know of no greater favor I could do you than to treat as she merits the woman who is your heart's delight. In order for you to see how erroneous your judgment was, I shall tell you first of all that one of my virtues lies in the very thing that made you burst forth so thoughtlessly in blame of me, because, since I have given my love to only one man, I always thought of pleasing no one else but him, and therefore I kept myself in that rigidity and harshness that you see, which, if I had striven to appear before the eyes of everyone, I should have been quite able to temper. For you must not believe that, even though I was born in these mountains, I lack the means and the skill to clean myself up; and even if I had not known them so well nor had the opportunity to learn them from others, I am convinced that you, since you are a lover of all women and have long lived among them, would have wished and known how to teach them to me. But I have never had the intention of living with more than one man and therefore, as long as in other things I gave him cause to love me, I have set aside all the vanities and charms that could have made me please many, judging that it was a good means to be loved by him for him to recognize in me this decency and honor, although, as men are naturally lovers of variety, I judged that it would be more pleasing to him when he came here to find this wildness and asperity to which his eyes are not so accustomed, in comparison with women in places near the city who are wont to adorn and to make themselves beautiful, than if he had found the beauties and adornments of the same kind in which he finds himself every day and every hour.[6] In this my artifice was double, because that by which I most thought to please him made me hope that I would please others less, something much desired by me because, since I am little desirous of having to do with different men every day and I love tenderly the man with whom I live now, and I know that those who consider things with their cortex as you did are more numerous than those who consider them with their medulla,[7] I am glad that if ever he should be of a mind to transfer me, he would not so easily find someone to whom I was pleasing and would almost of necessity be obliged to keep me with him.

So you see, Machiavelli, how much praise I deserve and how much dearer I should be held for that very cause that displeased you so much. Next time you will know better than to trust so much in yourself and in your opinion, and you will ponder more carefully before you judge, because many excuses are admissible in others that cannot be accepted in one of your wisdom and experience.

❖ LETTER 295
Lodovico Machiavelli to Niccolò Machiavelli
Adrianople,[1] 14 August 1525

To My Honored Father, Niccolò Machiavelli.
In Florence.
† Jesus. 14 August 1525.

Honored father, etc. You have been written to quite a lot in the past. This letter is to tell you about an account I have with Carlo Machiavelli that he has never been willing to settle. So I am thinking of going and taking care of my interests. In my other letter I wrote you that I had seven and a half pieces of cloth left out of the entire amount. Because these pieces of cloth are somewhat skimpy, I would have disposed of them better here than in Pera. Since Carlo Machiavelli was not very friendly to me, he went together with a certain Giovanbattista Masini and with Niccolò Lachi to the shops of those who they knew wanted them and told them that I had nothing but rejected cloth. If Carlo had behaved as a worthy man is supposed to behave, I would have disposed of them today, but I have been obliged to send them to Giovanni Vernacci in Pera. As if it was not enough for him to do me this injury, he did me another one. I wanted to leave fifteen days ago and accompany the goods and I wanted, before leaving, to settle the said account with him and for him to give me up to a hundred and twenty-three ducats that I am supposed to get from him to take care of my affairs; and there was never any way to get him to settle it. So I stayed behind and I shall stay here until people leave for Pera; and every day that I stay here I shall ask him if he wants to settle with me. If not, when I am in Pera I give you my word that the first thing I do will be this: I shall go and see the bailiff,[2] and he will have to come up there whether he wants to or not,[3] or arrange for me to be paid. I shall do him the honor that he deserves. For your information.

Whether you are in Rome or Florence, I beg you on receipt of this letter to write me what has happened to your affairs. It seems to me a great wonder that I have had no news at all of your affairs since the nineteenth of May, or from anyone over there. And yet a great many letters have come here from over there. For your information.

I also pray you that if you have done nothing about that scoundrelly priest,[4] on receiving this letter you see to it that I am avenged in some part for all the injuries he has done me. If you recall, you wrote me that I should make sure and do well in the Levant and you would make sure to be well off in Rome, and if you should succeed in this that the injuries could be avenged; I shall tell you that it was not possible to do any better with all the goods that I had. I really do not know how you may have done, though I judge that in comparison to me you have done much better. So you can imagine whether I feel like getting revenge. But it bothers me that the revenge that we could wreak with a few words, showing what a scoundrel he is and by that means throwing him out of that church, we are going to wait and do to our own loss, and pluck out two of our own eyes to pluck out one of our comrade's. It is all up to you. Similarly, in accordance with your advice, you know that I had to swallow that word of Cecco de' Bardi. But I do not want to discuss this any further. Let it suffice for you that if I have no other news, I shall go to Sant'Andrea before Florence and I shall punish that scoundrel. I shall not discuss it with you any longer, because I have written enough so that you must have understood me. I shall be quicker than you think, because I shall be there before the middle of January has gone by, if God lends me good health. Nothing else for this letter. Give my regards to Madonna Marietta and tell her that I have not written her for lack of time; the same to Bernardo. Greet the children on my behalf, and I send you my regards as always. God keep you from harm.

Yours,

Lodovico Machiavelli, in Adrianople

❖ LETTER 296
Niccolò Machiavelli to Francesco Guicciardini
Florence, 17 August 1525

Niccolò Machiavelli to Messer Francesco Guicciardini,
President of Romagna for the Pontiff.

Signor President. I received your letter of the twelfth yesterday, and in reply I shall let you know that Capponi[1] has returned and your Jacopo wanted to assume the burden of asking him; but, as you point out, I think there must have been a very good understanding between them. At any rate, you might make them an offer so that it can be seen that you want it, as long as they do not go too far from what is reasonable. Girolamo and I think you cannot offer less than three thousand ducats; but on this point you should fix whatever sum you like for it.

I like it that you like Messer Nicia, and if you put it on[2] during Carnival season we shall come and help you out. Thank you for the testimonials you gave; I beg you to keep them coming.

The superintendents of affairs in the Levant plan to send me to Venice to recover some lost funds.[3] If I am to go, I shall set off within four days and on my return trip I shall come through Modena to spend an evening with Your Lordship and to see our friends again.

I am sending you twenty-five pills made up four days ago in your name, and the list of ingredients for them is at the end of this letter. I can tell you that they have revived me. Start by taking one after dinner; if that causes a movement, do not take any more; if it does not, take two or three—at most, five. But I never took more than two, once a week, and when I felt heaviness in my stomach or in my head.

Two days ago I spoke to my friend about our affair[4]; I told him he would have to forgive me if I were entering too deeply into his important concerns but that it was he who had encouraged me, and, in short, I asked him what his intentions were about giving his son a wife. After a few formalities, he replied that he believed the matter had come to a point where young men felt demeaned if they did not obtain an extraordinary dowry and that he did not believe he would be able to restrict his son to an ordinary one. Then he said, after a little bit of reflection, "I think I can figure out on whose behalf you are speaking to me because I know where you have been[5] and this topic has been brought up through another intermediary." To which I replied that I did not know whether or not he had guessed correctly, but the truth was that this topic had never been mentioned between you and me; I proved this, speaking as effectively as I could, and said that if I were making a move, I did so for my own part and for the good that I wished both him and me. At this point I laid the cards on the table, yours and his, and discussed your respective situations, the nature of things as they are in the present and will be in the future, and so many items that I really awoke his curiosity. So he finally admitted that if the Magnificent[6] decided to marry a Florentine woman, he would be ill-advised were he not to obtain her from your family. Hence, I said that I could not see why you, as intelligent a man as he, would let yourself be passed over for some other citizen for two or three thousand ducats more despite the fact, since you have no sons and your wife has stopped giving you any more, that fate might cause it to turn out that the dowry would be larger than some other person's he might choose and so he might not gain anything other than the dowry. And since we had reached the Church of the Servites during the course of our discussion, I stopped in front of its portal and said, "I should like to say these final words to you in a memorable setting so that you will remember them: 'May God grant that you will have nothing to regret about this and that your son will not have little to be grateful to you for.'" So he said, "In God's name, this is the first time we have discussed this topic; we need to speak of it daily." To which I replied that I would never say anything to him about it again because it was sufficient that I had settled my debt. This is how I turned[7] my lance; there was no way to conceal what I knew he would discover. Now I shall wait for him to act and not let slip by any opportunity for driving this point home with general and specific discussions. But let us go back to the list of ingredients for the pills.

Prescription

Bitter Aloe	drams	1.5
Germander [8]	"	1
Saffron	"	.5
Selected Myrrh	"	.5
Betony	"	.5
Pimpernel	"	.5
Armenian Bole	"	.5

Florence, 17 August 1525
Niccolò Machiavelli

❖ LETTER 297
Filippo de' Nerli to Niccolò Machiavelli
Florence, 6 September 1525

To His Very Honored Messer Niccolò Machiavelli, as a Brother.
In Venice.

My very dear Niccolò. Since you left here,[1] Ludovico Alamanni has presented one letter of yours in particular to me, written by you on behalf of a friar who was supposed to preach in Modena since last January. The one who was supposed to make use of the letter, as the appropriate person, did not at first want to present it until I guaranteed it in every respect, as someone who knew your feelings about friars very well. It is enough that, as for that item, you are an all-too-worthy man, and I do not waste my time.[2] Let that be enough about the friar.

As for the part with the news, since the world has been transformed in so many ways since that time, it is therefore not necessary to speak otherwise about what you wrote then, and I would not know what other news to write you, unless I wrote to you that the Poggesis of Lucca have recently ransacked Bagni di Lucca, and since they had no other support or other forces, as you know, they withdrew with their booty and acted more like looters than like state recuperators.

I am very happy to know that you have been put on the ballot list and that gestures have been made to you, and the *accoppiatori*[3] have closed an eye. During the time I have been here, I have had innumerable confirmations of it. I was really very glad to hear whence such great favor has originated; since it comes from Barbary[4] and from some other kindnesses of yours, as you yourself testify in your letter, you enlighten me more from day to day. I do not understand the code about your sons and leave it to you to worry about whether they are dealing with *either servant girls or free ones* or perhaps concubines. If I had had news of it earlier, from either you or someone else, I should have rejoiced in it earlier; may it do you much good: God give you consolation in its time and place, and weep tender tears[5] about it as much as you see fit.

This absence of yours from among the dotards[6] here has clearly shown the people that you are the root of all evil. It is evident that you inherited your customs and manners completely from Tommaso del Bene; because now that you are not here, nothing is heard either of gambling or of taverns or of any other little thing. And thus we can tell whence all ill originated. Donato[7] has taken on the clothes of Cricca; Baccino is no longer to be seen; if Giovanni did it, I would not hold back; but most of the time either the place or the writings or a third person is lacking, and someone to bring the band together is always lacking because you are not here.

I am still here, and I shall go away two or three days after the fair. I shall wait for you in Modena; and there, at great leisure and without having to write, I shall inform you of many things that will perhaps please you. In the meantime, try to take care of things quickly, because here there is a lot of gossip among these merchants that you are passing your time at their expense entertaining literary people there. They need something more than fairy tales. You know that not everyone likes rumors, as you yourself have learned by experience: or else be ready to swallow that lump.[8]

I could not help but rejoice greatly with you, however, for all the good you are getting, for you know that I feel as if I am enjoying it myself because of our long-standing friendship. You certainly have struggled with fate for quite a while, and it has made you stretch your limbs and get the monkey off your back.[9] From what we hear by the letters from Venice, you have won two or three thousand ducats in the lottery,[10] for which your friends are all very happy, and it seems to them that what men have not provided for the merits of your qualities, fate has provided. Although this is a small thing compared with your merits, nevertheless a lot can be done with three thousand that come that way, especially without any obligation to anyone. May it do you much good. You have really wronged your friends and your relatives and those who love you by not letting us know of it here, for we had to learn of it from strangers' letters and by indirect routes, so that Count de' Mozzi[11] is all perplexed about it and does not know whether this thing should be believed in or not. But all in all he accepts it, seeing the letters written from there by very trustworthy merchants, and he also bases it greatly on the spells that you learned in Romagna; if it were not for this firm belief he has in this knowledge of yours, it would be hard to get him to believe it. I, on my part, am quite sure of it, because I do not think that the men who have written about it, who are not prone to gossip, would write such a falsehood. Once again, therefore, I am very glad, and may it do you much good. I pray you, in order to satisfy your friends, whenever such good luck should come to you again, let them know in such a way that they do not come to hear about it from the neighbors; and do it with such deftness that it is not announced publicly here, as happened with these three thousand that you have won now; because, there being some idea of changing the tax lists or to name some arbitrator, you might get some pain in the ass[12] from this report that would give you a much harder time[13] than it did Messer Nicia.

Donato has been sulking about you ever since I told him that you had written that he had closed up shop,[14] and he submitted a protest to the company. You are going along losing friends, to your detriment. I have nothing else for now. May the lottery help you, and Francesco del Nero and his companions come out well and at the proper time.

From Florence, 6 September 1525.
Yours, as a brother,
Filippo de' Nerli

❖ LETTER 298
Domenico Mazzuoli to Niccolò Machiavelli
Ferrara, 28 September 1525

To the Notable, Honored Messer Niccolò Machiavelli.
In Florence.

Notable man, Messer, etc. At the first opportunity that the Bologna customs agents have, your chest should be sent to you, because I sent it by that route on the day after your departure, with another small chest that is coming to Lady Costanza de' Conti, the wife of Lord Lorenzo Salviati. You will arrange to get it, and you will be so kind as to have either Calandro or Spina notify us of it. You have to pay for the freight or any other expense that may have been incurred between Bologna and there, as the aforementioned customs agents will write you. Yesterday evening I received from His Lordship the Governor of Modena[1] a letter that asked me to remind you that you have made him a promise to go and see him. I was too late, for in addition to reminding you of it, I would also have prayed you to. I remind you that, if there should be anything you need here, you should certainly ask it of us, because I shall be happier to do you a favor than you perhaps are to receive it. There is nothing further to say. I am at your orders. God fulfill all your desires happily.

From Ferrara, 28 September 1525.
Brother Domenico Mazzuoli

❖ LETTER 299
Niccolò Machiavelli to Francesco Guicciardini
Florence, 16–20 October 1525

Niccolò Machiavelli to Messer Francesco Guicciardini.

Signor President. I have not written you because as soon as I arrived in the country, I found my Bernardo sick with a double tertian fever. But, upon returning from the farm this morning to talk with the doctor, I found a letter from Your Lordship dated the thirteenth; from it I realize what mental anguish Messer Nicia's simple-mindedness and the ignorance of those people[1] have brought you. Although I believe that there are many ambiguous passages, still I shall do my best to satisfy you, since you have decided you want explanations for only two of them. *Fare a' sassi pe' forni* means only to do something a madman would do; hence, when my character says that if everybody were like Messer Nicia "we would be feeding the oven with stones," he means that we would be behaving like crazy people—so much for the first ambiguity. [2]

As for the toad and the harrow, [3] this indeed does require greater scrutiny. And, to tell the truth, I have delved through a great many tomes, just like Fra Timoteo, in order to discover the source for this harrow; at last I came across a passage in Burchiello [4] that I think is quite germane; it is in one of his sonnets where he says:

> Fearing that the empire might invade
> A linen kettle was sent as ambassador,
> The tongs and the paddle were given the chase,
> For four skeins were found missing,
> But the harrow of Fiesole dragged there . . .

This sonnet seems quite mysterious to me, and I think that, for anyone who scrutinizes it carefully, it is going to annoy our modern world. There is but this difference: whereas once we sent a linen kettle, the linen has now become a noodle [5]; so it seems to me that the world repeats itself and we are consistently the same. A harrow is a square wooden tool with a number of teeth that our peasants use whenever they want to break up the soil and even it out for sowing. Burchiello brings up the harrow of Fiesole as being the most ancient in Tuscany because, according to the *Second Decade* of Titus Livy, the people of Fiesole were the first to invent this implement. [6] And one day, when a peasant was making his land even, a toad, which was not accustomed to seeing such a big implement, watched in amazement and amusement what was going on; the harrow ran over the toad and scraped its back severely, and the toad rubbed the spot with its foot more than once. So, after the toad felt itself scraped hard by it, the toad said to the harrow as it passed over its back, "Don't bother to come back!" This cry gave rise to the expression that goes "as the toad said to the harrow"—used whenever you do not want someone to return. This is all I have found that is of any use; if Y[our] L[ordship] still has any uncertainty about this, let me know.

While you are working hard [7] there, we here are not sleeping; Ludovico Alamanni [8] and I have been dining these last few evenings with Barbera and discussing the play; hence, she has offered to come with her singers and sing the songs between the acts. I have offered to write lyrics [9] consistent with the action, and Ludovico has offered to provide her and her singers with lodging at the Buosi's house. So, you see we are applying ourselves diligently so that this celebration will have all it needs for perfection. My regards.

Niccolò Machiavelli

❖ LETTER 300
Niccolò Machiavelli to Francesco Guicciardini
Florence, after 21 October 1525

Niccolò Machiavelli to Messer Francesco Guicciardini.

I never think of Y[our] L[ordship] (and I think of you every hour) without considering how you might fulfill your wish in that matter[1] that weighs more heavily than anything else—as I am aware. Among the many fancies that have entered my mind, there is one that I have decided to write you about, not in order to advise you but to open a door through which you, better than anyone else, will know how to pass. Filippo Strozzi finds himself burdened with sons and daughters, and just as he seeks to do his sons ample justice, so he thinks it proper to do so for his daughters; he also believes, as do all wise men, that his eldest daughter[2] ought to show the way to the others. He tried, among various young men, to give her to a son of Giuliano Capponi with a dowry of four thousand florins, but he did not get what he wanted in return because Giuliano did not want to do it; whereupon—despairing of being able to do something advantageous on his own, unless he appeared with a dowry greater than he could later keep up with—Filippo applied to the pope for aid and assistance. At the latter's suggestion Filippo took the matter up with Lorenzo Ridolfi and concluded it with a dowry of eight thousand florins—four thousand of it paid for by the pope and four thousand by Filippo. Paolo Vettori, who wanted to arrange a distinguished marriage but was unable to see any prospect of coming up with a sufficient dowry, also applied to the pope, who, to satisfy Paolo, put in two thousand ducats of his own with his authorization.

My dear president, were you the first who had to break the ice in order to proceed in this direction, I might chance to be one of those who would go slowly about advising you to embark on it; but since two men, who are no better than you either in rank, merit, or any other human consideration, have already prepared the way for you, I shall consistently advise that, with courage and without any reservation, you do what they have done. With the pope's aid, Filippo has profited by a hundred and fifty thousand ducats, and he had no hesitation about asking the pope to subsidize him in his hardship; you who have not profited by twenty thousand need hesitate even less. Paolo has been subsidized countless times and in countless ways—not with positions but with actual cash—then, without reservation, asked the pope to subsidize him in this particular need. You who have given the pope succor with honor and profit, and not been a burden to him, ought to have even less hesitation about doing it. I need not remind you about Palla Rucellai, Bartolomeo Valori, or a goodly number of others whom in their need the pope has succored from his own purse; these examples ought to embolden you in your request and give you confidence about obtaining it. Hence, were I in your shoes, I should write a letter to your agent in Rome, who would read it to the pope, or I would write the pope and have your agent deliver it—secretly sending the agent a copy and enjoining him to see to it that he got a reply. I would like the letter to include how on his account you have striven for ten years[3] to earn honor and profit and that it seems to you that in both respects you have fulfilled that aim—though with the greatest of deprivation and peril to yourself—for which you give thanks first to God and then to the blessed memory of Pope Leo and His Holiness, to whom you owe everything. True, you know full well that if a person carries out ten deeds in an honorable fashion and then fails in one, that one effectively cancels out all the others—especially if it is a matter of some significance; for that reason, since it seems to you as if you have served in the role of a man with ability, you would not want to be a failure in any single one. After you had written a preamble such as this, I would point out to him what your situation is: that you find yourself with no male children but with four females, that you think it is time to marry off one of them, and that should you not marry her in a fashion consonant with your other accomplishments, you would feel as if you had never done anything of value. And then point out that only the evil ways and corrupt customs of the modern world run counter to your desire, since matters have come to such a point that, all other considerations aside, the richer and nobler a young man is, the larger the dowry he seeks; in fact, when they do not receive huge, even excessive dowries, they count themselves disgraced. So you have no idea how to overcome this difficulty because, were you to offer three thousand florins, which would be as much as you might be able to contribute—and such an amount would mean that four daughters would require twelve thousand florins—that is the entire profit gleaned from your perils and exertions. Hence, unable to go any higher and aware that your offer is half what young men are requiring, you have summoned up your courage—as the sole remedy—to do what his greatest friends, among whom you number yourself, have done: to apply to His Holiness for aid and assistance, since you cannot believe that he would deny you what he has bestowed upon others. And at this point I would disclose to him the young man whom you have in mind and that you know the dowry is all that is spoiling the arrangement; therefore, His Holiness must overcome this difficulty. Now, press him and charge him with the most efficacious words you can find so as to convince him how important you think the matter is; I feel certain that, if it is handled correctly in Rome, you will carry the day. Consequently, do not let yourself down, and, if both time and season permit, I would urge you to send your Girolamo there for this purpose, because it all boils down to asking boldly and evincing discontent if you are refused. Princes easily yield in granting new favors to those to whom they have granted old ones; or rather, if they refuse, they are so afraid of losing the benefits of their previous favors that they always rush to grant the new ones—should they be asked in the manner that I trust you will use in this case. Be prudent, etc.

Morone has been taken prisoner and the duchy of Milan is done for[4]: and just as he has awaited his hood,[5] so too will all the other princes—there is no remedy for it. *Thus is it imposed from above.*[6]

I see the fleur-de-lys of Alagna return,
and in his Vicar . . .[7]

You know the lines, read the rest for yourself. For once, let us have a merry carnival; arrange a room for Barbera with those friars, and if they do not go crazy
over her, I shall not want any money for it. Give my regards to Maliscotta and
let me know how far along the comedy is, and when you intend to put it on.

I received that raise[8] to a hundred ducats, for the *History.* I am just now beginning to write again,[9] and I vent my feelings by accusing the princes who
have all done everything they can to bring us to this situation. *Farewell.*

Niccolò Machiavelli
Historian, Comic Author, and Tragic Author[10]

❖ LETTER 301
Niccolò Machiavelli to Francesco Guicciardini
Florence, 19 December 1525

Niccolò Machiavelli to Messer Francesco Guicciardini.

Signor President. I have put off answering your last letter until today both
because it did not seem to me to matter much and because I have not been in
Florence much. Now, since your stable master has seen us and I thought I
might be able to send one safely, I have decided to put it off no longer. I cannot deny that your reservations, which cause you to be undecided about
whether or not to attempt that business by such a tack,[1] are good and presented sensibly; nevertheless, I shall tell you my view: one can err in being too
judicious as well as by being too hasty; in fact, quite often it is better to be
hasty. If Filippo and Paolo[2] had had these reservations, they would not have
accomplished their goals; and even if Paolo has no more daughters to set a
pattern for the others, Filippo does—but, as long as he can settle the first one
to his satisfaction, he gives no thought to his other daughters. And I do not
know whether or not what you say about consigning your one daughter to
Heaven only to consign the others to Hell is true, because, once you have
done so, you are in no worse position with the others than you are now in
with them all; in fact, your position is better because your future sons-in-law,
in addition to having you, will also have a respectable brother-in-law—and
you may turn up some who are less greedy and more respectable. Still, even if
none were to turn up, the kind available for the oldest daughter will not be
unavailable for the others. In short, I would try the pope just the same, and
even if I came up short the first time around, I would talk about my aim in
general terms, beg him to help me with it, find out where he would stand, and
proceed directly or hang back—depending upon how it went. I remind you of
the advice that Romeo gave the duke of Provence,[3] who had four daughters;
he urged him to make a distinguished marriage for the eldest, pointing out
that she would provide an example and precedent for the rest. So, he married

her to the king of France[4] and gave him half of Provence as dowry. Once he did this, he married the others off to three kings; as Dante says:

> He had four daughters, each a queen;
> The cause of all this was Romeo
> A pilgrim and of humble birth.[5]

I am delighted to hear about the disputes of those friars; I desire to decide upon them not here but there, on the spot—we shall go with whoever does the best for us. But I can certainly tell you that if rumor sends them into confusion, our presence will send them into a rage.

As for worldly matters, I have nothing to tell you, since after the duke of Pescara's death[6] everyone has cooled off, for they discussed new rapprochements and such before his death, but now that he is dead it seems someone else[7] has collected his wits somewhat: convinced that he has time, he gives his enemy time. In short, my conclusion is that this gang here will never ever do anything honorable and bold worth living or dying for; I observe so much fear in the citizens of Florence and such disinclination to offer any opposition to whoever is preparing to devour us—and I see no exception to my conclusion. Hence, whoever is forced to act upon consultation with them will act in no way other than has been tried heretofore.

19 December 1525
Niccolò Machiavelli, in Florence

❖ LETTER 302
Francesco Guicciardini to Niccolò Machiavelli
Faenza, 26 December 1525

To the Notable Niccolò Machiavelli, as an Honored Brother.
In Florence.

Honored Niccolò. I shall begin my answer to you with the comedy,[1] because it does not seem among the less important things that we have on our hands, and at least it is a discussion that is within our power, so that the time spent thinking of it is not wasted, and recreation is more than ever necessary amid so much tumult. I hear that those who are to perform are ready; but I shall see them in a few days, and since they are not in agreement about the argument,[2] which would not be understood, they have made another one,[3] which I have not seen; but I shall see it soon. Because I desire that it not be watered down, I do not think you can go wrong if you put together another one suited to the low intelligence of the audience, and in which they would be depicted rather than you. I am planning to have it performed a few days before Carnival, and it would make sense for you to arrive before the end of January with the intention of staying here until Lent.[4] The lodgings for the distinguished company[5] will be ready; but, if you please, let me know of your decision and seriously, because these are not matters to be neglected. I would not have gotten into this business, to tell the truth, if I had not definitely taken your coming for granted.[6]

Concerning public affairs, I do not know what to say because I have lost my bearings.[7] Even hearing that everyone is crying out against that opinion, which I do not like but seems necessary to me, *I hear nothing said.*[8] If I am not mistaken, we shall all know better the evils of peace when the opportune time for making war is past. I have never seen anyone who, when he sees bad times coming, did not seek in some way to try and protect himself, except for us, who want to await them unprotected in the middle of the road. Therefore, *if anything bad were to happen,* we say not that our sovereignty was taken away from us but that *it fell shamefully from our hands.*

You have made me look for a Dante throughout Romagna to find the tale or rather the story of Romeo,[9] and I finally found the text, but there was no gloss. I think it is one of those things that you are accustomed to having up your sleeve; *but let us get back to our business*[10]: your advice carries *so much weight with me* that it has no need of others' authority. The times seem unfavorable, for a month or two, for taking up such things, because I believe, or rather I am certain, that we have no less hung up our brains than our weapons, and therefore I shall have the leisure to think about it carefully, and meanwhile, if ever you should see some good opportunity, I know that you would not fail to do your duty as a true friend. I send you my regards while awaiting your reply.

In Faenza, 26 December 1525.
Yours, Francesco Guicciardini

L E T T E R S

1526

The letters between Machiavelli and Guicciardini at the beginnning of 1526 alternate between discussions of immediate political events and the possible production of *La Mandragola*. Toward the end of 1525, Guicciardini had been asking Machiavelli to explain some difficult spots in the play, because Guicciardini planned to sponsor a performance in Faenza during the carnival season of 1526 that would feature Machiavelli's Barbera and her theatrical company. Real political events, however, soon took precedence over fictional ones.

One consequence of Charles V's victory in the Battle of Pavia at the end of February 1525 was the imprisonment of Francis I in Madrid. On 14 January 1526, the two rulers signed the Treaty of Madrid. Under its terms, Francis agreed to give up all his interest in Italy, to restore Burgundy to the emperor, to marry Charles V's sister Leonora of Austria, the dowager queen of Portugal—her husband Emanuel the Great had died in 1521—and to leave his two sons, Francis and Henry, in Spain as hostages. Francis was released in February, left Madrid in March, and, by May, was renewing his challenge to the emperor in Italy. Quickly breaking the promise he made in the Treaty of Madrid, of which Clement VII was swift to absolve him, Francis I signed on to the League of Cognac with the pope, the duke of Milan—Francesco Sforza II—and Venice. Becoming a signatory led Francis I to the first of four offensives, which continued with his son Henry II throughout the sixteenth century, to fulfill the century-old French ambition of gaining a foothold in Italy. (This War of the League of Cognac did not end until the signing of the Treaty of Cambrai in August 1529, the so-called Ladies' Peace because it was negotiated and signed by Louise of Savoy and Margaret of Austria, the former acting as regent for her son, Francis I, and the latter acting as regent for her nephew, Charles V.)

❖ LETTER 20
Francesco Machiavelli[1] to Niccolò Machiavelli

Florence, 5 November 1500

To the Magnificent Niccolò Machiavelli,
the Florentine Ambassador to His Most Christian Majesty.
Via Lyons, at the Court.
In the name of God, 5 November 1500.

Your Magnificence Ambassador, etc. By the present letter I do not wish, my dear and honored Messer Niccolò, to renew in either you or me the sorrow of the losses[2] you and we have sustained, although ours was greater for having been in the more noble sex; we are saving it to be expressed orally, since I judge that will be within a short time, as we strongly desire it, and we know that you do the same. I inform you by the present letter that, although the late, beloved Giovan Battista is not in the house of Rinieri, in Lyons, everyone there is yours, and especially Maria, who must have arrived there by now with her husband Rinieri: her sons are there; there is such a residue of kindness and love in that house that all the relatives as well as the friends of the late beloved will always be greeted with love and good will, and every hospitality and favor will be given to them, and you can make yourself completely at home there. I know there is nothing new, and I thought I ought to write you this note, having in particular to send you your letters, which will be in this one.

I understand a relative of Stiatta Ridolfi, your colleague[3] Francesco della Casa, is ill, and Stiatta has asked me several times about him, claiming not to have news from you as to how he is and expressing surprise. I feel you have done your duty in everything, since I know that is your nature: I wanted to tell you, if it should be appropriate, although I know Your Excellency has gone on to Nancy,[4] and he to Paris.

I would desire, if you should have some opportunity (as I imagine you will), that you should inform His Lordship Messer Giulio[5] that I send him my regards and that I have promptly delivered every letter received from him. And because I know he will have a report from his friends as well as Niccolò as to the outcome of all his affairs, I shall refrain from wearying His Lordship and myself as well.

When you see Ugolino Martelli,[6] be so kind as to give my regards to him and greet him a thousand times on my behalf.

Today, Adovardo Buglione,[7] His Most Christian Majesty's steward, is leaving, bearing a dispatch from our Signoria for his return. To us a resolution seems to have been made that ought to be agreeable to His Majesty, as you will be notified by the public letter.

And in this letter I shall say no more to you. I am yours and send you my regards. Christ be, etc.

Yours, Francesco Machiavelli, in Florence

The pope, who first had sent Count Guido Rangoni, governor general
of the army of the Church, to Piacenza with his men at arms and five
thousand infantry, now sent the Florentine Vitello Vitelli, who was governor of Florence, with his infantry and men at arms, and Giovanni de'
Medici [Giovanni delle Bande Nere], whom he made the commander
of the Italian infantry; as deputy commander, his general in the army
and in all the states of the Church—with full and virtually absolute
power—the pope sent to Piacenza Francesco Guicciardini, at that time
the president of Romagna. And the Venetians, on the other hand, added
to their army, whose commander was the duke of Urbino and whose
quartermaster general was Pietro da Pesaro. (XVII, 3, p. 1638)

Guicciardini's title of "Luogotenente," deputy commander, was one by which
he was known throughout Italy.

This gathering storm in Lombardy soon enveloped Machiavelli. We do not
know exactly when he, too, arrived in Piacenza or what his exact function
was, but it is clear that he was there in mid-July, both from Letter 313, dated
13 July from Marignano, about thirty-two miles northwest of Piacenza, and
from Guicciardini's letter to Roberto Acciaiuoli, Florence's ambassador to
France, on 18 July: "Machiavelli is here. He came to reorganize the militia,
but, seeing how rotten it is, he has no hope of having any respect from it.
Since he is unable to remedy the faults of mankind, he will do nothing but
laugh at them." Acciaiuoli's replied on 7 August: "I am glad that Machiavelli
gave the orders to discipline the infantry. Would to God that he might put
into action what he has in mind, but I doubt whether it is like Plato's *Republic*. Hence it would seem to me better if he were to return to Florence and
carry out his duty of fortifying the walls because the time when we will need
them is rapidly approaching" (texts in Gaeta, p. 593).

During the summer of 1526, while Machiavelli was in Lombardy with the
papal forces, a revealing incident occurred. Giovanni delle Bande Nere, out of
admiration for Machiavelli's *Art of War*, allowed him to drill his three thousand
troops in the Lombard sun one sweltering day. After two hours at Machiavelli's command, the men were in hopeless disarray. Giovanni took pity on
them and deftly reordered them. The novella writer Matteo Bandello, who
witnessed the tangle, comments, "How great the difference is between someone who knows and who has not set in operation what he knows and someone who, as well as knowing, has often rolled up his sleeves and plunged in, as
we usually say, and has derived his thoughts and mental view from outward
deeds." But Bandello also saw in Machiavelli "an excellent and eloquent teller
of tales"—albeit a bawdy one (*Novelle*, II, pp. 83–84).

Despite Acciaiuoli's advice that Machiavelli should stay in Florence, he
spent most of the rest of 1526 traveling. Early in September, Guicciardini sent
him to Cremona. The city's capitulation at the end of September represented
a victory for the anti-imperial forces. Then Florence ordered him to Modena
to discover what Guicciardini thought Florence's policy should be once the

pope's truce was disclosed. The truce that Clement VII made at the end of 1526 resulted from another military and diplomatic failure. While events in Lombardy seesawed between victorious skirmishes for both camps, Clement was assailed at home. Plots against the pope had been led by members of the Colonna family (Cardinal Pompeo, Ascanio, and Vespasiano) in conjunction with Don Hugo de Moncada, the ambassador of Charles V to the pope. Late in August, a truce was concluded, but the Colonnesi broke it, entered Rome unopposed on the night of 19 September, and rampaged through the Vatican and St. Peter's Church. Clement VII was forced to seek refuge in Castel Sant'Angelo and then to agree to a truce. It established a four-month peace between his army and the emperor's army by withdrawing his troops from Lombardy; furthermore, it obliged him to pardon the Colonnesi, to withdraw his troops from the attack on Genoa, and to hand Filippo Strozzi over as a hostage. Guicciardini comments that this truce "severed all the plans for Lombardy and all the fruits of the victory at Cremona" (*Storia d'Italia*, XVII, 13, p. 1698). With no compunction, the pope soon shattered the agreement: he appointed Paolo Vitelli to lead his troops to destroy the territories belonging to the Colonna family and to prepare an attack on Naples (see Guicciardini, *Storia d'Italia*, XVII, 15).

❖ LETTER 303
Niccolò Machiavelli to Francesco Guicciardini
Florence, 3 January 1526

To Messer Francesco Guicciardini, etc.

Signor President. In answer to your most recent letter, I thought I could start it off in joy, yet I must begin it in sorrow since you had a nephew, for whom everyone yearned for so long a time, and his mother has died so soon thereafter—a truly unexpected blow, one deserved neither by her nor by Girolamo.[1] Nevertheless, since God has willed it so, so it must be; since no remedy for it exists, we must think about it as little as possible.

As for Your Lordship's letter, I shall begin at the point you do, about living happily amid such turbulence. I can tell you this: I shall go there come what may; nothing can hold me back except illness, may God protect me from it; I shall arrive when the month is up and at whatever time you may set in your letter. As for Barbera and the singers, I believe I can bring her for fifteen *soldi* to the lira unless some other consideration holds you back. I mention this because she has certain lovers who might block the way; still, one might contrive to keep them quiet. And that she and I have decided to come, you have this attestation: we have composed five new songs appropriate to the play[2] that have been set to music and are to be sung between the acts. As an enclosure to this letter, I am forwarding you the words so that you may look them over; either all of us or I alone shall bring you the music for them. If she decides to come, you will certainly need to send one of your grooms with two or three animals. So much for the play.

I have always been of the opinion that if the emperor intends to become *master of the situation,* he will never release[3] the king, for by holding on to him he keeps all of his enemies in a weakened position; consequently, they are giving him, and will give him, all the time he would like in order to get himself together. Thus he keeps first France and then the pope in hopes of an accord; he neither calls off the negotiations nor concludes them. And whenever he sees that the Italians are about to join with France, he takes up the negotiations with France again so that no agreement is reached—and he profits, as we have seen him already win Milan over to his side with these sleights of hand and come within an ace of winning over Ferrara.[4] Had he gone there, he would have succeeded; if that had happened, all Italy would have been done for. And, may our Spanish brethren forgive me, this time they have made a mistake, for when the duke[5] passed through Lombardy to return home, they ought to have stopped him and forced him to go to Spain by way of the sea; they ought not to have trusted him to go there on his own because they should have realized that many circumstances might arise—and did—that would prevent his return.

Four days ago we learned of a rapprochement[6] between Italy and France, and it is credible because, since Pescara is dead, since Antonio de Leyva[7] is ill, since the duke has returned to Ferrara, since the fortresses[8] of Milan and Cremona are still being held, since the Venetians are under no constraints, and since everyone is clear about the emperor's ambition, it seems in everybody's interest to protect themselves, and there is a good opportunity for them to do so. But at that point word came that the emperor and France had reached an agreement: France cedes Burgundy, marries the emperor's sister, renounces her four hundred thousand ducat dowry, gives her a dowry of the same amount, offers either his two younger sons or the dauphin as hostages, and hands over to him all claim to Naples, Milan, etc. For the reasons given above, many people find such an agreement credible and others do not; I, in fact, do find it credible that the emperor drew it up in order to prevent the rapprochement mentioned above; later on he will pick faults with it and break it. Now we shall have to wait and see what happens.

I understand what you are saying about your concern[9] and, since it is not the right moment, that you think you have time for reflection; my answer to this will be brief—with the sincerity required by the love and respect I bear for you. For as long as I can remember, people have always been either making war or talking about going to war; it is now being talked about and in a short while it will be declared; when it is over, people will start talking about it again, so that there will never be any time to reflect about a thing. And it seems to me that the present might do more for your concern than peaceful times would, because were the pope to consider scheming, or fear being schemed against, he must realize that he needs you—and badly—and consequently must want to satisfy you.

3 January 1525[6]
Niccolò Machiavelli, in Florence

❖ LETTER 304
Giovanni Manetti to Niccolò Machiavelli
Venice, 28 February 1526

To the Very Erudite and Excellent Messer Niccolò Machiavelli.
In Florence.
† In the name of God, 28 February 1525[6], in Venice.

Just these past few days, Your Excellency Messer Niccolò, my very honored master, I received a letter from you together with the *Decennale* that I had asked for, which made me very happy, and, after many other obligations, I am deeply obligated to you. Concerning this, let that suffice for now.

To satisfy Y[our] L[ordship]'s wish to hear about the performance of your *Comedy of Callimaco,*[1] I inform Y[our] L[ordship] that it was performed so well and so properly that a performance of the *Menaechmi* of Plautus, which was being staged in translation that same evening in competition with yours by another company of noblemen at great expense, although it is an ancient comedy, quite admirable, and was performed by good actors, was nonetheless considered a dead thing compared to yours. And so, seeing the former praised so much more highly than the latter, spurred on by shame, they requested your play's company with great insistence to be so kind as to perform it in their house, where their own had been performed. And thus, as they were very noble people, it was once again performed on another evening with the same intermezzi[2] as the first time, and it ended to the very great satisfaction of everyone. For this, applause was given abundantly, first of all to the writer and subsequently to the rest, who had gone to the trouble of doing it; I also was obliged to share in it[3] because I held the text[4] of the comedy in my hands behind the sets in the proscenium, so that it might go along more smoothly and to help out any of the performers if need be, which was not required. Let this be a source of satisfaction for Y[our] L[ordship]. It was so well received that the merchants of our colony[5] have made a promise to themselves, if only they can have something by you and no one else, that they will perform it this coming May first, if it were possible to have it in time. And so you are begged on behalf of everyone, if it is possible that Y[our] L[ordship] should deign to let us have either something already finished, or else if you should have composed it in your mind. And do not think that anyone else's writings would receive this request, because in truth they have a sweetness and flavor from which can be drawn delightful meaning and honorable satisfaction.

Since I received your letter, I have not been with His Serene Highness,[6] to be able to tell him what you demand of me. But I do think that, *as soon as* I speak to him, I shall do what Y[our] L[ordship] has asked me to do. You will be informed as to what comes of it.

I am sending you by the present courier, Mariano, three *para* of smoked roe wrapped in blue paper and canvas; this is some of the best that has been seen here this year. If it had been better, I would have been even happier to send it to you. This is so that you may be be so kind as to enjoy it for my sake; the courier has been taken care of for the delivery, so it is not necessary for you to pay anything.

If some sonnets, *stanze,* or *capitoli* in praise of women[7] should come into Y[our] L[ordship]'s hands, and if it should not be too much trouble, I pray Y[our] L[ordship] to deign to let me share in it as well as any other material, as long as it is of Y[our] L[ordship]'s writing. I once again send you my regards.

Giovanni Manetti

❖ LETTER 305
Niccolò Machiavelli to Francesco Guicciardini
Florence, 15 March 1526

To Messer Francesco Guicciardini.

Magnificent and honorable Messer Francesco. I have dawdled so long in writing you that Your Lordship has gotten ahead of me.[1] The reason for my dawdling was that I thought peace would be made and I believed that you would soon be returning to Romagna, and I delayed so I could talk to you in person, even though my head was full of fancies, part of which I got off my chest to Filippo Strozzi[2] four or five days ago. While writing him about some other topic, I got myself involved in discussing three hypotheses: one, that despite the treaty,[3] the king will not be set free; two, that if the king were to be set free, he would keep the treaty; three, that he would not keep it. I did not indicate which of these three I held to, but I did decide that any of them would result in war for Italy and that I could offer no remedy for such a war. Now, since I realize from your letter what you want, with you I shall go into what I was silent about with him—and all the more willingly since you have asked me about it.

Were you to ask me which of these three hypotheses I held, I cannot relinquish that fixed idea I have always believed in: the king is not going to be set free because everyone realizes that, should he carry out what he is capable of, he would cut off all the emperor's possible routes to the status[4] he has in mind for himself. I see neither motive nor reason sufficient to prompt him to let the king go. In my view he must let him go either because his council has been bribed—something at which the French are masters—or because he realizes the inevitability of this rapprochement between the Italian states and the Kingdom of France and he does not think he has either the time or the means to wreck it unless he sets the king free. The emperor also must believe that the king, once freed, will have to adhere to the terms; in this respect the latter must have been a prolific promiser and shown at every opportunity the causes for the hatred he bears the Italians and other reasons he could cite for assuring the emperor of his adherence. Nevertheless, every reason that might be cited does not prevent the emperor from being made to look foolish[5] if the king decides to be wise; but I do not believe he is going to decide to be wise. The first reason is that, until now, I have seen that every bad decision the emperor makes does not harm him and every good one the king makes does not do him any good. As I have said, it would be a poor plan for the emperor to set the king free; it would be a good one for the king to promise anything in order to be freed. Nevertheless, because he will adhere to the terms, the king's plan will have poor results and the emperor's plan will have good results.[6] I have written to Filippo[7] the reasons why the king will adhere to them; they are these: if he does not, he must leave his sons in prison; it will be necessary for him to exhaust his kingdom, which is already exhausted, and to exhaust his barons by sending them into Italy; and it will be necessary for him to turn immediately to painful tasks that, given examples from the past, he considers appalling. And why should he have to do these things to aid the Church and the Venetians who helped ruin him? I have written you, and I am writing you now, that the wrath the king must feel for the Spaniards is tremendous but that what he must feel for the Italians cannot be much less. Well do I know that it can be said—and it would be true—that if he permits Italy to fall because of this hatred, he might then lose his kingdom. But the fact of the matter is that this is how he intends the situation to be because, once he is set free, he will be between two problems: one, of having Burgundy taken from him, of losing Italy, and of being at the emperor's mercy; the other, of becoming virtually a parricide and someone who breaks his vows, in the problems mentioned above, to help out disloyal and capricious men who, at the slightest provocation, would cause him a second defeat once he had won. Consequently, I lean to the view either that the king will not be set free or, if he is, that he will adhere to the terms because the appalling prospect of losing his kingdom after having lost Italy is not likely—since, as you say, he has a French brain—to influence him in the same way as it might someone else. The other, which he will not believe, is that Italy would go up in smoke—and he might even believe that he could help it once it had purified itself of some of its sins and he would have gotten some of his sons back and become flush again. And were there to be an understanding between them about dividing the spoils of war, there would be all the more reason for the king to adhere to the terms, but all the more reason why it would be crazy for the emperor to restore to Italy someone whom he had removed—only then himself to be driven out of Italy. I am telling you how I think matters may be, but I am not at all arguing that it would be a more sensible decision for the king, because in order to humble so odious, alarming, and dangerous a power he would once more endanger himself, his sons, and his kingdom. It seems to me that the remedies are these: to arrange it so that as soon as the king gets out, he has someone close by who, with his authority and eloquence[8]—as well as those of whoever sends him—can make the king forget about the things of the past and think about new ones; to show the king Italy's unanimity; to show the king, should he decide to become the free king that he ought to want to be, that the plan would be successful. I believe that eloquence and prayers might be effective, but I believe that the facts would be more so.

However matters turn out, I believe that war in Italy is inevitable—and at hand; the Italians therefore need to see to it that France is on their side and, if they they cannot have France with them, to consider how they are going to handle this situation. It seems to me that in this instance we have one of two ways to go: either we can be at the mercy of whoever appears and receive him with money and buy our way out or we can arm ourselves in earnest and help our own cause out with these weapons. I personally do not believe that we can buy our way out or that money will suffice, because if it would, I would say, "Let's call a halt here and consider nothing else"; but money will not suffice, because either I am completely blind or he will first take your money and then your life. Hence, it would be a sort of revenge to arrange things so that he found us impoverished and wasted away, were self-defense to serve no other purpose. Therefore I do not think we ought to postpone arming ourselves or to wait on the king of France's decision, because the emperor has commanders for his troops, he has them in place, and he can start a war on his own terms whenever he pleases; we must, either overtly or covertly, assemble a military force or else one morning we shall wake up completely lost. I would recommend assembling a force covertly. I am going to tell you one thing that you will think absurd; I shall put forward a plan that you will consider either rash or ridiculous: nevertheless, these times of ours demand bold, extraordinary, and unusual decisions. You know—and anyone who knows how to reason about this world knows it, too—that the people are fickle and foolish; nevertheless, as fickle and foolish as they are, what ought to be done is frequently what they say to do.[9] A few days ago it was being said throughout Florence that Giovanni de' Medici[10] was raising a company of mercenaries in order to fight wherever he saw the best opportunity. This rumor alerted me to consider whether the people might not be saying what in fact ought to be done. I believe everyone is agreed that among Italians there is no leader whom the soldiers more willingly follow or whom the Spaniards fear more or respect more than Signor Giovanni. Everyone also agrees that he is brave and impetuous, has great ideas, and is a taker of bold decisions. Therefore we could get him to raise this mercenary company, secretly enlarging his forces and putting under his command as much infantry and cavalry as possible. The Spanish would believe we did so with cunning, and they might suspect both the pope and the king of France, since Giovanni is in the king's hire; and if this were to happen, it would certainly soon addle the brains of the Spaniards and change their plans, they who had counted on perhaps demolishing Tuscany and the Church without any resistance. It could change the king of France's mind too, causing him to opt for abandoning the treaty and choosing war, since he would realize that he was dealing with live people who, in addition to eloquence,[11] show him deeds. And if this remedy is unavailable to us and we still have to declare war, I do not know what else we can do; nothing else occurs to me. Tie a knot around your finger to remember this: should the king not be influenced by force and authority and by what is being done, he will keep the treaty and leave you in the lurch because, since he has come into Italy several times and you either have acted against him or stood by watching, he will not permit the same thing to happen to him again this time.

Barbera is there in Rome; if you can do her any service, I commend her to you, for she gives me far more concern than does the emperor.

15 March 1525[6]
Niccolò Machiavelli[12]

❖ LETTER 306
Filippo Strozzi to Niccolò Machiavelli
Rome, 31 March 1526

To His Very Dear Friend Niccolò di Messer Bernardo Machiavelli.
In Florence.

My dear Niccolò, I would not want you to think for anything that since I answer you late or do not answer your letters I hold you in low account, because in addition to being everyone's duty to esteem all those by whom you know you are esteemed, it is also a natural thing. Those who, in addition to bearing more than usual love and affection for you, have such character and qualities that everyone ought to make them better and closer friends, among which number you hold the principal place for me, deserve to be held in even greater account. But it is because I feel I have such great intimacy with you, which completely excludes such considerations, that is the sole cause that I take up my pen and let it fall in answering you according to my convenience. If I see that this excuse is accepted by you in the same way that it is stated by me, I shall continue this custom of mine in the future whenever I may get such letters from you. If you should feel otherwise, I would try to become accordingly more diligent, not failing to tell you and to answer you that, whenever there should be some action to be done for your benefit, you will find me just as prompt and diligent as anyone else. I am negligent about writing polite letters, but only with those persons who I am convinced will take it in good part, as I am convinced about you.

But so that the introduction is not more than all the rest, I shall come to the narration, and I shall tell you that I read your last letter of the 10th of this month to Our Lordship,[1] who listened to it with great attention, commended passages, since it seemed to him that you had touched on everything that could come to the mind of anyone who, without specific reports or notices, discussed such matters, and he was very pleased by it. It did not seem to me, however, that he was of the opinion that the first idea would come about, that is to say, that the king[2] would not be freed even though an agreement had been made saying he will be freed. Although such an idea would have more partisans today than it did then, seeing that there has not yet been news of his having been set free, and so it can be judged that this result has not yet occurred. But many things can have delayed this result, and will not prevent it. The advantage that the emperor gains by postponing it for a month longer in order to be more prepared and to find us more unready to prevent his passage does not seem to make up for the loss he incurs in the face of the king, adding this final oddity to the other insults and mistreatment he has given him. And so it is believed here that it is for some other reason rather than the one you have thought of. Once he is free, what he ought to do right away if he wanted to play according to the rules of the game can be very easily seen. But his not being considered prudent makes it very doubtful that the second idea argued by you, that is, that he would observe the agreement, is going to turn out to be true, especially for some time. There could be nothing more obviously harmful to Italy and to us than that; the danger is clear and evident to everyone. I find no one yet who knows how to remedy it, because the Venetians, with Our Lordship, Ferrara, and us, are not judged by most people to be sufficient to bar passage to the emperor if the king remains neutral.

I have seen what you propose in a letter to Guicciardini,[3] because mine has been shared with him and then his with me; in the final analysis, it is not satisfactory, because we can see no difference between going at it in such a way and leaving Our Lordship completely uncovered, because without money such a captain of fortune[4] would not be effective, if he should find opposition in Lombardy of the sort he would find. If O[ur] L[ordship] offers him money, the venture becomes his,[5] and going with all banners unfurled would be more approved for his reputation and to draw the Venetians into the same game, too. All in all, the king may not be wise, but the possibilities are limited. There then remains the possibility that the emperor may not recognize such a fine and great opportunity. So our fate is in the dice, but we have hard stakes.

But the day on which I am writing does not seem to allow this kind of talk. Therefore I shall pass on to the last part, where you recommend Barbera to me heartily, requesting kisses of me for your sake, with the permission of the lady, however; and since I have never been able to get it, I have not yet been able to kiss her. I became convinced afterward, when I had thought further about the matter, that in fact you did not want me to come to such a pass, since you had placed such a harsh condition on it.[6] Therefore I do not thank you very much for such generosity, since I recognized within it a subtle niggardliness. I excuse you, for I know now to my own misfortune what it means to love other men's daughters. I read her your *capitolo,* and I made her the most generous offers I was able to, in your name, intending to carry them to fulfillment if only I could. When I learned for what reason she had come, I began to speak with Giovan Francesco de' Nobili, my great friend and

Camillo's brother-in-law, about the matter, and I found no basis whatever for it, and Camillo has gone back over there again. And so she can leave on this business when she wants, as I said several days ago to Lorenzo Ridolfi, who is likewise her supporter. She will see if there is anyone who takes so much pleasure in music that a fixed stipend will be established for her, as she was given hopes of by someone, but I do not believe it is going to turn out. And so I believe that she is going to be back there before long. I have no other news.

The last day of March, 1526, in Rome.

Yours, Filippo Strozzi

❖ LETTER 307
Niccolò Machiavelli to Francesco Guicciardini
Florence, 4 April 1526

To Messer Francesco Guicciardini.

Your Magnificence, my honored superior. Today, around four o'clock, I received your letter of the first of this month. Since Roberto Acciaiuoli was absent, having left for Monte Gufoni, I immediately went to the cardinal[1] and informed him of His Holiness's intentions with respect to the matters Pietro Navarra[2] dealt with and of His Holiness's wish that he draw up so great and so bold a plan that it might inspire a populace cut from a mold such as ours and such that they might be counted on to defend themselves against any kind of serious and violent attack. His Most Reverend Lord said that he would have him come before him again this evening and that, with the most effective means he possessed, he would entreat and press him to come up with such results. Nevertheless, once we had discussed those plans that were presented,[3] it appears that if we want to stay with the old walls, they cannot be improved, because if we wanted to remove them, either we must enlarge Florence through the measures His Holiness Our Lord is familiar with or we must tear down the Santo Spirito district and restrict the city to being only in the level area. The first method's weakness is that you would need a huge garrison, one for which even the population of Cairo[4] would be too few; the second method has both something of the weak and something of the pitiless about it. It would be weak to let the houses of that district remain standing, because you would be leaving the city to an enemy more powerful than you are and better able to avail himself of the countryside than you, so that he could harrass you more than you could harrass him. The other method of demolishing the district, as everyone realizes, would be difficult and unusual. Consequently, we must keep the district's fortifications as they are; I do not want to write you just yet about what method to use because it has not yet been determined and because I do not want to anticipate my superiors' method. Suffice it to say that some of the walls of the said district on the far side of the Arno ought to be torn down, some ought to be extended, and some ought to be contracted. I think, and so does Signor Vitelli,[5] who has come for this purpose, that this site would be extremely strong—stronger than the level area; Count Pietro[6] declares and maintains the same thing, swearing on oath that, prepared with these measures, this city would become the strongest region in Italy. Tomorrow morning we shall meet to review everything—especially the overall plan; then the appointed representatives will meet again, examine closely whatever has been devised, put it down in writing and in a sketch, and forward it[7] to His Holiness Our Lord in Rome. It is my conviction that he will be delighted with it—especially the part dealing with the hillside, for which extraordinary measures have been devised. The part dealing with the level area is not out of the ordinary; but, since everybody knows how to fortify such sites, it is less important. Count Pietro will be here tomorrow and the next day, and we shall do our best to pick his brain as much as possible; I have held off in order to hear what he has to say, so that what happened to the Greek with Hannibal does not happen to me.[8] My thanks to you, etc.

4 April 1526
Niccolò Machiavelli

❖   LETTER 308
Niccolò Machiavelli to Francesco Guicciardini
Florence, 17 May 1526

To Messer Francesco Guicciardini.

I have not written you since I left there[1] because my head is so full of ramparts that nothing else could enter it. The law has been put into effect[2] for the organization in the manner and with the instructions that Our Lord in Rome has directed. People are watching for the announcement of the public officials in charge and going ahead with the undertaking until there arrives from Rome a replacement for Clemente Sciarpelloni,[3] who is said to be so unwell that he cannot attend to such matters. It will also be necessary to find a substitute for Antonio da Filicaia, who had a fit of apoplexy the day before yesterday and is in a bad way. People are surprised that the cardinal[4] has not had any communication concerning Clement, and they are beginning to suspect there may be some sort of objection; nobody wants to believe it, however, since the project has proceeded so far.

I have heard about the disturbances[5] in Lombardy, and we are all aware of how easy it would be to drag those scoundrels out of that region. For the love of God, let us not lose this opportunity and remember that Fortune, our bad counsel, and the worst kinds of officials would have driven not only the king but even the pope to prison; the bad advice of others and this same Fortune have taken him out. For the love of God, see to it now with such measures that His Holiness does not fall back into these same perils; you will never be secure from these perils until the Spaniards are somehow pulled out of Lombardy so that they cannot return. I have an idea that the emperor, once he realizes that the king is going to let him down, will make the pope some major offers; if you recall the poor support and the threats that were made to you in the past, you ought to turn a deaf ear to these offers. And remember, the duke of Sessa[6] used to go around saying *that the pontiff began to fear Caesar too late.* Now God has brought things to such a pass that, if this moment is not lost, the pope is in time to take the emperor. You are aware of how many opportunities have been lost: do not lose this one or, putting yourself in the hands of Fortune and Time, put your trust in having it again, because Time does not always bring identical circumstances and Fortune is not always identical. Were I talking to a man who was ignorant of secrecy or who was unaware of the world, I should discourse longer. *Free Italy from long-lasting anxiety*[7]; *eradicate those savage brutes, which have nothing human about them save their faces and voices.*

If the fortifications proceed, people here believe that I am to be given the position of supervisor and secretary, that I am to be given one of my sons[8] as an assistant, and that Daniello de' Ricci is to handle the money and all the accounts.

17 May 1526
Niccolò Machiavelli

❖ LETTER 309
Francesco Guicciardini to Niccolò Machiavelli
Rome, 22 May 1526

To the Notable Niccolò Machiavelli.

My very dear Niccolò. You have probably seen, by the announcement of the leadership, which must have been made by this time, that the fear[1] you had over there, which you wrote me about in your letter of the 17th, was groundless, because O[ur] L[ordship] is of the same mind and not about to lose his enthusiasm,[2] in my judgment. The replacement he has ordered for Antonio da Filicaia can bear excellent witness to that. Therefore hasten the material so that it can finally be gotten under way.

About things in general I say the same as you do. Of what you discuss, aside from its being quite true, it is very well known here what ill there is, and that matters that several powerful men have to join together in are always necessarily more lengthy than would be required. However, I hope that we shall not fail to get his due from each one, if not as quickly as one would want, at least not so delayed that it would be entirely too late.

In Rome, 22 May 1526.
Yours, Francesco Guicciardini

❖   LETTER 310
Niccolò Machiavelli to Francesco Guicciardini
Florence, 2 June 1526

To Messer Francesco Guicciardini.

Magnificent *Signor* President. It has been quite a few days since I have written you anything about the ramparts; now, I am going to tell you all that is necessary. Influenced by the opinion of Giuliano del Bene, who says in his letter that there is greater strength and less expense in including all those hillsides, it seems to us here that the pope has gone back to his belief about the high ground.[1] As concerns strength, no large city is ever strong, because its size causes those defending it to lose heart, occasioning a great deal of confusion; things do not happen this way in moderate-size cities. As concerns less expense, that is humbug, because del Bene is making many false assumptions. First, he maintains that escarpments can be dug into all the high ground extending from this side of Bonciani's house to the far side of Matteo Bartoli's house—according to del Bene, one thousand *braccia*,[2] but really sixteen hundred—whereas it is only necessary to construct walls around the others. He maintains that the escarpments can be used as a wall and that above them a rampart four *braccia* high and sixteen *braccia* thick can be built. This is false because there are innumerable spots where there can be no trench digging since they are level; further, all those spots where they can dig a trench would be unable to stand by themselves and would cave in so that they would have to be supported by a wall; eventually the ramparts would cost a mint and would make our city the laughing stock, and within a very few years they would have to be rebuilt—the expense would be huge and continual and involve very little honor. He maintains that the city might avail itself of eighty thousand ducats in additional property value—what nonsense; he knows neither what he is talking about nor where this additional value might be gotten from—so everybody thinks his plan improbable. Nevertheless, we shall build the model the pope has requested and send it to him. Until some special appropriation is granted for this feat, we must spend the money we have on hand; consequently the law stipulates[3] that the treasurer of the Signoria should pay out what money the city now has on hand, regardless of what account it is deposited in—whether that of the Signori or the officials. Nevertheless, unless Our Lord writes him and orders payment, Francesco del Nero will create problems about paying. The office has written the ambassador[4] about it. I entreat you to help the matter along and have the pope write him about it.

2 June 1526
Niccolò Machiavelli

❖ LETTER 311

Niccolò Machiavelli to Francesco Guicciardini

Florence, 2 June 1526

To Messer Francesco Guicciardini.

I did not have an opportunity to speak with L[orenzo] S[trozzi][1] until last Saturday; but since I was with him and discussing several matters, he broached the subject of his son with me so I had a chance to reproach him for paying so little attention to the affair that I had already brought to his attention. I said I was sure that since a rich marriage had already slipped by him, now one with a great deal of distinction—and one that would not be impoverished—was not going to slip by him and that, should he want to give his son a Florentine girl, I did not know where else he might be able to turn one up. He freely admitted to me that I was telling the truth, that you had approached him, and that he could not be more pleased; it pleased him so much that, even if the matter could not be arranged now, he thought he would be in time for one daughter—since you have four of them. His reasons for procrastinating were that his wife's health was better now than it was before and that his son had taken a better turn by associating with educated men and studying diligently; since previously his son did neither of these two things, he had given some thought to finding him a partner. His daughter, whom he wants to marry off first, was his third reason. Nevertheless, the matter pleases him so much that he has already talked to his son about you many times. When he had returned from Loreto, he took the opportunity of staying two days in Romagna with your Jacopo,[2] who displayed to him the prestige of your position, the dignity with which you have maintained it, and your reputation—he praised your accomplishments to the skies. These things all worked toward facilitating the matter, when it was discussed, because he suspected his son's mind to be set on a large dowry. As far as all these matters were concerned, he spoke in such a vein that I could not have wished for more. I did not fail to point out that his qualms were needless because his daughter is at such an age that she can remain unmarried for four or five years and that this match would help him marry his daughter off because the man who is after uncommon dowries has also to bestow them. I struggled with him for a while, and were he not a man tied up in knots, I would have great hope for this matter.

2 June 1526
Niccolò Machiavelli

❖ LETTER 312
Niccolò Machiavelli to Francesco Guicciardini
Florence, 2 June 1526

To Messer Francesco Guicciardini.

Although I am aware that your Luigi has written you his ideas about including the hill of San Miniato inside the wall,[1] I do not want to pass up a
chance to drop you a line about it because I consider it an extremely important matter. The most detrimental initiative a republic can undertake is to construct a stronghold,[2] or something that could be quickly fortified, within its
precincts. If you were to have the model that was left there in Rome placed in
front of you, you would realize that a fortress is created once San Miniato is
included and the rampart is built up there. Because the distance from the San
Miniato Gate to that of San Niccolò is so short, one hundred men could
make it a fortress in one day by digging a trench. Hence, if a powerful leader
should ever come to Florence because of some kind of disorder, as did the
king of France in 1494,[3] you would be enslaved with no remedy whatsoever
because, since he would discover the area cleared, you could not prevent him
from going into that area; since he would easily be able to close it off, you
could not prevent him from doing so. Consider this possibility carefully and,
with all your adroitness, avert it; argue for the digging of a trench, which offers strength and no danger, because once the plan for including San Miniato
has gotten under way, I suspect halting it would be too unpleasant.

I have written these three letters[4] to you separately so that you can make
use of them as you see fit.

2 June 1526
Niccolò Machiavelli

❖ LETTER 313
Niccolò Machiavelli to Bartolomeo Cavalcanti[1]
Marignano[2], 13 July 1526

[. . .] the quartermaster general's laden baggage wagons still stood in front
of his door; since they realized defeat was certain, they had no other alternative to advise: they went up to the duke[3] and concisely pointed out how
necessary it was to get themselves out of there if they did not want a rout.
Nothing could be done on this occasion except to complain bitterly about
this disarray and agree to submit to necessity. More with indications of fear
than with any other emotion, we struck camp before daybreak because the
duke had ordered the artillery leaders to head toward Lodi without stopping
unless a new order came from him[4]; the quartermaster general[5] sent his
driver to Lodi with their money and the better part of his possessions. There
remained in their encampment one tent for the enemy; one solitary man remained—one of their officers in charge of their horses who had not heard

that they were evacuating and came near to being taken prisoner. More than half the troops in the vanguard, both infantry and cavalry, made off for Marignano at more than a trot; whereupon, once the division commander became aware of this disarray, he asked some supply officers where they were going to set up camp; they replied, "At Marignano." He was astonished, since he had thought it had been planned for them to set up camp in San Martino. And not leaving the road, he did all he could, both with the duke and the quartermaster general, to make them follow the order that had been given—to no avail.[6] And so we made it to Marignano, where we are still. And surely, had the enemy known about the disarray during the evening and on the following morning, there is absolutely no doubt that they would have caused us grief and we risked the danger of having them instantaneously become masters of Italy.

Since then, these gentlemen have been in consultation; the duke maintains that he is discouraged about whether we can have any success with this infantry and that even if this first detachment of Swiss soldiers, which ought to be about five thousand men, were to arrive, he would initiate no campaign that might result in a battle. Therefore, we were to await the arrival of the troops who are supposed to come from France and Switzerland. Once the changes in the duke's ideas are taken into consideration, one naturally infers that, according to his previous speeches, he had no confidence in his troops and he was unwilling to run any risk; but the persistence of those who urged him on, who were in the majority and among his foremost men, caused him to opt for that choice—hoping all the while that perhaps some confusion might ensue among the enemy's forces to our benefit—given the enemy stronghold and that discontentment. Perhaps this was the reason why quite early in the morning he hurriedly set up the artillery and started that skirmish, determining that the more courage one demonstrated, the more the enemy might be frightened either into withdrawing or into not attacking us. But once evening descended and no reward had yet been reaped, he reverted to his basic nature and to his initial mistrust. Hence, since he was no longer willing that the other troops' excessive audacity damage his position, the result was the sudden and ill-advised departure and the great retreat of Marignano. So, as you see, here we are. In my opinion, it is best to do all we can to prevent confusion from being created until the reinforcements that have been promised to us come and the troops whom we must stir up both from the Kingdom of Naples and outside Italy make their move. It is impossible for us not to win this war, because if reinforcements come to us from France before our enemies in Austria receive theirs, this war will be over in two days. But should reinforcements suddenly come both to us and to them and should we be able to confine them narrowly with an encampment, in a very short time—if our money does not run out, it is necessary for theirs to do so, and if they should experience the widespread shortages, they will run out, since the countryside is against them—in a very short time, then, the German troops will be disbanded and victory will fall into our hands. But we must not wish for too quick a victory so that we may not suffer the fate of those courageous merchants who, wanting to become rich in a year, become impoverished in six months.

I have nothing more to say, unless I wanted to sadden you with tales of this region's poverty, which I do not want to do lest I perturb the happy disposition of you and your friends. Therefore, I shall end this letter entreating you to give my regards to Giovanni Serristori and the others and to read them this letter without making a copy of it or otherwise rendering it public. And may this letter serve as a reply to one in Latin that I received from you; the division commander read it and praised it greatly, and he is now completely devoted to you, since he thinks your accomplishments deserve it. *Again, farewell and love me, as you do.*

13 July 1526
Niccolò Machiavelli, in the field.

❖ LETTER 314
Agostino del Nero to Niccolò Machiavelli
Bologna, 21 July 1526

To the Notable, Honored Messer Niccolò Machiavelli.
At Marignano.
Jesus. In the name of God, 21 July 1526.

Honored foster father. Since your departure from Bologna,[1] we have not written to you because there was no need and also so as not to trouble you. This letter will just be to tell you that I have been asked by my honored Francesco to let you know that a certain sum of money will arrive there in two days, including around 7,000 Florentine gold ducats, for which I would like you to be so kind as to go to Messer Alessandro del Caccia's when it is being counted in order to be able to certify it to His Lordship the Lieutenant, so that he may see that I would not traffic in matters of this sort, that I know the ones I sent a month ago were sent to me thus, for I would feel ashamed as a scoundrel not to send the same ducats that have been sent to me. If possible, I would like you to bring His Lordship the Lieutenant, for him to see with his own eyes what kind of gold it is that I have sent to Messer Alessandro.

I have nothing to tell you about Florence, for your Bernardo has never written to me. I would have written to him several times, but I find myself so taken up by business that I have not been able to do it.

I imagine you have sold the horse at a good price by now. Nothing else. I send you my regards as always. Give my regards to His Lordship the Lieutenant and tell him that I am his devoted servant.

Yours, Agostino del Nero, in Bologna

❖ LETTER 315
Jacopo di Filippo Falconetti to Niccolò Machiavelli
Florence, 5 August 1526

To the Notable Niccolò Machiavelli.
In the Camp of the League.[1]

My very dear Niccolò, I send you my regards as usual, etc. This letter is in reply to one of yours, from which I learn that you have sold the horse and where I am to get the money. I have gotten paid and everything is fine. I also learn from the said letter that Barbera has never written you and that you would like to hear how she is. And so, as soon as I received your letter, I went to see the said Barbera; she had already written you and I believe you have received it. I could not help giving her a good piece of my mind; so she answered me that she was surprised at me and there was no man whom she esteemed more highly and at whose orders she was more completely, but also that she did you some occasional discourtesies to see if you love her. She would like you to get back to Florence quicker, because it seems to her when you are there that she rests completely assured.[2] Now you know her better than I do: I do not know if she should be believed completely. She excused herself to me by saying that she has not been in Florence; and I know that she is telling the truth in this, because I sent word to her several times, and as soon as she was back she came to the garden, because I had a Roman woman there. She told me she would write you every week, since she sees that you are glad to see them.[3] She begged me in particular to give you her regards, and she begs you not to be annoyed with her. I greeted Raffaello Corbinelli on your behalf, and he told me that if I should write you, he sends you his regards and he is entirely devoted to you. If I can do anything at all here, ask it of me, for you could do me no greater favor. God keep you.

5 August 1526.
Yours, Jacopo di Filippo, *Fornaciaio,*[4] in Florence

❖ LETTER 316
Francesco Vettori to Niccolò Machiavelli
Florence, 5 August 1526

My dear *compare.* I have had two letters from you within two days. Your last one, of the 31st of last month, is a long one, and I am obligated to you for writing me so clearly about how you are doing. Because there are many things of importance in the said letter and it is not possible to take care of them or deal with them from here, I have sent them on to Filippo[1] in Rome, informing him that he should handle them with his usual care; I am certain he will, if only he can get it deciphered. As soon as I got your letter, I had myself taken by Donato[2] to Barbera's house. Although she showed me the code,[3]

my age, my worries, my infirmities have so weakened my body and my imagination that I could not decipher it properly. I was therefore forced to use
Francesco del Nero's trust, but with a thousand remonstrances not to talk. I
believe that he will keep his word to me, because the poor man has other
worries at present than making quips and telling tales about this matter. I
promise you that he does not have an hour's rest, he is always in a bad mood,
full of complaints, and he cannot be spoken to. You know that in Florence
there are many who, when bad news comes, are stabbed through their hearts.[4]
But no one so much as he. I do not know how his brain holds up amid as
many things as he has to do. In brief, we interpreted the code, and I do not
want to talk about what happened or is going to happen there, but I just want
to tell you that the emperor is far too lucky. Leaving aside the matter of past
years, this has caused him to delay so long in starting the campaign that the
people of Milan were defeated; this also, that you arrived late and in disarray
at the walls of Milan, and you withdrew without seeing those who were driving you away; this also, that you took many days to decide to relieve the castle,
and afterward the decision was so long in taking place that it was necessary to
make a treaty first; this also, that the Genoans, who ought to be the worst enemies that the emperor had in Italy, remain under Antoniotto Adorno[5] and
aid any campaign of the emperor's both with money and in every other way;
this too makes the king of England, now that the emperor has taken a wife
other than his daughter,[6] think nothing of it and take no account of not being
esteemed, and makes the cardinal,[7] who is wont to be the proudest man in
the world, the most humble.

I had written up to this point yesterday evening in Donato's shop, on this
sheet, with a bad pen and worse ink, and I wanted to finish it, but that asshole
Donato insisted on closing up, and I had to go along with Donato. To return
to the emperor's good fortune, it is this that makes His Most Christian
Majesty[8] continue in both his disorders and irresponsibility, and so the pope
and the Venetians have begun to suspect that what arises from the king's nature and from his inability arises from his unwillingness. The said good fortune is the reason why all the Spaniards do all they can to exalt him, and he
on the other hand behaves in Spain in everything and for everything as the
Flemish want and takes away from the Spaniards what he can to give it to the
said Flemish. This is the reason why Ferrara does not come to an agreement
with the pope; and lastly, this has made the troops—I do not want to say
army—of the pope and the Florentines be routed by four hundred Sienese
recruits and no more[9]; yet they were five thousand paid infantrymen and at
least three hundred mounted warriors, all told.

You know that I am very unwilling to believe anything to be supernatu-
ral, but this time it seems to me to have been as extraordinary—I do not
want to say miraculous—as anything that has happened in war from '94 to
now. It seems similar to me to certain stories I have read in the Bible, when
fear entered into men and they fled they knew not from whom. Not more

than four hundred infantrymen went forth from Siena, for a quarter of our dominion was there, outlaws and confinees, and fifty light cavalry, and they put five thousand infantrymen and three hundred cavalry to flight as far as Castellina,[10] who, if only they had put a thousand infantrymen and a hundred cavalry together after their initial flight, would have recaptured their artillery within an hour; but without being pursued for more than a mile, they ran ten miles away. I have heard you say several times that fear is the greatest master there is, and in this it seems to me I have seen the surest evidence of it; or else this good fortune lasts for a certain time and then changes, and we do not know when it is going to begin to change. The pope undertook this campaign with reason, and if it fails no one will be able to say that he was moved by passion. I do not want to judge what is going to happen because I am too doubtful. Indeed, I do not want to conceal from you my delusion, that I would deem it one of the good pieces of news we could have if we should hear that the sultan of Turkey had taken Hungary and was heading toward Vienna, and that the Lutherans were coming out on top in Germany, and that the Moors, whom the emperor wants to drive out of Aragon and Valencia, were putting up a fight and were able not only to defend themselves but also to go on the offense.[11] Some men have come here from both Milan and Cremona who have told such tales about the imperial troops, the Spaniards as well as the Germans, that there is no one who would not prefer to have the devil rather than them. You understand your code: [. . .][12] as for the money, that it may be enough and plead in Rome and not here, where there are many problems, and therefore you must not stop pleading.

Compare, I do not approve of that going with the army toward the kingdom [of Naples], because, since the league has made such a campaign to relieve the castle, without having done so, but let it come to terms before their eyes; since the king and the pope have a fleet on the seas to keep Bourbon[13] from coming, and he came nonetheless; since a part of the league made a campaign against Siena and sent troops to be the victors and they were vanquished, I would not think that on the basis of this defeat and with so little glory they could fight their way out of a paper bag.[14] I would indeed agree, in order to plead with the king, to his being offered Milan and some other things [. . .]. I do not want to rack my brain over these fancies that distress me, and especially since I have a lawsuit going on with my sister-in-law that I have to help out with, although it is in her name, since it is my brother. Since it has to do with a sister of Matteo Strozzi, of such rank, with so many relations and riches, I have to proceed with caution; and so I am afraid I shall have to stake my possessions and my honor. We are having very poor harvests here, and we hear that they are worse elsewhere. So we judge that the year is going to be very bad, because of war, plague, and famine, and since in times of tribulation people turn toward God, having also heard the saints have conquered as a result of making prayers and processions, we have tried to obtain a

Jubilee for the middle of August from Our Lord, to be taken without money,[15] and fasts, confessions, and prayers will suffice to take it. I have nothing else to tell you in this letter, except to pray you to give my regards to Messer Francesco and yourself.

In Florence, 5 August 1526.
Francesco Vettori

❖ LETTER 317
Francesco Vettori to Niccolò Machiavelli
Florence, 7 August 1526

To My Dear *Compare*, Niccolò Machiavelli.
In the Army of the League.

My dear *compare*. Yesterday I answered two letters from you [. . .] of the 31st of last month. Then yesterday evening [. . .] another one of the 2nd was brought to me, in which you give news in great detail about the nature of the league's and the imperial armies. I showed it to the cardinal [and] Ippolito,[1] and Ippolito had high praise for it. In truth, if the money holds out, I am convinced that this war is going to come to a good end. But that is the problem, and I know well just how far we can go here, but in Rome I do not really know what can be done. You tell me that you would like to hear precisely how the Siena affair has turned out,[2] and so, *although the mind shudders at the memory,*[3] I shall do my best to write you.

The Sienese had sent 500 infantry and 50 light cavalry to capture Monte Rifre, Giovanni Martinozzi's[4] stronghold. The pope, when he heard this, felt that if he let this place be taken from him the libertines[5] would be encouraged too much and would then try to attack our borders, and that we would be obliged to spend money to defend them. Since you had raised the siege of Milan, judging that the war was going to go on for a long time, he decided to see whether he could assure himself of Siena at little expense by putting back the exiles, who asserted with certainty that when they entered Sienese territory, [. . .] the entire countryside would be [. . .] if they approached Siena, it would revolt [. . .]. He planned to send the count of Anguillara[6] with 100 cavalry all told and with 800 infantry who would have half pay, and the count of Pitigliano[7] with an equal number, and Gentile Baglioni with the same quantity. He arranged that they should only make a little show of calling up infantrymen here and bring out two artillery pieces, and a commissioner should be sent to Montepulciano.[8] This order having come here already decided, it was not possible to say no to it; but in a bit of discussion that took place, Luigi Guicciardini, as the most experienced and perhaps the wisest, said that they were going to lose because this was no longer a time when wars could be made with recruits,[9] who would make disorder in the supplies with their stealing and then would be the first to flee. The order should be carried out, and they were to try to rout the Sienese infantry who were at Monte

Rifre, where the infantry of Messer Gentile went with good leaders, according to the custom of those factions. But when they got near the enemy, they started to ask for full pay. Since there was no one there who could give it to them, they rebelled and so made it easy for those who were in Monte Rifre to withdraw with their artillery [. . .] the others who were coming [. . .] noise, began to pillage the entire area. And so they suffered greatly for supplies; and therefore they decided to see whether they could take Montalcino,[10] and they approached it without artillery and without ladders, and they were thrown back with losses and shame.

When the pope learned of this and, furthermore, that there was great dissension among the exiles,[11] he decided to make a treaty through Lord Vespasiano Colonna, since he felt he would have less shame in this way. When these exiles learned of this, they began to protest; and the pope had already let them know that they should not proceed further. They sent Domenico Placidi here and Aldello to Rome, to indicate that they were not happy about this treaty and they could not return there in safety with it, and that if they persisted in bringing the camp to the walls, the campaign would be won. The pope began to pay attention to them, especially because of the datary's[12] arguments, the latter being very inclined to put the exiles back,[13] and he ordered artillery and infantry to be sent there from here. In order for the Sienese, the exiles as well as those inside, to be less afraid and have greater confidence, when it came to drawing up a treaty Roberto Pucci was sent there, as a man who was more apt to make a peace treaty than to organize the war, because there was a commissioner from Parma there to organize it, [. . .] who was believed here to be a man [. . .]. The artillery was set up and [. . .] five thousand hired infantrymen, as well as many recruits. [. . .] our constables there were Jacopo Corso and Lord Francesco dal Monte, who after all have gained some reputation in war. Thirteen artillery pieces of various sizes were set up on this side, in a place where they offered little threat to the walls of Siena. The camp was quartered throughout that village, which was very handy for those who were there. Although many Florentines went there to look and they reported that the camp was in danger there, Roberto, when he was written from here, said that he heard the same thing from many people, but when he called the chiefs into consultation they all agreed, but especially Jacopo Corso said, that the camp was very safe and that there was nothing to fear. However, since that opinion came here from many people, it had been decided to withdraw the artillery and Gherardo Bartolini had been sent there for this. But he was not yet at Poggibonsi[14] when he began to encounter men who were fleeing and reported on the rout, which occurred as follows.

Our troops were quartered, as I have told you, in the village coming toward Florence, which is a long one and the road is about 20 *braccia*[15] wide. The commissioners, with a lack of foresight, had let those who sold the camp's necessities make sheds out of branches throughout the village, so that there were scarcely 8 *braccia* of the road's width left free. The artillery's guard was attacked on the 25th at one in the afternoon. About 200 of the Sienese issued forth from the gate of Fontebranda and 200 from the wicket of the same gate where the camp was. The escorts, or guards to speak more precisely, saw them issuing forth, but no sooner were they engaged in combat than the company of Jacopo Corsi and other Corsi who had come with the count of Anguillara began to flee. When the flight began, those who were selling things, in trying to escape, filled the street with mules and donkeys, with barrels and hampers, so that there was no one there who could ever make a stand. The horses of the counts of Pitigliano and of Anguillara, which were not accustomed, either they or their riders, to seeing anything but oxen, broke into a run; and if any foot-soldier wanted to stop, they scattered them, running at full gallop. Only Braccio Baglioni, with perhaps 50 light cavalry, ran toward the artillery and put the Sienese who were there to flight and captured a nephew of Lord Giulio Colonna, whom he took along as a prisoner to Castellina; but since he was not followed by anyone, he had to yield to fortune. Lord Francesco dal Monte caused a great disorder because, having one of his young sons with him, taking fright at the initial attack, he put him in the custody of two of his top men so that they would take him to safety. They began to flee with him, with the result that most of his company took to their heels. Seeing the others fleeing, Lord Francesco's infantrymen, who were all well-considered warriors and among the best in that camp, also took flight. So the said lord stayed to make something of a stand with five or six of his men, but it had no effect whatever.

Indeed, those cavalry and infantry, fleeing and not being pursued by any of the enemy, never stopped running until they were in Castellina, and they did not feel they were safe there until the gates had been locked. The artillery was lost and some materiel that was in those houses, but not much, for everyone strove to save as much as he could. As I told you in another letter, I believe that it has happened many other times that an army has fled before shouts, but for it to flee ten miles with no one pursuing it, I do not believe this has ever been read of or seen. This resulted from the ease with which our infantry could run away; for if they had had to flee through enemy territory, they would have never taken flight. Therefore I conclude that the analysis that you give is quite true, that the imperial troops in Milan have been made bold by past victories and by necessity; still I have faith, especially because of the good organization of the chiefs who are there, that things are going to go ahead well.

These French are finding it so hard to send their aid that people here are seriously beginning to doubt the will of that king. Although Roberto[16] writes inflamed letters, no one believes them, since we do not see results. You will be believed, however, when you write that Swiss or lancers are beginning to appear there on behalf of His Majesty.[17]

There are letters from Spain this morning, but quite old ones, which I believe are from the 9th of June. The emperor was in Grenada with very little money; coldness and indecision were seen concerning everything.

I sent your other letters to Rome; this one I have not sent. I have indeed recorded here the part that is in code, but since our friend is doing all that you tell me, [. . .] and then come what may.[18] For now nothing else is being done in Siena. These borders of ours are being guarded well, at some expense. They sent proclamations right away for none of their subjects to dare steal anything from the Florentines. Messer Andrea Doria[19] has captured Port' Ercole and Talamone and the strongholds and a few other little castles in that part of the Maremma[20] from them. I pray you give my regards to Messer Francesco, and I am your devoted servant. God keep you.

In Florence, 7 August 1526.

Francesco Vettori

❖ LETTER 318
Bartolomeo Cavalcanti to Niccolò Machiavelli
Florence, 11 August 1526

To Niccolò Machiavelli, Whom I Honor as a Father.
In Camp.

My honored Niccolò. The reason that I have not written you so often as you would perhaps have wished and as I certainly would have wanted to has been that, not having heard sooner whether several of my letters, some written to you and some to Guidotti,[1] had arrived, I did not want to write you once again in vain. But as soon as I heard that those had arrived, although belatedly, I could not help talking with you a bit by letter, although I am lacking matter for it; I miss your presence and your conversation, since they are very sweet and very wise, more each day, and I cannot help complaining about being deprived of them. You whetted my appetite at the beginning[2]; since then you have not satisfied me with even a couple of words, and yet my silence, if one can call silence not bothering you constantly with chattering and conversation of no importance, did not deserve this. Because you know very well that you should not expect letters from me containing great matters, since none are being dealt with here in any way, nor discussing present affairs, which first of all I do not hear about, and in any case I would not be so presumptuous and foolish as to dare discuss them. But one thing you know with complete certainty, and you cannot doubt it, is that I desire your letters very deeply and that to me they have the value of oracles, and so, for both these reasons, you could have been somewhat more generous with them to me. And if it should seem to you that your letter was still apt to satisfy me, because in truth *you were already looking ahead then,* nevertheless many things have happened since then *that may have altered your judgments and understanding of the war.* Therefore I can no longer go hungry, and I await your letters with the greatest desire, and I shall not add prayers in order to beseech them more readily, since it seems to me something unworthy of our friendship, to which you have always granted everything generously, and this, I hope, you will grant willingly. I am sorry not to have matter to discuss at length with you; for that I shall await the answer I shall write to those letters of yours that I am expecting, because from them I shall get a good deal of material, and perhaps in the meantime something will still happen to write you about. If that happens, I shall not lack diligence or any sense of duty toward you.

All your friends are well and greatly desire your letters. Aside from the taxes, here we are all in the peace of Caesar Octavian[3] and in the greatest calm. Siena is no longer giving us trouble. You are far away, and what do we lack? It remains for me to beg you to give my warmest regards to His Lordship the Lieutenant, and then to greet Giovanni Bandini, Fieravante, and our other friends on my behalf, and offer them my services. You stay well, and tell me if I can do anything at all for you.

From Florence, 11 August 1526.
Yours, Bartolomeo Cavalcanti

❖ LETTER 319
Francesco Vettori to Niccolò Machiavelli
Florence, 24 August 1526

To the Notable Niccolò Machiavelli, etc.

My dear *compare*. The last letter[1] I wrote you reported on how the Siena business had turned out, as you had requested. Since then I have received two letters from you, the latest from the 17th, but I cannot answer you precisely because, as soon as I got your letters, I sent them on to Filippo[2] in Rome, thinking that they could help the campaign, if they might be read there by Our Lord. Filippo writes me that he not only reads them but he also rereads them and appreciates them.

In your last letter you analyze for me three ways of pursuing the war, which have been discussed or, to put it better, spoken of there. I am not in favor of leaving Milan and going toward Alessandria, because you will have the same difficulty and greater in Alessandria that you have in Milan and Cremona and that you think you would have in Pavia, because you will go there with less glory. I would indeed be in favor of having these fleets sail toward Genoa, as they seem to me to be planning,[3] and of the marquess of Saluzzo's going in that direction by land with his infantry and men-at-arms, and I should think that if Fortune did not wish to aid the emperor unusually in this campaign, as it has in almost all the others up to now, making them revolt would succeed,[4] and that victory would definitely ensue from a revolution in Genoa. I do not believe experienced men in the militia would be very much in favor of guarding the borders of the Venetians and of the Church and attacking the Kingdom of Naples with the rest of the army, and leaving the emperor's forces in Lombardy intact, because you let the fortress of Milan be lost under your very eyes there, which was the cause that made you anticipate war. You were at the very gates of Milan and you retreated to Marignano faster than if you were running away; you tried Cremona, and fought and did battle with it, and that did not work out for you; the pope has undertaken the Siena campaign, and his troops were routed there. So would you believe that with so much misfortune you would succeed with anything in the kingdom [of Naples]? I admit that the people of the kingdom are very discontented, but those of Lombardy are worse and they are holding still. The cities that you could attack in the kingdom, especially the good ones, are on the plain, and they could be fortified. The emperor's men would not lack for ways to put two or three thousand good soldiers in them, with the result that you would have the same difficulty capturing cities there that you have here. And so you have to accept that the way to carry on war is to persist in the capture of Cremona; if that succeeds, you will be able, with the army that is there, to resist any lansquenets that came from Germany, attack Genoa with these fleets by sea and by land with the infantry and the men-at-arms that Saluzzo is leading; and if Genoa revolts, the fleets need to turn back the kingdom [of Naples] and keep it at bay, and Saluzzo needs to head toward Milan and you need to make two camps surrounding it. If it is true that in Milan they are suffering so much for foodstuffs that they are thinking at present of abandoning it, they will think of it all the more when they are surrounded more closely. If because of this difficulty they withdrew to Pavia and abandoned Milan, your army would find it much easier to besiege them in Pavia than it does in Milan, and they would have no way to be able to withdraw anywhere else. If they should have lost Genoa, they could receive neither money nor messages nor letters. Although they are bold and gallant men, I do not believe they are made of any other stuff than other men, all of whom want to live, and they would think of the same thing. It is true that this kind of war will be long and will cost intolerable amounts of money, but victory ought to result from it. But from the other kinds it cannot be seen that anything but harm or shame can result. If you were to tell me that you have to think where this money is going to come from, I should say that this campaign should be dispatched within three months and that, without the men-at-arms, with the Swiss and everything else there, there should be an expense of 160 thousand ducats per month, of which the king gives forty, so that the pope and the Venetians would be left to provide 120 per month. I think the Venetians can provide their share, that is, 60 thousand per month; the pope would be left with another sixty, which would make 180 thousand in three months, which is not an amount that could not be provided, and I believe I could even say from what sources and how he would get it. If it should be objected to me that these campaigns will not succeed, especially in so little time, I should tell you that if by the end of November the war is not, if not completely won, at least winding down, the pope is obliged to accept whatever conditions the emperor is willing to give him, which one can imagine are going to be very harsh. I know, *compare,* that I may be considered presumptuous to try and give my judgment about such important things, of which I have neither familiarity nor experience; but when I write to you, I feel as if I am talking with myself. For if I had to write or talk with someone else, I would do it with more restraint. I pray you to give my regards to the governor[5] and yourself.

In Florence, 24 August 1526.
Yours, Francesco Vettori

❖ LETTER 320
Donato del Corno to Niccolò Machiavelli
Florence, 28 August 1526

To Messer Niccolò Machiavelli.
In Camp, at Milan.
Jesus, 28 August 1526.

My honored chief, etc. I took care of Ser Mariotto's request, and if not exactly according to the plan sent me, it was all done smoothly and I went in person, the better to give satisfaction. Do not worry about Titone, for he has fallen silent, and especially because he who charms the devils, since you are not here, has taken me as his target, and keeps turning around me and tells me a jumble of tales, so that if I were not a worthy man and did not watch out, I would have lost my head several times. But I think so well and behave so discreetly that I believe I shall regain the reputation of not being considered a chatterbox. Even if things should be written to you by him or anyone else to put blame on me, do not be led into temptation, because they are doing it out of cursed envy, because they see that I am your agent and respondent, and I know how to keep the matter in good repute, and I behave so well that I pray God for your return that it may be a happy one, for you will not recognize my ways or customs, and I have decided that they will no longer get my slippers off me[1] at every step. But to return to Ser Mariotto, who is the reason for my writing to you now in the enclosed letter, he sends you a thousand regards, and looking together over a few little books belonging to you, he seemed to me so much in agreement with the order of my fancy that, seeing your business at a standstill because of your absence, I am afraid he may stir me to some venture with his craft. God keep you. Yours,

Donato del Corno, in Florence

❖ LETTER 321
Bartolomeo Cavalcanti to Niccolò Machiavelli
Florence, 18 September 1526

To My Niccolò Machiavelli, Honored as a Father.
In the Field.

My honored Niccolò. I wrote you on the 6th and sent you the letter along with some others of mine written to Guidetti of whose receipt I have so far had no notification whatever. Although at present I have no matter to write you about and I do not feel I should bother you with useless letters, nevertheless I have not been able to help writing you. I have decided rather to be noted by you for this importunateness than be blamed for laziness about writing. If, as I believe, you have gotten my letter of the 6th, you will have seen how much I long for your letters and how deeply. And I do not doubt that, as you have always done because of your kindness and our friendship, when you have an opportunity, you will satisfy this longing of mine, which grows all the stronger the more I consider the progress of this campaign.

You have returned from Cremona,[1] and I hope that you were as happy to have been in that place as I rejoice in your having returned from there safe and sound. But in any case, I was very glad for you to have gone there, judging that either you will have strengthened that army there and us here in some good hope for that campaign or you will have recognized the flaws in it and demonstrated them in such a way that they can have been corrected most easily and have provided for and remedied the ill that could come from them. We here see perhaps how useful a successful assault may be, but we are not really able to judge what may be born out of the opposite outcome, it seems so harmful to us in every way. Certainly harm will come to us all from that; but I really do not know if a successful assault will bring us all profit. However, the money will not have been spent in vain, especially that of the Venetians. The French must have been found again, if their chief has not indeed gotten lost, which, however, we do not believe, and today we hear that those troops are at Tortona.[2] God bring them back to camp right away, and make at least some of these many hopes come true.

Giovanni Serristori sends you a thousand greetings, and Averardo as well. Lelio de' Massimi, who is leaving tomorrow morning for Rome, sends you his best regards and is your devoted servant.

I await your letters with great longing and if they are as I hope, I promise you I shall get all dressed up right away and fill up a page for you. I shall say nothing else to you for now, except that I pray you to love and command me. God keep you well.

From Florence, 18 September 1526.

Yours, Bartolomeo Cavalcanti

❖ LETTER 322

Niccolò Machiavelli to Bartolomeo Cavalcanti

In the Field, around 6 October 1526

Dearest Bartolomeo. The reason why the pope started this war before the king of France sent his troops into Italy and attacked in Spain according to his agreement—and prior to the arrival of all the Swiss—was his reliance on the people of Milan and his belief that 6 thousand Swiss, whom the Venetians and the pope had dispatched at the first sign of rebellion in Milan, would be so

quick that they would arrive at the same time as the Venetians arrived with
their army. Furthermore, he believed that the king's troops, even if they were
not so quick, would at least be early enough to help the campaign to be won.
Added to these expectations was the stronghold's evident need of being relieved. Every one of these conditions, therefore, precipitated the pope's actions; with such high hopes we believed that this war ought to be over within
XV days; the capture of Lodi[1] intensified this expectation. Well, then, the
Venetian and papal armies did meet, but two of the most important premises
just mentioned did not come about because the Swiss did not come and the
people of Milan were useless. Hence, once we appeared before Milan, the
people did not stir; since we were minus the Swiss, we did not have the
courage to stay there and we withdrew to Marignano. We did not return to
Milan until the 5 thousand Swiss troops did come. Although previously their
arrival would have been useful, it was now harmful because they provided us
with the courage to return to Milan in order to relieve the stronghold[2]—but
it was not relieved; and since we were committed to remaining there, because
the previous retreat had been a disgrace, no one advised a second one. This resulted in the attack on Cremona being attempted with part of the infantry
but not all of it; we would have used it all had we still been at Marignano
when the stronghold had fallen. For these reasons, therefore, and in the expectation that it would be easy, our attack on Cremona was feeble; it was carried
out contrary to a rule of mine that says, "Risking all one's fortune without using all one's forces is an injudicious strategy."[3] As a result of the fortress being
there, the leaders believed that 4 thousand soldiers would suffice to win out.
Because it was a feeble one, this attack made Cremona more difficult, since
the army did not so much attack the weak spots as they did point them out;
thus, those within did not lose control of those areas but rather reinforced
them. Furthermore, they fixed their minds on defense; so, even though the
duke of Urbino later went there and 14 thousand soldiers were around there
too, that was not enough. Whereas had he been there at the outset with the
entire army and able to make several breaches simultaneously, we would have
had to take it in 6 days and perhaps we also would have won this campaign
because we would have had the glory of conquest[4] together with a greatly
enlarged army, because 13 thousand Swiss arrived. Thus, either Milan or
Genoa—or perhaps both—would have been seized and there would have
been no remedy for the enemy, the disorders in Rome[5] would not have occurred, and the reinforcements, which have yet to arrive, would not have been
in time. We have spent 50 days courting Milan, and the capture of Cremona
was drawn out, when all manner of destruction came raining down on our
backs. Consequently, our side has lost this war twice: once when we went to
Milan but did not remain and once when we made our drive toward Cremona but did not go there. The duke's faintheartedness was the reason for the
first loss, and the arrogance of us all was the reason for the second one, because, having been disgraced by the first retreat, nobody dared advise a second
one. Against the will of us all the duke was able to act badly; against the will

of us all he was not able to act well. These are the mistakes that have deprived us of victory; I say "deprived" because we did not conquer at the outset; if disorder on our part had not occurred, we might have postponed—and not lost—the campaign. This disorder is also of two sorts: first, the pope did not raise money at a time when with his influence he could have done so and with means that other popes have employed. The second sort of disorder is his having stayed in Rome in a situation where he could be taken like a baby—something that has so tangled this skein that not even Christ could un-snarl it. For the pope has withdrawn his troops from the battlefield, Messer Francesco is still on it, and the duke of Urbino is due to arrive today. Quite a few condottieri have remained—those with quite a difference of opin-ion—but they are all ambitious and insufferable; lacking anyone who knows how to mitigate their caprices and keep them united, they will be a ca-cophony of barking dogs. The result is an extremely widespread insouciance about their work, and Signor Giovanni[6] already wants to get out of there; I think he will leave today. Messer Francesco's promptness and conscientious-ness has set all this disorder right. In addition to this, if up until now money has been coming from Rome, now it will be lacking altogether; hence, I see little order in our houses, and if God does not help us out in the south, as He has already done in the north, then there are few remedies left to us. For, just as He interfered with the reinforcements from the Germans for the northern-ers with the destruction of Hungary,[7] so he will have to interfere with the re-inforcements from Spain with the destruction of the fleet; hence, we shall be in need of Juno to go and pray Aeolus on our behalf[8] and promise him the countess[9] and every lady Florence has, so that he might set loose the winds in our behalf. Were it not for the Turks, I unequivocally believe that the Spaniards would have come and observed All Saints' Day with us.

Since I saw the stronghold fall and reflected upon how the Spaniards have gone about hunkering down in three or four of these towns and made sure of the populace, I thought that this war would be a long one and, because of its length, a perilous one. For I know how difficult it is to capture cities when there are people inside them bent on defending them and how a re-gion can be captured in a day, but a defended city may require months—or years—to capture, as is pointed out in much of ancient history and in mod-ern times by Rhodes and Hungary.[10] This is why I wrote Francesco Vettori that I believed we would be unable to put up with this campaign unless we were to see to it that the king of France captured Milan—we ought to give it to him—or, as a tactical diversion, to see to it that the frontiers were pro-tected so that the Spaniards were unable to advance and might attack the Kingdom of Naples with their entire army[11]; I believe it could be captured before any of the cities in these parts. For here there were neither dogged defenders nor conquered people [. . .] as the man would like them to be. In addition, the war would foster strife, because the reinforcements that would have been gotten from the cities would have gotten wages, and the abun-dance coming from unravaged land would make these reinforcements go further. And without any new expenditures the pope could live securely in Rome and we would learn which the emperor valued more, Lombardy or the Kingdom of Naples. Were this solution not to be carried out, I consider the war to be lost because its duration is certain and during this duration perils can be said to be certain too—either because there is not enough money or because there are other unforeseen circumstances, such as have already cropped up. It seemed like a strange plan to me: for us to wear ourselves out on the battlefield and the enemy to loll about in the city and then, once the reinforcements arrive and find us exhausted, for him to lay waste to us just like the admiral and the king.

❖ LETTER 323
Francesco Guicciardini to Niccolò Machiavelli
Piacenza,[1] 30 October 1526

To the Notable Messer Niccolò Machiavelli, as an Honored Brother.
In Florence, or Wherever He Might Be.

My very dear Messer Niccolò. I got your letter from Modena[2] with the long report[3] about what occurred on the day that you left here. Because, as you know, it is my nature not to wish to decide important matters by myself, I had the council summoned, the main members of which were the bishop of Casale[4] and the treasurer, and the vice-legate, who knows the man, was also very graciously willing to take part; the ambassador of the duke of Milan was there, the lieutenant of the marquess of Mantua, and so many other important men that not so many take part in the council in the Venetians' camp. I read your letter, and it was all well-considered and discussed just as well as was done on the day when we deliberated not to relieve the fortress. I do not want to enter into details because I am not in the mood for fairy tales, and I am also obliged to speak with Messer Filicciafo, who has graciously spent all of today with me; but the argument was entirely over two points: the first, whether what Giannozzo did should be called revenge or betrayal; the other, even if it should be called revenge, whether it was honorable or not for someone of his rank.

But leaving aside gossip, our friend came here this evening, and he complained justifiably that while you were there you never deigned to call him commissioner, but you always referred to him as *podestà,* which he criticized you for doing in order to mock him and to make him lose prestige; in truth, he is very displeased about it. But his complaints had scarcely come to an end when I received a letter from the quartermaster there, informing me that this venerable man indicated he had spent on your account a good five ducats, between the things you had eaten and what had been thrown away on your account the evening before, and he requests the commune to reimburse him for this expense, claiming that he had nothing to do with you, but that he had quartered you there at my request, as I am sending you about in the service of Our Lordship[5]; and so, seeing myself named in this story, and that these dealings were not without blame on my part, I began to get angry with him about it; and because he disagreed presumptuously, I had to give him a piece of my mind,[6] almost as much of it, in fact, as I had to give to the brother. You see what a fine story this has been; you started it as a comedy and I have almost ended it as a tragedy, and so I have lost all the pleasure that I should have gotten from his business. So *farewell.*

From Piacenza, 30 October 1526.
Yours, Francesco Guicciardini

❖ LETTER 324
Filippo de' Nerli to Niccolò Machiavelli
Modena, 1 November 1526

To the Notable Niccolò di Messer Bernardo Machiavelli, as an Honored Brother.
In Florence.

You will see from the letter from His Lordship the Lieutenant how your fairy tale turned out. It was not enough for you to have repaid that poor man[1] who had honored you much more than your merits deserved in return for the honor that he did you, with the rank that you conferred on him and not to have ever called him by his name; for you were also the cause of his getting a chewing out that must have been a beautiful one. I told you that you were indeed dangerous people and not to be allowed in one's house; and the lieutenant also writes me about all the acrimony that he had with the *podestà* and the commissioner: think what they will say of me, who kept them many days, since they have said so many things about someone who kept them only one evening. All in all, you are dangerous people, and worse than charcoal.[2]

I would not wish, however, if you wanted to treat Count Guido[3] and me like the commissioner of San Donnino, with letters and gossip, for you to plan to do it also by not keeping your promise to us: so remember to send us the first two books of that history,[4] and they will be sent back to you at the end of fifteen days, and you will then be able to send back the others; and I pray you not to fail in this and to answer us about it. The way to send them is to roll them up in oilcloth and give them to Luca del Vantaggio so he can make a cover and to send them by passing couriers or horse trains. They can only come in complete safety.

Give my regards to all the dotards and especially to my Donato,[5] who if he makes sure this winter that, apart from cluttering up his shop next to the heater, you do not infect him also with belly-rumblings, would be a worthy man. Without saying any more, I am your very devoted servant and send you my regards, may Christ keep you from harm.

From Modena, 1 November 1526.
Yours, Filippo de' Nerli

❖ LETTER 325
Niccolò Machiavelli to Francesco Guicciardini
Florence, 5 November 1526

To Messer Francesco Guicciardini.

   Signor Lieutenant. I wrote Your Lordship a letter from Modena more suited
for Filicciafo's amusement than for anything else; thus, I must write you what
happened next. So I shall begin with my arrival at Modena when Filippo[1]
met me saying, "Is it possible, then, that I have never done anything right?" I
laughingly replied, "*Signor* Governor, do not be surprised at that; it is not your
fault but that of the year, because no one has done things well or anything
gone but the wrong way. Since the emperor did not in all this time send his
troops any reinforcements, even though he could have easily done so, he
could not have behaved worse; the Spanish could have sometimes played
some dirty tricks on us but did not know how; we could have won but did
not know how to; the pope had more confidence in a single quill full of ink[2]
than in a thousand foot soldiers, who would have been adequate for his protection; only the Sienese have behaved well, and we should not be surprised
that the crazies give a good account of themselves during crazy times.[3]
Hence, my Signor Governor, to have given a good account of ourselves
would have been a worse sign than having given a poor one." "Well, if that is
how it is," replied Filippo, "I am going to stop worrying about it and be quite
happy." And so the first act of the comedy came to an end. Count Guido[4] arrived shortly and when he saw me, he said, "Is the division commander still
angry?" I replied then he was not, since the cause of his anger was no longer
nearby. So as not to go into all the details, we talked for a while about this
blessed ill humor of yours; he said he would rather be exiled in Egypt than
serve in an army where you were. At this point I said what was called for, and,
in particular, we argued about the good and bad things that your presence had
accomplished, so that everyone readily agreed that it had accomplished more
good than harm. I remained in Modena for two days and talked with a
prophet who maintained, with witnesses, that he had predicted the pope's
flight and the campaign's futility; and again he says that all the bad times are
not yet over—both we and the pope will suffer greatly during them. We finally arrived in Florence, and the worst accusation I have heard against you is
that in letters written here to the cardinal[5] you pointed out how easy the
campaign would be and how certain victory would be; whereas, since I believe I have seen all the important letters Your Lordship has written, in which
there were judgments diametrically opposed to a certain victory, I have maintained that this is impossible.

5 November 1526
Niccolò Machiavelli

❖ LETTER 326
Jacopo Salviati to Niccolò Machiavelli
Rome, 5 November 1526

To the Notable Niccolò Machiavelli, My Very Dear Friend.

Notable man, very dear friend, etc. I wrote you as soon as I got your letter from Piacenza, and in reply to it I told you to come here when you liked,[1] that Our Lordship[2] was very happy about your coming but that you took so long to arrive in Florence that it was necessary for them to arrange for someone else in the position that was intended for you; and for now there is no question of replacing him, because it would be too great a hardship for him. Nevertheless, if any other occasion arises I shall recall you to O[ur] L[ordship], and I shall not fail in any of those duties and actions that are expected of a very good friend, even though I know this is not necessary for the affection that His Holiness bears toward you. *Nothing else. Farewell.*

From Rome, 5 November 1526.
Jacopo Salviati

❖ LETTER 327
Francesco Guicciardini to Niccolò Machiavelli
Piacenza, 12 November 1526

To the Notable Niccolò Machiavelli, as an Honored Brother.
In Florence.

My very dear Machiavelli. I have your letter of the 5th. The story of Borgo San Donnino was pure comedy, that of Modena was like a tragedy, yours of Rome has been like a fairy tale. I cannot tell you anything else about it except that Messer Cesare[1] writes that as soon as he had told the pope what I wrote him about the [. . .] His Holiness replied, "Write him that he should come, that it pleases me." Since then he wrote me that he had been written that he should postpone it and about the reason why they had had to make use of someone else for this task in the haste of the soldiers' departure from Rome with Lord Vitelli. I have written back to him once again, and I am of the opinion they will change their minds: I wanted that more for my sake than for yours, because, to tell you the truth, I think that you would have gotten little satisfaction from being in those little strongholds of the Colonnas where you would have had to stay: if I should hear anything else about it, I shall let you know, and I shall strive to get further information about it.

I pray you to write to me and I shall do the same. I shall not tell you anything new because for now there is nothing else, and Messer Filicciafo is my regular table companion. Looking back over these accounts of the expenses incurred in camp, I do not find any for which the pope can complain about me, except for the money that was given to Guidotti, and I hear that at his departure from here he complained to the entire house that I had given him very little, and he must have done the same over there. That was all I needed to know his nature and quality thoroughly. I am your servant.

In Piacenza, 12 November 1526.
Yours, Francesco Guicciardini

LETTERS

1527

Machiavelli's letters to his friends and his dispatches to Florence during the last two years of his life, but especially in those from 1527, expose his imagination of disaster. Machiavelli knew only too well that even though he was reveling in being once more able to act for Florence, Italy was immobilized. The situation was out of control. As Paolo Giovo put it, "We all shamefully plunged into a disaster that was hardly unforeseen"; it was a "prolonged moment of confusion" (Chastel, *Sack of Rome,* pp. 15, 17).

Officials in Florence were convinced that the imperial forces, bent on taking their revenge on Rome for breaking the truce that forced Clement VII to withdraw his army from Lombardy, were not going to bypass their city. On 3 February the Eight of Affairs ordered Machiavelli to Parma to advise Guicciardini, there with the papal army, that the situation in Florence was desperate: the city needed more forces from the league to defend it. Machiavelli's job was first to convince Guicciardini of this fact, though the latter needed little persuasion, and then to get military support from Francesco Maria della Rovere, the duke of Urbino. Machiavelli remained with Guicciardini; he did not return to Florence until 22 April. As the military headquarters moved southeast from Parma to Bologna to Imola and to Forlì, so did Machiavelli. (The correspondence exchanged between Machiavelli and the Eight during this mission is contained in *Leg.,* III, pp. 1617–1653.)

Toward the end of March, Clement and the imperial viceroy in Naples, Charles de Lannoy, agreed to still another truce. On the one hand, its terms stipulated that the pope would remove his army from the region around Naples, hand the city over to the emperor Charles V, pay Charles III de

Bourbon, constable of France, 60,000 ducats, and pardon the members of the Colonna family; on the other hand, it stipulated that there would be no fighting for eight months and that the imperial forces would leave the Church's lands and all Italy, provided that Venice and France respected the truce. Although the pope injudiciously disbanded his army, Charles de Bourbon did not disband his; instead, he resolutely made his way south toward Tuscany. Simultaneously, George Frundsberg was moving southeast into Romagna and Tuscany. (He was the leader of an advancing army of fourteen thousand German lansquenets that Giovanni de' Medici—Giovanni delle Bande Nere—had tried to prevent from crossing the Po in November 1526, when he was killed, much to Machiavelli's regret.)

In fact, the combined armies of Bourbon and Frundsberg joined near Piacenza, in February, and headed in the direction of Reggio; by early March they were ravaging the territory of Bologna. On 5 April Bourbon moved on Imola, the same day that Machiavelli wrote to Vettori telling him that Guicciardini would defend Romagna as long as he could pay for the army's support, "at sixteen *soldi* to the lira," but march the troops west for the defense of Florence as soon as the situation appeared hopeless. The pope, blindly trusting in his truce, "drawn up in Rome but not observed in Lombardy" (Letter 330), did nothing to stop Bourbon. Viceroy Charles de Lannoy, however, who had promised that the emperor would be bound by the truce, arrived in Florence on 6 April intent on compelling Bourbon to respect its terms. He was unable to do so. Indeed, it was doubtful that Bourbon could even have controlled his army by that point, except by assuring them they could pillage Rome and keep the booty. On 16 April, realizing that no help from the pope would be forthcoming, Guicciardini informed the Eight of Affairs that, on his own initiative, he was going to order all the troops at his disposal to Florence.

With the end approaching, Florence saw an opportunity to reject the Medici. On 26 April, during what is known as "the Friday tumult," a group led by Niccolò Capponi and Filippo Strozzi drove out the cardinal of Cortona, who was acting on behalf of young Ippolito and Alessandro de' Medici. The imperial forces, meanwhile, were intent on Rome, not Florence. They moved rapidly and were at Rome's gates by 6 May. In a bloody sack, with the lansquenets shouting "Vivat Luther Papa," Bourbon was killed and Clement was captured. In the aftermath, Florence, at Guicciardini's urging, sent Machiavelli on 22 May to Civitavecchia, where the pope had taken refuge, to discuss matters with Andrea Doria, the commander of the French fleet against Charles V. Machiavelli returned to a Florence once more governed as a republic. But he had little time left to enjoy it. He fell ill on 20 June, died the next day, and was buried the day after; his final resting place is now in the Basilica of Santa Croce. We do not know whether or not his sermon, known as the *Esortazione alla penitenza* (Exhortation to penitence), dates from this period, but it closes on a fitting note. Adapting the last two lines from the famous first sonnet in Petrarch's *Rime,* Machiavelli epitomizes the imagination of disaster that the letters, especially those exchanged with his son Guido, bespeak:

> And to repent and to clearly realize:
> What may please on earth is but a brief dream.

✤ LETTER 328
Niccolò Machiavelli to Guido Machiavelli
Imola,[1] 2 April 1527

To My Dear Son Guido di Niccolò Machiavelli.
In Florence.

My dearest son Guido. I received a letter from you[2] that has given me the greatest pleasure, especially since you write that you have quite recovered; I could not have had better news. If God grants you and me life, I believe that I may make you a man of good standing, if you are willing to do your share. For, besides the influential friendships I have now, I have made a new one with Cardinal Cibo[3]—it is so close that I am astonished at it myself—that will prove to be opportune for you. But you must study and, since you no longer have illness as an excuse, take pains to learn letters[4] and music, for you are aware how much distinction is given me for what little ability I possess. Thus, my son, if you want to please me and to bring profit and honor to yourself, study, do well, and learn, because everyone will help you if you help yourself.

Since the young mule has gone mad, it must be treated just the reverse of the way crazy people are, for they are tied up, and I want you to let it loose. Give it to Vangelo and tell him to take it to Montepugliano and then take off its bridle and halter and let it go wherever it likes to regain its own way of life and work off its craziness. The village is big and the beast is small; it can do no one any harm. Thus, we can observe what it wants to do without causing ourselves any problems, and whenever it comes to its senses, you will be on the spot to catch it again.[5] As for the rest of the horses, do whatever Lodovico[6] has told you to do. Thank God he has recovered and that he has sold them. Since he has sent some money, I know he has profited, but I am surprised and saddened that he has not written.

Greet Madonna Marietta for me and tell her I have been expecting—and still do—to leave here any day; I have never longed so much to return to Florence as I do now, but there is nothing else I can do. Simply tell her that, whatever she hears, she should be of good cheer, since I shall be there before any danger comes. Kiss Baccina, Piero, and Totto, if he is there; I would dearly appreciate hearing whether his eyes are any better. Live in happiness and spend as little as you can. And remind Bernardo, whom I have written to twice in the last two weeks and received no reply, that he had better behave himself. Christ watch over you all.[7]

2 April 1527
Niccolò Machiavelli, in Imola

❖ LETTER 329
Niccolò Machiavelli to Francesco Vettori
Forlì, 5 April 1527

To My Most Magnificent Francesco Vettori.
In Florence.

My honored Francesco. Since the truce[1] was concluded in Rome and we realized that the imperial troops had no intention of keeping it,[2] Messer Francesco wrote[3] to Rome that it was necessary to choose one of three alternatives. One, return to the war once more under such conditions that the whole world would know that we would never again discuss peace so that France, the Venetians—everybody—would fulfill their obligations with no hesitation or suspicion; in his letter he pointed out that there were still many remedies available, especially if the pope were willing to be helped. Two, if the first alternative were unsuitable, we might choose a second, which would be diametrically opposed to the first: to go directly into this peace with all due zeal and put ourselves in the hands of the viceroy[4] and in this manner let ourselves be ruled by Fortune. Third, were the first alternative to exhaust us and the second to make us afraid, we could choose a third, which at the moment it is of no import or need to discuss.[5] Today Messer Francesco received a reply from Rome: the pope opted for the second alternative, to throw himself into the viceroy's hands and into peace; if this decision succeeds, it will be our salvation now, and if it does not, it will cause everyone to desert us. Whether or not it will succeed, you can judge as well as we, but this alone I tell you: Messer Francesco has made this decision in any case to help out the affairs of Romagna—so long as he sees that they may be defended at sixteen *soldi* to the lira[6]; as soon as he realizes that they are unable to be defended, he will forsake them without any scruple whatsoever. With whatever Italian troops he can unearth and with whatever money he may have left, he will head in this direction to deliver Florence and her territory.[7] Rest assured that he will do it any way he can.

The imperial army is brave and large; nevertheless, if it does not come across deserters, it would not even fight its way out of a paper bag.[8] But the danger exists that out of inertia one city begins to surrender to him and, as one begins, all the others will go up in smoke; this is one of the conditions that makes defending this region risky. Nevertheless, if it is defeated, you—provided you do not lose courage—can save yourselves; through your defense of Pisa, Pistoia, Prato, and Florence you may reach a treaty with them that, though it may be painful, will not be absolutely fatal. And, because the pope's decision is still a secret as far as these allies are concerned—and for many other considerations—I beg you not to make this letter public. *Farewell*.

2 April 1527.
Niccolò Machiavelli, in Forlì

❖ LETTER 330
Niccolò Machiavelli to Francesco Vettori
Forlì, 14 April 1527

To My Most Honored and Magnificent Francesco Vettori.
In Florence.

Magnificent One. We here have always recommended the treaty for the same reasons that you there[1] have always recommended it. Since we have observed how France and the Venetians have behaved, how undisciplined our troops were, how absolutely hopeless it was for the pope to keep the war against the kingdom [of Naples] going, and how powerful and dogged the enemy has been, we have deemed the war lost, just as you, when I left you there, deemed it lost too. These observations have consistently led us to recommend a treaty, but we meant a treaty that would be stable and not, like this one—drawn up in Rome but not observed in Lombardy—questionable and equivocal; and we also meant for there to be a little money paid out. We would need this small amount either to be set aside for an equally questionable treaty while we remained unarmed or to be spent for arming ourselves while we remained without any money for the treaty. Consequently, whereas we assumed an unambiguous treaty would be our salvation, an equivocal one is absolutely destructive and ruinous.

People in Florence now write us that the treaty is practically settled; since the initial payment is sixty thousand ducats,[2] people count on the majority of it coming from the money we have here. We have thirteen thousand ducats in cash and seven thousand in credit with the Venetians. Should the enemy advance and start attacking Tuscany, we shall have to spend this money on the support of our troops here if we want to hold onto this wretched city; consequently, if you are counting on the treaty, you must rely on one that calls a halt to these armed forces and expenditures. Otherwise, if we enter into an equivocal treaty, which means we shall have to pay for both it and the war, neither one of them will be provided for: the result will be our loss and the enemy's profit; they are thinking only of war as they march toward us, and they are letting you get entangled between war and treaties. I am yours.

14 April 1527
Yours, Niccolò Machiavelli, in Forlì

❖ LETTER 331
Niccolò Machiavelli to Francesco Vettori
Forlì, 16 April 1527

To His Honored, Very Magnificent Francesco Vettori.
In Florence.

Magnificent one, etc. Today Monseigneur de la Motte[1] has been at the imperial camp with the treaty's final form drawn up in Florence; if Bourbon accepts it, he must call a halt to his army. If he makes a move, that is a sign that he does not accept it; hence, tomorrow will decide our affairs. Consequently, it has been decided here that, should he make a move tomorrow, we will plan for war absolutely and leave aside all thought about peace; if he does not make a move, we shall provide for peace without even a thought about war. Given this kind of north wind, you too must set sail[2] and, once you have decided on war, cut off any negotiations for peace and do so in such a way that the allies will openly come forward, because at this point we do not need any more limping but rather some recklessness: despair often discovers remedies that choice could not. Without artillery their troops are entering a rugged region,[3] so that if we, with whatever little life remains, join forces with the league's troops that are in place, the enemy will either withdraw from that territory in disgrace or be reduced to reasonable terms. I love Messer Francesco Guicciardini,[4] I love my native city more than my own soul[5]; and I tell you as a result of the experience I have had over sixty years[6] that I do not believe there were ever more difficult problems than these, where peace is necessary and war cannot be renounced, and where we have a prince[7] on our hands who can barely meet the needs of either peace by itself or war by itself. I send you my regards.

16 April 1527
Niccolò Machiavelli, in Forlì

❖ LETTER 332
Guido Machiavelli to Niccolò Machiavelli
Florence, 17 April 1527

To His Honored Father, Niccolò Machiavelli.
In Forlì.
Jesus.

Honored father, greetings, etc. In reply to your letter of 2 April, by which we learn that you are in good health, God be praised, and may he keep you so.
We did not write you about Totto because we had not yet gotten him back[1]; but we hear from the nurse that his eyes are not yet healed. But she says that he is getting better all the time; so do not worry about him. The young mule has not yet been sent to Monte Pugliano because the grass has

not yet grown back; but, however the weather turns out, he will be sent there anyway.

We learn from your letter to Madonna Marietta that you have bought such a beautiful chain for Baccina, who does nothing else but think of this beautiful little chain and pray God for you, that He should make you come back soon.

We are not worrying about the lansquenets anymore because you have promised us to try and be with us if anything should happen. And so Madonna Marietta is no longer worried.

We pray you to write to us if ever the enemy should think of coming and harming us, because we still have many things in the country[2]: wine and oil, although we have brought twenty or twenty-three barrels of oil down here; and the beds are there. You wrote to us to find out whether Sagrino was willing to take them into his house, and he has accepted. We ask you about this because it would take two or even three days' time to bring so much stuff to San Casciano.

We are all well, and I feel fine. I shall begin this Easter, if Baccio is better, to play and to sing and to do three-part counterpoint. If both of us stay well, I hope to be able to do without him within a month, may it please God. In Latin, I am getting to participles today. Ser Luca has read me almost all the first book of Ovid's *Metamorphoses*. I want to recite it all to you by heart as soon as you get home.

Madonna Marietta gives you her regards and sends you two shirts, two towels, two caps, three pairs of hose, and four handkerchiefs. She prays you to come back soon, and so do all of us. Christ be with you, and keep you in prosperity.

From Florence, 17 April 1527.
Yours, Guido Machiavelli, in Florence

❖ LETTER 333
Niccolò Machiavelli to Francesco Vettori
Brisighella, 18 April 1527

To My Honored, Very Magnificent Francesco Vettori.
In Florence.

Honored Francesco. These French troops[1] here in Brisighella have behaved miraculously; and so it will be a miracle if the duke of Urbino arrives tomorrow from Pianoro,[2] as it would appear from what his legate in Bologna[3] writes, and we, I believe, shall wait here to find out what he has done. And for the love of God, since this treaty cannot be made, if indeed you are unable to make it, break the negotiations off immediately; do so in such a way, with both letters and action, that our allies will help us out. For, just as the treaty, were it kept, would be a guarantee of our safety, so discussing it without concluding it would be a guarantee of our destruction. And that the treaty was necessary will be obvious if it is not concluded; if Count Guido[4] says anything different, he is an asshole.[5] There is only this one point I want to argue with him about: ask him if they could be restrained from entering Tuscany; if he says what he always has said in the past, he will say that it is impossible—the duke of Urbino will say the same thing. If it is true, then, that they could not be restrained, ask him how they could be driven out without fighting a battle and how Florence was capable of bearing the burden of two armies on its back when the friendly army was more insufferable than the enemy's. If he settles this problem for you, tell him he is right. But whoever profits from war, as these soldiers do, would be crazy to extol peace. Yet God will grant them more war than we would like.

18 April 1527
Niccolò Machiavelli, in Brisighella

❖ LETTER 334
Lodovico Machiavelli to Niccolò Machiavelli
Ancona, 22 May 1527

To His Very Honored Father, Niccolò Machiavelli.
In Florence.
† *Christ.* 22 May 1527.

Honored father, etc. My last letter was from Pera.[1] Since then I have not written you because there was no reason to. At present, [I write] to tell you that I arrived here in Ancona two days ago, and yesterday I had a high fever. We are stabled and shut in here because of the disease.[2] I should like you to tell me by this man who is going to return here whether my horses have been sold and if you have buyers at hand, because I have seven horses here. If there are buyers for the big horse, I remind you it cost me a hundred ten ducats, so do not sell it for less. So give me news by this man right away, for he will not waste any time there; and we shall not depart from here if the said man has not returned. I shall not go on longer, because there is no time and also I do not feel too well, for we crossed over from Ragusa in thirty hours, and men were falling dead in the streets there from the plague. I am very afraid on this account. God help me. I send you my regards as always. God keep you always from ill. Give my regards to Madonna Marietta and tell her to pray God for me; greet the entire family.

Yours, Lodovico Machiavelli,
outside Ancona

❖ LETTER 335
Doctor R. to Niccolò Machiavelli

To the Very Honorable Niccolò Machiavelli.
In the Country.

Honored Niccolò. From what I gather from your letter, Bernardo's illness must be over and his urine is much better and you can see that it is less red, and from this, since changes are somewhat to be feared, I judge that you should not move him because the air is better there than here. You will purge him and you will judge from day to day and you will see that the case will turn out happily. His sweat should be dried with hot cloths and do not let him stay afterward in the place where he has been sweating. Be of good cheer. I send you my regards.

Doctor R.[1]

Appendix

Letter A appears in the Appendix because it cannot be dated precisely. It can be placed between 8 November 1520 (when Machiavelli received the charge of writing the history of Florence) and 6 March 1525, the date when Minerbetti was transferred from the diocese of Torres to that of Arezzo (Gaeta).

❖ Letter A
Francesco Minerbetti[1] to Niccolò Machiavelli

Outstanding Man, Honored as a Brother.

Since I know, from mutual and long-standing goodwill, that you will share your late night studies willingly with me, and I presume that, in writing of the history of our native land from 250 on, which was the source of several forms of freedom, it has been necessary for you to find the succession of Charles, count of Provence,[2] the cousin and brother-in-law of good king Louis of France, and the said Charles was called into Italy by Urban IV[3] and then by Clement IV,[4] Roman pontiffs, as champion of the Church, and granted the kingdoms of Naples and of Sicily, to deprive the son of Emperor Frederick II,[5] the last king of Naples, in whose direct bloodline and succession was Robert, the son of Charles, surnamed "the Lame," who was the first-born son of the above-mentioned Charles the First; I find that this Charles II[6] had many legitimate children, and the first was Charles, who reigned for several years for him in Naples and is called by some writers Charles III, because Charles II "the Lame," his father, during the rebellion and wars [that] Charles the First fought on the island of Sicily, was taken prisoner by King James of Aragon, who kept him under guard in Spain until his death; after that a daughter, who was left as his heiress, came to an agreement with him and freed him on the understanding that he and his successors[7] should not disturb or try to recover the Kingdom of Sicily again, so that, returning to Naples and finding that entire kingdom loyal to his first-born son, Charles III, he joined him in matrimony with a queen of Hungary, who had been left heiress to that kingdom, and he established Robert, his second-born and brother of the said Charles II, king of Hungary, after him, and he gave great states and principalities in the realm to his other children. And you will find that two of

them died in the defeat at Montecatini at the hands of Uguccione da Fag-
giuola or that there were born of the above-mentioned third ones [. . .] the
2nd "the Lame" [. . .] and that were captains in that conflict [. . .] their succession, or others of that royal blood who had remained in Italy, who did not
succeed to the Kingdom of Naples, I find no one but Louis, prince of
Taranto, who took to wife Queen Joanna I, the daughter of the previously
mentioned King Robert, who joined her in matrimony to a second-born son
of the above-mentioned Charles III, king of Hungary, or his nephew, surnamed Andreasso,[8] because the said Robert, having lost all his other sons and
daughters, decided to restore the kingdom after himself to the succession of
King Charles III of Hungary, his older brother, so that his only daughter,
Joanna, might also reign. I find that this Andrew, surnamed Andreasso, when
he inherited the kingdom, by the marriage, was put to death fraudulently by
her, since she was in love with her cousin Louis,[9] the prince of Taranto, and of
the royal blood himself; his affairs, as well as hers, were always administered by
Nicola Acciaiuoli, the grand seneschal of that kingdom, and they sold Prato to
the Commune of Florence. Such hatred arose in the first brother of the said
Andreasso, whom some writers call Louis, king of Hungary, that *by dint of violence* he came to take the Kingdom of Naples, and he captured it by force of
arms, and I find that Queen Joanna and King Louis, her consort, fled by sea to
Avignon, an ancient and natural state and county of his grandfather, King
Charles the First, and after selling that to the apostolic see, which still owns it,
Joanna was called by several citizens [of the Kingdom of Naples], assembled a
great army, and with her husband, Louis, came to battle with the Hungarian
king, and by an agreement they kept the peace within the kingdom [of
Naples]. And King Louis of Hungary,[10] as the writers say, since he was unused
to the air and customs of Italy, where he could not maintain his Hungarian
soldiers, who were moreover frightened by a great pestilence [. . .] to the
realm. A short time afterward her husband King Louis died [. . .] another of
base rank, and she behaved in such a fashion that, either because of that or because she did not observe the conventions made with the said king of Hungary, she so provoked him that he gave up all claim to the Kingdom of Naples
and of Sicily to a disciple of hers named Charles, who excelled in ability and
military skills and was born of royal blood and her succession, either of
Charles the First her great-grandfather or of Charles III, her father. Finally, I
desire to understand this, *namely,* who were his father and grandfather, because
some modern writers do not say but call him Charles IV[11] of Durazzo, and I
have found letters of his written to our townspeople that are signed Charles
IV, king of Naples, Sicily, and Jerusalem. Note that, with the might and the
support of the said king of Hungary, this man came to Italy, and was crowned
by Pope Urban VI,[12] and gained the realm by force of arms, and by trial put
to death the said Queen Joanna and her husband, named Ottone, the lord of
Brescia, and other accomplices of theirs. After that, upon the death of King
Louis of Hungary, he was called by the barons and crowned king of that king-

dom, which had no legitimate male heirs, and in brief he was killed by treachery through the machinations of the old queen, in her bedroom, or else attacked, and afterward, in a brief span of time, he died, and *meanwhile* the citizens preserved the Kingdom of Naples for his only son, Ladislas, and Joanna II, surnamed Giovanella, who were under the dominion of their mother, according to what some writers say, and through her shrewdness and wisdom the barons were kept loyal to the said Ladislas. I believe that, since you are most diligent, you must have found who was the mother of the said Ladislas and what became of Joanna, called Giovanella, his sister, after his death.

Fr. F. † Archbishop of Torres.

*A*lthough Gaeta's edition is the basis of our translation, we have incorporated many of the suggestions made by Giorgio Inglese in his 1984 review of that text. We hesitate to rush into the complicated issue of what constitutes either personal letter or diplomatic correspondence. Nevertheless, because Inglese's suggestions seem so frequently to be accurate, we herewith present Letters B, C, and D, our translation of letters that he believes should have been included in Gaeta's edition (see Inglese, Review of *Opere,* p. 272). Letter E is one that Inglese included in his 1989 edition of the correspondence from Machiavelli to Vettori and Guicciardini (which is not in Gaeta's edition).

❖ Letter B

Letter Attributed[1] to Totto Machiavelli to Niccolò Machiavelli
30 December 1504

To the Outstanding Man Niccolò Machiavelli, Florentine Secretary.
In Florence.
Jesus. In the name of God, 30 December 1504

Honored brother, etc. I wrote you on the first and on the 10th, the 11th, and the 14th, and I have no reply from you to any of them. I wrote you what ought to be done about our nephew, Giovanni, and that the courier would stay three hours so you could see whether you might arrange something.

Remind Battista to sow a lot of beans, and likewise quite a bit of the spelt, since there is time to have quite a bit sown; if there should not be enough spelt, have them purchase a few *staia*[2] of it.

Nothing else for this letter. God keep you.

I told you that a piece of fustian sells for 22 sealed florins.[3]

[unsigned letter, in Totto Machiavelli's hand]

❖ LETTER C
Biagio Buonaccorsi to Niccolò Machiavelli[1]
5 September 1506

To His Most Honored Niccolò Machiavelli, Florentine Secretary,
with the Supreme Pontiff.
At the Court.

My very dear Niccolò. I have written to you several times, and your first letter should let me know you have received them; thus with the sculptor Michelangelo *acting as deputy* I have sent you the money for the courier, the same that was received in payment.[2] He told me he would be there next Sunday and would find you, since he also has some of his own business to do. It should not be too much trouble for you to say a word about this, too.

I believe two hundred infantrymen, from among those of Mugello, as you will understand, are to be sent to Livorno.

[The king of] Aragon[3] is expected in Piombino anytime now, since he set out as of the 22nd of last month and here no ambassadors have been named as yet, <this will turn out like the other times.>

Your household is well, and there has been nothing new here since the passage of the emperor, who is warming up day by day. The rest is going as usual.

Narbonne[4] got here last night, and his arrival was learned of only once he was at the inn; he was given as much honor as was possible and was immediately taken from the inn and lodged at the Tornabuoni's, and all the formalities were extended to His Reverend Lordship that should have been done at his arrival. He will leave after lunch today for Incisa, where he will be honored once again.

Nothing else. *From Florence, 5 September 1506.*
Brother Biagio

❖ LETTER D
Niccolò Machiavelli to Giovanni de' Medici (passages)[1]
29 September 1512

I shall respectfully remind Your Most Reverend Lordship of one more thing. . . . I therefore believe that it is necessary for your house to win friends over to your side and not to turn them away—and this is not the way. I should like to give you an example of it derived from your house. . . . Hence I repeat that I should like to make friends for your house, not enemies. And so I should see to it that there would be a discussion in the Balìa[2] in which it would be decided that you should have from the Commune of Florence for a certain period four or five thousand ducats per year as an imbursement to your house . . .

❖ LETTER E
Niccolò Machiavelli to Francesco Guicciardini[1]
Florence, 24 March 1526

To Messer Francesco Guicciardini.

On 24 March 1525[6], Machiavelli writes to Guicciardini that the populace is surprised that there is still no news about the king's release[2] and that the Spaniards have gone back to Pontremoli,[3] where they cannot remain—they must either beat a hasty retreat or go on ahead.

24 March 1525[6]
Niccolò Machiavelli

*A*lthough Gaeta omitted the following letter from his 1984 edition, he printed it in the earlier edition he prepared in 1961 for Feltrinelli (p. 509). We include it here as contemporary testimony concerning Machiavelli's final hours, because controversy and apocryphal stories cloud the circumstances of his death (see Ridolfi, *Life,* pp. 248–250; *Vita 7,* pp. 596–597, 609–613). It was not until three hundred years later that *"tanto nomini nullum par elogium"* (no epitaph is equal to so great a name) was inscribed on Machiavelli's monument in the Basilica of Santa Croce in Florence.

❖ LETTER F
Piero Machiavelli to Francesco Nelli[1]
Florence, 22 June 1527

To the Notable Francesco Nelli, Florentine Lawyer.
In Pisa.

My very dear Francesco. I have the lamentable duty of informing you that our father, Niccolò, died on the 22nd of this month, from pains in the belly[2] caused by some medicine that he took on the 20th. He allowed Brother Matteo, who kept him company until his death, to hear the confession of his sins.[3] Our father left us in the deepest poverty, as you know.

When you come back up here, I shall tell you a good deal face-to-face. I am in a hurry and shall tell you nothing else except that I send you my regards.

[22 June] 1527.
Your relative,
Piero Machiavelli

❖ LETTER G

Niccolò Machiavelli to Alamanno Salviati[1]

Florence, 28 September 1509

To the Noble Alamanno Salviati, Most Worthy Captain of Pisa,
Honored Patron, etc.
In Pisa.

Magnificent One, etc. Since I do not think I could make you a more welcome present[2] than giving you a report on matters in Padua[3] and on the emperor, I shall write you concerning what their situation is and what judgment is made, or can be made, about their outcome and intention. And should you recognize any presumption in my judgment, Your Magnificence will please excuse it, while taking for granted that I discuss it with him in confidence.

On the tenth day of this month, the emperor was with his army in the town of Santa Croce, about a mile from Padua. Since he wanted to set himself up in a place where it would be both easier to bombard the city and more convenient for intercepting any supplies that might come from Venice, and since he needed to go wide around the city to avoid certain swamps, he set up his billets at Bovolento on the river Bachillone, seven miles from Padua, where they plundered and slaughtered a good number of peasants who had taken refuge with their livestock.

Then he set up another camp at Stra, a country house situated at the confluence of the Bacchillone and the Brenta, about four miles from Padua. From there he drew closer to the city and began bombarding it on the twenty-first.

He garrisoned his army from the Portello gate to the one leading to Trevi, which is said to be a distance of three miles; the army took up a mile in width. They say this army of his consists of thirty thousand foot soldiers, about seventeen thousand of whom are Germans; the rest are troops brought there by the duke of Ferrara, the pope, and the king of France. Indeed, they say that fresh German infantrymen arrive every day without any pay other than the profits from booty in the present and hope for the future. Furthermore, there are twelve thousand or more cavalrymen with him; half are from Burgundy and Germany, the rest are all Italian and French. He has forty pieces of heavy artillery and up to one hundred medium and light pieces.

Your envoys arrived in camp on the twenty-first, and their letters date from the twenty-fourth. They report that at this time the greater part of his artillery has been sited, that he already has knocked down the entire wall from Santo Stefano to the Mercato Nuovo ^and^[4] that some of his heaviest artillery can shoot some three hundred pounds of iron. They make marvelous thrusts, and no fortification can withstand them; it was learned from people fleeing Padua that they have killed many people, among whom are said to be Lo Zitolo and Messer Peretto Corso.

They report that the emperor is resolved to storm the city and to act as a commander and as a soldier and that his camp is extremely united and has copious supplies of foodstuffs.

Your envoys write absolutely nothing about things going on within the city, except that they fire on the camp constantly and damage it quite a bit; Messer Luzio Malvezi went to Venice for money with a good escort and returned to Padua safely without much interference.

Such is the report from your ambassadors. We have also heard about their internal troop arrangements and defenses from a friar who came here from Padua eight days ago; he says the following. First, they have filled the moats around the city with water and have erected some bastions around the walls to protect the moats and walls from outside; then there is the inside wall, all around which they have stuck shafts eight feet[5] from the walls and from one shaft to the next they have made a chain with beams and timbers to be used as a fence; and they have filled in the area between the fence and the wall with earth, which they have pounded and heaped up as much as possible. In addition, still on the inside, they have dug a ditch of approximately twenty-eight feet in the French manner. Finally, they have then built a protective shelter sixteen feet high over the ditch; the part toward the inside is leveled in such a way that horses can run on it. Behind this {ditch}[6] ^shelter^ they have made wide clearings so that the horses can be driven onto it.

This friar reports a mass of munitions and artillery spread out over the ramparts, and in the casemates {above} of these ditches he says there are ten thousand hired infantrymen, four thousand cavalrymen, ten thousand men drawn from Venice, and more than four thousand peasants—all united and ready for defense; they show no fear of anything, and they rely on both the supplies laid in and the weather becoming bad for the siege.

Matters are in this state, as you see, and people here are arguing first about whether or not Padua has to be lost and then—whether or not Padua is lost—whether we have to fear {if} ^that^ the emperor will now upset affairs in Tuscany or Rome.

I shall pass over whatever people may be saying about whether Padua will be lost, because I see no one who knows anything about it discussing it and each person discusses it from his own viewpoint, but we shall discuss only whether we have anything to fear from either of the two outcomes mentioned above.

For now, the majority of those here are quite afraid of it, whether or not the emperor captures it, because they say if he takes Padua, his prestige will be so great that the king of France will side with him and he will come and get the crown without hindrance—we, and all the rest in Italy, will be at his disposal; if he does not take it, he will reach an agreement with Venice against the rest of us; and he will do the same thing because, since he is under arms and is uniting the armies, no one can see any opposition.

But I am of the opposite opinion, and I do not fear him whether or not he takes Padua. First of all, I maintain that if he does not seize it, he has to do one of three things: he withdraws to Germany and leaves matters here in the hands of others; or he withdraws to Vicenza and Verona, relieving himself, in large part, of the expenses for the infantry and, with the aid of the French, expecting to wage a fightable war with the Venetians during the course of this winter; or he actually reaches an accord with the Venetians.

In the first two cases, there is no need to fear him; as for the third, which is an agreement with the Venetians, such an agreement needs to be either with his allies' consent ^either^ against the wishes of all or of a part of them.

In the first instance, there is not much need to fear him, because his allies are going to keep him in order and they ought to want to save themselves completely—and their friends at least in part.

If he does it against his allies' wishes, I cannot see what harm it can do us, and I do not see even {that} how such an agreement can be reached with his interest and those of the Venetians in it, because, if we want to determine whether an agreement must ensue, we must first scrutinize the motives that prompt the parties and, if there are any, then to believe in them.

The motives that prompt the emperor concern where he may see honor and utility lying. What prompts the Venetians concerns where they might see they could gain time, avoiding for the moment those dangers that may threaten their freedom, and where they might lessen their expenses.

Now, I do not see what kind of agreement could arise among them against the allies' wishes that would be to the advantage of each of them and where there would be the two aims mentioned above.

First of all, for the emperor to get utility and honor out of it, the Venetians would have to give him either Padua or so much money that he could go with his army toward a profit that would compensate for the {profit from} ^campaign against^ Padua that he gave up. Given either of these two conditions, it seems to me that the Venetians gain neither time nor money, because whereas they have, in a manner of speaking, one enemy on their back, they will have three of them: France, Spain, and the pope. They have all but put their swords in it and will now pull them out, so that such an agreement does not get them out of danger or even free them from expenses; rather, it increases them, because, in addition to the large sums of money they would have to give the emperor, they would also have to continue paying the army they now find themselves with so that they do not remain at its mercy, since they cannot trust it.

Therefore, I do not know how or why they have to reach an agreement with an emperor who is unable to take Padua to double expenses and to find themselves in a bigger war than before. So, in conclusion, I do not see, first of all, how this agreement can be reached against the allies' will, and even if it were to be reached, I do not see how we have anything to fear from it.

Nor does it seem to me, either, that {thus} it might be reached with the consent of part of those allies mentioned above, since the prestige of the emperor in Italy is not in the interest of France, or Spain, or the pope for reasons that are so well known that they need not be commented upon. With the result that, if he does not take Padua, with or without an agreement, we do not have to fear him.

Nor need we fear him even if he does take Padua, because the emperor, once he has taken it, must do one of two things: either abide by the agreement reached at Cambrai or break it.

If he abides by the agreement, he will, first and foremost, have to agree with the allies about what to do with the Venetians and put an end to the Venetian war either through a pact with them or through all-out destruction of the Venetians. Destruction seems difficult: one difficulty arises because part of his allies wants Venice to stay as it is, especially the king of Spain and the pope—both of whom will aways feel that with Venice they are keeping a thorn in the side of the emperor and the king of France; the other difficulty is the season—it does not permit the water supply to be managed, and without it the army will fade away; hence it is necessary for them to opt for an agreement that the Venetians remain there living under their own laws, and having done this, he may then think about going to get the crown, which, even if it is settled, means there is not much to fear from him, as was pointed out above.

If he does not want to abide by the Cambrai agreement, he will first realize that he lacks one-third of the army he now has, because, considering his army, a third of it is not his, he has so many troops from France, the pope, and Ferrara; these troops, once Padua is taken, will draw closer together again because their captains will immediately become jealous of the emperor's prestige, since that is not to the advantage of any of them, as I have said. And the French, one might say, are at arms because they are ready with men at arms and with money and have the Swiss at hand so that the emperor will have so much to do, before he can come easily into Tuscany, that a great deal of time will go by, because I do not see how he can go beyond and leave his territory taken if he has not first settled all internal affairs. And settling them by force will take no small amount of time or expenses. And, I am sure, if ever the emperor found himself isolated and without people to subsidize him and was kept waiting by whoever might be able to spend money, he would find himself without an army in no time at all—which has happened to him on many campaigns and on many an occasion. And if anyone should say that the Venetians would subsidize him with money, it would make me laugh, because their wound has spilled so much blood that whenever it is partly stanched, it will seem to them that they are so weak that they will be unwilling to open it again, if their wounds hurt them as they do others.

I therefore see the situation in this way,[7] and while all these princes are alive, I am not very afraid—even if this opinion runs counter to most people's.

Both eager to hear your own letter and partly to delight you with this trifle,[8] I was prompted[9] to write you.

Farewell. Florence. The twenty-eighth of September 1509.

Your Servant Niccolò Machiavelli, Secretary

Notes

1. See Letter 286, n. 7, for the text of this letter.

2. When Machiavelli and his friends use *fortuna* and *virtù* in their correspondence, they challenge translators. Generally speaking, we have used "Fortune" when we believe the context implies that the writers are referring to the abstract idea—inherited from Latin and medieval writers—of that powerful, pervasive, and arbitrary force that militates against a person's intelligent foresight; we use "fortune" when we believe the writer refers to good or bad luck, although clearly "fortune" often results from the operations of "Fortune." Neither "Fortune" nor "fortune," however, can be separated from the multivalent word *virtù* because these correspondents frequently conjoin these two words. Because they can draw on a wide range of potential meanings, generally speaking we have left the word untranslated. Rarely is "virtue," in the sense of "moral excellence," a proper equivalent for *virtù*. The sense of "virtue" in the phrase "by virtue of," namely, that of "force," "power," or "authority," is closer to the use in Renaissance Italian. For Machiavelli in particular, *virtù* suggests a person's flexibility in initiating effective, efficient, and energetic action that is based on both a courageous assertion of the will and an ability to execute the products of one's calculations. As such, *virtù* "seems to be the heart of the Machiavellian ambiguities. . . . On the one hand *virtù* is that by which we innovate, and so let loose sequences of contingency beyond our prediction of control so that we become prey to *fortuna;* on the other hand, *virtù* is that internal to ourselves by which we resist *fortuna* and impose upon her patterns of order, which may even become patterns of moral order. . . . The more the individual relies upon his *virtù* the less he need rely upon his *fortuna* and—since *fortuna* is by definition unreliable—the safer he is. But if *virtù* is that by which we acquire power, the ideal type . . . is the individual who acquires it wholly by the exercise of his personal qualities and not at all as the result of contingencies and circumstances outside himself" (Pocock, *Machiavellian Moment,* p. 167). Kahn makes an important argument for relating these considerations to what she terms "Machiavellian rhetoric": "the problems of political innovation in the realm of contingency that the new prince encounters are rhetorical problems: problems that cannot be resolved by applying fixed moral principles on the one hand or mere force on the other, problems whose solutions are inextricable from the use of imitation, representation, and persuasion. Thus rhetoric is not simply an instrument of *virtù* but is also analogous to *virtù* in the sense that both are faculties for responding to the realm of contingency or fortune; and *virtù* is rhetorical because what counts as *virtù* is produced from within a rhetorical analysis of the

circumstances at hand and varies accordingly. Political innovation proves to be inseparable from rhetorical invention" (*Machiavellian Rhetoric,* p. 17).

3. Atkinson, p. 93. For the full bibliographical reference for this and all subsequent references throughout this text, see the Abbreviations and Works Cited at the back of this edition.

4. For a more detailed examination of the complex relationship between Machiavelli and Buonaccorsi, see Fachard, *Biagio Buonaccorsi,* and Sasso, *"Biagio."*

5. For a discussion of the technical as well as the looser uses of the word *compare,* see Najemy, *Between Friends,* p. 82, n. 59. It ought to be observed that in the Notes to the Vettori-Machiavelli exchanges the reader is referred to some—but not every—relevant passage in Najemy's *Between Friends.* Their letters during this period represent a lode rich in implications and interpretive potential. Najemy's study is an excellent, informative, and subtly argued one. It throws a bright spotlight on the interplay of these two figures and does their letters ample justice. So, readers would do well to consult his book, even when they are not specifically referred to it in the Notes.

6. See also Najemy, "Machiavelli's Service," pp. 107–108, where this letter is treated as an example of Machiavelli's "reluctance to respect the conventions and proprieties of the political system within which he worked . . . its unwritten rules of deference and hierarchy" (p. 103).

7. See also the relevant passages in Najemy, *Between Friends,* for his argument about Machiavelli's talent for empathy: e.g., pp. 134–35, 137–138, and 234–238.

8. Dionisotti, *"Letterario,"* translated by Olivia Holmes in Ascoli and Kahn, *Machiavelli and the Discourse of Literature,* p. 49; and in the Italian edition, Dionisotti, *"Machiavelli letterato,"* p. 264.

9. See Najemy, *Between Friends,* pp. 143–146, for a more detailed discussion of the implications of Vettori's challenge. *La Mandragola* would also be an excellent example of meeting Vettori's challenge, but the argument here is restricted to Machiavelli's political and historical writings.

10. Ficino, *Letters,* vol. 2, p. 30. In a slightly different translation, this sentence serves as an epigraph for Ian McEwan's 1992 novel *Black Dogs.*

11. The letter, which was probably written in September or October 1476, when Machiavelli was seven years old, is brief enough to quote its entirety:

> Giovanni, write to me sometime about what you have been doing in those matters common to us both, or what you want to be done by me; that is, my good Giovanni, if you know what you want at this time. At present I do not really know what I want; it may be that I do not really want what I know and want that which I do not know.
>
> However, I think that things are not settled for you under the benign influence of your Jupiter progressing in Pisces; but for me, under the malign influence of my Saturn retrogressing in Leo, they are far from settled.

Nevertheless, as we often observe, thanks should be given in all things to Him who, from His infinite goodness, converts all things to the good. (Ficino, III, 22)

For more on both this letter and Ficino, see Klibansky et al., *Saturn and Melancholy,* pp. 254–274, especially pp. 257–58. It was Ficino "who really gave shape to the idea of the melancholy man of genius and revealed it to the rest of Europe" (p. 255).

12. Callimaco echoes these thoughts in his opening soliloquy to act 4, scene 1, of *La Mandragola:* "How many men have gone to Hell! Why should you be ashamed to go there too? Face up to your destiny. Flee from evil, but if you can't, bear it like a man" (Machiavelli, *Comedies,* p. 231). On this passage from *La Mandragola,* see Hulliung, *Citizen Machiavelli,* pp. 210–211.

13. Young-Bruehl, "Biographer's Empathy," p. 11.

1497-1498

Letter 1

1. *Draft:* this entire draft is in Latin. Aside from several notations in his father's *Libro di ricordi,* we have little documentary evidence about Machiavelli's life prior to 1497. Two references occur in a legal context. His father, Bernardo, appointed his son Niccolò as representative to deal with the dowry of his daughter, Primavera (28 April 1494). When Machiavelli's sister became a widow, Primavera appointed him as one of her representatives to "'exact all payments of the Monte'—presumably, the *Monte delle Doti,* or state dowry fund" (Stephens and Butters, "New Light," p. 56; text, p. 65).

2. *[. . .]:* Gaeta indicates that there is an ellipsis in the text at this point; all subsequent ellipses will also be enclosed in square brackets.

Letter 2

1. *has:* this letter addresses its recipient in the third person, as befits a supplication to higher authority; in the second paragraph, however, and in the Latin phrases toward the end, it falls back into the *voi* (second person plural) form characteristic of Machiavelli's letters to people in authority or of high birth, even friends. The nature of the second person used will be indicated throughout the notes to these letters whenever it departs from the norm, since English does not make such distinctions.

2. *through our venerable ancestors:* text in Martelli, p. 46, reads "through our ancestors."

3. *unless your clemency:* text in Martelli, p. 47, reads "unless Your Clemency."

Letter 3

1. *9 March 1498:* it was the custom in Florence to begin each new year not on 1 January but on 25 March; Florentines used the designation "in the

year of the Incarnation." All dates in these letters are regularized according to modern practice; thus, although Machiavelli signed this letter "dated Florence, 9 March 1497," it should read 1498.

2. *you:* Machiavelli addresses Becchi as *voi*, the usual form of address in this correspondence.

3. *copies:* there is no reason to assume that Machiavelli sent the copies of Savonarola's two sermons, those of 11 and 18 February 1498, to Becchi, although Machiavelli clearly seems to have been in communication with him about how matters stood in Florence.

4. *Carnival:* these sermons, including the Carnival one of 25 February, can be found in Savonarola, *Prediche,* I, pp. 3–36, 37–67, and 68–98.

5. *brief:* it is dated 26 February 1498.

6. *Fra Domenico:* the loyal Fra Domenico da Pescia, who was to die with Savonarola. For the sermon of 1 March 1498, see Savonarola, *Prediche,* I, pp. 122–145.

7. *Exodus:* Exodus 1:12, quoted as in the Vulgate; the King James version reads, "But the more they afflicted them, the more they multiplied and grew"; see Savonarola, *Prediche,* pp. 146–175, for the first sermon at San Marco on 2 March.

8. *right-reason:* cf. Thomas Aquinas, *Summa Theologiae,* II, 2, q. 47, 2, where *cognitio* = *ratio* (Gaeta).

9. *Ascension Day:* on 4 May 1497, one year earlier, Savonarola, while he was preaching in Santa Reparata, was attacked by opponents who intended to assassinate him (Gaeta).

10. *Moses slew an Egyptian:* Exodus 2:11–12; for this sermon of 3 March, see Savonarola, *Prediche,* I, pp. 176–203 (Gaeta).

11. *in his behalf:* in their reply of 3 March to Pope Alexander VI's brief mentioned above, dated 26 February.

1499

Letter 4

1. *Messer Antonio Grimani:* an important Venetian statesman (1436–1523) who opposed Charles VIII's invasion in 1495 but later joined with France under Louis XII to foster Venetian expansion. Until his humiliating defeat at Zonchio (Navarino, modern Pylos, in Greece) in August 1499, he was Venice's general of the sea and procurator of St. Mark. He eventually regained his good name and became doge of Venice in 1521.

2. *Venetian Signoria:* throughout this letter Machiavelli refers to the Signoria of Venice; he does not specify to what branch of that republic's government he is referring (the Great Council; the senate, responsible for policy formation; the college, responsible for arranging the senate's agenda and carrying out its decisions; or the Council of Ten, responsible for security).

3. *sultan [of the Turks]:* Bajazet (Bayazid) II (1481–1512), who was constantly attacking Venice while simultaneously negotiating with Pope Alexan-

der VI about his brother Djem, whom the pope held as hostage in order to keep the Ottoman Empire at bay. Bajazet would rather have had Djem dead but settled for his being imprisoned until his death at Naples in 1495. Square brackets here and throughout this translation will indicate translators' emendations; square brackets also designate ellipses in Gaeta's text.

4. *agreement with Pisa:* the peace treaty that Ercole d'Este, duke of Ferrara, negotiated in April.

5. *duke:* i.e., Ludovico Sforza.

6. *archduke:* better known as Philip I the Handsome (*el Hermoso*) (1478–1506), he was the son of Maximilian I, the Holy Roman Emperor. He bore several titles: archduke of Austria and duke of Burgundy. He married Juana, the daughter of King Ferdinand and Queen Isabella of Spain, and established the Hapsburg dynasty in Spain; their children were Archduke Charles of Hapsburg, also known as Charles V (1500–1558), Holy Roman Emperor (1519–1556) and King of Spain as Charles I (1516–1556); and Archduke Ferdinand of Hapsburg, also known as Ferdinand I (1503–1564), Holy Roman Emperor from 1556 to 1564.

7. *pope:* Rodrigo Borgia, Alexander VI, pope from 1492 until 1503.

8. *King Frederick:* Frederick I of Aragon (1452–1504) was king of Naples (or of the Two Sicilies) from 1496 to 1501.

9. *arbitration:* that worked out by the duke of Ferrara concerning Pisa.

10. *Apulia:* the region around the port city of Bari in southeastern Italy, bordered by the Adriatic Sea and the Gulf of Taranto.

11. *prefect:* probably the prefect of Rome, the gonfalonier of the Holy Roman Church, Giovanni della Rovere (1457–1501); his brother Giuliano della Rovere (1443–1513) was a cardinal and was to become Pope Julius II in 1503.

Letter 5

1. *Antonio da Colle:* Antonio Guidotti da Colle was a notary in the Second Chancellery (Gaeta).

Letter 6

1. *temporizing . . . of time:* cf. the use of a similar phrase, common in the dispatches and writings of Florentine politicians, in *Prince,* 3; see Atkinson, p. 116, note to l. 203–204.

Letter 7

1. *Biagio Buonaccorsi:* The young Biagio Buonaccorsi (1472–1526) entered the Florentine chancellery in early August 1498, less than three months after Machiavelli did. Within two years he became coadjutor of the first chancellery. Though he was sent on fewer missions than Machiavelli, he was posted to Pisa during June and July 1500, to France from September 1501 to July 1502, to Mantua in May 1503, and to Rome from November 1505 to June 1506. While he was fulfilling these duties, he took notes (*Sunmario di cose*

seguìte da dì 6 di giugnio 1498 a dì X di settembre 1508) for what was to become an important contemporary document that objectively detailed the political events from 1498 to 1512: his *Diario de' successi più importanti seguìti in Italia, et particolarmente in Fiorenza dall'anno 1498 in sino all'anno 1512.* Although neither Machiavelli nor Guicciardini mentions it in their histories of Florence, Jacopo Nardi virtually incorporates Biagio's account into his *Historia della città di Fiorenza* (1494–1531). The *Sunmario* is also important for evidence that Leonardo da Vinci's designs for diverting the river Arno during Florence's attack on Pisa in 1504 were not the ones Machiavelli used. For more on Biagio, see Fachard, *Biagio Buonaccorsi;* Martelli, *"Preistoria";* and Sasso, *"Biagio."*

2. *governor:* Paolo Vitelli, who assumed command on 1 June (Gaeta).

3. *Monsignor Ascanio:* Cardinal Ascanio Sforza (1455–1505), Ludovico Sforza's brother. Originally a supporter of Pope Alexander VI, Ascanio sought Church reform and soon became the pope's enemy. His desire to become pope was never realized.

Letter 8

1. *there:* i.e., in Forlì.

2. *Her Excellency:* Caterina Sforza, Countess of Forlì.

Letter 9

1. *Napoli di Romania:* the Greek port of Nauplia (modern Nàvplion) in the eastern Peloponnesus, at the head of the Gulf of Argolis.

2. *Cattaro:* now Kotor, a port city on the Adriatic Sea in Montenegro (former Yugoslavia).

3. *Gulf of Morea:* Morea was a Renaissance name for the Peloponnesus; this would seem to refer to the Turks dragging ships from the Gulf of Megara to the Gulf of Corinth, across the Isthmus of Corinth.

4. *this Signoria:* i.e., Venice.

5. *Cavo Sant'Angelo:* the Italian name for a cape in the Venetian Peloponnesus, probably what is known today as Cape Malea on the southeastern tip of the Peloponnesus.

6. *Valona:* Vlone (Vlona, Vlore, Vlora; formerly Avlona), a port city in southern Albania on the Adriatic Sea.

7. *gulf:* the Adriatic Sea, then often referred to as the Gulf of Venice (Gaeta).

8. *Friuli:* a region of northern Italy, on the border of the former Yugoslavia.

9. *court:* i.e., of France.

10. *loaded up:* Inglese would render this as "were hoisting their sails."

11. *Uson:* since Cesare Borgia was on his way to Lyons, this town is probably Auxonne—or maybe Aubusson—though neither town is in the old region known as Berry, which comprises the modern-day *départements* of Cher and Indre.

Letter 10

1. *Messer Marcello:* Marcello Virgilio di Adriano Berti, who is frequently referred to as "Marcello" in the letters of Machiavelli's chancellery friends through 1510 and as "Marcello Virgilio Adriani" by twentieth-century commentators.

2. *Ser Antonio:* Antonio della Valle.

3. *9 o'clock:* translation of *insino alle 3 ore,* "until 3 hours" (after six in the evening).

4. *Gianiacopo:* Gian Giacomo Trivulzio (1441–1518) was a famous Milanese military commander whom Ludovico Sforza employed until the French threat became too great. Trivulzio then went over to the French, eventually entering Milan with them; his reward was to be named governor of Milan by Louis XII. Toward the end of his life he led the armies of the League of Cambrai against the Venetians at Agnadello in 1509 and helped the French defeat the Swiss at the Battle of Marignano in 1515.

5. *duke:* Ludovico Sforza, duke of Milan.

6. *that Signoria:* i.e., of Venice (Gaeta).

7. *Lunigiana:* the region around Luni, the former capital of Etruria in northwest Tuscany.

8. *to peck about:* translation of *sgallinare,* a familiar term for "pecking," i.e., picking up extra money by taking a mission.

Letter 11

1. *Chancellery Secretary:* translation of *cancielliere,* "chancellery secretary," here and throughout these letters, to avoid confusion with "chancery," i.e., a court of equity or the court of the Lord Chancellor of the United Kingdom.

2. *early October:* Ridolfi (*Life,* p. 264, n. 13; *Vita 7,* p. 441, n. 15) suggests 5 October as a reasonable date for this letter.

3. *opprobrium:* alludes to Paolo Vitelli's decision to withdraw his troops rather than to attack with them in early August (Gaeta).

4. *Piero Gambacorti's flight:* a Pisan military leader who fled to Lucca after Vitelli captured their stronghold of Stampace (Guicciardini, *Storie Fiorentine,* p. 181; Domandi, p. 168).

1500

Letter 12

1. *Roberto Acciaiuoli:* (1467–1547) after a career in the Church, he became active in Florentine politics, serving in Rome, which he knew well, and in France, where Machiavelli came across him again. Because his social rank was higher than Machiavelli's, he was sent as an emissary to Gonzalo Fernández de Córdoba, the great Spanish general who was threatening to aid Pisa in May 1505, despite the fact that Soderini would have preferred to send Machiavelli. In 1518 he was Florence's gonfalonier of justice and in 1522 a prior of liberty. Toward the end of Machiavelli's life, Acciaiuoli was sent to France as

both papal nuncio and Florentine emissary (1526–1527).

2. *Giovanni Folchi:* one of Machiavelli's friends, to whom he dedicated his *capitolo* "Dell' ingratitudine"; for Folchi's involvement in the Boscoli conspiracy in 1510, see Butters, *Governors,* pp. 210–211.

3. *jubilees:* although they could be proclaimed more often, every twenty-five years a papal proclamation would set aside a specific period of time of special solemnity; often the pope would grant an indulgence during this period to Catholics who performed certain acts of repentance and piety. Landucci says that on 25 December 1499, "The Jubilee began at Rome, and a number of northerners passed through Florence" (p. 175).

4. *this fellow:* may refer to Pope Alexander VI.

Letter 13

1. *Luca degli Albizzi:* Luca di Antonio degli Albizzi (1459–1502) served Florence in several political capacities (prior in 1490 and 1497 and one of the *Dieci di Balìa* in 1498) and on several diplomatic missions (commissioner to various cities from 1494 to 1496 and to the Florentine forces at Pisa from 1499 to 1500 and ambassador to France in 1501) (Gaeta). Biagio Buonaccorsi, who was with Luca degli Albizzi on his mission to Pisa in 1500, wrote a *"Delle cose fatte da Luca di Antonio degli Albizzi e dell'assalto dato a Pisa dai Fiorentini con le genti francesi nel 1500"* (see Fachard, *Biagio Buonaccorsi,* p. 8, n. 6).

2. *Totto:* Totto di Messer Bernardo Machiavelli (1475–1522), Machiavelli's younger brother, destined for a career in the Church (Gaeta).

3. *Messer Marcello:* Marcello Virgilio di Adriano Berti (Gaeta).

4. *what you desire:* from the official diplomatic correspondence it is clear that Machiavelli was constantly short of cash and repeatedly sought proper payment for his services, here an amount equivalent to della Casa's; see the following letter for this problem's resolution.

5. *Francesco:* della Casa.

6. *Cristofano:* this may be Cristoforo da Casale, mentioned in Letter 172, or Cristoforo Sernigi, mentioned in Letters 223 and 262 (Gaeta); Gaeta also lists three other "Cristoforos" known to be active in the Florentine chancelleries.

7. *Buondelmonti:* Rosso di Battista Buondelmonti, a member of an old, powerful Florentine family currently living in Lyons, an important French commercial center (Gaeta).

8. *La Ventura:* built by Paolo Vitelli during the siege of Pisa (Gaeta).

9. *Panciatica:* a faction friendly to the Medici, whereas the Cancelliera faction had a less aristocratic tinge to it. These events occurred in August 1500. Since Pistoia is only about twenty-three miles northwest of Florence, the Signoria was worried lest Cesare Borgia get involved, thus making the situation a potentially dangerous one. The Signoria sent Machiavelli to Pistoia on several occasions in 1501.

10. *hands of the Swiss:* the Swiss captured and imprisoned Luca di Anto-

nio degli Albizzi, one of the Florentine commissioners to Pisa, on 9 July 1500.

11. *Lorenzo Machiavelli:* probably Lorenzo di Niccolò d'Alessandro Machiavelli, who died in 1539 (Gaeta). Najemy (*Between Friends,* p. 76) refers to a Lorenzo di Niccolò Machiavelli, from another branch of Machiavelli's clan, who may have married one of Francesco Vettori's aunts.

12. *Brother Anfroi [Ancroi]:* also mentioned in Letter 18.

13. *Casa:* Filippo Casavecchia, one of Machiavelli's most loyal friends in the chancellery, remained faithful to him after Machiavelli fell from grace with the Medici in 1512, at which time references to him become more frequent. He was one of the first readers of *The Prince,* even before Machiavelli told Vettori about his study.

14. *Ser Antonio:* Antonio della Valle (Gaeta).

15. *by the Grazie:* where the woman alluded to lives (Gaeta).

16. *Ser Raffaello:* Raffaello Fedini (Gaeta).

17. *Gaddi:* Francesco Gaddi, a powerful official in the Second Chancellery, had been one of Machiavelli's rivals for his position in 1498, when Gaddi was a teacher of rhetoric at the university.

18. *Baccio:* perhaps Bartolomeo Ruffini (Gaeta).

Letter 14

1. *parity:* Machiavelli's brother was instrumental in finally getting Machiavelli's per diem allowance increased so that it would be equal to della Casa's. This parity gave Machiavelli more total recompense than della Casa, but he deserved it since he was the actual writer of the reports to Florence (Ridolfi, *Life,* p. 39; *Vita 7,* p. 63).

2. *florins:* in the early Middle Ages, the usual circulating medium of commercial exchange was a thin silver penny, or denarius; 12 of these equaled a solidus (called a soldo in Italian), and 20 soldi or 240 denari made a libra (called a lira in Italian). Neither the solidus nor the libra circulated. In 1252 Florence issued the *fiorino d'oro,* a gold florin with the city's patron saint, St. John the Baptist, on one side and their armorial lily on the other side; it was originally issued at a value of 20 soldi or one libra to the florin. By the middle of the fourteenth century, its value had risen to 60 silver soldi or 3 librae of silver denari. Two factors influenced this rise: other European mints debased their pennies by increasing the percentage of copper in them; simultaneously, there was greater pressure applied to gold as a solid base to support world trade. The Florentine gold florin was thought throughout the world of commerce to be solidly backed. As the demand for gold increased, the metal naturally rose in value. The florin did, too. Consequently, during the period covered by these letters, there was constant fluctuation in the value of a florin. By Machiavelli's day the regular gold florin was worth about 6 or 7 lire. This was also the value of a *scudo.* Other terms for Florentine money include the *fiorino largo,* or *fiorino d'oro [in oro],* so called because its circumference was enlarged and its weight was increased, which was worth about 7 lire in 1500 and 7 lire

and 10 soldi by 1531; and the *fiorino piccolo* or *fiorino di suggello,* called a "sealed florin" because it had been weighed, tested, and sealed in purses or boxes, which became debased as currency values fluctuated and was worth about 4 lire—the same value attributed also to the *fiorino di studio* (see Ridolfi, *Life,* pp. 182–183; *Vita 7,* pp. 285-286). In Letter 100, Totto Machiavelli suggests that in 1505 three sealed florins were equivalent to two gold ducats.

3. *Filippo Buondelmonti:* (1434–1522) a rich Florentine active in commercial and financial affairs and a doctor of civil and canon law. He participated in Florentine political life as a prior and member of the *Dieci di Libertà e Pace* and of the *Dieci di Balìa.* He was also an ardent supporter of the war against Pisa but a member of the pro-Medici faction against Piero Soderini (Gaeta).

4. *Gonfalonier:* Niccolò Zati (Gaeta).

5. *Primavera:* Machiavelli's sister.

6. *Nasi:* an important Florentine commercial family (Gaeta).

Letter 15

1. *Vespucci:* Machiavelli's trusted friend and assistant in the Second Chancellery (Gaeta).

2. *ten good men:* in May 1499, irritated by the lack of progress in the war against Pisa, Florence refused to elect members of the *Dieci di Balìa,* responsible for carrying out the war. The new *Balìa,* elected 19 September 1500, was composed of Francesco Gualterotti, Piero Soderini, Niccolò Zati, Giuliano Salviati, Antonio Del Vigna, Clemente Sernigi, Giovanni di Santi Ambrogi, Gioacchino Guasconi, Leonardo Guidotti, and Marco Baroncini (Gaeta).

3. *debtors' list:* translation of *a specchio* (literally "in the mirror"), the designation for those officially in debt.

4. *Modone . . . Friuli:* the modern Mesene(i), an important port in the Peloponnesus; Corfu is a port city on the island northwest of the Peloponnesus; Friuli is a district in northern Italy northeast of Venice. All this news is in the context of Venice's attempt to keep the Turks from reducing her power in the Adriatic and Mediterranean.

5. *King Frederick:* the scene quickly shifts to Naples and a discussion of Frederick of Aragon (1452–1504), who became king of Naples in 1496 and was striving to stave off attempts by King Louis XII, a Valois king who pressed a complicated genealogical claim to Naples through the Angevin line, and Ferdinand the Catholic, king of Spain from 1479 until 1516, who was capitalizing on the confused situation of his relatives in Naples in order to control Naples. Within two months Louis and Ferdinand would agree secretly to the Treaty of Granada, whereby they agreed to conquer Naples and to divide the territory between them. This deceit was not revealed until June 1501, when both kings initiated their Neapolitan campaign. King Ferdinand presents a problem of identification because of what he ruled: as Ferdinand V of Castile he jointly ruled that region with Isabella; as Ferdinand II he was king of Aragon from 1479 to 1516 and thus united the two kingdoms; as Ferdinand

III of Naples he ruled from 1504 to 1516. He was king of Sicily from 1468 to 1516. For the sake of convenience, he will be designated as "Ferdinand the Catholic" in these notes.

6. *Ten:* i.e., Ten of War (the Ten of War were often thus designated).

Letter 16

1. *His Most Reverend Monsignor Cardinal:* the Signoria dispatched Piero Soderini as its ambassador to Giovanni della Rovere (a prefect of Rome and captain general of the Church of Rome) and his brother, Cardinal Giuliano della Rovere.

2. *king:* this is the first of the coded material in Gaeta's edition. We follow his text, but in some instances it seems unclear to us exactly where the coded material begins and ends.

3. *you:* Soderini is using the plural *voi* here; its singular could be either *tu* or *voi*, but he tended to use the latter for more official communications, like the present one.

4. *Monsignor of Rouen:* Georges d'Amboise, archbishop of Rouen at this point in his career (Gaeta).

5. *Andrea Doria:* he was currently serving the della Roveres as the commander of their fortress at Senigallia; see Letter 317, n. 19.

Letter 17

1. *Albizzi:* Florence had wanted Luca di Antonio degli Albizzi to go to the French court with some new responses and information for Machiavelli and della Casa to present to Louis XII; Francesco Pepi, Bernardo Rucellai, and Giovanni Ridolfi all found ways to get out of going on what they considered to be an ill-fated mission to help Machiavelli and della Casa.

Letter 18

1. *20–29 October:* the dates for the writing and actual sending of the letter (Gaeta).

2. *Signor Marcello:* Marcello Virgilio Adriani.

3. *Biagio:* Biagio Buonaccorsi.

4. *Andrea and Giuliano:* Andrea di Romolo and Giuliano della Valle (Gaeta).

5. *they say at* ronfa: a play on the words *ronfa*, a sixteenth-century card game, and the Latin *rompha*, arthritis.

6. *Protesilaus:* a mythical Greek leader who was the first to jump ashore as the Greeks landed at Troy and was killed (*Iliad*, 2.695ff.); although many legends developed around him, here the sense is of an "eager-beaver" type.

7. *throws Venus:* the winning throw in ancient dice games, although there may be a more arch allusion here.

8. *Aretine:* probably Francesco d'Ottaviano d'Antonio di Arezzo, notary and "chancellor of the Reformed Council of the People of Florence" (Gaeta).

9. *Fedini:* Raffaello Fedini (Raffaelo di Matteo di Feo di Dino) (Gaeta).

10. *most impure:* an allusion to Cicero's condemnation of Sextus Clodius; see *De doma sua,* 18.48.

11. *Ottaviano Ripa:* chancellor of the Ten (Gaeta).

12. *Luca:* Luca Ficini (Gaeta); also known as Luca di Fabiano da Montegonzi. He served as a secretary to Antonio della Valle in the first chancellery in 1500; he is frequently mentioned in Biagio Buonaccorsi's *Ricordi;* see Fachard, *Biagio Buonaccorsi,* index.

13. *debtors' list:* translation of *a speculo,* in turn a translation of the Italian *dallo specchio,* "from the mirror"; see Letter 15, n. 3.

14. *Alfani:* Francesco Alfani (Gaeta).

15. *like Vulcan:* i.e., lame; perhaps, since Vulcan is the god of fire, lameness suggests figuratively the flickering nature of fire.

16. *friends:* a list of men in the chancellery who will be identified in their proper context below.

17. *Via Flaminia:* the long Roman highway built from Rome to Fano on the Adriatic and north along the shore to Pesaro and Rimini; begun when Gaius Flaminius was censor in 220 B.C. This was roughly the route that Cesare Borgia followed during his second campaign, but Faenza, loyal to its ruler, Astorre Manfredi, staunchly defended itself against Borgia, who spent the winter nearby and did not proceed to Bologna.

18. *[six years]* . . . *a great share:* an allusion to *Aeneid,* 2.5–6, as Aeneas recounts the horrors of Troy and its fall. The square brackets are in Gaeta's text.

Letter 19

1. *Primavera:* a sister of Totto and Machiavelli who was born around 1465 and was married to Francesco Vernacci; their son Giovanni was born in 1486. Machiavelli took an avuncular interest in the boy; their correspondence provides a glimpse into Machiavelli's concern for his family, especially as Giovanni pursues his commercial career in far-flung locations.

2. *boy:* since adolescence was considered to end at twenty-five (see Dante, *Convivio,* 4:24), Totto refers to Giovanni as a "boy" (Gaeta).

3. *discharge:* permission for Machiavelli to return to Florence from France was not granted until December 12. Gaeta also points out that the Signoria never actually sent Machiavelli any money while he was in France.

4. *Leonardo Guidotti:* a member of the newly elected *Dieci di Balìa* (see Letter 15) with a career in Florentine politics that began in 1490 (Gaeta).

Letter 20

1. *Francesco Machiavelli:* son of Piero di Francesco Machiavelli; a commissioner to Arezzo in 1510 (Gaeta).

2. *losses:* the reference is to the deaths of both Machiavelli's father, on 10 May 1500, and his sister.

3. *colleague:* della Casa, sick with a fever, had left Machiavelli in Melun on 14 September and gone on to Paris (Gaeta).

4. *Nancy:* translation of *Nanci,* though Machiavelli had followed the

peripatetic French court to Nantes, so Francesco may be confused on this point (Gaeta).

5. *Giulio:* Giulio de' Scorciatis, an official of Ferdinand I of Aragon whom Louis XII had appointed as chamberlain in his court (Gaeta).

6. *Ugolino Martelli:* Ugolino di Niccolò Martelli was a Florentine official in France with the Florentine delegation who had been active in Florentine political affairs since 1480 (Gaeta).

7. *Adovardo Buglione:* Edouard Bouillon was a *valet de chambre* of Charles VIII and Louis XII and at the time the letter was written was serving as a French ambassador to Florence; he left for France in October 1500 (Gaeta).

Letter 21

1. *16th hour:* i.e., 10 A.M.

1501

Letter 22

1. *Cei:* (1471–1505), a member of the faction against Savonarola who wrote a volume of erotic poetry (Gaeta); see also Letter 53, n. 1. For more on Cei, see Dionisotti, "*Letterato,*" pp. 246–247 (translated, in Ascoli and Kahn, *Machiavelli and the Discourse of Literature,* pp. 34–35).

2. *sodomy:* Pulci did not want to be suspected of being a homosexual; the other poets mentioned (Pacifico Massini di Ascoli and Phaedrus, i.e., Tommaso Inghirami) also wanted to avoid such suspicion (Gaeta).

3. *Vitellius . . . Sardanapalus:* the former was Aulus Vitellius, emperor of Rome in 69 A.D., infamous for his debauched reign; alluded to in *Prince,* 17 (Atkinson, p. 272, n. 47–51). The latter is said to have been an effeminate, immoral ruler who burned his palace when Nineveh, the capital of his Assyrian empire, was threatened with defeat in the ninth century B.C.; see Byron's poem "Sardanapalus."

4. *Salii:* priests of a minor college (literally "the jumpers") connected with the annual rites of Mars usually held in March and October at the beginning and end of the campaign season; their sacred processions involved ritual dances and singing followed by magnificent feasts.

5. *Bacchantes:* the frenetic followers of Bacchus/Dionysus, the god of wine.

6. *take me in:* Vespucci has the pope imaginatively quote the opening speech of Sinon the Greek, who lets the Trojans capture him so that he can persuade them to bring the wooden horse within the city walls; *Aeneid,* 2.69–70.

7. *Sulla:* considered a typical example of a Roman dictator, he ruled Rome from 82 to 79 B.C. and proscribed many of his opponents, most of whom were killed, after he initiated a policy of using military force against the state in a civil war; for the conjunction of Sulla and proscriptions, see Cicero, *Epistulae ad Atticum,* 9.10.6 (Gaeta).

8. *renegade:* translation of *marrano,* literally a Jew falsely converted to Christianity; there were rumors that Pope Alexander VI was a *marrano;* Gaeta believes the sense here is really "scoundrel" or "renegade."

9. *Rota:* a tribunal of the Papal Curia through which the pope governs the Church.

10. *seven o'clock:* translation of *da l'avemaria ad una ora.*

Letter 23

1. *archduke:* see Letter 4, n. 6.

2. *Kingdom of Naples:* French and Spanish armies entered the Kingdom of Naples and began their attack early in July.

3. *Maréchal de Gié:* Pierre de Rohan (1451–1513), a general for Louis XI and Charles VIII; he saved the latter from defeat at the battle of Fornovo, July 6, 1495, thus enabling Charles to return to France after his successful descent into Italy, when he "was allowed to conquer Italy with chalk" (*Prince,* 12; Atkinson, p. 221).

4. *Robertet:* Florimond de Robertet, secretary under Charles VIII and Louis XII and treasurer of France (Gaeta).

5. *high-handedly:* translation of *alla gianizola* (*alla giannizzera,* "Janissary fashion").

Letter 24

1. *first:* i.e., to predict the campaign against the Kingdom of Naples. See Letter 23, n. 2.

2. *ambassador:* Pier Francesco Tosinghi (Gaeta).

3. *[?]:* per Gaeta's text.

Letter 25

1. *cardinal of Capua:* Giovanni Lopez, whom Pope Alexander VI made cardinal in 1496; he died August 5, 1501 (Gaeta).

2. *cardinal of Lisbon:* Giorgio da Costa, whom Pope Sixtus IV had made cardinal in 1476; he died in 1508 (Gaeta).

3. *14 thousand:* presumably ducats; no indication in text.

4. *all:* i.e., the money.

5. *cardinal of Modena:* Giovan Battista Ferrari, whom Pope Alexander VI made a cardinal on September 28, 1500 (Gaeta).

6. *Monreale:* Giovanni Borgia the Elder (1446–1503), a nephew of Pope Alexander VI, who advanced his career; he was archbishop of Monreale in 1483 and cardinal in 1492.

7. *Cardinal d'Este:* Ippolito I (1479–1520) (Gaeta).

8. *died of:* although modern commentators are less quick to judge, contemporaries accused both Pope Alexander VI and Cesare Borgia, either with or without the other's complicity, of poisoning many of their enemies. Among the alleged victims of the infamous *cantarella,* concocted perhaps from white

arsenic, are Prince Djem, brother of Sultan Bajazet; Virginio Orsini, the head of that noble family in Rome; the rich Pedro d'Aranda, bishop of Calahorra; Francesco d'Almeida, bishop of Ceuta; Juan Borgia, cardinal of Monreale; the wealthy Cardinal Giovanni Michiel, bishop of Porto, patriarch of Constantinople, and a nephew of Pope Paul II; and, in 1503, one that Vespucci mentions, Cardinal Giovan Battista Ferrari, bishop of Modena.

9. *Great Standard-bearer:* Cesare Borgia; his father made him captain-general and gonfalonier of the Holy Roman Church on 29 March 1500.

10. *Ser Antonio . . . Ottaviano:* Antonio della Valle, Biagio Buonaccorsi, Luca Ficini, Ottaviano da Ripa (Gaeta).

11. *Saint Bartholomew:* celebrated in Rome on August 25, though it falls on August 24.

12. *Boethius:* (?480–?524) author of *The Consolation of Philosophy,* who also wrote a treatise, *De musica.*

13. *Phaedra . . . Lippi:* Tommaso Inghirami, Pietro Marso, M. Antonio Sabellico, and Aurelio Lippi Brandolini (Gaeta).

14. *wedding plans:* the wedding between Lucrezia Borgia, the pope's daughter (formerly married to Giovanni Sforza, duke of Pesaro, and to Alfonso of Aragon, duke of Bisceglie—both marriages ended at the direction of the pope, the former in humiliation and the latter in murder) and Alfonso I d'Este, duke of Ferrara, occurred on December 30. For the Este family it was a political decision to save their house from the ravages of Cesare Borgia.

15. *Vitellozzo:* one of Cesare Borgia's condottieri and henchmen; while his troops were laying siege to Piombino, Cesare Borgia joined the French army in its attack on Naples.

16. *Piombino:* Giulio Cesare da Varano was lord of Camerino, Guidobaldo da Montefeltro was duke of Urbino, and Jacopo d'Appiano was prince in Piombino.

Letter 26

1. *Lomel:* Lomello, a town south of Milan and about twenty miles west of Pavia, was important during the latter years of Imperial Rome and into the Middle Ages (Inglese).

2. *Ser Luca:* Luca di Antonio degli Albizzi (1459–1502), together with Francesco Soderini, was an ambassador to France; Biagio served them as secretary during this mission, which lasted from September 1501 to July 1502. Inglese, however, identifies this person as Luca Ficini; see Letter 18, n. 12.

3. *cardinal:* Georges d'Amboise (Gaeta).

Letter 27

1. *Valori:* (1464–1526) at the time the letter was written Valori was a Florentine commissioner in Pistoia.

2. *Lanfredini:* Lanfredino Lanfredini.

3. *city . . . hill:* allusion to Christ's "Sermon on the Mount"; Matthew

5:14; the Douay version reads, "seated on a mountain" (Gaeta).

4. *since you left:* Machiavelli had accompanied Valori, then the Florentine commissioner, to Pistoia, leaving Florence on 18 October and returning to Florence on 26 October. Machiavelli had already been sent to Pistoia on 2 February, 13 July, and earlier in October, because of the unrest between the Cancellieri and Panciatichi factions.

5. *Antonio:* Antonio Giacomini (Gaeta); since he is generally referred to as Antonio Giacomini, that designation is used in this translation. At times, however, as in Letters 103 and 104, he is referred to as Antonio Tebalducci. To adopt the alternative "Giacomini-Tebalducci," used in some indices, seems unnecessarily confusing.

6. *Bernardo:* perhaps Bernardo Ricci (Gaeta).

Letter 28
1. *Albizzi:* for more on Luca di Antonio degli Albizzi, see Letter 13, n. 1.
2. *Ugolino:* Ugolino Martelli (Gaeta).

I 5 0 2

Letter 29
1. *Urbino:* Soderini was still trying to persuade Cesare Borgia that Florence wished to sign a treaty of friendship with him, although it was pledged to France.

Letter 30
1. *Lorenzo di Niccolò Machiavelli:* see Letter 13, n. 11.

2. *Valentino's troops:* they seized a mule train carrying goods for Marco and Jacopo di Piero Brinciassi, two Florentine merchants, and took them to a fortress held by Alessandro Spannocchi, Cesare Borgia's secretary and treasurer (Gaeta).

3. *Martino dello Scarfa:* the son of Giovanni di Martino dello Scarfa (Gaeta).

Letter 31
1. *charming letter:* probably on the occasion of his brother Piero Soderini's election as gonfalonier for life in Florence (Gaeta).

2. *ability:* translation of *virtute,* the modern Italian *virtù.*

Letter 32
1. *essay:* refers to a dispatch Machiavelli sent the Ten of Liberty and Balìa dated 7/8 October (Gaeta); excerpted in AG, I, pp. 121–123; *Leg.,* I, pp. 338–344.

2. *more forthright:* Machiavelli had noted that Cesare Borgia (here, "His Lordship") "always kept circling at a distance" from the subject of a treaty with Florence (*sempre girò largo, Leg.,* I, p. 342) (Gaeta).

Letter 33

1. *Ricci:* Bernardo de' Ricci (Gaeta).
2. *spirit of yours:* a good thumb-nail sketch of Machiavelli's character.
3. *Leonardo:* Leonardo Guidotti (Gaeta).

Letter 34

1. *safe-conduct:* so that Florentine traders could maintain their traffic "coming and going to the Levant," Machiavelli had been asked to obtain safe-conducts for Florentine merchants and their goods through territory controlled by Cesare Borgia (Gaeta). Once Cesare Borgia lost Fossombrone, 21 October, Machiavelli was able to do so.
2. *M. Alessandro:* Alessandro Spannocchi; see Letter 30, n. 2 (Gaeta).

Letter 35

1. *around midnight:* translation of *circa ore 6,* "around 6 hours [after 6 P.M.]."
2. *Madonna Lessandra:* Biagio's wife, Alessandra Ficino (Gaeta).
3. *Madonna Gostanza:* the wife of Antonio della Valle (Gaeta).
4. *grow new feathers on sparrows:* Gaeta suggests a double meaning; given the context, evidently sexual in nature.
5. *Ser Snail:* her husband.
6. *Ser Tightass:* a nickname for Antonio della Valle (Gaeta).
7. *Fedini:* Raffaello Fedini (Gaeta).
8. *I am not angry:* this paragraph may be what Ridolfi has in mind when he says that Biagio sometimes writes to Machiavelli "with the jealousy of a lover" (Ridolfi, *Life,* p. 56; *Vita 7,* p. 90).
9. *Lorenzo:* Lorenzo Machiavelli (Gaeta); see Letter 13, n. 11.
10. *Ricci to go to France:* Vespucci discussed this in Letter 33 (Gaeta).
11. *ambassador:* Luigi della Stufa (Gaeta).
12. *rustle up:* translation of *sgallinare* (see Letter 10, n. 8).
13. *Your Leonardo:* Leonardo Guidotti (Gaeta).
14. *Fracassa:* a nickname (from a familiar farce character) for Gaspare Sanseverino, captain of a mercenary company (Gaeta).
15. *the code:* large sections of this letter, as can be seen, are in code.
16. *our friend:* Bernardo de' Ricci (Gaeta).
17. *Pandolfo:* Pandolfo Petrucci (1452–1512), the ruler of Siena; da Colle's mission to him is discussed above in the main letter. Since Machiavelli was sent to Siena in 1503 to deal with him, see that year's Headnote for more on Petrucci.
18. *Postscript:* written by Agostino Vespucci.
19. *Giovanni:* Giovanni Vespucci (Gaeta).
20. *wrote you in Latin:* i.e., Letter 33.
21. *Campriano:* another member of the chancellery (Gaeta).

Letter 36

1. *Piero Guicciardini:* (1454–1513) a member of one of Florence's most

distinguished patrician families and, at the time the letter was written, also a member of the Ten. He was the father of Francesco Guicciardini, a historian of Florence, a political figure, and a person with whom Machiavelli corresponds at length.

2. *His Lordship . . . the king:* references to Cesare Borgia and Louis XII.

3. *Grechetto:* Giovanni Greco da Gianina, whom Cesare Borgia had sent to Florence to recruit troops.

Letter 37

1. canna: Gaeta notes that 1 *canna* equals 4 *braccia* or 2.3 meters; thus Buonaccorsi's 7.5 *braccia* equals roughly 5 yards. For the sake of simplicity, a *braccio* will be assumed to equal 2 feet for the purpose of linear measurement in these letters. It is generally believed that in Machiavelli's Florence a *braccio* equaled 21.7 inches for a land surveyor and 23 inches for a builder.

2. *nuptial gift:* discussed in the first paragraph of Letter 41 (Gaeta).

3. *Sardigna:* a refuse dump beyond Florence's Porta S. Frediano.

4. *to go rustling about:* translation of *sgallinare.*

5. *my appropriation:* for more on these money matters, see the first paragraph of Letter 14 and the postcript to Letter 35, dated 18 October (Gaeta).

6. *His Lordship:* Pandolfo Petrucci, according to Gaeta; but Inglese identifies him as Cesare Borgia.

7. *His Lordship:* Cesare Borgia.

Letter 38

1. *Lorenzo di Giacomino:* the writer's Italian is characterized by semiliterate spelling and syntax.

2. libbra: a variable measure of weight, equivalent to slightly more than 12.7 ounces (362 grams x .035).

Letter 39

1. *my election:* he hoped to be chosen as *podestà* of Orvieto.

Letter 40

1. *the rank:* permanent gonfalonier of justice for life in Florence.

2. *you:* here Soderini uses the formal *voi.*

3. *Most Illustrious Prince:* Cesare Borgia (Gaeta).

4. *His Excellency's men:* for details, see Letters 30 and 54 (Gaeta).

Letter 41

1. *marry off my girl:* see Letter 37, paragraph 4 (Gaeta).

2. *we usually get:* seems to refer to a bonus or gratuity.

3. *Cianchera:* evidently a nickname ("Gimpy") for a bowlegged person.

Letter 42

1. *Ser Alessandro:* Alessandro Braccesi was sent to Rome pending the arrival of the new ambassador, Giovan Vittorio Soderini, Piero's brother (Gaeta).

2. *constables:* derived from the Latin *comes stabuli,* 'count of the stable,' 'master of the horse'; in these letters it generally refers to an officer in charge of a local militia, supervising some men and horses, not a simple policeman.

3. *Borgo:* Borgo San Sepolcro (Sansepolcro) (Gaeta). The town was strategically important because it controlled a gap in the Apennines through the Val di Marecchia.

4. *What you desire:* probably a financial supplement for Machiavelli.

Letter 43

1. *Jacopo Salviati:* within three months he would succeed Machiavelli as Florence's ambassador to Cesare Borgia.

2. *loan:* a compulsory public loan issue (Gaeta).

Letter 44

1. *too bold a conclusion:* in particular, the remarks in the reports sent from Imola on 15 and 23 October (Gaeta) (*Leg.,* I, pp. 361–365; 383–388; excerpts in AG, I, pp. 126; 127–128). As Ridolfi points out (*Life,* p. 56; *Vita 7,* p. 90), it was precisely because of Machiavelli's bold conclusions that Valori (Letter 42) valued Machiavelli's reports; this respect would not continue were Machiavelli to follow Biagio's advice to restrict his reports to facts only. The quotation from Machiavelli's *Legations* about checking his facts, cited in the Headnote, addresses this issue and the Signoria's sense of urgency to have as many—and as fresh—facts as possible at their immediate disposal. The quote continues, "I am endeavoring to make use of my time and not to fritter it away. . . . Whoever has time but bides his time is on a quest for better bread than is made from wheat; be that as it may, he does not always find a ready-made opportunity" (*Leg.,* I, p. 427). A bit ruffled by the impatience of the Signoria, Machiavelli rises to the occasion: "Your Lordships look for many dispatches from me and up to now it seems to me that I have satisfied this demand—if all my letters have been read" (*Leg.,* I, p. 428); see Najemy, "Machiavelli's Service," p. 106–107, on this remark and Biagio's advice. Perhaps in an effort to placate Biagio and his superiors, Machiavelli says one month later, of Cesare Borgia's relations with Vitellozzo, that Cesare Borgia "accepts everything; nobody knows what course he may follow, for it is difficult to figure it out and understand it. If I have to express an opinion on this matter based on the facts alone, his words, and those of his principal ministers, I can expect only the worst [for Vitellozzo]" (*Leg.,* I, p. 458).

2. *league's forces:* those of the group that had met at the Diet of Magione.

3. *answering you:* here and below, the letter concerned is Letter 43 (Gaeta).

4. *Niccolò and Albertaccio:* Niccolò di Alessandro Machiavelli and Albertaccio Corsini (Gaeta). Niccolò di Alessandro Machiavelli is Machiavelli's cousin, who was a member of the Signoria and the Ten, a prior for the *Arti,* a commissioner in Pistoia in 1500 and in Cortona in 1505 (Gaeta). Najemy, *Between Friends,* p. 76, n. 44, notes that between 1496 and 1512 he was elected to the *Consiglio degli Ottanta* (Council of Eighty) and that he was "on the foreign

policy committee of the Ten in the summer of 1512, during the dramatic days that led to the collapse of the republic; see Butters, *Governors and Government,* p. 161."

5. *leave:* Machiavelli states his desire to return in a letter to the Ten on 23 October (*Leg.,* I, p. 388) (Gaeta).

6. *Ser Andrea:* for the tiff between della Valle and Andrea di Romolo over a backgammon game, see Letter 37 (Gaeta).

Letter 45

1. *negotiations:* these negotiations are elaborated on in a postscript to a letter the Ten wrote Machiavelli on 28 October (*Leg.,* I, p. 398) (Gaeta).

2. *Cortona:* a town about seventy-five miles southeast of Florence, on the way to Arezzo.

Letter 47

1. *rustled up:* translation of *sgallinare.*

2. *ducats:* despite the discrepancy, these probably are the ducats referred to in the first sentence of Letter 46.

3. *French troops:* those sent by Georges d'Amboise, Louis XII's governor in Milan, as part of the French effort to bolster Cesare Borgia. The latter requested this aid because of the conspirators' success, especially at Fossombrone.

4. *Messer Alessandro:* Alessandro Spannocchi, Cesare Borgia's secretary and treasurer (Gaeta).

5. *Our friend:* Bernardo de' Ricci (Gaeta); see Letter 35, the section that Biagio wrote on 18 October.

6. *Piero:* Piero Soderini (Gaeta).

Letter 49

1. *showing up:* according to Inglese, this would be translated as "leaving the office."

2. *hall:* Gaeta refers to Ridolfi, *Life,* p. 271, n. 28, *Vita 7,* p. 454, commenting that he believes that the "hall" refers, in part, to the offices of the second chancellery.

3. *Piero del Nero:* the brother-in-law of Machiavelli's wife, Marietta Corsini; a member of the Ten in May 1500 and a captain at Pisa in 1511 (Gaeta).

4. *Giovambattista Soderini:* Giovan Battista di Paolo Antonio Soderini, Piero's nephew; see Letter 119.

Letter 50

1. *wonderful things:* in Letter 49, about the reorganization in the chancellery (Gaeta).

2. *as I wrote you:* in Letter 49 (Gaeta); Alessandro is Alessandro Nasi.

3. *loan:* Jacopo Salviati discusses this in Letter 43.

4. *raring to go:* see Letters 130 and 132 for an incident in which the Bishop of Volterra's being "raring to go" proved dangerous.

Letter 51

1. *you:* Berti addresses Machiavelli with the familiar *tu.*

Letter 52

1. *post-box:* a little box with a tilting lid that could serve as a portable desk, in which documents, maps, and other materials could be carried (Gaeta).

2. *Lorenzo:* Lorenzo Machiavelli (Gaeta); see Letter 13, n. 11.

3. *Leonardo:* Leonardo Guidotti (Gaeta).

4. *loan:* Jacopo Salviati discusses this in Letter 43.

5. *reduction:* see the first paragraph of Letter 50.

6. *150:* see the penultimate paragraph of Letter 37.

Letter 53

1. *Francesco Cei:* see Letter 22, n. 1.

2. *Agostino:* Agostino Vespucci (Gaeta).

3. *Pulci:* Raffaello Pulci (Gaeta).

Letter 54

1. *you:* Soderini addresses Machiavelli, here exceptionally, as *voi,* probably as a consequence of the letter's official nature.

2. *list:* Machiavelli did so, at the end of a dispatch dated 13 November (Gaeta) (*Leg.,* I, pp. 426–432; excerpts in AG, I, pp. 133–134; the list is not included).

3. *His Most Christian Majesty:* Louis XII.

4. *Monsignor of Volterra:* Francesco Soderini.

5. *His Excellency:* Cesare Borgia.

6. *[not]:* textual emendation in Gaeta.

7. *thereabouts:* this matter was mentioned in Letters 30 and 40 (Gaeta).

8. *Tommaso:* Tommaso di Paolantonio Soderini (1470–1531) (Gaeta).

Letter 55

1. *8th:* see the three dispatches in *Leg.,* I, pp. 416–424 (Gaeta): two are dated the 8th, one the 10th; and the dispatch dated the 13th in *Leg.,* I, pp. 426–432 (there are excerpts in AG, I, pp. 129–134).

2. *France:* see the third paragraph of Letter 50.

3. *bishop:* Francesco Soderini, Bishop of Volterra, the brother of Piero Soderini, the new gonfalonier of Florence (mentioned in the next paragraph), was Florence's ambassador to France.

4. *Alessandro:* Alessandro Nasi (Gaeta).

5. *raise:* in Machiavelli's per diem.

6. *Totti:* the messenger, Tommaso Totti (Gaeta).

7. *His Lordship:* Cesare Borgia.

8. *singles . . . doubloons:* translation of *scempi* and *doppioni,* referring to the ducats.

Letter 56

1. *Brisighella area:* a town near Imola, on the road from Florence to Ravenna via Faenza. Compare this account with that in the first paragraph of Letter 63.

2. *captain of Brisighella:* Dionigi Naldi, Cesare Borgia's captain of the infantry of the Val di Lamone (Gaeta).

3. *Sant'Arcangelo:* Sant'Arcangelo di Romagna (Gaeta), near Rimini.

Letter 57

1. *in Arezzo:* evidently an expression referring to something obvious; here, an ironic equivalent of "like fun (you say)."

Letter 58

1. *onions:* a joking way to request more frequent letters, because many of the Ten wished to receive more of Machiavelli's reports. Biagio wanted to get more of Machiavelli's letters, too: he believed he deserved them as a friend; more importantly, he believed he could then act more effectively on Machiavelli's behalf among their superiors in the Signoria (Gaeta).

2. *Madonna Marietta is angry:* eight weeks earlier, Machiavelli had told her he would be gone for only one week; Ridolfi (*Life,* p. 59; *Vita 7,* p. 94) points out that she went to stay with her brother-in-law, Piero del Nero, in order not to be alone.

Letter 59

1. *you:* Soderini addresses Machiavelli here as *tu.*

Letter 60

1. *you:* Soderini addresses Machiavelli here as *tu.*

2. *His Illustrious Lordship:* Cesare Borgia.

Letter 61

1. *[. . .]ay:* textual omission; "ay" stands for the ". . . rno" in the text, on the assumption that it is a fragment of *giorno,* hence "day."

2. *Filippo:* Filippo Rucellai, see the next paragraph and Letters 98, 99, and 100, all written by Totto Machiavelli.

3. *stamps:* translation of *bolle,* probably tax stamps.

4. *Alessandro Spannochi:* Cesare Borgia's secretary and treasurer.

Letter 62

1. *yours:* here again Soderini uses the formal *voi,* probably in consequence of the letter's official nature.

2. *bishop of Urbino:* Gian Pietro Arrivabene (Gaeta).

3. *His Excellency:* Cesare Borgia.

Letter 63

1. *compare:* a friend or comrade, originally from the Latin *compater,* someone who has served as a godfather to one's child.

2. *Brisighella area:* see Letter 56, which tells the same story in much the same words.

Letter 64

1. *you:* Soderini addresses Machiavelli with the familiar *tu* here.

Letter 65

1. *cold fish:* translation of *cheppia,* a kind of shad.

2. *in motion:* in the context, evidently a bowel movement.

3. *Luca:* Luca Ficini (Gaeta).

4. *Monsignor:* Francesco Soderini, Bishop of Volterra, Florentine ambassador to the French court (Gaeta).

5. *this office:* of the second chancellery (Gaeta).

6. *cursing God:* see Letter 58, n. 2, on his wife's anger.

7. *onions:* see Letter 58 for the metaphorical use of "onions" for Machiavelli's dispatches (Gaeta).

Letter 67

1. *list:* see Letter 54 and the list detailing the number of infantrymen, cavalry, and weaponry that constituted Cesare Borgia's army.

2. *damask:* the ducats were for Machiavelli, who complained constantly of his lack of money; the damask cloth was a gratuity for a member of Cesare Borgia's staff, his secretary and treasurer Alessandro Spannocchi, in connection with the safe-conduct mentioned in Letters 30 and 61.

3. *discharge:* ever since Machiavelli's report to the Ten of 23 October, he had been trying to be relieved of his duties with Cesare Borgia and to be allowed to return to Florence (Gaeta).

Letter 68

1. *Pier Francesco di Corbizzo:* a relative of Corbizzo dei Corbizzi, a powerful figure in Romagna who had been murdered by the Naldi faction on 5 February 1499 (Gaeta).

2. *Salvestro di Bossi:* a Florentine man of arms who had been captured by Vitellozzo Vitelli at Anghiari; Cesare Borgia incarcerated him in the fortress at Forlì (Gaeta).

1503

Letter 69

1. *event:* see the Headnote for 1502 for Cesare Borgia's capture of the main conspirators and his treatment of them at Senigallia.

2. *first . . . second:* see *Leg.,* I, pp. 507–510, 511–513 (Gaeta).

Letter 70

1. *after 23 January 1503:* the dating is examined in Ridolfi, *Vita* 7, pp. 435–436. To accept this as the approximate time Machiavelli wrote this letter seems appropriate, given the internal evidence: Accolti became bishop of Ancona, hence no longer a "Messer," in 1505; the cardinal of San Pietro in Vincula became Pope Julius II in November 1503; the phrases "one of those courtiers" and "letters were forwarded through the ambassador" indicate that Machiavelli was no longer in Romagna with Cesare Borgia, since he began his return trip to Florence on 20 January; from the context, Totto seems to be in Rome (Gaeta).

2. *San Pietro in Mercato:* a benefice of the Machiavelli family (Gaeta).

3. *Our Niccolò:* Niccolò di Alessandro Machiavelli (Gaeta); see Letter 44, n. 4.

Letter 71

1. *brother:* translation of *fratello carnale,* which denotes a brother born of both the same parents. Guglielmo was a Florentine in Cesare Borgia's service (Gaeta).

2. *His Lordship the Duke:* Cesare Borgia.

Letter 72

1. *Soderini:* Cardinal Soderini was an equally interested observer of the papal election that the Ten sent Machiavelli to Rome to report on. Machiavelli was also dispatched to try and hire Gian Paolo Baglioni as a condottiere for Florence.

2. *Niccolò:* Niccolò di Alessandro Machiavelli, one of Machiavelli's relations, who was currently a member of the Signoria (Gaeta); see Letter 44, n. 4.

3. *our jurisdiction:* i.e., in the chancellery.

4. *given birth:* to Machiavelli's third-born son, Bernardo, named after Machiavelli's father (Gaeta).

Letter 73

1. *Angelo Tucci:* a stationer who, during November and December, was one of the priors; for his anger at Machiavelli, see Letters 84 and 85, based on Tucci's Letter 82 (Gaeta).

Letter 74

1. *Battista Machiavelli:* one of the godfathers of Machiavelli's new son, Bernardo; see the last paragraph of Letter 80.

2. *Totto:* Machiavelli's brother, an ecclesiastic (Gaeta).

3. *Cardinal de' Medici:* Giovanni de' Medici, the future Pope Leo X (Gaeta).

4. *San Clemente:* Giacomo Serra, cardinal of San Clemente (Gaeta).

5. *Minerbetti:* Francesco Minerbetti, a Florentine canon and later bishop of Arezzo (Gaeta); see Appendix Letter A.

6. *archbishop:* Rinaldo Orsini (Gaeta).

Letter 75

1. *Messer Lorenzo Pucci:* a member of the papal datary and later a bishop and a cardinal (Gaeta).

2. *Messer Giorgio:* Giorgio dell'Antella (Gaeta).

3. *damp weather:* this paragraph is written with a double meaning evidently clear to Machiavelli.

Letter 76

1. *Your reply:* see *Leg.,* II, pp. 609–612, 618–623 (Gaeta); excerpts in AG, I, pp. 149–150.

2. *yesterday: Leg.,* II, pp. 633–635 (Gaeta).

3. *safe-conduct:* with the intention of joining and reinforcing his troops in Romagna, Cesare Borgia had asked Florence for a safe-conduct; much to the new pope's relief, Florence denied it—even though Cardinal Francesco Soderini and Georges d'Amboise, cardinal of Rouen, favored the request.

4. *being strong:* Gaeta refers to Sasso, *"Machiavelli e Cesare Borgia,"* pp. 188–189, n. 173, for commentary on this passage and a belief that Biagio and those in Florence probably misjudged the situation between the pope and Cesare Borgia. Sasso further points out that, diplomatically speaking, it was precarious for Machiavelli to recommend against Florence's granting the safe-conduct when two powerful cardinals, particularly Francesco Soderini, were urging Florence to grant it.

5. *plasma:* a kind of translucent quartz or silica.

Letter 77

1. *infected people:* Machiavelli feared having contracted the plague; see Letter 78 (Gaeta).

2. *Caesar . . . Dolabella:* Publius Cornelius Dolabella (c. 80–43 B.C.), a noted spendthrift and Cicero's son-in-law, joined Caesar at Pharsalia, and Caesar wanted him to be consul as a result.

Letter 78

1. *Pera:* now known as the Beyoglu quarter of Istanbul, lying north of the Golden Horn and west of the Bosphorus. At that time it was a center for European commerce and international relations; over the last two hundred years it has become the heart of Istanbul.

Letter 79

1. *your:* Soderini uses the familiar *tu.*

2. *kingdom [of Naples]:* Louis XII and Ferdinand the Catholic of Spain were still vying for control of Naples. The French army headed south in July but delayed in Rome on the news of Alexander VI's death. Gonzalo Fernández de Córdoba was preparing for an attack that came at the Battle of the Garigliano on 28 December, when he wiped out the French forces.

Letter 80

1. *Alessandra:* Biagio's wife.

2. *cardinal:* Francesco Soderini.

3. *ambassadors:* Machiavelli recommended in his dispatch of 1 November that six ambassadors be sent to Rome to honor the election of Julius II and to render him obeisance, as Florence had done previously on the occasion of the election of Sixtus IV and Alexander VI; see *Leg.,* II, p. 593 (Gaeta).

4. *Lodovico:* Lodovico Corsini, Machiavelli's father-in-law (Gaeta).

Letter 81

1. *debtors' list:* translation of *da specchio.*

2. *to be made:* see Letter 74 concerning potential church benefices for Totto.

3. *Messer Battista:* Battista Machiavelli (Gaeta).

Letter 82

1. *Agnolo Tucci:* see Letter 73. Ridolfi comments that he was "one of the *Signori,* a man of low birth, [who] asked to be personally informed on the Pope's policy in Romagna, and made a fuss because he did not get a quick reply" (Ridolfi, *Life,* p. 74; *Vita* 7, p. 117).

2. *You:* Tucci uses the *voi* form here; since later in this letter (see note 6) he addresses Machiavelli with the *tu,* it may be supposed that the *voi* here is intended as a plural.

3. *every other place:* after taking Faenza on 20 November, the Venetians were advancing toward Imola; see the Ten's reports to Machiavelli in *Leg.,* II, pp. 666–668 (Gaeta).

4. *faction:* Florence feared that the Venetians and Julius II had reached some sort of an agreement during the conclave for the pope's election (Gaeta).

5. *armed troops:* those led by Gian Paolo Baglioni in Romagna.

6. *Make:* Tucci uses the intimate form here (*"Fàllo"* in Gaeta's text); see note 2 above.

7. *Farewell:* the signature is barely decipherable. The first letter seems to be *A;* see opening sentence of Letter 85 (Inglese).

Letter 83

1. *Marietta Corsini:* Machiavelli's wife. On this letter, see Ridolfi, *Life,* pp. 274–275, n. 40; *Vita* 7, pp. 461–462.

2. *You:* like Machiavelli's brother, Totto, Marietta uses the *voi* form in addressing her husband.

3. *daughter:* Primerana, Machiavelli's daughter, his first child (Gaeta).

Letter 84

1. *Volterra:* Cardinal Francesco Soderini, the former bishop of Volterra; for Machiavelli's acting "as a go-between for the transaction of business by the Soderini brothers," see Lowe, *Church and Politics,* p. 61–62.

2. *satisfied:* a reference to Machiavelli's habitual requests for more money.

3. *Girolami and Matteo Strozzi:* Raffaello di Francesco Girolami and Matteo Strozzi were two of the six ambassadors that Machiavelli had recommended be sent to Rome to honor the election of Julius II and to render him obeisance.

4. *with Rouen:* Georges d'Amboise, cardinal of Rouen.

5. *for his brother:* see Letter 73 (Gaeta).

6. *Your Niccolò:* Niccolò di Alessandro Machiavelli; see Letter 44, n. 4.

Letter 85

1. *man:* by a typographical error in his text, Gaeta has *vit* instead of *vir* here.

2. *signature:* modern editors cannot understand the signature either; see note to Letter 82 (Inglese).

3. *now that Faenza has been lost:* the content and tone of this reply seem to substantiate that Tucci wrote Letter 82 (Gaeta). The sarcasm of the first paragraph, what Najemy calls Machiavelli's *cattiveria,* may indicate that Machiavelli is smarting at the demands made on him in Florence by people for whom he has little esteem; see Najemy, "Machiavelli's Service," pp. 107–108.

4. *Both of them:* Pope Julius II and Georges d'Amboise, cardinal of Rouen (Gaeta).

5. *Gianpaolo:* Gian Paolo Baglioni, whom Florence, through Machiavelli's intercession, wanted to use directly in Romagna to fight for its interests, not only France's (Gaeta).

1504–1505

Letter 86

1. *Compare:* the cardinal had wished to be one of Bernardo Machiavelli's godfathers; see Letter 90.

2. *your letters:* sent while Machiavelli was on a mission to France (Gaeta). Soderini uses the *voi* form, unlike his brother, Piero; his use of *tu* in Latin, in the postscript to this letter, corresponds to Latin usage, in which *tu* is simply a singular and *vos* a plural.

3. *plan:* this may refer to Machiavelli's plans for organizing a Florentine militia; Ridolfi thinks it is possible that Machiavelli's ideas on this subject solidified while he was in Rome (*Life,* 80–81; *Vita 7,* 127–128).

Letter 87

1. *24 March 1504:* "1503" is the date in the text, and Gaeta connects this letter to Letter 70; see also Letter 97, with an identical text (dated 24 March 1505 by Gaeta); nevertheless, as Inglese points out, the text reads 23 March.

Letter 88

1. *Most Reverend Monsignor:* Cardinal Giovanni de' Medici (Gaeta).

2. *benefice:* the request for an ecclesiastical benefice for Totto Machiavelli (Gaeta).

Letter 89

1. *Bartolini:* Leonardo Bartolini (Gaeta).

2. *Messer Raimondo:* Raimondo Raimondi, who served Cardinal Soderini in the conclave of 1503 (Gaeta).

3. *verses:* these may be the *Serenata,* "*Salve, donna . . .*" (Martelli, "*Memento*"), or, as Gaeta is inclined to believe, the *Strambotti,* "*Io spero e lo sperar . . .*" and "*Nasconde quel con che . . .*"

4. *Serristori:* see Letter 161, n. 1.

Letter 90

1. *militia:* the cardinal is an ardent supporter of Machiavelli's plans to reorganize the Florentine militia so that citizens will constitute it; see Letter 86.

2. *suspicious:* although in the following two quotations Guicciardini is writing about the year 1505, the fears and objections among powerful Florentine politicians to Machiavelli's and Piero Soderini's militia projects were fairly consistent at this time: "During this period the gonfalonier . . . aimed at setting up an infantry militia in our territory and wanted to make its leader Don Micheletto [Miguel de Corella], an extremely cruel, greatly feared, and dreadful man who had been in Valentino's service. To make his way easier, the gonfalonier decided to engage him as a sheriff in our rural districts. And because the gonfalonier suspected that the citizens might not approve of this idea if it were put before a consultative meeting (*pratica*) of the Ten, he first of all adroitly had chancellor Machiavelli probe the minds of *Messer* Francesco Gualterotti, Giovan Battista Ridolfi, Piero Guicciardini, and other leaders. Realizing that they were opposed to hiring Don Michele, the gonfalonier had the hiring put before the Eighty for a vote without having it first submitted to any deliberation whatsoever. Since the Eighty happened to be benighted, the gonfalonier won the hiring on the second and third ballot. The leading citizens were greatly angered because they suspected that his desire to have Don Michele was rooted in some evil scheme, and that this man was a tool that might enable the gonfalonier either to take over as despot or, were he in some trouble, to eliminate those citizens who were his enemies. Although much ill was spoken against this hiring, it nevertheless had to go into effect because the Eighty had passed it" (*Storia d'Italia,* I, 226; *Storie Fiorentine,* p. 281; Domandi, p. 257). For more on the "suspicious" nature of the opposition as it related to Bernardo Rucellai, Guicciardini states: "During this period Bernardo Rucellai, the gonfalonier's arch enemy, . . . secretly left the town; . . . since he had probably not conferred with anyone about his plan and the reasons that motivated him, people made various inferences. Some considered that he had left because, once he realized that the battalions were set up and Don Michele was hired, he feared that the gonfalonier sought to harm his enemies with illegal and despotic measures . . . and he believed he would be the first among the leaders to be struck down . . . . Others thought that Bernardo was so discontented with the gonfalonier that he had held some discussions

with the Medici or Pandolfo Petrucci about overthrowing the government" (*Storia d'Italia,* I, 228; *Storie Fiorentine,* p. 283; Domandi, pp. 258–259). On Don Michele, Miguel de Corella, see Dionisotti, *"Machiavelli, Cesare Borgia, e don Micheletto,"* and Sasso, *"Machiavelli, Cesare Borgia, Don Micheletto."* The question of whether or not Machiavelli's militia was, in effect, a plan for a private army to be established for Soderini as a proto-prince is reviewed succinctly in Black, "Machiavelli, Servant," pp. 89–94. There he considers the arguments put forth by Italian and Anglo-Saxon critics ranging from Carlo Dionisotti and Sergio Bertelli to R. Pesman Cooper, R. Devonshire Jones, and H. C. Butters (with relevant bibliographic citations).

    3. *Aloys d'Ars:* Louis d'Ars, bailiff of Vitry; after he held out against the Spanish at the fortress of Venosa, in Basilicata, he was released and left immediately for France (Gaeta).

    4. *road between:* Lowe, *Church and Politics,* p. 61, cites this clause and the one in the previous paragraph about the army being raised not "for private, but public convenience" (*non paretur ad commodum privatum sed publicum*) as examples of the fact that Francesco Soderini and Machiavelli "shared a common political outlook and used the same vocabulary for the discussion of political affairs and policy."

Letter 91

    1. *Bartolomeo d'Alviano:* a member of the Liviani family who were lords of Casigliano; Bartolomeo was one of Gonzalo Fernández de Córdoba's condottieri who left the Spanish general in the Kingdom of Naples after the Battle of Garigliano and headed for Rome, where he joined with Jacopo d'Appiano, Gian Paolo Baglioni, the Orsini, and Pandolfo Petrucci, and was thought to be planning an attack on central Italy and Tuscany.

    2. *Valori has written:* from France, where he was still serving as the Florentine ambassador (Gaeta).

    3. *Libbrafratta:* the Florentine attack on Pisa in May was headed by Gian Paolo Baglioni, Marcantonio Colonna, and Jacopo Savelli. Antonio Giacomini was the Florentine commissioner general until September; he laid waste to Pisa and Lucca and captured Libbrafratta.

Letter 92

    1. *Vespucci:* a doctor of arts and medicine, and professor of astronomy at the University of Padua (Gaeta).

    2. *letter:* since Machiavelli's letter is lost, we cannot tell precisely what it was about.

    3. *now another:* i.e., although the course, and hence the influence of the stars, is fixed, a wise man can change the effect of the stars by modifying his own behavior. Gaeta points out that Ptolemy is said to have stated, "The wise man will contol the stars." See Letter 121, n. 23, for Machiavelli's rejection of this notion.

Letter 93

1. *Battista Dini:* perhaps Battista di Francesco di Piero Dini, a prior in July and August 1501 (Gaeta).

2. *Ambassador:* in Rome.

3. *in public:* translation of *in piazza,* that is, to be seen in or to be heard on the public square for everyone to know about.

4. *here:* in Rome.

5. *Rome:* For another letter attributed to Totto and written later this year on 30 December, see Appendix Letter B.

Letter 94

1. *waters:* a reference to the Florentine plan to divert the waters of the Arno. For more discussion of this project, see Fachard, *Biagio Buonaccorsi,* pp. 126–130; he shows, from evidence in Buonaccorsi's *Sunmario* and *Diario,* that Machiavelli and Leonardo did not work together on the plan because it was based on the ideas of an architect named Colombino and an engineer named Giovan Berardi. See also Masters, *Science of Power,* chapter 1 and appendix 1, for the argument that Machiavelli's criticisms of Colombino and Berardi were based on expertise Machiavelli derived from his acquaintance with Leonardo da Vinci.

2. *recruitment:* of soldiers for the *Ordinanza*—the citizen militia—that Machiavelli had been advocating; see Letters 86 and 90.

3. *person:* the cardinal is making excuses for his brother Piero's lack of immediate support for Machiavelli's militia plans; Piero's policies would soon change.

Letter 95

1. *enmity:* as the next sentence shows, Valori is disappointed at not receiving more letters from Machiavelli (as are most of Machiavelli's correspondents); thus what Valori means here is that by becoming a godparent to Machiavelli's son, Bernardo, Valori seems to have alienated Machiavelli; otherwise he would have heard from him more often.

2. *Giacomini:* Antonio Giacomini; he was soon to be named as the Florentine commissioner general in their war against Pisa.

Letter 96

1. *Ser Latino:* probably Latino Giovenale Manetti (Gaeta).

Letter 97

1. *Soderini . . . Machiavelli:* the text of this letter is the same as that of Letter 87.

Letter 99

1. *Filippo:* the Filippo Rucellai mentioned in Letter 98 (Gaeta).

Letter 100

1. *sealed florins:* "*fiorini di suggello*" in the text; see Letter 14, n. 2, for more on money.

Letter 101

1. tavolaccino: literally, "little table or plank," an official servant or bailiff of the Signoria. Totto wants Machiavelli to have this official sequester the harvest of the lands of the church (the revenues of the church of S. Maria a Cigoli) as an intermediate step toward seizing the benefice—a not uncommon ploy.

2. *cardinal of Volterra:* Francesco Soderini.

Letter 102

1. *someone else:* Biagio is referring to Pandolfo Petrucci and Bartolomeo Alviano and the preparations for the defense of the Florentine stronghold, Campiglia, against Alviano's attack (Gaeta).

2. *the advance:* the prepayment of the condottiere's salary (Gaeta).

3. *Marchese:* Francesco Gonzaga (Gaeta).

4. *Chaumont:* Charles d'Amboise, lord of Chaumont, the French governor of Milan, to whom Niccolò di Girolamo Morelli had been sent as Florentine ambassador (Gaeta). Florence was still counting on French support for the Pisa campaign.

5. *leave:* Machiavelli's permission to return from his mission to Pandolfo Petrucci.

Letter 103

1. *Antonio Tebalducci:* the addressee of this letter and the next one is better known as Antonio Giacomini; see Letter 27, n. 5.

2. *Ercole:* Ercole Bentivoglio (Gaeta).

3. *Marco Antonio:* Marcantonio Colonna (Gaeta); the same Marcantonio as below, a Florentine condottiere.

4. *Iacopo:* Iacopo Savelli (Gaeta).

5. *Annibale:* Annibale II Bentivoglio (Gaeta).

6. *Luca:* Luca Savelli.

Letter 104

1. *authorized:* because of severe criticism in Florence, Giacomini had threatened to abandon his troops and return home without permission (Gaeta).

1506

Letter 105

1. *you:* Berti addresses Machiavelli as *tu*.

2. *infantry:* Guicciardini's description of the early stages of planning for

this infantry is interesting: "During this same period people started an initiative for setting up the battalions. In the olden days these battalions had existed in our territory when people fought wars not with mercenary and foreign soldiers but with our own citizens and subjects. . . . After [14]94, during our misfortunes, there were occasions when many people said that it would be good to return to the usages from the olden days; however, it was never brought before any consultative body—no initiative was planned or undertaken. Subsequently, Machiavelli set his mind on it and convinced the gonfalonier; realizing that he was persuaded, Machiavelli began to delineate the measures in detail. But because it was necessary for the prestige and preservation of so great a measure that it be backed by the Council and, bearing in mind that because it was a new and unusual proposal the people might not support it unless they had seen some test of it beforehand or unless the leading citizens had agreed to it, the gonfalonier (who correctly suspected that a consultative meeting would not back it) began to enlist men throughout the rural districts—Romagna, Casentino, Mugello, and the most bellicose spots—without any consultations and with the authority of the Signoria. Those men who seemed suited to this service were grouped under leaders and began drilling on holidays and put into formations according to the Swiss model; nothing was done in Florence because this was so new and unusual a measure that it had to be executed gradually" (*Storie Fiorentine*, pp. 281–282; Domandi, pp. 257–258).

3. *Dicomano:* a town northeast of Florence where Machiavelli recruited two hundred men; see his letter to the Ten, of 5 February, in *Leg.*, II, pp. 929–930 (Gaeta).

4. *Scarperia and Barberino:* two more towns in the Mugello district.

5. *Borgo and Vicchio:* Borgo San Lorenzo, the main town in the Mugello; also located there is Vicchio, the birthplace of Fra Angelico and a town in which Benvenuto Cellini lived.

6. *Banchi:* a constable (Gaeta). In an appendix Fachard prints a letter Biagio Buonaccorsi copied in which a priest from Sansalvi describes the hardships the troops commanded by Simone Banchi and Machiavelli caused the local civilian population (*Biagio Buonaccorsi,* pp. 269–271).

7. *Bastiano:* Bastiano da Castiglione, a constable and one of the militia leaders (Gaeta).

8. *Carnival:* on 15 February (Gaeta); see the Headnote for Landucci's glowing description of this event.

Letter 106

1. *Filippo:* Filippo di Alessandro Machiavelli, who was made *podestà* of Pistoia; see Letter 108 (Gaeta).

2. *Consalvo:* the Spanish general Gonzalo Fernández de Córdoba.

3. *Panzano:* a town southwest of Florence in the wine-producing region of Chianti.

4. *Folchi:* Giovanni Folchi (Gaeta).

Letter 107

1. *Ercole Bentivoglio:* captain general of Florence; see the Headnote for 1504–1505.

2. *poem:* Machiavelli's *Decennale primo;* although written in 1504, it was not published until February, by Agostino Vespucci, Machiavelli's assistant in the chancellery, at Vespucci's own expense. It was dedicated to Francesco Guicciardini's father-in-law, Alamanno Salviati, who opposed Machiavelli's efforts to pass legislation to organize a citizen militia—despite the fact that Salviati had defeated the citizens of Arezzo in their 1502 uprising against Florence.

3. *Pharaoh:* a reference to Exodus 14.

Letter 108

1. *Battista Machiavelli:* Battista di Buoninsegna di Guido Machiavelli; the Battista mentioned in the first line was a godfather of Machiavelli's son Bernardo and obviously not the Battista who is writing this letter (Gaeta).

2. *Valona . . . Ancona:* Vlone (Vlona) is a port in southern Albania; Ancona is an important Italian port on the Adriatic.

3. *Romena:* near Arezzo (Gaeta).

4. *company:* Brunaccino wished to lead the troops Machiavelli was raising in Romena (Gaeta).

Letter 109

1. *4 March 1506:* Martelli, p. 1094, dates this letter 4 March 1507; for the question of dating, see Rubinstein, *Machiavelli,* pp. 15–16, and Ridolfi, *Vita 7,* pp. 482–483.

2. *letter:* unfortunately, this letter has not been preserved.

3. *write wisely . . . justice:* the cardinal's emphasis on "justice," which in this military context connotes "discipline" as well as the notion of "justice," echoes passages at the beginning of two other works Machiavelli wrote that year: one is from the *Discorso dell'ordinare lo stato di Firenze alle armi* (Discourse on the organization of the Florentine state for arms): "everyone knows that whoever talks about empire, kingdom, princedom, or republic and whoever talks about men who command—beginning with the highest rank and descending to the captain of a brigantine—talks about justice and arms. You have little judicial authority and no weapons at all" (Machiavelli, *Arte della guerra,* p. 95, and *Altre opere storiche e politiche,* p. 99); the other is from the *Provvisione prima, per le fanterie, del 6 dicembre 1506* (First provision for infantry, of 6 December 1506): "all republics that have maintained and enlarged themselves in the past have always had two primary means of support, namely justice and arms, so that they could control and govern their subjects and could defend themselves against their enemies" (Machiavelli, *Arte della guerra,* p. 101, and *Altre opere storiche e politiche,* p. 105; AG, I, p. 103). Furthermore, the emphasis on "justice" echoes a letter that Soderini wrote to his brother, the gonfalonier Piero Soderini, on the same day as this one in support of Machiavelli's idea of a citizen militia.

On these questions, see Rubinstein, *Machiavelli,* pp. 14–16. See also Najemy, "Machiavelli's Service," p. 110, which states that when Machiavelli wrote that Florence had "little judicial authority and no weapons at all," he was demonstrating a "lack of restraint that must have seemed gratuitous even to those who agreed with him." Najemy's argument is that Machiavelli's "was certainly not a partisan criticism; indeed, it implicated everyone, indiscriminately, in a collective failure from which—or at least such was the implication—only Machiavelli's truth could save the republic."

4. *things written:* it is assumed that Cardinal Soderini had already read either an early or a final draft of Machiavelli's *Discorso dell'ordinare lo stato di Firenze alle armi.*

Letter 110

1. *In Poppi:* near Bibbiena, in the Casentino, where Machiavelli was recruiting troops for the citizen militia.

2. Compendium: a pirated edition, by Andrea Ghirlandi da Pistoia, of Machiavelli's *Decennale primo* (whose initial title was *Compendium rerum decennio in Italia gestarum*). Because Agostino had published the *Decennale primo* at his own expense, he was protecting his investment.

3. *teeny, tiny little signatures:* translation of *quinternucci,* diminutive of *quinterni,* groups of five sheets of paper folded together in the making of a book.

4. *fine of two* grossi: i.e., if Andrea did not answer the subpoena.

5. *8 o'clock:* translation of *a le 2 ore,* i.e., two hours after six in the evening.

6. *share:* i.e., of the printed texts (Gaeta).

7. *Messer Donato:* Donato Marinelli, from Arezzo (Gaeta).

8. *them:* i.e., the Eight (Gaeta).

9. *story:* translation of *cantafavola,* a far-fetched tale or children's story; the word is of popular origin, meaning literally "a sung tale"; see also Letter 144, n. 9. Here it is Vespucci's playful characterization of Machiavelli's *Decennale primo;* see Machiavelli's later use of the term in Letter 178 to dismiss one of his poems as "doggerel" and Letter 176, n. 8.

10. *six in the morning:* translation of *le 12 ore,* i.e., twelve hours after 6 p.m.

11. *Ser Francesco:* Francesco Ottaviani, chancellor of the *Riformagioni* (Gaeta); the *Riformagioni* were responsible for dealing with laws or decrees recently promulgated by Florence's legislative councils.

12. *Soderini:* Cardinal Francesco Soderini.

13. *know it:* the correct readings were: v. 77: *piena* ("full," rather than "pain"); v. 103: *s'incavuglia* (necessary for the rhyme, although both verbs are obscure); v. 147: *La diffidenza che nacque tra loro* ("The mistrust that arose between them," rather than "The difference that came between them"); v. 334: *sfrenato* ("unbridled," rather than "slashed"); v. 416: *del sangue* ("*with* the blood," rather than "the blood"); *La Puglia* (or *Le Puglie*) is simply Apulia, the region in southeastern Italy of which Bari is the capital (although the term is used to refer to all of southern Italy).

Letter 111

1. *In Florence:* evidently a mistake; there is no evidence where Totto was when he wrote this letter.

Letter 112

1. *Ridolfi:* probably Giovanni di Tommaso Ridolfi, captain and commissioner of Arezzo in 1502 and 1503; he was commissioner general in the recent 1506 campaign against Pisa (Gaeta).

2. *emperor . . . Hungary:* Maximilian I (1459–1519), Holy Roman Emperor from 1493 to 1519, and Ladislas II (1456–1516), a weak ruler and pawn of his nobles, king of Bohemia (1471–1516) and of Hungary (1490–1516).

3. *Gonsalvo:* Gonzalo Fernández de Córdoba, the Spanish general who conquered the Kingdom of Naples in 1504.

4. *king of Aragon:* Philip I the Handsome (1478–1506), son of Maximilian I (see Letter 4, n. 6); his father-in-law was Ferdinand the Catholic, king of Spain.

5. *king of England:* Henry VII (1457–1509) reigned from 1485 to 1509. Machiavelli's practice here and throughout his letters is to refer to "England" or "France," meaning not the nation but the king or ruler of a dominion. In translating these passages, we have added "king of" for clarification both in this letter and in subsequent ones.

6. *Valentino . . . Spain:* Pope Julius II imprisoned Cesare Borgia in November 1503, but he escaped to Naples, where Gonzalo had him transferred to Spain in April 1504 (Gaeta).

7. *Swiss soldiers:* Renaissance commentators were wildly enthusiastic about the Swiss infantry: "when [the military leaders of Europe] saw the Swiss at close quarters in Italy they were . . . impressed by their martial bearing. Their machine-like drill, their march discipline, and their air of comparative refinement reminded scholars of the soldiers of antiquity" (Taylor, *Art of War,* p. 58). It is no wonder Guicciardini noted that the new recruits from Florentine territory were "put into formations according to the Swiss model" (see Letter 105, n. 2).

8. *bailiff of Dijon:* Antoine de Baissey led the Swiss and German troops at the battle of Fornovo, 6 July 1495, which led to Charles VIII's withdrawal from Italy; the bailiff remained a powerful military adviser to King Louis XII; he served as ambassador to the Swiss.

9. *Monseigneur d'Argenton:* Philippe de Commynes (?1447–1511), a French political adviser and chronicler, whose *Memoirs* are a valuable source for the reigns of Louis XI (1461–1483) and Charles VIII (1483–1498).

10. *recent agreement:* urged by Pope Julius II and signed at Blois on 22 September 1504, it stipulated that Louis XII, Maximilian I, and Philip of Burgundy would attack Venice. Although nothing came of the treaty, it was not publicly announced until the following year at Haguenau, a town north of Strasbourg in Alsace. Rouen is Georges d'Amboise, the cardinal of Rouen.

11. *king of France:* this paragraph refers to the commitment of Louis XII to marry his daughter, Claude de France, to his cousin Francis of Angoulême, the son of Charles, count of Angoulême, and Louise de Savoie. Francis was

the future Francis I, king of France from 1515 to 1547. Since Francis was born in 1494, the marriage did not take place until 1514. Gaeta points out that this commitment broke a provision of the 1504 agreement signed at Blois, under which Claude de France would have married the grandson of Emperor Maximilian, Archduke Charles of Hapsburg, who was later Holy Roman Emperor Charles V and King Charles I of Spain.

12. *Monseigneur de Cisteron:* Pierre Le Filleul, bishop of Sisteron and Aix (Gaeta). Sisteron is in the Alpes de Haute Provence; it was once a bishopric, though it is now a small, unimportant town.

13. *king of the Romans:* Maximilian I had not yet been crowned emperor of the Holy Roman Empire, so this is the correct designation for him (Gaeta).

14. *coming into Tuscany:* at the instigation of Ludovico Sforza, Maximilian entered Italy in the autumn of 1496, intending to attack Pisa; his supporting fleet was destroyed, and he withdrew in ignominy.

15. *information . . . dependents:* Florence knew little about whatever policy the German princes might follow (Gaeta).

16. *Count Palatine:* the elector of the Palatinate, Philip of Wittelsbach, defeated during the contest for the succession in the Landshut (Gaeta).

17. *supply . . . incursion:* this had been agreed upon at a diet convened in Cologne, but most of the German princes asssumed they were supporting the emperor's efforts in the succession of Hungary (Gaeta).

18. *Alexander:* on 15 January 1495, Pope Alexander VI reached an accord with Charles VIII, after the latter's invasion of Italy (1494–1495).

19. *sermons:* translation of *bibbie;* in addition to "sermons," the word also means "bibles." Machiavelli chooses a politely self-effacing image for this lengthy disquisition on current international politics, one reminiscent of his analytical letters to Vettori about similar topics when he is in exile and remote from the behind-the-scenes details.

Letter 113
1. *In Court:* see the Headnote.

2. *Marietta:* Machiavelli's wife, Marietta Corsini.

3. *courier:* Machiavelli had paid for the courier to bring a dispatch from Rome to Florence and had asked the Ten to reimburse Biagio for it; see *Leg.,* II, pp. 957–958 (Gaeta).

4. *Monsignor:* Francesco Soderini, cardinal of Volterra (Gaeta).

5. *Tedesco:* Giovanni Tedesco, one of the constables (Gaeta).

6. *Bastiano da Castiglione:* another constable.

7. *Biagio:* For a letter Biagio wrote to Machiavelli dated 5 September, which chronologically follows Letter 114 from Francesco del Nero and precedes Letter 115, see Appendix Letter C.

Letter 114
1. *great captain:* Gonzalo Fernández de Córdoba.

2. *galleys:* Venetian galleys had intercepted and then seized goods that Totto Machiavelli and his business associate, the writer of this letter, shipped

from Vlone (in present-day Albania) to Lecce (an Italian port on the Adriatic Sea south of Brindisi). Piero Soderini had written to Gonzalo on 30 July to see if he would help in restoring the confiscated material (Gaeta).

3. *His Catholic Highness:* Ferdinand the Catholic, king of Spain.

Letter 115

1. *Michelangelo:* at the insistence of Pope Julius II, who had even written to the Florentine Signoria on 8 July, Michelangelo Buonarroti had decided to return to Rome, which he had left in April (Gaeta). We are not accustomed to reading about the great sculptor in the context of such an infra dig task.

2. *courier:* see Letter 113.

3. *court:* Buonaccorsi had accompanied the Florentine ambassador, Alessandro Nasi, the "Alessandro" of the next sentence, to Rome in 1505 (Gaeta). The mission lasted from November 1505 to June 1506; Biagio was Alessandro's secretary—see Fachard, *Biagio Buonaccorsi,* pp. 101–105.

4. *passage:* see Letter 113, where Maximilian I's passage into Italy, i.e., invasion, is in question.

5. *He:* refers to Jacopo Doffi.

6. *what you write:* Machiavelli had written to the Ten that he put no credence in the reports about Maximilian's entry into Italy and that the Venetians had circulated such reports in order to dampen Julius II's enthusiasm for his own military plots (*Leg.,* II, pp. 958–959; 963) (Gaeta).

7. *His Catholic Majesty:* Ferdinand the Catholic, king of Spain, who had become king of Naples in 1504.

8. *Sisteron:* Pierre Le Filleul; see Letter 112, n. 12.

Letter 116

1. *taken:* see Letter 114.

2. *Billi:* the Florentine representative in Naples (Gaeta).

Letter 117

1. *Serristori:* Lorenzo Serristori (*Leg.,* II, p. 973) (Gaeta). Ridolfi (*Life,* p. 95; *Vita 7,* p. 151) comments that Biagio is sending Machiavelli extracts from the chancellery's log books.

2. *de' Ricci:* the Ten sent him on a mission to Emperor Maximilian on 11 September to verify reports they had received about the latter's plans to invade Italy (*Leg.,* II, p. 974) (Gaeta).

3. *His Catholic Majesty:* Ferdinand the Catholic, king of Spain, who had become king of Naples in 1504. Because Ferdinand was suspicious of the conduct of Gonzalo Fernández de Córdoba, his strongman in Naples, the king went to Naples at the end of October.

4. *Gualterotti:* Giovan Vittorio Soderini, Piero's brother, Alamanno Salviati, and Francesco Gualterotti (Gaeta).

5. *da Castiglione:* one of the constables; he was recruiting troops in the region west of Florence in the Arno Valley.

6. *lord of Piombino:* Jacopo d'Appiano (Gaeta).

7. *Michelangelo:* see Letter 115, n. 1.

8. *Guicciardini:* Piero Guicciardini, father of Francesco, the historian, statesman, and eventual correspondent of Machiavelli.

Letter 118

1. *ambassadors for Piombino:* Giovan Vittorio Soderini, Alamanno Salviati, Niccolò de Nero (cf. those mentioned in Letter 117, n. 4), and Giovan Battista Ridolfi (Gaeta).

Letter 119

1. *Giovan Battista Soderini:* Piero's nephew, Giovan Battista di Paolo Antonio Soderini (1484–1528). He had a long history of opposition to the Medici (he was exiled in 1512 and banished for his role in a conspiracy in 1522), although at one point, between 1506 and 1508, there was the possibility that a Medici-Soderini alliance would be cemented through a marriage between him and Clarice de' Medici, Lorenzo the Magnificent's granddaughter. Soderini rejected the proposal. Bullard suggests he "did not dare risk the ire of the people which that much hypocrisy would assuredly have aroused" (*Strozzi and the Medici,* p. 50).

2. *Wherever He May Be:* Machiavelli was in Perugia with the papal court from 13 to 21 September; he had joined the pope in Nepi, about twenty-five miles northeast of Rome, and stayed with him through his progress northeast into Perugia and Bologna.

3. *Filippo di Banco:* In his review, Inglese identifies him as Filippo Casavecchia, according to the entry in the *Dizionario biografico degli Italiani.*

4. *Piombino:* they would like to go with the Florentine ambassadors, to await the arrival of Gonzalo Fernández de Córdoba and Ferdinand the Catholic, king of Spain.

5. *one . . . sun:* i.e., each has his reason for going or his obstacles to going; there may also be a reference to astrological signs, which were often consulted prior to making travel plans (Gaeta).

6. *at the same time:* evidently a reference to Machiavelli's urgent efforts for the organization of a nonmercenary militia composed of Florentine citizens and Piero Soderini's simultaneous temporizing activities, due to political pressure from his opposition. In his review, Inglese notes the proverbial cast of the expression, citing Pulci, *Morgante,* XI, 100, v. 2.

7. *decision:* it seems that Filippo was expecting a court decision in a law suit (Gaeta); according to Inglese, in his review, this would be Filippo Casavecchia.

Letter 120

1. *Tedesco:* one of the recruiting constables; see Letter 113.

Letter 121

1. *13–21 September:* In his review, Inglese wonders if this ought not to be extended to the 27th.

2. *recognized it:* referring to Letter 119, Machiavelli remarks that this cryptic letter, initialed and not signed, arrived with Biagio's scribblings on it, so that he had to read further to determine who wrote it. Until fairly recently it was thought that this letter was written to Piero Soderini after his flight from Florence in 1512; see Martelli, *Rinascimento* #9, and Ridolfi and Ghiglieri, "*I Ghiribizzi.*"

3. *obstacles . . . too little "light":* Machiavelli here picks up allusions in Soderini's letter: see Letter 119, n. 5. Gaeta believes that Machiavelli had altered the allusions to mean that Filippo (Casavecchia, according to Inglese) was "impeded" by having a dearth of wisdom ("light") and Soderini by having too much.

4. *nuisance:* Machiavelli would have February 1507 to work out his plans for a citizen militia; see Letter 119, n. 6 (Gaeta). Nevertheless, there seems to be the ring of a popular saying to it (Raimondo).

5. *apprehension:* see Letter 119, n. 7 (Gaeta).

6. {*He who . . . does*}: the manuscript of the letter contains a number of marginal comments; they are translated within brackets and inserted where sense dictates—as close to the original placement as possible.

7. *opportunity:* i.e., to write this letter (Gaeta).

8. *remind me not to do:* Inglese here recalls the second sentence of Letter 119, "I have nothing to tell you, and I do not want you to write me any answer."

9. *purpose:* the ultimate "purpose" may well have been for Giovan Battista to see to it that his uncle the gonfalonier read this letter (Gaeta).

10. *savored:* translation of *gustare;* the sensory element suggests intuition as well as mental effort in such consideration. Machiavelli's "savoring" of books and experiences results in no surprise that an action with one aim in mind could lead to something other than the one intended.

11. *navigation:* similar uses of the nautical image, based on the compass—*bussola*—idea, occur in *Discourses,* I, 7, 52, 56, 59; III, 3, 9, 30; see, too, Letter 331, n. 2; for Guicciardini's use of the image, see Letter 302 (Raimondo).

12. *ports it has guided you to:* Machiavelli's first draft has "what status it has honored you with"; the alteration tightens the comparison and avoids flattering someone who had not achieved the status of his uncle (Gaeta).

13. *acting . . . same end:* cf. "Hence it turns out, as I have said, that two people functioning differently can produce the same result; and that given two people functioning similarly, one can fulfill his goal and the other can not" (*Prince,* 25, 69–73; Atkinson, p. 365). The example of Pope Julius II that follows here ("this pope's actions") is also discussed in *Prince,* 25, 91–125; Atkinson, pp. 367, 369.

14. *outcomes:* Machiavelli does not adduce the example of Julius II consistently. His dispatches from the scene are a good place to start. On 12 September he wrote the Ten from Perugia that the pope had told him that if neither Louis XII or Maximilian would come to his aid, "were there no remedy in this situation, it might be easy for him [Julius II] to put a lower value on

harm to the Church or danger to others than on his own disgrace" (*Leg.*, II, p. 977)—Machiavelli's subtle way to show how the pope was justifying what Machiavelli would come to consider the pope's impetuosity, as he put his honor before that of the Church by initiating this campaign against Giampaolo Baglioni in Perugia and Giovanni Bentivoglio in Bologna. The next day Machiavelli informed the Ten that "although the troops of the Church are billeted within these walls and those of Giampaolo are at a greater remove, nevertheless the Pope and his court are at Giampaolo's mercy and not the reverse; if the latter will do no evil to the man who has come to deprive him of his state, it will be thanks to his good nature and human kindness. How this matter will end I do not know" (*Leg.*, II, p. 980). The example of Julius and Giampaolo occurs again in *Discourses,* I, 27. In the latter instance, however, Machiavelli reversed his emphasis on Baglioni's "good nature and human kindness" and spoke of his "cowardliness" and "baseness" (*viltà*); Baglioni "gave no thought to his being a person who committed incest and publicly murdered his relatives." Gaeta quotes the comment of Sasso, *Osservazione,* that the antithesis between the impetuous and circumspect, a point Machiavelli makes in *Prince,* 25, 91–125, about the character of Julius II, might be one a careful reader—perhaps Piero Soderini—would grasp were he eventually to see this letter.

15. *cloy it:* for this marginal note, see the final clause of the third sentence from the end of this letter. *Discourses,* I, 37, opens with the sentence, "A pithy saying of ancient writers was that mankind gets distressed by the bad and cloyed with the good," and Machiavelli quotes this same passage later in *Discourses,* III, 21, though he reverses the order of the elements—"gets cloyed with the good and distressed by the bad."

16. *victory:* to illustrate the principle that "some people would be amazed were they to realize how some military leaders, despite the fact that they have adhered to opposite activities, have nevertheless achieved similar results," in *Discourses,* III, 21, Machiavelli writes: "we find that upon entering Spain Scipio, with his human kindness and mercy, made that region his ally immediately and made himself adored and admired by its people. On the other hand, we find that upon entering Italy Hannibal, with diametrically opposed means, namely, cruelty, violence, pillage, and all manner of perfidy, achieved the same result as Scipio did in Spain, because all the cities in Italy revolted in favor of him and the entire population followed him." Machiavelli refers to the Second Punic War (218–201 B.C.) and the activities of Publius Scipio Africanus Major and the Carthaginian general Hannibal; as Machiavelli shows in a subsequent paragraph, all of Italy did not go over to Hannibal's side.

17. *friend of youth:* see *Prince,* 25, 130–138; Atkinson, pp. 369, 371: "I am absolutely convinced that it is better to be impetuous than circumspect, because Fortune is a woman and you must, if you want to subjugate her, beat and strike her. It is obvious that she is more willing to be subjugated that way than by men with cold tactics. Therefore, like a woman, she always befriends the young, since they are less circumspect and more brutal: they master her more boldly." The notion occurs again in two of Machiavelli's literary works:

Clizia, IV, 1: "O Fortune, since you are a woman, you ought to be the mistress of young men"; and *Capitolo di Fortuna,* vv. 73–75, which suggests in its last line that "audacity and youth stand [Fortune's] test the best." See the relevant passages in Pitkin, *Fortune Is a Woman.*

18. *fortresses:* the examples used here are also discussed in *Prince,* 20, "Whether Fortresses . . . Are Useful or Useless," 135–155; Atkinson, p. 327; and in *Discourses,* II, 24, "Fortresses Generally Are Much More Harmful Than Useful."

19. *Emperor Titus:* Titus (39–81 A.D.), emperor from 79 to 81; in *Discourses,* I, 10, he is cited as an example of someone who did not need "the soldiers of the praetorian guard or a crowd of legions to protect him, because his character, the goodwill of the people, and the love of the Senate protected him." To describe the attributes of Titus, the son of Vespasian, Machiavelli relies on the end of Suetonius, *Divus Titus,* 8.1.

20. *means:* with many of these marginalia it is often unclear what is the proper place for insertion; Inglese is especially concerned about the integration of this remark into the letter with Gaeta's emendation of the negative.

21. *disarmed:* this does not mean unarmed. The only escort the pope had when he entered Perugia was that of the Swiss Guard, numbering 150 men (Gaeta). In *Discourses,* I, 27, Machiavelli notes that Julius II, "borne along by the wild enthusiasm characterizing all his deeds, placed himself and the unpretentious guard he had with him in the enemy's hands."

22. *Fates:* cf. *Prince,* 25, 44–47, 83–88; Atkinson, pp. 363, 367: "I maintain that, without our having noticed him altering his character or any of his traits, we can see a prince thriving today and ruined tomorrow . . . since he has always prospered by keeping to one path, he is unable to leave it. Therefore when the moment has arrived for the circumspect man to act impetuously, he does not know how to do so; hence, he is destroyed"; and *Capitolo di Fortuna,* vv. 70–71: "whatever evil that befalls, you charge / to Her from whom it comes."

23. *wise man:* see Letter 92, n. 3, for the attribution of this belief to Ptolemy; see, too, Thomas Aquinas, *Summa Theologiae,* I, q. 115, art. 4 *ad tertium* (Raimondo). With "but such wise men do not exist" in the next sentence, Machiavelli rejects this belief. He opens *Prince,* 25, however, with these words: "I am not unaware that many men have been, and still are, convinced that wordly affairs are controlled by Fortune and God, so that even prudent men are unable to rule them and have, indeed, no remedy against them. . . . Nevertheless, since our free will ought not to be destroyed, I think it may well be true that Fortune is the mistress of half of our actions, but that even so she leaves the control of the other half—or nearly that much—to us" (1–5, 14–18; Atkinson, pp. 361, 363).

24. *I believe . . . under her yoke:* this long passage has many specific echoes in Machiavelli's work. For the first two sentences, cf. "[man] is incapable of deviating from what nature predisposes him to do" (*Prince,* 25, 82–83; Atkinson, p. 367); "we cannot oppose what our nature has predisposed us to do" (*Discourses,* III, 9); and *Capitolo di Fortuna,* vv. 112–114. As for the statement

"the man who matches his way of doing things with the condition of the times is successful," cf. "I also believe that the prince who makes his way of doing things consistent with the condition of the times may be successful. . . . Since Fortune is fickle and men are fixed in their ways, I therefore conclude that men are successful when they act harmoniously with Fortune and unsuccessful when they act inharmoniously with her" (*Prince*, 25, 51–53, 126–130; Atkinson, pp. 365, 369); "the reason for men's bad fortune or good fortune depends upon their making their way of doing things consistent with the times" (*Discourses*, III, 9); and finally *Capitolo di Fortuna*, vv. 100–105. With the phrase "anyone wise enough to adapt. . . . " cf. "yet were he to alter his character according to the times and circumstances, Fortune would not change" (*Prince*, 25, 88–90; Atkinson, p. 367). Two interesting discussions of this letter in connection with Machiavelli's other works can be found in Ferroni, "*Cose vane*," pp. 221–226, and Martelli, *Rinascimento* #9.

25. *Hannibal . . . Scipio:* Machiavelli returns to the example he used earlier; see n. 16 above.

Letter 122

1. *Tedesco:* a constable mentioned in Letters 113 and 120.

2. *Bibbona:* a town on the Mediterranean coast, on the way from Florence to Piombino (here the king of Aragon is Ferdinand the Catholic).

3. *Two days:* again, Ridolfi (*Life*, p. 95; *Vita* 7, p. 151) believes Biagio is sending Machiavelli extracts from the chancellery's log books.

4. *duke of Ferrara:* a conspiracy against Duke Alfonso I of Ferrara, the husband of Lucrezia Borgia, was formed by Giulio d'Este, the natural son of Alfonso's father, Ercole I; by Ferrante d'Este, a brother of Alfonso and Giulio; by Albertino Buschetto, count of San Cesaro; and by Gherardo Roberto, Alfonso's son-in-law. The marchioness of Mantua was Isabella d'Este, the wife of Francesco Gonzaga. See Cartwright, *Isabella d'Este*, I, 265–266, for more detail both about this grisly feud, which began over a beautiful handmaiden of Lucrezia Borgia, and about the conspiracy, which runs the gamut from the partial blinding of the handsome Giulio to beheadings and reprieves. Isabella d'Este was forced to release Giulio, and he was imprisoned until 1559; he is said to have been wearing clothes that were in fashion in 1506.

Letter 123

1. *some days ago:* Letter 119, dated 12 September.

2. *Filippo:* Filippo Casavecchia (Inglese).

3. *Consalvo:* Gonzalo Fernández de Córdoba, who was going to Piombino to join Ferdinand the Catholic, king of Spain; the Florentine ambassadors would await them both there.

Letter 124

1. *Francesco:* Francesco del Nero (Gaeta).

2. *ambassadors:* see Letters 118, n. 1, and 119, n. 4.

3. *two letters:* official, not personal, correspondence; see *Leg.,* II, pp. 995–998 (Gaeta).

4. *Genoa:* the situation here had its ramifications for Florentine foreign policy: a quarrel between the aristocratic faction and the popular party led to the expulsion of Gian Luigi Fieschi and the nobles, who appealed to and received the support of Louis XII and the popular party, which relied on Emperor Maximilian I. Louis informed the Florentine ambassador that he would help Florence out in the war against Pisa if the situation in Genoa worsened and he had to enter Italy, which he did in April 1507.

5. *man from Aix:* Pierre Le Filleul, bishop of Sisteron and Aix. See Letters 112, n. 12, and 115, n. 8.

6. *king to Chaumont:* Charles d'Amboise, lord of Chaumont, the French governor of Milan.

7. *Lapi:* Machiavelli had sent his letter of 21 September to the Ten from Perugia with him (Gaeta).

Letter 125

1. *Giustiniano and "Your Comrade":* the former appears in Letters 113 and 122 but has not been otherwise identified; neither has the "comrade" (Gaeta).

2. *blessing:* there appears to be a joking use of ecclesiastical language here and elsewhere in this letter (Gaeta).

3. *here:* i.e., Florence (Gaeta).

4. *vows:* Machiavelli is in Cesena, about nine miles southeast of Forlì, as the Florentine representative to the papal court.

Letter 126

1. *Castrocaro:* Tosinghi was commissioner general there, a town about sixty miles northeast of Florence near Forlì.

2. *12 noon:* translation of *ad ore 18.*

3. *de' Pazzi:* Cosimo de' Pazzi, bishop of Arezzo, had preceded Julius II to Forlì (Gaeta).

Letter 127

1. *Ruffini:* Bartolomeo Ruffini (Gaeta).

2. *request:* made in a letter to the Ten dated 3 October, *Leg.,* II, p. 1008 (Gaeta).

3. *article:* probably a letter, unlocated, in response to Letter 123 (Gaeta); Inglese thinks it is more likely a paragraph about Soderini inserted in a letter to Biagio.

4. *Alessandro to San Giorgio:* from Alessandro Nasi to Raffaello Riario, cardinal of San Giorgio in Velabro (Gaeta).

5. *Alamanno:* Alamanno Salviati, to whom Machiavelli had dedicated his *Decennale,* is now repaying Machiavelli by referring to him as a *ribaldo,* "rascal."

6. *Uguccioni:* the name of a family of Florentine merchants (Gaeta).

7. *archduke:* Philip I the Handsome (1478–1506) (Gaeta); he died 25 September.

8. *king of Aragon:* Ferdinand the Catholic, referred to later in this paragraph as "His Majesty."

9. *little son:* Archduke Ferdinand of Hapsburg, then three years old (Gaeta), the younger brother of Archduke Charles of Hapsburg, who was the future Holy Roman Emperor Charles V and King of Spain Charles I. Archduke Ferdinand became the Holy Roman Emperor Ferdinand I from 1556 to 1564; his father was Philip the Handsome (Philip I of Spain).

10. *enemies:* an allusion to the struggle for the throne of Castile upon Queen Isabella's death in 1504, when Philip I the Handsome and his wife Juana, the daughter of King Ferdinand the Catholic and Queen Isabella of Spain, were in Flanders and Ferdinand the Catholic ruled Castile until the couple's return in June 1506.

11. *Consalvo:* the Spanish general Gonzalo Fernández de Córdoba.

12. *His Most Christian Majesty:* Louis XII, king of France.

13. *legate:* i.e., Machiavelli, and his potential to "take priestly vows and become a thoroughly modern curial ecclesiastic" (see Letter 125 above).

14. *Gian Paolo's contract:* Giampaolo Baglioni was the ruler in Perugia whom Julius II challenged; as a condottiere in 1503, he had failed to join his troops with those of Louis XII at the Battle of Garigliano and thus contributed to the French defeat. Thereafter Louis considered him pro-Spain (Gaeta).

15. *Messer Mercurio:* Mercurio Bua (Gaeta).

16. *Chaumont:* Charles d'Amboise, lord of Chaumont, the French governor of Milan.

17. *Ludovico:* Ludovico Pico della Mirandola, while he was in Cesare Borgia's employ, had seized his brother Giovan Francesco Pico della Mirandola's possessions in 1502 (Gaeta).

18. *Madam Margaret:* Margaret, the daughter of Maximilian I, was to marry Filiberto, duke of Savoy, after the death of her first husband, Juan of Aragon, pretender to the Spanish throne, but Filiberto died in 1504 before the marriage could be celebrated. Had this marriage occurred, Henry VII, the Tudor king of England, would have controlled the low countries (Gaeta).

19. *Mademoiselle d'Angoulême:* refers to Marguerite d'Angoulême, the daughter of Charles d'Orléans, older sister of King Francis I, and future wife of King Henry of Navarre, following the death of her first husband, Charles IV, duke of Alençon (Gaeta).

20. *Gelderland:* Charles Egmont, duke of Gueldre (1470–1538), was fighting the Hapsburgs with the aid of France to regain territory lost by his father Charles the Bold of Burgundy (Gaeta).

21. *duke of Savoy:* Charles III (1504–1553) (Gaeta).

Letter 128

1. *Piero di Francesco:* brother-in-law of Machiavelli's wife, Marietta Corsini; see Letter 49, n. 3 (Gaeta).

2. *Francesco:* for the issue of the galleys with goods belonging to Totto Machiavelli and Francesco del Nero that were seized by the Venetians, see Letters 114, n. 2, and 116, n. 1.

3. *painter:* Gaeta notes that Ridolfi, *Vita 7,* p. 481, n. 31, wonders if this is a reference to an unknown portrait of Machiavelli.

4. *King Philip:* see Letter 127, n. 7.

Letter 129

1. *censures:* papal censures involved the loss of ecclesiastical sacraments, church services, and benefices. Both Machiavelli and Cardinal Soderini were in Cesena; Machiavelli reported this issue over the censure of the people of Bologna in his letter to the Ten sent from Cesena on this same day, *Leg.,* II, p. 1013 (Gaeta).

2. mazuco: whooping cough; he died on 25 September.

3. *Ramazzotti . . . Morattini:* Melchiorre Ramazzotti from Bologna had left the service of Giovanni Bentivoglio, who ruled Bologna, and gone over to the pope's side; Giovanni Morattini was from Forlì (Gaeta).

Letter 130

1. *fright:* Cardinal Soderini and his mule fell down a ravine during the entry of Pope Julius II into Colombaria, but he was unharmed; recall Letter 50 and Soderini's being "raring to go."

Letter 131

1. a duobus incompetibilia: a restriction against holding more than one benefice with a cure of souls (i.e., not a "sinecure") at the same time. Evidently the young man was seeking dispensation from this restriction because he already held one such benefice.

2. *France:* Tosinghi was the Florentine ambassador to the court of Louis XII in 1500; the meeting with then Cardinal Giuliano della Rovere would have occurred in September 1501 (Gaeta).

Letter 132

1. *Wherever . . . He Is:* the phrase indicates Biagio's frustration at not receiving more regular letters from Machiavelli.

2. *della Stufa:* Luigi Agnolo di Lorenzo della Stufa had been an ambassador to France in 1502 and a member of the Ten in 1504 (Gaeta).

3. *Ciachi:* no such correspondence survives.

4. *Martelli:* a Florentine merchant (Gaeta).

5. *added . . . letter of the 5th:* this naval metaphor refers to Machiavelli's lobbying efforts on behalf of the militia contained in his letter to the Ten on 5 October from Cesena, describing a military review and parade of the troops of Julius II; he elsewhere remarks that if the Ten could see these troops they "would not be ashamed of their conscripts or consider them worthless" *Leg.,* II, pp. 1011–1012 (Gaeta).

6. *Bernardo:* Bernardo Nasi replaced Piero Guicciardini in the Ten (Gaeta); Piero, the father of the historian, statesman, and eventual correspondent of Machiavelli, Francesco Guicciardini, was opposed to Machiavelli's plans for a citizen militia.

7. *Pepi:* Francesco Pepi, Florentine ambassador to Julius II (Gaeta).

8. *danger:* see Letter 130, n. 1.

9. *Ruffini:* Bartolomeo Ruffini (Gaeta).

Letter 133

1. *Lattanzio Tedaldi:* a friend of the humanists Marsilio Ficino and Callimaco Esperiente (Gaeta).

2. *Man:* the text has *"viso"* ("face") instead of *"viro,"* evidently a typographical error.

3. *you:* Tedaldi addresses Machiavelli as *tu*.

Letter 134

1. *obtain:* see the first paragraph of Letter 131.

Letter 135

1. *His Lordship the Governor:* Cosimo de' Pazzi, bishop of Arezzo and governor of Romagna (Gaeta).

2. *Gualterotti:* Francesco Gualterotti and Jacopo Salviati were chosen as Florentine ambassadors to France on 26 September (Gaeta).

Letter 136

1. *Messer Francesco:* this event is described in *Leg.,* II, pp. 1033–1034; Francesco Pepi had Vespucci along as his assistant while he was acting as Florentine ambassador to Julius II (Gaeta).

2. *shit blood:* translation of *cacare il sangue,* which seems not to be meant literally and might mean "made him very ill."

3. *Baccio di Ruffino:* Bartolomeo Ruffini (Gaeta).

4. *Ser Luca:* Luca Ficini (Gaeta).

5. *shit blood:* same phrase as above, though in context the meaning here is "won't have a hard time."

6. *entrance:* Pope Julius II entered Bologna on 30 November (Gaeta).

Letter 137

1. *Giovanni da Empoli:* writing from Bologna because he was in the service of Cardinal Soderini at the court of Pope Julius II (Gaeta).

2. *Messer Raimondo:* Raimondo Raimondi, Cardinal Soderini's treasurer, was awaiting the announcement that he would be a godfather to the child that Marietta Corsini Machiavelli was expecting; see the last paragraph of Letter 138.

Letter 138

1. *Carlo Albizzi:* Carlo di Zanobi Albizzi, abbot of Santa Maria of Taglifiume, was a Florentine doctor of canon law (Gaeta).

2. *Most Reverend Monsignor of Pavia:* Francesco Alidosi, bishop and cardinal of Pavia, the papal treasurer (Gaeta).

3. *in my place:* Machiavelli had asked Albizzi to be godfather to the child (Ludovico) that Marietta was carrying.

Letter 139

1. *magistracy:* the new magistracy, nine officers of the Florentine ordinance and militia, responsible for overseeing military affairs, for which Machiavelli wrote the order for the *Provvisione prima, per le fanterie, del 6 dicembre 1506* (First provision for infantry of 6 December 1506).

Letter 140

1. *Marco:* Marco della Palla (Gaeta).

2. *Bolognese lire:* the Bolognese lira was worth about six quattrini (Gaeta). One quattrino was equal to four denari; see Letter 14, n. 2.

3. *the Nine:* the nine officers of the Florentine ordinance and militia; see Letter 139.

4. *one or more:* a direct quotation from the *Provvisione prima, per le fanterie, del 6 dicembre 1506* (First provision for infantry of 6 December 1506) that Machiavelli wrote; see Machiavelli, *Altre opere storiche e politiche,* p. 108.

5. *position:* Machiavelli held on to both positions, but Vespucci did not become one of the coadjutors—Ser Francesco di Ser Tommaso Tommé from San Gimignano was elected chancellor (Gaeta).

6. *Basilio:* Basilio da Bagno, the abbot of San Felice (Gaeta); he was a Camaldolese monk and friend of Machiavelli; see Lowe, *Church and Politics,* pp. 238–239, n. 23.

7. *bed board:* translation of *una proda di letto;* it seems to denote some form of assistance.

8. *German cardinal:* Melchiorre Mekaw, bishop of Bressanone (Gaeta). Bressanone (Brixen, in German) is a town in the Alto Adige, north of Bolzano.

9. *Messer Giovanni:* Giovanni Bentivoglio (Gaeta).

10. *Nobili . . . Luca:* Giovan Battista de' Nobili and Luca Ficini (Gaeta).

1507-1508

Letter 141

1. *Giovanni Ridolfi:* see Letter 112.

Letter 142

1. *Lorenzo Berardi:* in dealing with practical matters about Machiavelli's landholdings, Berardi writes a syntactically confusing letter containing many grammatical and spelling errors.

2. *Gaza:* probably a tenant on a *colonia,* a farm governed by a profit-sharing lease arrangement (Gaeta).

3. *has . . . belongings:* translation of *ha fatto mazzi de' sua salci,* "has gathered

up his willows in bunches," a proverbial expression meaning "has packed up his belongings and departed" that is also found in Luigi Pulci's mock epic *Il Morgante* (Gaeta).

Letter 143

1. *at seven:* translation of *a ore una di notte,* "at one hour of the night."

2. *Buggiano:* a town between Pescia and Montecatini (Gaeta), about thirteen miles west of Pistoia.

Letter 144

1. *"If I grieved . . . grieve again":* a slight misquotation of Dante, *Inferno,* 26, v. 19: *"Allor mi dolsi, e ora mi ridoglio"* ("I grieved then and now I grieve again" [G]).

2. *friendships:* on this issue, in the context of this letter, see Najemy, "Machiavelli's Service," pp. 109–112.

3. *Tarquinius:* Lucius Tarquinius Collatinus was the husband of Lucretia, who was raped by Sextus Tarquinius, the son of Lucius Tarquinius Superbus—not "the son of Sextus." Tarquinius Superbus was the last king of Rome, and the story of Lucretia's rape is traditionally associated with the fall of the monarchy; Tarquinius Collatinus was one of Rome's first consuls and was considered the founder of the Roman Republic, c. 509 B.C.

4. *Marius and Sulla:* Caius Marius (157–86 B.C.), a famous Roman general, a plebian who became tribune, praetor, and consul. Lucius Cornelius Sulla (138–78 B.C.), also a Roman general, served under Marius and became consul in 88 B.C. He and Marius then disagreed over who should be the military commander against Mithridates VI in the First Mithridatic War in Asia Minor (88–84 B.C.): Sulla was favored by the senate and Marius by the populace. Their rivalry turned into civil war. Because Sulla marched his army on Rome, his faction won. Marius fled Rome; when Sulla went to Asia Minor, he returned and massacred his enemies.

5. *Caesar . . . Pompey:* Julius Caesar (100–44 B.C.) was the nephew of Marius's wife and hence allied with the popular faction; Sulla forbade his marriage to Cornelia, the daughter of the Marian party's leader, Cinna. Early in his career, Pompey (106–48 B.C.) fought for Sulla. His connection with Caesar began in 60 B.C., with the formation of the First Triumvirate with Caesar and Crassus; in 59 B.C. Pompey married Caesar's daughter, Julia. With her death in 54 B.C., their alliance broke down and the two became bitter enemies. Civil war broke out in 49 B.C. as Caesar, after his lengthy campaign in Gaul, crossed the Rubicon, a stream separating Italy from Cisalpine Gaul. His decision was sparked by Pompey's and the senate's decision to deprive him of his power base in the army and to force him to proceed politically for the consulship.

6. *Antony and Octavius and Lepidus:* the Second Triumvirate, established in 43 B.C., was given enormous power to restore the public welfare after Cae-

sar's death; these powers were renewed for five more years in 37 B.C. In the power struggle between Mark Antony, Octavius (Caesar's adopted son and heir), and Lepidus, the Roman Republic fell and Octavius became the first Roman emperor, as Augustus (63 B.C.–A.D. 14).

7. *Dietisalvi and Piero di Cosimo:* Machiavelli discusses the 1466 conspiracy of Dietisalvi Neroni against Piero di Cosimo de' Medici in his *Florentine Histories,* 7, 10–20. Cosimo, at his death in 1464, urged his heir Piero to hire Neroni to look over the Medici's account books and to heed his advice. More interested in being a benefactor than a banker, Piero followed Neroni's advice to call in many of the Medici loans, thereby causing panic among a large number of creditors. Amid this uproar, Neroni conspired with others envious of the Medici's power and influence to unseat Piero. Despite constitutional changes urged on Florence by the conspirators—Neroni, Luca Pitti, Agnolo Acciaiuoli, and Niccolò Soderini, an uncle of Piero and Francesco Soderini—Piero faced them down and passed on a stable firm to his son Lorenzo.

8. *Giuliano and Francesco de' Pazzi:* Machiavelli discusses the 1478 conspiracy of the Pazzi, a rival Florentine banking firm, against Lorenzo de' Medici, in which his younger brother Giuliano de' Medici was killed, in his *Florentine Histories,* 8, 2–9, and *Discourses,* 3, 6. In 1478 Francesco and his brother Girolamo, along with Pope Sixtus IV's nephew Girolamo Riario, his kinsman Cardinal Raffaello Riario, and a mercenary captain named Battista da Montesecco, spearheaded a conspiracy to murder the two Medici before the altar in the cathedral church of Santa Reparata (the Duomo). The city rose up in support of Lorenzo de' Medici. The humanist and poet Angelo Poliziano also wrote a famous account of this conspiracy; translated in Kohl and Witt, *The Earthly Republic,* 305–322.

9. *story:* translation of *cantafavola;* see Letter 110, n. 9.

10. *prevented it:* a reference to Machiavelli's having lost out to Vettori as ambassador to Maximilian's court, because "many well-thought-of men" (see the first passage from Guicciardini, *Storie Fiorentine,* quoted in the Headnote for 1507) in the Signoria had opposed Machiavelli's appointment.

11. *Manelli:* he may belong to a family that Guicciardini discusses in *Storie Fiorentine,* in regard to a sordid murder trial occurring in 1506 (Gaeta); see *Storie Fiorentine,* pp. 287–289; Domandi, pp. 262–264.

Letter 145

1. *unfortunate:* Alessandro is consoling Machiavelli for his disappointment at not having been named ambassador to Germany (Gaeta). "Cure" and the medical imagery are carried throughout the paragraph.

2. *you:* Nasi addresses Machiavelli as *tu.*

3. *Germany:* Nasi uses the derogatory *Todescheria* rather than *Germania.*

4. *social standing:* Guicciardini used the phrase *tanti giovani da bene,* "many decent young men," in the same context; see the first passage from his *Storie Fiorentine* quoted in the Headnote for 1507.

Letter 146

1. *Miguel de Corella:* in April 1506, Don Micheletto (Miguel de Corella, Michele Coreglia), a Spanish lieutenant whom Cesare Borgia had employed several years earlier to make soldiers out of peasants in Romagna—which he did ruthlessly—was appointed to lead Florence's citizen army. His appointment was renewed in early 1507. See Letter 90, n. 2, for more on this military leader.

2. *Firenzuola:* a town about thirty miles northeast of Florence, in the Appennine valley of the Santerno.

Letter 147

1. *Michele Corella:* the same Don Micheletto who wrote Letter 146.

2. *part:* as if in answer to the accusation of his partisanship, Don Micheletto seems to be playing here and elsewhere in this letter on two senses of the word *parte:* "part" and "party."

3. *Our Most Exalted Lordships:* i.e., the Signoria.

4. *more . . . coat:* proverbial expression meaning "first things first."

5. *servants of Marzocco:* the name given to the lion rampant bearing a lily shield, a patriotic symbol of Florence.

6. *Castrocaro and Modigliana and Marradi:* towns east of Firenzuola, in the direction of Faenza and Forlì.

7. *Bagnacavallo:* a town in Romagna between Imola and Ravenna.

8. *horse's hoof:* i.e., by a hairbreadth.

9. *how . . . Don Michele?:* a self-dramatizing aside on the writer's part.

10. *Miguel de Orella:* his own way of spelling his name.

Letter 148

1. *answered:* in Casavecchia's *capitolo* (a humorous poem in terza rima): *"Machiavel mio, le tue buone vivande"* ("Machiavelli mine, your good victuals"). Machiavelli's "little epistle" has not been found (Gaeta).

2. *spiritual:* see the tone of the first paragraph of Letter 144.

Letter 149

1. *Redhead: il Rosso* in the original; if this is a real person, he has not been otherwise identified.

2. *Guicciardini:* Piero (Gaeta); in the disputes within the Signoria over the power Soderini sought to gain, Piero Guicciardini was known for his prudent caution in arguing on the side of the more fractious Alamanno Salviati and Giovan Battista Ridolfi. But Piero was an outspoken opponent of Machiavelli's citizen militia. He refused to accompany Salviati when the Signoria elected them both as representatives to Maximilian's court, and thus Vettori was sent in June.

3. *real:* a reference to Maximilian's possible invasion of Italy. Gaeta believes that Nasi did not put much credence in the possibility of this invasion or in the actual strength of the emperor's army.

4. *woe . . . men:* cf. "Woe unto the world because of offences! for it must needs be that offences come; but woe to that man by whom the offence cometh!" (Matthew 18:7); the Douay version substitutes "scandals" for "offences" and "nevertheless" for "but" (Gaeta).

Letter 150

1. *desire:* Machiavelli had asked Acciaiuoli, the Florentine ambassador to Rome, to help him find a successor to Don Micheletto (Miguel de Corella) as head of the citizen militia; see Letter 147. The Ten cashiered him in October, and he was assassinated in Milan in February 1508 (Gaeta).

2. bargello: the title given the chief of police in medieval and renaissance Florence; the office was scorned by condottieri because they believed they were destined to greater glory in the military.

3. *Sophi:* specifically, the term referred to the king of Persia, but here it appears to be a more general term for "the Turks" (Gaeta).

4. *Rinaldo said:* Acciaiuoli quotes from memory verses from Luigi Pulci's romantic chivalric epic, *Morgante,* III, 30, vv. 7-8 (Gaeta); Rinaldo's friend Dodone, or Dudone, is dubbed "the man with a club," but it is Rinaldo's friendship for him that is important here.

5. *Zeffi:* probably Giovan Francesco Zefi, who brought out an edition of Pliny the Younger and translated the letters of St. Jerome into Italian (Inglese).

Letter 151

1. *Bolzano:* Maximilian's court was in this town in the Tyrolean Alps.

2. *Francesco:* Francesco Vettori, the Florentine ambassador to Maximilian's court. Ridolfi reads this sentence and the next as evidence of a strong rapport between Machiavelli and Soderini. He suggests that were this not an "official" document Machiavelli might be freer in his remarks and that one can find a hint of pride as well as bitterness reading between the lines (*Vita 7,* p. 618). For more on Vettori's role in the negotiations and in writing the diplomatic dispatches, see Jones, "Vettori and Machiavelli," and Jones, *Vettori,* pp. 15–31. For the view that the letter was Machiavelli's attempt to be recalled from what he believed to be a useless mission, see Black, "Machiavelli, Servant," p. 88.

Letter 152

1. *Cesare Mauro:* a scholar whom Machiavelli had met in Germany and evidently asked to find some manuscripts so that Machiavelli could verify some facts of a political and military nature when he was drafting his thoughts on the German mission (Gaeta).

2. *mouse:* an allusion to Horace, *Ars poetica* (*Epist. Ad Pisam* 2.3) v. 139, which in turn is based on Phaedrus, *Fables,* 4.22.1, and Plutarch, *Life of Agesilaus,* II.

3. *man from Herculanum:* refers to someone from a city east of Capua (near Naples) in an ancient Samnite region of Italy.

4. *Venafro:* Pandolfo Petrucci, the prince of Siena, hired a professor in

the Studium of Siena, Antonio Giordani da Venafro, as his minister; Machiavelli thought very highly of Venafro's abilities: see *Prince*, 22; and Gaeta points out that Machiavelli called Venafro the "foremost among his [Petrucci's] men" (*Leg.*, II, p. 910).

5. *Bartolo . . . De Belleperche:* a list of famous jurists: Bartolo da Sassoferrato (1314–1357), Baldo degli Ubaldi (1327–1400), Cino da Pistoia (1270–1336/1337), Giovan Cristoforo Porcio (15th century), Pierre de Belleperche (d. 1308) (Gaeta).

6. *"woe . . . wretched":* an allusion to the fall of Rome, as described in Livy, Book Five.

7. *Antimachus:* a turgid, pompous late-Greek epic poet.

8. *Signor Francesco:* Francesco Vettori (Gaeta).

Letter 153

1. *orders:* the issue is the search for a successor to Don Micheletto (Miguel de Corella) as head of the militia; see Letters 147 and 150 (Gaeta).

2. *Santa Reparata:* the cathedral of Santa Maria del Fiore, the duomo; the meaning here is, wait until the three of us—Casa being Filippo Casavecchia—are in Florence (Gaeta).

3. *bench-sitting:* i.e., lengthy and private discussion on public benches, where gossip was traditionally exchanged (Gaeta).

4. *six o'clock:* translation of *hora vero ante primam*.

Letter 154

1. *Mariotto:* Mariotto d'Amerigo, a broker in Rome, received an order from the Signoria to give a receipt to Acciaiuoli for 500 ducats made out in the name of Lorenzo and Totto Machiavelli (Gaeta); on Lorenzo di Machiavelli, see Letter 13, n. 11.

Letter 155

1. *matter:* see Letter 154, n. 1.

2. *Lorenzo Machiavelli:* see Letter 13, n. 11.

Letter 156

1. *summary:* perhaps Machiavelli's *Rapporto delle cose della Magna* (Gaeta).

Letter 157

1. *Pisans:* Machiavelli had left for Pisa on 16 August.

2. *laying waste:* the Florentine policy of laying waste to the Pisan countryside (Gaeta).

3. *you:* Soderini addresses Machiavelli as *tu,* as is usual for him.

Letter 158

1. *in camp:* with the Florentine troops in the campaign against Pisa.

2. *di Banco:* here and in the postscript, according to Inglese, Filippo Casavecchia is the man concerned.

3. *feast:* 8 September 1508 (Gaeta).

4. *San Niccolò:* near Poppi (Gaeta), a town on the Arno in the Casentino.

Letter 160

1. *Carducci:* he became the constable of Vico Pisano in May 1509 (Gaeta).

Letter 161

1. *Niccolò Serristori:* In the last paragraph of Letter 89 Serristori is described as someone who "is completely devoted to" Machiavelli.

2. *Jonah:* since Machiavelli's letter, to which this is an answer, is lost, there is no way to trace this biblical allusion (Gaeta).

3. *Fuggers:* a family from Bavarian Swabia of merchant princes and financiers, especially for the House of Hapsburg; Jakob II, "the Rich" (1459–1525), lent money to Maximilian I and acted as a papal banker through the branch in Rome opened in 1493; their correspondence and their newsletters are a great source of information about life in late sixteenth-century Europe.

4. *Kingdom Come:* translation of *in Santo Celso.*

5. *sanctuary:* in this case, diplomatic and not ecclesiastical sanctuary (Gaeta); i.e., immunity.

6. *cronies:* specifically, Machiavelli and Niccolò di Alessandro Machiavelli (Gaeta); on the latter, see Letter 44, n. 4.

1509

Letter 162

1. *Captain General:* Biagio uses the title jokingly, even though Machiavelli had a great deal of freedom of action in his work with the Ten and the Nine (Gaeta). Fachard, *Biagio Buonaccorsi,* discusses this letter and the next in the context of the official correspondence between Biagio and Machiavelli, pp. 50–52.

2. *4 chancellors:* the three other commissioners to the camp at Pisa were Alamanno Salviati, Antonio da Filicaia, and Niccolò di Piero Capponi (Gaeta).

3. *pope:* Biagio now begins discussing the actions of the signatories of the recent League of Cambrai.

4. *Tarlatino and Romeo:* two Florentine riders (Gaeta).

5. *his towns:* in Apulia, the "heel" of Italy, the Venetians occupied the ports of Monopoli, Polignano, Trani, Brindisi, Otranto, and Gallipoli (Gaeta).

6. *expense:* in addition to the actual military expenses, Florence had made separate agreements to pay off Louis XII, Ferdinand the Catholic, and Maximilian I for the latter's tacit agreement not to interfere in the war against Pisa. Because Florence was not an official signatory of the anti-Venetian League of Cambrai, these payments were a bribe (what Machiavelli calls "stuffing each [country]'s throat and whatever mouth remained open," *Decennale secondo,* vv.

155–156) for Florence's freedom to pursue the war against Pisa (Gaeta).

7. *bridge:* actually, it was no more than pilings set up to cut off the Arno and prevent supplies from reaching the besieged Pisa (Gaeta).

8. *down there:* Machiavelli was at the mouth of the Fiumemorto with about one thousand militia troops (Gaeta); the canal was eventually closed on 7 March.

9. *That wind . . . comes up:* this paragraph is to be read figuratively: it seems to refer to the attacks on Machiavelli launched by Piero Soderini's opponents (Gaeta).

10. *commissioner of Cascina:* Niccolò Capponi (Gaeta); Cascina is a town on the Arno about eight miles east of Pisa.

11. *grumbling and complaining:* so committed to his militia was he that Machiavelli was too busy to write; he "'hovered everywhere throughout the armies'" and "the soldiers recognized his authority more than that of the [regular Florentine] commissioners" (Ridolfi, *Life,* pp. 106–107; *Vita 7,* pp. 169, 171). Embittered, Capponi eventually filed an official complaint with the Ten about not receiving enough information from Machiavelli.

12. *Baldovino:* Fachard, *Biagio Buonaccorsi,* p. 49, identifies Baldovino as one of Biagio's best friends.

Letter 163

1. *case:* see Letter 162, n. 11.

2. *superior:* Piero Soderini (Gaeta).

3. *Ser Francesco:* Francesco Serragli (Gaeta).

4. *bridge:* see Letter 162, n. 7.

5. *first day of Lent:* i.e., the last day of the Carnival season.

Letter 164

1. *yours:* here Soderini uses the formal *voi.*

Letter 165

1. *Consalvo and one of his nephews:* Gonzalo Fernández de Córdoba and Pedro de Córdoba, the son of Gonzalo's brother Alonso (Gaeta).

2. *His Most Christian Majesty:* Louis XII.

3. *Rucellai and Giuliano:* Giovanni di Bernardo Rucellai and Giuliano de' Medici (Gaeta).

4. *superior:* Piero Soderini (Gaeta).

5. *Piombino:* refers to Jacopo d'Appiano, the prince of Piombino, acting as an agent for a possible peace treaty with Pisa.

Letter 166

1. *Lattanzio Tedaldi:* A friend of the humanists Marsilio Ficino and Callimaco Esperiente (Gaeta).

2. *you:* Tedaldi addresses Machiavelli as *tu,* as is usual for him.

3. *possession:* Pisa's surrender was signed in Florence on 4 June; Ma-

chiavelli countersigned it, along with Marcello Virgilio di Adriano Berti. Florence's army actually entered Pisa on Friday, 8 June (Gaeta).

4. *auspicious:* apparently based on evidence from a horoscope.

5. *seven o'clock . . . six-thirty:* translation of *le 12 ore e 1/2 . . . 13 ore passate.*

Letter 167

1. *three in the afternoon:* translation of *le 21 ore.*

2. *your battalions:* i.e., Machiavelli's own citizen militia.

3. *restored:* translation of *ut non cunctando sed accelerando restitueritis rem florentinam,* a reference to the judgment of Ennius (*unus homo nobis cunctando restituit rem,* "one man by delaying restored the state to us") in his *Annales,* quoted by Cicero in his *De senectute,* IV.10; it refers to the Roman consul and general Quintus Fabius Maximus, known as *Cunctator,* "the Delayer," because he sought to avoid direct contact with Hannibal during the Second Punic War, 218–201 B.C.

Letter 168

1. *Niccolò di Alessandro Machiavelli:* see Letter 44, n. 4.

2. *Alamanno:* Alamanno Salviati (Gaeta).

Letter 169

1. *Barga:* a town about twenty-five miles north of Lucca, on the Serchio River.

2. *Pontedera:* a town on the Arno, about twelve miles east of Pisa.

3. *noble city:* Pisa.

4. *weighty things:* Casavecchia is referring, with the phrase *cose gravi,* to reputation and public opinion in connection with Machiavelli's career, not to physical gravity.

5. *ideas:* i.e., Machiavelli's ideas about a citizen militia.

6. *Every day . . . had:* Casavecchia may be somewhat of a prophet himself. Ridolfi ends his biography by commenting on the aptness of this remark for defining Machiavelli's place in history: "A prophet, but an unarmed prophet like Savonarola, he too had to submit to the fate to which he had condemned his fellows, even if it were only his effigy and his books that went on the pyre. It was inevitable that he should rise again from the pyre *post fata* and take his revenge with those weapons which equip unarmed prophets and make them invincible" (*Life,* p. 254; *Vita 7,* p. 398). For the danger of Machiavelli's thinking of himself as a prophet, see Najemy, "Machiavelli's Service," p. 115.

7. *province:* i.e., the territory under Casavecchia's jurisdiction (Gaeta).

Letter 170

1. moggia: a measure of dry weight—since one *moggio fiorentino* weighs about 16 ½ standard U.S. bushels, Casavecchia claims to have ordered 660 bushels of mortar.

2. libbre: approximately 1596 modern pounds, in terms of standard U.S. weight.

Letter 171

1. *Pietro Corella:* see also Letters 146 and 147 from Don Micheletto (Miguel de Corella, Michele Coreglia) for examples of the epistolary style of a Spanish mercenary.

2. *when . . . death's door:* translation of *quando fuse state con la candela alla boca,* "even if he had a candle in his mouth," recalling the idiomatic expression *essere alla candela,* "to be at the brink of death."

3. *Anziano:* perhaps Azzana, near Pisa (Gaeta).

4. *turned into a monk:* i.e., become as peaceful as a monk (Gaeta).

Letter 172

1. *Transpadana:* on the other side of the Po; the "affairs" refer to Venetian counterattacks after their defeat at Vailà (or Agnadello of the Battle of Ghiaradadda, since the town is on the Adda) and the subsequent occupation of Venetian territory by Louis XII's and Maximilian's troops. The Venetians succeeded in retaking Padua (17 July) and also Treviso (Gaeta).

Letter 173

1. *letter:* for Machiavelli's letter to Salviati, dated 28 September 1509, see Appendix Letter G.

2. *obliged:* the tone of the opening sentence, plus the compliment later for the "quite beautiful" discussion, may be Salviati's covert way of acknowledging that he understands the situation both in Padua and, more importantly, in Florence; that is, Florence and Soderini are completely behind what may well be a policy Machiavelli devised and persuaded others to follow; see Rubinstein, "Politica imperiale," and Luzzati and Sbrilli, *"Massimiliano d'Ausburgo."* For the argument that this letter is heavy with irony and sarcasm and an "eloquent testimony of the loathing which Machiavelli—in Salviati's view a godless, arrogant intellectual—inspired among the Florentine conservative patriciate," see Black, "Machiavelli, Servant," p. 98.

3. *part:* Luzzati and Sbrilli, *"Massimiliano d'Ausburgo"* p. 854, indicate a three-syllable, illegible crossing-out at this point.

4. *His Most Christian Highness . . . His Catholic Majesty:* i.e., Louis XII, Pope Julius II, and Ferdinand the Catholic.

Letter 174

1. *Wherever He May Be:* Machiavelli was in search of Maximilian I, so that he could deliver the first payment of Florence's indemnity in order to have a free reign in Pisa.

2. *Verona:* Machiavelli had recently heard that Vicenza had rebelled in favor of Venice and that Verona—exactly where Machiavelli was headed in his quest for the emperor—was rumored to be doing likewise (Gaeta).

3. *bench-sitters:* translation of *pancacce,* roughly equivalent to our notion of people hanging around bars "mouthing off" from their barstools.

Letter 175

1. *suit:* see Letter 176, n. 2.

2. *Giovan Vittorio:* Giovan Vittorio Soderini (1460–1528) held numerous posts in Florence as prior, commissioner, and ambassador—indeed, he was an ambassador to Maximilian I in 1509. In 1512 he shared his brother Piero's exile in Perugia, although he returned to Florence in 1513 (Gaeta).

Letter 176

1. *Luigi Guicciardini:* Francesco's eldest brother. In addition to being the recipient of Machiavelli's famous Letter 178, Luigi Guicciardini received an important letter from his son Niccolò. Dated 29 July, probably in 1517, it is one of the earliest reactions to *The Prince* by one of Machiavelli's contemporaries; see Stephens and Butters, "New Light," pp. 61–62; text, pp. 68–69.

2. *lawsuit:* Ridolfi hazards a guess that the legal matter concerned ecclesiastical benefices involved in a suit at Rome and that it somehow related to Machiavelli's brother Totto's coming ordination as a priest (5 January 1510); Totto had renounced his claim to their father's house in Florence and the country property at Sant'Andrea in Percussina (*Life*, p. 113; *Vita 7*, 181–182); oblique references to this matter crop up in letters to Machiavelli written in 1510.

3. *Jacopo:* because he was sick, Luigi was in Mantua to visit him (Gaeta); a younger brother of Francesco.

4. *Giovanni:* Giovanni Borromei, with whom, following his instructions from the Ten, Machiavelli had taken lodgings (Gaeta).

5. *Pandolfini:* Francesco di Pier Filippo Pandolfini was the Florentine representative to the French cardinal, Georges d'Amboise, in Milan; Pandolfini sent his dispatches to Borromei, who in turn forwarded them to Florence (Gaeta).

6. *Lang:* Matthäus von Wellenburg Lang, bishop of Gurk, secretary to Maximilian I; Machiavelli's credentials were addressed to Lang (Gaeta). Gurk, the seat of a former bishopric, is a town in Carinthia, Austria, north of Klagenfurt, not far from the Italian border. For his reception in Florence in 1512, see Landucci, pp. 263–264.

7. *Francesco:* Machiavelli's future friend and correspondent, Francesco Guicciardini.

8. *writing:* a reference to the *capitolo* entitled *Dell'ambizione* that Machiavelli dedicated to Luigi Guicciardini (Gaeta); in Letter 178, Machiavelli calls this his "doggerel," *cantafavola* (see Letter 110, n. 9). For more concerning Machiavelli's state of mind while writing this letter, see Najemy, "Machiavelli's Service," p. 116.

Letter 177

1. *Strozzi:* late in 1508 Filippo Strozzi had married Clarice de' Medici, despite Piero Soderini's active opposition to the wedding. He sought to squelch the wedding plans because he viewed the marriage alliance as a strengthening of the opposition that centered on a Medici ascendency to

power within Florence. The Eight of Guard fined Strozzi and exiled him to Naples for three years; some believed Machiavelli was instrumental in his banishment, but this allegation is not mentioned in Bullard, *Strozzi and the Medici,* pp. 45–60, or in Guicciardini, *Storia d'Italia,* pp. 235–241; *Storie Fiorentine,* pp. 326–332; Domandi, pp. 297–303.

2. *illness:* perhaps a sexually transmitted disease.

3. *Lanfredini:* Lanfredo Lanfredini (Gaeta).

Letter 178

1. *Hell's Bells, Luigi:* although this story may well have been "dreamed up," it certainly is not an "irreproachable letter" of the type that Machiavelli would draft and send to the Ten (see the second paragraph of Letter 176). Rebhorn, *Foxes and Lions,* pp. 242–244, has a provocative discussion of this letter.

2. *first thing I noticed . . . their ends:* elements of her description might remind a Renaissance reader of a grotesquely ironic play on standard iconographic images associated with *occasio,* opportunity, or Fortuna. Few people, however, would want to seize this opportunity by the forelock.

3. *I'll be damned:* translated according to a suggestion in Inglese.

4. *Giovanni:* Giovanni Borromei; see Letter 176, n. 4 (Gaeta).

5. *doggerel:* translation of *cantafavola,* see Letter 110, n. 9. Inglese is perplexed about the reason why Machiavelli would have sent the poem "Dell'Ambizione" to Gualtieri before letting the dedicatee, Luigi Guicciardini, see it.

Letter 179

1. *Venafro:* the prince of Siena, Pandolfo Petrucci, hired him as his minister. Machiavelli admired him—see Letter 152, n. 4.

2. *cardinal:* evidently Cardinal Soderini.

Letter 180

1. *Pigello Portinari:* secretary to Maximilian I, though a Florentine. He had tried to get the Signoria to help him with affairs he had pending both in Florence and in Rome (Gaeta).

2. *Stefano del Benino:* a Florentine merchant, perhaps a relative of Neri del Benino (see Letter 217), a brother-in-law of Giovanni Machiavelli (Gaeta).

3. *Most Reverend Monsignor:* Georg von Neideck, bishop of Trent (Gaeta).

Letter 181

1. *matter:* the exact nature of this assertion is unclear: it may refer to a charge that Machiavelli's father, Bernardo, was illegitimate, and hence Machiavelli was disqualified from holding public office, or it may refer to a charge that Bernardo was *a specchio,* i.e., that he had incurred debts—a situation that would make his children ineligible for office. This latter view is well-argued by Ridolfi (*Life,* 112–113; *Vita 7,* 180–181) and seems a more probable explanation.

2. *judged:* i.e., against Machiavelli (Gaeta).

3. *wont to say:* although Machiavelli often teases Biagio about being overly concerned for his welfare, Machiavelli seems, indeed, to have heeded Biagio's advice and tarried "wherever he may" have been, probably at Mantua or Bologna, during his return trip to Florence; he arrived 2 January 1510.

4. *eight in the evening:* translation of *hora secunda noctis.*

1510–1512

Letter 182

1. *good instruction:* aware of Piero Soderini's private instructions to Machiavelli, the cardinal wrote a carefully worded letter affirming the need to prevent a rift between Louis XII and Julius II, "to keep that prince, Louis XII, in good union with His Holiness the Pope." See Lowe, *Church and Politics,* pp. 84–85, concerning the point that Machiavelli was really a private envoy expressing the Soderinis' beliefs, but especially the cardinal's, that good relations with France had to be maintained at all costs. Guicciardini would maintain that such an attachment was too costly and led to the Florentine republic's downfall (*Storie Fiorentine,* p. 299; Domandi, p. 273).

2. *ambassador:* Angelo Leonino, bishop of Tivoli (Gaeta).

3. *Girolami:* Cardinal Soderini's personal representative at the French court (Gaeta); it is more likely that he was his agent there.

Letter 183

1. *Bartolomeo Panciatichi:* a merchant and banker from Pistoia residing in Lyons, through whom Machiavelli sent his correspondence to Florence (Gaeta).

2. *Acciaiuoli:* Roberto Acciaiuoli, Florence's new ambassador to Louis XII (Gaeta).

3. *marquess of Mantua:* Francesco Gonzaga II (1466–1519), the fourth marquess of Mantua, husband of Isabella d'Este.

Letter 184

1. *Roberto:* Roberto Acciaiuoli, the Florentine ambassador en route to the French court (Gaeta).

2. *Filippo:* Filippo Casavecchia (Gaeta).

3. *overthrow Genoa:* the July campaign of Marcantonio Colonna; another attempt was made in September (Gaeta).

4. *Mons. d'Auch:* as François Guillaume de Clermont, cardinal archbishop of Auch, was preparing to leave Rome for France, Julius II had him arrested and locked up in the dreaded Castel Sant'Angelo (Gaeta).

5. *duke of Ferrara:* Alfonso I (1476–1534), husband of Lucrezia Borgia. Since Ferrara was the only city standing in the way of Julius II regaining control of Romagna and the papal states, the pope prepared to launch a campaign against Ferrara. By September he was in the region personally leading the attack.

6. flussi *or* primera: card games.

7. *Bologna:* it was the pope who moved on Bologna; his triumphal entry occurred seven weeks later, on 22 September.

8. *kingdom:* the Kingdom of Naples (Gaeta).

9. *nephew:* Archduke Charles of Hapsburg, the future Charles V, Holy Roman Emperor from 1519 to 1556 and King Charles I of Spain from 1516 to 1556.

10. *Francesco:* a familiar signature; it indicates the heightened degree of friendship between the two; Vettori was a godfather to one of Machiavelli's children who died in infancy.

Letter 185

1. *Lecce:* a provincial capital and an important port on the Adriatic, southeast of Brindisi.

Letter 186

1. *[in the Chancellery]:* the square brackets indicate Gaeta's belief that this "friend" was in the chancellery.

Letter 187

1. *D. Marcello:* this is the last direct reference to Marcello Virgilio di Adriano Berti in these letters; but see Letter 191, n. 6 and Letter 257, nn. 5–6, for possible allusions to him.

2. *lose her:* Biagio's wife Lessandra, the niece of Marsilio Ficino, died less than two months later; Biagio enters her death in his *Ricordi,* 16 October 1510 (Fachard, *Biagio Buonaccorsi,* p. 20).

Letter 188

1. *Modena and Ferrara:* a reference to the Ten's dispatch to Machiavelli dated 22 August that contained false news that the pope's armies had taken Ferrara and Reggio Emilia and a factual report of the same armies' entry into Modena (*Leg.,* III, pp. 1302–1306) (Gaeta).

2. *circumstances:* in the same dispatch, the Ten expressed fear that the pope, in his attempt to gain control of northern Italy, might attack Siena, thereby applying pressure on Florence; they emphasized their point by adding, "these matters in our judgment are not to be neglected" (*Leg.,* III, p. 1304) (Gaeta).

Letter 189

1. *Modena:* the pope arranged a treaty so that the city would come over to his side.

2. *Swiss:* they were no longer allied to the French and had passed over to the service of Julius II (Gaeta).

3. *Girolami:* Giovanni Girolami (Gaeta).

Letter 190

1. *Ser Antonio:* Antonio della Valle (Gaeta).

2. *eager:* Pope Julius II sought to separate Florence from France and threatened an invasion of Tuscany under Giampaolo Baglioni; there was even some thought given to restoring the Medici so that the pope could count on the city's support. These matters are alluded to in the Ten's dispatch of 22 August, mentioned in Letter 188, nn. 1–2, and detailed in the rest of this paragraph.

3. *Piombino:* i.e., Florence had become afraid of sharing the fate of Piombino and the rest of the cities mentioned (Gaeta).

4. *Vada:* a port south of Leghorn.

5. *Sarteano:* near Siena.

6. *great galley:* translation of *galeazza,* a three-masted ship with high sides, armed with cannon—it was larger than a *galea,* or galley.

7. *Savona . . . Nice:* all these ports were in the westernmost reaches of the Italian Riviera; Villefranche and Nice have since become part of France.

8. *Polesine:* the region along the Po, between Rovigo and Ferrara.

9. *Legnago:* a town on the Adige, halfway between Verona and Rovigo.

10. *Carpi or Mirandola:* towns west of Ferrara, on the other side of the Po.

Letter 191

1. *you:* the question mark indicates that Gaeta does not know the identity of this correspondent; whoever this correspondent may be (see n. 6), he uses the familiar *tu* with Machiavelli.

2. *end [?]:* per Gaeta's text.

3. *Percussina:* Machiavelli's country house at Sant'Andrea in Percussina, southwest of Florence, where he later retired during his exile.

4. *"Without . . . victor":* the writer recalls a passage from Livy, 35.49.13, that Machiavelli himself uses later in Letter 243 and *Prince,* 21 (76–78; Atkinson, p. 335); "Quinctius" is Titus Quinctius Flaminius, the victor at Cynoscephalae (197 B.C.).

5. *departure:* the condottiere Marcantonio Colonna left Florence's service and joined Julius II's army in his attack on Genoa (Gaeta).

6. compare: this does not seem to be Buonaccorsi; Ridolfi believes it may be Marcello Virgilio di Adriano Berti or Piero Soderini (Gaeta). Inglese, agreeing with Sergio Bertelli, thinks it is more likely Machiavelli's anonymous friend in the Florentine chancellery who wrote Letter 186—both as a friend and as a copyist for Marcello Virgilio.

Letter 192

1. *Gallarate:* a town about fifteen miles northwest of Milan.

2. *duke:* Alfonso I d'Este, duke of Ferrara, who had not accepted the truce that Julius II signed with Venice (Gaeta); see Letter 184, n. 5.

3. *Panciatichi:* Bartolomeo Panciatichi (Gaeta), writer of Letters 183, 189, and 193.

4. *Roberto:* Roberto Acciaiuoli (Gaeta).

5. *Ambassador:* he was the Florentine ambassador to Charles d'Amboise, lord of Chaumont, the French governor in Milan (Gaeta); d'Amboise (1473–1511), who was a nephew of cardinal Georges d'Amboise, was soon to become commander of the French troops in Italy.

Letter 193

1. *Cei:* an adviser to the Florentine colony in Lyons (Gaeta).

Letter 194

1. *Messer Giovan Pietro:* Bertelli identifies him as Giovan Pietro Machiavelli, Totto's cousin, to whom he ceded the parish church of Sant'Andrea in Percussina in 1515 (Gaeta).

Letter 195

1. *Giovanni Girolami:* in August he had brought to the Signoria Cardinal Soderini's recommendation that Florence mediate between Louis XII and Julius II; he returned to Blois during the second week of September, around the time of Machiavelli's departure for Florence (Gaeta).

2. *nation:* i.e., France (Gaeta).

3. *Alamanni:* he had entered the service of Cardinal Briçonnet and acted as Charles VIII's right-hand man with Florence during the king's Italian expedition between 1494 and 1495. He gave financial assistance several times to Florentine ambassadors to the French court (Gaeta).

4. *Trémoïlle:* Louis de la Trémoïlle, the first chamberlain of Louis XII (Gaeta).

5. *articles:* these were drawn up by Charles de Haultbois, bishop of Tournai, and the theologian Godefroy Boussard; Louis presented them to an assembly of French clergy at Tours (Gaeta). The king had convened a general council of the Church in an attempt to depose Pope Julius II.

6. *hot buns:* i.e., hot news.

7. *Jeanne:* a courtesan with whom Machiavelli had contact (Gaeta).

Letter 196

1. *Jeanne:* the same courtesan mentioned in Letter 195 (Gaeta).

2. *La Riccia:* a Florentine courtesan whom Machiavelli frequently visited (Gaeta); tradition has it that the "cupid" referred to in the name of the Via dell'Amorino, just east of the present-day Piazza dell'Unità Italiana, helped Machiavelli in his affairs with this "Curly-Haired Woman." La Riccia is also mentioned in Letters 225, 229–230, 246, and 262. As evidence of Machiavelli's unpopularity among certain Florentines, Stephens and Butters report that there was an "anonymous denunciation of Machiavelli . . . dated 27 May 1510" claiming that he "committed an unnatural sexual act with a certain Lucretia, known as *La Riccia,* a courtesan"; it "was dismissed as unproven" ("New Light," p. 57; text, p. 66).

3. *certain:* apparently a play on the meaning of the word *chiaro,* used in

Italian to mean both "certain" and, in connection with accounts, "paid up quickly" or "open and aboveboard."

4. *ambassador:* Giacomo Suardino (Gaeta).

5. *dealings:* a possible play on words, because *condotte* can also mean "tubes" or "pipes."

6. *friend:* an allusion to Louis XII, to whose court Maximilian had sent Pigello Portinari (Gaeta).

7. *Casa . . . Luigi:* Filippo Casavecchia, Francesco del Nero, and Luigi Guicciardini (Gaeta); Inglese suggests that "Francesco" may well be Vettori instead of del Nero.

8. *to consecrate you:* a possible play on *votarvi,* which can mean both "to offer you up as a vow" and "to empty you" or "to drain you."

Letter 197

1. *favor:* Florence had asked Louis XII for permission to hire an Italian condottiere in Lombardy in anticipation of the end of Muzio Colonna's contract and his expected transfer to the service of Julius II (Gaeta).

2. *Messer Teodoro:* Teodoro Trivulzio, a member of a Milanese family that had served extensively in the armies of Louis XII (Gaeta).

3. *you . . . employed:* the past participle indicates that the "you" here was plural.

4. *Tamerlane:* since the general of the Tartars had died in 1405, his name here is used to represent the Tartars in general (Gaeta).

5. *plague:* translation of *el canchero,* cancer.

6. *everyone:* translation of *tutto el mondo,* "all the world," a gallicism—evidently Acciaiuoli had spent too much time in France.

Letter 198

1. *Gian Giacomo:* Gian Giacomo Trivulzio (Gaeta); on Chaumont's death, early in 1511, he shared command of the French troops in Italy with Gaston de Foix, the nephew of Louis XII.

2. *prince of Melfi:* Troiano Caracciolo was a candidate for condottiere put forth by some Florentines but rejected by the Signoria (Gaeta).

3. *You:* as in Letter 197, a plural form is used.

4. *friend:* Louis XII (Gaeta).

5. *you:* translation of *l'uom,* "the man"; evidently a gallicism for *l'on,* "one."

6. *letter of August 29th:* from the Ten to Acciaiuoli (*Leg.,* III, pp. 1322–1323) (Gaeta).

7. *employ him:* Gaeta quotes from the above letter (*Leg.,* III, p. 1323) and points out that its wording requesting the "favor" of a native Italian condottiere is a bit subtle; Antonio della Valle, writing to Machiavelli from France, warns Machiavelli to tread carefully on this sensitive issue (*Leg.,* III, p. 1325).

8. *Vettori:* Francesco Vettori (Gaeta).

9. *in the square:* translation of *di piazza,* signifying "in the marketplace," i.e., "in public life."

10. *Finale:* Carlo Domenico del Carretto, called the cardinal of Finale because he belonged to a family from the Marches by that name (Gaeta).

11. *Valori:* Bartolomeo Valori (Gaeta).

Letter 200

1. *you:* Nasi uses the *tu* form with Machiavelli.

2. *maneuvers:* refers to enrolling infantry and cavalry for the militia; Nasi was then in Pisa as Florentine military commander (Gaeta).

3. *Taddeo:* Francesco Taddei had been gonfalonier in May 1502 and a member of the Ten in 1505 (Gaeta).

4. *Lord Jacopo:* Jacopo d'Appiano (Gaeta).

5. *Janus:* because the Roman god of the year is shown with two faces, each looking in the opposite direction (hence our "January"), Nasi is suggesting the two-faced, hypocritical nature of Corsellini.

Letter 201

1. *governor:* François de Rochechouart, the French governor of Genoa. Machiavelli had no doubt asked for his mediation in the talks with Grimaldi and for permission to spend some time in Genoa (Gaeta).

Letter 202

1. *In Camp:* note what happens shortly after this letter is written: Soderini is asked to resign as gonfalonier four days later and Giuliano de' Medici enters Florence five days later.

2. *You know who:* Piero Soderini (Gaeta).

3. *four o'clock:* translation of *ora 22*.

4. *Brother Biagio:* this is the last letter Machiavelli received from Biagio, who probably deserves better than to be described as a "functionary who was a man of letters" (Fachard, *Biagio Buonaccorsi,* p. 164, quoting Chabod). Fachard, *Biagio Buonaccorsi,* pp. 157–158, even cites one of Machiavelli's official letters in which he unflatteringly describes Biagio as being *"guasto o ver inamorato"* ("smitten or really infatuated"). Biagio, too, was forced to leave active political life with the return of the Medici. His only official function after 1512 was as secretary to Filippo Strozzi when the latter was Florence's ambassador to France from October to December 1515. Biagio's *Ricordi* indicates that he spent much of his latter life as a copyist. He copied a commentary by Marsilio Ficino on the epistles of St. Paul, Pico della Mirandola's commentary on Girolamo Benivieni's famous *"Canzone d'Amore,"* and some works by Filippo Beroaldo and Xenophon. Of more immediate interest is the fact that he made three copies of Machiavelli's *Prince* and two of his *Art of War.* Furthermore, in a prefatory letter to a copy of *The Prince* that Biagio made for his patron, Pandolfo Bellacci, Biagio urged Bellacci to be a "fierce defender [of Machiavelli] against all those who, whether out of malice or envy and according to the custom of these times, might be bent on gnawing on him or tearing him to pieces" (quoted in Fachard, *Biagio Buonaccorsi,* p. 158). Biagio's

steadfast loyalty is graphic proof that *The Prince* had already been under heavy attack even while it was circulating in manuscript form. Some forty poems that Biagio wrote contribute to the notion of him being a man of letters; they have recently been published; see Fachard, "Liriche." Ridolfi's hypothesis that there was some kind of quarrel between the two seems to be the only explanation for why Biagio's friendship for Machiavelli went unrequited and for why there was so little contact between them once the Medici returned to power *(Life)*.

Letter 203

1. *Noblewoman:* it is impossible to identify this woman definitively. The fact that Machiavelli explains some geographical locations leads Gaeta to suggest it might be Isabella d'Este, wife of Francesco Gonzaga. Inglese is convinced by Brian Richardson's article in *La Bibliofilia* 84 (1982), pp. 271–276, that this is Isabella d'Este.

2. *wishes:* Machiavelli writes this letter in the third person, as befits the formality of the occasion and the rank of the recipient.

3. *meeting in Mantua:* the one in early August that sealed the fate of the pro-Soderini faction in Florence.

4. *viceroy:* Ramón de Cardona (Gaeta). Originally Raymond Folch was a soldier under Gonzalo Fernández de Córdoba; he was made duke of Cardona, and later Ramón de Cardona became viceroy of Naples and the commander of Spanish and papal forces. Although the loser at the Battle of Ravenna, Cardona won Milan for the Holy League and successfully led the forces against Florence and the sack of Prato.

5. *ten miles:* translation of *dieci miglia;* approximate calculations make this equivalent to about 9.5 miles, although by modern roads Prato is some thirteen miles north of Florence.

6. *eighteen miles:* translation of *diciotto miglia.*

7. *Florence:* Gaeta suggests that more detailed descriptions of these events can be found in Biagio Buonaccorsi, *Diario* (Fachard, *Biagio Buonaccorsi,* pp. 22–25); Francesco Guicciardini, *Storia d'Italia,* XI, 2–4; and Francesco Vettori, *Sommario della Istoria d'Italia,* included in his Scritti.

8. *defense:* to show how Machiavelli shaded this passage, Gaeta quotes the following passage from Guicciardini, *Storia d'Italia,* XI, 3, p. 1065: "Given the disposition of almost all the people for maintaining popular government, there was no doubt what the council would decide. Hence, it was a surprising agreement both that the council would consent to the return of the Medici as private citizens—but that they would deny the Gonfalonier's removal from the government—and that if the enemy should persist in its demand [for Soderini to be dismissed], then with our wealth and our lives we should apply ourselves to the defense of our liberty and our shared native land."

9. *postponing:* Machiavelli comments on this point in *Discourses,* II, 27, where he implies that all would not have been lost if Soderini had more readily agreed to Cardona's proposal (Gaeta). Despite Machiavelli's long association

with Soderini's policies, he held firm to the belief that Soderini's fatal flaw was his inability to act decisively.

10. *defenders:* these were led by Luca Savelli, "an old condottiere who had acquired no distinction in the science of military affairs as a result of either age or experience" (Guicciardini, *Storia d'Italia,* XI, 3, p. 1065).

11. *chimeras:* "the gratitude offered to him several days earlier by the people" is written in the margin of the manuscript (Gaeta).

12. *envoys:* Baldassare Carducci and Niccolò del Nero (Gaeta).

13. *cowardice:* Machiavelli is in reluctant agreement with Guicciardini's judgment, quoted in the Headnote, about the militia's cowardice.

14. *guard:* an armed group including Anton Francesco degli Albizzi, Gino Capponi, Bartolomeo Valori, and Paolo Vettori, Francesco's brother—some of whom had secretly met Giuliano de' Medici several months earlier at Vettori's country house, La Paneretta, on the outskirts of Florentine territory near Siena—entered the Palazzo della Signoria and "suddenly ordered the public officials who, according to law, had the broadest authority over the gonfaloniers to be assembled; they demanded that the officials legally remove Soderini from office, otherwise they threatened to deprive him of his life" (Guicciardini, *Storia d'Italia,* XI, 4, p. 1068; Gaeta also cites Vettori, *Sommario,* pp. 339–340 in this context).

15. *fell:* Machiavelli omits his own role in these activities: Soderini sent Machiavelli to Francesco Vettori, who was then commanding the forces defending the city, as his personal envoy to seek a safe conduct out of Tuscany; see Vettori, *Sommario,* pp. 339–340 (Gaeta).

16. *regulations:* according to the regulations, the term for gonfalonier was limited to one year—Giovan Battista Ridolfi was chosen—and the life term for the office was abolished; the Grand Council was retained, "but to the Council of the Eighty, ... so that the best-qualified citizens might always participate in its councils, [were] added in perpetuity all those men who had hitherto administered the principal offices either of foreign or domestic policy, ... [the] Gonfalonier of Justice or members of the Ten of the *Balìa* ... [and] all those who had been appointed by the Council of Eighty as either ambassadors to princes or general commissioners during wartime. In all other respects the organization of the government was left unchanged" (Guicciardini, *Storia d'Italia,* XI, 4, p. 1070).

17. *legate:* a reference to Cardinal Giovanni de' Medici, who entered Florence on 14 September.

18. *Ramazzotti:* Melchiorre Ramazzotti, from Bologna, was a military leader whom the Medici hired (Gaeta).

19. *palle:* reference to the "balls" on the Medici coat of arms, which had six red balls on a gold field—as well as the lily of France granted to the family by the French King Louis XI. Some commentators say the balls had their origin as representing coins, from the family's banking origins; others say they originated as pills, from *medici,* meaning "[medical] doctors."

20. *reinstated:* "through the decree of these men, the government was re-

turned to the form that it was accustomed to having prior to the year 1494; a military guard was established within the palace, and the Medici recovered their former prestige, but governed much more peremptorily and with much more absolute power than were their forefathers accustomed to having" (Guicciardini, *Storia d'Italia,* XI, 4, p. 1072). Gaeta notes that the system of government set up by Lorenzo de' Medici in 1480 was based on a Council of Seventy that appointed the members of the Signoria and the Eight of Pratica, among other public officials, and that deliberated over matters of domestic and foreign policy. For passages from a letter Machiavelli wrote to Cardinal Giovanni de' Medici on 29 September 1512, see Appendix Letter D.

21. *governed:* on this point, see Marietti, "Machiavel Historiographe," pp. 82–84.

1 5 1 3

Letter 204

1. *Francesco:* see the Headnote; Inglese believes that Gaeta's text incorporates a scribal error in its first line because Machiavelli would not refer to Francesco's brother by using his last name; elsewhere Machiavelli usually writes "your Paolo" when discussing him.

2. *universal rejoicing:* once Cardinal Giovanni de' Medici was elected Pope Leo X, the prison doors were opened and the conspirators were released into a Florence wild with celebration and rejoicing over the ascendancy they believed that this powerful city would now enjoy throughout Italy.

3. *suspicious:* Machiavelli perhaps believes that the Medici, with their power in Florence and Rome now consolidated, will be less interested in seeking revenge on the former supporters of Soderini. This may also be a way of reminding Francesco Vettori of their ties, both personal and political, which were nurtured during their service together in Germany under Soderini's aegis.

4. *Messer Totto:* Machiavelli is enlisting Francesco Vettori's support for his brother, Totto.

5. *Florence:* presumably Machiavelli is no longer able to write his letters from the *Palazzo della Signoria;* in Letter 212 he talks of "being restricted to my farm." While in Florence he lived on the left bank of the Arno, between the Ponte Santa Trinita and the Ponte alla Carraia. To get there today, go to the corner of the Via dei Coverelli and the Via del Santo Spirito. Machiavelli's house is the one "across the street from the *sgraffito* house, at nos. 5–7.... The *sporti* (protruding additions) to the house that jut out over *Via dei Coverelli* were added in the fifteenth century" (Holler, *Florence Walks,* p. 177).

Letter 205

1. *torture:* Machiavelli was subjected to six turns of the rope during his twenty-two day prison term.

2. *when the pope was elected:* 11 March, two days before Machiavelli wrote

enlisting Francesco Vettori's help; Francesco Vettori acted quickly on Machiavelli's behalf.

3. *those people:* the Medici.

4. *different standing:* Francesco Vettori always expected to be relieved of his post in Rome, in part because he believed Leo X trusted Matteo Strozzi and Jacopo Salviati, thanks to their long-standing Medici sympathies.

5. *Filippo:* Filippo Casavecchia (Gaeta).

6. *Poggibonsi:* a town about twenty-two miles southwest of Florence.

7. *Cavalcanti:* a papal chamber servant (Inglese).

Letter 206

1. *your Paolo:* Paolo Vettori; Machiavelli is grateful for Paolo's help in easing Machiavelli's situation in Florence.

2. *lying on the ground:* i.e., in a state of uselessness and abandonment—a turn of phrase Machiavelli often uses in subsequent letters.

3. *I came here:* Machiavelli's use of "here" in this context is, perhaps deliberately, ambiguous: it seems to refer to "this life" but also to Florence itself.

4. *to thrive:* Machiavelli's need for money has been an underlying theme throughout these letters, beginning with the very first one.

5. *Filippo:* Casavecchia.

6. *little Brancacci:* Giuliano Brancacci (Gaeta), a mutual friend.

7. *Giovanni:* implicated in the Boscoli conspiracy, Giovanni di ser Antonio di ser Battista was incarcerated in the Fortress of Volterra (Gaeta).

8. *gossip-monger:* translation of *cicale,* literally "cicadas"; the term was in general use in this sense as early as Antonio Pucci, but it is also found in Luigi Pulci, Lorenzo de' Medici, and, more contemporaneously with Machiavelli, Aretino and Ariosto.

9. *Donato:* Donato del Corno (Gaeta); Tommaso del Bene was a secretary and courier for the foreign policy committee of the Ten.

10. *yesterday:* because Landucci notes (p. 268) that "Our Lady of Santa Maria Impruneta was brought into Florence, and a great procession was made in her honour"—an event that occurred on 18 March to celebrate the election of Giovanni de' Medici to the papacy—and Machiavelli says that it happened "yesterday," Inglese suggests that the dating of this letter may be off by one day.

Letter 207

1. *he:* i.e., the pope; the following "he" is Totto Machiavelli.

2. *profitable:* on 13 May, Francesco Vettori points out to his brother Paolo that "if you considered how many relatives, how many servants, and how many friends the pope has, you would realize how impossible it is to get anything at all from him" (quoted in Bullard, *Strozzi and the Medici,* pp. 74–75).

3. *others:* Francesco Vettori writes Paolo on 5 May: "I am here for nothing and I dare not ask His Holiness for the slightest favor either for myself or for others" (Gaeta).

4. *city:* refers here and throughout this letter to Florence.

5. *want as a youth:* this is in response to Machiavelli's being "born in poverty" (Letter 206). It is worthwhile being alert to the antiphony that develops between Machiavelli and Francesco Vettori in their subsequent correspondence.

6. *Siena:* Giovanni Todeschini Piccolomini (Gaeta), a potential candidate for the papacy, was the cardinal from Siena. Inglese, however, would repunctuate this sentence so that it reads, "Siena [was elected] because of his old age, Naples did not want it at that time, even though he was old, because he had too many relatives." This would make "Siena" refer to Pius III, Francesco Todeschini Piccolomini, who was pope for fifteen days in 1503.

7. *Naples:* Olivero Carafa (Gaeta), another potential candidate, was from Naples.

8. *heads of the council:* refers to Cardinals Bernardino Carvajal (cardinal of Santa Croce) and Federico Sanseverino, two of the four schismatic cardinals who, at the instigation of Louis XII, convened a general council at Pisa in 1511 to depose Pope Julius II (see the Headnote for Machiavelli's involvement in this attempt). Guicciardini slyly treats this example of Leo's "happiness" in the context of "God might already be beginning to approve of this pontificate" because Leo got control of these two schismatics so easily. Concerning these two cardinals, Guicciardini comments further that "since they had been legally removed from office, and the Lateran Council had confirmed this removal, they should no longer function in cardinal's attire." On their way to Rome, Sanseverino foolishly "relied on the Pope's clemency." The two "voluntarily made their way to Pisa where they were received in honor, and then led away to Florence where they were courteously kept prisoner in such a way that they had no means of escape—for that is what the Pope desired" (*Storia d'Italia,* III, pp. 1096–1097). Gaeta notes that the two cardinals publicly submitted to Leo on 27 June.

9. *Roberto:* Roberto Acciaiuoli, the Florentine ambassador to France (Gaeta).

10. *His Most Christian Majesty:* Louis XII.

11. *Donato:* Donato del Corno.

Letter 208

1. *And I . . . doubt?":* cf. Dante, *Inferno,* IV, 16–18 (Gaeta). Noticing Vergil's pallor as they stand at the brim peering into the "blind world" of Limbo, the first circle of Hell, Dante wonders how he can have the strength to descend if even Vergil seems afraid. Machiavelli makes a deferential compliment in response to Vettori's fears concerning his precarious political situation and his powerlessness, expressed in Letter 207.

2. *rope:* Machiavelli's direct, if not nonchalant, reference to his torture indicates a sound instinct to put his experience behind him as quickly as possible.

3. *but:* Inglese would begin a new sentence here with the transition "I

implore you . . . ." He also believes, noting Landucci's entry for 8 April (p. 268), that this letter was written in the evening of 8 April but that following a Florentine custom Machiavelli dated it the 9th.

4. *unscrolled:* the play on words refers to Totto's being added to the list of Leo X's household members, his staff of "familiars."

5. *politics:* Max Weber, in "Politics as a Vocation," describes a person who fosters "his inner balance and self-feeling by the consciousness that his life has meaning in the service of a cause," an apt depiction of Machiavelli. Nevertheless, whether or not the language of political discussion can ever effect any kind of conformity between "the opinions and ideas we have" and the capriciousness of "matters" and external events is an issue basic to *The Prince* and to the dialogue between Machiavelli and Vettori in these early letters exchanged by them. This point is well-argued in Najemy, *Between Friends.*

6. *territory:* part of Machiavelli's punishment was to be confined to Florentine territory for one year.

7. *pontiff:* Leo X sought a reconciliation with the Soderinis: even before he was elected pope, he and Francesco Soderini, the cardinal of Volterra, had mended fences; Leo called Piero Soderini from Siena to Rome and proposed a marriage alliance between the two families, but it never actually took place (Gaeta).

8. *archbishop:* Cosimo de' Pazzi; his successor was Giulio de' Medici (named 9 May), Leo X's cousin and the future Pope Clement VII (Gaeta).

Letter 209

1. *9 April:* following their reading of the *Apografo Ricci,* Inglese, *Lettere,* p. 117, n. 19, and Najemy, *Between Friends,* pp. 110–111, n. 21, believe that the date of this letter was incorrectly copied and that it should be dated 19 April; thus the "two letters" Vettori refers to in the first sentence would be Machiavelli's Letters 208 and 210, and this letter and Letter 210 would be reversed.

2. *truce:* the one signed at Orthez.

3. *His Catholic Majesty:* the king of Spain.

4. *the Eight:* Vettori assumes that since his brother Paolo stood a good chance of being elected to the Eight of Ward, the *Otto di Guardia,* who "had jurisdiction over Machiavelli's legal status," he could influence the group to permit Machiavelli to travel to Rome (Najemy, *Between Friends,* p. 117).

Letter 210

1. *Tommaso:* Tommaso del Bene (Gaeta)

2. *a fish out of water:* translation of *come un barbio intronato,* "like a dazed barbel" (a fresh-water fish); a similar expression occurs in Pulci, *Morgante,* 20, 48, v. 4.

3. *Capponi's bench:* it became customary for the wealthier merchants to build benches that faced the open piazzas so that in the cool of the evening the populace might socialize, gossip, even flirt and discuss marriages.

4. *horn:* because of an erroneous scribal transcription, Inglese believes

this sentence should read "Donato del Corno has opened another shop where they sell doves . . . ." The reference to a shop "at the sign of the horn where they sell doves" would be another allusion to homosexuality (Raimondi).

5. *Riccio:* presumably an obliging young man who had acquired something of a reputation (Gaeta).

6. *Brancaccino:* a familiar diminutive for their mutual friend Giuliano Brancacci; see the second paragraph of Letter 206 for more on him.

7. *tears:* an adaptation of the closing tercet of Petrarch's sonnet #102, *"Cesare, poi che l' traditor d'Egitto."* Machiavelli heightens the personal emotion of his last line by substituting *sfogare,* "to give vent to," for Petrarch's *celare,* "to conceal."

8. *Salviati . . . Strozzi:* Florentine ambassadors to the papal court who outranked Vettori.

9. *to please me:* this persistent belief in Giuliano de' Medici's interest in Machiavelli leads Machiavelli to plan on dedicating *The Prince* to him, but Machiavelli's intentions will be frustrated by Giuliano's lack of interest in being a "new prince" with military projects and by his early death.

10. *cardinal of Volterra:* Francesco Soderini.

Letter 211

1. *our Bernardo:* Francesco Vettori's uncle, who supported the Medici and was active in the government of Florence.

2. *government:* the popular government of Soderini's gonfaloniership (Gaeta).

3. *this one:* the Medici government (Gaeta).

4. *agreed . . . truce:* see the Headnote for the agreement at Blois and the Treaty of Orthez.

5. *Cestello:* now a monastery in Borgo San Frediano (Gaeta). Najemy, however, points out that in the sixteenth century it was situated in the Borgo Pinti (*Between Friends,* pp. 118–119).

6. *past three years:* i.e., since the Holy League was formed in 1510 (Gaeta).

7. *defended Pamplona:* Spain occupied Navarre during the summer of 1512, and the French, once Henry VIII had withdrawn his support of Ferdinand the Catholic, unsuccessfully attacked Pamplona in December 1512 (Gaeta).

8. *in Italy:* in early March, Spanish forces under Ramón de Cardona occupied Parma and Piacenza (Gaeta); for more on Cardona, see Letter 203, n. 4.

9. *he:* Louis XII.

10. *Castile:* Ferdinand the Catholic became the regent of Castile for his grandson, Archduke Charles of Hapsburg, the future Holy Roman Emperor Charles V and King of Spain Charles I, after the child's mother Juana went mad on the death of her husband, Philip I the Handsome; see Letter 127, n. 10.

11. *alliance:* refers to one made with the Gascon family of Albret. Jean d'Albret married Catherine de Foix and the Kingdom of Navarre came as

part of her dowry. (Jean d'Albret's sister, Charlotte, was Cesare Borgia's wife, and Catherine de Foix's cousin, Gaston de Foix, was the French commander killed at the Battle of Ravenna in April 1512.) Under the provisions of the Treaty of Orthez, Louis XII withdrew his support of Jean d'Albret.

12. *he:* Ferdinand the Catholic.

13. *experience of last year:* the Battle of Ravenna, 11 April 1512 (Gaeta).

14. *duke:* the son of Ludovico *"Il Moro"* Sforza, Massimiliano Sforza (1493–1530) was twenty when he took possession of the duchy of Milan at the end of December 1512 (G, with Inglese's correction).

15. *without flattery:* a sincere expression of admiration for Machiavelli's political acumen, consonant with the opinion of many of Machiavelli's contemporaries. Coupled with the postscript, this may be Vettori's intimation that other officials in Rome, to whom he would show the reply, might come to value Machiavelli's "judgment" as well.

16. *[P.S.]:* The square brackets are Gaeta's; he reminds us that Ridolfi, *Vita 7,* p. 508, finds this postscript "typical" of Francesco Vettori.

Letter 212

1. *Francesco Vettori:* See the notes that follow for variants contained in a draft of this letter that Gaeta includes in an appendix. He and most commentators agree that what we have translated is the definitive text.

2. *According . . . 21st:* the draft contains the following lengthy text here:

> Amid all my blessings I have never received anything that gave me as much pleasure as your discussions because I have always learned something from them. Imagine, therefore, now that I find myself removed from any other happiness, how very pleased I was by your letter—all it lacks is your presence and the sound of your live voice. While I have been reading it, for I have read it several times, I have consistently forgotten about my wretched situation and I seem once more to be back among those activities into which, to no avail, I put so much drudgery and I spent so much time doing. And even though I have vowed not to think about matters of state or to discuss them, as my coming to the farm and eschewing conversation bear witness, nevertheless I am obliged to break all my vows in order to answer your questions, because I think I am bound more to the abiding friendship I have with you than to any other tie I may have to anyone else; particularly when you do me as much honor as you do toward the end of your letter, since, to tell you the truth, I have taken some pride in it—it is true that *to be praised by a man who is praised is no small matter.** I am afraid, however, that my points may seem to you not to have their former pungency; for this I hope you will forgive me, because I have given up thinking about all these political goings-on, and furthermore I have heard no details about what is now happening in these matters. And you are aware of how well matters—particularly these—can be assessed in the dark; however, what I have to tell you will be based either on the foundation of your com-

mentary or on my conjectures. If the latter are erroneous, I trust that, for the reasons given above, you will forgive me.

[* An allusion to, but not a quotation from, Cicero, *Epistulae ad Familiares* 5.12.7, repeated in 15.6.1. The remark is made by Hector, quoted in a fragment by Naevius, a poet and playwright of the third century B.C. Cicero repeats this comment in *Tusculanae Disputationes* 4.31.67.]

3. *to you:* the draft inserts "when all its particulars are carefully scrutinized."

4. *your hesitation . . . question of:* the draft has "nothing gives you more anxiety than the assumption you make about."

5. *it is undeniable . . . wise:* the draft has "Spain has always seemed to me to have more cunning and good fortune than wisdom and common sense."

6. *other deeds . . . shall go:* the draft has "deeds at length, but going into."

7. *would . . . intentions:* the draft has "could act or be certain that he ought to act."

8. *man:* the draft has "prince."

9. *year:* 1512 (Gaeta).

10. *pope:* Julius II (Gaeta).

11. *treaty:* the Treaty of Orthez, signed by Louis XII and Ferdinand the Catholic on 1 April, is still being discussed.

12. *can be:* the draft has "is."

13. *and France was always . . . in check:* the draft has "And if Spain were to say that France did not advance then because he had first this doubt, then that one, I would reply that all those doubts he had then he would have always, because the pope was always going to be against Naples reverting to France and France was always going to have doubts about the pope and the other powers (since he was aware of his ambition)—that they might unite." There is no new paragraph after this text in the draft.

14. *I would counter:* the draft has "what would I counter?: that."

15. *France thought . . . degree:* as a consequence of the success of Julius II in forcing the French through the Holy League to withdraw from northern Italy.

16. *Gonsalvo:* Gonzalo Fernández de Córdoba.

17. *all this:* the draft has "all these deeds."

18. *Whenever . . . a thousand:* the draft has "And when it seems to me that a man has committed such a serious mistake, I assume that he will commit a thousand."

19. *I do not . . . cheese:* translation of *io non beo paesi,* "I do not savor wine by the estate on which it is grown," meaning trusting in its reputation rather than savoring the wine itself (Gaeta)—an image of appearance (shadow) as opposed to a matter of reality (substance).

20. *conclude:* the draft has "wish to conclude."

21. *discuss . . . discover:* the draft has "discuss this as if he made a wise decision. Arguing from such a premise and honestly wishing to discover."

22. *I shall assume:* the draft has "I shall discuss it assuming."

23. *Spain:* the draft has "he."

24. *counting:* the draft has "by chance counting."

25. *would mount:* the draft has "makes."

26. *bishop of Gurk:* Matthäus von Wellenburg Lang, bishop of Gurk, secretary to Maximilian I.

27. *got out of:* the draft has "left."

28. *Fuenterrabía:* a city in Spain, on the Bay of Biscay at the mouth of the Bidasoa River near Irún, at the western end of the modern border with France.

29. *well-placed person:* Francesco Guicciardini, who was appointed Florence's ambassador to Ferdinand the Catholic in January 1512. For Guicciardini's similar judgment about Ferdinand's troops, see *Storia d'Italia,* XI, 9, p. 1099. Guicciardini served in Spain until 1514.

30. *that with this truce . . . or to remove:* the draft has "his plan has been to remove."

31. *and danger:* this text is lacking in the draft.

32. *yielded:* i.e., to a new French offensive; see Letter 211, n. 7 (Gaeta).

33. *event:* the draft inserts another sentence here: "It is unlikely that he would have wanted to risk running this danger."

34. *Spain:* the draft has "he."

35. *one thing . . . to another:* translation of *el mangiare insegni bere,* "eating may teach how to drink."

36. *etc., both:* the draft has "as you say he should have done."

37. *I am therefore . . . his army:* the draft has "Indeed, I believe France would perhaps not have done it because he must have already reached an agreement with the Venetians and then, as a result of distrusting both Spain and his armies."

38. *others:* there is not a new paragraph in the draft.

39. *to him . . . in peace:* the draft has "in it for him."

40. *Lombardy:* the draft has "the dukedom."

41. *So Spain . . . in it:* the draft has "So Spain sees no security on this account."

42. *emperor:* here the draft inserts "so that seeking to reach an agreement with his allies would be a dream."

43. *old wrongs . . . favors:* compare Letter 219, n. 4, below with *Prince,* 7, 302–303; Atkinson, p. 175; the former contradicts the apparent thrust of this remark and the passage in *The Prince.* The notion occurs again in *Discourses,* III, 4, where Machiavelli states that "new favors" never cancel out "old injuries"—all the less so when the new favor is thought to be less important than the previous injury. Cf. Guicciardini, *Ricordi,* whose C 25 would agree with this latter formulation; cf. also Isocrates, *Philippus,* 37.

44. *of others:* a thought echoed in *Prince,* 21, 109–111; Atkinson, p. 339. As these notes suggest, much of this letter is relevant to the *Prince.*

45. *since . . . ratify it:* the draft has "and gives them time to nullify it if it does not please them once they have ratified it."

46. *them:* translated following Inglese's suggestion that the antecedent is "Venice and France." The draft, however, reads "France."

47. *France:* the draft has "them."

48. *lap:* see *Prince,* 3, 251; Atkinson, p. 119, for the same expression applied to allies who had thrown themselves into the lap of Louis XII.

49. *attack:* the draft has "proceed against."

50. *armies . . . last year's:* the draft has "larger and more organized armies than last year's."

51. *Therefore . . . either to:* the draft has "Therefore, I believe his aim has been this: he believes that with this treaty he can either."

52. *either pursuing . . . peace:* the draft has "namely, either pursuing the war or making peace against their will."

53. *a middle way:* Machiavelli's style is often interpreted as designed to reinforce the conclusion that diametrically opposed alternatives are the only ones he offers or supports. Examples of his willingness, in contexts that he deems appropriate, to follow a middle way can be found in *Prince,* 19, 411–418; Atkinson, p. 315, and the last sentence of *Discourses,* II, 27.

54. *His Catholic Highness's . . . progress:* Ferdinand was one of Machiavelli's primary models for a "new prince" in *The Prince.* This summary paragraph adumbrates both the first paragraph of *Prince,* 21, devoted to Ferdinand, "How a Prince Should Act to Obtain Prestige" and the end of *Prince,* 18: "A certain contemporary prince, whom it is better not to name, proclaims nothing but peace and trust, yet he is an extremely dangerous menace to both. Had he respected either, he would have been deprived—many times over—of either his reputation or his power" (Atkinson, p. 285). Most commentators believe that this is a not-too-veiled allusion to Ferdinand the Catholic. Some of these same ideas occur in *Discourses,* III, 34. Guicciardini's *Ricordi,* C 77 (B 51) and C 142, express similar opinions about Ferdinand. The draft reads "this King's methods."

55. *hence . . . kingdom [of Naples]:* refers to "attacks" on the North African coast from Oran in Algeria to Tripoli in Libya (Gaeta). The "partition" was done in conjunction with Louis XII (Gaeta): Machiavelli discusses it at greater length at the end of this paragraph. The draft has "the result of this is the war in Granada, the attacks on Africa, the entrance into the kingdom [of Naples]."

56. *activities:* "Thus [the king of Spain] has consistently planned and executed great projects which have always kept the minds of his subjects in suspense and wonder—concentrated upon the outcome of the events" (*Prince,* 21, 29–32; Atkinson, p. 333).

57. *he always . . . ardently:* this sentence, with its ardent seizing of the initiative, specifies a character trait that Machiavelli greatly admires. The draft has "he starts things off ardently."

58. *either . . . artifice:* it is worth being alert to these disjunctions, especially as they prepare for the "force or fraud" alternative of *The Prince.* In place of "artifice," the draft reads "deception."

59. *And always . . . the outcome:* the draft has "What he has done he will

always do; and the result of all these moves will prove to you that this is the truth."

60. *Julius alive:* Julius II died on 20 Frebruary; Leo X was elected on 11 March. The draft has "that Julius was alive."

61. *of his death . . . election:* the draft has "that he died and the other was elected."

62. *common sense:* the draft adds "at all."

63. *any obligations . . . younger days:* i.e., before Giovanni de' Medici became Pope Leo X (Gaeta). The draft has "any favor done for him during [Leo's] younger days or by any relationship they may have had."

64. *war:* the draft has "wrangling."

65. *peace:* the draft ends here.

66. *higgledy-piggledy:* translation of the idiom *uno pesce pastinaca,* "indecisive." For a subtle discussion of the implications of this "sting ray," a fish sold in the markets without any apparent head or tail, see Najemy, *Between Friends,* pp. 126, 135.

67. *restricted:* this letter, dated 29 April, is "from Florence," as are most of these letters—even the famous one of 10 December. They may be written "as if" from Florence or they may have been composed partly at his home in Florence (see Letter 204, n. 5) and partly at his farm in San Casciano.

Letter 213

1. *skim the surface:* translation of *scagliare,* "to scale," "to flake," "to fling," "to hurl."

2. *campaign:* see the Headnote; Louis XII had recently been defeated at the Battle of Novara.

3. *House:* the Medici family.

4. *I believe:* this is an important sentence for a clear view of Machiavelli's perspective. First, foresight is an essential component of a "prudent man," that is, a leader with *virtù;* see *Prince,* 3, 85–89, Atkinson, p. 109; *Prince,* 13, 121–123, Atkinson, p. 243; and *Discourses,* I, 18, where a "prudent man . . . sees trouble at a great distance and in its initial stages"; cf. Letter 219, n. 6, on the king of Spain's ability to see problems "at a distance." Second, a "prudent man" with that foresight seeks "constantly . . . to aid the good and to thwart the evil in plenty of time." Thus, to do evil is clearly not a good. Finally, there is the impersonation—the donning of the persona, the wearing of the actor's mask—so that Machiavelli may more acutely feel and act as might someone else. The psychological insight of this remark and its translation into practice ("as to the treaty, it could occur . . . without me," in the next paragraph) greatly sharpen Machiavelli's political analyses in these letters and in his major works; see the discussion of empathy in the Introduction, p. xxix.

5. *English:* in fact, the French lost at the so-called Battle of the Spurs; the treaty referred to in the next sentence is the one drawn up on 5 April in the name of Ferdinand the Catholic, Henry VIII, Leo X, and Maximilian I at Mechlin (Mechelen, in northern Belgium)—see the Headnote.

6. *last year:* at the Battle of Ravenna on 11 April 1512.

7. *lack of territory:* a hint at a concentration of Medici power that might lead to a powerful state (Gaeta).

Letter 214

1. *Giovanni:* Machiavelli's beloved nephew; see Letter 19, n. 1. The letters to Vernacci (Letters 217, 234, 248–250, 252, 255–256, 258–259, 266) are particularly significant because they frequently provide a direct and immediate sense of Machiavelli's real, inner being. As Ridolfi notes, "with men like Vettori whom [Machiavelli] regarded as his equals in intellect though superior in rank and fortune, [Machiavelli] would hide behind his usual mask, now jocular, now over-bold, now cynical, and occasionally don his curial robes; but with his nephew he always showed his miseries naked and shamelessly" (*Life,* 162–163; see also *Vita* 7, p. 524, n. 31).

2. *innocence:* Machiavelli denied any complicity in the Boscoli conspiracy. The confession of Giovanni Folchi, one of the conspirators, says nothing about Machiavelli's involvement in the Boscoli plot; when describing the recently instated Medici rule, Machiavelli is alleged to have said merely "that it appeared to him that this regime (*stato*) would not be governed without difficulty, because it lacked someone to stand at the tiller, as Lorenzo de' Medici had properly done" (see Stephens and Butters, "New Light," p. 58–59; text, p. 67). Butters notes, "Niccolò also said that he thought the League an ephemeral creation which could easily fall apart" (*Governors,* p. 211).

3. *Lorenzo Machiavelli:* see Letter 13, n. 11.

4. *consul:* Giuliano Lapi; cf. Letter 217 (Gaeta).

Letter 215

1. *Jacopo:* Jacopo Salviati (Gaeta).

2. *Brancacci:* Giuliano Brancacci (Gaeta).

3. *Trent:* during the diplomatic mission to Maximilian I, 1507–1508 (Gaeta).

4. *last battle:* at Novara (Gaeta).

5. *duke:* i.e., remove Massimiliano Sforza from the duchy of Milan. Many Medici partisans, especially in Rome, believed that Giuliano de' Medici might become king of Naples and Lorenzo II, the future duke of Urbino and dedicatee of *The Prince,* might become duke of Milan.

6. *I . . . disposal:* he is not convinced that Ferdinand the Catholic can influence English foreign policy to further Spanish goals (Gaeta).

7. *[not]:* the negative is Gaeta's emendation.

Letter 216

1. *Parma and Piacenza:* after the Battle of Ravenna and the entry of Swiss forces, the retreating Louis XII lost control of these two cities in the valley of the Po. Ramón de Cardona occupied the cities on Massimiliano Sforza's behalf and, upon Julius II's death, gave them over to Sforza, who in turn restored them to Leo X (Gaeta).

2. *past popes:* Calixtus III, Alfonso Borgia (1455–1458); Pius II, Aeneas

Silvius Piccolomini (1458–1464); Sixtus IV, Francesco della Rovere (1471–1484); Innocent VIII, Giovanni Battista Cibo (1484–1492); Alexander VI, Rodrigo Borgia (1492–1503); and Julius II, Giuliano della Rovere (1503–1513).

3. *to make trouble:* Maximilian I's grandiose plans for extending his dominion included having himself crowned pope.

Letter 217

1. *you:* Machiavelli uses the familiar *tu* here.

2. *Lorenzo Machiavelli:* see Letter 13, n. 11.

3. *Neri del Benino:* see Letter 180, n. 2.

4. *ill in every other respect:* a direct statement of Machiavelli's despair.

Letter 218

1. *yours:* this letter of Machiavelli's is lost (Gaeta).

2. *this side of the sea:* see the Headnote for the landing of the English army at Calais and the subsequent "Battle of the Spurs."

3. *Casa:* Filippo Casavecchia (Gaeta).

4. *His Most Christian Highness:* Louis XII.

5. *King Federigo:* King Frederick, from the Aragonese line, king of the Two Sicilies, was deposed in 1501 (Gaeta).

6. *new Turkish ruler:* Selim I, who succeeded Bajazet II in 1512 (Gaeta).

7. *simpering:* translation of *lezii* (*lezio* in the singular); Inglese, *Lettere,* p. 160, n. 15, believes it is the plural of *lezzo,* "stench" or "filth."

Letter 219

1. *S. Andrea:* the first letter dated from a village in Percussina near San Casciano in Val di Pesa, about nine miles southwest of Florence, where Machiavelli was, as he says in signing this letter, "on the farm." The Vettori family, too, owned property in San Casciano.

2. *lansquenets:* German mercenary infantrymen or pikemen, *Landsknechts,* who took their name from medieval German serfs who served their knights on foot without benefit of armor; it was from this group that Maximilian I first formed his permanent infantry—derived from "servant of the land" and not, as is sometimes thought, from "a knight who carried a lance." For more on the term and on Emperor Maximilian's attempt to create a standing army through his lansquenets, see Oman, *History of the Art of War,* pp. 75–77.

3. *attacking the Church:* almost six weeks after the French defeat at Novara, Louis XII sent the bishop of Marseilles, Claude de Seyssel, to Rome so that he could open negotiations on ecclesiastical problems (Gaeta). Seyssel (?1450–1520), also known as "Monsieur d'Aix," wrote an important political treatise, *La Monarchie de France,* in 1515; see the translation by J. H. Hexter in the edition prepared by Donald R. Kelley (New Haven: Yale, 1981).

4. *to be forgotten:* see Letter 212, n. 43.

5. *old, exhausted, sickly king:* Louis XII would live for about sixteen more months.

6. *distance:* see Letter 213 above, n. 4.

7. *to dominate them:* Machiavelli refers to this in the penultimate paragraph of this letter as "the sweetness of domination"; see *Discourses,* I, 37 (Gaeta), the first paragraph.

8. *Duke Charles:* Charles the Bold (1433–1477), duke of Burgundy; the Swiss Confederation defeated him at Grandson in March 1476 and again at Morat in June 1476, thereby ending Burgundian resistance to France.

9. *Lorini:* when Swiss and French troops led by Charles de Beaumont marched on Pisa in June 1500, Pellegrino Lorini was a Florentine diplomat sent to inform the commander that Louis XII now wanted Pisa to be returned to Florence (Gaeta).

10. *graft:* the images of the Swiss "taking root" and grafting themselves onto Italy is reminiscent of the language in *Prince,* 7, 25–35; Atkinson, p. 157, discussing Cesare Borgia's putting down roots to hold onto Romagna.

11. *Casa:* Filippo Casavecchia.

12. *ass:* Gaeta believes that this refers not to Machiavelli's poem *Dell'asino d'oro* (The Golden Ass) but rather to an inconclusive reply or discussion.

13. *Brancacci:* Giuliano Brancacci, a mutual friend.

Letter 220

1. *Filippo:* Filippo Casavecchia.

2. *benefices:* see Letter 219, n. 3, regarding Seyssell, who is referred to as "this ambassador" two sentences later.

3. *Lateran:* the schismatic popes called the Council of Pisa in 1511, and Julius II called the Lateran Council in 1512.

4. *to break it:* in May 1513 (Gaeta).

5. *league:* a league drawn up at Mechlin on 5 April in the name of Ferdinand the Catholic, Henry VIII, Leo X, and Maximilian I.

6. *Thérouanne:* besieged in July.

7. *bishop of Gurk:* translated according to Inglese's suggestion to emend Burgense, "Burgos," with Gurgense, "the bishop of Gurk," who is Matthäus von Wellenburg.

8. *viceroy:* Ramón de Cardona.

9. *Vicenza:* in conjunction with the French attacks on Asti and Alessandria in Lombardy, Bartolomeo d'Alviano, commanding the Venetian army, also attacked in Lombardy. He captured Bergamo, Brescia, and Cremona, but after the defeat of the French at Novara, Alviano was obliged to retreat to Padua, where Ramón de Cardona, at the head of the army of the Holy League, besieged him.

10. *matter of the council:* under Florentine pressure, the French had to move the council from Pisa to Milan (Gaeta).

11. *Brescia:* during the war between France, Julius II, and the Holy League, Brescia rebelled from France in February 1512, and the French

commander, Gaston de Foix, after defeating Giovan Paolo Baglioni and the Venetians, moved on to Brescia; he arrived on 17 February and brutally sacked the city on the 19th. Gaston de Foix was also the victor at the Battle of Ravenna on 11 April 1512.

12. *young king:* Henry VIII of England.

13. *injuries . . . forgotten:* Vettori picks up one of Machiavelli's themes; see Letter 212, n. 43.

14. *a year ago:* see Letters 211, n. 7, and 212, n. 29, on the situation in Spain, which had occupied the Kingdom of Navarre during the summer of 1512.

15. *rout:* at Novara on 6 June.

16. *Pellegrino:* Lorini; see Letter 219, n. 9.

17. Politics: of Aristotle; Gaeta refers to Sasso, *Pensiero politico,* pp. 29–30, n. 32, for the belief that the clause "if you read the *Politics* well" would have "profoundly irritated" Machiavelli, because he had, in fact, read Aristotle and found nothing relevant to this topic. See Letter 222, n. 7.

18. *like this one:* i.e., set up as was the Swiss Confederation.

Letter 221

1. *Donato del Corno:* a mutual friend; on this effort see Butters, *Governors,* p. 241, who also notes that Soderini's government considered del Corno a dangerous Medici partisan in August 1512 (pp. 163–164).

2. *Signor Giuliano:* Giuliano de' Medici, the duke of Nemours, who was now in Florence while his brother Giovanni was Pope Leo X in Rome. Within three years Machiavelli dedicated *The Prince* to him.

3. *in the bag:* del Corno wanted to be *imborsato,* that is, to have his name put into the election bag of Florentine citizens eligible for office. The *accoppiatori's* power lay in the fact that they were the public officials, magistrates, responsible for forming a government: they drew up a list of eligible voters and put their names in election bags, deciding who could be *imborsato.*

4. *scrutiny:* the "scrutiny" process that the proper officials carried out to determine the qualifications of a voting citizen so that he might be eligible for a particular office.

5. *recognized:* translation of *veduto,* "seen"—referring to a name that had actually been drawn out of an election bag and hence "seen" or "recognized" as being someone the *accoppiatori* officially designated as eligible for office. One customary means for the Medici to govern tightly was to ensure that only men sympathetic to their cause were *imborsati* and then *veduti.*

6. *Pepi:* a Florentine diplomatic figure; for more information on him, see Letters 132, n. 7, and 136, n. 1.

Letter 222

1. *fox . . . lion:* an allusion to the Aesop fable that describes the fox collapsing in fear the first time it sees a lion, taking courage the second time, and approaching it and conversing with it the third time; depending on the edi-

tion used, the fable is #10, #42, or #136. Latin translations had recently appeared in both Milan (Bonaccorso di Pisa), in 1480, and Venice (Aldus Manutius), in 1505 (Gaeta). Najemy notes that versions by Ermolao Barbaro or Lorenzo Valla could have been available to Machiavelli; see *Between Friends*, pp. 168–169. For more on the fox and lion image, see Rebhorn, *Foxes and Lions*, and Pitkin, *Fortune Is a Woman*, ch. 2.

2. *king of Spain:* see *Prince*, 16, 46–48; Atkinson, p. 263, where Machiavelli repeats the judgment that Ferdinand the Catholic was not generally considered "generous" by his contemporaries.

3. *friar:* Savonarola, who in turn is quoting from God's condemnation of false prophets (Ezek. 13:10) (Gaeta).

4. *Thérouanne:* the news of the English victories at Thérouanne and in the "Battle of the Spurs" at Guinegate on 16 August had yet to reach Machiavelli (Gaeta).

5. *objective:* this passage is relevant to the thorny question of dating the *Discourses;* see Baron, "Machiavelli the Republican," and Sasso, *"Composizione,"* as they relate to *Discourses*, I, 12, and II, 4, 12. The following judgment that Machiavelli makes about Venice is relevant to *Discourses*, I, 6 (Gaeta).

6. *Casa:* Filippo Casavecchia.

7. *confederated republics:* see Letter 220, n. 17; *divulse* comes from the Latin *divellere*, "to tear away," but the point, as it is expanded in *Discourses*, II, 4, is that the Confederation of Swiss Republics was separated into autonomous districts or cantons. For Machiavelli, this type of organization exhibits an inherent weakness. In this letter, Machiavelli further objects to the Swiss unwillingness "to create subject nations." Behind Machiavelli's incredulity and scepticism in both this letter and the *Discourses* lies his conviction that a unified republic requires a centralized authority as part of its governance for it to be truly powerful, which definitionally means expansion and hence the creation of "subject nations." Sasso, *Pensiero politico*, p. 29, n. 32, calls attention to Machiavelli's irony: it is not that Machiavelli does not know what Aristotle has to say but rather that Machiavelli wishes to direct attention to topics of more pith: "what might reasonably exist, what exists, and what has existed."

8. *Etruscans:* the Etruscans, as well as the Aetolians and the Achaeans mentioned in the next sentence, were united into loose confederations—the Achaean League and the Aetolian League—similar to that of the Swiss.

9. *best armies:* the basis for Machiavelli's definition of an "armed populace" as the best army rests on his recent experience as first secretary of the Nine. See also *Prince*, 12–13 (Gaeta).

10. *mixed armies:* i.e., those composed of both mercenaries and a citizen militia; see *Prince*, 13, 109–113, and Atkinson, p. 243. Machiavelli discusses some of these same examples in *Prince*, 5–6, and *Art of War*, end of Book I (Gaeta).

11. *King Louis: Prince*, 13, 90–120; Atkinson, pp. 241, 143, treats in greater depth the reasons for the failure of recent French military policy under Louis XII (Gaeta).

12. *owes to Pope Julius:* see *Discourses*, I, 12; II, 22 (Gaeta).

Letter 223

1. *Sernigi:* see Letter 13, n. 6, and Letter 262, where he is mentioned ironically.

2. *Panzano:* Frosino da Panzano is a mutual friend mentioned in Letters 224 and 231. See Najemy, *Between Friends,* p. 216, for a discussion of an elaborate play on words here to the effect that the "cards," or letters they are writing to one another, are "always superseded by events and thus obsolete before they arrived at their destination."

3. *events:* between August and November there were the English victory at Guinegate on 16 August; the signing of an accord between French commander La Trémoïlle and an invading Swiss army at Dijon in September, according to which Louis XII gave up his claims to Milan and paid the Swiss an indemnity of 600,000 ducats; the campaign by the viceroy of Naples, Ramón de Cardona, on behalf of the Holy League against Venice at the end of September, and his defeat of the Venetians under Bartolomeo d'Alviano at Vicenza on 7 October; the formation in Lille of a league between Ferdinand the Catholic and Maximilian I, against France, on 17 October; and Louis XII's renunciation of the schismatic synod on 26 October, which paved the way for his reconciliation with Pope Leo X (Gaeta). The reconciliation was effected by the Treaty of Corbeil in early November, and the French king adhered to the Lateran Council in mid December.

4. *Borgo:* Vettori lived in the vicinity of the present-day church of SS. *Michele e Magno* in the *Borgo Santo Spirito* "quite near" the Vatican Palace and the square before St. Peter's Basilica (Gaeta).

5. *Janiculum:* one of the seven original hills of Rome, on the right bank of the Tiber River.

6. *Brancacci:* Giuliano Brancacci, a mutual friend; see especially Letters 226 and 231.

7. *O[ur] L[ordship]:* Pope Leo X.

8. *Cardinal de' Medici:* Giulio de' Medici.

9. *Giuliano the Magnificent:* Giuliano de' Medici, the duke of Nemours.

10. *Piero Ardinghelli:* one of Giuliano's secretaries and chancellors (1470–1526). He had originally been a partisan of Soderini's republican government, but his Medici sympathies appeared as early as 1503. Machiavelli's dislike of him will erupt in Letter 224.

11. *Ser Sano . . . Girolami:* Sano is mentioned in Letters 226, 227, 228, 230, and 269, where there are allusions to his homosexuality. Tommaso may allude to someone referred to in Book II of Vettori's *Viaggio in Alamagna,* an anecdotal account of the legation that Vettori and Machiavelli headed to the court of Maximilian I in 1508 replete with·Boccaccio-like short stories. Giovanni Rucellai (1475–1525), the son of Bernardo Rucellai, an active opponent of Piero Soderini, was Leo X's cousin, an ecclesiastic, humanist, and author; his *Rosmunda,* written in 1515, borrowed from *Antigone* by Sophocles. Girolami was an agent of Cardinal Francesco Soderini.

12. *Florus . . . Procopius:* Florus wrote in the second century; there are discrepancies between Livy and this *Epitome,* although its praise of the Roman people made it a popular school text. Sallust (86–35 B.C.) is important for writing monographs with a specific, limited scope (the conspiracy of Catiline, the Jugurthine war); Plutarch (c. A.D. 50–120) is famous for his twenty-three pairs of virtuous character traits—his example is known, of course, to all the writers mentioned in this note. Appian (Appianus Alexandrinus) in the second century wrote an account, primarily in praise of Roman imperialism, of Rome from its founding through the reign of Trajan (d. A.D. 117). Tacitus (c. A.D. 56–c. 117) was a stylist whose works (*Germania, Annals,* and *Histories*) generally sought to show the corruption of his Rome when compared with republican Rome. Suetonius (c. A.D. 69–140) is famous for his *De vita Caesarum,* twelve biographies from Julius Caesar to Domitian (d. A.D. 96). [Aelius] Lampridius and [Aelius] Spartianus are purported to be among the writers (*Scriptores Historiae Augustae*) of the *Historia Augusta,* a compilation of biographies of Roman rulers from A.D. 117 to 284—these are alleged to be by various hands, although some modern scholars consider the work to be a forgery. Herodian in the third century wrote a history of Roman rulers that covers the period from 180 to 238. Ammianus Marcellinus in the fourth century wrote a sequel modeled on Tacitus—it was a history covering the period from 96 to 378. Procopius wrote in the sixth century, chiefly about the Byzantine emperor Justinian.

13. *two pontiffs:* namely, Alexander VI, pope from 1492 to 1503, and Julius II, who reigned from 1503 to 1512; Vettori omits the reign of Pius II, which lasted less than a month.

14. *Bibbiena:* Bernardo Dovizi (1479–1520, called *"Il Bibbiena"* because he was from that small town about twenty miles north of Arezzo), a Medici follower, was made a cardinal 23 September 1513, the same day as Giulio de' Medici. He is the humorist of *The Courtier* and the author of a popular, frequently imitated comedy, *La Calandria* (1513).

15. *recall me:* i.e., home to Florence from Rome (Gaeta).

16. *Sed fatis trahimur:* "but we are drawn along by the Fates"; see Seneca, *Epistulae,* 107.11, where the author says he is using Cicero's translation of lines from Cleanthes; but St. Augustine quotes them as Seneca's own (*De civitate Dei,* 5.8).

Letter 224

1. *"Divine . . . late":* Machiavelli elegantly acknowledges receipt of Vettori's last letter by quoting from Petrarch's *Trionfo dell' eternità,* v. 13—a line that Machiavelli altered in his *Serenata,* v. 120, to read, archly, "Love's favors were never late"—which is more than could be said of whatever favors Vettori might bestow. See Najemy, *Between Friends,* pp. 222–223, for the wordplay on *grazie* and a patron's favors.

2. *good steward:* Machiavelli states that he has exercised good stewardship because he has not passed Vettori's letters around; therefore they have not been read by the wrong people.

3. *Filippo and Paolo:* Filippo Casavecchia and Paolo Vettori.

4. *Amphitryon's books:* an allusion to a novella in *ottava rima* popular in the fifteenth and sixteenth century, *Geta e Birria,* based on a comedy by Plautus, *Amphitruo,* in which Amphitryon loads his servant Geta down with books and sends him to his wife Alcumena to warn her of his imminent return (unaware of Jupiter's attempt to spend a night of deceitful love with her). The servant's name in Plautus is Sosia, but in Terence's *Phormio,* where there is a similar incident, the servant's name is Geta. For a suggestive examination of the implications of this identity ("I looked like Geta"), see Najemy, *Between Friends,* pp. 221–230, based on his more detailed "Machiavelli and Geta."

5. *November:* Gaeta follows Ridolfi's suggested emendation of "November" for "September" in the text.

6. cricca: a card game, in which the object is to get three of a kind.

7. *got us to agree:* Giovanni Machiavelli, along with Filippo Machiavelli and Francesco Vettori, "paid the 1000 gold florins which Niccolò was obliged to find as surety for his undertaking not to leave the Florentine dominion," part of his punishment after the Boscoli conspiracy in December 1512 (Jones, *Vettori,* p. 104).

8. *north . . . blowing:* although Gaeta believes this to be an allusion to the Boscoli conspiracy, Inglese points out that a literal interpretation is equally valid—people need wood to burn because it gets colder then.

9. *flay an ox:* the point is that Tommaso—a friend of Machiavelli's from his early days in the chancellery, when del Bene was a secretary to the Ten—and his crew stacked the wood so tightly that Machiavelli's load looked much smaller. Similarly, Gaburra, apparently a butcher whom Vettori knew, and his band do more than merely butcher an ox: they try to tenderize the meat by beating it to a pulp.

10. *Prato:* Battista Guicciardini was the *podestà* of Prato (Gaeta); the Spanish took him prisoner as he tried to escape the sacked city. The city's defeat paved the way for the fall of Florence and the return of the Medici. Since about forty per cent of the Florentine troops at Prato were from Machiavelli's citizen militia, it is striking that he uses so cavalier a tone about both their defeat and his own subsequent disasters.

11. *make my way:* translation of *trasferiscomi poi in su la strada,* as Machiavelli sets up his famous line in the next paragraph (see n. 13), when he "nourishes himself" on ancient writers and *tutto mi trasferisco in loro,* "I absorb myself in them completely."

12. *slum around:* translation of *io m'ingaglioffo;* Gaeta glosses this as *m'incanaglisco* (I associate with the rabble); but see Rebhorn, *Foxes and Lions,* p. 245, n. 22, where his translation is "I become a knave."

13. *completely:* translation of *tutto mi trasferisco in loro,* literally, "I transfer myself into them completely"; Machiavelli uses the same verb (*mi trasferisco*) in the preceding paragraph of this letter, when he speaks of going to the inn after his morning in the woods. See also Introduction, p. xxiv.

14. *understood:* Dante, *Paradiso,* V, vv. 41–42.

15. *His Magnificence Giuliano:* there is little evidence to prove that the duke of Nemours was ever very interested in Machiavelli's plight; he died on 17 March 1516. It should be noted that the summary of *De Principatibus* Machiavelli has just given coincides with the first ten chapters of *The Prince* as we now have it. For the relation of this remark to the questions of dating the composition of *The Prince* and why Machiavelli changed his mind and dedicated it to Lorenzo II de' Medici, who became duke of Urbino on 8 October 1516, see *Prince*, Atkinson, pp. 23–25; Clough, "Yet Again," to be contrasted with Butters, *Governors*, pp. 223–225; Ridolfi, *Vita 7*, pp. 256–258, 525–527; Sasso, *Pensiero politico*, p. 331, and *"Scopo pratico*," pp. 81–109 (Gaeta). For more recent discussions, see Martelli, *"Logica Provvidenzialistica*," and Najemy, *Between Friends*, pp. 177–184.

16. *currying it:* this remark has given rise to a theory that *The Prince* may have been written on two separate occasions. In Letter 228 Vettori says, "I have seen the chapters of your work . . . but since I do not have the entire work, I do not want to make a definitive judgment." In addition to the works cited in the note above, see Sasso, *Pensiero politico*, pp. 314–315, n. 39, and *Principe due redazioni;* Martelli, *"Occasione"* (Gaeta).

17. *Soderinis:* Cardinal Francesco Soderini and his brother Piero; see Letter 208, n. 7 (Gaeta).

18. *Bargello:* this is now a national museum, but at that time it was a prison where Machiavelli had been tortured during the aftermath of the Boscoli conspiracy.

19. *this regime:* the Medici regime, recently restored in Florence (Gaeta).

20. *to you:* concerning the advisability of Vettori's presenting *The Prince* to Giuliano de' Medici, Vettori says in Letter 226, "When I have seen it, I shall tell you my opinion about presenting it or not to the Magnificent Giuliano, as it may seem to me."

21. *Ardinghelli:* see Letter 223, n. 10; later, in a letter dated 14 February 1515, he advised Giuliano de' Medici to avoid all contact with Machiavelli—see Clough, "Yet Again," p. 39, for that text. In so doing Ardinghelli was following the advice of cardinal Giulio de' Medici, who strongly recommended against any contact with Machiavelli on Giuliano's part.

22. *poverty:* a classical commonplace; see Juvenal, III.153, and Plautus, *Stichus*, vv. 176–177 (the soliloquy of Gelasimus opening act I, scene 3). The word "contemptible" is a translation of *contennendo*, a strong word from the Latin *contemnere;* Machiavelli uses the word twice in *Prince*, 14, 18; Atkinson, p. 247, "despised"; and *Prince*, 16, 51; Atkinson, p. 265, "poor and despised."

23. *stone:* an allusion to *Inferno*, VII, 16–66, Dante's description of the fourth circle of Hell, where the avaricious and the wasteful are condemned like Sisyphus to the task of pushing weights around, because both are guilty of too great an interest in wordly goods. Significantly for this context, Dante continues with Vergil giving his famous description of Fortune as the handmaiden of God's providence, turning and ruling the Earth's sphere as the angels turn and rule that of the planets. Cf. also Vergil, *Aeneid*, VI, 616: *"saxum*

ingens volvunt," at the point in the Tartarus section of Hades where Aeneas comes upon those who "roll a great stone" as part of their eternal punishment. Machiavelli's phrasing is closer to Vergil's Latin than to Dante's Italian. (For a provocative discussion of this image and its relation to Lucretius, *De rerum natura,* III.995–1002, and to Latin literature in general, especially Terence and Ovid, see Raimondi, *"Sasso"* [Gaeta].)

24. *forty-three years:* although Machiavelli was forty-three when his "honest and faithful" service to Florence ended in November 1512, Inglese notes that Machiavelli was born on 3 May 1469, so his age would be forty-four and a half at the writing of this letter.

Letter 225

1. *Donato del Corno:* see Letter 221.

2. *Gianfigliazzi:* a pro-Medici political figure in Florence; see Butters, *Governors,* index.

3. *cold comfort:* see Butters, *Governors,* p. 241.

4. *Michelozzi:* Machiavelli's successor as secretary of the second chancellery (Gaeta); according to Butters, he was one of "the secretaries who were deep in Medici counsels . . . a serviceable secretary to Lorenzo de' Medici, and now he assumed the same role for his son Giuliano, keeping him informed about the activities of the Signoria and the Dieci" (*Governors,* p. 208).

5. *Ardinghelli:* see Letter 224, n. 21. Butters goes on to point out that while he was in Rome Giuliano allowed only Michelozzi and Machiavelli's enemy Piero Ardinghelli to use Giuliano's "name to recommend friends" (*Governors,* p. 209).

6. *gratis:* for reference to this loan remaining unpaid, see Letter 254, beginning of the second paragraph.

7. *Riccio:* a young homosexual (Gaeta).

8. *pitchmen:* a quotation important for Rebhorn's argument; see *Foxes and Lions,* p. 38.

9. *friar:* Francesco da Montepulciano; on this passage, see Stephens, *Fall,* pp. 77–78, with notes.

10. *La Riccia:* see Letter 196, n. 2.

Letter 226

1. *in women:* Vettori uses the pejorative term *femmina,* usually applied to women of ill-repute. Inglese, *Lettere,* p. 209, n. 2, suggests that this is an allusion to Pulci, *Morgante,* IV, 48, v. 3; Najemy, *Between Friends,* p. 246, n. 11, concurs because in Pulci there is a conflict between pleasure and politics—Rinaldo professes no interest in attempting to conquer a kingdom—and in Vettori that same conflict is implied by his initial silence on political matters.

2. *Gianfigliazzi . . . Ser Sano:* see Letters 223, n. 11, and 225, n. 2.

3. *via dei Banchi:* then one of Rome's commercial centers (Gaeta).

4. *seen it:* see Letter 224, n. 20.

5. *Piero:* Piero Soderini.

6. *anyone:* this paragraph of close analysis of Machiavelli and Piero Soderini's relationship does not minimize the bonds of friendship but rather emphasizes the belief "that continuing links with the Soderini were recognised openly as grave political disadvantages for anyone wishing to remain in Florence" (Lowe, *Church and Politics,* p. 76)—which was where Machiavelli wished to serve.

7. *Piero:* Piero Ardinghelli (Gaeta).

8. *farthings:* translation of *carlini.*

9. *hermit:* Friar Francesco da Montepulciano; see Letter 225 (Gaeta).

1514

Letter 227

1. *of the Safi and of Prester John:* i.e., Persia and Ethiopia (Gaeta).

2. *Ser Sano:* Ser Sano was an intermediary between Jacopo Gianfigliazzi and Vettori (Raimondi); see notes to Letters 223, n. 11.

3. *to the next:* at least twenty-five years, unless, as Gaeta suggests, it is a figure for a long period of time. Raimondi suggests that Machiavelli is jokingly picking up on Vettori's remark that Giuliano, having seen Ser Sano once, twice, thrice in a week, said he was "depraved" (second paragraph of Letter 226).

4. *Valencia:* in the early sixteenth century, Valencia was the center for trade between Spain and Italy—a city as well-known for its wealth as for its corruption (Gaeta).

5. *crazy by night:* this is also a saying that Machiavelli attributes to Castruccio Castracani; see *Vita di Castruccio Castracani,* in Machiavelli, *Altre opere storiche e politiche,* p. 272.

6. *boon companion:* translation of *buon compagno;* Vettori will use this phrase in his reply, but with a different shade of meaning—see Letter 228, n. 3.

7. *Mona Smeria:* perhaps one of the women—*femmine*—whom Vettori was frequenting (Raimondi); the allusion also occurs in a sonnet, "*Manze d'ovile e cavoli fioriti,*" by Burchiello, a poet in whose humor Machiavelli took much delight (Gaeta); see Letter 299, n. 4, for more on that poet. On this letter, and on the general role of "frivolous matters" in these letters, as well as Machiavelli's appreciation of Burchiello, see Ferroni, *"Cose vane."*

Letter 228

1. *women:* again, as in Letter 226, the pejorative *femmine.*

2. *Bossi:* Gian Alberto di Donato Bossi, born c. 1460, the author of *Institutiones Gramatice* (Inglese).

3. *play around a bit:* translation of *buona compagna;* Vettori uses a phrase that Machiavelli used in the previous letter. Vettori's phrase, however, is akin to the way Machiavelli has Callimaco use it to characterize Sostrata, the mother of Messer Nicia's wife, Lucrezia, in *Mandragola,* I, 1 (Machiavelli, *Comedies,* pp. 168–169). Machiavelli also uses *buon compagno* in the play's prologue to describe Callimaco, more in the manner of his use in Letter 227 of a "well-rounded,

easy-going, boon companion" (Machiavelli, *Comedies*, pp. 156–157).

4. *O[ur] L[ordship]:* Pope Leo X.

5. *what you will:* translation of *a che è buona la paglia,* "whatever straw is good for."

6. *woman:* both uses of "woman" in this paragraph translate *femmina.*

7. *work:* i.e., *The Prince;* see Letter 224, n. 16; Vettori's offhand reference to it must have disappointed Machiavelli, especially when Vettori, three paragraphs later, seems to get more pleasure from Machiavelli's letters than from his treatise.

Letter 229

1. *twenty-third:* Inglese points out that Gaeta's text follows the *Apografo Ricci* but that Vettori's letter (Letter 228) is dated the 18th; see Letter 235, n. 1.

2. *notes:* Ridolfi believes that these are notes for a projected wide-ranging work of history that culminated in *The Florentine Histories,* presented to Pope Clement VII in 1525 (*Life,* pp. 90, 278–279; *Vita 7,* pp. 142, 472–474). Referring to the dedicatory letter that Agostino Vespucci wrote for a 1506 edition of Machiavelli's *Decennale Primo,* Ridolfi argues that as early as 1506 Machiavelli was amassing copies and extracts of chancellery documents as source material because, even then, he was planning a history of Florence. Inglese, *Lettere,* pp. 221–222, n. 3, wonders whether the lost notes may explain why the *Decennale secondo*—a work projected to describe events from 1504 to 1514—actually ends with the events of 1509.

3. *chains:* see Petrarch, *Trionfo d'Amore,* I, vv. 159–160 (Gaeta); from the *Triumphus Cupidinis.*

4. *"O Heaven . . . Neptune":* *Adelphoe,* l. 790 (Gaeta). A line expressing the older father's realization that he is a victim of a comic deception, enabling his younger son to go against his strict wishes in an affair of the heart (V, 3). Machiavelli assumes that Vettori will relish the irony of this hyperbolic wail, in the context of Machiavelli's recreation of the scene in Rome.

5. *"majesty . . . abode":* see Ovid, *Metamorphoses,* II, vv. 846–847 (Gaeta). The context, beginning a series of witty sexual allusions, is Jupiter transforming himself into a bull (since majesty and love do not go well together) so he can possess Europa; Vettori will use this phrase in Letter 230.

6. *swan . . . gold:* this continues the sexual innuendo with reference to the myth of Jupiter changing himself into a swan so that he can possess Leda, which results in the births of Castor, Pollux, and Helen, and then changing himself into a shower of gold so that he can possess Danae, which results in the birth of Perseus (Gaeta).

Letter 230

1. *dignity and love:* Vettori picks up the phrase that Machiavelli uses in Letter 229.

2. *wife:* Vettori's wife was Lena di Pietro Capponi (Gaeta).

3. *she:* Costanza.

4. *"and I . . . gestures":* a slightly altered quotation of Petrarch, *Trionfo d'Amore,* III, 91–93 (Gaeta); again, from the *Triumphus Cupidinis.*

5. *Piero:* Piero di Paolo Vettori (1500–1517) (Gaeta).

6. *wise men:* see the penultimate paragraph of Letter 229.

7. *Francesco:* Anton Francesco degli Albizzi (Gaeta).

8. *he:* Anton Francesco.

9. *in the bag . . . recognized:* see Letter 221, nn. 3 and 5, for the terms *imborsato* and *veduto* in Donato's "scrutiny" hopes.

Letter 231

1. *yarn:* translates *novella* in order to convey the sense of *novella* as both "rumor" and "short story." For a more detailed study of Machiavelli's literary devices in these letters, see Bardazzi, "Tecniche narrative."

2. *say:* Machiavelli thus leaves it open whether this Brancacci is a fictive name or the real Giuliano Brancacci, who is actually in Rome, not Florence. For the possible identification of Machiavelli with Brancacci, who is the fictive narrator of this short story, see Najemy, *Between Friends,* pp. 272–273.

3. *into the woods:* the possibility of this identification is increased by the fact that "to go into the woods" translates *"andare a la macchia,"* with a pun on Machiavelli's nickname.

4. *Via del Canto de' Mozzi:* Najemy, *Between Friends,* p. 273, believes this is the present-day Via del Parione.

5. *Santo Ilario:* Saint Hilarius (Saint Mirth); see Najemy, *Between Friends,* p. 274.

6. all over heaven: a quotation from Ovid, *Metamorphoses,* IV.189 (Gaeta). This line occurs at the end of the description of Vulcan trapping Mars and Venus in a net during their lovemaking and displaying the ensnared couple for the ridicule of the rest of the gods: an appropriate context for the "landing of a young thrush" and the eventual unmasking of the seducer. Vettori quotes the same line in Letter 281; again, the context is an arch one. With similar phrasing, Ovid repeats the same comment on the fame of Vulcan's capture of Mars and Venus in *Ars amatoria,* II.561.

7. *regret it:* *Decameron,* III, 5 (Gaeta). The subject for the third day is how people get what they want through their own efforts; the fifth story involves a lady deciding to accept a lover, with the play on action and regret for inaction. Machiavelli alters the quotation to suit his meaning and to emphasize the antithesis with a "not" that is absent in Boccaccio.

Letter 232

1. *February–March:* Ridolfi, *Life,* p. 298, n. 36; *Vita 7,* p. 525, n. 36, believes this letter is either "a fragment or more probably a postscript to a letter to Vettori" and that it was written during a stay in Florence. Neither Inglese, *Lettere,* p. 232, nor Najemy concurs. The actions of "the Magnificent Lorenzo" in early 1514 were nothing like those that Machiavelli describes; see Butters, *Governors,* pp. 236–245, and Stephens, *Fall,* pp. 83–95. In addition,

Machiavelli never mentions Vettori. Najemy, *Between Friends,* pp. 277–278, n. 2, argues for its having been written in August and September 1513 or during the period when Machiavelli was readying *The Prince* for publication.

2. *Lorenzo the Magnificent:* Lorenzo II became the governor of Florence about six months prior to this letter. Ridolfi, *Life,* p. 164; *Vita 7,* p. 257, refers to this "portrait of Lorenzo" as evidence of Machiavelli's conviction that Lorenzo II de' Medici "rather than the unwarlike Giuliano" was a better model for Machiavelli's "new Prince"; thus, it is not surprising that he would dedicate *The Prince* to Lorenzo II.

3. *his grandfather:* Lorenzo de' Medici.

4. *others:* i.e., among the Medici supporters in Florence (Gaeta); Inglese adds that he treated people with detachment.

Letter 233

1. *16 April:* the *Apografo Ricci* (see Letter 235, n. 1) provides a draft version of this letter, which is published both in Gaeta's 1961 edition of Machiavelli's letters and in Inglese, *Lettere,* pp. 236–237. Significant differences are indicated in the following notes.

2. *mover:* translation of *motore;* the draft reads *mobile.* The "disorders" referred to are those that might ensue if Louis XII and Ferdinand the Catholic renewed their agreement, the Treaty of Orthez. Guicciardini dryly comments (note the force of "more") on a new provision: Louis agreed "very secretly, while the truce was in effect, not to disturb the government of Milan . . . the King of Spain divulged and formally proclaimed this condition throughout all Spain. People were unclear which was more true—the denial of Louis or the affirmation of Ferdinand," *Storia d'Italia,* XII, p. 1159.

3. *in the year past:* translation of *come l'anno passato;* the draft reads *come anno.*

4. *to lose:* the draft then reads "in both these instances his destruction is implicit. Therefore the situations offer him no advantage . . . ," continuing with the next paragraph.

5. *master:* the draft reads "its master."

6. *King Philip's second son:* the draft reads "to the archduke's son." The final version is more specific. Machiavelli refers to Philip I the Handsome (*el Hermoso,* 1478–1506), the son of Maximilian I, the Holy Roman Emperor, and Mary of Burgundy. Philip bore the titles of archduke of Austria and duke of Burgundy. He married Juana, the daughter of King Ferdinand and Queen Isabella of Spain, and established the Hapsburg dynasty in Spain. Machiavelli is alluding to Louis XII's announced aim of linking the fortunes of France and Spain through the marriage of his daughter, Renée, to one of Philip's two sons, that is, the grandsons of Ferdinand the Catholic: either to Archduke Charles of Hapsburg (Charles of Ghent) or to Archduke Ferdinand of Hapsburg, Philip's second son—see the Headnote.

7. *dolt:* translation of *babbione;* the draft reads "if he were not such a half-wit [*zugo*]."

8. *it:* the draft continues "to the archduke's son, that is more rational."

9. *emperor:* Archduke Ferdinand of Hapsburg was still a minor at this time—he was born in 1503 (Gaeta).

10. *Spaniards:* the draft here contains a paragraph, its final one, that is deleted from the version that Machiavelli sent:

Therefore, all things considered, it seems to me that the king of Spain cannot tolerate such a situation in Italy and he cannot change it with any safety. As for matters beyond the mountains [in France], in order to make them change their appearance, he must transfer the war [an ellipsis follows in the text of the *Apografo Ricci*]. To do so he needs to be careful that the war—but not the fear of war—is taken out of France, because every time the king of France is on the other side of the mountains without a war—or without the fear of it—he will be so bold that Ferdinand will be unable either to withstand him or to control him. How this can be done, I know not, and I see countless problems in that idea, because in order to carry it out, it would be necessary for the king of France, the emperor, and the Swiss to be tied together on a string, and for them all to let go when Ferdinand says, "Let go," and for them all to pull when he says, "Pull." Now, were anyone to ask me: "how do you think he can pull it off?" I would answer that I have no idea—and were I able to think something up, I would not like to tell him about it.

11. Monte: the officials of the Florentine system for public financing of the town's debt, "the mountain." The *Monte redivisibile* ("redeemable") would issue to private citizens credits, which drew interest and were negotiable, in amounts equal to their contributions to the "mountain" of public debt. Thus Florence created a public bank in Florence with an accumulation, a "mountain," of money and assets.

12. *forty florins . . . or less:* Machiavelli fears a tax demand of forty florins, a heavy one for an income of ninety florins.

13. *to write:* Vettori did write, claiming that Machiavelli "is poor and worthy, no matter what anyone says to the contrary, and I can vouch for him. . . . He has heavy tax to pay and little income; he has no money and many children" (Ridolfi, *Life*, p. 157; *Vita 7*, p. 246).

Letter 234

1. *In Pera:* now known as the Beyoglu quarter of Istanbul, lying north of the Golden Horn and west of the Bosphorus. When the letter was written, it was a center for European commerce and international relations; during the last two hundred years it has become the heart of Istanbul.

2. *Lorenzo:* Lorenzo Machiavelli (Gaeta); see Letter 13, n. 11.

3. fiorini di suggello: "sealed florins"; for more on money, see Letter 14, n. 2.

4. *in your behalf:* marriage for his nephew is also a topic in Letters 255 and 256.

Letter 235

1. *16 May 1514:* Giuliano de' Ricci, Machiavelli's grandson and literary executor, between 1573 and 1594 made a transcript of Machiavelli's letters known as the *Apografo Ricci.* About this letter he says that he omitted the first part because it dealt with an illicit love affair by Vettori.

2. *conjectures:* in the fifth paragraph of Letter 233.

3. *stronger than himself:* i.e., King Louis XII of France.

4. *dowry:* see Letter 233, n. 6.

5. *a year ago:* Letter 212 (Gaeta).

6. *King Charles:* Charles VIII was king of France from 1483 to 1498.

7. *treaty:* the League of Venice, concluded 31 March 1495, provided for the mutual defense of the signatories: Spain, Venice, Milan, the pope, and Maximilian I against the then Louis d'Orléans, the future King Louis XII.

8. *half of it:* under the provisions of the Treaty of Granada, concluded on 11 November 1500, sometimes referred to as the "Partition Treaty," Louis XII would conquer and appropriate the northern part of the Kingdom of Naples with the title of king of Naples and Jerusalem, and Ferdinand the Catholic would get the southern part of the Neapolitan territory as duke of Apulia and Calabria.

9. *Genoa:* in April 1507.

10. *League of Cambrai:* signed on 10 December 1508; its original signatories were Maximilian I, Louis XII, and Ferdinand the Catholic; later Pope Julius II, the Marquess of Mantua, and the dukes of Savoy and Ferrara joined it, too.

11. *Messer Gian Giacomo:* Trivulzio (1441–1518) was a marshal of France and the French governor of Milan; he commanded the League of Cambrai's army in the defeat of the Venetians at Agnadello (Vailà, or the Battle of Ghiaradadda) in May 1509 and in several victories over the forces of Julius II.

12. *treaty:* the Holy League, signed in October 1511, between Spain, the Venetians, and Pope Julius II; Henry VIII of England signed it in November.

13. *Sanseverino:* Cardinal Federico Sanseverino was one of the leaders of the schismatic council and its representative to the French military forces, with whose leaders the cardinal had frequent disagreements (Gaeta).

14. *viceroy:* Ramón de Cardona (Gaeta). Originally, Raymond Folch was a soldier under Gonzalo Fernández de Córdoba; he was made duke of Cardona, and later Ramón de Cardona became viceroy of Naples and commander of the Spanish and papal forces. He was indirectly responsible for the Medici's restoration in Florence because of his victory at Prato.

15. *cardinal:* Giovanni de' Medici (Gaeta). Reminiscent of Cesare Borgia's having "erred in this choice": namely, of not trying to stop the election of Pope Julius II in 1503; see *Prince,* 7, n. to lines 251–258; Atkinson, p. 171, and n. to lines 291–292, 302–304, p. 175.

16. *others:* i.e, errors.

17. *match:* between Louis XII's daughter Renée and Archduke Ferdinand of Hapsburg, the future Ferdinand I (1503–1564), Holy Roman Em-

peror from 1556–1564.

18. *in his hands:* Guicciardini expresses a similar judgment in *Storia d'Italia,* XII, 4, p. 1159.

Letter 236

1. *forgot them:* Ridolfi has "many doubts about the reply to these letters" because "Sant' Andrea was on the road to Rome and very near the post where the horses were changed; so that Machiavelli had no need to wait until he went to Florence to send off the letters." Because it is clear from Letter 237 that Machiavelli never sent these letters, Ridolfi believes Machiavelli "either never wrote that reply, or it was so expressive of his strong feelings that he decided not to send it" (*Life,* p. 297, n. 12; *Vita 7,* p. 519, n. 12). That Machiavelli's feelings are already "strong" is evident in the second paragraph of this letter. Even Vettori's reaction to this letter acknowledges that Machiavelli seems "excessively afflicted" by his current situation.

2. *my lice:* recalling the end of the third paragraph of Letter 224, where Machiavelli says that he is "cooped up among these lice," his cronies in San Casciano.

Letter 237

1. *in the bag:* see Letter 221, n. 3.

2. *freely:* i.e., without expecting any compensation.

3. *friend:* Piero Ardinghelli (Gaeta).

4. *time . . . lesser arts:* i.e., when the lesser artisans' guilds, the *arti minori,* were to elect their own gonfalonier (Gaeta).

Letter 238

1. *creature:* although Machiavelli never mentions her name, Ridolfi is "convinced" that she was the widowed sister of Niccolò Tafani, mentioned in Letter 240; see *Life,* p. 160; *Vita 7,* pp. 250–251. Ridolfi notes that Machiavelli uses the word *creatura* and not Vettori's *femmina.*

2. *fiftieth year:* Machiavelli was actually forty-five.

3. *tender thoughts:* perhaps he is referring to the sonnet "The youthful archer many times has tried . . . ," which he sends to Vettori in Letter 247, dated 31 January 1515.

4. *Cyprus:* Homer refers to Aphrodite as "the Cyprian"; hence Venus became associated with the island.

5. *discuss . . . better:* a curious remark for someone who must "take a vow of silence" if he cannot "discuss politics" (Letter 208).

Letter 239

1. *old game:* Horace, *Epistulae,* I.1.2–3 (Gaeta). Just as Horace feigns renouncing poetry so that he can take up philosophy, in the poetic letters to which this is an introduction, Vettori cleverly turns the allusion to Horace so that he can chaff Machiavelli about renouncing politics for love and singing its

praises. The foil involved is what was given to gladiators upon their discharge. See Najemy, *Between Friends,* p. 296, for a suggestion that Vettori, unaware of the irony involved, may be playfully alluding to Machiavelli's breaking away from his "patron,"Vettori, in the same way Horace did from his Maecenas.

2. *to answer:* Vettori is about to raise issues concerning the complex political situation in Italy during the second half of 1514; for more detail on these questions, see Guicciardini, *Storia d'Italia,* XII, 1–9 (Gaeta).

3. *pope:* Najemy believes that Vettori concealed the fact that it was Cardinal Giulio de' Medici's idea to sound out Machiavelli and that the pope's position was to side with the coalition against France—exactly what Machiavelli would advise him not to do in Letter 241 (*Between Friends,* pp. 297–305). In the next paragraph, however, Vettori sends a hint, strong enough for Machiavelli to pick up, that Leo X will see Machiavelli's response.

4. *marriage and peace:* see Letter 233, n. 6. Gaeta observes that Guicciardini, *Storia d'Italia,* XII, 6, and Vettori, *Sommario in Scritti,* pp. 155–156, are helpful concerning this treaty.

5. *shop:* i.e., the Florentine chancellery.

Letter 240

1. *Tafani:* see Letter 238, n. 1. This entire letter is in Latin.

2. *two Niccolòs:* Niccolò Machiavelli and Niccolò Tafani (Gaeta).

3. *for me alone:* Machiavelli quotes Ovid, *Metamorphoses,* XIII.507. The context is Hecuba's grief on learning that her daughter, Polyxena, had been sacrificed by Neoptolemus, obeying the command of his father, Achilles's shade, to kill Polyxena, whom he loved. For the Trojan people, the agony was now over; Machiavelli, however, hoped Vettori would supply the first part of v. 508: *in cursuque meus dolor est,* "and my pain continues to flow."

Letter 241

1. *10 December:* Ridolfi has resolved the question of dating; see *Life,* p. 297, n. 21; *Vita 7,* p. 520, n. 21. Giving more latitude to the dating of this letter, Inglese, *Lettere,* pp. 165–166, assigns a date of "3/14 December 1514?." Since the upshot of Machiavelli's advice in this memorandum-letter is to side with France, it is strange that Vettori did not inform Machiavelli that Pope Leo X was leaning toward Spain—see Letter 239, n. 3.

2. *insults:* Ferdinand the Catholic signed the Treaty of Orthez in April 1513 without consulting Henry VIII; see the Headnote for 1513.

3. *armed forces:* a proposition discussed in *Prince,* 3, with the example, again, of Louis XII; see l. 217 ff.; Atkinson, p. 117.

4. *Castile:* Henry VIII's sister, Mary Tudor, had been betrothed to Charles, prince of Castile—the future Archduke Charles of Hapsburg, Holy Roman Emperor Charles V, and King of Spain Charles I—from 1508 to 1514; then Henry married her off to Louis XII. It is worth reiterating the fact that throughout this correspondence the writers refer to a ruler or a country interchangeably. Thus "king" may mean England, and "England," as in this case,

may mean King Henry VIII.

5. *these two:* Inglese, *Lettere,* p. 258, breaks this sentence at this point and begins a new one with "For anyone wishing . . ."

6. *these passes:* see *Discourses,* I, 23 (Gaeta).

7. *would belong to them:* see *Prince,* 3, ll. 145–160; Atkinson, p. 113. For this context and that of Letter 243, see also the opening paragraph of *Prince,* 12.

8. *Duke Charles:* Charles the Bold, duke of Burgundy (1433–1477); see Letter 219, n. 8.

9. *group:* Pope Leo X signed a secret agreement with Ferdinand the Catholic in Bibbiena, on 21 September, that denied support for any potential attack on Milan, Genoa, and Asti in northern Italy (Gaeta). Najemy remarks that the pope would be astounded, if not enraged, by this section of Machiavelli's memorandum-letter: "Only two years had passed since the Spanish troops restored Leo and his family to Florence and removed the pro-French popular republic that had kept the Medici in exile for eighteen years. And here was Machiavelli advising Leo to throw his support, not merely to France, but also to the cause of a *'rebellione de' popoli'* in Lombardy, and possibly Tuscany as well" (*Between Friends,* p. 301).

10. *coastline:* along both the Adriatic and Tyrrhenian seas (Gaeta).

11. *yours:* he means those troops that Florence supplied.

12. *waiting:* i.e., until they could openly take their position (Gaeta).

13. *duke of Ferrara:* Alfonso I d'Este (1476–1534) was duke of Ferrara from 1505 to 1534.

14. "you know . . . is nigh": Machiavelli quotes Matthew 24:32; the context is that of Christ disclosing to his disciples the signs of His second coming: "Now learn a parable of the fig tree; When his branch is yet tender, and putteth forth leaves, ye shall know that summer is nigh."

15. *league:* the Holy League against Louis XII of France, signed in October 1511, between Spain, the Venetians, and Pope Julius II; Henry VIII of England signed it in November.

16. *as the Venetians did:* i.e., in the wars during 1509 subsequent to the formation of the League of Cambrai in December 1508, especially at Agnadello (Vailà or the Battle of Ghiaradadda) in May 1509.

17. *without parallel:* for more thoughts on the Swiss, see *Prince,* 12–13 (Gaeta).

18. *importance:* for more on Ferdinand the Catholic, see *Prince,* 21 (Gaeta).

19. *territory of France:* specifically, the territory around Avignon and in the Vaucluse that was once under papal authority (Gaeta).

20. *contempt:* see *Prince,* 16, 86–94; Atkinson, p. 267; and *Prince,* 19, "how to avoid contempt and hatred," and 21, "obtaining prestige."

21. *Pope Julius II:* in this context, see remarks in *Prince,* 2, 7, 13, 16, and 25 (Gaeta).

22. *now:* see *Prince,* 11, 71–101; Atkinson, p. 215.

23. *neutral:* see *Prince,* 21, 80–103; Atkinson, p. 337.

24. *[always]:* the square brackets are Gaeta's; all the square brackets in the

remainder of this letter are his emendations.

25. *as enem[ies]:* for more on the theme of "an enemy of the loser and an enemy of the winner," see Letter 243 (Gaeta).

26. *emperor:* see *Prince,* 23, 30–45; Atkinson, p. 351.

27. *otherwise:* Gaeta notes that at this point the text of the letter contains the annotation: "An enemy of the loser and an enemy of the winner: one because of a desire for revenge, the other because of a desire for profit. Motives that are not discovered sooner are discovered later." The theme that Machiavelli mentions about Julius II remaining neutral, at the end of the third paragraph from the end of this letter, is taken up at the beginning of Letter 243.

Letter 242

1. *one:* this letter has been lost (Gaeta).

2. *another one:* i.e., Letter 240 (Gaeta)

3. *the other one:* Letter 241 (Gaeta).

4. *Monsignor de' Medici:* only after the fact, and not in Letter 239, where the subject was first broached, does Vettori inform Machiavelli that Cardinal Giulio de' Medici asked for what becomes the memorandum-letter, Letter 241.

5. *recently published:* Sigismondo Mayr published Giovanni Pontano's *De fortuna* in Naples in 1512. See Najemy, *Between Friends,* pp. 308–309, for the implications of this allusion.

6. Gonzalo: Gonzalo Fernández de Córdoba.

7. *who . . . too:* Vettori alludes to Vergil, *Aeneid,* I. 198–199, in his attempt to comfort Machiavelli, just as Aeneas was trying to comfort his men after they were washed up onto the shores of Carthage. He hopes, with Aeneas, *"forsan et haec olim meminisse iuvabit"* ("one day, perhaps, you will recall even these adversities with pleasure," v. 203). For more on this allusion, see Rebhorn, *Foxes and Lions,* p. 241, and Najemy, *Between Friends,* pp. 309–310.

8. *drawn:* see Letter 221, nn. 3, 4, 5.

9. frati: Vettori uses the word *frati,* "brothers" or "monks," in place of "ducats."

Letter 243

1. *considerations:* see the last three paragraphs of Letter 241.

2. contempt and hatred: Machiavelli's Latin here, *contemptum et odium,* echoes the chapter title of *Prince,* 19, *"De contemptu et odio fugiendo."*

3. *"Nothing . . . dignity":* Machiavelli recalls a passage from Livy 35.49.13 that he uses in *Prince,* 21 (76–78; Atkinson, p. 335); see Letter 191, n. 4.

4. *all things . . . again:* a conviction replete with implications for the study of history and of historical necessity.

5. *detail:* Machiavelli still has in mind the reasons that he delineated in Letter 241.

6. *lesser of two evils:* see *Prince,* 21, 123–125; Atkinson, p. 339 and n., with its cross references to *Discourses,* I, 6, and I, 38, the opening lines of *Mandragola,* III, 1 (Machiavelli, *Comedies,* pp. 202–203), as well as Cicero, *De off.,*

3.1.3. Guicciardini's thoughts in *Storia d'Italia,* XII, 4, are quite similar: "It is the duty of a wise prince, in order to avoid the greater evil, to opt for espousing the lesser evil for the sake of the good and the useful; he must not try to extricate himself from one danger and one confusion only to rush into other more serious or more disgraceful ones" (p. 1157). Interestingly enough, the context of this quotation is Guicciardini's discussion of the signing of an accord between the French commander, La Trémoïlle, and an invading Swiss army at Dijon in September 1513, according to which Louis XII gave up his claims to Milan and paid the Swiss an indemnity of 600,000 ducats. Vettori alluded to this event in Letter 223.

7. *squares:* translation of *due case,* which Gaeta annotates as an image from chess, indicating that the pope is in the enviable position of making two moves (Gaeta); Inglese notes that the literal sense of "two houses" is equally appropriate—namely, Rome and Avignon.

Letter 244

1. *enclosed:* the previous letter, Letter 243.

2. *fifteenth:* Letter 242.

3. *letters:* because Sasso believes Machiavelli despises the ostentatious display of erudition, he sees heavy irony in this reference to Vettori's hauling in Pontano to belabor the obvious; see *Pensiero politico,* p. 30, n. 32.

Letter 245

1. See . . . racks me: Gaeta notes that it is based on Ovid, *Remedia amoris,* vv. 161–162, which reads, "Why did Aegisthus yearn to commit adultery? / The reason is apparent: he was idle." Inglese notes that vv. 136–137 are equally appropriate: "Avoid idle ways, idleness makes you love."

2. *Mino da Siena:* see Fiammetta's story, in *Decameron,* VIII, 8, about Zeppa di Mino, who lived in Siena. His best friend seduced his wife, so Zeppa made love to his friend's wife on top of a chest in which he had trapped the husband. Revenge was tit for tat, and from then on the men agreed each to have two wives and the wives agreed each to have two husbands. Najemy, *Between Friends,* pp. 315–316, suggests the relevance of Sacchetti's eighty-fourth story in his *Libro delle trecento novelle,* written circa 1390.

3. *Cardinals:* Bibbiena was Bernardo Dovizi (*Il Bibbiena,* 1479–1520), a Medici follower, who was made cardinal on 23 September 1513, the same day as Giulio de' Medici (the other cardinal whom Vettori mentions).

1 5 1 5 - 1 5 1 9

Letter 246

1. "Ah, Corydon . . . seized you?": see Vergil, *Eclogues,* II.69 (Gaeta). Only momentarily does Vettori here employ the persona of the clumsy, love-sick, rather comical shepherd Corydon as he begins to reassure himself that, since Alexis has spurned him, he can find another youth to requite his

love (Vergil was imitating Theocritus, *Idylls,* II.72–76). Inglese would give an exclamatory rather than an interrogatory sense to the quotation from Vergil.

2. *La Riccia:* a courtesan friend of Machiavelli.

3. *women:* the pejorative *femmine.*

4. *Filippo:* Filippo Casavecchia (Gaeta) or Filippo Machiavelli (Inglese).

5. *Lorenzo Machiavelli:* see Letter 13, n. 11.

6. *Donato:* Donato del Corno (Gaeta).

Letter 247

1. *youthful archer:* Love (Cupid); see notes to Letter 238. Ridolfi thinks Machiavelli's love for the sister of Niccolò Tafani may also have led to the sonnet *"Se sanza a voi pensar solo un momento . . ."* (If I could help thinking of you for but a moment) and the *Serenata "Salve, donna, tra le altre donne eletta . . ."* (Hail, lady, elect among other ladies); Ridolfi, *Life,* p. 304, n. 31; *Vita 7,* p. 539, n. 32. See Najemy's discussion of this sonnet in *Between Friends,* pp. 325–328; in fact, his ninth chapter, "Poetry and Politics," is relevant for what he terms Machiavelli's "dialogue with the poets" (p. 337).

2. *this sonnet:* a graceful sonnet in reply to Vettori's "fucking" of Letter 246.

3. *skiff . . . tempest:* on the comfort that Machiavelli finds in Donato del Corno and La Riccia, based on the second paragraph of Letter 246, and the implications of "skiff" (*legno*), see Najemy, *Between Friends,* pp. 321–325.

4. O Nymph . . . enemies: a translation of Ovid, *Metamorphoses,* 1.504–507. The text of Machiavelli's letter contains two slight variants: for their implications, see Najemy, *Between Friends,* pp. 321–325.

5. And just . . . me: Machiavelli implies that just as Apollo got nowhere with Daphne, so he is having no success with the woman who is his "sole haven and refuge"—perhaps a metaphorical reference to glory and fame.

6. *cannot be censured:* Machiavelli uses the verb *imitare,* but more in the sense of following an example than of slavish mimicry; he is asserting his identity with nature and thus implying less control over it than strict imitation would warrant. On this famous paragraph, see Ferroni, *"Cose vane";* Martelli, *"Cultura di Machiavelli,"* useful on the literary tradition of combining "weighty matters" with the "petty"; and Najemy, *Between Friends,* pp. 329–330.

7. *Your . . . control:* the people referred to in this sentence are Paolo Vettori, Giuliano de' Medici, and Pope Leo X; for the events referred to in this paragraph, see the Headnote. Baron, *"Principe* and the Puzzle," pp. 98–101, contains an important argument concerning how the remainder of this letter proves that chapter 26 of *The Prince* was written between January and March 1515.

8. *countless problems:* Machiavelli addresses the problem of being the on-site governor of a new princedom in *Prince,* 3, 77–79; Atkinson, p. 107, and note. There are also many echoes throughout *Prince,* 6 of the analysis in this letter. Machiavelli's solution, suggested in this letter's next two sentences, is for Giuliano to consolidate the new cities into one large body; the phrase *tutti uno corpo* occurs in this context and that of *Prince,* 3, 72–73; Atkinson, p.

107, see note. Gaeta refers to Sasso, *"Scopo pratico,"* pp. 84–95, for how this paragraph relates to the question of the philosophical as opposed to the practical nature of *The Prince,* raised by Clough, "Yet Again."

9. *Milan . . . Ferrara:* Parma and Piacenza were part of Milan; Modena and Reggio, part of Ferrara (Gaeta).

10. *His Lordship:* Pope Leo X.

11. *on all occasions:* the illustrative examples from Cesare Borgia's life that Machiavelli uses in *The Prince* do not always coincide with this assertion. Machiavelli's zeal in this letter to provide advice on a situation that is so close to the thrust of advice to a "new" prince in *The Prince* may have caused him to overlook what he says of Ramiro in chapter 7, ll. 158–178, and nn. As seems clear from the following sentence, Machiavelli may have in mind Vettori's brother Paolo, since he was close to Giuliano de' Medici, as someone whom Giuliano might actually appoint as his on-the-spot representative in one of the cities where Giuliano is to become the new governor. Certainly Paolo would not want to play Ramiro to Giuliano's Cesare if Paolo, too, were to have his "body laid out one morning in two pieces on the public square . . . with a block of wood and a bloody sword beside it" (*Prince,* 7, pp. 174–176; Atkinson, p. 167). See Najemy, *Between Friends,* pp. 330–334, for the argument that Machiavelli is "rewriting" *Prince,* 7.

12. *your Paolo's case:* although Machiavelli coolly refrains from any ingratiating, self-serving remarks in this paragraph, if he ever had high hopes for himself through Paolo Vettori, they were soon to be dashed. Piero Ardinghelli, one of Giuliano's secretaries and chancellors—and no friend of Machiavelli—wrote from Rome to Giuliano in Florence: "Yesterday Cardinal [Giulio] de' Medici questioned me very closely about whether I knew if Your Excellency had taken Niccolò Machiavelli into your service; since I answered that I had no knowledge of it or belief in it, His Most Reverend Lordship said precisely these words to me: 'I do not believe it either; since there is no report from Florence about it, I would remind him that it is neither to his advantage nor ours. This must be something fabricated by Paolo Vettori . . . write him that, for my part, I counsel him not to get involved with Niccolò; I do not say this in order to instruct him about what he ought to do but because I am prompted out of love for him, etc.'" (Ardinghelli's letter is dated 14 February; text cited from Clough, *Researches,* p. 39; see also Ridolfi, *Vita 7,* p. 254; cf. *Life,* p. 162). Clough suggests that Machiavelli may have been thought useful as a princely adviser to Giuliano de' Medici, because his contemporaries thought that his brother, Pope Leo X, might carve out a new state in Lombardy for Giuliano to govern. On the basis of Marchand, *"Ghiribizzi,"* it is also possible that Machiavelli could have been thought useful as a military adviser to Giuliano in bolstering the Florentine militia. For how Ardinghelli's letter squelches Machiavelli's hopes, see Baron, "*Principe* and the Puzzle," pp. 99–100.

13. *And . . . Macone:* the second of these two lines of verse is a quotation from Pulci, *Morgante,* I, 38, v. 8; the first line Machiavelli conflates from *Morgante,* I, 35, vv. 5–6, and I, 37, v. 6. The context is Orlando's slaying of two

Moorish giants. *"Macone"* was a literary name for Muhammad, the founder of Islam. The emphasis is on loyalty in adversity, although Machiavelli may have hoped Vettori would understand a pun on Machiavelli's own name; see Najemy, *Between Friends,* pp. 320–321.

Letter 248

1. *In Pera:* now known as the Beyoglu quarter of Istanbul; see Letter 234, n. 1.

2. *you:* as usual, Machiavelli addresses Vernacci as *tu* here and in Letters 249, 250, and 252; when Vernacci replies in Letter 253, he uses the formal *voi* as an expression of respect.

Letter 249

1. *you:* Machiavelli addresses Vernacci as *tu.*

2. *as are you:* Machiavelli is more self-revelatory with his nephew than with almost any of his other correspondents.

Letter 250

1. *You:* Machiavelli addresses Vernacci as *tu.*

2. *As . . . so:* another poignant glimpse into Machiavelli's state of mind, which he evidently chose to share only with his nephew.

Letter 251

1. *Captain of the Papal Galleys:* Vettori was appointed captain of the papal galleys in 1513 (Gaeta). We know little more than that in this capacity Paolo Vettori sent Machiavelli to Leghorn to execute some commissions for him.

Letter 252

1. *you:* Machiavelli addresses Vernacci as *tu.*

2. *Bernardo and Lodovico:* Machiavelli's older sons.

Letter 253

1. *you:* typically, although Machiavelli writes to Vernacci using the intimate *tu,* the latter replies with the formal *voi* as an expression of respect.

Letter 254

1. *Ludovico:* Ludovico di Piero Alamanni (1495–1556), better known as Luigi Alamanni, was an important literary and diplomatic figure as well as a member of the Florentine group of humanists who met at the *Orti Oricellari* (Rucellai Gardens). He opposed the Medici and was part of a failed plot against Cardinal Giulio de' Medici in 1522. He fled to Venice and then to France. King Francis I welcomed him, sent him on diplomatic missions, and acted as his literary patron. He returned briefly to Florence in 1527, but, with the end of the Second Republic and another return of the Medici, he hastened to France in 1530 to bask in French adulation. He is not to be confused

with his older brother, Lodovico di Piero (1488–1526), an aristocratic, pro-Medici politician who wrote one of the numerous reports on Florentine constitutional problems, *Discorso di Lodovico Alamanni sopra il fermare lo stato di Firenze nella devozione de' Medici* (Lodovico Alamanni's discourse on assuring the government of Florence's devotion to the Medici) dated 25 November 1516; see Gilbert, *Machiavelli and Guicciardini,* p. 101 and index.

2. *Donato del Corno:* at issue is the long-term attempt to get his name on the list of those eligible for political office; see Letter 221 and subsequent references in Machiavelli's letters to Francesco Vettori.

3. *Lord Giuliano:* this loan to the duke of Nemours is referred to in the third paragraph of Letter 225.

4. *Buoninsegni:* a member of Cardinal Giulio de' Medici's household, with administrative duties, and a very influential adviser to Pope Leo X on financial matters (Gaeta).

5. Orlando Furioso: the first edition of Ariosto's poem was published in Ferrara by Giovanni Mazzocchi dal Bondeno in April 1516 (Gaeta).

6. *poets:* Gaeta says this alludes to a gallery of mediocre sixteenth-century poets on display in the *Orlando Furioso,* 46, 12–19. The edition available to Machiavelli had only forty cantos; the poem was forty-six cantos long in the third edition (Ferrara, 1532). It may be, however, that this collection of poets appeared in an earlier canto and, in the numerous revisions that Ariosto made, was thought to be more appropriate in a later canto.

7. Ass: Machiavelli's *Dell'Asino [d'oro]*—"Golden" was a later addition, in imitation of Apuleius and perhaps of Angelo Firenzuola—was probably written in 1517; whether or not Machiavelli would have followed through on his promise here to include Ariosto among a similar list of second-rate poets we cannot know. Machiavelli left the poem incomplete. Nevertheless, the joke is a good one. (The allusion in VII, 43–51, to "an animal unlike the others that nature made with more art" has been inconclusively interpreted to refer to Ariosto and to the duke of Urbino, Lorenzo II de' Medici.)

8. *together with:* the names mentioned in this paragraph are related to the discussions in the Rucellai Gardens; important background about this cénacle can be found in Gilbert, "Composition" and "Rucellai and the *Orti Oricellari";* Cantimori, "Rhetoric and Politics"; Spini, *Rinascimento;* Von Albertini, *Florentinische Stattsbewusstsein,* pp. 67–85; and Bertelli's introductory note to *"Discursus florentinarum"* in Machiavelli, *Arte della guerra.* As for some of the men mentioned, Cardinal Giovanni Salviati (1490–1533), the son of Jacopo Salviati and Lucrezia de' Medici, and Pope Leo X's nephew, was in a good position to receive papal patronage; Filippo de' Nerli (1485–1556) was ardently pro-Medici throughout his life, one of the priors in 1517 and 1522, a governor of Modena from 1523 to 1527, and the author of *Commentarii de' fatti civili occorsi dentro la città di Firenze dal 1215 al 1537* (Commentaries on the civil events that occurred inside the city of Florence from 1215 to 1537), which, incidentally, is a source for information about the meetings at the Rucellai Gardens; Zanobi Buondelmonti (1491–1527) was ardently

anti-Medici—enough so to be a member of the conspiracy against Cardinal Giulio de' Medici in 1522, along with Luigi Alamanni and Battista della Palla—and was obliged to flee to Lucca, to Garfagnana with Ariosto (whom Alfonso I, the duke of Ferrara, had appointed governor with headquarters at Castelnovo di Garfagnana), then to Venice, and finally to France; Buondelmonti returned to Florence in 1527 and was present at Machiavelli's death (Machiavelli dedicated *The Discourses* to him and Cosimo Rucellai and *The Life of Castruccio Castacani of Lucca* to him and Luigi Alamanni, and he made Buondelmonti one of the interlocutors in his *Art of War,* along with Fabrizio Colonna, Cosimo Rucellai, Luigi Alamanni, and Battista della Palla); della Palla at one point was quite friendly with Giuliano de' Medici and hoped to become a cardinal through Giuliano's help. On the latter's death, in March 1516, della Palla vainly hoped that Leo X would make him one. After the failure of the conspiracy against Cardinal Giulio de' Medici in 1522, della Palla fled to France; along with Buondelmonti, he was with the imperial army that advanced on Florence in 1527. After the downfall of the Second Republic in 1530, he was arrested and died in prison (Gaeta).

Letter 255

1. *you:* Machiavelli addresses Vernacci as *tu* here and in Letters 256, 258, and 259.

2. *to get married:* marriage for his nephew was also on Machiavelli's mind in Letter 234, of April 1514, and in the next letter.

Letter 256

1. *you:* Machiavelli addresses Vernacci as *tu.*

2. *fourth of November:* see the last paragraph of Letter 253.

3. *caviar:* see the second paragraph of Letter 253.

4. *camlet:* see the last paragraph of Letter 252.

Letter 257

1. *In Genoa:* during Lent, a group of Florentine merchants employed Machiavelli to handle their affairs in Genoa; see the Headnote and *Leg.,* III, pp. 1503–1508 (Gaeta).

2. *I:* this correspondent may be Francesco Lenzi, a signer of a letter to Machiavelli detailing his responsibilities, *Leg.,* III, p. 1508, or a Francesco del Pugliese mentioned in a letter from Giuliano Brancacci to Francesco Vettori, dated 3 March, about this trip and quoted in *Leg.,* III, p. 1503 (Gaeta).

3. *your:* whoever this correspondent may be, he addresses Machiavelli with the familiar *tu.*

4. *Salvago:* Stefano Salvago, a merchant from Genoa; see *Leg.,* III, p. 1508 (Gaeta).

5. *Messere:* Marcello Virgilio di Adriani Berti (Inglese).

6. *Dioscorides:* a Greek writer on medical subjects of the first century A.D., whose works had been published in 1499 and were published in Marcello Virgilio's Latin translation in October 1518; see Letter 296, n. 8.

Letter 258

1. *you:* Machiavelli addresses Vernacci as *tu.*

1520

Letter 259

1. *you:* Machiavelli addresses Vernacci as *tu.*

2. *the Six:* the *Sei alla Mercanzia* (Gaeta), a group responsible for supervising commercial relations.

Letter 260

1. *Giuliano:* Giuliano de' Medici, the duke of Nemours, died 17 March 1516 (Gaeta).

2. *company:* the humanist group that met in the Rucellai Gardens to discuss relevant topics—in this case, constitutional reform. Zanobi Buondelmonti was one of them, as was Battista della Palla; at this point, both men were pro-Medici; see Letter 254, nn. 1 and 8.

3. *something else:* this is the earliest hint that Machiavelli will receive a commission on 8 November to write "the annals and chronicles of Florence" (Gaeta).

4. *comedy: La Mandragola* (The Mandrake); it is assumed that a performance in Florence generated so much interest that the pope ordered one in Rome. This letter helps establish a *terminus ad quem* for dating one of the best comedies of the Italian Renaissance; a manuscript is dated 1519.

5. *esteems it:* Ridolfi notes that "Leo was the sort of man who might more easily be won by a coarse comedy than by a *Prince:* he would have enjoyed the jokes and rejected what was bitter" (*Life,* p. 179; *Vita 7,* p. 280).

6. *Santa Maria in Portico:* another name for Cardinal Bibbiena; see Letter 223, n. 14. In *The Courtier* he plays the role of the humorist. Taking his material from Plautus's *Menaechmi* and four tales from *The Decameron* in which Calandro/Calandrino is involved, he produced his witty, bawdy, learned comedy *La Calandria (The Follies of Calandro)* in Urbino at the court of Francesco Maria della Rovere, during the Carnival of 1513. Gaeta thinks that Machiavelli, through the willing hands of della Palla, probably sent his respects to the cardinal in the form of a greeting from his character Messer Nicia, in *La Mandragola,* to Bibbiena's character Calandro, in *La Calandria.*

7. *Salviati:* Jacopo Salviati.

8. *Carnesecchi:* he is mentioned among those attending the discussions at the Rucellai Gardens in the penultimate paragraph of Letter 254.

Letter 261

1. *Lucca:* Machiavelli was in Lucca to work on a bankruptcy case on behalf of some Florentine merchants. "He was to represent these creditors and make sure that business debts should take precedence over gambling

ones, inquire into the bankrupt's assets and so forth" (Ridolfi, *Life,* p. 180; *Vita* 7, pp. 281–282); see *Leg.,* III, pp. 1511–1544.

2. *Madonna Marietta:* Machiavelli's wife.

Letter 262

1. *edge to edge:* Machiavelli's letter has been lost.

2. torrone: a nougat candy, often popular at Christmas, that is a specialty of Lucca; but it seems also to be a play on the word for "big towers."

3. *Sernigi:* see Letter 13, n. 6, and Letter 223, n. 1.

4. *noon-time friends:* the discussions of the habitués of the Rucellai Gardens. The "Filippo" may be Filippo Strozzi; Gaeta identifies him as Filippo Casavecchia, noting that Casavecchia is the only friend from Machiavelli's days in the chancellery to be mentioned in this collection of letters after the Medici returned to power in 1512.

5. *San Leo and Montefeltro:* towns in the duchy of Urbino; San Leo was important to Florence because it was a hill town, with a fortress, which Florence wanted to control, in the region of Montefeltro, west-southwest of the Republic of San Marino in the Marches.

6. *Roberto:* Roberto Acciaiuoli, the *podestà* of Pistoia (Gaeta); see Letter 12, n. 1.

7. *Trojan:* probably the *Historia destructionis Troiae* by Guido delle Colonne, which had been translated into Italian by Filippo Ceffi and published in Venice in 1481; it was derived from the *Roman de Troie* by Benoît de Sainte-Maure (Gaeta).

8. *to get his revenge:* translation of *dare il suo resto,* a play on *resto,* "remainder" or "change," and *resti,* "remains."

9. *Saint James's eve:* 24 July (Gaeta).

Letter 263

1. *Luigi . . . Francesco:* Luigi Alamanni (a dedicatee of the *The Life of Castruccio Castracani of Lucca,* along with Zanobi Buondelmonti), Francesco Guidetti, Jacopo da Diacceto, and Anton Francesco degli Albizzi (Gaeta).

2. *apothegms:* the reference is to the pithy, terse maxims and sententious remarks attributed to Castruccio at the end of the *Life;* by and large, these "sayings" are taken from Diogenes Laertius, *Lives of the Philosophers,* although one is based on an earlier *Castruccii Antelminelli Castracani lucenis ducis vita* by Niccolò Tegrimi (Modena, 1496) and one on Dante, *Inferno,* XXI, 41; Buondelmonti will object to these later in the sentence.

3. *history:* the projected *Florentine Histories* (Gaeta).

4. *prayer:* the speech Machiavelli constructs for Castruccio on his deathbed (Gaeta).

5. *know about:* the project to have Machiavelli commissioned to write a history of Florence (Gaeta).

Letter 264

1. *substance:* Machiavelli is here drafting the exact conditions under

which the university officials—those of the Florentine Studio—would hire him to write a history of Florence. The head of the Studio was Cardinal Giulio de' Medici, and its chief administrator was Machiavelli's brother-in-law, Francesco del Nero. Instead of this draft, the actual contract is dated 8 November. In it Machiavelli's salary is specified as 100 *fiorini di studio,* the equivalent of 57 *fiorini di suggello*—in other words, slightly more than half the amount he received while serving in the chancellery. With an order of 15 October 1525, this salary was practically doubled: "to Machiavelli where there were 100 *fiorini di studio* there are 100 *ducati d'oro*"; see Gaeta and Ridolfi, *Life,* pp. 182–183; *Vita 7,* pp. 284–286. For more on money, see Letter 14, n. 2.

Letter 265

1. De re militari: Machiavelli's *Arte della guerra* (Art of war); see the Headnote.

2. *Justin:* Marcus Justinus, who prepared a widely read Latin summary of Pompeius Trogus, *Historiae Philippicae,* in the third century A.D.

3. *Quintus Curtius:* in about the middle of the first century A.D. Quintus Curtius Rufus wrote the history of Alexander the Great referred to here.

4. *Lucrezia:* Lucrezia di Lorenzo de' Medici, the wife of Jacopo Salviati (Gaeta); their son, Cardinal Giovanni Salviati, was a frequenter of the *Orti Oricellari.*

5. *ass:* translation of *pesce,* "fish,"

6. *Corneto and Montalto:* Corneto is the name then given to Tarquinia; Montalto is Montalto di Castro. Both these towns are northwest of Civitavecchia on the Mediterranean coast.

7. *His Most Reverend Monsignor:* Cardinal Giulio de' Medici; he left for Rome on 6 November (Gaeta).

1521

Letter 266

1. Monte: see Letter 233, n. 11.

2. *florins:* see Letter 14, n. 2.

3. Badìa: this would seem to be the *badìa fiorentina,* the city's first monastery, which may have accepted sums of money for safekeeping.

Letter 267

1. *discussing it:* i.e., with anyone else.

2. fiorini di suggello: see Letter 14, n. 2. Soderini's tone of "affectionate familiarity," along with his gentle twit about exchanging historical writing for political activity, indicates that he still took a warm interest in his good friend's career; see Lowe, *Church and Politics,* pp. 77–78.

Letter 268

1. Monte: see Letter 233, n. 11.

2. Badia: see Letter 266, n. 3.

3. *caviar:* see Letter 253.

Letter 269

1. *Pachierotto . . . Ser Sano:* two well-known Florentine pederasts (Gaeta).

2. *bishop:* Teodoro Pio (Gaeta). Machiavelli will pick up on this "fine specimen of a man," from whom he "could learn a thousand fine tricks," at the beginning of the last paragraph of Letter 270.

Letter 270

1. *help her out:* although some scholars doubt that Machiavelli wrote it, Gaeta notes that a similar sentiment opens the *Discorso o dialogo intorno alla nostra lingua* (Discourse or dialogue concerning our language): "whenever I have been able to do my *patria* honor, I have done so willingly, even at the expense of personal loss and danger, because a man has no greater duty in his life than that toward his *patria*" (since the entire burden of the dialogue is to vaunt the language of Florence and Tuscany over Italian in general, *patria,* "native land," has been left untranslated here).

2. *Ponzo:* Fra Domenico da Ponzo, at first one of Savonarola's adherents, later an opponent (Gaeta).

3. *Fra Girolamo:* Savonarola.

4. *Frate Alberto:* perhaps a reference to Frate Alberto da Imola in Boccaccio, *Decameron,* IV, 2, or to Frate Alberto da Orvieto, whom Pope Alexander VI sent to Florence in 1495 and who advised the pope to command Savonarola to appear in Rome, under some pretext, so that Savonarola could be imprisoned. In context, however, the characteristics attributed to the fictional and the historical figures are not mutually exclusive (Gaeta).

5. *to steer clear of it:* rather than adhere to the goal of classical and medieval ethical theory, which was to eradicate evil, Machiavelli seeks both to find a preacher to teach "the way to go to the Devil" and to learn "the way to Hell," i.e., to find ways to live with evil—a measure of his distance from his predecessors.

6. *Rovaio:* Giovanni Gualberto, known as *Il Rovaio,* "the north wind" (or, because of a familiar expression, "the hangman").

7. *thick and fast:* for the joke that Machiavelli cooked up with Guicciardini, and its implications, see Rebhorn, *Foxes and Lions,* pp. 228–249.

8. *Martelli:* unknown; all we can assume is that he must have been quite a storyteller.

9. *hard to find:* this sentence could refer to Machiavelli's apprehensions about embarking on writing his *Florentine Histories.* Specifically, it might indicate his awareness of the ironic twist of fate that had turned a steadfast defender of Republican Florence into someone hired by a Medici cardinal to write a history of Florence—one who can ill afford to be too censorious of the Medici's role in Florentine history. See also Najemy, "Lessons."

10. *lodgings:* Machiavelli was staying with Sigismondo Santi, chancellor

of Teodoro Pio, a bishop. Although Machiavelli and Guicciardini were about to trick Santi, the latter was a greatly admired friend of Guicciardini: see Ridolfi, *Guicciardini,* index; Guicciardini calls him "a skillful man greatly trusted by the pope," *Storia d'Italia,* XVI, 8, p. 1574.

11. *hump does not lie:* the supposition is that Teodoro Pio was "deformed" both physically and spiritually, so that his hump was taken as an external indication of his inner condition (Gaeta). Machiavelli deftly answers Guicciardini's remark that Pio was a "fine specimen of a man, someone you could learn a thousand fine tricks from" (last paragraph of Letter 269).

12. *bucketful:* refers to the "tricks" that Guicciardini mentions in the last paragraph of Letter 269, as we might refer to someone's "bag of tricks."

Letter 271

1. *advice:* i.e., Machiavelli's requests for advice about some serious and some not so serious topics, in Letter 270.

2. *M. Gismondo:* Machiavelli's host in Carpi, Sigismondo Santi (Gaeta).

3. for you . . . among you: an inversion of the affirmation in Matthew 26:11, when Christ tells his disciples of his forthcoming death: "For ye have the poor always with you; but me ye have not always" (Gaeta).

Letter 272

1. *Lysander:* Spartan general and statesman; although he was one of the most competent of Sparta's leaders, his pride, ambition, and autocratic principles made him unpopular with his contemporaries and subsequent commentators (d. 395 B.C.).

2. *brotherly:* translation of *fratesco,* "monkish," but a word that also evokes *fratello,* "brother."

3. *Republic of Clogs:* the organization of the Minorite Friars.

4. *plowmen:* in other words, we are not turned from the tricksters into the tricked.

5. *ancestors:* translation of *maggiori,* a word recalling Farinata's imperious *"Chi fur li maggior tui?"* ("Who were your ancestors?") in Dante, *Inferno,* X, v. 42. With Dante's answer comes Farinata's prediction that Dante will be exiled from Florence and suffer ignominy from his native land—perhaps Guicciardini's warning to Machiavelli to be cautious, now that matters appear to be going in his favor.

6. *lord consuls:* refers to the officers or consuls of the wool guild; see the Headnote.

Letter 273

1. *18 May:* although this is in chronological order, the sense of this letter would seem to mean that Guicciardini received it before he wrote Letter 272 to Machiavelli and that Machiavelli's Letter 273 is a response to Guicciardini's Letter 271 (see Ridolfi, *Life,* p. 191; *Vita* 7, p. 298; and Inglese).

2. *sky:* the crossbowman's arrival has caused a sensation in Carpi (Gaeta).

3. *king:* see the end of the second paragraph of Letter 270.

4. giulios: silver coins minted by Julius II, pope from 1503 to 1513.

5. *Pope Angelico:* in 1515, a monk named Teodoro di Giovanni Scuta-riotto turned up in Florence, claiming to be the Pope Angelico who Savonarola had promised would eventually come. He turned out to be a fake and was condemned to ten years in prison. He escaped in 1520 and sought refuge on the island of Polvese in Lake Trasimeno (Gaeta).

6. *Soncino:* Paolo da Soncino, from Milan, who had been the vicar-general of the order during the previous year (Gaeta).

Letter 274

1. Shittus!: a compromise translation of *cazzus,* a word Machiavelli made up from the Italian *cazzo,* penis, plus the Latin ending *-us,* to produce a humorous expletive.

2. *fellow:* Sigismondo Santi (Gaeta).

3. *thirty thousand devils:* an allusion to Pulci, *Morgante,* V, 44, 2 (Gaeta); the context is of Rinaldo boasting to his friend Dodone that even if the villain should be Death or thirty thousand ("devils" being understood), he will fight back.

4. *Albanian:* someone who feigns ignorance and does not reply appropriately when asked a question is called an Albanian; the phrase also occurs in a sonnet by Burchiello, "*La violente casa di Scorpione,*" and in Pulci, *Morgante,* III, 48, 1, at a point when Rinaldo plays dumb (Gaeta).

5. *shitless:* translation of *il culo mi fa lappe lappe* (my ass is going gurgle, gurgle); the burbling sound of water suggests what the bowels are doing. For a similar use of the phrase in a battle scene, see Pulci, *Morgante,* XXIV, 125, v. 8.

6. *partition:* see the Headnote for the goal of Machiavelli's mission, to get the friars to split up their congregation so that Florence could control them more easily.

7. Histories: it would appear that Machiavelli had already begun work on his *Florentine Histories.*

Letter 275

1. *military art:* Machiavelli's *Art of War* had been published on 16 August (Gaeta).

2. *pleasing to you:* the cardinal's high opinion of Machiavelli's work is matched by the high opinion of his father, Jacopo Salviati, of Machiavelli's abilities. In a letter dated 3 May 1525, Jacopo writes to Giovanni: "as a secretary and as someone by whom you might be advised, I would like Niccolò Machiavelli above all others. I have spoken about this matter to Our Lordship [Pope Clement VII] and he is undecided; I shall see if I can get him to make up his mind" (as quoted in Ridolfi, *Vita* 7, p. 330; *Life,* p. 212).

Letter 276

1. Signor Gonfaloniere: Vettori had assumed the office on 1 November (Gaeta); he was responsible for protecting the government, while Florence's attention was focused on both the attempt to drive the French out of Milan and the death of Pope Leo X.

1522–1524

Letter 277

1. *affliction:* Machiavelli's brother, Totto, lay dying at the time (Gaeta).

2. *If . . . master:* i.e., were I not busy with my duties as gonfalonier (Gaeta).

Letter 278

1. *two* mog[g]ia: approximately thirty-three standard U.S. bushels; see Letter 170 for equivalents of dry measure.

2. *grain:* translation of *grano;* it usually refers to wheat.

3. *fifty-four* staia: a *staio* in Florence is the equivalent of 24.4 liters, so the workers would have threshed approximately thirty-seven standard U.S. bushels.

4. *six* mog[g]ia: approximately ninety-nine standard U.S. bushels.

5. *twenty* staia: approximately fourteen U.S. bushels.

6. *twenty-seven* staia: approximately eighteen and one-half U.S. bushels.

7. *ten* staia: approximately seven U.S. bushels.

Letter 280

1. *San Quirico alle Sodora:* one of Totto Machiavelli's parish churches (Gaeta).

Letter 281

1. *16 April:* we follow the text Gaeta prints: it is a draft, and not the complete text, that Ridolfi first printed in *La Bibliofilia,* 71 (1969), pp. 260–263, and Inglese, *Lettere,* pp. 303–306, provides. Vettori actually dates this letter 17 April 1522, but Ridolfi gives good reasons for assigning the above date.

2. *aurei:* probably refers to *fiorini d'oro;* see Letter 14, n. 2.

3. cardinal: according to Ridolfi (*Bibliofilia,* 71, p. 260), Cardinal de' Medici. It is in part the known date of his departure that permits rectification of Vettori's dating of this letter.

4. Francesco del Nero: the brother-in-law of Machiavelli's wife, hence the uncle of young Giovanni (Inglese).

5. nuns' convent . . . San Clemente: according to Inglese (who cites L. A. Ferrai, *Lorenzino de' Medici,* Milan, 1891, pp. 8–9), these "nuns" were in fact prostitutes (*Lettere,* p. 308, n. 2).

6. *to all the heavens:* in an equally flippant context, Vettori quotes Ovid, *Metamorphoses,* 4.189; see Letter 231.

7. Lodovico: born in 1504 (Inglese).

8. Aeneas . . . things: an allusion to Vergil, _Aeneid,_ XII. 440, where Aeneas, who has had a wound inflicted by Turnus soothed through the intervention of Venus, says to his son Ascanius that the example of Hector and Aeneas should inspire him to greatness.

9. nothing wrong: from this point on, the text of the final version, as published by both Ridolfi and Inglese, differs significantly from that of the draft, probably because Vettori decided not to include some personal material in his letter and to substitute more objective comments about Roman politics, which Machiavelli had asked him for in any case. Here is a translation of the final version's ending, based on Inglese's text:

> . . . _and he took him along with him in order to avoid the contagion._
>
> _You get too upset about our sons' habits, my Niccolò, and you claim that bachelors, and husbands who have no sons, are lucky. One must remember what pleasures, what advantages are derived from sons, and not always complain if they fail in some duty or do something against the rules; for if you act that way, you will live in too great torment and anxiety._
>
> _You are living in the country, I take refuge at home. Indeed, I have caught some sort of mild fever that it is difficult to cure, particularly in these times, when almost all the doctors are out of the city. I am troubled, however, because it is said by some that I pretend to be ill in order to avoid the plague; and that was told to the cardinal and will perhaps be written to him, and although I have gone so far that it must not be believed of me, still something of what they hear always remains in people's ears, and so inexperienced people take pleasure in serving a powerful friend, but experienced ones are fearful._*
>
> _I should like to write you some news, as you ask. The secretary of Count Alberto di Carpi,_† _who does not go along with the French parties, has arrived from France. He has related that the king told him_‡ _that he has decided to send his army into Italy within two months, come what may, and that on this account he has given the sum of a hundred thousand ducats to the Swiss; even our merchants have written something about this, and the king himself has indicated in writing to the pope_§ _that he no longer wants peace or truces with the emperor and the English king,_** _unless the duchy of Milan is given back to him. However, these things are not believed, since the emperor has raised a very powerful army in Spain, and the king of England is preparing an army and a great fleet to attack the French. The emperor has sent money from Spain to Prospero Colonna_†† _so he can satisfy the Spanish infantry. Nothing certain is known about the Turk, following the capture of Rhodes._‡‡ _A few days ago, a certain Sicilian_§§ _who was headed for France to urge the king to invade Sicily was arrested near Rome by order of the pope, and he said that many of the island's top-ranked people were conspiring to hand it over to him._*** _He had with him a letter from Cardinal Soderini_††† _about this matter and many others to the benefit of the French. Those who work for the emperor in Rome_‡‡‡ _are crying out to the pope and accusing the cardinal of being an enemy of the Church, the pope, and peace. Up to now the pope has not taken any decision; Soderini_ §§§ _is especially_

fearful. I have nothing else to write. Farewell.

[* fearful: from Horace, *Epistles,* I, 18, 86–87 (Inglese). † di Carpi: the French ambassador to the papal court (Inglese). ‡ him: i.e., Alberto di Carpi. § *pope:* Adrian VI (Inglese). ** emperor . . . king: Charles V, the Holy Roman Emperor, and Henry VIII. †† Colonna: Prospero Colonna (1452–1523), an old and celebrated military leader, was in command of the imperial forces in Italy at the time (Inglese). ‡‡ Rhodes: Rhodes had fallen to the Turks on 25 December 1522 (Inglese). §§ Sicilian: one Francesco Imperiale, an émigré (Inglese); see Guicciardini, *Storia d'Italia* XV, 3, pp. 1448–1449). *** him: i.e., the king of France. ††† Cardinal Soderini: Francesco Soderini, the brother of ex-Florentine gonfalonier Piero Soderini. ‡‡‡ emperor in Rome: in particular, the duke of Sessa (Inglese); Luis Fernandez de Córdoba was emperor Charles V's ambassador to Rome; see Letter 308, n. 6. §§§ Soderini: he was in fact imprisoned in the Castel Sant'Angelo and was pardoned only by the next pope, Clement VII, who was elected on 19 November (Inglese).]

Letter 283

1. *trouble:* Ridolfi believes that Machiavelli was seeking payment for his *Florentine Histories* from his brother-in-law, who was chief administrator of the Florentine Studio that had hired Machiavelli (*Life,* p. 314, n. 22; *Vita 7,* p. 560, n. 22) (Gaeta).

Letter 284

1. *five* moggia: approximately eighty-three standard U.S. bushels.

2. *sixteen and a half* staia: approximately eleven and one-half standard U.S. bushels.

3. *twenty-three and a third* staia: approximately sixteen standard U.S. bushels.

4. *four* moggia: approximately sixty-six standard U.S. bushels.

5. *sixteen and a half* staia: approximately eleven and one-half standard U.S. bushels.

6. *thirteen* staia: approximately nine standard U.S. bushels.

7. *one* staio: approximately one-third of a standard U.S. bushel.

8. *twelve and a half* staia: approximately eight and one-half standard U.S. bushels.

9. *five* moggia: approximately eighty-three standard U.S. bushels.

10. *four and a half* staia: approximately three standard U.S. bushels.

11. *churches:* these churches had been Totto Machiavelli's benefices (Gaeta).

Letter 285

1. *history:* there is no solid evidence that this was the *Florentine Histories.* Giuliano de' Ricci, Machiavelli's grandson and literary executor, who made a

transcript of Machiavelli's letters (*Apografo Ricci*), summarizes the first part of this letter, but he is silent about whether or not the *Florentine Histories* are what was referred to in the opening sentence of his transcription (Gaeta).

1 5 2 5

Letter 286

1. *Fornaciaio:* see the Headnote for a discussion of this first performance of *Clizia.*

2. *patricians:* in the audience was Ippolito de' Medici, whom Giulio de' Medici, now Pope Clement VII, had put in charge of Florence along with Alessandro di Lorenzo de' Medici; the thirteen-year-old Ippolito was under the watchful eyes of Silvio Passerini, cardinal of Cortona (Gaeta).

3. *spectacles:* a quotation from Poliziano, *Stanze,* I, v. 1 (Gaeta).

4. *fooling around:* translation of *mondare nespole,* "peeling medlars"; the armies were those of Charles V and Francis I, which met two days later at the Battle of Pavia (Gaeta).

5. *to say . . . spade:* translation of *per recare le mille in una, e per dire più tosto zuppa che avere a dire pane e vino,* "to bring a thousand things back to one, and to say soup rather than to have to say bread and wine."

6. *dotards:* translation of *la barbogeria,* a familiar expression, used frequently in this correspondence, in reference to the group of Machiavelli's cronies.

7. *22 February 1525:* this chummy letter to Machiavelli should be compared with an extract from a letter that Nerli wrote to Machiavelli's brother-in-law, Francesco del Nero, dated from Modena on 1 March:

> Since Machia is a friend and relative of yours and a very good friend of mine, I cannot help saying, on this occasion that you have given me to write you, how aggrieved I am about what daily reaches my ears concerning him, because recently and during this carnival period I have had so many complaints that I am no longer affected by all this city's wicked ways. And were it not that these great, almost unbelievable things that have been going on lately in this poor old region have provided material for discussion more than mere gossip, I am certain that people would talk about nothing else but him, given that a paterfamilias of such character is galloping off (*andare alla staffa*)—I do not want to say with whom—and has written a comedy that, according to what I have heard, has some fine things in it. From now on, my Francesco, we are going to be left behind (*rimarreno nella fossa*). And not later but sooner I beseech you that, without bringing me into it any further, you take whatever steps you can to put these matters right and for you to beg him on my behalf to be so kind as to answer a letter of mine, sending me as well the comedy that was put on in Fornaciaio's garden. [Text in Gaeta]

Letter 287

1. *book:* a copy of *Florentine Histories* that Machiavelli wanted to present to Pope Clement VII (Gaeta); Vettori refers to this book later in this paragraph as *Historia.*

2. *times are opposed:* because of the defeat of the French at the Battle of Pavia on 24 February (Gaeta).

Letter 288

1. *In Romagna:* Machiavelli was with Guicciardini in Faenza to discuss support for his idea of a national militia with which the pope might stand up to Emperor Charles V.

2. *drawn up:* evidently a part of the 120 gold ducats that Clement VII paid Machiavelli, when he presented the *Florentine Histories* to the pope (Gaeta).

3. *Baccina's dowry:* Machiavelli's daughter, Bartolomea, married Giovanni de' Ricci; her son Giuliano de' Ricci was later responsible for the collection and classification of Machiavelli's papers (Gaeta).

4. *sultan:* Suleiman II the Magnificent (reigned from 1520–1566) added to his territory land from the present-day Iraq, Hungary, Albania, Aden, Algeria, and the former Yugoslavia, as well as established Ottoman naval supremacy in the Mediterranean.

5. *Adrianople:* the modern Turkish city of Edirne on the Maritsa River, near the border with Bulgaria.

Letter 289

1. *O[ur] L[ordship]:* Pope Clement VII.

2. *His Lordship the President:* Francesco Guicciardini, who had been named "President" of Romagna; Pope Clement VII had invited his opinion on the national citizen's militia and had learned of his reservations. Gaeta points out that Guicciardini's letter had been addressed to Cesare Colombo, his agent in Rome.

Letter 290

1. *friar:* this would appear to be a reference to the friar whom Guicciardini mentions in a letter to Cesare Colombo, dated 26 July from Faenza (Gaeta).

2. *His Excellency the President:* Guicciardini.

3. *stipend:* being "well disposed" results in an order of 15 October practically doubling Machiavelli's pay for the *Florentine Histories;* see Letter 264.

4. *pigeon:* i.e., a "deal."

5. *from there:* from Faenza; Machiavelli left on 26 July (Gaeta).

Letter 291

1. *letter:* Letter 288 (Gaeta).

2. *Mariscotta:* a courtesan in Faenza with whom Machiavelli spent some time while awaiting the pope's decision concerning the militia in Romagna (Gaeta).

Letter 292

1. *Colombaia:* Guicciardini had asked Machiavelli to visit two properties that Guicciardini had bought sight unseen and to write him about

them. Finocchieto was in the Mugello, near Santa Maria a Chiassi. In July 1527 Machiavelli went there for peace and quiet and wrote his *Consolatoria, Accusatoria,* and *Defensoria.* In a letter dated 24 November 1527, he wrote his brother that it was "a wild, lonely place" (Gaeta).

2. Finocchieto: a diminutive form of "fennel." The joke of "beginning with fennel" is that it customarily came at the end of a meal; that practice is referred to in Pulci, *Morgante,* XVIII, 198, v. 4; XIX, 62, v. 5; and XXV, 291, v. 3.

3. *Arabia Petraea:* "rocky Arabia," the northwestern part; its capital was Petra, on the slope of Mt. Hor, today in southwest Jordan north of Aqaba.

4. *Iacopo . . . Girolamo:* Guicciardini's brothers (Gaeta).

5. *your letter:* i.e., Letter 291; the "Maliscotta" is the same as the "Mariscotta" of Letter 291.

6. *your lady:* Guicciardini's wife, Maria di Alamanno d'Averardo Salviati; they were married in 1508 (Gaeta).

7. *Averardo:* Averardo Serristori.

Letter 293

1. *third:* i.e., Letter 292.

Letter 294

1. *Finocchieto:* Guicciardini writes this letter adopting the persona of the property on which he asked Machiavelli to check in Letter 292. Inglese, *Lettere,* p. 321, suggests that it may have been enclosed with Letter 293.

2. *you:* in adopting the persona of "Madonna Finocchieto," Guicciardini uses the *tu* form instead of the usual *voi* of his correspondence with Machiavelli.

3. *Barbera:* Barbera Raffacani Salutati; see the Headnote. She is also mentioned in Vasari's *Life of Domenico Puligo.*

4. *mercy:* translation of *pietà,* which connotes both "pity" and "piety."

5. *season:* translation of *condirebbe,* which suggests "dressing," i.e., putting a dressing of oil and spices on a salad—a play on the idea of "unction" expressed in *pietà.*

6. *But I have never . . . every hour:* Guicciardini's sentence is so complex that it is difficult to reproduce in English because of the absence of gender endings. His model is Latin rhetoric. The irony of such elegant language in the mouth of a plain, unadorned country "lass" is intentional—for the recipient's admiration.

7. *medulla:* Guicciardini/Finocchieto reflects contemporary thinking about the functions of various areas of the brain in human thinking; here he is essentially contrasting superficial with deeper thought.

Letter 295

1. *Adrianople:* Edirne; see Letter 288, n. 5. Ludovico had several unpleasant encounters with the law. Earlier this year, on 11 May, Machiavelli issued a decree in which he "set him legally free of dependence upon him" (Stephens

and Butters, "New Light," p. 63).

2. *bailiff:* translation of *bailo,* a title generally given to a representative of the Venetian ambassador to the court of Byzantium, who served as governor of the Italian colony there.

3. *whether . . . or not:* translation of *se crepasi,* "even if he should burst."

4. *priest:* a priest who refused to vacate one of the parish churches under the patronage of the Machiavelli family (Gaeta).

Letter 296

1. *Capponi:* Niccolò Capponi, see Letter 162, nn. 2 and 10; his son Pietro married Guicciardini's eldest daughter, Simona. The reference to three thousand ducats later in the paragraph concerns the dowry negotiations (Gaeta).

2. *put it on:* Machiavelli must have sent Guicciardini a copy of *La Mandragola,* perhaps one printed in Rome in 1524; it was to be performed during the 1526 Carnival season in Modena (Gaeta).

3. *lost funds:* see the Headnote.

4. *our affair:* a plan to marry off one of Guicciardini's daughters; as will emerge from Letters 300 and 311, the "friend" is Lorenzo Strozzi (Gaeta).

5. *you have been:* i.e., with Guicciardini in Faenza (Gaeta).

6. *the Magnificent:* Ippolito di Giuliano de' Medici (Gaeta).

7. *turned:* translation of *volto,* but the *Apografo Ricci* reads *rotto,* "broke" (Inglese) (see Letter 235, n. 1).

8. *Germander:* translation of *Carman deos,* for which there are two suggested readings: *Camedrios,* from the Greek *chamaidrys,* "germander," and *Cardam[omum] Dios[coridis],* related to cardamom of Dioscorides Pedanius, famed in pharmacology for his *Materia medica,* first century A.D.

Letter 297

1. *left here:* to go to Venice on his commission from the wool guild. The "Ludovico Alamanni" in the main clause is the man more frequently referred to as "Luigi Alamanni."

2. *I do not . . . time:* translation of *io non mondo nespole,* "I do not peel medlars"; see Letter 286, n. 4.

3. *accoppiatori:* public officials, magistrates, reponsible for forming a government by drawing up a list of eligible voters and putting their names in election bags; see Letter 221. An indication of the acknowledgment of Machiavelli's reentry into Florentine public life is that the *accoppiatori* had declared him *imborsato,* eligible to be selected.

4. *Barbary:* not the Barbary Coast, but a flippant, if not malicious, reference to favors that came Machiavelli's way, thanks to Barbera Raffacani Salutati.

5. *tender tears:* translation of *lagrimatene di tenerezza,* an allusion to *La Mandragola,* III, viii (Machiavelli, *Comedies,* pp. 218–219), where Messer Nicia, who has just been told that his wife, Madonna Lucrezia, will have a baby boy after her night with Callimaco, says *Io lacrimo per la tenerezza,* "I'm crying for joy."

6. *dotards:* translation of *la barbogeria;* see Letter 286, n. 6.

7. *Donato:* Donato del Corno, here and at the beginning of the last paragraph.

8. *to swallow that lump:* translation of *o béccati quello aglio,* "or peck (pick) up that garlic," a variant on the idiomatic expression *mangiare l'aglio,* "to swallow one's rage."

9. *get . . . back:* translation of *gittare il pidocchio nel fuoco,* "to throw the louse into the fire."

10. *lottery:* Gaeta believes that the exaggerated figure for his winnings indicates that this is merely kidding on Nerli's part.

11. *Count de' Mozzi:* evidently a familiar name; it means "shorty" or "stumpy."

12. *some . . . ass:* translation of *qualche porro di dietro,* "some leek (i.e., the vegetable) up the behind," an expression Messer Nicia uses in *La Mandragola,* II, iii (Machiavelli, *Comedies,* pp. 190–191), referring to a possible fine or tax (Gaeta).

13. *harder time:* translation of *far sudare gli orecchi,* "to make your ears sweat."

14. *closed up shop:* translation of *dètte le faccelline,* "passed on the torch."

Letter 298

1. *Governor of Modena:* Francesco Guicciardini.

Letter 299

1. *those people:* people in Faenza; the letter of the thirteenth has been lost, but Guicciardini obviously asked Machiavelli for some explanations of some difficult passages in the text of the copy of *La Mandragola* that he had sent—see Letter 296.

2. *ambiguity:* see *La Mandragola,* II, iv (Machiavelli, *Comedies,* pp. 190–191).

3. *toad . . . harrow:* see *La Mandragola,* III, vi (Machiavelli, *Comedies,* pp. 216–217); Machiavelli is using a proverbial expression for an unwelcome return.

4. *Burchiello:* a Florentine barber, Domenico di Giovanni (1404–1449), called *Il Burchiello* because he had a barge (*burchio*) on the sign over his shop, wrote a series of humorous sonnets and nonsense verses. Gaeta quotes, from an edition printed in Venice in 1553, some lines that, even when paraphrased in the quotation of poetry, are "quite [as] inscrutable" to us as they were to Machiavelli.

5. *noodle:* translation of *maccheroni;* the double sense of "noodle" is operative in both languages. Gaeta comments that Machiavelli's remark is an allusion to Cardinal Giovanni Salviati, who had been ordered to Madrid on a mission to Charles V, the mission on which Machiavelli almost accompanied him: see the Headnote. The cardinal botched the job of taking advantage of concessions the pope had made in order for Charles V to marry his cousin, Isabella of Portugal. Guicciardini's dry comment on the mission is that the cardinal "was no more energetic or resolute than his master," i.e., the pope

(Guicciardini, *Storia d'Italia,* XVI, 9, p. 1580). Prior to the cardinal's departure, he received a stern letter from his father, Jacopo Salviati: "I hear that you have a very indecorous retinue and that with no consideration for the world at large your servants publicly and in everyone's presence talk of nothing but wickedness and sodomy and every kind of evil. I would remind you that you are going to lands where such things are an abomination and the greatest disgrace, and that you are considered better than you are. And hence I beg and charge you, for the honor of God and the sake of your own soul, to be so good as to discipline yourself and your retinue so that at least it does not set a bad example; and I guarantee you that the affairs of the Church are in such a state that her priests and prelates by doing the very best they can—and by not practicing such customs—will endure the greatest travail in saving the Church. I pray you, I order you by the authority that a father has over his sons, to be so good as to attend to this and to all other matters that concern the honor of God" (as quoted in Ridolfi, *Vita 7,* p. 566, n. 22). Ridolfi goes on to comment: "It is clear that the writer of such advice would never have proposed to his son . . . that he should take Machiavelli as his secretary, if his behaviour had been reprehensible" (*Life,* p. 317); Jacopo did so in a letter to the cardinal dated 3 May 1525; see Letter 275.

   6. *according . . . implement:* twitting pedants, Machiavelli continues the joke: Livy never wrote a *Second Decade.*

   7. *working hard:* on the forthcoming production of *La Mandragola* (Gaeta).

   8. *Alamanni:* better known as Luigi Alamanni.

   9. *lyrics:* Machiavelli worked carefully on the lyrics for the intermezzos, in the expectation that they would be performed at a production to take place in Faenza under Gucciardini's patronage. It never occurred because Pope Clement VII summoned Guicciardini to Rome early in January 1526. Machiavelli composed a canzone on a carpe diem theme for the nymphs and shepherds to sing, rhymed a prologue at Guicciardini's suggestion, and added four short canzoni to serves as intermezzos. Two of these canzoni duplicate ones from *Clizia*—those after acts one and three; the other two are unique to *La Mandragola.* Their dulcet harmony jars with the script's caustic irony. The songs thus comment trenchantly on the action; they are appropriately pungent additions to the text. For more on this topic, Gaeta suggests Einstein, *Italian Madrigal,* I, pp. 250–251; Osthoff, *Theatergesang,* I, pp. 213–249, II, p. 68; H. C. Slim, *Gift,* II, pp. 344–349; Pirrotta and Povoledo, *Due Orfei,* in *Music and Theatre,* pp. 143 ff., and Ridolfi, *Vita 7,* pp. 574–576, n. 9.

Letter 300

   1. *that matter:* the plan to marry Guicciardini's daughter Simona to Pietro Capponi and the dowry negotiations; see Letter 296.

   2. *eldest daughter:* Marietta Strozzi, who married Lorenzo Ridolfi, a brother of Cardinal Niccolò Ridolfi (Gaeta).

   3. *ten years:* the ten years of service to the two Medici popes, Leo X and now Clement VII; Guicciardini had been governor of Modena, Reggio, and

Parma, as well as president of Romagna (Gaeta).

4. *Milan is done for:* for Girolamo Morone and his attempt to involve the Marquess of Pescara in a league against Emperor Charles V, to drive Spain out of Italy, see the Headnote.

5. *hood:* refers to being taken out of action and tamed, as is a falcon when it is hooded after the hunt (Gaeta).

6. Thus it is . . . above: *sic datum desuper,* perhaps an allusion to Seneca, *Epistulae,* 8.74.8.

7. *in his Vicar:* Machiavelli is alluding by memory, with slight variants, to a speech that Hugh Capet gives in Dante, *Purgatorio,* XX, vv. 86–87; he assumes that Guicciardini would complete the line "and in his Vicar, Christ is made captive." Alagna is Anagni, a town about forty miles east-southeast of Rome and the birthplace of four popes, including Boniface VIII (pope from 1294 to 1303), who had a palace there. It was there that Guillaume de Nogaret, the envoy of Philip IV of France, Philip the Fair (1268–1314), humiliated the pope. Throughout his papacy, Boniface feuded with Philip by issuing bulls to prevent royal taxation of the clergy and the extension of royal authority. Boniface was seized and his palace plundered; tradition has it that one of Nogaret's men, Sciarra Colonna, slapped the pope. Boniface is supposed to have said then, "If I am betrayed like Christ, I am ready to die like Christ." Just as Dante made Hugh Capet condemn his posterity so that Dante could in turn condemn France, Machiavelli expresses his pessimism about Italy's ability to curb the increasing power of Emperor Charles V by siding with France.

8. *raise:* see Letter 290, n. 3.

9. *to write again:* according to Ridolfi, Machiavelli is "summarizing and digesting the extracts of letters compiled in his office [before the return of the Medici in 1512] when he was planning to continue the historiographical tradition of the Florentine chancellors." These extracts and summaries could go back to the period of the first *Decennale* or be fragments of what might have been Book IX of the *Florentine Histories* (*Life,* pp. 225, 322; *Vita 7,* pp. 350, 578–579). Ridolfi's thesis is referred to above in the notes for Letters 117, 122, and 229; see *Life,* pp. 278–279, *Vita 7,* pp. 472–474. Inglese is not convinced by Ridolfi's arguments for the allusion to the *Nature di uomini fiorentini* being a fragment of Book IX of the *Florentine Histories.*

10. *Tragic Author:* Italy's tragic situation is addressed in the last chapter of *The Prince;* indeed, it is the implicit subject of all Machiavelli's major political and historical works. Ridolfi comments on the switch from the calculated advice to Guicciardini about how to draft his dowry letter to the pope to these last three paragraphs and the arresting signature: "*Sic datum desuper.* The tragedy was now in its fifth act and Italy was its subject. All its tragic force is contained in this brief prose of Machiavelli, with its sudden passage from the 'particular' to the apocalyptic universal judgment on the ruinous policies of princes, and from the illuminating prophecy expressed with miraculous foresight in a line of Dante, *nel Vicario suo Cristo esser catto* [and in his Vicar, Christ

is made captive], to the carefree carnival spirit. Here is all Machiavelli, and here he is more than ever the symbol of his times and of Italy. Appropriately he signs this letter half seriously and half in jest: '*Niccolò Machiavelli, istorico, comico e tragico*'" (*Life,* p. 219; *Vita 7,* p. 342).

Letter 301

1. *such a tack:* to get the pope to help him offer a suitable dowry for his daughter, Simona, to marry Pietro Capponi; see Letters 296 and 300 (Gaeta).

2. *Filippo and Paolo:* Filippo Strozzi and Paolo Vettori; see Letter 300 (Gaeta).

3. *duke of Provence:* the allusion is to Dante, *Paradiso,* VI, vv. 127–143. The context indicates that there are several reasons why Machiavelli brings in the story of Romieu de Villeneuve, the seneschal at the Provençal court of Raymond Berangar IV (1209–1245), count of Barcelona and marquess of Provence during the first half of the thirteenth century: first, to play on the fact that both Raymond and Guicciardini had four daughters; and second, to point out a parallel that Dante assumed his readers would recognize. Raymond treated his seneschal's loyal service badly; as Dante felt ill-used by Florence, so, too, did Machiavelli.

4. *king of France:* Louis IX, Saint Louis (1214–1270), married Margaret of Provence, Raymond's eldest daughter, in 1234. Raymond's other three daughters also married rulers: Henry III of England; Richard, Earl of Cornwall (1209–1272), Henry III's brother; and Charles of Anjou (1226–1285).

5. *A pilgrim . . . birth:* translation of *persona umile e peregrina.* Machiavelli is citing Dante, *Paradiso,* VI, 133–135, from memory, according to Gaeta. As the legend would have it, Romieu arrived at court dressed as a pilgrim returning from Santiago de Compostela, with its famous shrine to Saint James.

6. *death:* the marquess, not the duke, of Pescara died on 3 December; see Letter 300, n. 4 (Gaeta).

7. *someone else:* Pope Clement VII (Gaeta).

Letter 302

1. *comedy: La Mandragola;* the scheduled performance in Faenza did not occur; see Letter 299, nn. 1, 2, 3, 7, 9.

2. *argument:* i.e., the prologue of *La Mandragola;* it had been written for a production in Florence and seemed inappropriate for an audience in Faenza.

3. *another one:* Machiavelli wrote the opening canzone, "*Perché la vita è breve,*" and sent it along with four others for the intermezzos to be performed in Faenza; see Letter 303. The line in the fourth stanza, "*il nome di colui che vi governa*" (The name of him who reigns there) (Machiavelli, *Comedies,* pp. 154–155), is a compliment to Guicciardini, not to Lorenzo II de' Medici, and the reference in the last line of that stanza, "*godere e reingraziare—chi ve lo ha dato*" (Congratulation—offer him who has granted it), is to Pope Clement VII (Gaeta, and Ridolfi, *Life,* pp. 303, n. 21; *Vita 7,* p. 537, n. 21; p. 573, n. 5). Gaeta reminds us that Ridolfi also believes that Guicciar-

dini might have taken umbrage at the lines in the prologue's seventh stanza, *"ancor che facci sergieri a colui, / che può portar miglior mantel che lui"* (Our author doesn't give a fig / For lackeys of the biggest wig) (Machiavelli, *Comedies,* pp. 160–161).

4. *Lent:* in 1526, the Carnival season ended 13 February (Gaeta).

5. *company:* translation of *baronìa,* "the barony," evidently to designate Barbera and her company (Gaeta).

6. *granted:* according to the *Apografo Ricci,* there should be an ellipsis here to indicate a passage that has been omitted (Inglese).

7. *bearings:* for Machiavelli's use of the compass—*bussola*—image, see Letter 121, n. 11.

8. nothing said: a reference to Pope Clement VII's attempts to form a league, soon to be known as the League of Cognac, against Charles V, signed the following May. Guicciardini played a significant role in working out the league's details; see Letter 305, n. 1 (Gaeta).

9. *Romeo:* see Letter 301, nn. 3–5.

10. business: that of arranging the marriage and dowry of Guicciardini's daughter, Simona; his three other living daughers were named Lucrezia, Laudomina, and Lisabetta; see Letters 296, 300, and 301 (Gaeta). Guicciardini may be humorously alluding to Messer Nicia's line in *La Mandragola,* II, ii (Machiavelli, *Comedies,* pp. 184–185), where Nicia is trying to show off his Latin.

1 5 2 6

Letter 303

1. *Girolamo:* Francesco Guicciardini's brother Girolamo married Costanza di Angelo Bardi. Their son, Angelo, was born in 1525 and in 1561 was the first publisher of his uncle's *Storia d'Italia* (Gaeta).

2. *play:* see Letters 299, n. 9, and 302, n. 3.

3. *release:* Charles V did, however, release Francis I under the terms of the Treaty of Madrid; see the Headnote.

4. *Ferrara:* see Guicciardini, *Storia d'Italia,* XVII, 2–3. "[Clement VII] refused to include the Duke of Ferrara in this agreement [the League of Cognac], albeit that the King of France and the Venetians wanted him to be; in fact, the Pope succeeded in having the agreement stipulate, although in general terms, that the members of the League would be committed to helping him recover those cities that were in dispute with the Church" (XVII, 3, p. 1637).

5. *duke:* Alfonso I d'Este (Gaeta).

6. *rapprochement:* part of the negotiation for the forthcoming League of Cognac; see the Headnote. Gaeta notes that Venice sent Andrea Rosso to France and the pope sent Paolo Vettori. He became ill and in turn was replaced by Capino da Capo, a diplomat in the service of Federico II Gonzaga, marquess of Mantua.

7. *Antonio de Leyva:* a Spanish general (1480–1536), one of Charles V's best; a defender at Pavia.

8. *fortresses:* Spain used the Morone conspiracy (see the Headnote for 1525) as a pretext to take over all the important fortresses in the territory of Milan, except those at Milan and Cremona (Gaeta).

9. *concern:* that of arranging the dowry for the marriage of Guicciardini's daughter, Simona, to Pietro Capponi; see Letters 296, 300, 301, and 302 (Gaeta).

Letter 304

1. Comedy of Callimaco: one of the two productions in Venice during February; see the Headnote. During the same period, a company of Venetian gentlemen were also putting on the *Menaechmi* of Plautus, with Cherea, the actor from Lucca, in the lead. Because they were unable to draw the same crowd as Machiavelli, they asked that *La Mandragola* be done in their theater, the Ca' Morosini a Sant'Aponal, by the Florentine group (Gaeta). Ridolfi sums up the importance of these Venetian triumphs for *La Mandragola:* "this comparison with the ancient author in an age when the ancients were axiomatically the best . . . marked the greatest triumph of Machiavelli's comic muse" (*Life,* p. 225; *Vita 7,* p. 350).

2. *intermezzi:* i.e., the songs Machiavelli had composed for performance between the acts by Barbera and her troupe.

3. *it:* i.e., the applause.

4. *held the text:* i.e., Manetti was the prompter.

5. *colony:* the Florentine merchant community in Venice (Gaeta).

6. *His Serene Highness:* the doge (Gaeta).

7. *praise of women:* Ridolfi says, "It seems rather unlikely that he would send a poem expressly written for the purpose, although it would not be the first time that verses of this kind were composed without the direct inspiration of love. The inspiration in this case would have come from three pairs of smoked roes which Manetti sent to the greedy poet" (*Life,* p. 321, n. 14; *Vita 7,* p. 577, n. 14). Gaeta defines the "smoked roes" as "a kind of caviar made from the salted and pressed eggs of mullet or tuna."

Letter 305

1. *ahead of me:* i.e., with another letter. Guicciardini was in Rome, directing the diplomatic activity that culminated in the signing of the league on 22 May.

2. *Filippo Strozzi:* this letter is now lost; it was dated 10 March; see Letter 306 (Gaeta).

3. *treaty:* the Treaty of Madrid between Charles V and Francis I dated 14 January; see the Headnote.

4. *status:* that of political arbiter in Europe (Gaeta).

5. *to look foolish:* in connection with Machiavelli's belief that Charles V would be a fool to release Francis I—and his incredulity at its being done—see Machiavelli's epigram "*Sappi ch'io no son Argo quale io paio,*" (Know that I am not the Argus that I seem to be) (Machiavelli, *Il teatro e gli scritti letterari,* p. 365).

6. *good results:* for Machiavelli's operative principle in this analysis, cf. *Prince,* 3, pp. 261–267; Atkinson, p. 121.

7. *Filippo:* Filippo Strozzi (Gaeta).

8. *eloquence:* translation of *persuasioni;* here and in the last sentence of this paragraph, Machiavelli is relying on the traditional function of rhetoric, especially eloquent, forceful rhetoric, to persuade someone to accept the speaker's positions and beliefs.

9. *what they say to do:* interestingly enough, this trust in what the people say, whether or not as a result of Machiavelli's "eloquence," sets a standard for Guicciardini as he tries to influence the pope's policy in Rome. Clement VII, however, rejected this idea, perhaps because he was "jealous" of Giovanni de' Medici or because he resented "the boldness of a plan greater than he was" (Ridolfi, *Life,* p. 226; *Vita 7,* p. 353).

10. *Giovanni de' Medici:* Giovanni delle Bande Nere (1498–1526); "of the black bands" (probably because his soldiers added black stripes to his white banner upon learning of Pope Leo X's death in 1521) was the son of Caterina Sforza and Giovanni de' Medici (*Il Popolano*), a member of the younger branch of the Medici family. Machiavelli apparently trusted him, as head of a mercenary army, to follow the precepts of *Art of War* and *The Prince,* 26. Later in 1526, during the war of the League of Cognac, Giovanni commanded the league's infantry. He was killed in battle in November. He was alleged to have said of Machiavelli, "Niccolò knew how to write things well and [I] knew how to do them" (Ridolfi, *Life,* p. 323, n. 34; *Vita 7,* p. 581, n. 34).

11. *eloquence:* translation of *persuasioni;* see n. 8 above.

12. *Machiavelli:* For the summary of a letter from Machiavelli to Guicciardini that would come at this point chronologically, see Appendix Letter E.

Letter 306

1. *Our Lordship:* here and in the last sentence of this paragraph, Pope Clement VII; the letter of the tenth has been lost.

2. *king:* Francis I of France.

3. *Guicciardini:* i.e., Letter 305 (Gaeta).

4. *captain of fortune:* the mercenary leader Giovanni delle Bande Nere (Giovanni de' Medici) (Gaeta).

5. *his:* i.e., becomes the responsibility of the instigator, Pope Clement VII (Gaeta).

6. *it:* i.e., getting Barbera's permission.

Letter 307

1. *cardinal:* From 1524 to 1527 the cardinal of Cortona, Silvio Passerini, was the papal representative in Florence, administering the city in the name of the two young Medici boys, Ippolito and Alessandro (Gaeta).

2. *Pietro Navarra:* a Spanish refugee and expert military engineer, whom Pope Clement VII, fearing an imminent attack from France, sent to Florence to plan the city's fortifications; see the Headnote.

3. *presented:* because of his reputation as a military expert, Machiavelli's

voice seemed to be important in these consultations, even though he had no official position (Gaeta).

4. *Cairo:* the population of the Egyptian capital was legendary at this time; cf. Ariosto, *Orlando Furioso,* 15, 61, 63, in the wake of Astolfo's triumph over the giant Caligolante.

5. *Signor Vitelli:* Paolo Vitelli, head of the Florentine army (Gaeta).

6. *Count Pietro:* Pietro Navarra, count of Alvito.

7. *forward it:* the *Relazione di una visita fatta per fortificare Firenze* (A report of a visit made to fortify Florence) (Gaeta).

8. *so that . . . to me:* an allusion to Cicero, *De Oratore,* II.18.75–76. Catulus, a military officer, tells that Hannibal was said to have listened politely to Phormio, a Greek peripatetic philosopher, expatiating on the duties of a military commander and on military matters in general. When the lecture was over, Hannibal promptly rejected Phormio's ideas as those of a madman. Cicero's anecdote explains a blunder that Machiavelli seeks to avoid: unless one has practical experience, teaching theory is useless.

Letter 308

1. *I left there:* late in April, Machiavelli was summoned from Florence to Rome to discuss Florentine fortifications. He impressed Pope Clement VII and Francesco Guicciardini, who wrote to his brother Luigi on the 27th: "Machiavelli has left with the orders for the supplies and officers to be carried out; people are to start the fortifications in the way that you will learn from him . . . Machiavelli was the man who fostered this plan, hence please be obliged to treat him well during his stay and in the other matters that may be required because he has earned his share full well" (Ridolfi, *Vita 7,* p. 580, n. 26; cf. *Life,* p. 322, n. 26).

2. *into effect:* Machiavelli's *Provvisione per la istituzione dell'ufficio de' cinque provveditori delle mura della città di Firenze* (Provision for the creation of the office of the five superintendents for the walls of the city of Florence).

3. *Sciarpelloni:* one of Florence's condottieri (Gaeta).

4. *cardinal:* Silvio Passerini; Clement is Pope Clement VII (Gaeta).

5. *disturbances:* those in Milan over Spanish killings on 24 and 25 April; see Guicciardini, *Storia d'Italia,* XVI, 1, and XVII, 4 (Gaeta).

6. *duke of Sessa:* Luis Fernandez de Córdoba, duke of Sessa, was Charles V's ambassador to Rome (Gaeta).

7. *anxiety:* Machiavelli's fiercely urgent paragraph ends with an allusion to Hannibal's dying words (according to Livy 39.51.9 [G]); "eradicate . . . voices" is Machiavelli's own Latin addition to Livy. For the last part of this paragraph, see Baron, "*Principe* and the Puzzle," p. 87.

8. *sons:* Bernardo (Ridolfi, *Life,* p. 322, n. 28; *Vita 7,* p. 580, n. 28).

Letter 309

1. *fear:* see the second paragraph of Letter 308 concerning Machiavelli's worry that Pope Clement VII would lose the immediate opportunities Fortune offered him to defend Italy against Emperor Charles V.

2. *not . . . enthusiasm:* i.e., the pope is squarely behind creating the new

magistracy, the Curators of the Walls.

Letter 310

1. *high ground:* Machiavelli argued against the pope's idea of enclosing the area around San Miniato within the walls of Florence; see Letter 312 (Gaeta).

2. braccia: see Letter 37, n. 1, on translation of linear measurements.

3. *law stipulates:* Machiavelli should know, since he wrote the *Provvisione per la istituzione dell'ufficio de' cinque provveditori delle mura della città di Firenze* (Provision for the creation of the office of the five superintendents for the walls of the city of Florence) (Machiavelli, *Altre opere storiche e politiche,* pp. 240–242).

4. *ambassador:* Galeotto Medici (Gaeta).

Letter 311

1. *L[orenzo] S[trozzi]:* "his son" is Giambattista, who eventually married Maria di Bindo Altoviti (Gaeta, based on information from Ridolfi).

2. *Jacopo:* when Pope Clement VII summoned Guicciardini to Rome, he left his brother Jacopo in charge of Romagna, of which Francesco had been president (Gaeta).

Letter 312

1. *inside the wall:* see Letter 310.

2. *stronghold:* Machiavelli discusses the issues connected with constructing fortresses, for which he sees few positive reasons, in *Prince,* ch. 20, and *Discourses,* II, 24; part of Guicciardini's comment on the latter takes issue with Machiavelli's position: "Fortresses are often useful to those who hold them: for protecting themselves against conspiracies, for escaping to during revolts, and for recovering lost territory (*Considerazioni,* in Guicciardini, *Scritti Politici e Ricordi,* p. 119). See also Hale, "To Fortify or Not."

3. *1494:* Charles VIII marched into Florence on 17 November 1494: "his entry had as much grandeur, magnificence, and beauty as any event that had taken place in Florence for a long time . . . he came as a conquerer of the city in triumph" (Guicciardini, *Storie Fiorentine,* p. 103; Domandi, p. 98).

4. *letters:* Letters 310, 311, and 312.

Letter 313

1. *Bartolomeo Cavalcanti:* this firm anti-imperial believer (1503–1562), exiled in 1530 after the fall of the Florentine republic in 1527, sought refuge with Cardinal Ippolito d'Este in France and in Rome. He is known for his *Discorsi sopra gli ottimi reggimenti delle republiche antiche e moderne* (Venice, 1574), a translation of Aristotle's *Rhetoric* into Italian, and an *Orazione alla militare ordinanza fiorentina* given in the Church of Santo Spirito on 3 February 1530 (Gaeta).

2. *Marignano:* notwithstanding the famous battles fought there in 1515 and 1859, it is known today as Melegnano; it is about ten miles southeast of Milan.

3. *duke:* Francesco Maria della Rovere, duke of Urbino, in command of the Venetian army. See the Headnote for the assemblage of troops in Lombardy immediately after the signing of the League of Cognac.

4. *from him:* while the imperial army, under the leadership of Charles III de Bourbon (1490–1527), Constable of France, Alfonso del Avalon (1500–1546), Marquess del Vasto, and Antonio de Leyva, besieged and finally took the fortress at Milan, the anti-imperial forces took Lodi, about twenty miles southeast of Milan, on 24 June and marched on Milan. At the first sign of imperialist resistance in Milan, the papal forces called off their attack, on 7 July. Francesco Maria della Rovere, the duke of Urbino, was ordered to retreat southeast to San Martino and Marignano. There he was to await the arrival of Swiss reinforcements promised by Ottaviano Sforza, bishop of Lodi, and Gian Giacomo de' Medici of Marignano, commander of the fortress of Mus (Guicciardini, *Storia d'Italia,* XVII, 6; Gaeta).

5. *quartermaster general:* Pietro da Pesaro (Gaeta).

6. *to no avail:* seeing Guicciardini's complaints about this action, Francesco Maria della Rovere, the duke of Urbino, "replied in an agitated voice that as long as he had the staff [the insignia of his generalship] in his hands, he would not let anyone else use his authority; he would go to Marignano to set up camp. Hence with a great deal of dishonor and with very loud yells from all their soldiers, both armies would borrow Caesar's words—though with a contrary meaning—'I came, I saw, I fled,' and the army was led to Marignano to set up camp" (Guicciardini, *Storia d'Italia,* XVII, 6, pp. 1656–1657; Gaeta).

Letter 314

1. *Bologna:* Machiavelli had apparently stopped at Bologna on his way to Marignano (Gaeta).

Letter 315

1. *Camp of the League:* Machiavelli was at Badìa di Casaretto, near Milan (Gaeta).

2. *rests . . . assured:* translation of *dormir co' gi occi vostri,* "she sleeps with your eyes."

3. *them:* i.e., her letters.

4. Fornaciaio: Falconetti was known as *Il Fornaciaio* ("the brickmaker" or "the kiln-operator"); see Headnote for 1525.

Letter 316

1. *Filippo:* Filippo Strozzi (Gaeta).

2. *Donato:* Donato del Corno (Gaeta).

3. *code:* the one Machiavelli used to correspond with his friends in Florence (Gaeta).

4. *stabbed . . . hearts:* i.e., take it deeply to heart.

5. *Adorno:* under the articles of the League of Cognac, he ought to have

made an act of submission to Francis I of France and brought Genoa into the anti-imperial camp (Gaeta).

6. *daughter:* Charles V had married his cousin Isabella of Portugal (1503–1539) in March 1526; Charles was supposed to marry Henry VIII's daughter, Mary I, queen of England and Ireland, "Bloody Mary" (1516–1568), who eventually married the son of Charles V and Isabella of Portugal, Philip II of Spain (1527–1598).

7. *cardinal:* Cardinal Thomas Wolsey (1475?–1530), archbishop of York and lord chancellor of England. He reversed England's policy of allying itself with France and sided with Charles V, in the hope, said his detractors, of getting the emperor to back him as a candidate for pope. He had been instrumental in the proposed marriage of Charles V and "Bloody Mary."

8. *His Most Christian Majesty:* Francis I, king of France.

9. *no more:* after the Battle of Pavia, in February 1525, an antipapal, popular government was set up in Siena. On 17 June Clement VII sent a contingent of papal and Florentine forces, twelve hundred cavalry and eight thousand infantry, to force a change of government to one favorable to his concerns; Virginio and Ludovico Orsini commanded the army. An internal revolt failed to materialize, so a force of four hundred men obliged the papal forces to withdraw on 25 June (see Guicciardini, *Storia d'Italia,* XVII, 7, 9, and the following letter, 317; Gaeta).

10. *Castellina:* Castellina in Chianti, about twenty-seven miles south of Florence.

11. *offense:* only the first of these hopes had any substance. On 28 July, Suleiman the Magnificent (1496?–1566), after crossing the rivers Save and Drave, captured the Peterwardein fortress, "where, despite both mountains and the obstacles of rivers, he understood that all Hungary was most clearly in danger" (Guicciardini, *Storia d'Italia,* XVII, 9, p. 1676). Peterwardein is on the south bank of the Danube but north of the Save. It is now in Serbia (former Yugoslavia). For having opposed the Inquisition, fifteen to twenty thousand Moors in Valencia were scattered. Although Charles V gave them the alternative of conversion or exile, he was forced to compromise because he needed their money to finance his activities (Gaeta).

12. *[. . .]:* it has not been possible to decipher the code that Vettori used here (Gaeta).

13. *Bourbon:* Charles III de Bourbon, constable of France, who had gone over to the side of Emperor Charles V, managed to bring reinforcements to the imperial troops at Genoa just prior to the league's attack. To Vettori's dismay, he did so without being hindered by the French fleet (Gaeta).

14. *fight . . . bag:* translation of *si potessi sforzare uno forno,* "as if they could break into an oven"; cf. Machiavelli's use of a similar expression in Letter 329.

15. *without money:* i.e., indulgences will be granted without payment (Gaeta).

Letter 317

1. *cardinal [and] Ippolito:* Cardinal Silvio Passerini and Ippolito de' Medici (Gaeta); Martelli, p. 1239, omits the word "and."

2. *has turned out:* this is the campaign against Siena, alluded to at the end of the second paragraph of Letter 316.

3. *although . . . memory:* Vettori quotes the opening line of Aeneas's narration to Dido of the fall of Troy (*Aeneid,* II.12).

4. *Martinozzi:* a papal sympathizer who fled into political exile after the popular government had been set up in Siena (Gaeta).

5. *libertines:* Guicciardini says of these partisans of the independent popular government in Siena, "those who claimed to want freedom referred to themselves popularly as 'the libertines'" (*Storia d'Italia,* XVI, 4, p. 1544; Gaeta).

6. *count of Anguillara:* Virginio Orsini (Gaeta).

7. *count of Pitigliano:* Ludovico Orsini (Gaeta).

8. *Montepulciano:* a town about forty-two miles southeast of Siena.

9. *recruits:* with drafted troops, not professional ones (Gaeta).

10. *Montalcino:* a fortified hill town about twenty-four miles south southeast of Siena.

11. *exiles:* i.e., the political outcasts of Siena (Gaeta).

12. *datary:* Gian Matteo Giberti, bishop of Verona; an important adviser to Pope Clement VII, who, along with Guicciardini, was a powerful formulator of papal policy. Technically, a "datary" was an officer of the curia responsible for dating, registering, and dispatching all the bulls and documents that a pope issued; he could also grant some petitions, dispensations, and benefices.

13. *put the exiles back:* i.e., in Siena.

14. *Poggibonsi:* a town about twenty-seven miles south of Florence, seventeen miles northwest of Siena.

15. braccia: see Letter 37, n. 1, on linear measurements.

16. *Roberto:* Acciaiuoli, the Florentine ambassador to King Francis I of France (Gaeta).

17. *His Majesty:* Francis I.

18. *come what may:* the lacuna is due to a passage in code that has not been deciphered; the "friend" referred to might be the duke of Urbino, the king of France, the marquess del Vasto, or some other important personage from the league (Gaeta).

19. *Messer Andrea Doria:* (1468?–1560), an admiral, statesman, and doge of Genoa, whom they called "Liberator of Genoa" and "Father of Peace." At this point, from 1524 to 1528, he was the high admiral of the Levant and the commander of the French fleet against Charles V; in 1528 he switched his allegiance to Emperor Charles V, took over Genoa, and established a new government there; see Letter 16, n. 4.

20. *Maremma:* a region of southwestern Tuscany that was once a marshland; these two small seaports are about twenty miles south of Grosseto.

Letter 318

1. *Guidotti:* Leonardo Guidotti (Gaeta).

2. *at the beginning:* probably Machiavelli's Letter 313 (Gaeta).

3. *peace of Caesar Octavian:* the peace that eventually prevailed in Rome, under the rule of Augustus Caesar (63 B.C.–A.D. 14).

Letter 319

1. *last letter:* Letter 317.

2. *Filippo:* Filippo Strozzi (Gaeta).

3. *planning:* the forces of the league decided to renew their efforts to lift the siege of the fortress at Milan, held by the imperial army. They left Marignano on 22 July and set up camp at Lambrate, between the abbey of Casaretto and the Lambro River, but, because they could not reach an agreement about the plan of attack, Francesco II Sforza surrendered and handed the fortress of Milan over to Charles III de Bourbon, the constable of France. Francesco Maria della Rovere, the duke of Urbino, then decided to attack the imperial army laying siege to the fortress at Cremona. Under the command of Malatesta Baglioni, the army of the league began this campaign in early August; they encountered such stiff resistance that the duke had to divert some troops from the siege of Milan. Cremona finally fell on 23 September, but the duke of Urbino left before the fortress was officially handed over "and went to Mantua . . . to see his wife [Eleonora Gonzaga]" (Guicciardini, *Storia d'Italia,* XVII, 13, p. 1698). The pope's navy was concentrated at Civitavecchia and Leghorn, in an effort to take Genoa. The marquess of Saluzzo, Michele Antonio (1495–1528), was in the hire of King Francis I of France and commanded five hundred lancers in Piedmont (Gaeta).

4. *succeed:* i.e., the people of Genoa, so that they would go over to the league's side, against Emperor Charles V (Gaeta).

5. *governor:* Francesco Guicciardini (Gaeta).

Letter 320

1. *get my slippers off me:* i.e., trip me up.

Letter 321

1. *Cremona:* Guicciardini had sent Machiavelli to Cremona on 9 September to press the league's forces either to attack decisively or to abandon the siege and move on Genoa; see *Leg.,* III, pp. 1591–1592. There is even Machiavelli's signature on a map of attack decided upon at a meeting of military leaders in which he participated on 13 September (Gaeta).

2. *Tortona:* a town near Alessandria, about equidistant between Milan and Genoa.

Letter 322

1. *Lodi:* 24 June, see Letter 313, n. 4.

2. *stronghold:* the fortress of Milan.

3. *"Risking . . . strategy":* see the opening sentence of *Discourses,* I, 23: "Risking all your fortune without using all your forces was never considered

a judicious strategy" (Gaeta).

4. *conquest:* the victory at Cremona, 23 September (Gaeta).

5. *disorders in Rome:* see the Headnote for the plots against Pope Clement VII led by members of the Colonna family.

6. *Signor Giovanni:* Giovanni delle Bande Nere, Giovanni de' Medici (Gaeta).

7. *Hungary:* a reference to the Battle of Mohàcs, in southern Hungary, which the Turks won on 29 August (Gaeta).

8. *Juno . . . behalf:* see *Aeneid,* I.65–75, where Juno is imploring Aeolus, king of the Winds, to destroy Aeneas and his band as they are crossing the Tyrrhenian Sea—the same sea that the Spanish reinforcements would have to cross; they reached Naples on 1 December.

9. *countess:* this may be the countess of Antonio Castellani, wife of Piero Altoviti (Gaeta); she serves as a counterpart for Juno's promise, if Aeolus grants her request, to give him her loveliest nymph, Deiopea (v. 72).

10. *Rhodes and Hungary:* both, until recently, had withstood onslaughts from the Turks: Rhodes resisted for two hundred years, falling in 1522; Hungary resisted from the reign of Sigismund (1387–1487) to the reign of Louis II (1516–1526) (Gaeta). Inglese, however, notes that Hungary may be an example of "how a region can be captured in a day," based on the example of the Battle of Mohàcs, mentioned in n. 7 above.

11. *army:* for Vettori's position on an attack against the Kingdom of Naples, see the last paragraph of Letter 316 and the second paragraph of Letter 319.

Letter 323

1. *Piacenza:* Guicciardini had withdrawn with the papal troops to Piacenza on 7 October (Gaeta).

2. *Modena:* Machiavelli had followed Guicciardini to Piacenza and gone on to Florence. On his return trip he stopped in Borgo San Donnino, and for two days in Modena, on some business for Guicciardini (Gaeta). •

3. *report:* Machiavelli must have recapitulated what he wrote to Cavalcanti, about the members of the Colonna family and the uprising in Rome in September; see the Headnote.

4. *bishop of Casale:* Bernardino Castellari, known as *della Barba,* "the bearded one" (Gaeta).

5. *Our Lordship:* i.e., the pope.

6. *piece of my mind:* Guicciardini uses the idiomatic expression *lavar[g]li un bucato,* the modern Italian *dargli una lavata di capo,* "wash his head for him," which permits him to continue the image with *poco manco sapone,* "[with] almost as much soap."

Letter 324

1. *poor man:* the commissioner of Borgo San Donnino referred to in the second paragraph of Letter 323; Filippo de' Nerli was governor of Modena.

2. *worse than charcoal:* i.e., you cannot be dealt with without getting one's hands dirty (Gaeta).

3. *Count Guido:* Count Guido Rangoni, governor-general of the army of the Church.

4. *history:* Machiavelli's *Florentine Histories* (Gaeta).

5. *Donato:* Donato del Corno (Gaeta).

Letter 325

1. *Filippo:* Filippo de' Nerli, governor of Modena (Gaeta).

2. *quill full of ink:* i.e., the treaty that Pope Clement VII signed late in August prior to the revolt in Rome that the Colonnesi stirred up in September; see Letter 322, n. 5.

3. *crazy times:* see Letter 316, end of the second paragraph and n. 9, and Letter 317, paragraphs two through nine and nn. 2, 5, 11, 13. For the "craziness" of the people from Siena, see *Asino,* I, vv. 22–24 (*Scritti letterari,* pp. 269–270); there Machiavelli draws on the legend that people who drink from one of the famous fountains in Siena, the *Fonte Branda,* will go mad.

4. *Count Guido:* Count Guido Rangoni, governor-general of the army of the Church. The "divisional commander" is Guicciardini; the problems between the two are discussed in Ridolfi, *Guicciardini,* pp. 160–163.

5. *cardinal:* Silvio Passerini (Gaeta).

Letter 326

1. *when you liked:* once Pope Clement VII broke the truce and decided to punish the members of the Colonna family (see the Headnote), Machiavelli wrote Salviati to see if he could join the troops drawn from Florence for that campaign.

2. *Our Lordship:* Pope Clement VII.

Letter 327

1. *Cesare:* Cesare Colombo (Gaeta).

1527·

Letter 328

1. *Imola:* Machiavelli was there to arrange for the billeting of the league's troops, which were gradually separating from the imperial forces (*Leg.,* III, p. 1644).

2. *you:* Machiavelli uses the familiar form *tu* to address his young adolescent son; Guido was old enough to be "greeted" by Giovanni Vernacci—see Letter 253, dated 26 October 1517, penultimate paragraph.

3. *Cardinal Cibo:* the cousin of Pope Clement VII, papal legate in Bologna, whom Machiavelli had frequently visited during his recent stay in Bologna.

4. *letters:* these may be on his mind because Cardinal Cibo was an ad-

mirer of letters and because Machiavelli knew that his son had some talent; Gaeta notes that Guido wrote one comedy and translated one by Terence.

5. *again:* a glimpse of the gentle side of Machiavelli, which few would suspect from the remarks of his detractors.

6. *Lodovico:* Machiavelli's second son, then in the Levant on business for the second time. In Florence—vulnerable to attack from the imperial army—were his eldest son Bernardo; Guido and Piero, both students; Bartolomea, the Baccina of the next paragraph, who eventually married Giovanni Ricci, Machiavelli's literary executor; and the infant Totto, who was born in late 1526 or in early 1527 (he is not "there" because he was sent to a wet nurse [see Letter 332], though he did not live long) and was named for Machiavelli's brother, who died in 1522. "It was Guido perhaps whom [Machiavelli] loved best, delicate in health with a quiet, studious nature; perhaps he of all those children might one day have understood what kind of man his father was" (Ridolfi, *Life*, pp. 238–239; *Vita 7*, pp. 373–374).

7. *you all:* the concern and intimacy expressed in this letter mitigate the reading of this final expression as merely a conventional one.

Letter 329

1. *truce:* i.e., that the pope signed in Rome in March; see the Headnote.

2. *keeping it:* the truce was broken despite the efforts of Charles de Lannoy; see the Headnote.

3. *wrote:* on 29 March, Guicciardini wrote to the papal datary, Gian Matteo Giberti, bishop of Verona (Gaeta).

4. *viceroy:* Charles de Lannoy.

5. *discuss:* Guicciardini's third alternative was flight (Gaeta).

6. *to the lira:* i.e., as long as there is a serious possibility of defense (Gaeta).

7. *territory:* on April 25, the league's forces moved south from their camp at Rubiera, a town about seven miles west of Modena, to Barberino di Mugello, about nineteen miles north of Florence, and then on to Incisa, about eleven miles southeast of Florence, in an attempt to cut off any attack on Florence by Charles de Bourbon's army.

8. *paper bag:* there is a similar phrase in Vettori's Letter 316.

Letter 330

1. *there:* Machiavelli left Florence in February to go to Forlì to be with Guicciardini; he is specifying that there seems to be general agreement, with reservations, in both places about the treaty Pope Clement VII and Charles de Lannoy signed in March.

2. *ducats:* see the Headnote for this provision of the treaty.

Letter 331

1. *Monseigneur de la Motte:* Charles Choque de la Mothe-des-Noyers, Bourbon's secretary and lieutenant (Gaeta).

2. *set sail:* for Machiavelli's other uses of a nautical image, see Letter 121, n. 11.

3. *rugged region:* i.e., the Apennines in Tuscany (Raimondo).

4. *Guicciardini:* Machiavelli was writing this on the same day that Guicciardini informed the Eight, to its and Machiavelli's great relief, that he was ordering his troops out of Romagna and into Tuscany to defend Florence. "It is worth noting that Guicciardini, who was never satisfied and always ready to criticize and reprove everybody, Pope, cardinals, governors, had nothing but praise for Machiavelli in these last days . . . an extraordinary thing for him—he speaks of friendship between him and Machiavelli" (Ridolfi, *Life*, p. 327, n. 30; *Vita* 7, p. 588).

5. *soul:* there is a similar phrase in the *Florentine Histories*, III, 7, in the context of Machiavelli's nostalgic admiration for the Florentines, who created a magistracy of the *Otto Santi*, "the Eight Saints," to carry out courageously the War of the Eight Saints against Pope Gregory XI and his oppressive legate (1375–1378). In writing his *Florentine Histories*, Machiavelli consistently emphasizes such patriotism in the great men from the Florentine past. Inglese points out that the reading "more than my own soul" has become an accepted one for what in reality is a textual crux. Since the *Apografo Ricci* has a conspicuous erasure here, Inglese thinks it is hopeless to conjecture what the actual text may be, though he offers "more than Christ" as a possibility.

6. *sixty years:* Machiavelli was fifty-eight years old (Gaeta). Ridolfi believes the discrepancy was a result of Machiavelli's feeling "the weight of those years, and on top of them, all the labours he had endured, all the disappointment he had suffered, all the small miseries which depress unspeakably, great men and poets" (*Life*, p. 241; *Vita* 7, p. 378).

7. *prince:* i.e., Pope Clement VII.

Letter 332

1. *back:* see Letter 328; Totto was with a wet nurse (Gaeta).

2. *in the country:* i.e., at San Casciano (Gaeta). Ridolfi notes that getting the wine and oil into Florence would be useful if there were to be a siege; furthermore, the government had reduced the duty on products entering the city in order to build up supplies (*Life*, p. 243; *Vita* 7, p. 381).

Letter 333

1. *troops:* reinforcements from Francis I of France, led by the marquess of Saluzzo, Michele Antonio. Brisighella is a town about seven miles west of Faenza.

2. *Pianoro:* a town about ten miles south of Bologna; thus Francesco Maria della Rovere, the duke of Urbino and commander of the Venetian army, was about fifty-eight miles from Brisighella.

3. *legate in Bologna:* Innocenzo Cibo, the cousin of Pope Clement VII, whom Machiavelli had met when he was in Bologna.

4. *Count Guido:* Count Guido Rangoni, governor-general of the army of the Church.

5. *asshole:* translation of *cazzo,* "prick."

Letter 334

1. *Pera:* see Letter 234, n. 1.

2. *disease:* they were quarantined because of an outbreak of plague in Ragusa (Dubrovnik), from which they had sailed to Ancona.

Letter 335

1. *Doctor R.:* For a letter that Machiavelli's son Piero wrote to his uncle, Francesco Nelli, about Niccolò's death, see Appendix Letter F.

APPENDIX

Letter A

1. *Francesco Minerbetti:* Francesco di Tommaso Minerbetti, bishop of Torres in 1514, bishop of Arezzo from 1525; see Letter 74, n. 5.

2. *count of Provence:* the confusion of Minerbetti's letter is matched by that of the story of the lines of succession among the various houses competing for rule over the Kingdom of Naples and the Two Sicilies. In the final analysis, the struggle for succession in the kingdom was important because it established a pattern that was repeated throughout the Italian peninsula for more than two centuries: whenever there was a dynastic dilemma, to the detriment of the balance of power in Italy, some other foreign power was invited in to help settle the matter. The story in Naples begins with facts that do not square with Minerbetti's account. The first king of Naples was Charles I, who lived from 1226 to 1285; he was the son of Louis VIII, king of France from 1223 to 1226. Charles was the count of Anjou and Provence (1246–1250) and accompanied his older brother, Louis IX, Saint Louis, who was the French king from 1226 to 1270, on the Sixth Crusade (1248–1250). In 1246 Saint Louis gave Anjou as appanage to his younger brother, Charles; hence the period from 1268–1442 is referred to as the "rule of the Angevins" in Naples and the Two Sicilies. Charles I defeated Manfred at Benevento (1266) and at Tagliacozzo (1268) and became a powerful but harsh ruler—so harsh that the "Sicilian Vespers" occurred during his rule, in 1282. The Spanish drove him out of Naples in 1284.

3. *Urban IV:* Urban IV, pope from 1261 to 1264.

4. *Clement IV:* Clement IV, pope from 1265 to 1268.

5. *Frederick II:* Frederick II (1194–1250) was Holy Roman Emperor from 1215 to 1250 and king of Sicily from 1198 to 1212.

6. *Charles II:* Charles II (1246–1309) was the son of Charles I; although he ruled as king of Naples from 1285 to 1309, the Spanish held him prisoner from 1284 to 1288. Through the efforts of two kings of Aragon, James I

(*"Jaime el Conquistador"*), king of Aragon from 1213 to 1276, and his grandson James II ("the Just"), who was king of Sicily from 1285 to 1291, Spain entered the struggle for control of the entire southern area of the Italian peninsula. It was the claim of the descendants of Charles that led to the conflicting claims of the House of Anjou and the House of Aragon; these ultimately became the claims of France and Spain for the right to rule the Kingdom of Naples.

7. *successors:* for more on the dynastic complications and the competing rights to claim control of Naples, see the genealogical chart describing "the French claim to Naples" in Burd's edition of *The Prince,* p. 78; Benedetto Croce, *History of Naples;* and the relevant entries in *Webster's Biographical Dictionary.*

8. *Andreasso:* The suffix *-asso* probably represents an attempt to give his name ("Andreas") a Germanic sound rather than to suggest anything pejorative; he is usually referred to as Prince Andrew of Hungary.

9. *Louis:* also known as Louis I, count of Provence from 1339 to 1384 and duke of Anjou from 1360 to 1384. Joanna I adopted him as her successor to the throne; he was titular head only from 1382 to 1384.

10. *King Louis of Hungary:* Louis the Great, king of Hungary from 1342 to 1382.

11. *Charles IV:* this is probably Charles III, more generally known as Charles of Durazzo (1345–1386); he was the great-grandson of Charles II and king of Naples from 1381 to 1386. Charles III was succeeded by his son Ladislas, who ruled from 1386 to 1414, and then by Joanna II, who ruled from 1414 to 1435. At that point the Angevin line became extinct and the claim went to the House of Aragon: Alfonso I, the Magnanimous, who ruled Naples from 1442 until 1458; his natural son Ferrante (Ferdinand) I, who ruled from 1458 until 1494; and Ferrante (Ferdinand) II, who ruled from 1495 until 1496, when he was driven from Naples by Charles VIII, who was reasserting the Angevin claim through a mutual ancestor, Charles II.

12. *Pope Urban VI:* Urban VI, the first pope during the Great Schism, reigned from 1378 to 1379.

Letter B

1. *Attributed:* according to Bertelli's edition; see bracketed indication at the end of this letter. The source of this letter is Bertelli, *Opere di Niccolò Machiavelli,* vol. 5, p. 109, no. 78.

2. staia: see Letter 278, n. 3.

3. *florins:* see Letter 14, n. 2, on "sealed florins."

Letter C

1. *Machiavelli:* the source of this letter is Hurlimann, "Lettre 'privée,'" p. 183.

2. *payment:* For more on Michelangelo's status as courier, see Letter 113, n. 3.

3. *Aragon:* a letter to Machiavelli from the Ten, dated 7 September, confirms the fact that Ferdinand the Catholic was expected to land in Italy any

day: *Leg.*, II, p. 969. Two days later Florence sent four representatives to receive the king of Spain, whom they expected to land at either Piombino or Livorno: *Leg.*, II, pp. 974, 976. The king was headed toward Naples, where he remained until June 1507, so that he could keep a closer eye on the actions of his general, Gonzalo Fernández de Córdoba, who had conquered the Kingdom of Naples in 1504.

4. *Narbonne:* François Guillaume de Clermont Lodève Castelnau, archbishop of Narbonne, a nephew of Cardinal Georges d'Amboise, arrived with the bishop of Aix, Pierre Le Filleul, on their way to meet Pope Julius II. They left for Incisa in Val d'Arno, about twenty miles southeast of Florence, on the way to Perugia. Machiavelli reports to the Ten from Perugia, where he was with the pope, that the two emissaries arrived in Corciano, about six miles west of Perugia, on 12 September: *Leg.*, II, p. 979.

Letter D

1. *(passages):* the source of this letter is J.-J. Marchand, *Machiavelli: scritti politici*, pp. 303–304, n. 23.

2. *Balìa:* on 16 September 1512 the people of Florence consented to the appointment of a special magistracy, the Balìa, to reform the city's government. Cardinal Giovanni de' Medici took care to see that most of its members were loyal to his house. He angered many of his loyalists, however, by also recommending men from the aristocratic *ottimati*—men who Machiavelli knew would be opposed to his having any political office. This activity accounts in part for some of the vehemence of Machiavelli's *Ricordi ai palleschi,* probably written shortly after these passages to Cardinal de' Medici; see Headnote for 1510–1512.

Letter E

1. *Francesco Guicciardini:* This letter is included as Letter 62 in Inglese, *Lettere*, p. 350. It is a summary, not a transcription, of a letter found in the *Apografo Ricci.*

2. *release:* from his Spanish prison, according to the terms of the Treaty of Madrid between Charles V and Francis I.

3. *Pontremoli:* a town, in the region of Massa Carrara, along the Ligurian Coast in the northwest corner of Tuscany, about nineteen miles north of La Spezia.

Letter F

1. *Nelli:* mentioned briefly in Letter 175, he was the thirteen-year-old Piero's maternal uncle.

2. *belly:* Ridolfi believes that Machiavelli suffered from chronic appendicitis or a gastric ulcer and that he exacerbated the condition by taking some of his famous pills (see the end of Letter 296), so that he died of peritonitis (*Life*, pp. 329–330; *Vita* 7, 594–595).

3. *sins:* many of Machiavelli's detractors seek to discredit this statement because they want to minimize evidence of his being a practicing Christian. In the

citations given above, however, Ridolfi argues cogently for accepting it as fact.

Letter G

1. *Alamanno Salviati:* highly regarded by the Pisans, Salviati was in Pisa acting as governor for the victorious Florentines. This letter, first published in 1986, is taken from Luzzati and Sbrilli, *"Massimiliano d'Ausburgo."*

2. *present:* cf. the "little gift," as Machiavelli calls *The Prince* in its Dedicatory Letter to Lorenzo de' Medici, the duke of Urbino. In reality, his intelligence and analytical ability constitute the "gift" and the "present." Luzzati and Sbrilli believe that Machiavelli signed the letter, but the body is written in someone else's hand—perhaps that of Agostino Vespucci (*"Massimiliano d'Ausburgo,"* p. 828). The closely reasoned, syllogistic clarity of this letter is nevertheless characteristic of Machiavelli's style in both *The Prince* and his diplomatic reports.

3. *Padua:* Maximilian I sought to besiege that city after the Venetian victory in July; the siege lasted until shortly before Salviati's response (Letter 173).

4. *^and^:* a typographic indication, for this letter only, that the word or words enclosed are to be found either above or below the line, or in the margin of the letter.

5. *feet:* translation of *braccia,* here and in the rest of the paragraph; see Letter 37, n. 1, concerning linear measurement.

6. *{ditch}:* a typographic indication, for this letter only, that the word or words enclosed are legible, though crossed out.

7. *in this way:* Machiavelli was both analytic and prophetic; the situation turned out very much "in this way," as described in the closing lines of *Decennale secondo,* vv. 211–215 (*Scritti letterari,* p. 266): "having stayed for several days in Padua with his mind free, weakened and exhausted Maximilian withdrew his troops; forsaken by the League, he longed to wend his way back to Germany."

8. *trifle:* Luzzati and Sbrilli, *"Massimiliano d'Ausburgo,"* p. 842, compare this ostensible self-effacement with the "sermons" of a similarly analytical letter about current political arrangements—see the last paragraph of Letter 112. It is addressed to Giovanni Ridolfi, a similarly powerful political figure; neither man, however, was a Soderini partisan.

9. *prompted:* perhaps a self-conscious emphasis, if Machiavelli took the initiative and wrote this letter of his own volition.

Abbreviations

AG
Niccolò Machiavelli. *The Chief Works and Others.* Trans. Allan Gilbert. 3 vols. Durham, N.C.: Duke University Press, 1965.

Atkinson
Niccolò Machiavelli. *The Prince.* Ed. and trans. James B. Atkinson. New York: Macmillan Publishing, 1985.

Domandi
Francesco Guicciardini. *The History of Florence.* Trans. Mario Domandi. New York: Harper Torchbooks, 1970.

Gaeta
Niccolò Machiavelli. *Opere: Lettere.* Ed. Franco Gaeta. Vol. 3. Turin: Unione Tipografico-Editrice Torinese, 1984.

Inglese
Giorgio Inglese. Review of *Opere: Lettere,* by Niccolò Machiavelli, ed. Franco Gaeta, vol. 3. *La Bibliofilia* 86 (1984): 271–280.

Inglese, *Lettere*
Giorgio Inglese. *Niccolò Machiavelli: Lettere a Francesco Vettori e a Francesco Guicciardini.* Milan: Biblioteca Universale Rizzoli, 1989.

Landucci
A Florentine Diary from 1450 to 1516 by Luca Landucci Continued by an Anonymous Writer Till 1542 with Notes by Iodoco del Badia. Trans. Alice de Rosen Jervis. London: J. M. Dent; New York: E. P. Dutton, 1927.

Leg.
Niccolò Machiavelli. *Legazioni e commissarie.* Ed. Sergio Bertelli. 3 vols. Milan: Feltrinelli, 1964.

Martelli
Niccolò Machiavelli. *Tutte le opere.* Ed. Mario Martelli. Series "Le Voci del Mondo." Florence: Sansoni, 1971.

Raimondi
Niccolò Machiavelli. *Opere.* Ed. Ezio Raimondi. Milan: Ugo Mursia, 1971; 7th ed., 1976.

Works Cited

Ascoli, Albert Russell, and Victoria Kahn, eds. *Machiavelli and the Discourse of Literature.* Ithaca: Cornell University Press, 1993.

Bandello, Matteo. *Le novelle.* Ed. Gioachino Brognoligo. Vol. 2. Bari: Laterza, 1928.

Bardazzi, Giovanni. *"Tecniche narrative nel Machiavelli scrittore di lettere." Annali della Scuola Normale Superiore di Pisa,* 3d ser., 5 (1975): 1443–1489.

Baron, Hans. "Machiavelli the Republican Citizen and Author of *The Prince.*" In *Search of Florentine Civic Humanism: Essays on the Transition from Medieval to Modern Thought.* Vol. 2. Princeton, N.J.: Princeton University Press, 1988. 101–151.

Baron, Hans. "The *Principe* and the Puzzle of the Date of Chapter 26." *Journal of Medieval and Renaissance Studies* 21, 1 (Spring 1991): 83–102.

Bertelli, Sergio. *Opere di Niccolò Machiavelli.* In *Epistolario.* Vol. 5. Milan: Giovanni Salerno, 1969.

Black, Robert. "Machiavelli, Servant of the Florentine Republic." Eds. Gisela Bock, Quentin Skinner, and Maurizio Viroli. *Machiavelli and Republicanism.* Cambridge: Cambridge University Press, 1990. 71–99.

Bullard, Melissa Meriam. *Filippo Strozzi and the Medici: Favor and Finance in Sixteenth-Century Florence and Rome.* Cambridge: Cambridge University Press, 1980.

Burd, L. Arthur. Il Principe *by Niccolò Machiavelli.* Oxford: The Clarendon Press, 1891; rpt. 1968.

Butters, H. C. *Governors and Government in Early Sixteenth-Century Florence, 1502–1519.* Oxford: The Clarendon Press, 1985.

Cantimori, Delio. "Rhetoric and Politics in Italian Humanism." *Journal of the Warburg and Courtauld Institutes* 1 (1937): 83–102.

Cartwright, Julia. *Isabella d'Este, Marchioness of Mantua 1474–1539: A Study of the Renaissance.* 2 vols. New York: Dutton, 1905.

Chastel, André. *The Sack of Rome, 1527.* Trans. Beth Archer. Bollingen Series, 35, 26. Princeton: Princeton University Press, 1983.

Clough, Cecil H. *Machiavelli Researches. Annali dell'Istituto Universitario Orientale (sezione romanza),* 9, 1 (1967): 21–130.

Clough, Cecil H. *Machiavelli Researches. Pubblicazioni della Sezione Romanza dell'Istituto Universitario Orientale, Studi* [Naples] 3 (1967).

Clough, Cecil H. "Yet Again Machiavelli's Prince." *Annali dell'Istituto Universitario Orientale (sezione romanza)* 5 (1963): 201–226.

Croce, Benedetto. *History of the Kingdom of Naples.* Ed. H. Stuart Hughes. Chicago: The University of Chicago Press, 1970.

Dionisotti, Carlo. *Machiavelli and the Discourse of Literature.* Eds. Albert Russell Ascoli and Victoria Kahn. Ithaca: Cornell University Press, 1993.

Dionisotti, Carlo. *"Machiavelli, Cesare Borgia, e don Micheletto." Machiavellerie: Storia e fortuna di Machiavelli.* Turin: Einaudi, 1980. 3–59.

Dionisotti, Carlo. *"Machiavelli letterato." Machiavellerie: Storia e fortuna di Machiavelli.* Turin: Einaudi, 1980. 227–266.

Einstein, Alfred. *The Italian Madrigal*. 3 vols. Princeton: Princeton University Press, 1949.

Fachard, Denis. *Biagio Buonaccorsi: sa vie, son temps, son oeuvre*. Bologna: Boni, 1976.

Fachard, Denis. *"Liriche edite e inedite di Biagio Buonaccorsi."* Studi di Filologia Italiana 31 (1973): 157–206.

Ferroni, Giulio. *"Le 'cose vane' nelle lettere di Machiavelli."* La rassegna della letteratura italiana 76 (1972): 215–264.

Ficino, Marsilio. *The Letters of Marsilio Ficino*. 3 vols. New York: Gingko Press, 1985.

A Florentine Diary from 1450 to 1516 by Luca Landucci Continued by an Anonymous Writer Till 1542 with Notes by Iodoco del Badia. Trans. Alice de Rosen Jervis. London: J. M. Dent; New York: E. P. Dutton, 1927.

Gilbert, Felix. "Bernardo Rucellai and the *Orti Oricellari*." *Journal of the Warburg and Courtauld Institutes* 12 (1949): 101–131. Rpt. in Felix Gilbert. *History: Choice and Commitment*. Cambridge: Harvard University Press, 1977. 215–246.

Gilbert, Felix. "The Composition and Structure of Machiavelli's *Discorsi*." *Journal of the History of Ideas* 14 (1953): 135–156. Rpt. in Felix Gilbert. *History: Choice and Commitment*. Cambridge: Harvard University Press, 1977. 115–133.

Gilbert, Felix. *Machiavelli and Guicciardini: Politics and History in Sixteenth-Century Florence*. Princeton: Princeton University Press, 1965.

Gilmore, Myron P., ed. *Studies in Machiavelli*. Florence: Sansoni, 1972.

Guicciardini, Francesco. *The History of Florence*. Trans. Mario Domandi. New York: Harper Torchbooks, 1970.

Guicciardini, Francesco. *The History of Italy*. Trans. and ed. Sidney Alexander. New York: Macmillan Publishing, 1969.

Guicciardini, Francesco. *Opere: Storia d'Italia*. Ed. Emanuella Scarano. Vols. II (I–IX) and III (XI–XX). Turin: Unione Tipographico-Editrice Torinese, 1981; rpt. 1987.

Guicciardini, Francesco. *Scritti politici e ricordi*. Ed. Roberto Palmarocchi. Bari: Laterza, 1933.

Guicciardini, Francesco. *Storie Fiorentine dal 1378 al 1509*. Ed. Roberto Palmarocchi. Bari: Laterza, 1931.

Hale, J. R. *The Literary Works of Machiavelli*. London: Oxford University Press, 1961.

Hale, J. R. "To Fortify or Not To Fortify? Machiavelli's Contribution to a Renaissance Debate." Ed. J. R. Hale. *Renaissance War Studies*. Hambledon Press, 1983. 189–210.

Holler, Anne. *Florence Walks*. New York: Holt, Rinehart, Winston, 1983.

Hulliung, Mark. *Citizen Machiavelli*. Princeton: Princeton University Press, 1983.

Hurlimann, Guido. *"Une lettre 'privée' de Machiavel à Piero Soderini."* La Bibliofilia 74 (1972): 181–183.

Inglese, Giorgio. *Niccolò Machiavelli: Lettere a Francesco Vettori e a Francesco Guicciardini*. Milan: Biblioteca Universale Rizzoli, 1989.

Inglese, Giorgio. Review of *Opere: Lettere,* by Niccolò Machiavelli, ed. Franco Gaeta, vol. 3. *La Bibliofilia* 86 (1984): 271–280.

Jones, Rosemary Devonshire. *Francesco Vettori: Florentine Citizen and Medici Servant*. London: University of London, Athlone Press, 1972.

Jones, Rosemary Devonshire. "Francesco Vettori and Niccolò Machiavelli." *Italian Studies* 23 (1968): 93–113.

Kahn, Victoria. *Machiavellian Rhetoric: From the Counter-Reformation to Milton*. Princeton: Princeton University Press, 1994.

Klibansky, Raymond, Erwin Panofsky, and Fritz Saxl. *Saturn and Melancholy: Studies in the History of Natural Philosophy, Religion, and Art.* London: Nelson, 1964.

Kohl, Benjamin G., and Ronald G. Witt. *The Earthly Republic.* Philadelphia: University of Pennsylvania Press, 1978.

Lowe, K. J. P. *Church and Politics in Renaissance Italy: The Life and Career of Cardinal Francesco Soderini (1453–1524).* Cambridge: Cambridge University Press, 1993.

Luzzati, Michele, and Milletta Sbrilli. *"Massimiliano d'Ausburgo e la politicia di Firenze in una lettera inedita di Niccolò Machiavelli ad Alamanno Salviati."* Annali della Scuola Normale Superiore di Pisa, Classe di Lettere e Filosofia 3d ser., 16, 3 (1986): 825–854.

McCanles, Michael. *The Discourse of* Il Principe. Malibu, Calif.: Undena Publications, 1983.

Machiavelli, Niccolò. *Arte della guerra e scritti politici minori.* Ed. Sergio Bertelli. Milan: Feltrinelli, 1961.

Machiavelli, Niccolò. *The Chief Works and Others.* Trans. Allan Gilbert. 3 vols. Durham, N.C.: Duke University Press, 1965.

Machiavelli, Niccolò. *The Comedies of Machiavelli.* Ed. and trans. David Sices and James B. Atkinson. Hanover, N.H.: The University Press of New England, 1985.

Machiavelli, Niccolò. *Legazioni e commissarie.* Ed. Sergio Bertelli. 3 vols. Milan: Feltrinelli, 1964.

Machiavelli, Niccolò. *Le legazioni e commissarie.* Ed. L. Passerini and G. Milanesi. Vol. 5. Florence: Tipografia Cenniniana, 1876.

Machiavelli, Niccolò. *Opere.* Ed. Ezio Raimondi. Milan: Ugo Mursia, 1971; 7th ed., 1976.

Machiavelli, Niccolò. *Opere: Istorie fiorentine e altre opere storiche e politiche.* Ed. Alessandro Montevecchi. Vol. 2. Turin: Unione Tipografico-Editrice Torinese, 1971.

Machiavelli, Niccolò. *Opere: Lettere.* Ed. Franco Gaeta. Milan: Feltrinelli, 1961.

Machiavelli, Niccolò. *Opere: Lettere.* Ed. Franco Gaeta. Vol. 3. Turin: Unione Tipografico-Editrice Torinese, 1984.

Machiavelli, Niccolò. *The Prince.* Ed. and trans. James B. Atkinson. New York: Macmillan Publishing, 1985.

Machiavelli, Niccolò. *Il teatro e gli scritti letterari.* Ed. Franco Gaeta. Milan: Feltrinelli, 1965.

Machiavelli, Niccolò. *Tutte le opere.* Ed. Mario Martelli. Series *"Le Voci del Mondo."* Florence: Sansoni, 1971.

Marchand, J.-J. *"I Ghiribizzi d'ordinanza del Machiavelli."* La Bibliofilia 73, 2 (1971): 135–150.

Marchand, J.-J. *Niccolò Machiavelli: I primi scritti politici (1499–1512).* Padua: Antenore, 1975.

Marietti, Marina. *"Machiavel historiographe des Médicis."* Les Ecrivains et le pouvoir en Italie à l'époque de la Renaissance. Ed. A. Rochon. 2d ser. Paris: Sorbonne, 1974.

Martelli, Mario. *"I 'Ghiribizzi' a Giovan Battista Soderini."* Rinascimento 9 (1969): 147–180.

Martelli, Mario. *L'altro Niccolò di Bernardo Machiavelli.* Quaderni di Rinascimento. Florence: Sansoni, 1975.

Martelli, Mario. *"La logica provvidenzialistica e il capitolo XXVI del Principe."* Interpres 4 (1982): 262–384.

Martelli, Mario. *"Memento su un'edizione dell'epistolario machiavelliano."* La Bibliofilia 73 (1971): 61–79.

Martelli, Mario. *"Da Poliziano a Machiavelli: Sull'epigramma 'dell'Occasione' e sull'occasione." Interpres* 2 (1979): 230–254.

Martelli, Mario. *"Preistoria (Medicea) di Machiavelli." Studi de Filologia Italiana* 29 (1971): 377–405.

Martelli, Mario. *"Schede sulla cultura di Machiavelli." Interpres* 6 (1985–1986): 303–306.

Masters, Roger D. *Machiavelli, Leonardo, and the Science of Power.* Notre Dame: University of Notre Dame Press, 1995.

Najemy, John M. *Between Friends: Discourses of Power and Desire in the Machiavelli-Vettori Letters of 1513–1515.* Princeton: Princeton University Press, 1993.

Najemy, John M. "The Controversy Surrounding Machiavelli's Service to the Republic." *Machiavelli and Republicanism.* Eds. Gisela Bock, Quentin Skinner, and Maurizio Viroli. Cambridge: Cambridge University Press, 1990. 101–117.

Najemy, John M. "Machiavelli and Geta: Men of Letters." *Machiavelli and the Discourse of Literature.* Eds. Albert Ascoli and Victoria Kahn. Ithaca: Cornell University Press, 1993.

Najemy, John M. "Machiavelli and the Medici: The Lessons of Florentine History." *Renaissance Quarterly* 35, 4 (Winter 1982): 551–576.

Oman, Sir Charles. *A History of the Art of War in the Sixteenth Century.* 2d ed. London: Methuen, 1937.

Osthoff, Wolfgang. *Theatergesang und darstellende Musik.* 2 vols. Tutzing: Hans Schneider, 1968.

Pirrotta, Nino, and Elena Povoledo. *Music and Theatre from Poliziano to Monteverdi.* Trans. Karen Eales. New York: Cambridge University Press, 1982.

Pitkin, Hanna Fenichel. *Fortune Is a Woman: Gender and Politics in the Thought of Niccolò Machiavelli.* Berkeley: University of California Press, 1984.

Pocock, J. G. A. *The Machiavellian Moment.* Princeton: Princeton University Press, 1975.

Raimondi, Ezio. *"Il sasso del politico." Politica e Commedia.* Bologna: Il Mulino, 1972. 165–172.

Rebhorn, Wayne A. *Foxes and Lions: Machiavelli's Confidence Men.* Ithaca: Cornell University Press, 1988.

Ridolfi, Roberto. *The Life of Francesco Guicciardini.* Trans. Cecil Grayson. New York: Knopf, 1968.

Ridolfi, Roberto. *The Life of Niccolò Machiavelli.* Trans. Cecil Grayson. London: Routledge and Kegan Paul, 1963.

Ridolfi, Roberto. *Vita di Niccolò Machiavelli. (Settima edizione italiana accresciuta e riveduta).* Florence: Sansoni, 1978.

Ridolfi, Roberto, and Paolo Ghiglieri. *"I Ghiribizzi al Soderini." Bibliofilia* 12 (1970): 53–74.

Rubinstein, Nicolai. *"Firenze e il problema della politica imperiale in Italia al tempo di Massimiliano I." Archivo Storico Italiano* 116 (1958): 161–166.

Rubinstein, Nicolai. "Machiavelli and the World of Florentine Politics." *Studies on Machiavelli.* Ed. Myron P. Gilmore. Florence: Sansoni, 1972.

Sasso, Gennaro. *"Biagio Buonaccorsi e Niccolò Machiavelli." La Cultura* 18 (1980): 195–222.

Sasso, Gennaro. *"'Filosofia' o 'scopo pratico' nel Principe." Studi su Machiavelli.* Naples: Morano, 1967.

Sasso, Gennaro. *"Intorno alla composizione dei Discorsi." Giornale Storico della letteratura italiana* 134 (1957): 514 ff.

Sasso, Gennaro. *"Machiavelli, Cesare Borgia, Don Micheletto e la questione della milizia."* *Machiavelli e gli antichi e altri saggi.* Vol. 2. Milan and Naples: R. Ricciardi, 1988. 57–117.

Sasso, Gennaro. *Machiavelli e Cesare Borgia, Storia di un Giudizio.* Rome: Edizioni dell'Ateneo, 1966.

Sasso, Gennaro. *Niccolò Machiavelli: Storia del suo pensiero politico.* Bologna: Società Editrice Il Mulino, 1980.

Sasso, Gennaro. *"Il Principe ebbe due redazioni?"* *La Cultura* 19 (1981): 52–109.

Sasso, Gennaro. *"Qualche osservazione sui 'Ghiribizzi al Soderino' di Machiavelli."* *La Cultura* 11 (1973): 129–167.

Savonarola, Girolamo. *Prediche sopra l'esodo.* Ed. Pier Giorgio Ricci. 2 vols. Rome: Belardetti, 1955–1956.

Slim, H. Colin. *A Gift of Madrigals and Motets.* 2 vols. Chicago: University of Chicago Press, 1972.

Spini, Giorgio. *Tra rinascimento e riforma, Antonio Brucioli.* Florence: La Nuova Italia, 1940.

Stephens, J. N. *The Fall of the Florentine Republic, 1512–1530.* Oxford: The Clarendon Press, 1983.

Stephens, J. N., and H. C. Butters. "New Light on Machiavelli." *English Historical Review* 97 (January 1982): 54–69.

Taylor, F. L. *The Art of War in Italy, 1494–1529.* Cambridge: Cambridge University Press, 1921.

Young-Bruehl, Elisabeth. "The Biographer's Empathy With Her Subject." *Academy Forum: The Journal of the American Academy of Psychoanalysis* (November 1992): 9–11.

Vettori, Francesco. *Scritti storici e politici.* Ed. Enrico Niccolini. Bari: Laterza, 1972.

Von Albertini, Rudolf. *Firenze dalla republica al principato: Storia e coscienza politica.* Preface by Federico Chabod. Turin: Einaudi, 1970.

Von Albertini, Rudolf. *Das florentinische Staatsbewusstsein in Ubergang von der Republik zum Prinzipat.* Bern: Francke, 1955.

Weber, Max. "Politics as a Vocation." *From Max Weber: Essays in Sociology.* Ed. H. H. Gerth and C. Wright Mills. New York: Oxford University Press, 1946.

List of Correspondence

1506

1507–1508

1513

Index

For the sake of simplicity and usefulness to the reader, this Index does not include "Niccolò Machiavelli" and "Florence" among its items. Modern studies and their authors are not included here. Items from the Introduction, Headnotes, and Notes are indicated in **bold face**.

www.ingramcontent.com/pod-product-compliance
Lightning Source LLC
Chambersburg PA
CBHW021930110726
47901CB00003B/785